War and Empire

War and Empire

The Expansion of Britain, 1790–1830

Bruce Collins

Longman
is an imprint of

Harlow, England • London • New York • Boston • San Francisco • Toronto
Sydney • Tokyo • Singapore • Hong Kong • Seoul • Taipei • New Delhi
Cape Town • Madrid • Mexico City • Amsterdam • Munich • Paris • Milan

PEARSON EDUCATION LIMITED

Edinburgh Gate
Harlow CM20 2JE
United Kingdom
Tel: +44 (0)1279 623623
Fax: +44 (0)1279 431059
Website: www.pearsoned.co.uk

First edition published in Great Britain in 2010

© Pearson Education Limited 2010

The right of Bruce Collins to be identified as author
of this work has been asserted by him in accordance
with the Copyright, Designs and Patents Act 1988.

ISBN: 978-0-582-49422-0

British Library Cataloguing in Publication Data
A CIP catalogue record for this book can be obtained from the British Library

Library of Congress Cataloging in Publication Data
Collins, Bruce.
    War and empire : Britain, 1790–1830 / Bruce Collins. – 1st ed.
        p. cm.
    Includes bibliographical references and index.
    ISBN 978-0-582-49422-0 (pbk.)
    1. Great Britain–History, Military–19th century.   2. Great Britain–History,
Military–18th century.   3. Great Britain–Colonies–History, Military.
4. Imperialism–History–19th century.   5. Great Britain–History–1789–1820.
6. Great Britain–History–1800–1837.   I. Title.
    DA68.C65   2010
    941.07′3—dc22

                                                        2009050191

10   9   8   7   6   5   4   3   2   1
14   13   12   11   10

Set in 10/13.5 pt Sabon by 35
Printed and bound in Malaysia (CTP-VP)

The Publisher's policy is to use paper manufactured from sustainable forests.

Contents

List of maps		vii
Acknowledgements		viii
Preface		x

PART ONE War, empire and British identity   1

1	War and empire: the contested connection	3
2	British militarism	25

PART TWO The war against Republican France   59

3	Containing France in Europe, 1793–95	61
4	The expanded contest, 1793–97	91
5	The Irish rebellion, 1796–98	109
6	Renewing alliances and positioning for peace, 1798–1801	135

PART THREE Military imperialism in India   153

7	India: Military efficiency and Mysore, 1790–92	155
8	Imperial expansionism and Mysore, 1798–99	171
9	Expansionism against the Marathas, 1802–05	193

PART FOUR The war against Napoleon   227

10	The quest for objectives, 1803–08	229
11	The Iberian Peninsula commitment, 1808–12	254
12	Victory in Spain and France, 1813–14	280

PART FIVE Britain's global reach   317

13   The war of 1812   319
14   The Waterloo campaign: lessons learned?   347
15   Completing British paramountcy in India, 1814–19   364

PART SIX The impact of war   393

16   Instruments of power   395
17   Aristocracy and British military culture   419
18   Interventions overseas, 1820–30   439
19   Britain as a global power, 1815–30   464

Index   491

List of maps

1 The Netherlands campaign, 1793–95   xi

2 Naval warfare in European waters, 1792–1815   xii

3 Naval warfare in the Caribbean and America   xiv

4 Ireland, 1798   xv

5 Imperial possessions in India, 1783   xvi

6 The Deccan in 1803   xvii

7 The war against Holkar   xviii

8 The Iberian peninsula   xix

9 The American–Canadian border region   xx

10 The southern Netherlands and the Waterloo campaign   xxi

11 British possessions in India, 1818   xxii

Acknowledgements

This book has been long in the making. My initial explorations of the phenomenon of British power projection occurred at the University of Glasgow where I was encouraged and strongly supported by the late Geoffrey Finlayson and Keith Robbins. Christopher Black has offered advice and a sounding board for many years. My interest in British overseas policy benefited from conversations with David Gillard. Since leaving Glasgow, I have been an academic dean/director of school in five different universities and colleges of higher education, an experience which has led me to be less ready to write loftily of military blundering and poor decision-making among those faced with uncertainty and confusion. For many years, I tested early versions of work for the follow-up volume to this one on tolerant audiences at symposia organized by the British Commission for Military History; I must offer a general 'thank you' to participants at many meetings. Tony Hayter and Ian Beckett were extremely helpful when I began work on more strictly military history. I have also gained from brief conversations over many years with Brian Holden Reid. The Third Wellington Congress at the University of Southampton in July 2006, organized by Christopher Woolgar, provided an excellent occasion for exchanges of views on an extremely diverse range of topics. This book has been completed after my return to teaching and research in 2004, following long periods of academic administration. I have been extremely fortunate to be a member of such an intellectually vigorous and committed group of historians as those at Sheffield Hallam University. Many of them have put up with my preoccupations with apparent interest and good humour. Collectively they have provided a congenial and academically lively setting for historical inquiry and writing. I have particularly benefited from conversations with Peter Cain, Roger Lloyd-Jones, Merv Lewis and Matthew Roberts, and owe a great deal to Peter's encouragement.

I owe an enormous debt to Andrew MacLennan at Longman for the interest he took in the larger project of which this is a part. Christina

Wipf-Perry at what is now Pearson Longman has been immensely patient over the finalization of the typescript, which has had to be slimmed down considerably during the last year. I have benefited from the detailed comments of two anonymous readers' reports, as well as the encouragement and comments of Hamish Scott, the joint editor of the series of which this volume forms a part. Elizabeth O'Reilly has assisted the final process of tying the text together with great good humour and efficiency. My final thanks go my wife, Linda Nash, who has invariably supported me and who read the typescript and commented most helpfully on it.

Bruce Collins
December 2009

Publisher's acknowledgements

We are grateful to the following for permission to reproduce copyright material:

Maps

Maps 1–5 and Map 10 reproduced with permission of Edward Stanford Ltd; Map 6 adapted from *The Anglo-Maratha Campaigns and the Contest for India*, Cambridge University Press (Cooper, R 2003) p. 83 reproduced with permission of Cambridge University Press; Map 7 adapted from *Wellington in India*, Greenhill Books (Weller, J 1993); Map 8 adapted from *Wellington in the Peninsula*, Greenhill Books (Weller, J 1992); Map 9 adapted from *British Generals in the War of 1812*, McGill-Queen's University Press (Turner, W.B. 1999) reproduced with permission of Professor W.B. Turner; Map 11 adapted from *Raj. The Making and Unmaking of British India*, Little Brown (1997) p. 75, reproduced with permission of Ian Hyslop.

In some instances we have been unable to trace the owners of copyright material, and we would appreciate any information that would enable us to do so.

Preface

This book explores British involvement in a particularly intense phase in the history of warfare and the British use of military and naval power to uphold and advance Britain's expanding worldwide interests. Some of the ground covered has been extensively examined over many years, but many aspects of Britain's global military efforts have been patchily analysed or written up in detail long ago. My aim in drawing so much war-making into one volume, and bringing naval and military activities together is, first, to demonstrate the sheer scale and reach of Britain's projection of power in this period. The treatment is necessarily selective. It is difficult, for example, to convey the sheer extent of naval warfare, since so much combat at sea involved fighting between single ships or small numbers of ships and so much resource was devoted to blockading. Much effort went into defending or capturing or recapturing Caribbean islands. A large part of the army spent its time in unnoticed garrison duties worldwide. Moreover, restrictions of space limit the scope for going into the details of battles. I seek instead to convey the extent, challenges and complexity of Britain's projection of power by striking a balance between somewhat rarefied strategic analyses and the necessary assessment of selective individual campaigns. My second purpose is to consider the impact of this period of warfare on the nature of the British state. I am interested in how, at the national level, Britain became both the world's leading commercial country and yet operated as a global military and naval power. Rather than examine how the armed services were subject to internal social and cultural divisions and to external political and cultural criticism – all themes which are receiving increasing and stimulating attention from researchers – I look outwards to assessing how successful the armed services were in maintaining their prestige and influence through the development of a form of militarism compatible with British political and cultural mores. I am concerned to establish the contexts in which the armed services operated and the larger role they played within the UK, as well as in the wider world.

MAP   xi

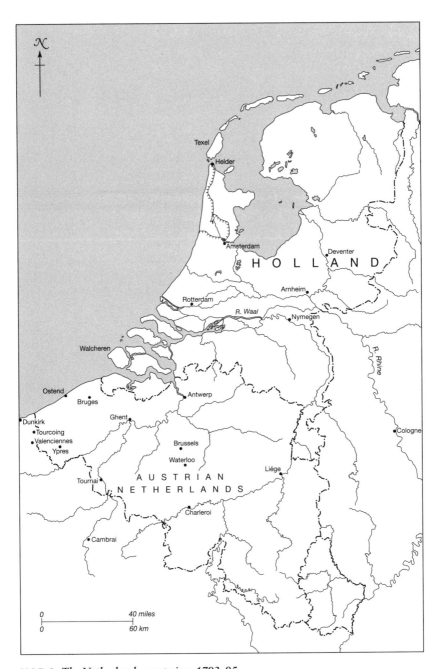

MAP 1 *The Netherlands campaign, 1793–95*

Source: adapted and reproduced with permission of Edward Stanford Ltd

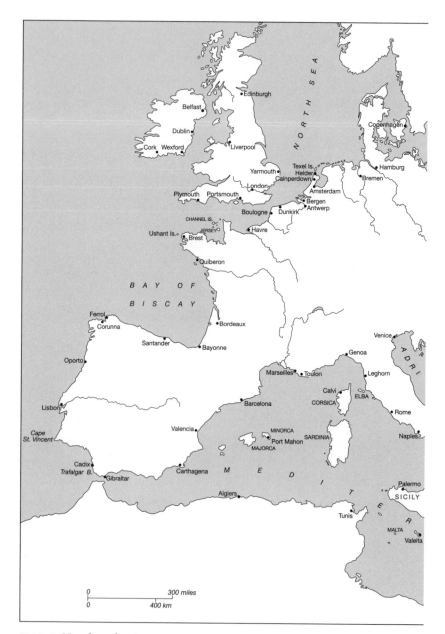

MAP 2 *Naval warfare in European waters, 1792–1815*

Source: adapted and reproduced with permission of Edward Stanford Ltd

MAP xiii

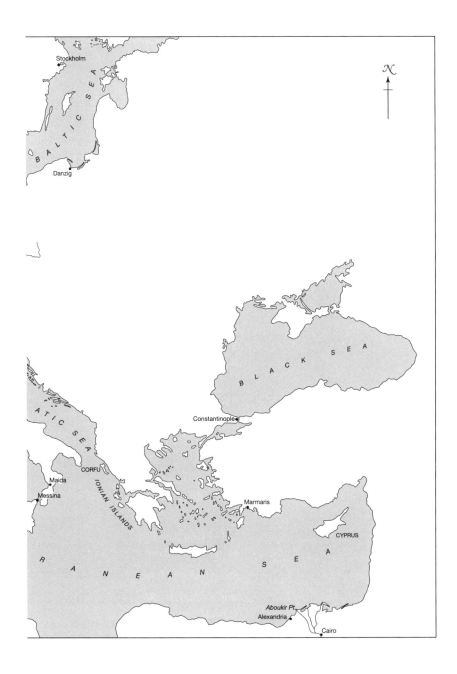

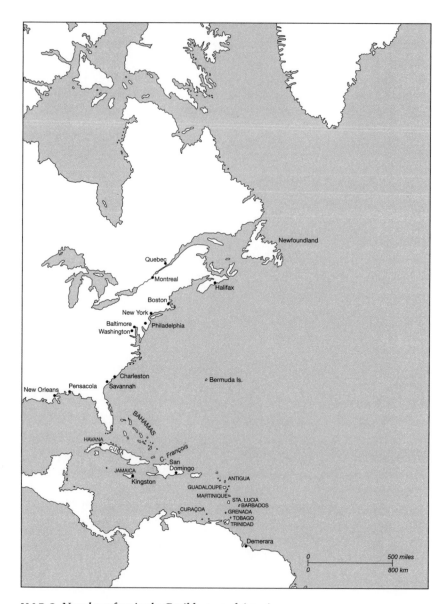

MAP 3 *Naval warfare in the Caribbean and America*

Source: adapted and reproduced with permission of Edward Stanford Ltd

MAP xv

MAP 4 *Ireland, 1798*

Source: adapted and reproduced with permission of Edward Stanford Ltd

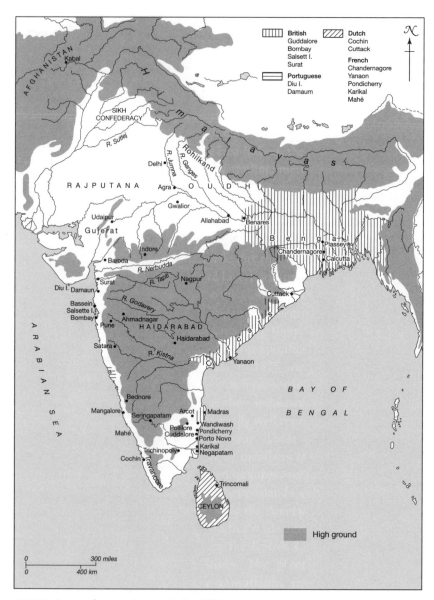

MAP 5 *Imperial possessions in India, 1783*

Source: adapted and reproduced with permission of Edward Stanford Ltd

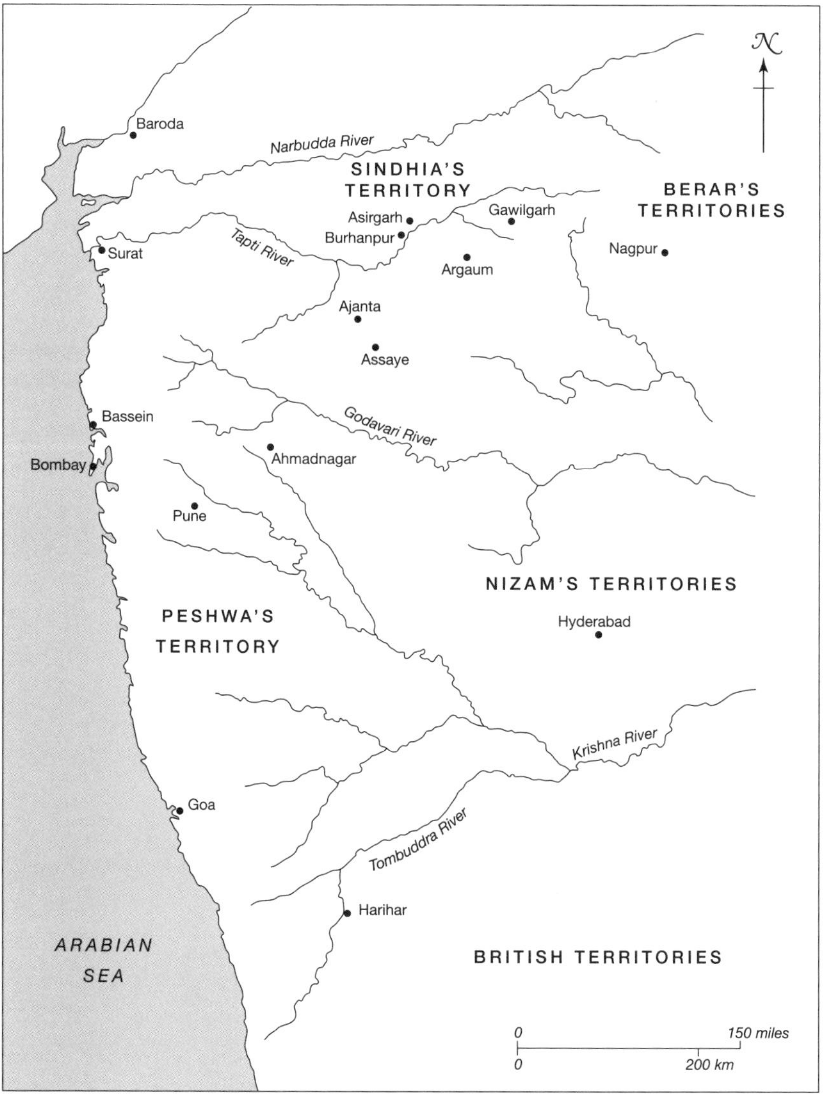

MAP xvii

MAP 6 *The Deccan in 1803*

Source: adapted from *The Anglo-Maratha Campaigns and the Contest for India*, Cambridge University
Press (Cooper, R 2003) p.83, reproduced with permission of Cambridge University Press

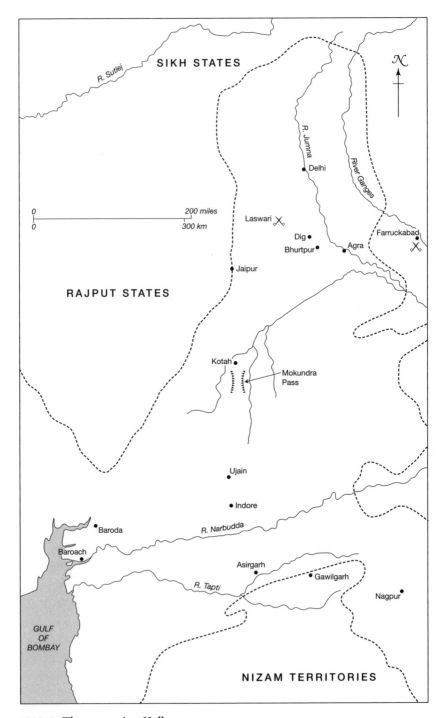

MAP 7 *The war against Holkar*

Source: adapted from *Wellington in India*, Greenhill Books (Weller, J 1993)

MAP xix

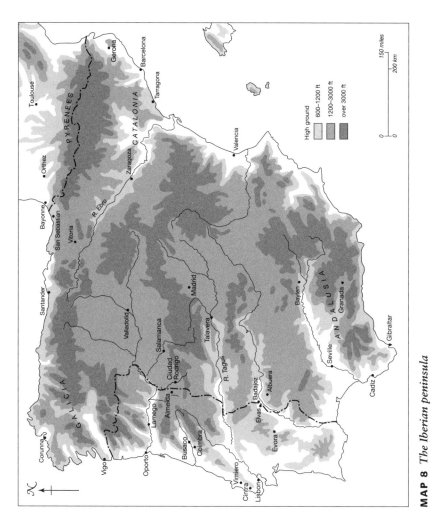

MAP 8 *The Iberian peninsula*

Source: adapted from *Wellington in the Peninsula*, Greenhill Books (Weller, J 1992)

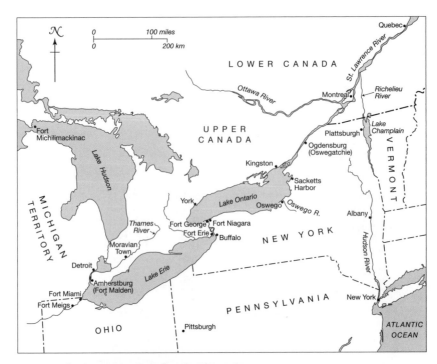

MAP 9 *The American–Canadian border region*

Source: adapted from *British Generals in the War of 1812*, McGill-Queen's University Press (Turner, W.B. 1999) reproduced with permission of Professor W.B. Turner;

MAP   x x i

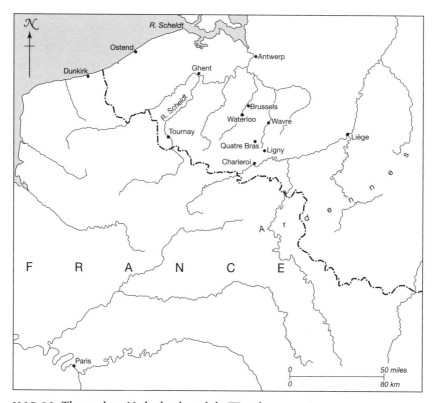

MAP 10 *The southern Netherlands and the Waterloo campaign*

Source: adapted and reproduced with permission of Edward Stanford Ltd

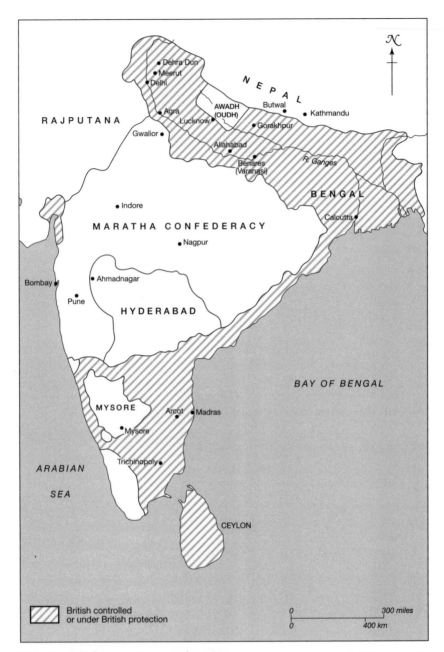

MAP 11 *British possessions in India, 1818*

Source: adapted from *Raj. The Making and Unmaking of British India*, Little Brown (1997) p.75, reproduced with permission of Ian Hyslop.

PART ONE

War, empire and British identity

CHAPTER 1

War and empire: the contested connection

During the period 1790–1830, Britain vastly expanded its existing empire. At the same time, it was heavily engaged in warfare across much of the globe. Whether and how far these two developments were linked and interdependent will be the core concern of this book. With hindsight the British have typically disavowed such a connection. 1926 the prime minister, Stanley Baldwin, denied that any relationship existed: 'The empires of old [were] . . . created by military conquest and sustained by military dominion. They were of subject races governed by military power. Our empire is so different from those.'[1] Such a reassuring gloss on the imperial experience exemplifies an enduring view that commerce and investment drove imperial policy, and that there was an endemic tension between a nation so focused on commercial progress and an interest in or commitment to militarism. Critics of British imperial policies conceded the existence of a contradiction, but insisted that Britain pursued her self-interest while embodying that contradiction. In 1787, Alexander Hamilton, one of George Washington's leading wartime aides, wrote of Britain: 'Commerce has been for ages the predominant pursuit of that country. Few nations, nevertheless, have been more frequently engaged in war.'[2] Others, however, insisted that war sat uneasily with the maintenance of British economic interests. Lord Stormont, a prominent former ambassador, warned the House of Lords in 1791 during a debate on India that 'The expense of a war . . . was a great disadvantage to a commercial country', adding that 'great caution ought to be taken how a nation, like Great Britain, . . . whose chief object it was, to promote its commerce, and consequently its prosperity' became involved in war.[3]

Given such objections to the notion that Britain's overseas expansion depended upon the effective use of military and naval power, any exploration of the dynamic relationship between war and empire should start by considering the principal arguments against militarism as a driver of imperial expansion. Those arguments arose from the political attachment in London to limited government and restricted expenditure, the confused management of Britain's overseas interests, and a range of ideological objections to expanded overseas commitments and to empire itself. A further set of reservations has been raised concerning the nature and strength of national political and popular support for war and expansion. Contentions that foreign wars galvanized national sentiment have been rebutted with counter proposals that national mobilization reflected instead the strength of people's attachments to their localities, and that much patriotic and nationalistic sentiment focused on liberties and rights, not on might. A further obstacle to the interdependence of imperial expansionism and the successful conduct of war has long been the reputation the British had for military inadequacy. This chapter will therefore conclude with a review of claims that Britain's military record was far too weak to sustain a world-conquering role.

Dilemmas of imperialism

The apparent contradiction between Britain's commercial preoccupations and the use of war to advance the country's interests was widely debated in the eighteenth century. Many in the governing elite and Enlightenment intellectuals in Britain doubted whether war even qualified as a necessary evil. Economic development and diversification indicated that the growth of commercial interests and the middle classes would reduce both the predilection and ability of governments to resort to war. War was described instead as the province of monarchs and aristocracies, with their quest for territorial possessions and the prestige, privileges, perquisites, and profits to be secured through rulership rather than commerce. Thus when France went to war with Britain in February 1793, Charles James Fox, the leading Whig politician of his age and persistent critic of royal influence, insisted that the hostilities stemmed from the efforts of George III and his submissive prime minister, William Pitt the Younger, to increase monarchical power.[4]

The tension between Britain's projection of military and naval power overseas and the celebration of commercial society was strikingly revealed during the mid- and late 1770s, when the British government confronted the rebellious American colonies by despatching the largest army ever to that date sent overseas from Britain. Three influential British writers of the late eighteenth century doubted the war-making capacity of an increasingly middle-class society. Edward Gibbon, the first volume of whose magisterial *Decline and Fall of the Roman Empire* appeared in 1776, questioned in 1775 whether the forces then deployed could quash the Americans.[5] His analysis of Rome's empire underscored the need for a cohesive and 'national' army locked into the metropolis and its values if an increasingly affluent society were to sustain a mighty and wide-flung empire.[6] While Gibbon provided an example of how an imperial state might lose its military capability, Adam Smith's *Inquiry into the Wealth of Nations*, also published in 1776, concluded that empires based upon military authority were financially irrational. Smith pressed the case for jettisoning the mercantilist mind-set which viewed colonies as essential to European maritime states' resources and power. Even though he predicted that political inertia rather than economic rationality would ensure empires' survival, Smith saw commercial societies as inherently incapable of sustaining imperial armies.[7]

The third commentary on empire and war came in Tom Paine's *Common Sense*, published in 1776 to advance the case for American independence. Paine asserted that monarchies were tyrannies founded ultimately upon medieval conquest, and that commercial republics ruled by the middle classes and skilled artisans would govern for 'the public good', thereby promoting peace.[8] Republicanism denied claims that royal rule, whose virtues had been re-emphasised since 1689, would provide stability, a constraint upon mere factionalism and localism, and a constitutional order founded upon the central principle of parliamentary supremacy.[9] Paine's claims inspired radicals throughout the late eighteenth and nineteenth centuries in their deep hostility to standing armies and their association of war with monarchical and aristocratic power.

These claims met with various rebuttals. One was that Britain, with considerable difficulty, had developed since the Revolution of 1689 the only constitutional monarchy and the leading Protestant state among the Great Powers of Europe. As commercial activity stretched British interests across the globe, British governments responded to increasing potential challenges from imperial rivals by strengthening London's role in naval and military defence arrangements and preparations, as well as in wider issues of colonial governance. Such measures in the 1770s and early 1780s met failure in America, success in India, and a mixed outcome in Ireland.[10] War and the extension of control over colonies resulted from international rivalries arising from the rapid progress of commercialization. War and commercial interest thus became intimate bedfellows not polar opposites.

A second counter-argument was that British governments prevented the army from garnering excessive power or authority from war and deliberately avoided the creation of a self-consciously 'professional' army separated from civil society. By fostering an officer corps which had close and deep ties with the landowning elite and those attached to it, such as the clergy of the Church of England, politicians felt confident that a 'civil-ianized' army would pose no praetorian threat to the state.[11] This struggle to limit the domestic role of the army and the generally non-militaristic thinking of the elite encouraged a third argument, that military power was a subsidiary factor in the making of the empire. Even the experience of the American Revolution did not diminish a British conviction that theirs was indeed an empire of liberty. After the wars of 1776–83, interest in empire focused not on any military lessons to be learned, but upon the regulation and expansion of imperial trade and the readjustment of Britain's con-stitutional relationship with its colonies.[12]

Underpinning counter-arguments to the intellectual assault upon war-like monarchies was a preoccupation among the British 'political nation' with countervailing power. Authority in London over policy-making was extremely fragmented, the legacy of historical inertia and deliberate efforts to prevent undue concentrations of influence. British territorial possessions in India were controlled by the East India Company, not the crown. But there was also a working model of empire as a loose collection of interests and territories whose tighter control might merely, as in the American case, intensify disagreements.[13] If much administrative attention in London was given to the army and navy, which together accounted for 60% or so of the national government's annual expenditure in the later eighteenth century, there was little debate over the armed services' imperial role or capabilities. Moreover, colonial issues tended to be dealt with in *ad hoc* ways. When problems exploded in North America during the late 1760s, a third Secretary of State was appointed to run a new American Department. So, too, when controversy flared over the East India Company's administration in India, Pitt's government created in 1784 a political and bureaucratic framework for supervising Indian policies, with a middle-ranking ministerial post – the President of the Board of Control – being established to work with and supervise the East India Company, which remained as the ruling authority in India until 1858. The colonies, originally overseen by the President of the Board of Trade, were handed over to the department responsible for military strategy and policy in the 1790s to form the portfolio for the newly created Secretary of State for War and the Colonies. Only in 1854 was a separate Colonial Office established at Whitehall. While bureaucracies do not define the world, they help describe the ways in which politicians envisage the world. Not only did the offices in Whitehall discourage imperial visioning, the Treasury's increasing scrutiny of departments' spending in the late eighteenth century reinforced ministers' habitual reluctance to maintain large defence establishments in peacetime and sustained bureaucratic pressure to cut government expenditure at the conclusion of any war.[14]

Even in wartime, the governing establishment regularly reaffirmed its civilian character. The tone was set, for example, in 1794, when, for a commemorative service at Portsmouth, George III indicated that 'a proper Sermon may be preached on the late victory, wherein may with great propriety be made some remark on a nation attached to religion, good government and obedience to law, in opposition to those hurried on by anarchy, irreligion and every horrid excess'.[15] When the king proclaimed a day of thanksgiving on 29 November 1798 for the battle of the Nile, the service in Anglican churches throughout the country included the prayer:

Continue, we beseech Thee, O Lord, to go forth with our fleets and armies. Inspire . . . the leaders with wisdom and courage and the men with loyalty and intrepidity. Support them in the hour of danger with the recollection, that the battle is for more than gain or glory – for religion and for public liberty, for the independence of their country, for the rights of civil society, for the maintenance of every ordinance, divine and human, essential to the well-being of man.[16]

The primacy of civil and providential concerns was unambiguous.

Equally clear was the absence of concerted political pressure for imperial expansion. For example, there was no major debate on an Indian issue in the House of Commons from 1793 to 1803.[17] As Major-General Sir Arthur Wellesley, later the Duke of Wellington, privately noted of opinion in Britain in 1805: 'The real truth is that the public mind cannot be brought to attend to an Indian subject.'[18] When ministers in London and the Company's directors became alarmed at the pace of expansionism in India, they induced the ailing Lord Cornwallis to return to India in 1805 as governor-general to halt the extension of British territories. Cornwallis advanced a sternly cautious argument:

it is not the opinion only of the Ministers, or of a party, but of all reflecting men of every description that it is physically impracticable for Great Britain, in addition to all other embarrassments, to maintain so vast and so unwieldy an empire in India, which annually calls for reinforcements of men and for remittances of money, and which yields little other profit except brilliant Gazettes.[19]

Later in the nineteenth century the Cambridge historian, J.R. Seeley, famously dismissed expansionism in India as only loosely connected to national political purposes because it was undertaken not by the British state but by British employees of the East India Company: 'Our acquisition of India was made blindly. Nothing great that has ever been done by Englishmen was done so unintentionally, so accidentally, as the conquest of India.' The expansionist impulse came allegedly from those serving in the sub-continent rather than from the metropolis.

Here then was a range of arguments against the notion that a contradiction existed between Britain's commercial expansion and her frequent recourse to war in the late eighteenth and early nineteenth centuries. The empire was one of liberty and the government was constricted in its powers; it was not administered centrally; the army was constitutionally constrained; the army and navy were geared to defending Britain's global interests; expansionism in India was unimportant in British thinking and policy-making. War and empire-building were essentially peripheral to British public consciousness and policy.

This mix of attitudes and arguments cast a long shadow. Nineteenth-century British accounts of imperial expansion from the 1740s focused on almost anything other than military might. The military and naval side of the imperial saga in the nineteenth century seemed to be consigned to books addressed mainly to schoolboys and aimed at conveying exemplary messages of courage, endurance and daring, or to campaign memoirs rushed out to exploit public interest in individual interventions. Victorians learned of Trafalgar, the Peninsular War and Waterloo as episodes in a long-endured international rivalry with France. Those imperial campaigns gaining public notice in Victorian Britain were defensive, brief, and, despite occasional initial setbacks, successful. They formed parts of no distinguishable pattern or sequence of activity, but rather epitomized the heroism, endurance, and resilience of individuals or small groups.[20]

One hundred years of intervening scholarship has revolutionized the way we think about the empire's origins and workings, but the role of force in those processes remains remarkably shadowy. The distortion has become embedded in most general histories of modern Britain, which generally fail to mention the army and navy even as institutions. Accounts of nineteenth-century Britain tend to cite the army's allegedly feeble performance in the Crimean war as an instance of the blighting effects of aristocratic government and the need for reform.[21] Otherwise, the army appears merely in a defensive role as the guarantor of order in times of domestic crisis, notably in 1819, 1831–32, 1837–39, and 1848. About the only active role at all commonly mentioned for the armed services is the Royal Navy's involvement in exploration and in the suppression of the slave trade, suitably civilianized missions compatible with the highest ideals of Victorian thinking about Britain's world role as the purveyor of Christianity, commerce and civilization.[22] Niall Ferguson's lively and best-selling *Empire* very occasionally mentions the part played by the army and navy in British expansionism, but offers scant discussion of this essential instrument of imperial aggrandisement compared with far lengthier attention given to other factors which explain how and why Britain established so vast an empire.[23] There are fine chapters on aspects of military and naval strategy and the sequence of colonial wars in the eighteenth-century volume of the *Oxford History of the British Empire*, but they form a small part of the whole analysis and they do not focus essentially on power projection.[24] The imposing multi-authored and multi-volume histories of the empire produced by Cambridge University Press in the 1930s and by Oxford University Press in the 1990s both include chapters on imperial *defence* as their principal assessments of naval and military developments in the nineteenth century.[25] They reflect the notion that military and naval planning and power were used reactively to secure the empire through local frontier pacifications and extensions which involved motives and means far removed from territorial aggression. Alan Frost has carefully analysed the quest for commodities, and the harbours and bases to sustain the traffic in them, during a period, 1764–1815, which he characterizes as encouraging 'perhaps the most extraordinary imperial expansion in world history'.[26] Military and naval action, however, play little direct role in the processes he describes.

As Christopher Bayly has concluded, the extraordinary imperial acquisitions which Britain made in the forty years following the loss of the thirteen American colonies in 1783 'have continued to be treated almost as aberrations of war'. In most accounts, conquest invariably appeared – if it appeared at all – as a mild and brief precursor to the establishment of British rule. Bayly observes that 'domestic and imperial historians have both implied that what the British do during wars should not be taken too seriously'. British commentators could regard the nineteenth-century empire, when disposed of in the mid-twentieth century, as no more than 'an expensive *cordon sanitaire* for the trading posts and financial centres which they were really interested in'.[27] To argue that the history of empire without the history of war resembles *Hamlet* without the prince might seem exaggerated; but it is certainly *Macbeth* without the dagger. The ambition might be throbbing and the opportunity might be tempting, but without the will to strike and the instrument to strike with, the end cannot be attained. In other words, Alexander Hamilton was correct in drawing attention to the contradiction between Enlightenment hypotheses about the behaviour of commercial societies and the behaviour of a war-making imperial power.

War and national identity

Rejecting the 'liberal' view of an inherent incompatibility between war and commercialization, some contemporaries and later historians have detected positive synergies between war and commercial, increasingly literate, and increasingly nationally self-conscious societies. Looking back on the beginnings of a new age, Carl von Clausewitz in the 1830s claimed that, with the French Revolution, 'Suddenly war again became the business of the people'.[28] The interaction between war and the development of national identities has been reassessed by historians in the last twenty years. The thrust of their work, however, has been to delineate the emergence of a sense of Britishness, using responses to the recurrent wars against France and the extent of mobilization for war as measures of popular identification with a British nation, not to suggest that prolonged warfare created a newly militaristic ethos. Indeed, for Linda Colley, such consciousness energized political activism to broaden civic inclusivity at home, especially during the period of reform in 1828–33. Overseas, the most significant imperial crusade in this reformist surge was the distinctly non-militaristic pressure to abolish slavery.[29]

Two issues have arisen from the exploration of the wartime formation of an enlarged sense of national identity. One is how far the linkage between war and nationalistic sentiment predated the French Revolution. The imperial theme won popular interest and support first in the 1740s with Admiral George Anson's circumnavigation of the world offering the allure of high adventure as well as delivering a blow against the Bourbon enemy. 'Rule Britannia' became a popular song during the same war against France, advancing the three principal claims that 'Britons' existed as a unified people, that their mission was to 'rule the waves', and that they were distinguished from continental enemies in not being 'slaves', free as they were from despotism. The first national anthem came in 1745 when 'God Save the King' became a patriotic rallying cry against the Jacobite rebels seeking to restore the Catholic Stuarts to the British throne.[30] The wars of the 1740s and 1750s seemed to confirm the view that the British empire was essentially an empire of the seas and trading posts serviced occasionally by hinterlands – what Seeley later called a 'world Venice' – and not a territorial empire.[31] National feeling rose again during the Seven Years' War (1756–63), appealing generally to the middle classes, rural and urban, who were attracted to assertions of Britain's independent spirit when demonstrated by overseas successes, particularly against France.[32]

The American war of 1776–83 provoked arguments over military mobilization which have led Stephen Conway to distinguish between ideas of national unity and a sense of shared, if contested, 'Britishness'. Objections to the American war sharpened discussion about the meaning of British liberties and rights. Apart from those who supported the Americans' case for greater representation, or decried the extra taxes needed for the war, many in Britain opposed specific measures taken to recruit soldiers and sailors through impressments or bounties which lured men from essential civilian work. Calling out the militia appeared as objectionable to some as creating a standing army. On the other hand, summoning volunteers and creating a citizens' defence force appealed to some radicals, who saw the right to bear arms as a step towards widening political involvement and representation. But, once France and then other continental powers entered the war from 1778, the conflict became more popular, with expressions of dogged commitment to an increasingly global struggle. Even so, the government remained suspicious of forms of military recruitment which might strengthen their political opponents. For their part, the opposition criticized the disproportionate recruitment of Scots into the armed forces as creating a subordinate group politically obedient to the ministry, and attacked the recruitment of Irish Catholics as a threat to Protestantism. When the British gained a striking naval victory at the Saintes in April 1782, public relief and celebration were palpable, expressing reassurance that Britain's true empire, that of the seas, remained intact. Yet disputes over the political and social impact of mobilization and how it affected national 'character' remained vigorous. For example, when militia service was imposed in 1797 in Scotland it provoked widespread rioting. Supporters argued, among other things, that militia service maintained an ancient cult of manly courage threatened by the corruptions brought by commerce. Opponents insisted that the militia was unacceptably dominated by the socio-political establishment and acted as a conduit for recruitment into the loathed standing army.[33]

Eighteenth-century wars thus fostered debates about the meanings of national identity, even if opinions differed widely over the definitions offered. In 1787, Alexander Hamilton, the proponent of a strong American union in a dangerous world, stressed that the 'the wars in which that kingdom [Britain] has been engaged have, in numerous instances, proceeded from the people'. He asserted that there had been 'almost as many popular as royal wars', with the nation and its representatives either dragging the country into war or prolonging wars when interest would have decreed the cessation of hostilities.[34]

A second issue arising from the wartime formation of an enlarged sense of national identity was how far national consciousness was aroused by external threats and was manifested in wartime organizational demands and imperatives rather than in ideological commitments. Professor J.E. Cookson has stressed that 'national defence remained heavily dependent for a long time on what local leaders could accomplish by voluntary effort'. While the aggregate figures for volunteering and recruitment were even more impressive for the period of warfare from 1793 to 1815 than they had been for the American wars, the level of participation in the armed forces rose and fell over time as the threat of French invasion flowed and ebbed. When volunteering increased sharply in 1798–99, it did so in response to immediate threats of French invasion and took on a nationalistic rather than simply loyalist tinge. The end of the war and massive demobilization after 1815 created a swing against manifestations of military involvement or nationalistic fervour. So, too, if images of John Bull took on a patriotic hue in 1800–15, they represented the national icon as a lover of freedom and hater of autocracy rather than as an uncritical supporter of the prevailing British order. After 1815, John Bull became once again the overtaxed, put-upon embodiment of freedom which had been common in the 1780s and 1790s. Mobilization in the national cause strengthened local power structures more than it extended national institutions.[35] Strong local attachments remained compatible with national pride, which itself was a volatile response to periodic naval and military victories. The conduct of mid-eighteenth-century warfare might best be seen, as Stephen Conway argues, as a process of social, political, denominational and regional partnership-building to overcome a multiplicity of internal differences and divisions.[36]

Such internal differences made it difficult to describe a straightforward national ideal. Eighteenth-century ideas of Britishness may have been bound together by little more than a common desire not to be ruled by the kings of France, or they may have been inspired by an affirmation of Protestantism. On the other hand, admiration for France, if not for its territorially acquisitive rulers, remained strong. Again, those most exercised by a Catholic 'threat' were British religious nonconformists who were often excluded or patronized by the governing establishment at home.[37] Intense disputes about the 'true' meanings of Britishness thus proliferated. The true Briton might insist that consent came before obedience, individualism before corporatism, liberty before deference. The debate, once started, acknowledged that definitions, however vigorously contested, were significant because the identity which people struggled to define had deeper meaning.[38] Yet from widespread wartime discussions about national identity, one factor seemed clear: militarism was a marginal consideration, defining Britons by its absence rather than its centrality.

If militarism figured little in idealistic debates about Britishness, wartime service in the militia and volunteers helped to raise national consciousness. At the height of the war scare in 1757 a new system required all 18- to 45-year-old men to be available for balloting to meet the quota numbers required for the militia from each county. Yet men selected in each county were permitted to find or pay £10 for substitutes, and this practice was widespread. During wartime, militia service became full-time.[39] Governments, however, remained suspicious of the military reliability of militia drawn by ballot from the whole population or made up by substitutes from among the poor. The threat of French invasion in 1778–79 led the government to foster the formation of volunteers, intended solely for local defence and organized on a temporary basis. Successful volunteering in years of danger was followed by a decline in numbers and disbandment with the return of peace. Volunteers were again organized from 1794 and became very significant in 1797–1801, with over 110,000 of them enrolled in 1800. There were varying tax concessions, exemptions from the militia ballot, payments for active service, and government supplies of arms, clothing and accoutrements to attract volunteering. These forces remained part-time (unlike the wartime militia) and could stimulate middle-class militarism. In 1797, Walter Scott, then a young advocate, enthusiastically helped form a volunteer company, the Royal Edinburgh Volunteer Light Dragoons, of 100 gentlemen who paid for their own horses and uniforms; Scott became 'quite a military man', flourishing in an atmosphere of military drilling and organization.[40] But most volunteers by 1800 were probably poor men whose martial skills and political reliability were not necessarily of the highest order.[41] Given doubts about soldiers' reliability, the authorities posted them away from their home districts and in the process broadened their British horizons; the Glamorgan Regiment of Militia, for example, spent only two years in Wales during its twenty-one years' service during the period 1793–1816.[42] The volunteer movement stimulated patriotism and interest in the military, but paradoxically arose because governments distrusted the national loyalties of militiamen compelled to serve in wartime.

Even if wartime recruitment into the army and militia promised to develop soldiers' sense of Britishness, the political and military establishment remained uncertain about the depth of the troops' national attachments. When, in April 1797, military reinforcements were required for Ireland, the Duke of York as commander-in-chief stressed that 'as almost the whole of the recruits of the infantry of the line are Irish it would be by no means a politick measure to send any of the regular battalions to Ireland'. Instead, he despatched to Ireland five regiments of non-regulars recruited in England and Scotland. Again, the Duke noted in September 1797 that maintaining order in Scotland might best be ensured with non-Scottish soldiers: 'Though there is not the least reason to doubt that the Scotch Fencibles would do their duty perfectly well in Scotland, yet I have thought it more advisable in case of accident to bring so many Scotch Fencible Regiments of Cavalry as possible southward and to relieve them by the English Fencibles'.[43]

Despite such doubts and the widespread disavowal of militarism as a characteristic of Britishness, military and naval success contributed in two ways to promoting national identity. Wartime mobilization was instrumental in forging national consciousness for at least some participants. And an enduring model of a civilianized British militarism, even if ignored or rejected by many in Britain, emerged by the 1820s from Britain's prolonged engagement in global campaigning, as a hallmark of the officer caste and among members of the landed elite.

The development of a 'positive' connection between British identity and military prowess certainly took practical shape in military recruitment. Britishness initially sat uneasily with Jacobites' loyalties or with their rebellions in Scotland in 1715 and 1745. Yet Jacobitism's appeal palled when Britishness was being fanned by hostility to France and to Catholicism during the war of the Austrian Succession. By 1830 Scotland as a whole supplied 13.6% of the British army's NCOs and soldiers, considerably more than its 9.5% share of the UK population.[44] Ireland remained more problematic for military policy-makers for far longer, since even the Protestant minority did not necessarily regard themselves as British. Fears for the British government's control over Ireland continued throughout the eighteenth and into the early nineteenth centuries. Yet to regard the British imperium over Ireland as the product of a garrison state raises its own difficulties. The number of British troops maintained in Ireland varied considerably over time, with the proportion of all troops stationed in the UK assigned to Ireland falling occasionally well below the Irish share of the national population. Many among the Catholic majority fought loyally in the British army, which lifted all restrictions on their receiving commissions up to the rank of colonel in 1793. Irishmen participated significantly in the British military-imperial adventure. In 1830 Ireland provided 42.2% of the NCOs and soldiers of the British army, from 32.2% of the UK's population. The British army thus acted both to control Scotland (until the 1770s) and Ireland and to integrate some of their male inhabitants into a prominently British institution. With some 55.8% of the troops in 1830 coming from two countries which contributed 41.7% of the UK's population, this was a successful if particular way of asserting Britishness.[45]

British military incompetence

In February 1944, Winston Churchill reflected gloomily on the fortunes of the Anglo-American force which had landed on the Italian coast at Anzio, intending to break through to Rome only to meet vigorous and bloody German resistance: 'I had hoped that we were hurling a wild cat on to the shore, but all we got was a stranded whale.'[46] The contrast between the aggressive expectations of power projection and the floundering reality of many military British interventions would have been familiar to students of the wars of 1793–1815, including Churchill.

Widespread criticism was customarily heaped on British military performance in the late eighteenth century and early nineteenth century. Some of that criticism was politically motivated. Charles James Fox, who spent two decades from 1784 opposing George III and his prime minister, William Pitt the Younger, dismissed the continental campaign which ended in April 1795 as one 'of defeat, of disaster, and almost irretrievable ruin' chronicled in 'almost daily gazettes crowded with calamity and ruin'.[47] John Fortescue, the pre-eminent early twentieth-century historian of the British army, wrote idealistically of the army as an autonomous organization whose standards and skills should be maintained and improved unsullied by politicians' inept interference. He attributed the failure of the campaign of 1793–95 to incompetent leadership at every level. Junior officers obtained their commissions through purchase or connections and they took little serious interest in their duties except when stimulated by the prospect of dashing into battle. Many battalion commanders lacked experience and owed their positions to jobbery or a capacity to raise new regiments among their labourers, tenants and local networks. Too few generals were assigned to the army and their defects were exposed by the rigorous demands of the campaign. Meanwhile, the minister responsible back in London, Henry Dundas, stood in Fortescue's dock as the worst possible exemplar of the opinionated yet ill-informed politician, incapable of the consistent or realistic management of complex and widely dispersed forces and ever prone to chasing after opportunistic but chimerical objectives. Throughout the 1780s and early 1790s, the prime minister, William Pitt the Younger, was guilty of 'scandalous neglect' of the army.[48] Adding to this dire litany, Arnold Harvey has stressed that for the 1800s 'Britain's main asset in the war was her wealth'. Her armed services were scarcely outstanding; 'the officer corps had not yet become properly professional', with instead a generally poor calibre of officers, who lacked technical competence, particularly in grasping the interrelationships of numerous military elements to the whole, and who were excessively subject to political interference. And at the top of the command pyramid in the 1790s and 1800s sat generals who were simply incompetent.[49]

More generally, Britain's global projection of power has seemed to owe little to military efficiency. According to Bruce Lenman, Britain's 'use of military power to create an Empire was often faltering and uncertain' in the period 1763–93. Edward Ingram argues that the victory at Waterloo in 1815 marked an exceptional British success in an otherwise mediocre record in war, from defeat in 1783 through repeated reverses in the four conflicts against France in 1793–1814, to failure to shape events in Greece in the 1820s and to resolve the Egypt–Ottoman dispute of 1832, to humiliation in Afghanistan in 1842. Victories at sea meant nothing in this analysis: 'One of the most overrated symbols of Great Britain is the Royal Navy, and the established, or should one say Establishment, history of its performance in the Napoleonic Wars is a fraud.' Britain, in this view, failed to protect her key trade with Europe during the wars of 1793–1815, could not command the seas because most of her overseas bases were not self-sufficient, and did not command interior lines of communication.[50] Analysing what he terms 'the age of battles' from 1648 to 1815 in Europe, Russell Weigley noted: 'It is one of the most impressive achievements of history that the British erected so much wealth and power on a foundation of no more than a collection of wooden, square-rigged sailing ships, at their biggest about 200 feet or seventy metres in length.' The British simply exploited two power vacuums to build their eighteenth-century empire. First, the indigenous peoples of North America, the Caribbean islands, and India 'did not yet possess the social cohesion or the sense of nationhood, apart from their relative backwardness in military technology, that would have enabled them to halt European aggression'. Secondly, the British confronted and defeated such opponents because they faced no real challenge from any competing European naval power in the mid-eighteenth century when they projected their own forces across the far oceans. 'It was not sea power as an instrument of war that built the British Empire . . . so much as sea power as a means of moving into power vacuums.'[51] Such an interpretation virtually removes the 'military factor' from any significant role in forming either the empire or Britishness.

Of course, ample evidence can be found to support the case for military inadequacy. When the British went to war with France in 1793 they did not secure their first clear victory in a significant land battle until 1801, and that was in Egypt against an isolated and demoralized opponent. The next did not come until 1806, in southern Italy, in a minor battle which was followed by a British evacuation. The big interventions in Flanders in 1793–95 and 1799 ended ignominiously with British withdrawals; the campaign of 1799 has been described by its most recent historian as disastrously managed.[52] Ten years later an expedition to Holland, commanded by the 2nd Earl of Chatham, became a byword for futility and for massive losses suffered through disease. Even in the Peninsular War, Wellington's early victories were followed by reversals and retreats, and only from May 1813 did a self-sustaining sequence of advances unfold. Wellington repeatedly complained of the shortcomings of senior officers, starting with the generals who superseded him in Portugal in 1808 and continuing with some of those sent to the peninsula from 1809. Despite his rigid insistence on officers having to be gentlemen, he was scathing in 1812 about his cavalry, led by the mostly gentlemanly cadre of his officer corps, deploring the 'trick our officers of cavalry have acquired of galloping at everything, and then galloping back as fast as they gallop on the enemy. They never . . . think of manoeuvring before an enemy – so little that one would think they cannot manoeuvre, excepting on Wimbledon Common'. Nor did experience of war improve military organization. Five weeks before Waterloo in 1815, the field marshal complained: 'I have got an infamous army, very weak and ill equipped, and a very inexperienced Staff.'[53] A recent, well-received history of the battle of Waterloo repeatedly reminds us of the British officer corps' heroic amateurism.[54] Despite Wellington's extraordinary achievements, the aura of profound and subsequently continuing incompetence has been hard to shake off, while the British reputation for inept and unprofessional generalship has retained a powerful hold on popular perceptions and shaped serious scholarship on many aspects of British military history.

Despite their reputation for military incompetence, or more positively, for being 'a polite and commercial people', the British fought for longer than any other people except the French in the years 1790–1815.[55] Indeed, the forty years from 1790 to 1830 covered in this book saw Britain not only expand its industries, commerce and urban population but also wage a war, mount a campaign, or force a boundary extension somewhere in the world in every year except 1820–22 and 1828–30. No comparable period in British history witnessed so warlike and so expansionist a record. That record cannot be reconciled with our prevalent historiographical concentration on a non-militaristic or anti-militaristic state.

Conclusion

This book seeks to explain how the dramatic expansion of Britain's global interests came about and how it was influenced by and in turn shaped the ways in which British policy-makers and the socio-political establishment at home wrestled with this recurrent tension between their commitment to civilian government and international peace and their acquisition of enlarged global responsibilities. The contention of this book is that war and the use more generally of military and naval force was central to that process. Britain was clearly not a country primarily or principally organized for the purposes of war. Its society and economy were fluid and dynamic in this period and it is perfectly reasonable that our historical image of a country undergoing major agricultural, commercial, industrial, demographic, cultural, political and social changes should be formed from a complex mosaic rather than from bold delineations.

But among this multiplicity of developments it is equally reasonable to insist that British governments ensured the country's security and interests in a competitive and often dangerous world by deploying and using considerable military and naval power. In many circumstances and at critical times, Britain acted aggressively to acquire additional possessions or extend its political influence. Very rarely, if ever, did such expansionism emanate from public enthusiasm for imperial ventures. Nor was the political elite in London united in any commitment to or pressure for imperial acquisitions. Quite the contrary, it is easy to see how the study of political debate and policy-making at home leads to a largely parochial view of Britain's role in the wider world other than its interest in international trade and finance. Yet a London-centric concentration on government policy-making fails to

capture the extent and reach of British expansionism and the pervasiveness of the application of force to attain objectives which were often
defined locally by British officials or officers, irrespective of grand designs
drawn up or, more frequently not drawn up, in the metropolis. At the
same time, some leading politicians and senior officers in the navy and the
army, which were the state's two most prominent and well-funded organizations, vigorously pursued expansionist aims. A key issue to be explored
is how far such expansionism was simply responsive to particular pressures
or developments, or wartime challenges, or arose from more persistent
impulses from London. But the British impact on the wider world and the
extension of the empire cannot be understood without grasping the extent
and frequency of the British use of military and naval force, whether its
application arose from metropolitan or peripheral reactions.

Before examining the process of British power projection over the period
1790–1830, we need to consider an alternative position: that there were
significant British stakeholders in empire, that the impact of the French
Revolution upon the conduct of war needs to be seen in a less dramatic
context than is typically the case, that British military capability was far
more consistently robust than many standard accounts suggest, and that
the association between aristocratic domination and the British armed
forces created a particular and viable form of militarism. The book will
then proceed to demonstrate Britain's widespread and persistent use of
force from 1790 to 1830. Why and how war was used by politicians as
an instrument of policy will be assessed across a wide range of contexts
and conflicts. In order to determine how competent the British were as
practitioners of war requires careful and detailed attention to the full
range of challenges which the army and Royal Navy were deployed to
overcome. Only by appreciating Britain's effectiveness as a military and naval
power can the fundamental underpinnings of the empire be understood.

Notes and references

1 P.J. Marshall, 'Imperial Britain', *Journal of Imperial and Commonwealth History*, XXIII (1995), 379–94; quote at p. 391.

2 Alexander Hamilton, James Madison and John Jay, *The Federalist* (London, 1971), p. 23 (no. VI).

3 *The Times*, April 12, 1791, p. 2.

4 L.G. Mitchell, *Charles James Fox* (London, 1997), pp. 108–35.

5 Ian Simpson Ross, *The Life of Adam Smith* (Oxford, 1995), p. 264.

6 Edward Gibbon, *Decline and Fall of the Roman Empire*, 7 vols (London, 1903 edn), Vol. I, pp. 9–12, 63–65; Vol. II, pp. 199–206.

7 Adam Smith, *An Inquiry into the Nature and Causes of the Wealth of Nations*, 2 vols (London, 1910 edn), Vol. II, pp. 192, 426–30.

8 Eric Foner, *Tom Paine and Revolution* (Oxford, 1976), pp. 74–78, 87.

9 Janice Potter, *The Liberty We Seek. Loyalist Ideology in Colonial New York and Massachusetts* (Cambridge, MA, 1983), pp. 167–69, 179–80; Brendan McConville, *The King's Three Faces: The Rise and Fall of Royal America, 1688–1776* (Chapel Hill, NC, 2006), pp. 212–19, 253–55, 286–99.

10 P.J. Marshall, *The Making and Unmaking of Empires: Britain, India, and America c.1750–1783* (Oxford, 2005), pp. 161, 366–79.

11 John Brewer, *The Sinews of Power: War, Money and the English State, 1688–1783* (London, 1989), pp. 40, 42–63; Alan J. Guy, 'The army of the Georges 1714–1783' in David Chandler with Ian Beckett, *The Oxford History of the British Army* (Oxford, 1996), pp. 92–111, esp. 97, 104.

12 Vincent T. Harlow, *The Founding of the Second British Empire 1763–1793*, Vol. II *New Continents and Changing Values* (London, 1964).

13 H.V. Bowen, 'British conceptions of global empire, 1756–83', *Journal of Imperial and Commonwealth History*, XXVI (1998), 1–27. These issues are further explored in Marshall, *The Making and Unmaking of Empires*. He argues (pp. 373–79) that 'the British' were expanding their empire in India while trying to stiffen their control over the American colonies in parallel developments; there was no single model of empire and no sense of a shift to India as compensation for the loss of America.

14 J.E.D. Binney, *British Public Finance and Administration, 1774–1792* (Oxford, 1958), pp. 253–54; C.J. Bartlett, *Castlereagh* (London, 1966), p. 136; Norman Gash, *Mr. Secretary Peel* (London, 1985 edn), p. 93.

15 A. Aspinall (ed.), *The Later Correspondence of George III*, 5 vols (Cambridge, 1968), Vol. II, p. 220.

16 By His Majesty's Special Command, *A Form of Prayer and Thanksgiving to Almighty God* (London, 1798), pp. 7–8. (I have modernized eighteenth-century capitalization here and throughout.)

17 P.J. Marshall, *The Impeachment of Warren Hastings* (Oxford, 1965), pp. 187–88.

18 J.R. Seeley, *The Expansion of England* (London, 1895 edn), p. 207; Duke of Wellington (ed.), *Supplementary Despatches and Memoranda of Arthur, Duke of Wellington, India, 1797–1805*, 12 vols (London, 1858–65), Vol. IV, p. 539.

19 Charles Ross (ed.), *Correspondence of Charles, First Marquis Cornwallis*, 3 vols (London, 1859), Vol. III, p. 545.

20 John M. Mackenzie, *Propaganda and Empire: The manipulation of British Public Opinion 1880–1960* (Manchester, 1984), pp. 178–83, 203–15; Jeffrey Richards, 'Popular imperialism and the image of the army in juvenile literature' in John M. MacKenzie (ed.), *Popular Imperialism and the Military, 1850–1950* (Manchester, 1992), pp. 80–108. The works of W.G. Fitchett might be taken as exemplars: *Fights for the Flag* (London, 1898), *Deeds That Won the Empire* (London, 1899), *The Tale of the Great Mutiny* (London, 1901). There is little on the military history of British expansionism in Bernard Porter, *The Absent-Minded Imperialists: What the British Really Thought about Empire* (Oxford, 2004), pp. 48–50, 80–81. For the Anglocentric approach to British fighting against Napoleon and increasing jingoism in late Victorian history textbooks, see Valerie E. Chancellor, *History for their Masters: Opinion in the English History Textbook 1880–1914* (Bath, 1970), pp. 122–23, 135–38; Seeley, *Expansion of England*, pp. 10, 205, 207.

21 Harold Perkin's classic analysis, *The Origins of English Society, 1780–1880* (London, 1969), contains no index references to the army or navy; even its long chapter discussing the lineaments of 'The Old Society' ignores those powerful institutions. A more recent social history, Edward Royle's *Modern Britain: A Social History 1750–1985* (London, 1987), similarly omits any mention of the army or navy. Asa Briggs's long-enduring *The Age of Improvement, 1783–1867* (London, 1959) offers an extensive discussion on the impact of war, 1793–1815, but has relatively little on either the army and navy, or on the extent of fighting. An exceptionally wide-ranging discussion of British identities over time has no index references to the army, navy or militarism. Keith Robbins, *Great Britain: Identities, Institutions and the Idea of Britishness* (London, 1998).

22 For example, Norman Gash, *Aristocracy and People: Britain 1815–1865* (London, 1979), pp. 5–7, 214–17, 300–04; Norman McCord, *British History 1815–1906* (Oxford, 1991), pp. 53–54; Boyd Hilton, *A Mad, Bad, and Dangerous People? England 1783–1846* (Oxford, 2006), pp. 558, 570–71, 586–87, 612–13.

23 Niall Ferguson, *Empire: How Britain Made the Modern World* (London, 2004 edn), pp. 144–45, for example, offers an extremely short account of the role of force in India. An enduring classic makes relatively brief mention of military and naval power in the early nineteenth century: Ronald Hyam, *Britain's Imperial Century, 1815–1914: A Study of Empire and Expansion* (London, 2002 edn), pp. 1–73. Other influences on expansionism figure far more prominently than military and naval power in Bill Nasson, *Britannia's Empire: Making A British World* (Stroud, 2004), pp. 68–102. T.O. Lloyd, *The British Empire 1558–1995* (Oxford, 1996 edn) has a chapter 'Expansion without effort 1815–1854' which scarcely mentions warfare or naval activity.

John Darwin's more general analysis, *After Tamerlane: The Rise and Fall of Global Empires, 1400–2000* (London, 2007) is strong on geopolitics and economic developments, but has relatively little on military and naval 'factors'. A similar point is made in a useful literature review: Jeremy Black, 'Britain as a Military Power, 1688–1815', *Journal of Military History*, 64 (2000), 159–77.

24 Bruce P. Lenman, 'Colonial wars and imperial instability, 1688–1793', N.A.M. Rodger, 'Sea-power and empire, 1688–1793', Michael Duffy, 'World-wide war and British expansion, 1793–1815' in P.J. Marshall (ed.), *The Eighteenth Century* (Oxford, 1998), pp. 151–207. A stimulating exploration of Britain's maritime world includes an acute analysis of the relative unimportance of the navy to the empire: Stephen Conway, 'Empire, Europe and British naval power' in David Cannadine (ed.), *Empire, the Sea and Global History: Britain's Maritime World, c.1760–c.1840* (London, 2007), pp. 22–40. David French *The British Way in Warfare 1688–2000* (London, 1990), provides a fine, closely worked reassessment, but does not examine imperial conflicts for this period.

25 W.C.B. Tunstall, 'Imperial defence, 1815–1870' in J. Holland Rose, A.P. Newton, E.A. Benians (eds), *The Cambridge History of the British Empire*, Vol. II (Cambridge, 1940), pp. 806–41; Peter Burroughs, 'Defence and imperial disunity' in Andrew Porter (ed.), *The Nineteenth Century*, Vol. III of *The Oxford History of the British Empire* (Oxford, 1999), pp. 320–45.

26 Alan Frost, *The Global Reach of Empire: Britain's Maritime Expansion in the Indian and Pacific Oceans 1764–1815* (Melbourne, 2003), pp. 3–6, 11–12, 143–46, 191, 206–07, 292–93, 313. There is some discussion of naval operations in 1776–83 on pp. 91–96, 111.

27 C.A. Bayly, *Imperial Meridian: The British Empire and the World, 1780–1830* (Harlow, Essex, 1989), pp. 248–49. An exception is Jeremy Black, *Britain as a Military Power, 1688–1815* (London, 1999). He argues (pp. 267, 271–82, 288–93) that, despite shortages and impediments, Britain became 'the strongest state in the world' by 1815, as a result of success in the wars of 1793–1815.

28 Carl von Clausewitz, *On War*, edited and translated by Michael Howard and Peter Paret (Princeton, NJ, 1989), pp. 589–93.

29 Linda Colley, *Britons: Forging the Nation, 1707–1837* (London, 1994 edn).

30 J. Thomson, 'Rule Britannia' in Francis Turner Palgrave (ed.), *The Golden Treasury* (London, 1954 edn), p. 140.

31 Seeley, *The Expansion of England*, p. 334.

32 Bob Harris, ' "American idols": empire, war and the middling ranks in mid-eighteenth-century Britain', *Past and Present*, 150 (Feb. 1996), 111–141; Kathleen Wilson, *The Sense of the People: Politics, Culture and Imperialism in England, 1715–1785* (Cambridge, 1995).

33 Foner, *Tom Paine and Revolution*, pp. 64–65; Stephen Conway, *The British Isles and the War of American Independence* (Oxford, 2000), pp. 118–22, 157–65, 316–25, 353–55; Stephen Conway, 'The politics of British military and naval mobilization, 1775–83', *English Historical Review*, 112 (1997), 1179–1201. John Robertson, *The Scottish Enlightenment and the Militia Issue* (Edinburgh, 1985), pp. 133–35, 150–51.

34 Hamilton, *The Federalist*, pp. 23–24.

35 J.E. Cookson, *The British Armed Nation, 1793–1815* (Oxford, 1997), pp. 91–94, 245, 253–54, 261–63; Miles Taylor, 'John Bull and the iconography of public opinion in England c.1772–1929', *Past and Present*, 134 (1992), 93–128.

36 The case for the compatibility of the intensification of both local and national pride is made by Stephen Conway, 'War and national identity in the mid-eighteenth-century British Isles', *English Historical Review*, 116 (2001), 863–893; *War, State, and Society in Mid-Eighteenth-Century Britain and Ireland* (Oxford, 2006).

37 Hilton, *A Mad, Bad, and Dangerous People?*, pp. 238–39.

38 For a sophisticated review of the literature, see J.C.D. Clark, 'Protestantism, Nationalism, and national identity, 1660–1832', *Historical Journal*, 43 (2000), 249–76.

39 Ian F.W. Beckett, *The Amateur Military Tradition 1558–1945* (Manchester, 1991), pp. 62–89; Gary Steppler, *Britons, to Arms!* (Stroud, 1992), p. 8.

40 Steppler, *Britons, to Arms!* pp.14–16, 21–24, 73; John Sutherland, *The Life of Walter Scott* (Oxford, 1995), pp. 66–68.

41 Beckett, *The Amateur Military Tradition*, pp. 81–88.

42 Bryn Owen, *Welsh Militia and Volunteer Corps, 1757–1908*, Vol. II, *The Glamorgan Regiments of Militia* (Caernarfon, 1990), pp. 38–41, 45–49, 53–58, 66–67.

43 Aspinall (ed.), *The Later Correspondence of George III*, Vol. II, pp. 565, 621; Owen, *Glamorgan Regiments*, pp. 47–48, 54.

44 Christopher Duffy, *The '45* (London, 2003), pp. 88, 145, 543, 562–63; Edward Spiers, *Army and Society, 1815–1914* (London, 1980), p. 50; Robert Clyde, *From Rebel to Hero: The Image of the Highlander, 1745–1830* (East Linton, 1995), pp. 150–53.

45 Spiers, *Army and Society*, p. 50. Disproportionate recruitment from disadvantaged minorities is not atypical of armies more generally; in the U.S. army in 1989 some 25% of active-duty recruits were black, while only 14% of the enlistment-age population was black (J.K. Galbraith, *The Culture of Contentment* (London, 1992), p. 131).

46 Roy Jenkins, *Churchill* (London, 2002 edn), p. 729.

47 *The Times*, 22 January 1795, p. 1.

48 John Fortescue, *A History of the British Army, 1763–1793*, 13 vols (London and New York, 1899–1930), Vol. IV: 96–97, 124–26, 295–98, 302–03, 322; J.W. Fortescue, *The British Army 1783–1802* (London, 1905), pp. 3, 9 13–16, 28–30.

49 A.D. Harvey, *Collision of Empires: Britain in Three World Wars, 1793–1945* (London, 1992), pp. 3, 128–30, 192–93.

50 Lenman, 'Colonial Wars and Imperial Instability', p. 167; Edward Ingram, *Commitment to Empire: Prophecies of the Great Game in Asia 1797–1800* (London, 1981), pp. 1–2, 6.

51 Russell Weigley, *The Age of Battles: The Quest for Decisive Warfare from Breitenfeld to Waterloo* (London, 1991), pp. 162, 230–31.

52 Piers Mackesy, *Statesmen at War: the Strategy of Overthrow, 1798–99* (London, 1974).

53 Elizabeth Longford, *Wellington: The Years of the Sword* (London, 1969, reissued 1972), pp. 184–85, 215, 255–59, 325, 472–73. See also Correlli Barnett, *Britain and Her Army, 1509–1970: A Military, Political and Social Survey* (Middlesex, 1974).

54 Alessandro Barbero, *The Battle: A New History of the Battle of Waterloo*, translated by John Cullen (London, 2005), pp. 28, 187–91. The view that British generals were 'blimps and boneheads' was widely current as late as 1942, and has been thoroughly revised by Davis French, 'Colonel Blimp and the British Army: British Divisional Commanders in the war against Germany, 1939–45', *English Historical Review*, 111 (1996), 1182–1201.

55 Paul Langford, *A Polite and Commercial People: England 1727–1783* (Oxford, 1999), pp. 617–31, 719–25.

CHAPTER 2

British militarism

The case for overseas expansion and a commitment to military efficiency prevailed by the 1810s despite doubts about the value, political morality, and viability of empire. Significant groups in Britain pressed for overseas action. So, too, the limitations of British military and naval capability need to be weighed against exaggerated expectations of military efficiency and scale created by the French Revolution. Moreover, the idea of military competence needs assessing against the challenges of higher command posed by Britain's global interests and role. Despite the anti-militarism of much British political rhetoric and practice, and despite the drive to constrain the military which informed British governance, pressures to use war as an instrument of policy and the relative effectiveness of British armed forces need equal acknowledgement. This chapter will argue that war was central to the expansion of empire in this period by considering prevailing assumptions about Britain's military performance and therefore reputation.

Four issues merit attention. First, the challenges of higher command were more generic and deep-rooted in the nature of war-making than many accounts allow. Secondly, comparisons with the French military experience of the 1790s, particularly regarding the size of armies and the character of the officer corps, will provide a broader framework in which to assess supposed British incompetence. Thirdly, the sheer enlargement in the scale of war-making in the 1790s and the proliferation of overseas commitments created a particular form of British militarism. Finally, British military leaders, whose values critics always linked to monarchy and aristocracy, looked less socially anachronistic in the face of burgeoning French military professionalism than is often alleged.

Stakeholders of empire

Forging a national consciousness and tying the consciousness of national interests to the cause of empire were stimulated by various interest groups with a positive commitment to Britain's global role.[1] The most prominent were the East India Company, which held a monopoly on trade between the East Indies and Britain (though not, in practice, any monopoly on trading by British subjects within the East Indies); the West Indies' interests involved in sugar-production and slave-trading; members of the governing elite; and the armed services.

The East India Company enjoyed significant political power in London and unique links with the British establishment. For example, the First Lord of the Admiralty in the 1770s, Lord Sandwich, had exceptionally close connections with the Company,[2] while Pitt the Younger (prime minister 1783–1801 and 1803–06) and Lord Liverpool (prime minister 1812–27) both had forebears who rose high in the Company's service. The number of MPs with direct East India Company connections increased in the parliaments of the 1770s and 1780s, reaching forty-five in the parliament of 1784–90. These MPs were divided on the specifics of Indian policy, but were united on the importance of India. In 1825 some seventy-seven MPs had Indian interests and were typically men possessing considerable wealth and a willingness to use it to extend their influence and status at home. The East India Company's directors, usually well represented in parliament, normally appointed 338 cadets each year. These posts, mainly in the Company's army, were much desired by members of the ruling establishment as places for their young kinsmen or supporters' kinsmen.[3]

The economies of Britain's Caribbean islands directly depended on imperial regulation and protection. After the American Revolution, West Indian merchants pressed London for a free trade agreement with America, in order to revive the traffic between the British Caribbean islands and the thirteen former mainland colonies. The plantation economy also depended upon the security of the transatlantic trade routes to sustain extraordinarily high levels of slave imports. During the period 1771–90 an estimated 577,000 African slaves were imported into the British colonies in the New World, compared with 369,500 going into France's possessions. By 1789, all the British West Indian islands together held 465,000 slaves, compared with 657,000 in the southern states of the USA. Only 50,000 whites, heavily concentrated in Jamaica and Barbados, lived in the British West Indies. Following the Enlightenment attack on slave trading in the 1790s and that trade's eventual abolition in 1807, the

British government switched from protecting slave-trading to preventing other countries from profiting from that now illegal trafficking. The government was also required to protect and police the Caribbean, for the war brought a boom in sugar prices in the 1790s and a subsequent surge in exporting. Only after 1815 did prices fall again and then world over-production, spurred by the earlier boom in prices, led to a slump in prices in the 1820s.[4] In terms of their commodity output, their need for secure trade routes and their control over a vast labour force, the sugar planters formed a distinctive interest group in imperial policy-making. Although the West Indies lobby in the House of Commons declined in size in the later eighteenth century, to only nine MPs in 1784–90, the West India Committee negotiated commercial issues directly with ministers. The importance of West Indian interests was readily accepted in national policy-making, the defence of the West Indian islands automatically becoming a major commitment in any war against France. In the campaigns of 1793–98 to defend the British West Indies and to conquer French and other colonies there, the British lost far more troops dead and wounded than in the infinitely more celebrated campaigns of the Peninsular War. The protection of merchant convoys from the West Indies was a major priority. In 1809, the British maintained 21,400 troops in the Bahamas, Jamaica and the Leeward Islands, more than were stationed in Ireland and almost as many as were sent that year to Portugal under the future Duke of Wellington. Of those troops, 7,900 were Africans enrolled in West India regiments.[5]

In addition to such interest groups, it has been argued by Cain and Hopkins that the financial and, in the late eighteenth century, still-emerging service sectors of the economy became increasingly involved both with the political establishment – drawn heavily from the landed gentry and aristocracy – and with Britain's world role. This linkage was especially important for and in London, described accurately by Adam Smith as 'the greatest mercantile city in the world'. In 1822, a French observer with a strong interest in reviving his own country's navy commented:

The metropolis of the British empire contains, within its circumference, the most frequented parts of the universe . . . The vessels of a hundred various countries display their colours on the Thames, even in the heart of this immense city . . . The citizens of London are justly proud on viewing the merchant fleets, which daily arrive from sea, or sail down the river . . . They cannot contemplate so interesting a scene without recognising that commerce and the empire of the sea have produced the wealth and grandeur of this great city.[6]

Particularly important in Britain's overseas policy-making was the raising and financing of the National Debt, standing at £133 million in 1763, £245 million in 1783, and £700 million in 1815, with this ballooning commitment being managed by the Bank of England. The number of fundholders soared from perhaps 100,000 in the 1780s to 250,000 in 1815.[7] Investment in that debt and the management of it tied many in London financial circles, and investors beyond, to the national cause and insulated the political establishment from criticisms of the costs of war. Added to these were contractors who secured major government contracts, especially in wartime, and those who bought government bonds. Many became MPs and all benefited from the massive expansion of government spending which occurred during war.[8]

Pitt the Younger, among prime ministers, had strong backing in the City of London. When George III appointed him in highly controversial circumstances, the Corporation sent the king an address congratulating him on his action. Throughout his premiership, Pitt remained essentially a man of Whitehall and Westminster whose rare socializing beyond those confines was in the City, attending to his duties as Master of Trinity House, dining at the East India Company, the Marine Society, the Lord Mayor's banquet, and occasional livery companies. He belonged to the City of London Volunteer Corps. His principal hinterland, beyond his family and political associates, was London finance.[9] The city also became the stage for national commemoration. A lord mayor of London, the print publisher John Boydell, donated in 1790 large paintings of heroic naval images from the early 1780s to be hung prominently for public viewings in the Common Council Chamber of the Corporation of the City of London. Nelson's funeral at St Paul's cathedral was the culmination of a massive pageant, following from the decision in 1795 to make the cathedral the national pantheon for heroic naval and military commanders.[10]

The governing establishment was thus in part involved in war and the extension of empire. By 1800, the lure of overseas service was beginning to inspire ambitious young men. One politician who played an overtly aggressive role in expanding British rule in India, Richard Wellesley, dramatically exemplified what many others aimed for when they ventured, if on a humbler plane, into the wider world. He went to India in 1797–98 expecting to save large sums from his annual income as governor-general, which he duly did, supplemented by a substantial annuity from the East India Company. But, early inspired by imperial adventure (having in 1780 won the University Prize for Latin Verse at Oxford with an elegy on Captain Cook's death), he also hungered to enhance his political reputation and authority. Within a few months of reaching India, he confided in his wife back in London: 'I am in the midst of great projects . . . my plans are of vast extent, but no more than circumstances demand. I shall be most anxious to know what Dundas, Pitt, Grenville and the Speaker think of what I am doing and what I mean to do.' A few months later he informed Lord Grenville, the Foreign Secretary, that his predecessor's administration in India had been 'careless' and 'timid with respect to all our foreign relations' and had been 'little feared or respected by any branch of the civil or military service'. In jocular vein, he referred to their joint dream (they had been close friends as undergraduates) of 'governing the world' and his own intended contribution to that end. A first step was made with the defeat of Tipu Sultan of Mysore in 1799: 'behold me covered with glory. I cannot adequately convey the enthusiasm and admiration of everyone here. I have done in two months something which took three years in Cornwallis' time . . . The whole plan was mine.' Wellesley continued on his expansionist course, giving a suitably grand public gloss to his achievements in 1804: 'The position in which we are now placed is suited to the character of the British nation, to the principles of our laws, to the spirit of our constitution, and to the liberal and comprehensive policy, which becomes the dignity of a great and powerful empire.'[11] Service to the state, while furnishing offices and wealth, provided the means to exercise authority, responsibility, and power. Wellesley's priorities and values, and the yardstick of his success, owed little specifically to India but flowed essentially from his impassioned quest for approval and reward in the metropolis.

Although Richard Wellesley's was an extreme and indeed melodramatic case, his arrival in India coincided with a far more general trend. Service in the army, navy and imperial posts was rapidly becoming a serious career for men hungry for financial reward and enhanced social and/or political status, while also initiating and executing policies of their own. In exploring the relationship between war, empire and national identity, it helps if we recognize from the outset that pride in military and naval service and commitment to empire were more widespread among establishment and professional groups than is usually acknowledged. One particular group was the landowning elite in Ireland, many of whose members were psychologically spurred to ambition as semi-colonial outsiders trying to make their mark on the imperial metropolis and whose experience of rulership led them into an easy acceptance of a British right to rule alien peoples. From such a background came the Wellesley brothers and, for example, Lord Castlereagh who, as Foreign Secretary from 1812 to 1822, helped shape post-Napoleonic Europe. When in March 1815 the

Congress of Vienna issued a declaration against Napoleon, three of the four British signatories were from the Anglo-Irish aristocracy: Field Marshal the Duke of Wellington, Richard Wellesley's brother, Lieutenant-General Lord Stewart, Castlereagh's half-brother, and Lord Clancarty. The fourth, Lord Cathcart, was a Scottish general.

Leaders were not in politics simply to gain, protect, or extend country estates and to secure titles and social prestige. High office provided income, patronage and enhanced status, but it also attracted men from the landowning elite with the opportunity to apply their energy, ambition and even talent to the exercise of power and the extension of the authority of the state. Those who rose highest and stayed at the top longest were 'men of business' who ensured the continued working of the machinery of state. Politicians, administrators and generals continued to be driven by organizational, personal and reputational imperatives to expand British political influence and military control. In 1818 Thomas Munro, a senior official who became governor of Madras in the 1820s, offered an explanation:

Englishmen are as great fanatics in politics as Mahomedans in religion. They suppose that no country can be saved without English institutions. The natives of this country have enough of their own to answer every useful object of internal administration, and, if we maintain and protect them, our work will be easy.[12]

One of Wellington's complaints about the Spanish elite was that personal and political rivalries, fostered but not created by the collapse of the Spanish regime in 1808, subsumed the whole process of government. Generals, nobles, officials, and parliamentarians bickered and struggled for position without any guiding sense of common purpose or commitment to the efficient conduct of business. All suffered from a lack of 'vigour'.[13]

For many of those politicians and officials who dominated the British establishment, conducting the business of the state and maintaining the state's authority were absorbing ends in themselves; the defence and extension of the state's global interests and responsibilities offered an additional and rewarding challenge to at least some of that elite. Any organization, large or small, engenders strong commitments to its preservation, development and growth. Service to the state as an organizational entity exerts an exceptionally powerful influence upon many of those employed by it. Such organizational dynamics were reinforced in this particular case by the social distinction gained through political leadership and by the importance attached to controlling territory by a landowning, rent-raising elite. Inheriting or acquiring, improving and then passing on landed estates were central to aristocratic status and life. The territorial possessions of the state – their defence, economic development and extension – were an extension on a grand scale of this customary impulse to accord primacy to the territorial imperative.

The French comparison

The criticism that empire was unpopular or marginal in the late eighteenth century was matched by the more enduring criticism that the British failed to keep pace in the 1790s and 1800s with the military advances created by the French Revolution. The common charge has been that the British army was simply left behind by the intensification in the 1790s of developments emerging from the so-called 'military revolution' of the previous two hundred years.[14] According to critics, British military operations were on a small scale and the British failed to rival the military advances made by continental European states in accelerating the pace of campaigning, expanding the size of armies, and organizing army battalions into divisions and divisions into corps. Such improvements, capping a long process of change, were implemented most dramatically by the French, whose armies in 1794, in Eric Hobsbawm's phrase, 'were about to enter on twenty years of almost unbroken and effortless military triumph'.[15] While 'effortless' would have struck millions of ordinary French soldiers who suffered death, wounding, or captivity in two decades of strenuous campaigning as curious, the claim conveys a widespread assumption about the inability of France's enemies to embrace the character and consequences of this long military revolution. Such a failure reinforced the image and reality that Britain was incapable of forging an empire by military force.

Yet the relationship between the French revolutionary armies and eighteenth-century military practice remains complex. For example, if we consider tactics, the revolutionaries, in giving priority to the initial attack, built upon earlier efforts to prepare soldiers for the central clash of arms that characterized battle. One purpose of the elaborate drilling and training which eighteenth-century troops received was to prepare them to grasp victory quickly in decisive battles. This priority did not necessarily result from exultant martial *élan*. Frederick the Great of Prussia, for instance, needed quick battlefield successes because he was numerically and financially vulnerable to more populous and wealthier neighbours. The battles themselves were intensely fought with high levels of casualties. The revolutionary wars of the 1790s did not deliver bloodier battles than the armies earlier in the century experienced; they simply delivered more of them, by speeding the pace of campaigning and, for the French, by rapidly replacing casualties with fresh conscripts.[16]

British generals did not fail to display a suitably aggressive spirit when the opportunity for battle offered itself, but were handicapped by lack of experience of large battles and intensely paced campaigns. Examples from their most recent involvement in major wars, in 1775–83, were instructive. The British conveyed to North America the largest army ever sent overseas from Britain up to that date, raising their troop presence throughout North America from 7,000 in April 1775 to some 50,000 by February 1778.[17] Yet these forces fought few and small battles. The largest commitment of British troops to a land engagement, at Brandywine Creek on 11 September 1777, saw each side field only about 12,000 men. On 16 August 1780, one hour's fighting at Camden, South Carolina, delivered what has been described as 'the most crushing victory that British arms every achieved over the Americans in the Revolutionary war'.[18] Yet Lord Cornwallis commanded only 2,233 officers and men, merely 817 of them being regular British soldiers (excluding staff).[19] Even though many British troops serving in North America and the Caribbean in 1780 engaged in expeditions and extensive patrolling and skirmishing, fewer than 1,000 of those 55,000 soldiers participated in any formal battle during the entire year and that tiny battle only lasted for one hour.[20] Wherever the British fought in this global struggle, throughout the campaigning in India in 1778–84 and in the prolonged defence of Gibraltar, besieged by the Spanish in 1780–83, British armies never joined battle with more than 10,000 men in a single, consolidated force.

British military efforts paled beside the force concentrations achieved by their opponents in the two largest engagements of the War of American Independence. Both of those turned out to be massive assaults on besieged positions. At Yorktown in 1781, the French and Americans assembled a force of 16,700 soldiers. The French land commander, the Comte de Rochambeau, a soldier of thirty-seven years' standing, had reputedly taken part in fourteen sieges and his army was well equipped for another one. These land forces were backed up by the French fleet, headed by 36 ships of the line, with its 15,000 seamen.[21] An even greater enemy concentration was amassed in a failed effort to secure Spain's main Spanish objective of regaining Gibraltar. A prolonged siege having failed, the French and Spanish attacked Gibraltar in September 1782 with perhaps 40,000 troops and 200 heavy guns on land, the fire power of 47 ships of the line, and over 200 guns on 10 specially devised battering ships. Although the vastly outnumbered British warded off this assault and, in a major naval achievement, brought an armada of supply ships into Gibraltar during October to relieve the hard-pressed garrison, they never rivalled the French and Spanish in the concentrations of force assembled.[22] Their capacity for modern war seemed circumscribed.

When Britain was drawn into fighting on the continent in 1793, it faced a French revolutionary state which mobilized unprecedentedly large numbers of soldiers for its armies. The *levée en masse* of 1793, consolidated in successive years to provide high and repeated inflows of new manpower, enabled French generals to maintain the offensive momentum of a campaign even after a battle in which they might have suffered 10,000 casualties. In contrast, an Austrian or British commander would pause, if not withdraw, on receiving such a setback in lost manpower. But the *levée en masse* did not mean that the French armies fought in new ways dependent upon an aroused citizenry's commitment, however brilliantly galvanized and coolly channelled, rather than on detailed military skill. The highly effective enhancements made in French battlefield practices – the approach to battle commonly being in column followed by deployment in line, and with deliberate emphasis upon the attack and the bayonet – required and resulted from systematic training. The French victory at Valmy on 20 September 1792 has often been heralded as the result of revolutionary passion and thus as the dawn of a new era. Yet the French vastly outnumbered the Prussians, who probed towards their enemy's defensive position in the expectation that the French army would flee. The French stood their ground because the centre of their position was held by regulars; on the flanks, about three-eighths of the infantry were regulars, while many of the volunteers were relatively experienced soldiers who had served since 1791. The leading generals had been senior officers under the Bourbons – Kellerman, the commander of the army had joined the army in 1752 and served in six campaigns – and ensured that their men deployed in a strong defensive position. Crucial to cowing the Prussians into calling off their probe was French effectiveness during an artillery duel lasting seven hours or so; the French artillery, long distinguished for its calibre, was composed entirely of regulars. The casualties resulting from this probe involving 51,000 French and 34,000 Prussian troops were 480 for the two sides together. Dysentery and food shortages, not revolutionary ardour, obliged the Prussians to withdraw ten days later.[23] British generals could scarcely be expected to perceive immense revolutionary challenges in what they confronted on the continent when the French revolutionary army prevailed through customary advantages buttressed by a sudden accretion of manpower.

Of course, the French army changed profoundly in the wake of the Terror of 1793–94. The removal of aristocrats and the expansion of the army meant that 55% of all officers by 1794 had been corporals in the royal army of 1789. But these men, the master practitioners of drill, imposed the formal disciplines into which they had been so thoroughly inducted, even if they may also have been inspired by revolutionary ideology. Nor has the extent of tactical reform been unquestioned. For example, the French of the 1790s, in developing the eighteenth-century preference for the offensive, probably relied no more heavily on the bayonet than their predecessors had done, although they increased the use of battlefield artillery in attack and light troops to cover their retreats.[24]

The intensification of fighting brought on by the French in the 1790s resulted partly from a more ruthless management of logistics and personnel. Despite proclaiming a political mission to liberate the peoples of countries they invaded, French armies by 1794 needed to advance in order to gain supplies because ample and carefully distributed supplies no longer accompanied French armies on the march. Senior officers were motivated by the prospect of prompt and severe punishment for failure as much as by ideological enthusiasm. During 1793 and 1794 alone, 352 French generals were dismissed from the army and 84 were guillotined.[25] For ordinary soldiers, career opportunities were dramatically boosted. Whereas only 10% of all regimental officers in 1789 had served as privates, 77% of sous-lieutenants commissioned in the period 1802–14 started their careers as privates. NCOs and junior officers had strong career incentives to perform aggressively and with sustained vigour. But this fact had limited explanatory value in assessing British military efficacy, for few accused the British soldier and his leaders at company level, whatever their defects, of fighting without courage and tenacity. Moreover, as the revolutionary regime moved into a Napoleonic dictatorship the French officer corps became less socially fluid. Extremely few soldiers commissioned from the ranks in 1802–14 rose higher than captain, whereas one-third of captains directly commissioned as officers went on to senior rank. Napoleon encouraged a rapprochement with the old aristocracy, and nominated *Ancien Régime* nobles' sons for commission. Moreover, the sons of officers he had enobled began to come forward for military preferment by the 1810s. The officer corps above the rank of captain began to look far less distinctive in character from other armies' higher ranks, the longer Napoleon reigned.[26]

In sum, it is difficult to see how far any other country copied or wished to replicate the French Revolutionary model by executing generals, raising ill-educated masters of drill to higher command, living by systematic plunder, and pressing offensives without regard to casualties because human cannon-fodder could so readily be replaced. These were scarcely the characteristics of a professional 'modern' army that the British would wish to emulate.

One defining characteristic of French revolutionary warfare – and subsequent 'modern' wars – was the involvement of national populations in fighting. Although Frederick the Great developed a form of conscription on a relatively large scale in mid-eighteenth-century Prussia, the raising of mass armies was first seen in 1793–94 in the defence of the new and apparently fragile French republic against Europe's leading powers. It was difficult to arouse equivalent commitment in Britain where invasion threats were occasional and localized, given the country's island geography. But, when such threats loomed, as they did in 1799 and in 1803–05, mass mobilization occurred in Britain as effectively as it did in France. The key difference, however, was that the French republic and empire demanded from its citizens continuing subservience to the nation's war effort. For two decades following 1792, the French state repeatedly waged war, with unprecedented consequences for domestic political control, and a massive drain of casualties. This high level of loss was sustained periodically over a number of years, and not simply when France itself, as in 1792–94 and 1813–14, came under serious threat of invasion. No similar losses of manpower afflicted Britain, the nearest equivalent probably being the devastation suffered by the Spanish people in their national struggle of 1808–13. On the other hand, revolutionary fervour among French soldiers sagged by 1795 and a more restricted system of conscription evolved. When the annual take-up of men eligible for active service increased rapidly from 1809, the number of men marrying, and thereby gaining exemption, soared. For Britain, the parallel experience was the continuing heavy expenditure on the Royal Navy and the accompanying extension of the national debt, demonstrating that the British state could raise unprecedentedly large financial resources for the war effort.[27]

While British governments put substantial financial resources into maintaining the world's largest and most widely distributed navy, the British army did not expand in size or increase the geographical scope of its operations in parallel with continental European experience. By the end of the Napoleonic era, the battle of Leipzig (1813) involved about 400,000 men on the two sides, a total of truly unrivalled magnitude. Napoleon's offensives dazzled by their speed, their coordination of corps operating independently of each other, and the extent of the French imperial armies' reach. The invasion of Russia in 1812 confirmed the emperor's ambition to mount simultaneous and sizeable operations as far apart as Madrid and Moscow. The advance of 600,000 men into Russia, while over 250,000 troops were simultaneously engaged in Spain, displayed war-making on a scale unmatched until the First World War. Again, however, the gap between British effort and the new realities of continental warfare was less extreme than aggregate figures indicate. In sharp contrast to 1914–18, these really vast armies were not maintained in being for years on end. Indeed, the Grand Army in Russia had ceased to exist as an operational entity within seven months of its formation. Moreover, as Rory Muir has pointed out, very large-scale battles cited by historians to demonstrate the expanded arena of warfare were in fact infrequent, and fighting between forces of this size was not prolonged.[28]

Disparaging British military efforts because of their limited scale has been easy rather than accurate. Of course, the British never deployed more than 30,000 of their own troops in battle at one time in Europe and their campaigning, if often courageous, rarely, if ever, dealt sudden decisive blows. But British officers were deeply involved in organizing and leading far larger allied armies, especially in Spain and south-western France in 1809–14 and in Belgium in 1815. If we cast the net farther afield, the scale of operations launched by British armies in India was formidable. For example, the invasions of Mysore in 1792 and 1799 each involved 46,000–47,000 troops drawn from widely dispersed areas of southern and central India. The campaigns against the Marathas in 1803–05 and in 1817–19 stretched across 1,500 miles and involved numerous armies, separately raised and separately run, totalling over 100,000 troops. By March 1815 the attack on Nepal involved 49,000 troops and 56,000 camp followers.[29] Britain's global involvement created many quite different and specific military challenges, often entailing close cooperation between the army and navy, while Indian campaigning and military garrisoning has to be factored into any assessment of the scale of British military commitment and effectiveness.

The British approach to land warfare, typified by the steady accumulation of fighting resources, careful coalition-building, and often cautious if not tentative probes, was not as anachronistic as initial assessments have suggested. Recent analyses of Napoleonic warfare depict war more as process than as a set of discrete, identifiable events. Russell Weigley has argued in addition that allegedly decisive battles failed to yield results. Far from marking a new age of warfare, the conflicts of the 1790s and 1800s, according to Weigley, represented the last instalment of a system of war glorifying decisive battle. Weigley depicts the pursuit of victory in a single, culminating battle as a peculiar phenomenon of warfare arising in the early seventeenth century and ending with Waterloo. Subsequent large-scale wars, notably the American Civil War and the First World War, demonstrated how attrition and prolonged, bloody campaigning prevailed over sudden, annihilatory battle. One can build on that argument by stressing that even Napoleon's repeated battlefield victories were followed by mounting resentment and resistance that led defeated foes to reform their armies, regroup their resources, re-forge their alliances, and resume their armed struggle against French expansionist power and Napoleon's dynastic ambitions. Dramatic decisions in battle did not settle the under-lying political instability which revolutionary doctrines and Napoleonic adventurism unleashed. Both the Peninsular War and the Russian cam-paign of 1812 showed the increasing difficulties of subduing countries through battlefield success.[30] Indeed, Brian Bond has argued that the classic phase of Napoleonic warfare, with speedy campaigns, brilliant manoeuvre operations and politically as well as militarily decisive battles occurred only during 1805–07.[31]

Thus the classic model of French Revolutionary and Napoleonic military organization and war planning did not last. We have seen how the French officer corps became less open to men from ordinary social backgrounds by the 1810s. During the decades after 1815, the armies of Europe reverted to patterns of recruitment and values which had prevailed under the *Ancien Régime*. The real consolidation of the changes brought about by the wars of 1793–1815 did not occur, therefore, according to Gunther Rothenburg, until the Prussians' lightning campaigns of the 1860s and the new approach to military organization, planning, and mass mobil-ization embedded by Helmuth von Moltke as chief of staff from 1857.[32] The full integration of civilian populations with the military through conscription, and the forging of an overriding sense of national political purpose infusing both army and state, became government priorities, at least in unified Germany, in the late nineteenth century, whereas this had not been true in the four or five decades following Waterloo. Even so, it should be stressed that the highly 'modern' German army at the end of the nineteenth century possessed plenty of 'pre-modern' characteristics. Although the officer corps expanded significantly to match the sheer size of the con-script army, the proportion of officers who were aristocrats was about 50% in the 1860s and 30% in the 1910s, with a far higher proportion dominating the senior ranks. Politically, the army remained responsible essentially to the emperor, subject to very limited parliamentary supervision or control.[33] This army, whose organization and operations were subject to the most rigorous staff planning and technological sophistication of any in the late nineteenth-century, remained far removed from the French revolutionaries' ideal of a 'nation in arms' deployed as an instrument of popular political will.

British military leadership

Comparisons between a rigid and backward-looking British army with a dynamic French army have typically focused on the defects of the British officer corps. Yet blanket critiques of leadership often serve as a convenient avoidance of more careful analysis of the challenges facing Britain as a military power. Isolating defective leadership as an explanation for relatively poor British military performance suffers from the genuine difficulty of assessing the efficiency of leadership in any large, complex organization.

The difficulty of making such assessments is well illustrated by judgements on the modern American army's officer corps, the most rigorously selected and trained in world history. Assessments of American senior commanders in the Iraq war include the description of the first head of Central Command in 2003, General Tommy Franks, as someone who reduced all strategic issues to tactical initiatives, and of Lieutenant General Ricardo Sanchez, who became the commander in Iraq, as 'a fine battalion commander who never should have commanded a division, let alone a corps or a nationwide occupation mission'. The occupation mission seemed to be driven by 'a relentless focus on minutiae', summarized by a State Department official as 'All trees, no forest'.[34] Yet the pitfalls of high command remain difficult to counter through prior training. A detailed study of American senior army officers in the first Gulf War of 1991 concluded that American officers commanding companies, battalions and brigades generally dealt capably with the demands of technologically complex and fast-moving operations. In contrast, officers commanding divisions and corps were more typically cautious and even tentative in their approach. Apart from the generic explanation that there was greater risk of failure at the higher levels of command, the more precise explanation was that senior commanders had no training in leading large military entities in battle conditions over a sustained period, whereas exercises including simulated action formed part of the standard training for commanders of smaller units.[35] This modern analogy helps explain the contrast between the often exemplary performance of British battalions in fighting during the eighteenth and nineteenth centuries, sustained by middle-ranking officers and NCOs with long experience in their posts,[36] and the image of a frequently dithering and ineffectual higher command.

The gap between high competence at battalion level or in staff work and senior command was and remains a difficult one to bridge. Appointments to high command continued to be bedevilled by difficulties in assessing how individuals would cope with enlarged responsibilities. One of Wellington's complaints in the Peninsular War was that few officers possessed the experience and resoluteness to take on large subordinate commands.[37] Even the Royal Navy, whose officer corps has suffered less from historians' subsequent critiques and whose promotion procedures were more rigorous than the army's, faced similar challenges. In 1806, Admiral Lord St Vincent reviewed with a leading Whig politician the difficulties of finding admirals suitable for wartime commands: 'There is such a deficiency of nerves under responsibility that I see officers of the greatest promise and acquired character sink beneath its weight.' Two admirals – Lord Gardner and Sir Edward Thornborough – were 'brave as lions in the presence of an enemy' but could not cope with the demands of directing a prolonged blockade in the difficult seas around Brest. Added to the gruelling demands of sustained fleet operations were the challenges of naval diplomacy. St Vincent cautioned that Sir Richard Strachan, though excellent for any 'hardy enterprise', 'has neither the temper nor head piece for negotiation'. By contrast, when St Vincent took over the political leadership of the Admiralty in early 1801, Cuthbert Collingwood wrote privately: 'No man in England is more capable of conducting the naval department than he is.' Not the least of his virtues was his devotion to business – he had 'little taste for pleasure' – and his capacity to work with rarely more than four or five hours of sleep a night.[38] In fact, St Vincent failed to excel in political high office.

St Vincent's ascent to the cabinet leads to reflections upon the distinctive role played by officers in parliament. Serving officers were permitted to sit as MPs in the nineteenth century and officers formed a substantial proportion of the House of Commons. This tendency both ran counter to the argument that a professional officer corps should be separated from political institutions, and helped strengthen the impression of British military amateurism because the officer corps was not organizationally separated from politics. The contrary argument is that senior officers require political understanding and that the institutional arrangements of politics simply shape the ways in which the interaction between armies and their larger societies occur.[39]

Reformers stressed the dangers of corruption in the early nineteenth-century relationship between the army and politics. But it could equally well be argued that the absence of MPs with personal experience of the armed services limits informed assessments of defence issues coming before parliament. In the USA it has been argued in recent years that the worlds of the armed services and politics have become so far separated – except for a miniscule group of elite officers who take on specialist staff appointments – that there are real dangers to policy-making in the mutual lack of understanding between the vast majority of middle-ranking and senior officers and politicians in the Congress. One study has suggested that when Congress and the administration contained high proportions of military veterans among their members, politicians were more cautious about going to war but pressed for the large-scale deployment of force in such wars, whereas when there were fewer veterans within the decision-making elite, the uses of force were more frequent, more piecemeal, and less successful.[40] Finally, there is the moral dimension to the political decision to use force. At the height of American protests against the Vietnam War, the service records of the 234 sons of members of Congress who were of military-service age revealed that no more than 28 had gone to Vietnam, only 19 had been involved in combat, and only one had been wounded.[41] The British establishment in Britain's imperial age was never thus insulated from direct engagement by its members in the heart of conflict. On the other hand, army officers' political connections fostered an image of incompetence because military decisions were politicized when officers belonged to rival factions. Instead of being treated as matters of professional judgement or misjudgement, errors of omission or commission made by senior military or naval officers were typically seized upon by political opponents in order to embarrass the party associated with the erring commander. A vibrant press and print trade immediately conveyed criticism in parliament to the wider public sphere, thereby disseminating ideas of bumbling admirals and generals which may have greatly exaggerated reality.

The aura of ineffectiveness and inefficiency surrounding the British army, or at least its officer corps, while providing an ample target for recurrent satire, ridicule, disgust or contempt, has, more seriously, discouraged systematic attention to the challenges facing the British projection of power globally, deflected historians from comparisons with continental European military competences, and deflated the importance of military involvement to the consolidation of the British establishment.

British militarism reconsidered

British militarism in the 1790s and 1800s might be generally depicted in negative terms. The British were slow to adopt many elements of military modernity. In rigorous planning of resource mobilization and the implementation of some form of conscription, Britain lagged behind the leading European states. The creation of a modern staff system was also long delayed. But the British had more complex challenges to overcome in their military and naval planning and operations than those faced by any other European government, challenges which arose from the sheer extent and scale of the British empire.

Given that British naval and military imperialism was global, not merely Asian, and dynamic, not merely defensive, the British developed a distinctive approach to warfare, exemplified by the conduct of war following the resumption of fighting against France in 1803. Five characteristics may be distinguished. First, Britain alone engaged in global operations. Within ten years they fought in Denmark, Italy, Portugal and Spain, in North America, the West Indies and South America, in southern Africa, extensively in the Indian sub-continent, and in the East Indies. No other European power was so active so widely. This extraordinary activity depended upon a second distinctive characteristic, the scale and pervasiveness of naval operations. In the years 1809–13 the Royal Navy had between 685 and 773 warships of all sizes, manned by 130,000 to 145,000 sailors, in service around the world. At any one time a further 200 warships were in reserve or being repaired.[42] This provided the basis for an unprecedented projection of naval and military power. A third distinctive characteristic, contradicting much mythology about British military effectiveness, flowed from this wide dispersal of force and operations. Naval and military command was normally devolved to an extent very rarely, if ever, approached by continental European powers. For a country possessing an apparently weak military tradition, authority in naval and military decision-making was surprisingly broadly distributed, as it had to be where operations and campaigns were so typically distant from metropolitan centres of command and control. Given the breadth and relatively circumscribed scale of these operations, British governments tended to accept, as a fourth characteristic, the lessons of war as process. Victories in battle were almost invariably regarded as contributions to a drawn-out process of wearing down enemies and weighing the balance of advantage in Britain's favour. Their most dramatic impact was to provide booster-jabs to maintain political and public commitment to war.

Success in campaigns or battles owed a great deal not only to national support for or engagement in war but also to the widespread mobilization of resources and manpower across the empire. A fifth characteristic of British warfare was therefore its armies' use of local manpower drawn from extremely mixed national and racial groups. The bitter accusation that George III attempted to smash the American rebellion from 1776 by despatching German mercenaries to crush a people rightly struggling to be free has reverberated down the centuries. However, it has been pointed out that the army sent to North America had the lowest percentage of non-British troops of any major expeditionary force sent overseas since the late seventeenth century. Nor did Americans complain when one-quarter of the French troops sent to America in May 1780 turned out to be Germans. Dependence on troops enlisted from various countries was, in fact, standard eighteenth-century practice. The British relied on mixed forces even for operations within the UK, nearly one-third of the small army sent to destroy the Jacobite rising in 1745–46, for example, being recruited from Hesse.[43] Nor did the emergence of revolutionary warfare reduce the dependence on multi-national forces. Napoleon's Grand Army invading Russia in 1812 drew half its strength from outside France, including men from twenty-five countries, with substantial contributions from Italy, the German states and Poland.[44]

British armies outside Europe were even more multi-ethnic in character. The East India Company depended upon locally recruited sepoys who by 1809 numbered 128,000 indigenous troops, serving under British officers and alongside British battalions. Not only did the British raise troops from their dependent peoples within India. In expanding into Nepal in 1815, they also recruited Gurkhas from their opponent's army into their own forces. To meet its wartime global commitments, Britain by 1815 had also raised four regiments in Ceylon, one in west Africa, and nine in the West Indies.[45] In the West Indies, the death-rate for European soldiers often reached 20–25% a year, the result of poor health among recruits dispatched there, the impact of malaria and yellow fever once there, and the habitual dependence of British troops upon rum. To counter such losses among white soldiers, the British recruited African slaves and ex-slaves, who had better immunity to malaria and yellow fever and were not as addicted to rum as British soldiers were. The British government thus became the largest single purchaser of slaves in the Caribbean of the early 1800s.[46] Similar shortages of local white manpower led to the formation of a multiracial force in Southern Africa. Having experimented with using Khoikhoi as soldiers in 1796, the British established the Cape Regiment in

1806, enlisting 800 men in it. During the campaign against the Xhosa in 1811–12, the force sent into the Zuurveld consisted of 900 Boer militia, 700 Africans of the Cape Regiment, and 500 British troops, a curiously mixed force by any contemporary standards.[47] The recruitment, training, organizing, and leading of such extraordinarily multiracial forces was an unparalleled military accomplishment.

The British also faced challenges in mounting operations in the midst of civilian populations over whom they ruled. How they mobilized such populations caused great problems in the early 1780s. When the British took over coastal South Carolina in 1780–81, for example, they controlled a region boasting the highest *per capita* white household wealth anywhere in the British empire. The British assigned slaves sequestered from patriots to constructing and repairing equipment and barracks, and used some 5,000 slaves to grow food for the army, but these actions brought such social and economic uncertainty, disruption, and, in places, breakdown, that increasingly embittered planters opposed British rule.[48] In May 1781, Lieutenant-General Lord Cornwallis concluded: 'The perpetual instances of the weakness and treachery of our friends in South Carolina, and the impossibility of getting any military assistance from them, make the possession of any part of the country of very little use, except in supplying provisions for Charleston.'[49] British presence and practices simply intensified internal conflict and created a pattern of localized civil wars.

The collapse of British authority and failure to hold the loyalty of subject populations was particularly dramatic in the southern India war sparked by Haidar Ali of Mysore's invasion of the Carnatic and the Madras presidency. On the one hand, some 200,000 local people fled from the Carnatic countryside into Madras's Black Town, and wealthy Europeans stripped their country houses of furniture and even doors and window blinds before fleeing to the anticipated safety of Fort St George.[50] Yet at a council of war in December 1780, Lieutenant-General Sir Eyre Coote saw no hope of mobilizing wider support in the south: 'We have not only to combat against Haidar, but against the whole Carnatic; and have therefore no Reason to hope for least Assistance in any Part of the Road we may march, or any Part of the Country we may go into.' Colonel Lord Macleod commented on 'the hostile Mind of all the Natives of the Carnatic to the English Interest, and of the Attachment to Haidar Ali'.[51] A senior official attributed this disastrous situation to 'A Degeneracy of Character, and overlove of Riches, a Want of public Spirit, and even of the common Feelings of Humanity towards the People who lived under our Government', resulting in 'a dissipated Revenue' and 'the Torrent of

Corruption' in Madras.[52] Military failure cut deeper than simple battlefield reversals because the inability to contain enemy forces exposed wider defects of British rule.

While British militarism should be analysed in the light of the standards of military organization and conduct set by the French Revolution, the distinctive traditions, challenges and opportunities faced by the British need to be carefully weighed in any comparison with the French model. The spread of British interests and operations in itself made for a distinctive approach to war-making. Moreover, the principles behind the British practice of war – creating regional alliance systems, avoiding systematic plunder, attempting to live with and alongside civilian populations, recruiting from among local peoples – informed a quite cautious but, the British hoped, collaborationist relationship between British forces and civilian populations. British expansionism rarely evinced that tumultuous combination of vaulting ambition, liberationist ideology, and coercive plunder which so typically characterized French empire-building.

Military ethos

Setting aside generalized military cultures and looking instead at the armed forces themselves, we confront the persistent claim that a significant aristocratic presence and a pervading aristocratic ethos within the British army officer corps delayed its professionalization until at least the late nineteenth century, if not well into the latter part of the twentieth century. The emphasis on bravery and dash, it has been suggested, confirms the essentially amateur nature of the aristocratic military tradition.

As Britain entered the 1790s, the recent legacy of warfare was largely confined to America and India, where battle severely tested officers' endurance and skills, but exposed only a small number of senior officers to fighting. For example, some 27% of the 1,924 British officers and men engaged at Guilford Court House on 15 March 1781 were killed, wounded or missing. Of the five senior officers present, Cornwallis had a horse shot under him, his second-in-command, Brigadier-General O'Hara, suffered bad wounds (and his son, an artillery lieutenant, was killed), and Lt. Col. James Webster died of his wounds. The Guards battalion's 481 officers and men suffered 45% casualties, with eleven of the nineteen Guards officers present being killed or wounded.[53] In India, Mysore's invasion of Madras resulted on 10 September 1780 in a disaster at Conjeveram which, according to critical officials, 'cannot be parralleled [sic] since the English had possessions in India'.[54] An army of 3,853 officers and men was destroyed; of the eighty-six European officers present, no fewer than thirty-six were killed in action or died of their wounds, and another thirty-four were wounded.[55] Such limited and bloody events offered little experience upon which future generations of officers might build.

The British could comfort themselves that their only two major defeats in America were inflicted by overwhelmingly larger enemy forces. The capitulation at Yorktown brought no disgrace to the 200 British officers who surrendered there.[56] Many of them went on to highly successful careers, with 16 being listed in the *Oxford Dictionary of National Biography*, including Cornwallis and his deputy Charles O'Hara, who became governor of Gibraltar, Harry Calvert, who became Adjutant-General of the British army, and Gerard Lake, who became commander-in-chief in India. More generally, only a tiny part of the British army experienced defeat; 5,930 troops plus officers surrendered at Yorktown and its dependent garrisons, whereas the vast majority of the troops in North America remained on garrison duties to the end of the war. By September 1781, the British Parliament paid for 149,000 men embodied in the army and militia, with other British forces being charged to the Irish Parliament and the East India Company. Only 35,641 troops (plus 2,684 paroled under the Convention of Saratoga) were then serving in the American ex-colonies.[57]

If the wars of 1776–84 vindicated British courage, they also exposed British dilemmas over command and coordination. George III in 1777 wanted tougher measures in America in order to hasten the war's end, arguing that heavier casualties on both sides in the short run would prove less cruel than a prolonged war.[58] Because neither the king, nor the responsible ministers, nor the generals in the field took final decisions over strategic priorities, coordinating British military dispositions in America caused major problems, especially in 1777, while the theatre commander-in-chief was much criticised in 1780–81 for indecision and vague oversight. The system of command in India proved even more defective. For much of 1776–83, the Madras presidency army was disrupted by intense clashes between the presidency's commanders-in-chief and members of its council or governors.[59] When news of the Dutch declaration of war on Britain reached India in 1781, Sir Eyre Coote, the senior commander in India, argued with Lord Macartney, the governor of Madras, over military priorities. While the governor pressed to implement the home government's decision to seize Dutch colonies, the general objected that the Company could not wage war simultaneously upon Mysore and upon the Dutch.[60] Macartney left Coote to carry on the war started by the attack on Madras launched by Haidar Ali, the ruler of Mysore in 1780.

Independently of his commander-in-chief, he launched his own expedition in January 1782 to oust the Dutch from Ceylon, having informed London in October that the 'overthrow of Indian Princes is among us a slighter gratification and a lesser object of national policy than advantages over European enemies'.[61] By the summer of 1782 relations between governor and commander-in-chief were further soured when Warren Hastings, as governor-general in Calcutta, extended Coote's powers.[62] Macartney deeply resented this enhancement in the commander-in-chief's authority, informing a prominent member of the Supreme Council:

It is the constitution[al] system of the Co's [Company's] Government that the commander-in-chief should have the sole and exclusive conduct and control of all military operations, and the entire . . . command of all the forces under their authority to the utmost possible extent of his wishes. I rather believe such a commission of latitude is not suitable to the constitutional system of any civilised country upon earth . . . you will find I believe the prince of Condé, Marshall Turenne, Prince Eugene, and the Duke of Marlborough were never trusted with such a discretion.[63]

On Coote's death in 1783, relations were no better with his successor in Madras, Major-General James Stuart, whose dismissal Macartney secured.[64] The most important lesson of warfare in southern India in 1780–84 was the need to address the system of command. A similar argument could be made for the American war. The greatest failures – the surrender at Saratoga in 1777 and the failure of the forces at Yorktown in 1781 – flowed from poor strategic coordination and the failure to co-ordinate the movements of widely separated armies.

Despite flaws in British military performance and shortcomings in command in the 1770s and 1780s, the British army by the 1810s had proved itself to be as dedicated to the profession of arms as any contemporary armed service.[65] Its officer corps contained numerous experienced middle and senior battalion soldiers dedicated to their duties. At the same time the purchase system allowed others to move from regiment to regiment, gaining experience of different fighting units and a wide range of personal and professional networks. During wartime, promotion could be reasonably rapid, even for those who could not afford to purchase senior rank. Admittedly, it could be argued that excessive attention was paid to discipline and drill, which were rigorously scrutinized at periodic regimental inspections; but both were vital to efficient battlefield performance and unit cohesion under fire. This was entirely comparable to the emphasis given to drill in the leading continental armies; as has been noted, the French revolutionary levies were carried forward by strenuous training and not simply by ideological or nationalistic fervour. One participant in the defence of Gibraltar in 1780–83 attributed British success to the efficiency of officers 'of approved courage, prudence, and activity; eminent for all the accomplishments of their profession, and in whom we had unbounded confidence'.[66]

More formal means of inculcating professional attributes were provided with the establishment of the Royal Military College in the 1800s, and by the 1810s well-trained officers entered staff positions in Wellington's army in the Iberian peninsula. By the 1810s, regimental pride was well developed, and there were plenty of British units which displayed the aggressive and self-confident *esprit de corps* associated with Napoleon's Imperial Guard. Competition for senior posts was intense and clear, if non-publicized, selection occurred. Networking was vital, and if the clubbable characteristics sought were what might be labelled aristocratic in tone, the fact of behavioural stereotyping does not differ from that of modern organizations which insist upon their own cultural norms and spend considerable effort moulding their managers into bonded teams, behaving, thinking, and reacting in standard and predictable ways. Part of Wellington's insistence on appointing 'gentlemanly' officers – a vague term which did not exclude middle-class men – was the need to assure the smooth conduct of military business based upon shared assumptions and attitudes. There is no evidence that social background made any difference to professional commitment. Napoleon himself frequently complained of the inefficiency of his marshals and generals when left to their own devices in the peninsula, and at least some of them slipped into lives of considerable self-indulgence once they gained imposing rank buttressed by revenue-generating estates. Napoleon's senior generals did not display a professionalism superior to British generals. Both Sir John Moore and Wellington outmanoeuvred and out-fought Soult, who was one of Napoleon's ablest marshals; and William Beresford halted Soult at Albuera, forcing the French into a tactical withdrawal. Wellington outwitted and defeated five other marshals – Jourdan, Masséna, Marmont, Ney and Victor – in the peninsula. Much of the success of Napoleonic warfare in fact depended upon the coordinating energy, strategic insight, and swiftness in execution displayed by Napoleon himself.

The British army's reputation as, allegedly, amateur by European standards arose because it was so small and thus dependent upon continental allies. Failures to land effective blows against the French in 1793–95 were attributed by Pitt to unreliable allies and the inability of their commanders to work together. In the Flanders campaign of 1794, the British corps was one of the few which kept to the agreed plan of advance, but the British government despaired of the Austrians' insistence on providing the commander-in-chief, because, it was said, any failure to do so would be a public humiliation for the Habsburgs' standing as the military and political leaders of central Europe. A history of the campaign of 1794–95 concluded that 'the enemy were formidable only in their numbers, and to their numbers alone were they indebted for their conquests'.[67] A War Office memorandum of 1804 asserted: 'France is superior to Great Britain only in population, and the consequent facility of raising large armies. In all the other qualities which constitute the strength of Empires; in military discipline, in security of frontier, in naval power, in wealth, in knowledge, in courage and in reputation, Great Britain is either equal, or superior, to France.'[68] In 1805 Wellington already argued – before he had sight of the Iberian peninsula – that British soldiers were second only to French troops in their efficiency and capability, basing his assertion on the British record in India. Disasters did occur, but often resulted from an over-confident commitment to maintaining the momentum of offensive action, and an over-readiness to fight an enemy whose strength was underestimated. Moreover, none of the reverses was large-scale or strategically damaging. Throughout the wars of 1793–1815 the British were periodically to withdraw in the face of superior French numbers, but they were never defeated on a field of battle by a French army. Once Wellington was able to deploy an army on the continent on a continuing basis, its performance was no less professional than that of the French armies in the Iberian peninsula.

A positive public image of British military proficiency was not the by-product merely of the Peninsular War. The war for American independence, however unpromising when considered with hindsight, offered high points with which contemporaries embellished British pride in military achievement, most notably the defence of Gibraltar against Spain and France. Pictures and then prints immediately proliferated to commemorate this sublime act of defiance, especially the emasculation of the floating batteries on the night of 13/14 September 1782. Public bodies and institutions commissioned paintings; 60,000 people visited the studio of John Singleton Copley, one of the period's leading 'realist' artists, to view his depiction of the triumphant event. The imagery familiar to the upper and middle classes, the political elites and the electorate celebrated determination and resistance, a stern display of British resolve and character. The assaults against Gibraltar under General Eliott were patriotically embellished in 1800 as 'the most formidable operations that ever were made for the capture of a place. The eyes of all Europe were fixed upon Eliott and his brave garrison, which baffled the united efforts of France and Spain, and have gained the most elevated place in modern military history.'[69]

The extension of the British empire from the 1780s to the 1820s depended not solely on trade, entrepreneurship, the drive of British emigration, or a capacity to invest, but also on the ability to project and assert British power worldwide. Far from occupying overseas power vacuums, the British presence was maintained against a multiplicity of foes in extremely demanding geographical, climatic and political environments. The lack of any imperial grand design should not disguise the importance and complexity of 'local' political and military planning and preparation which underpinned imperial expansionism. Beyond that, and back home, this sustained period of warfare had implications which historians have begun to map out, for the resilience of the lander elite, and for definition of British nationhood. But the involvement of the political establishment in war and expansion went deeper than is usually depicted and contributed to the development of a distinctive British military culture which has proved to be of enduring significance. What follows, therefore, is a reassessment of what happened in the process of Britain's acquiring a new empire and how the British succeeded in claiming that theirs was a non-military imperium. At the same time, any definition of British identity needs to include an understanding of the development in this period of a distinctive British military culture which, while malleable over time, had enduring strength.

War and empire: the central connection

Two of the most contentious themes in the analysis of imperial history have been the tensions between central and peripheral impulses – was empire driven on by the conditions of turbulent frontiers or by decision-making in London? – and between economic and geopolitical motives.[70] A further refinement in the assessment of metropolitan impulses to expansionism arose from the argument that the imperial ambitions of the governing establishment were the by-product not of middle-class commercialism but of aristocratic atavism. The aristocratic ideal linked war and empire.

One strong connection between central and peripheral impulses to imperial expansion was provided by the widespread willingness of military and naval commanders, either while planning operations from

Britain or conducting such operations overseas, to apply force and accept high risks. Given the cumulative way in which advantage or disadvantage accrued to one or the other side during a war, British wars were often conducted in an opportunistic manner. Military and naval commanders operating far from London frequently found themselves left to devise a strategy, discern an opening, or develop an initiative. They could usually take decisions by reference to two lodestars of eighteenth-century British policy, hostility to France and its interests and allies, and the promotion of British commercial gain. These underlying purposes were fully internalized by military and naval officers who, in their distant postings and without reference to London, often shaped their own local strategies confident that, barring unanticipated disasters, they would win metropolitan approval. William Cormack concluded that political support for the Royal Navy underpinned its ability to act under clear rules without executive tyranny, thereby making a vital contribution to its effectiveness; the victories of a navy sustained by popular support and political commitment 'represented the triumph of British Parliamentary Government over the French Revolution'.[71] Military and naval commanders pressed the agenda and interests of their own organizations, within the broad strategic contexts suggested, or likely to be approved, by ministers, when they operated abroad. Individual commanders might be impelled by a mixture of motives: professional pride, the quest for honour and honours, an appetite for prize-money, the drive to exercise professional talents in the heat of war, and an ambition to outwit and defeat the enemy. But by pressing forward their separate organizations' capacities and interests, their actions expanded the empire. Commercial advantage might be cited to gain approval for their activities, but military and naval forces, once deployed overseas, often acquired an imperialistic momentum of their own.

Success in conducting such wars was the responsibility of an officer corps which formed one of the largest single professional groups in Britain. Willingness to take risks testified to that officer corps' self-confidence, which in turn was reinforced by public enthusiasm for victories and an underpinning faith in the armed services' competence. The effects of professional commitment within the officer corps and the development of marked fighting skills permeating it were frequently commented upon. One young official in India reflected in 1791 on British advantages:

in India, where dominion changes every day, where the powers among which it is divided have only had a short existence . . . and where it is not certain how soon all of them may be overthrown, a nation like the

*English, whose strength does not depend on the qualities of one man,
whose government is fixed on solid foundations, and whose military
character is so infinitely superior to that of its competitors, need not fear
that by gaining an increase of territory and force, it will stimulate those
to combine against it who were afraid to do so when it was in a weaker
condition.*[72]

The close link between military force and empire was spelled out in 1800
by Lieutenant General James Stuart, commander-in-chief of the Bombay
army, to the cabinet minister responsible, Henry Dundas:

*Commercial pursuits first made us visit India; but a scene of brilliant
exploits, little connected with commerce, led to the establishment of an
extensive empire, which must now be supported by a just combination
of military strength, with objects relating to trade. Hence the
encouragement of military and commercial exertion, is the chief
object of national concern. By this means we have acquired, and
by these means we must maintain our dominion over this country.*

In 1805 Major General Sir Arthur Wellesley, later the Duke of Wellington,
travelling back to England after nine years in India, informed the then
responsible minister, Lord Castlereagh: 'The English soldiers are the main
foundation of the British power in Asia.' He proceeded further in responding to Castlereagh's inquiries about the more flexible and extensive use of
subject peoples as imperial soldiers:

*Bravery is the characteristic of the British army in all quarters of the
world; but no other quarter has afforded such striking examples of the
existence of this quality in the soldiers as in the East Indies. An instance
of their misbehaviour in the field has never been known; and particularly
those who have been for some time in that country cannot be ordered
upon any service, however dangerous or arduous, that they will not
effect, not only with bravery, but a degree of skill not often witnessed
in persons of their description in other parts of the world.*

Part of that distinguished behaviour flowed from their feeling 'that they
are a distinct and superior class to the rest of the world which surrounds
them' and their impulse to live up to 'their high notions of their own superiority'. British rule in India rested not on trade or wealth; instead, British
soldiers provided 'the foundation of the British strength in Asia'.[73] The
point was generalized by a reviewer in the conservative *Quarterly Review*
in 1811:

All history proves that one state conquers another not by superior freedom or virtue, but by possessing more numerous, braver, better organized, and better commanded armies, with a more vigorous system of military policy, and more constancy in repairing disasters in war.

The first historian of the Peninsular War, Sir William Napier, a soldier himself, wrote of Wellington's defeat of Napoleon: 'England stood as the most triumphant nation of the world. She rejoices in the glory of her arms!'[74]

Widespread confidence in the ability of British soldiers and sailors, and belief in the disproportionate impact their deployment could have, contributed to the formation of the British establishment's world view. The experience of war in the 1790s, and Wellington's own record as a general and then as military adviser to governments for nearly four decades after Waterloo, indicated that exercising military and naval power in this protracted period of Great Power wars and imperial campaigning was typically far more difficult than these confident declarations suggested. Nevertheless, statements such as these support the conclusion that the army and navy did not merely provide occasional heroes for the popular imagination but were persistent and dynamic stakeholders of empire. Since this view runs counter to much contemporary and subsequent criticism of the army and navy, their role as instruments of global power projection requires the extensive reassessment which this book offers.

Notes and references

1 For a wide-ranging discussion of ideas of empire, see P.J. Marshall, *The Making and Unmaking of Empires: Britain, India and America c.1750–1783* (Oxford, 2005), pp. 158–206.

2 N.A.M. Rodger, *The Insatiable Earl* (London, 1993), p. 92.

3 P.J. Marshall, *The Impeachment of Warren Hastings* (Oxford, 1965), p. 25; Douglas M. Peers, *Between Mars and Mammon: Colonial Armies and the Garrison State in Early Nineteenth-century India* (London, 1995), pp. 19–20, 47.

4 Michael Duffy, *Soldiers, Sugar and Seapower: The British Expeditions to the West Indies and the War against Revolutionary France* (Oxford, 1987), pp. 14, 17, 379, 390; *Historical Statistics of the United States*, US Bureau of the Census (Washington DC, 1960), p. 12. Earlier links are analysed in Andrew Jackson O'Shaughnessy, *An Empire Divided: The American Revolution and the British Caribbean* (Philadelphia, 2000), pp. 15–17, 20–21, 205–10.

5 Vincent T. Harlow, *The Founding of the Second British Empire 1763–1793*, Vol. II *New Continents and Changing Values* (London, 1964), pp. 255–61; Sir John Knox Laughton (ed.), *Letters and Papers of Charles, Lord Barham*, 3 vols (London, 1907–11), Vol. III, p. 277; A. Aspinall (ed.), *The Later Correspondence of George III*, 5 vols (Cambridge, 1967), Vol. III, p. 625; John Fortescue, *The County Lieutenancies and the Army 1803–1814* (London, 1909), pp. 305, 307.

6 Charles Dupin, *A Tour through the Naval and Military Establishments of Great Britain* (translated London, 1822), pp. 32–33.

7 P.J. Cain and A.G. Hopkins, *British Imperialism 1688–2000* (London, 2001 edn), p. 79; Boyd Hilton, *A Mad, Bad and Dangerous People? England 1783–1846* (Oxford, 2006), p. 130.

8 John Brewer, *The Sinews of Power: War, Money and the English State, 1688–1783* (London, 1989), pp. 206–10.

9 William Hague, *William Pitt the Younger* (London, 2004), pp. 158, 160, 165; John Ehrman, *The Younger Pitt: The Consuming Struggle* (London, 1996), pp. 84–90.

10 Alison Yarrington, *The Commemoration of the Hero 1800–1864: Monuments to the British Victors of the Napoleonic Wars* (New York, 1988); Margarette Lincoln, 'Origins of public maritime history: The Royal Navy and trade 1750–1815', *Journal of Maritime Research* (May 2002); Marianne Czisnik, *Horatio Nelson: A Controversial Hero* (London, 2005), pp. 97–118.

11 Iris Butler, *The Eldest Brother* (London, 1973), pp. 35, 151–52, 177, 201, 323.

12 Rev. G.R. Gleig, *The Life of Major General Sir Thomas Munro, Bart.*, 2 vols (London, 1830), Vol. III, pp. 252–53.

13 Duke of Wellington (ed.), *Supplementary Despatches and Memoranda of Field Marshal Arthur, Duke of Wellington*, 12 vols (London, 1858–80), Vol. VII, pp. 12, 491; Vol. VIII, pp. 25, 42, 44–45, 66–67.

14 Geoffrey Parker, *The Military Revolution: Military Innovation and the Rise of the West, 1500–1800* (Cambridge, 1996 edn).

15 Eric Hobsbawm, *The Age of Revolution, 1789–1848* (London, 1962), p. 91.

16 An excellent asssessment is Alan Forrest, 'The French Revolutionary and Napoleonic Wars' in Geoff Mortimer (ed.), *Early Modern Military History, 1450–1815* (Basingstoke, 2004), pp. 196–211; Tim Blanning, *The Pursuit of Glory: Europe 1648–1815* (London, 2007), p. 604.

17 Piers Mackesy, *The War for America, 1775–1783* (London, 1964), pp. 524–25.

18 Franklin and Mary Wickwire, *Cornwallis: The Imperial Years* (Chapel Hill, NC, 1980), p. 162.

19 Charles Ross (ed.), *Correspondence of Charles, First Marquis Cornwallis*, 3 vols (London, 1859), Vol. I, p. 56.

20 The totals are drawn from Mackesy, *The War for America*, p. 524. The definition of battle excludes sieges, minor engagements and movements in the presence of the enemy.

21 Don Higginbotham, *The War of American Independence* (Boston, 1983 edn), p. 382; Lee Kennett, *The French Forces in America, 1780–1783* (Westport, CT, 1977), pp. 12, 136, 142, 144, 165.

22 Jonathan Dull, *The French Navy and American Independence: A Study of Arms and Diplomacy, 1774–1787*, (Princeton, NJ, 1975), pp. 374–76.

23 Colonel Ramsay Weston Phipps, *The Armies of the First French Republic*, 5 vols (Oxford, 1929–39), Vol. I, pp. 121–30, Vol. II, pp. 14–28.

24 T.C.W. Blanning, *The French Revolutionary Wars, 1787–1802*, (London, 1996), pp. 116–28, 270.

25 Blanning, *The French Revolutionary Wars*, p. 126.

26 Samuel F. Scott, *The Response of the Royal Army to the French Revolution* (Oxford, 1978), pp. 184, 193, 204; Rafe Blaufarb, 'The social contours of meritocracy in the Napoleonic officer corps' in Howard G. Brown and Judith A. Miller (eds), *Taking Liberties: Problems of a New Order from the French Revolution to Napoleon* (Manchester, 2002), pp. 126–46, esp. pp. 141, 143–46.

27 Richard Cobb, *The People's Armies*, trans. by Marianne Elliott (New Haven, CT, 1987), pp. 616–17; Louis Bergeron, *France Under Napoleon*, trans. by R.R. Palmer (Princeton, NJ, 1981), pp. 110–11; Elie Halevy, *England in 1815* trans. by E.I. Watkin and D.A. Barker (London, 1961 edn), pp. 365–83; J.E. Cookson, *The British Armed Nation, 1793–1815* (Oxford, 1997), pp. 259–63.

28 Rory Muir, *Tactics and the Experience of Battle in the Age of Napoleon* (New Haven, CT, 1998), pp. 7–9; David Chandler, *The Campaigns of Napoleon* (London, 1966), pp. 144–58.

29 John Pemble, *The War for Nepal: John Company at War* (Oxford, 1971).

30 Russell F. Weigley, *The Age of Battles: The Quest for Decisive Warfare from Breitenfeld to Waterloo* (London, 1993), pp. 536–39.

31 Brian Bond, *The Pursuit of Victory: From Napoleon to Saddam Hussein* (Oxford, 1996), pp. 32–33, 36.

32 Gunther E. Rothenberg, *The Art of Warfare in the Age of Napoleon* (Indiana 1978, reissued 1980), pp. 16–21, 241–45.

33 David Blackbourn, *The Fontana History of Germany, 1780–1918* (London, 1997), pp. 376–77, 406–07.

34 Thomas E. Ricks, *Fiasco: The American Military Adventure in Iraq* (London, 2006), pp. 127, 173–74.

35 William E. Odom and Robert Dujarric, *America's Inadvertent Empire* (New Haven, CT and London, 2004), p. 73.

36 J.A. Houlding, *Fit for Service: The Training of the British Army, 1715–1795* (Oxford, 1981), pp. 105–16.

37 Wellington (ed.), *Supplementary Despatches*, Vol. VIII, p. 254; Vol. IX, pp. 277, 308.

38 Craig Hardin, Jnr. (ed.), 'Letters of Lord St Vincent to Thomas Grenville, 1806–07' in Christopher Lloyd, ed., *The Naval Miscellany* (London, 1952), Vol. IV, pp. 482, 485–86; Captain C.H.H. Owen, RN, 'Letters from Vice–Admiral Lord Collingwood' in Michael Duffy (ed.), *The Naval Miscellany* (Aldershot, Hants., 2003), Vol. VI, p. 172.

39 Hew Strachan, *The Politics of the British Army* (Oxford, 1997), pp. 17–19, 27, 42–43.

40 Odum and Dujarric, *America's Inadvertent Empire*, p. 94.

41 Gerard J. DeGroot, *A Noble Cause? America and the Vietnam War* (Harlow, 2000), p. 315.

42 Michael Lewis, *The Navy in Transition, 1814–1864: A Social History* (London, 1965), p. 64.

43 David French, *The British Way in Warfare, 1688–2000* (London, 1990), p. 87; Kennett, *French Forces in America 1780–1783*, p. 22; Rothenberg, *The Art of Warfare*, p. 17; Christopher Duffy, *The '45* (London, 2003), p. 131.

44 Rothenberg, *The Art of Warfare*, pp. 158–62.

45 *Army List 1815* (London, March 1815), pp. 399–414, 417, 420–23, 447–72, 486–90.

46 Roger Norman Buckley, *Slaves in Red Coats: The British West India Regiments, 1795–1815* (New Haven, CT and London, 1979), pp. 22–28, 52–62, 134–38; Roger Norman Buckley, *The British Army in the West Indies: Society and the Military in the Revolutionary Age* (Gainesville, 1998), pp. 117–24, 282–93; Vincent Harlow and Frederick Madden (eds), *British Colonial Developments 1774–1834: Select Documents* (Oxford, 1953), pp. 88–89.

47 Timothy Keegan, *Colonial South Africa and the Origins of the Racial Order* (Leicester, 1996), pp. 83, 85–86, 315.

48 Russell R. Menard, 'Financing the Lowcountry export boom: capital and growth in early Carolina', *William and Mary Quarterly*, 3rd series, Vol. LI (1994), pp. 659–76; Works Project Administration, *South Carolina* (New

York, 1941), pp. 31–33; Sylvia R. Frey, *Water From the Rock: Black Resistance in a Revolutionary Age* (Princeton, NJ, 1991), pp. 82–85, 89–94, 106, 121–26, 132; Robert Olwell, *Masters, Slaves, and Subjects: The Culture of Power in the South Carolina Low Country 1740–1790* (Ithaca, NY, 1998), pp. 229–30, 239, 249–51; Lawrence S. Rowland, Alexander Moore, George C. Rogers, Jr., *The History of Beaufort County, South Carolina*, Vol. I, *1514–1861* (Columbia, SC, 1996), pp. 208, 210–12, 215–23; Kenneth Morgan, 'Slave sales in colonial Charleston', *English Historical Review*, 113 (1998), 905–27.

49 Ross, ed., *Correspondence . . . Cornwallis*, Vol. I, 99, 503–04.

50 William Hodges, RA, *Travels in India During the Years 1780, 1781, 1782 and 1783* (London, 1793), pp. 5–7.

51 *Second Report from the Committee of Secrecy Appointed to Enquire into the Causes of The War in the Carnatic* (n. p., 1782), *Supplemental Appendix to the First Report*, p. 37.

52 *Ibid.*, p. 77.

53 Wickwires, *Cornwallis*, p. 309. The battle is fully described on pp. 292–310. See also John Fortescue, *A History of the British Army, 1763–1793*, 13 vols (London, 1899–1930), Vol. III, pp. 368–75.

54 *First Report from the Committee of Secrecy*, Appendix 9, Smith and Johnson, 1 October, 1780.

55 Fortescue, *A History of the British Army*, Vol. III, pp. 435–42.

56 Howard C. Rice (ed.) *The American Campaigns of Rochambeau's Army*, 2 vols (Princeton, NJ, 1972), Vol. I, p. 149.

57 Mackesy, *The War for America*, pp. 524–25.

58 Ira D. Gruber, *The Howe Brothers and the American Revolution* (Chapel Hill, NC, 1972), pp. 232–35, 252–55.

59 William Fullarton, *A View of the English Interests in India* (London, 1787), pp. 33–35.

60 C. Collin Davies (ed.), *The Private Correspondence of Lord Macartney*, Camden 3rd Series, Vol. LXXVII (London, 1950), pp. 39, 159, 169.

61 Admiral Sir Herbert Richmond, *The Navy in India 1763–1783* (London, 1931), pp. 162–64, 171–72.

62 Davies, *Correspondence . . . Lord Macartney*, pp. 90–94; T.A. Heathcote, *The Military in British India: The Development of British Land Forces in South Asia, 1600–1947* (Manchester, 1995), pp. 49–50.

63 Davies, *Correspondence . . . Lord Macartney*, p. 55.

64 Davies, *Correspondence . . . Lord Macartney*, p. 67.

65 For a fuller discussion, see Strachan, *Politics of the British Army*, pp. 8–17.

66 John Drinkwater, *A History of the Late Siege of Gibraltar* (London, 1785),
     p. 287.

67 Captain L.T. Jones, *Historical Journal* (London, 1797), p. 183.

68 'Memorandum on extending the service of East India Troops, written in
     1804', WO 1/902, The National Archives, London.

69 *A Universal Biographical and Historical Dictionary* (London, 1800),
     Eliott entry.

70 One model is offered in Ronald Hyam, *Britain's Imperial Century,
     1815–1914: A Study of Empire and Expansion*, (Basingstoke, 2002 edn),
     pp. 285–90.

71 William S. Cormack, *Revolution and Political Conflict in the French Navy
     1789–1794* (Cambridge, 1995), pp. 301–02.

72 Gleig, *The Life of Major General Sir Thomas Munro*, Vol. III, p. 65.

73 Montgomery Martin (ed.), *The Dispatches, Minutes, and Correspondence of
     the Marquess Wellesley*, 5 vols (London, 1838), Vol. V, p. 172; Wellington,
     ed., *Supplementary Despatches*, Vol. IV, p. 525. Peers has stressed that
     expansionism in India should not be attributed to proconsular initiatives
     alone but to the militarized state peculiar to India. Peers, *Between Mars and
     Mammon*, pp. 37–38, 45–46.

74 *Quarterly Review*, 1811, Vol. V: 405–06; Sir W.F.P. Napier, *A History of the
     Peninsular Campaign, 1807–1814*, abridged by W.T. Dobson (London,
     1889), p. 408.

PART TWO

The war against Republican France

CHAPTER 3

Containing France in Europe, 1793–95

Continental commitment

B ritain's role in the world has long been disputed: was Britain primarily a European power or a country whose interests were principally global? The two realms could be linked by arguing that, from the late 1680s to the 1810s, Britain developed and projected military and naval power worldwide not essentially to acquire an empire, but to contain and periodically confront France. For most European policy-makers in the eighteenth century, France posed a geopolitical threat, because of its advantages of geographical concentration and size, large population, economic diversity, and possession of a highly centralised state and, in its British opponents' eyes, because of its despotic government, its expansionist challenge to vital British commercial interests in the Low Countries, and its espousal of Roman Catholicism. John Lynn has noted that from 1661 to 1815 the French state was at war for 90 of the 155 years, either with external forces or against internal insurgents.[1]

In confronting France in the 1790s, William Pitt the Younger repeatedly stressed that his objective was neither European nor global. In 1799 he declared:

We are at war with armed opinions; we are at war with those opinions which the sword of audacious, unprincipled, and impious innovation seeks to propagate amidst the ruins of empires, the demolition of the altars of all religion, the destruction of every venerable and good, and liberal institution under whatever form of polity they have been raised.

When asked in the House of Commons in February 1800 to state his ministry's war aims succinctly, he insisted: 'We alone recognized the necessity of open war, as well with the principles, as the practice of the French revolution.' He boasted, in November 1800, that such commitment had yielded unprecedented gains since 1793:

Reviewing . . . the circumstances and success of this war, with the events of former wars . . . I cannot think that the present yields, in the importance of its success, to the most brilliant period of our history . . . Its advantages have been as extensive, as solid, and as important as any that ever were purchased by our armies.

The government had not only protected British possessions overseas and the British constitution, but had 'destroyed the maritime power, and taken the most valuable maritime possessions' of France.[2] Pitt's quest for security thus expanded the empire in the West and East Indies as urged by Henry Dundas, one of his most powerful colleagues, in July 1793: 'Success in those quarters I consider of infinite moment, both in the view of humbling the power of France, and with the view of enlarging our national wealth and security.' In August 1796, when Spain was about to join France, Dundas, despite the increased allied threat in European waters, requested naval reinforcements for Jamaica: 'I cannot too often repeat, what I sincerely feel, that the loss of Jamaica in the present moment and state of the country would be complete ruin to our credit and put you at once at the feet of the enemy.' He claimed to prefer a French landing in Ireland or Britain to one in Jamaica, since French success in the latter would enable them to assert naval superiority in a vital part of the Caribbean, cripple trade, damage national prestige, and undermine the money markets' confidence in British national securities, thereby choking off the principal means of funding the war.[3]

The idea that a tension existed between a continental commitment and a formal global strategy emerged explicitly in reaction to the suffering and loss incurred on the Western Front in 1914–18. It was claimed that Britain's 'way in warfare' had always been to bring pressure to bear by indirect means on an enemy's trade and colonies, and that Britain would most effectively use her sea power by launching amphibious raids on an enemy's coasts. Bottling up trade and seizing colonies would reduce an opponent's economic strength and thereby sap its war-making capability. Unanticipated interventions would draw off enemy forces, weaken their central front, and encourage rebellions against, or resistance to, an enemy regime.[4] The argument against such a claim was that peripheral campaigns, however much damage they might inflict, have never decided major wars. Drawing upon his own experience of the Napoleonic wars, the influential Prussian theorist of war, Carl von Clausewitz, concluded in the 1830s:

governments and commanders have always tried to find ways of avoiding a decisive battle and of reaching their goal by other means or of quietly abandoning it. Historians and theorists have taken great pains, when describing such campaigns and conflicts, to point out that other means not only served the purpose as well as a battle that was never fought, but were indeed evidence of higher skill . . . Recent history has scattered such nonsense to the winds . . . only a great battle can produce a major decision.[5]

British governments' preference for distant campaigns against their enemies' colonies and colonial trade over continental commitments was well entrenched by the late eighteenth century. Britain never sent large forces to co-operate closely with the main European states. Frederick the Great of Prussia, noting this preference, dismissed the British in 1771 as a European power: 'I admire the tranquillity of the British Government, in the present situation in Europe. It smacks too much, however, of unpardonable indolence, of complete lethargy.' In 1780, in the midst of a Franco-Spanish war upon her empire, Britain conducted a policy which struck Frederick as exemplifying 'Stupid vanity; ignorance of the interests and strengths of the other powers of Europe; pride in carrying, alone, "Neptune's trident".' The defeat at Yorktown in 1781 would 'help diminish the insufferable arrogance with which they treat every other nation'.[6] Given the isolation which Britain endured in the wars of 1778–83, devoid of any continental ally, such views may be understandable. Yet the renewed outbreak of war with France seemed to indicate a quite opposite tendency. According to Professor Rodger: 'When war again broke out in 1793, the British had been cured of their obsession with colonies. Once again they recognized that the real peril lay close at hand, and once again they concentrated their fleets in European waters to face it.'[7]

In fact, the relationship between Britain's interest in a stable balance of power in Europe and British commercial and territorial expansionism beyond Europe remained fluid and ill-defined. The tension between Pitt's focus on Europe and Dundas's quest for colonies was resolved by diplomatic and naval primacy being accorded to the first and military might being applied to the second. Throughout the 150 years separating the end of the Seven Years War in 1763 and the British Expeditionary Force's sailing to France in 1914, Britain rarely despatched even small armies to engage in European campaigns; and the longest commitment apart from the Peninsular War of 1809–14 was to Flanders, for two years in 1793–95. Britain made only a limited effort to engage in major continental campaigning in its long wars of 1793–1815. Moreover, the scale of the continental military commitment is suggested by the fact that, for example, in May 1809 Britain sent 22,000 troops back to the Iberian peninsula at the beginning of what was to prove her most sustained continental engagement of the war. Allowing for the 40,000 troops assigned in 1809 to the expedition to the Low Countries which failed in Walcheren, these forces formed small contingents out of the 366,000 regular soldiers deployed across the globe, especially when supplemented within the United Kingdom by some 65,000 militia who were capable of active military service, as well as 388,000 local militia and volunteers.[8] Although the regular forces included 128,000 sepoys embodied in India, total manpower deployed vastly exceeded the numbers ever assigned to continental European operations. The empire's military manpower requirements, consisting in May 1809 of 22,000 British troops on Mediterranean islands and Gibraltar, 21,400 in the West Indies, 8,000 in North America, 25,000 in India, 5,800 at the Cape of Good Hope, circumscribed continental commitments. And 1809 witnessed an unusually heavy commitment of troops to continental expeditions.

Nor did financial subsidies compensate for a lack of manpower allocated to continental Europe, since they were relatively limited until 1808 and the following years. Only Austria received large loans in 1795 and 1797 and a substantial grant of over £1 million in 1800. Total subsidies to all countries remained small in the five years 1803–07 inclusive. When the purse strings loosened in 1808, financial assistance went to Portugal, Spain, Sicily, and Sweden, with the single exception of a grant to Austria in 1809. The financial floodgates did not open until 1813 with the formation of the grand coalition. Even then the total amount given to Austria, Prussia, and Russia was less in 1813 than the sum allocated to Sicily and Sweden. Only in 1814 and 1815 did British funding flow into the treasuries of the great European powers to support large-scale continental campaigning. During the entire period 1793–1816, Britain granted £65.8 million to her allies, with £20 millions of that going out in 1814 and 1815 alone and nearly £14 millions of it being granted to Austria, Prussia, and Russia in those last two years of fighting. Compared with the aggregate expenditure of £830 million on its army, navy and ordnance in the years 1793–1816, the British government's allocation to its allies represented a relatively small commitment. The total cost of maintaining the army in the peninsula added £80 millions, or under 10% of total wartime military and naval spending.[9] Even with the costs of expeditions to the Netherlands in 1793–95 and 1799, less than 20% of all wartime spending on the armed services and subsidies were directed to land operations on the continent, where any late eighteenth-century statesman understood that the European balance would be decided.

Of course, Britain applied considerable naval effort to influencing the European balance of power, with its main battle fleets bottling up enemies' great fleets. But much naval effort was directed against enemy merchant shipping as frigates and smaller warships scoured the sea lanes and coasts within and far beyond European waters. Indeed, naval morale and efficiency depended on prize-money derived from frigate and small-ship warfare. Naval activity thus took three distinct forms: fleet blockading, raiding against mercantile shipping and enemy non-line warships, and punitive expeditions and invasions. While most ships of the line were concentrated in the seas around Europe, there was a considerable deployment of smaller ships across the globe. When, for example, the British retook Martinique in 1809, they allocated only 6 line ships to that task. But the expeditionary force included also 9 frigates and 28 smaller warships, making up a far more considerable fleet – of 43 fighting ships – than counting only the line ships would indicate.[10]

When war with France broke out, Britain faced strategic challenges without having a clear view as to the likely length or nature of the conflict. Ministers continued to portray themselves as dedicated to essentially defensive purposes. The sequence of responses to European strategic challenges flowed from Britain's inability to shape the scale and nature of a continental European land war. While very substantial naval resources were dedicated to European waters, there were strong pressures to direct energies to the capture of French colonies overseas as well as the colonies of European powers unfortunate or misguided enough to become French subordinates or allies. Once established overseas, the British undertook further campaigns to stabilize, protect, or extend their frontiers. Colonial warfare, just like Britain's quest for a balance of power in Europe, came to be depicted as essentially reactive and defensive. Many contemporary intellectuals poured cold water on the whole enterprise of empire; most politicians prioritized European diplomacy; military effort remained limited, even in the principal seat of war; mass mobilization was defensive and strengthened localism as much as national consciousness. The framework of opinion and policy-making as Britain went to war in 1793 scarcely prefigured Britain's wide-ranging imperial expansionism and the establishment of Britain as the first global military power.

In order to understand the ways in which Britain resolved its strategic challenges, enhanced its military experience, and advanced its imperial agenda, it is necessary to examine the course of the war against Revolutionary France and the stages by which the realm of conflict within that war spread.

Strategic choices

Although antagonism between Britain and France was a fundamental given in international relations from the mid-seventeenth century to 1815, the longest war the two countries fought, from 1793 to 1815 with only a brief break, began almost as a by-product of a French effort to defeat Austria and the subsequent failure of the Germanic powers to crush the revolution in 1792. The French army thwarted the Prussians at Valmy (20 September 1792), defeated the Austrians at Jemappes (6 November 1792), and entered Brussels in the Austrian Netherlands on 14 November. The sudden French advance created a crisis in international relations, partly because British ministers, as Edmund Burke stressed, regarded the Low Countries 'as necessary a part of this country as Kent'.[11] For the opposition, Charles James Fox agreed with the government's contentions that access to the Low Countries was vital to British interests but argued that such access, and the ending of the French occupation, could be settled by negotiation. Such prospects were diminished by French military success and by the revolutionaries' proclamation of a republic in the autumn of 1792.[12] The French declaration of war upon Britain on 1 February 1793 signalled a French appreciation of the extent of Britain's concern for the Low Countries' political fate. Yet when war came, the British government – committed to the Netherlands' independence from France as what the responsible minister, Henry Dundas, termed one of the 'uncontrovertible maxims of British policy'[13] – remained confident that Prussia and Austria could constrain French expansion with limited British involvement.

The war raised three immediate challenges for Britain. Would the home front remain stable? How much effort should be devoted to a continental land war? How should naval power be used to bring maximum advantage to Britain? The revolution's universalist claims posed a potential threat to confidence in the robustness of public commitment to fighting at home. There has been much debate about how far revolutionary enthusiasms and ideology within the British Isles threatened the political establishment. Protest against the prevailing political order proliferated in the mid-1790s. The most serious protest appears to have been in 1792, before the war, and that was exacerbated by high food prices, resulting from poor harvests, in September. Literary and more general public enthusiasm for revolution was, nevertheless, widely manifested by intellectuals and publicists, with Tom Paine publishing *The Rights of Man* in two parts in the spring of 1791 and early 1792 as a reprise of his much admired assault on monarchy, British institutions and colonial policy in *Common Sense* back in 1776. As the war worsened and French revolutionary fervour intensified, government law officers took such critiques seriously enough to make strenuous efforts in 1794–95 to prosecute and convict those they claimed were plotting or simply desiring or 'imagining' the king's death. A young barrister, Spencer Perceval, later prime minister, made his name as a junior counsel for the crown in various cases aimed at throttling 'seditious' publications, including the trial of the printers of Paine's *Rights of Man*, and alleged encouragements to regicide.[14] Local manifestations of republicanism recurred, despite government repression, and a naval mutiny at the Nore in May 1797 briefly worried the authorities.

Yet, without dismissing the importance of republican sentiments and reformist pressure, a good case can be made for the resilience of the prevailing order. Burke famously wrote in 1790 of the apparent chorus of sympathy in Britain for revolutionary principles:

Because half a dozen grasshoppers under a fern make the field ring with their importunate chink, whilst thousands of great cattle, reposed beneath the shadow of the British oak, chew the cud and are silent, pray do not imagine that those who make the noise are the only inhabitants of the field; that, of course, they are many in number; or that, after all, they are other than the little, shrivelled, meagre, hopping, though loud and troublesome, insects of the hour.[15]

In November 1792 the Association for the Preservation of Liberty and Property against Republicans and Levellers (the APLP) was formed and became the best supported of all late eighteenth-century pressure groups. Numerous public meetings protested against Tom Paine's works and demonstrated their loyalty to the regime in 1792–93. The more vigorously radicalism spread, or was thought to spread, from France, the greater became the drive for the establishment to rally round the ministry. The government's position was buttressed in various ways. Politically, the majority of Whigs joined the ranks of the government's supporters in July 1794. On the policy front, efforts were made to rebut suggestions that the national debt incurred by war drained the economy. In 1794, the Secretary of the Board of Trade, George Chalmers, produced an enlarged and revised edition of a book on the development of Britain's wealth, originally published just after the American conflict, to demonstrate that the immense overhang of debt from all previous wars had not impeded Britain's economic progress. Indeed, rapid past recoveries from wartime falls in trade and economic activity showed how resilient the economy inevitably proved to be and how the country readily carried the accumulated burden of the national debt. Thus, for example, exports of British manufactures to all countries increased by over 40% from the six-year average of 1768–74 to the six-year average of 1786–92, while tax receipts also rebounded after 1784.[16] On a more celebratory level, victories in the West Indies and at sea enabled the government to stage public celebrations in May and June 1794. Similar events followed, and parades, commemorations, funerals for military and naval commanders, and the erection and installation of monuments to them, all added to the stock of loyalist activity and symbolism. The rallying of middle-class support also took practical shape in the rapid growth of the militia and volunteer corps during the mid-1790s. Other evidence of support for the regime was shown by the ease with which the government raised money – for example, the £18 million in four days for the so-called Loyalty Loan of December 1796.[17] By the end of the 1790s the king was increasingly depicted as a symbol of national purpose and unity, representing both moderate reform and conservatism, derived from accessible paternalism.

While continental fighting depended upon an Austrian alliance, the government built up its armed forces at home to deter invasion and to secure order. Starting with an army of only 17,000 regular troops stationed in Britain, in early 1794 ministers planned for 52,000 militia men (16,000 of them in Ireland), raised strictly for home duties, 40,000 British fencibles, available for service in Ireland, and formal status for volunteer companies of artillery, cavalry and infantry. The regular army expanded, to a planned total of 175,000 men, while a further 34,000 planned foreign mercenaries boosted that figure. Many of these new regulars served in defensive rather than offensive roles, both at home and especially in the colonies abroad. When the ministry discussed cooperation with Austria for a land campaign against eastern France, the British commitment (including Germans under British command) totalled only about 40,000 men. The Austrians planned to deploy 312,000 men on that front and to provide the bulk of a mobile force of 170,000 for an invasion of France.[18] Given the unwillingness of men in a relatively high-wage economy to serve in the army or navy, and the extent of imperial commitments, Britain could scarcely play a major role in continental campaigning.

Ministers in London sought to gain maximum advantages from the limited resources available. Much hinged on the effectiveness of what

British forces could achieve in three widely separated spheres in which Britain operated as a regional power. First, the Low Countries constituted probably the most frequently and intensely fought-over region in the world for about five hundred years down to 1945. The British had major trading and Hanoverian interests in northern Europe, and fiercely opposed French expansionism, especially in the direction of the River Scheldt. The Austrian Netherlands (essentially modern Belgium) and the Dutch Republic stood as bulwarks against French power. For their part, the French had various motives for invading the Low Countries, ranging from a high-minded drive to liberate oppressed neighbours, through the gnawing material need to seize food, to the greedy quest for the Austrian Netherlands' rich industrial resources and tax revenues, to the traditional thrust of Great Power politics to overawe and dominate their borders and exert influence over the German states loosely strung together in the Holy Roman Empire. Overcoming these aims was seen by the British as essentially the responsibility of the other German powers themselves. The Duke of Richmond, head of the Ordnance whose responsibilities covered the artillery and engineers, sought to avoid 'endless war against fortified Towns' in Flanders.[19]

A second theatre emerged from discussions throughout the 1790s over the desirability and effectiveness of using British sea power to succour royalist or counter-revolutionary risings in France. This form of warfare first occurred in the Mediterranean, where Britain became a significant power from the 1790s. The most dramatic intervention occurred at Toulon, the great French Mediterranean naval port, where local political turmoil was intensified by disaffection in the naval base and economic problems surrounding the arsenal and dockyard, ending with a rebellion by arsenal workers. French naval commanders clashed with the city authorities, who decided to accept British naval intervention essentially to tame their own fleet. Without any prior authorization from London, Admiral Lord Hood, the commander-in-chief in the Mediterranean, offered British protection, initially insisting that the city declare for the Bourbons. William Pitt, in an expansive mood optimistic beyond even his own normally sanguine thinking, envisaged pouring 60,000 men into Toulon during late 1793 and 1794, and operating from there to sustain the royalists further inland as well as on the coast. Yet he anticipated that no fewer than 50,000 of those troops would be supplied by Austria, Naples, Sardinia (Piedmont) and Spain, buttressed by Swiss mercenaries, with Britain acting as an impresario of continental war in her traditional style.[20]

A different approach found particular favour with Henry Dundas, one of Pitt's most influential cabinet ministers who was to take on the new post of Secretary of State for War and the Colonies in 1794. Long interested in India, the management of government patronage, and supporting ambitious Scotsmen seeking careers outside their native land, he persistently pressed for attacks on enemy colonies and equally vigorously rejected arguments for a concentration of naval forces in the Channel as a protection against French invasion.

It was not, therefore, surprising that the biggest British military effort during 1793–97 occurred not in Europe but in the West Indies. Britain's position as a power in that region contrasted sharply with her position in Europe. The French held six islands, intermingled with the eleven under British control, and were readily exposed to British attack, especially since they had no major troop concentrations and a smaller population than the British islands'. Moreover, the Royal Navy had defeated the French navy in the Caribbean in the early 1780s despite the unprecedented challenge of being opposed in 1780–83 by all three of the European naval powers coming after Britain in importance: France, Spain and Holland. With France enjoying no military or naval advantages, the British undertook various campaigns which transformed the regional balance of power. Yet it was unclear whether ministers in London at the time regarded the conquest of French (and later Spanish) West Indian islands as a means of crippling their opponents' home economies, as a way of gaining a bargaining advantage for the eventual round of peace negotiations, or as economic and strategic objectives in themselves.

Binding these principal theatres of strategic operations together was the recurrent preoccupation with the effective deployment of naval power. In 1793 the three main fleets, each speedily mobilized to provide 20–25 ships of the line, were in the Channel, the Mediterranean, and the reserve at Portsmouth and Plymouth; in addition, the two Caribbean squadrons were substantially strengthened. The Channel and Mediterranean fleets were tasked with blockading the two principal French naval bases at Brest and Toulon respectively, and with protecting vast convoys of British merchant ships. The only high-seas battle of the early years of the war – the Glorious First of June in 1794 – occurred because the French fleet from Brest sought to protect a huge grain convoy sailing to France from America, not because France was attempting to deploy naval power more strategically.

The limitations of French naval power decisively shaped the war at sea. Concentrating French naval forces was extremely difficult, given the long distances between their Mediterranean and Atlantic seaboard ports. The French also had far fewer ships than the Royal Navy possessed and deficiencies in naval stores. As soon as war broke out, Sir Charles Middleton, a former Comptroller of the Navy, predicted that the French would not appear at sea in fleets but would maintain 'numerous and active squadrons' at their ports, ready to pounce upon British trade and to seek out naval supplies. He envisaged the French using flying squadrons to capture St Helena and the Cape, to raid British trading routes from the Leeward Islands, the Newfoundland fisheries and Quebec, and to intercept merchant shipping returning from the Baltic in July to September, laden with materials essential to the building and running of ships. In defending Britain's home trade in the Channel and the North Sea, frigates and smaller cruisers would prove far more important than line ships in confronting France's 'war against trade'.[21]

This French threat to shipping explains the prominence British authorities accorded to early British victories in small-ship engagements, for those successes served as public warnings to France and celebrated the British ability to counter the threat. On 17 June 1793, for example, Captain Edward Pellew fought and captured a French frigate, bringing it back to Portsmouth as a prize, the first capture of a significant enemy warship in the war. Only eight days after his return he was knighted by George III at Britain's premier naval base. Captain James Saumarez received the same accolade after capturing a French frigate off Cherbourg in mid-October.[22] In 1794, George Chalmers, an active publicist on the government's behalf, emphasized the unprecedented triumph at Toulon, the rash of successes in small-warship encounters against the French, and the hefty trawl of French merchantmen and other cargo vessels and privateers. Those blows outweighed, he stressed, the French seizure of 236 privateers and merchant vessels amongst Britain's 15,000 merchant ships.[23] More impressively, during the four years 1793–1796 inclusive the Royal Navy captured or drove to destruction 61 enemy frigates (including five Dutch and two Spanish vessels) in small-ship engagements, excluding actions in which line ships were also involved and excluding those frigates seized or destroyed at Toulon. The annual tally rose year by year, with the French losing fifty-four frigates in 1793–96 compared with the twenty-three frigates they lost throughout the conflict of 1778–83.[24] This demonstrated a compelling response to the French campaign against British maritime trade.

One problem raised by maritime commercial warfare was that British trading interests needed very wide-ranging protection. The average annual value of British manufactured exports in the six years 1786–92 totalled £14,754,000. Of that total over half went outside Europe, with £5,350,500 going to the USA, the West Indies, and British North America in declining order of importance, and £1,922,000 going to the East Indies. British naval activity had to be widely dispersed in order to protect such extensive and substantial trade. Moreover, Britain's manufactured exports to Europe, worth £5,466,000, were extremely widely dispersed. While £2,613,700 went to the German states, Holland, Flanders, and France, some £2,221,000 went to the Atlantic seaboard of southern Europe and the Mediterranean (Spain, Portugal, Gibraltar, and the Italian states), and over £550,000 went to the Baltic countries.[25] Given this pattern of trading, it is difficult to see how a fleet concentration in the Western Approaches, a strategic option much canvassed by naval historians, would have won acceptance from those involved in trading with such diverse destinations and therefore been a viable policy to politicians.[26]

Yet how far an even greater focus on home waters might have enabled Britain to shape events on the continent is less clear than the demonstration that substantial naval effort was concentrated in home waters suggests. There is no evidence that British blockades or British seizure of the colonies held by France or its subordinates sapped French capacity to fight on land. Nor did the imposition of British naval superiority in the Channel and its approaches in itself induce continental powers to ally themselves to Britain. The consequences of naval power boosted British government revenues (through extra-European trade) and depressed French revenues (from the loss of such trade). But the struggle in home waters arose because the Royal Navy, like virtually all organisations concentrating on its service rival, sought to constrict the French fleet's operations and to capture French warships. The naval effort occurred in home waters almost in isolation from any larger concern for war-making except the fear that any French fleet securing operational freedom might endanger the British Isles, even though any such naval threat was in reality extremely generalized other than as an impediment to British trade.

The Low Countries 1793–94

When Britain went to war against the French after only ten years of peace, military advice within the Cabinet came from the third Duke of Richmond who was Master General of the Ordnance from 1784 until late 1794. The duke had last seen active service in 1762 and had opposed government policy during the wars of 1776–83. In discussing military strategy with Pitt in April 1793, he tried to concentrate on possible opportunities in north-west France, where expeditions might assist French royalists opposing the new regime. This admirable desire to focus on one strategic point had the unfortunate defect of ignoring the fundamental issue upon which

Britain went to war, namely the security of the Low Countries. The prime minister, in contrast, airily considered a whole range of strategic options, hoping to assemble a striking force mobile enough to influence events in the Netherlands and then shift to the Mediterranean during the late summer, establishing itself there in sufficient strength to enable some of its numbers to be detached to the Caribbean from October. Pitt also envisaged expeditions to the East Indies. The duke objected that this smacked of unreality: there were too few troops; they needed time – six months in the case of fresh recruits – for proper training and acquiring the ability to act in large bodies; and they would soon suffer from too much attrition to supply the strength for a rapid sequence of widely dispersed operations. The shortage of readily deployable forces became clear when the Duke of York's forces on the continent totalled 17,000 German mercenaries and only 6,500 British soldiers. Thus, when war broke out in 1793, strategic thinking had not progressed from the practices prevailing during the American war: heavy reliance on foreign mercenaries because war aims exceeded Britain's reserves of manpower; failure to coordinate military advice and opportunities; and a predilection for setting unrealistic political objectives.

The diplomatic situation, however, differed dramatically from that of 1779–83. The League of Armed Neutrality, created by Russia and drawing in the Baltic powers, disappeared under a convention between the British and St Petersburg. More importantly, Britain negotiated a large number of bilateral agreements, thus ending her increasing isolation from Europe which had begun in 1778. Some of them – notably that with Austria and, importantly for the future in the Mediterranean, that with the Kingdom of the Two Sicilies (Naples) – involved positive cooperation in wars with France, while others committed countries to supporting or assisting Britain's objectives without entering any war.[27]

Despite the range of alliances and agreements, the main fighting against France fell to Austria's lot. The only state capable of countering France in western Europe was the Habsburg empire. Though hard pressed by the costs of a major war against the Ottomans in 1788–91 and by acute political challenges in Hungary and the Netherlands by 1790, Vienna maintained sound finances and a peacetime army in 1791 of 304,000 men, while ruling around 24.5 million people, compared with France's 28 million.[28] From April to November 1793 British forces under the Duke of York cooperated in an essentially Austrian war in Flanders. By August 1793 the Austrians had 93,000 troops in the Low Countries, compared with 22,000 under British command and 15,000 Dutch. The Austrians deployed a further 38,000 men on the Rhine, while Prussia had 46,000 men at the central point of the allied front stretching from the North Sea coast to Switzerland; Prussian success lay in freeing Mainz from French control.[29] Austrian victories in the spring provided the basis for further advances in July–August by which time the French Republic began to look distinctly vulnerable. But the British decision to attack Dunkirk proved over-ambitious, resulting in 10,000 casualties among 'British' forces, partly because the logistical demands could not be met with the speed and careful planning required and partly because a lack of allied coordination permitted the French to strengthen Dunkirk. Both the British and the Austrians, in their respective spheres of operations, had to pull back by November when winter forced their armies into quarters. By then, the ascendancy of the Jacobins and their Committee of Public Safety promised to provide new energy and efficiency in the French army.

In contrast with this reinvigorated approach to war-making, the British land campaign of 1793–95 has generally been lambasted as a byword for incompetence and ineptitude. Yet the problems which it raised were more complex than any such broad characterization might indicate. Pitt's diplomatic objective was to keep the Austrians and Prussians fighting, in order to halt French expansionism and create buffer states on France's eastern borders; from January 1794 Pitt also sought the restoration of a strongly constitutional monarchy in France.[30] Within these limited objectives, operations in 1793 yielded some British successes, including the capture of the fortified border town of Valenciennes. By early November 1793, the British covered the country from Nieuport to Ypres while lodging the bulk of their forces in Bruges and Ghent. The weather had become so bad that casualties from sickness mounted among the troops and the horses, with those of the artillery 'dying like rotten sheep'. The Duke of York was confident, however, that there would be no winter campaigning because the French had 'abandoned almost all their outposts and are breaking up the roads everywhere, in order to render any attack upon them impossible'.[31] But planning for 1794 proved frustrating. In reviewing the lessons of 1793, York accepted 'the absolute necessity' that 'a well digested plan for the next campaign should be arranged and settled between the different Allied powers', especially the Austrians and the British. As the year ended, however, York reported 'the very great unwillingness' of the Prince of Coburg and the Prince Hohenlohe 'to undertake anything'. In turn, the Austrians complained particularly of their inadequate supplies, and seemed to have made no arrangements for establishing magazines for the campaign of 1794.[32] The Austrian Netherlands did not provide a benign environment for Austrian war-making, since local protest in 1789 had been suppressed with considerable vigour as, for example, in Antwerp, and disregard for local rights. The Austrians, had, for a time evacuated their dependency, retaking it from December 1790 to June 1791.[33] They would willingly have exchanged it for territories in southern Germany.

Austrian failure explains Britain's military difficulties in 1794. With the benefit of hindsight, Carl von Clausewitz later argued that the entire strategic dispositions were at fault. Because the Austrians had a fragile grip on the Netherlands, the Prussians should have been assigned to fight alongside the British rather than along the Upper Rhine. As they had demonstrated in 1787, the Prussians held a stronger stake than Austria did in the security of the United Provinces against radical politicians and French influences, while some of their territories, near Nijmegen and Arnhem, abutted the United Provinces.[34] Yet Prussian efforts proved un-inspiring. In April 1794 Prussia, in return for a major British subsidy, agreed to provide 62,400 men deployable at the discretion of Britain and the Dutch Republic. This plan failed because the Prussian commander of the field army retained ultimate responsibility for his forces' dispositions, while delays in remitting the substantial monthly payments to Berlin meant that troops were unavailable for campaigning in Flanders during June and July. By September, cash tranches to Prussia had yielded no results, with Lord Malmesbury, the special envoy to Berlin, complaining:

The disgraceful failure of every military operation His Prussian Majesty has undertaken since the year 1791 has destroyed the reputation of the Prussian army, and the duplicity and versatility of his Cabinet put an end to all confidence and good faith.[35]

In the same month, the British ministry stopped advances to Austria (whose government found it hard to raise loans on the London money markets) for lack of a satisfactory Austrian military effort in campaigning on the Meuse. Trying to prop up allies with financial backing or guarantees thus offered no simple panacea to Britain's military dilemmas in waging a continental war.

The real obstacle to a continental commitment was that neither prin-cipal ally shared Britain's preoccupation with the security of the Scheldt waterway. Britain expended much effort in 1793–95 in trying to dissuade Austria from pursuing its preferred policy of bartering its suzerainty over the Austrian Netherlands for concessions in southern Germany. Equally, and whatever the merits of Clausewitz's strategic analysis of 1793–94, Prussian interests did not prioritize the Low Countries. Prussia made significant territorial gains against Poland in 1793 and nearly half its army operated in these new territories during 1794. When the final carve-up of Poland occurred in 1795, Prussia had increased its territory by 50% and its population by even more. Its ruling elites were absorbed by the administrative, legal, and military tasks of integrating such acquisitions into the Prussian state, and by the sale of lands taken from the Polish crown or sequestered from rebel nobles. The critical strategic issue for 1794 concerned not British military competence but the extent to which Prussia would be even half committed to operations against France and the relative determination of Austria to pour resources into the western campaign when her rivals in the east were intent on demolishing the very state – Poland – which in the 1760s had been territorially larger than France or the Habsburg's Germanic lands and the fourth most populous European country, and which many Austrians regarded as a vital buffer against Russian and Prussian expansionism.[36] Nor did the United Provinces, deeply divided by the revolution of 1787 which pitched the established, conservative Patriots against revolutionary Liberators, respond uniformly to rising radicalism and expansionism in France as if such tendencies were undesirable, threatening, and to be resisted.

The failed campaign of 1794–95

When British campaigning started, over three weeks late, on 25 March 1794, manoeuvring occurred around Valenciennes, Cambrai and Tournai. Although there was periodic fighting and a good deal of skirmishing, no battle occurred until 16–18 May around Tourcoing. The French victory there, particularly humiliating for the British contingent, was not decisive in a strictly military sense, but was quite enough to lead the Austrians to swing their attentions from France to new opportunities for intervention in Poland, where a nationalist rising, starting on 25 March 1794, liberated Warsaw on 20 April. Those events stimulated the intervention of first Prussia and then, at the end of May, Austria, as the last stage unfolded in the dismemberment of Poland by its voracious neighbours. The British in Flanders staged a holding operation on 22 May, and on 26 June the allies attacked French posts but were flung into a retreat of 30 miles, leaving Brussels to the French. At this point, the allied strategy collapsed. The Prussians failed to provide their contracted numbers – indeed any numbers at all – and the Austrians did not meet their targets for concentrated troop strengths. Far worse, the allies' retreat led them in two divergent directions. Whereas the British headed north, attempting to keep in contact with the coast and their source of supplies and reinforcements and their potential escape route if they needed an exit strategy, the Austrians headed eastwards towards the Rhine. By contrast, the French increased their numbers and imbued their generals with intensified determination to succeed. Some 17 French generals were executed in 1793, and no fewer than 67 met a similar fate in 1794.[37] Such intimidation helps explain the drive behind the French advances of 1794, particularly as the winter wore on.

Once the allied armies had divided, the separated Anglo-German force faced three difficulties. First, in conducting a steady retreat it cut itself off from the coast and supplies. During July the British lost access to Ostend, through which they had been able earlier to channel reinforcements. On 22 July a large amount of stores were destroyed when they evacuated Antwerp, the major port on the tidal River Scheldt whose independence from France had been the principal objective of the entire campaign. Second, the retreating army repeatedly found it impossible to hold positions in the face of overwhelming French numbers, withdrawing twice across rivers in September in the face of French armies three times their own size. By 11 October, they withdrew to Nijmegen and Arnheim. Continuing French pressure forced the evacuation of Nijmegen on 7–9 November and resulted in the British taking up cantonments upon the Waal, where they faced the hardships of the winter weather.[38] The French had been probing the River Waal in late December; by 10 January the river had iced over, and they were able to cross wherever they wished. This forced the British to retreat once again, this time in savage cold which inflicted appalling casualties. One officer commented on a day's march on 14 January: 'We could not proceed one hundred yards without perceiving the dead bodies of men, women, and horses, in every direction.'[39] Thirdly, the local Dutch population became increasingly disaffected from the ruling house of Orange and explicitly pro-French by mid-October 1794. Indeed, the area around Deventer, where the British encountered the worst of the freezing winter weather, was also one of longstanding anti-Orange political principles.[40] The lack of local support and succour the British received should have been entirely predictable. These factors, reinforced by a breakdown in local commissariat arrangements, forced the British to pull back into Germany, reaching Bremen on 26 March, and eventually evacuating through the port of Bremerleche, from which 200 ships sailed on 24 April 1795.[41]

This agonizing retreat was scarcely the unremitting collapse of traditional historiography. The British withdrew about 100 miles from the Cambrai area to Oosterhout between 26 April and 5 August 1794; a further 70 miles to Deventer by 19 January; and a final 120 miles from Deventer to Bremen from late January to 26 March. This was scarcely a rout inflicted by the French. During the entire campaign from April 1794 to 14 January 1795, the Anglo-German army suffered about 3,300 operational casualties, as recorded in one officer's formal account of the campaign. Some 940 of them were suffered in the battle around Turcoing on 16–18 May, and another 434 losses (nearly all of them missing, as prisoners) resulted when one regiment was trapped in a minor engagement on the Waal on 20 October.[42] While these returns exclude the losses from illness, disease, and the terrible freezing weather of January, they indicate that the British army did not suffer military humiliation at French hands. Quite the contrary, the British adopted a common system of infantry drill for the first time, thus improving the leadership of battalions, used infantry lines of two men deep where no enemy cavalry threatened, increasingly deployed light companies to try to counter the French use of *tirailleurs*, or skirmishers, and engaged their cavalry effectively. They depicted themselves as engaged in 'a constant scene of skirmishing' with their enemy in which they acquitted themselves well against their opponents. The worst problems arose from the prolongation of campaigning into the harsh winter and the shortages of food, clothing and medicine which followed.[43]

Contemporary British accounts of the campaign depicted British bravery rather than military ineptitude. One account insisted that British forces displayed their 'usual bravery' and were 'irresistible with the bayonet, where the numbers are any thing near equal'.[44] Official despatches on, for example, the French advance between the Leck and Waal rivers on 14 January 1795 stressed that the Anglo-German troops' behaviour was 'as steady as it was spirited' against 'very superior numbers'.[45] Another described the campaign: 'This dreadful trial of courage, patience, and military skill . . . deservedly excited the admiration of all Europe.'[46] These qualities could not, however, prevail against French numbers; as one military history of the campaign published some years later stressed, 'the enemy were formidable only in their numbers, and to their numbers alone were they indebted for their conquests'.[47] The British campaign of 1794–95 sank once allied numbers plummeted. The allies committed 80,000 troops, instead of a planned 190,000, to the Austrian Netherlands by late June, whereas the French, in line with the general surge in their conscription of military manpower, commanded 300,000 men.[48] There was nothing the British could do to counteract the emergency *levee en masse* of 1793 which lifted the French army from 156,000 men in 1789 up to 983,000 men in arms, including those assigned to home defences, in

1793.[49] The disparity of numbers ensured French victory once the Austrian and the Anglo-German armies withdrew on divergent routes. Whether or not British generalship was lax or incompetent – so recurrent a theme in British military historiography – had relatively little to do with the campaign's progress or impact.

The French seizure of the Netherlands during the winter of 1794–95 profoundly affected the future course of the war and Britain's role in it. By taking over the United Provinces, France secured control of the centre of Europe's, especially northern Europe's, financial markets. The Austrian Netherlands, the United Provinces and German territories taken in 1794–95 were 'all rich, fertile and populous countries' which, together with French acquisitions in Italy and on the Spanish border, added an estimated 13 million people in these neighbouring states to France's population of 28 millions. That was a gain nearly equivalent to the 15.9 million people of the United Kingdom in 1801.[50] In addition to achieving such augmentations in financial power, territory and people, the French increased their naval power by about 30 ships of the line belonging to the Dutch navy.[51] France, already mighty, had suddenly become much mightier, by far and away the most populous and richest European power. Even more menacing to Britain, France had the opportunity of controlling the Dutch colonial empire. The British withdrawal from the Low Countries and then from the continental mainland thus opened the way to a new phase of campaigning. Naval competition became a challenge once more, and intensified when in late 1796 Spain allied itself to France. Globally, the British faced the urgent need to prevent the French from seizing the Dutch overseas empire. Pitt's war planning had concentrated well into late 1795 on wearing down the French government in the expectation that it would collapse from financial or military pressures. That expectation was no longer sustainable. Even though the *levee en masse*, by exposing so many Frenchmen to the grim hazards of war, could not be maintained on its initial scale,[52] it had ensured the regime's survival and dramatic expansion. An apparently fractious, fragile, and fanatical regime achieved in 1794–95 what the Bourbons had failed to gain in over a century of regal ambition.

Naval warfare and the legacy of 1778–83

In looking beyond Europe to Britain's global role, we enter a different realm of British power projection. The Royal Navy was a mighty and frequently tested instrument of war. Its experience of the wars of the American Revolution had not been uniformly positive, but helped forge the successful navy of the 1790s which, unlike the army, operated on the grand scale and positioned itself for major confrontations with the enemy. It met the biggest single challenge of combating the combined power of the three largest fleets in Europe after its own; by 1780, France, Spain and the Netherlands were all at war with Britain. No more serious concentration of enemy numbers faced the Royal Navy in its history. Although the navy lost control of North American waters at a critical moment in September 1781, thereby enabling the French with their American allies to force the surrender of a small British army at Yorktown, naval power proved decisive in wearing out the French and Spanish. When the British fleet warded off a planned Franco-Spanish attack on England's south coast in 1779, Lord North, the prime minister, gleefully reported that the French had pulled back, despite 'their great preparations, their immense expenses, their boastings, their menaces, and their having in fact an opportunity of attacking us which they never had before.'[53]

Positive naval successes followed the expansion of the Royal Navy in 1780. Sir George Rodney led a fleet to resupply the Gibraltar and Menorca garrisons with provisions for two years.[54] By late February 1780, Rodney's fleet had destroyed or captured nine Spanish and French ships of the line, with more line of battle ships taken in a single action than in either of the two previous great wars. In February 1781, the Dutch Caribbean island of St Eustatius fell to Rodney, yielding the British goods and ships valued at perhaps £3 million, a sum equivalent to the annual exports of all the American colonies in the early 1770s. Rodney boasted to his wife, 'there never was a more important stroke made against any state whatsoever'.[55] Edmund Burke noted that the illuminations in London celebrating this victory were the biggest he had ever seen.[56]

The only battle, on land or sea, to achieve classic status from the wars of 1776–84 was at the Saintes where Rodney broke a French effort to concentrate forces for an invasion of Jamaica, which in 1774 accounted for as much British investment wealth as all thirteen American colonies together.[57] By the time Rodney called off the engagement at the Saintes on 12 April 1782, his fleet had been closely manoeuvring against the French fleet for four days and suffered debilitating damage from French fire against the British sails, masts and rigging.[58] Improvements in gunnery may have been crucial to victory, although only some of Rodney's line ships had had their guns adjusted to achieve an enhanced range and less recoil, thereby doubling the standard rate of fire.[59] In many ways, the Saintes was a mêlée battle prefiguring the naval battles of 1797–1805. Rodney captured five ships of the French line, a significant haul by any previous standards, and prevented a Franco-Spanish invasion of Jamaica.[60] The naval war thus ended on a high note for Britain. In all, the French lost sixteen ships of the line to enemy action, capture and wreckage at sea in 1782, compared with five such losses in the three years 1779–81 inclusive.

Counterbalancing impressive operational achievements were well-publicized defects, particularly of command. The 'failure' to engage the French fleet off Ushant in 1778 provoked a politically poisonous controversy. Defects of command at the Saintes allegedly prevented a decisively destructive battle from being gained. But a line of battleships was extremely difficult to manoeuvre, and senior officers enjoyed no opportunities between wars of gaining practice in fleet operations.[61] Owing to the half-pay system, the movement of ships for refitting and between different fleets, and the greater financial attractions in serving in frigates, which preyed on merchant shipping or enemy small ships singly or in twos and threes and offered more occasions for gaining prize-money, it was also difficult to develop teamwork among officers. A comparison between three battles fought in the West Indies during the years 1780–82 shows that of the 25 captains and admirals at the battle between the islands of Martinique and Dominica on 17 April 1780, only one other than Rodney was present at the Saintes two years later; and he commanded a frigate not a ship of the line at the later engagement. Of the 41 senior officers present at the Saintes, only 11 had been at the battle of St Lucia one year earlier in April 1781, but not necessarily in the same ships, and only one, Rodney himself, had been present two years earlier.[62]

Added to practical difficulties concerning command, the larger strategic argument concerning naval warfare has been N.A.M. Rodger's insistence that the only way the Royal Navy might have achieved a decisive victory was in the Western Approaches to the English Channel.[63] By concentrating fleet numbers and effort there and adopting a more defensive strategy than the one the ministry applied in 1778–82, the British might have created an opportunity to destroy their opponents' fleets. But the suggestion that North America and some West Indian islands might have been jettisoned (to be recaptured later) in order to concentrate naval strength glosses over the increased importance which those possessions had acquired since the 1750s. George III emphasised the West Indies' significance to Lord Sandwich in September 1779: 'our islands must be defended, even at the risk of an invasion of this island. If we lose our sugar islands, it will be impossible to raise money to continue the war'.[64] The more global British interests had become, the more difficult it was to focus military or naval strength at any one place. Intense financial and political pressure existed in London to protect specific interests across the world.

Naval successes offered much to crow about. The *Annual Register for 1783* enumerated the warships of all the powers either taken or destroyed during the wars. The balance-sheet of losses and gains in firepower was as if Britain at the end of the war had retained its full strength in warships of 1778, while the French and Spanish had lost the equivalent of one-quarter of their line of battle ships of that year.[65] The British lost sixteen line ships in 1777–83, but only one to enemy action and that was retaken in 1782. In contrast, Britain's opponents lost twenty-nine line ships, fourteen of which were added to the Royal Navy. The Spanish also lost nearly one-third of the frigates they possessed in 1780. The naval war ended on a politically satisfying high note for the British, since fifteen of the allied losses of ships of the line occurred between April and December 1782.[66] Such success came at a price. It has been estimated that some 176,000 men were enlisted in Royal Navy ships in the years 1774–80 and that 19,800 seamen died in the years 1776–80, mostly of sickness and disease.[67] Extrapolated for the entire war, this level of naval casualties matched the Americans' total losses of 25,000 dead during their war for independence from Britain. But the naval effort indicated that if the French and Spanish from 1779, reinforced by the Dutch from 1780, had been unable to defeat a vastly overstretched Royal Navy then they would be unlikely ever to do so. Moreover, British dominance in fighting at sea began in the early 1780s, not in 'the age of Nelson'; the Spanish lost seven line ships as a result of combat on 16 January 1780, while in 1782 the French lost the same aggregate number at the Saintes and in Mona Passage one week later.

One other legacy of the wars of the American Revolution was the expectation of victories at sea. George III wrote to Lord Sandwich, the minister responsible for the navy, on 8 July: 'I sigh for an action. I know it must turn out to the advantage of this nation, and procrastination is the worst evil that can befall us at present.' In September 1779, when the Franco-Spanish fleet sailed into the Channel, George impressed upon the First Lord of the Admiralty that 'the enemy must not quit the Channel without having received hard blows'. Sandwich told the commander-in-chief, Admiral Sir Charles Hardy that 'a battle is inevitable' and the Channel a good place for it:

I need not tell you that the eyes of all the world are upon you, and that no man in this kingdom ever had such an opportunity as yourself of serving his country, his connections, and himself.[68]

The obvious rejoinder, that attack would be foolhardy in the light of Franco-Spanish numerical superiority, elicited the reflection that large fleets suffered from diminishing returns in battle efficiency. Sir Thomas Pye, commander-in-chief at Portsmouth, argued in early July that thirty British ships of the line would suffice against a combined Franco-Spanish fleet of forty ships or more, because thirty ships of the line, stretched along four miles, were as many as any admiral 'can manoeuvre with propriety'; a Franco-Spanish battle fleet exceeding thirty would encounter 'anarchy and confusion' since the Spanish, Admiral Pye claimed, were not good at managing fleets and the allies were not accustomed to operating together.[69] The naval war in 1778–82 helps explain the Royal Navy's aggressive fighting ethos of the 1790s because it stimulated expectations of a decisive naval battle and thoughts about the optimal size required for a battle fleet.

The Mediterranean 1793–95

Unlike the army, the Royal Navy entered the long wars in 1793 strong on recent fighting experience and high on professional self-confidence. Its immediate task was to provide concentrated fleets at key strategic points, in order to thwart French commerce and prevent any possible French counter-attack against Britain or its West Indian colonies. Among Dundas's strategic priorities for offensive operations, as formulated in July 1793, assistance to royalist outbreaks by coastal interventions in France came a distinct third behind the drive to free the Netherlands and the quest for French colonies in the East or West Indies. But, when war began, the Admiralty decided to keep a close check on the large French fleet at Toulon, despatching four squadrons to the Mediterranean from early April.[70] By the time Lord Hood, as commander-in-chief, arrived off Toulon in mid-August, he had a substantial naval force of twenty-two line ships, and twenty-nine other warships under his orders. It almost immediately became the instrument for opening up a second 'front' against the French mainland. The allies were invited by counter-revolutionaries to take over the port, doing so on 27 August at a time when Lyons and Marseilles – temporarily as it soon transpired – had fallen to local rebellions.[71] Captain Horatio Nelson, serving in the Mediterranean fleet, informed his wife:

What an event this has been for Lord Hood. Such a one as History cannot produce its equal. That the strongest place in Europe and twenty-two sail of the line etc. should be given up without firing a shot, it is not to be credited.[72]

The Foreign Secretary, Lord Grenville, privately concluded in September that the capture of Toulon would be 'decisive of the war'.[73] This Anglo-Spanish intervention soon, however, encountered grave political and military difficulties. Pitt's hopes of building up a garrison of 60,000 faded as only 17,000 allied troops – merely 2,100 of them British – were assembled by late November.[74] Under pressure from an increasingly large French counter-force, the allies withdrew on 18–19 December. Yet the French navy suffered major losses, with thirty-three warships of all kinds being captured or destroyed, and eleven more damaged. Although the suddenness, scale and crush of the withdrawal meant that the British could not remove all the French vessels in the harbour,[75] the loss of thirteen French ships of the line exceeded the loss later suffered by France at Trafalgar, and greatly exceeded that inflicted at the battle of the Glorious First of June 1794, near the western approaches to the Channel. Moreover, the massive loss of building timber impeded the revolutionary navy's capacity to recover.[76]

But the limited effect of this intervention on French politics justified critics' general scepticism of coastal interventions as a form of warfare. In fact, the Austrians did not accept that Toulon merited particular attention or the diversion of any of their forces from northern Italy. The relatively small number of reinforcements gathered into Toulon during the autumn, largely from Naples, and conveyed from there to Toulon by the Royal Navy, merely replaced sick and injured troops. When the allies had to withdraw in the face of a massive French build-up, they had demonstrated once more the dual need to set strategic priorities and to deploy adequate manpower. The lack of troops meant that the allies failed to move inland and take control of the routes through the mountains, which would have provided the only way of consolidating their hold on Toulon. The First Lord of the Admiralty, Lord Chatham, the prime minister's older brother, agreed that Toulon should have been given absolute priority or abandoned earlier, but insisted that: 'My opinion was treated with no great respect.' John Ehrman suggests that the government failed, as it did over Dunkirk as well, to acquire sufficient military intelligence of the precise geography and political situation at Toulon, or to secure an Austrian commitment to supply troops before becoming heavily committed to its retention.[77] Lord Loughborough, the Lord Chancellor, whose nephew and heir was adjutant-general at Toulon, insisted more positively that the intervention had crippled the French base and its Mediterranean fleet at little cost to Britain. As in the Low Countries, excessively cautious allies – in this case, the Neapolitans and Spanish – had let the British down.[78] An official on the spot, Gilbert Elliott, described the 6,800 Spanish troops as 'worse than useless', running away in action, while the 4,800 Neapolitans had no experience of being under fire: 'The superiority of the English is something beyond one's imagination. In looks and dress and discipline and courage they are a higher order of beings.'[79] Unfortunately, there were very few of them.

The withdrawal from Toulon necessitated the acquisition of a new base in the Mediterranean. Unfortunately, the British had lost the island of Menorca back to the Spanish (who were now their ally) in 1782. They enjoyed access to Leghorn, the main port of Tuscany, but such access would always be subject to the inter-state diplomacy of northern Italy. The preferred option was Bonaparte's birthplace, the island of Corsica, which had only recently become French. In 1794 Pascal Paoli led an anti-French rebellion, recognizing both the vital importance of British support and the need to offer the British some form of suzerainty in order to protect the island against France when and if its independence were secured. Possessing useful supplies – the French obtained naval timber and stores from the island – and a port, Calvi, 109 miles from Antibes in southern France, Corsica made a desirable, as well as an attainable, base. Lord Hood immediately turned his attention to the island, and from 9 February to 10 August British forces took the key coastal towns of St Fiorenzo, Bastia, and Calvi. The navy played a prominent role in bombarding Bastia and Calvi and in landing forces to assault those towns, giving rise to a continuing historiographical emphasis upon naval energy and activism contrasting with the army's hyper-cautious, if not supine, approach to operations.[80]

The first two years of war thus saw the British achieve significant victories at sea and a significant advance in the Mediterranean. These gains balanced the failed intervention in the Low Countries and the recriminations within the army over that failure. If the collapse of the allied front in the Austrian Netherlands resulted from Austria's strategic decisions and Prussian indifference, there were enough deficiencies in British military logistics and command to raise doubts about the army's competence. In more distant theatres, despite the lessons of the American War of Independence, the coordination of command, particularly in army–navy joint operations, depended on the personal chemistry of the respective commanders rather than any system. Overall, the British did not conduct war-making in 1793–95 in any new or reformulated ways. But their achievements in naval warfare far exceeded any previous maritime accomplishments.

Notes and references

1 John Lynn, *The Wars of Louis XIV, 1667–1714* (London, 1999), pp. 362–67.

2 William Pitt, *Orations on the French War* (London, 1906), pp. 290–91, 345, 376, 378.

3 Cyril Matheson, *The Life of Henry Dundas* (London, 1933), p. 182; Julian S. Corbett and H.W. Richmond (eds), *Private Papers of George, Second Earl Spencer*, 4 vols (London, 1913–24), Vol. I, p. 318.

4 Michael Howard, *The Continental Commitment* (London, 1972).

5 David French, *The British Way in Warfare, 1688–2000* (London, 1990), pp. xv–xvii; Carl von Clausewitz, *On War*, edited and translated by Michael Howard and Peter Paret (Princeton, NJ, 1989) pp. 259–60.

6 David Fraser, *Frederick the Great* (London, 2000), pp. 544, 598–99.

7 N.A.M. Rodger, 'Sea-Power and Empire, 1866–1793' in P.J. Marshall (ed.), *The Eighteenth Century* (Oxford, 1998), pp. 169–83; p. 182.

8 Rory Muir, *Britain and the Defeat of Napoleon, 1807–1815* (New Haven, CT, 1996), p. 381; Christopher D. Hall, *British Strategy in the Napoleonic War, 1803–15* (Manchester, 1992), pp. 90–93, 191–93; J.W. Fortescue, *The County Lieutenancies and the Army, 1803–1814* (London, 1909), pp. 305–06.

9 John M. Sherwig, *Guineas and Gunpowder: British Foreign Aid in the Wars with France, 1793–1815* (Cambridge, MA, 1969), pp. 345, 352–55, 365–68.

10 William Laird Clowes, *The Royal Navy: A History*, 7 vols (London, 1897–1903), Vol. V, p. 283.

11 T.C.W. Blanning, *The Origins of the French Revolutionary Wars* (London, 1986), pp. 138–42, 158–59.

12 L.G. Mitchell, *Charles James Fox* (London, 1997 edn), pp. 129; Jeremy Black, *British Foreign Policy in the Age of Revolutions, 1783–1793* (Cambridge, 1994), pp. 460–71.

13 Matheson, *The Life of Henry Dundas*, p. 182.

14 John Barrell, *Imagining the King's Death: Figurative Treason, Fantasies of Regicide, 1793–1796* (Oxford, 2000), pp. 21–27, 29–30, 367; Denis Gray, *Spencer Perceval* (Manchester, 1963), p. 11. There is a fine general discussion in James P. Epstein, *Radical Expression: Political Language, Ritual, and Symbol in England, 1790–1850* (Oxford, 1994).

15 Edmund Burke, *Reflections on the French Revolution and Other Essays* (London, 1910), p. 82.

16 George Chalmers, *An Estimate of the Comparative Strength of Great Britain* (London, 1794), pp. xxii, 276–81.

17 John Ehrman, *The Younger Pitt: The Reluctant Transition* (London, 1983), pp. 329, 639; Harry T. Dickinson, 'Popular Loyalism in Britain in the 1790s' in Eckhart Hellmuth (ed.), *The Transformation of Political Culture: England and Germany in the Late Eighteenth Century* (Oxford, 1990), pp. 503–33; Marilyn Morris, *The British Monarchy and the French Revolution* (New Haven, CT, 1998), p. 187; Blanning, *Origins*, pp. 147–52; Boyd Hilton, *A Mad, Bad, and Dangerous People? England 1783–1846* (Oxford, 2006), pp. 65–74.

18 Ehrman, *The Younger Pitt: The Reluctant Transition*, p. 331.

19 Ehrman, *The Younger Pitt: The Reluctant Transition*, pp. 268, 282–97.

20 William S. Cormack, *Revolution and Political Conflict in the French Navy 1789–1794* (Cambridge, 1995), pp. 175–85, 189–98, 202–3, 205–07; Ehrman, *The Younger Pitt: The Reluctant Transition*, p. 306.

21 Sir John Knox Laughton (ed.) *Letters and Papers of Charles, Lord Barham*, 3 vols (London, 1907–11), Vol. II, pp. 365–67.

22 William James, *The Naval History of Great Britain*, 6 vols (London, 1847 edn), Vol. I, pp. 96, 99, 103–05.

23 Chalmers, *An Estimate of the Comparative Strength*, pp. cxiv–cxvii.

24 Clowes, *The Royal Navy*, Vol. IV, pp. 114–15, 552–55, 558–60.

25 Contemporary figures indicate what was knowable at the time. Chalmers, *An Estimate of the Comparative Strength*, pp. xxvii–xxviii.

26 N.A.M. Rodger, 'Sea-Power and Empire, 1866–1793' in P.J. Marshall (ed.), *The Eighteenth Century* (Oxford, 1998), pp. 169–83; Stephen Conway, 'Empire, Europe and British Naval Power' in David Cannadine (ed.), *Empire, the Sea and Global History: Britain's Maritime World, c.1760–c.1840* (London, 2007), pp. 22–40.

27 For international relations throughout the period, see H.M. Scott, *The Birth of a Great Power System 1740–1815* (London, 2006).

28 T.C.W. Blanning, *Joseph II* (London, 1994), p. 4; P.G.M. Dickson, 'Count Karl von Zinzendorf's "new accountancy": The structure of Austrian government finance in peace and war, 1781–1791', *International History Review*, XXIX (2007), 22–56; Colin Jones, *The Longman Companion to the French Revolution* (London, 1988), p. 287.

29 Clausewitz, *On War*, pp. 630–31.

30 Jennifer Mori, *William Pitt and the French Revolution, 1785–1795* (Keele, 1997), pp. 144–50.

31 A. Aspinall (ed.), *The Later Correspondence of George III*, 5 vols (Cambridge, 1968), Vol. II, pp. 117–19.

32 Aspinall (ed.), *The Later Correspondence of George III*, Vol. II, pp. 135, 137.

33 *The Annual Register . . . for the Year 1789* (London, 1802 edn), pp. 41–52.

34 Clausewitz, *On War*, pp. 630–31.

35 Peter Jupp, *Lord Grenville 1759–1834* (Oxford, 1985), p. 173.

36 Paul W. Schroeder, *The Transformation of European Politics 1763–1848* (Oxford, 1994), pp. 144–45; Piotr S. Wandycz, *The Lands of Partitioned Poland 1795–1918* (Seattle, 1974), pp. 3, 6, 11, 14–16. A fine summary analysis is Brendan Simms, *The Struggle for Mastery in Germany, 1779–1850* (Basingstoke, 1998), pp. 54–67.

37 Blanning, *The Origins of the French Revolutionary Wars*, pp. 120, 126.

38 *The Times*, 6 January 1795, p. 4.

39 *The Times*, idem.; Captain L.T. Jones, *An Historical Journal of the British Campaign in the Continent* (Birmingham, 1797), pp. 101, 115–19, 121, 131, 156, 159, 167, 170, 174.

40 Jonathan Israel, *The Dutch Republic: Its Rise, Greatness, and Fall, 1477–1806* (Oxford, 1995), pp. 1105, 1120.

41 *The Annual Register 1795* (London, 1800), p. 56.

42 Jones, *An Historical Journal*, pp. 40–41, 46, 133.

43 Jones, *An Historical Journal*, pp. 92, 134, 155, 81–83, 91, 94–99, 108–11, 143–44, 171; G.J. Evelyn, ' "I learned what one ought not to do": The British Army in Flanders and Holland, 1793–95', in Alan J. Guy (ed.), *The Road to Waterloo* (London, 1990), pp. 16–22.

44 Jones, *An Historical Journal*, pp. 131, 134–35.

45 *The Times*, 20 January 1795, p. 2: The despatches of General Count Walmoden, commanding the allied army, and Lieutenant General William Harcourt, his deputy.

46 *Annual Register 1795*, p. 55.

47 Jones, *An Historical Journal*, p. 183.

48 Jones, *An Historical Journal*, p. 77.

49 The figures are in Colin Jones, *The Longman Companion to the French Revolution* (London, 1988), p. 156.

50 *Annual Register 1795*, p. 53.

51 *The Times*, 24 February 1795, p. 1.

52 Jennifer Mori, 'The British Government and the Bourbon Restoration: The occupation of Toulon, 1793', *Historical Journal* 40 (1997), pp. 699–719.

53 J.R. Barnes and J.H. Owen (eds), *The Private Papers of John, Earl of Sandwich . . . 1771–1782*, 4 vols (London, 1932–38), Vol. III, pp. 96–98.

54 David Spinney, *Rodney* (London, 1969), pp. 300–02; Barnes and Owen (eds), *The Private Papers of . . . Sandwich*, Vol. III, pp. 194, 204.

55 Piers Mackesy, *The War for America, 1775–1783* (London, 1964), pp. 378–79; H.M. Scott, *British Foreign Policy in the Age of the American Revolution* (Oxford, 1990), pp. 223, 231, 291.

56 P.J. Marshall and John A. Woods (eds), *Correspondence of Edmund Burke*, Vol. VII (Cambridge, 1968), p. 413.

57 Kenneth Morgan, *Slavery, Atlantic Trade and the British Economy, 1660–1800* (Cambridge, 2000), pp. 50–54, 57.

58 This analysis is based on evidence in Barnes and Owen (eds), *The Private Papers of . . . Sandwich*, Vol. IV, pp. 157, 235, 258–59; Spinney, *Rodney*, pp. 443–44.

59 Laughton (ed.), *The Letters and Papers of . . . Barham*, Vol. I, pp. 271–87.

60 Barnes and Owen (eds), *The Private Papers of . . . Sandwich*, Vol. IV, pp. 249, 259, 264; Dull, *The French Navy and American Independence*, pp. 268–69, 284.

61 N.A.M. Rodger, *The Insatiable Earl*, (London, 1993), p. 239.

62 Data in Clowes, *The Royal Navy*, Vol. III, pp. 454, 482, 520.

63 Rodger, *The Insatiable Earl*, pp. 271–74; Rodger, 'Sea-Power and Empire, 1688–1793' in Marshall (ed.), *The Eighteenth Century*, pp. 169–83.

64 Barnes and Owen (eds), *The Private Papers . . . Sandwich*, Vol. III, p. 163.

65 *The Annual Register for 1783* (London, 1800), pp. 297–300.

66 Clowes, *The Royal Navy*, Vol. IV, pp. 109–16.

67 Clowes, *The Royal Navy*, Vol. III, p. 339.

68 Barnes and Owen (eds), *The Private Papers of . . . Sandwich*, Vol. III, pp. 41–42, 61, 87, 92–93; Mackesy, *The War for America*, p. 211.

69 Barnes and Owen (eds), *The Private Papers of . . . Sandwich*, Vol. III, pp. 33–37.

70 French naval power at Toulon had challenged the British in earlier eighteenth-century wars. Rodger, 'Sea-Power and Empire, 1688–1793' in P.J. Marshall (ed.), *The Eighteenth Century*, p. 177.

71 Ehrman, *The Younger Pitt: The Reluctant Transition*, pp. 298–318; Clowes, *The Royal Navy*, Vol. IV, pp. 202–08.

72 Geoffrey Rawson (ed.), *Nelson's Letters* (London, 1960), p. 71.

73 Ehrman, *The Younger Pitt: The Reluctant Transition*, p. 303.

74 Colonel Ramsay Weston Phipps, *The Armies of the First French Republic and the Rise of the Marshals of Napoleon*, 5 vols (Oxford, 1929–35), Vol. III, p. 110.

75 Clowes, *The Royal Navy*, Vol. IV, pp. 203, 211.

76 Rodger, *The Command of the Ocean*, p. 427.

77 Clowes, *The Royal Navy*, Vol. IV, p. 210; Malcolm Crook, *War and Revolution in Toulon, 1750–1820* (Manchester, 1991), pp. 145–48; Ehrman, *The Younger Pitt: The Reluctant Transition*, pp. 315, 318.

78 Marshall and Woods (eds), *The Correspondence of Edmund Burke*, Vol. VII, pp. 524–25.

79 Countess of Minto, *Life and Letters of Sir Gilbert Elliott, First Earl of Minto from 1751 to 1806*, 3 vols (London, 1874), Vol. II, pp. 191–92.

80 Rodger, *The Command of the Ocean*, pp. 430–31.

CHAPTER 4

The expanded contest, 1793–97

The war against France became globalized in two stages. In 1793–94, British ministers agreed to attack the French West Indian islands in order to gain political leverage in Europe, to put pressure on Paris, and to neutralize French power in the Caribbean. The key objective of ruining French overseas trade, which was heavily dependent upon the West Indies, was however difficult to balance against the costs. Holding the islands taken from France turned out to be far more expensive in manpower and money than the British estimated would be the case. An intended *coup de main* became an increasingly damaging military drain by 1795–97. On the French side, aggrandizement in Europe, especially with the effective takeover of the Netherlands in 1795, easily compensated for Caribbean losses. Worse for Britain, the capitulation of the Low Countries to France opened the way to an extension, not contraction, of France's global empire. The British government therefore was compelled to expand the war from early 1795 to prevent France – now an expansionist power rather than a revolutionary regime teetering on the brink of collapse, as it appeared to be in 1793 – from gaining Dutch possessions which might threaten British interests. Even more than the Caribbean intervention, this new initiative deployed the strength, self-confidence, and strong war-fighting record of the Royal Navy to best advantage.

The Caribbean

When war broke out in 1793, the Royal Navy's immediate dispositions indicated Britain's strategic concern for the Caribbean. Since no line ships were stationed in Jamaica and the Leeward Islands together, a squadron of seven ships of the line left England on 24 March 1793 before any reinforcements went to the main naval concentrations in the Mediterranean and Channel.[1] When the principal French West Indian islands of Guadeloupe and Martinique did not, under the somewhat distant promise of royalists' influence, throw themselves under British protection, the ministry decided upon a major expedition to capture them.

Two calculations gave prominence to the West Indies. Britain had massive economic interest in the region to protect. In 1789–90, some 22% of British imports came from the West Indies, which also accounted for 10% of British exports and re-exports. Sugar and coffee were vital consumer goods and cotton was an important raw material. London merchants took half Britain's West Indian trade, affording a cogent example of the metropolis's stake in this region and the pressure its interests could bring upon government. Bristol, Liverpool and Glasgow had large and growing stakes in that same trade. Protecting this interest loomed especially because privateering flourished in the Caribbean, and the very advantage enjoyed by so much of the plantation economy – proximity to the sea – made it vulnerable to depredations from opportunistic or systematic predators. Secondly, powerful blows could be struck in the Caribbean against French commercial might. About one-third of France's overseas trade in the 1780s came from the area, the proportion having risen steadily during the previous century. The French West Indies accounted for more of France's total sugar imports than did the British West Indies for Britain's, and very high proportions of French colonial sugar and coffee were re-exported to the rest of Europe.[2]

Economic reasons for intervention were sharpened by calculations over timing, which in turn were conditioned by the state of the war in Europe. In early September 1793, the British force under the Duke of York pulled back from its siege of Dunkirk and in mid-October the French beat the Austrians at Wattignies. The loss of allied momentum and their settling down into winter quarters encouraged the use of the winter months to engage in colonial campaigning. The global situation in late November 1793 was not unfavourable, since the French armies had halted their offensives, Toulon remained in British hands (at least until December), and Spain provided an ally. Equally auspicious was the parlous condition of the French navy. Politics swept professionalism aside in the republic's continuing purges of the officer corps during 1793. Inexperience among seamen and artillerists, as well as officers, led to frequent collisions in sailing and poor accuracy in cannonading in the mid-1790s. Strategy, self-interest and the enfeebled state of the French navy thus indicated that attractive opportunities might be available in the Caribbean for 1793.

Reinforcing British calculations about the Caribbean was the opportunity which the French possession of only six islands opened to the Royal Navy. The most obvious target was Saint Domingue, which covered the western third – much of it mountainous and little developed – of the second largest island in the West Indies. In 1788, nearly 40,000 of the 55,000 whites and approximately 500,000 of the 594,000 slaves in the six French West Indian colonies lived in that single colony. It was fabulously rich, accounting for 40% of France's foreign trade and producing two-fifths of the world's sugar and half the world's coffee. Another factor giving significance to Saint Domingue was its relative proximity – some 100 miles at the islands' nearest points – to Jamaica, itself the largest of Britain's Caribbean colonies, possessing one of the world's greatest harbours in Kingston and some 256,000 slaves in the late 1780s.[3] Finally, royalist plantation-owners offered potential support locally for British intervention.

The other five principal French colonies were in a great arc of small islands consisting mainly of extinct volcanic mountains. At the centre of command of the eastern Caribbean Martinique boasted the great harbour of Fort-de-France on its western side, dubbed by Sir Charles Grey 'the finest harbour in the universe'. Enjoying a healthy climate, it supported over 100,000 people, over 300 sugar estates and a booming trade. In 1794 it also contained massive military stores.[4] South of Martinique the French held St Lucia, a mountainous island possessing a fine natural harbour on its western or lee side, away from the prevailing Atlantic winds. Only about 100 miles north-west of Britain's naval base at Barbados, it in turn commanded access to Martinique. St Lucia's strategic position explains why the island changed hands fourteen times from the seventeenth century before finally remaining British in 1814.

Although the strategic targets were limited in number and obvious in priority, the conduct of operations against them raised immense challenges. The main centres of British white population – Jamaica (with 23,000 of the 50,000 whites in Britain's West Indian colonies in the late 1780s) and Barbados (with 16,000 whites), were about 1,150 miles apart and held too few Europeans, too widely dispersed, to provide a recruiting ground for troops. Their colonial legislatures jealously guarded their prerogatives, which meant they staunchly refused to pay higher taxes for their own defence. Within the Windward Islands, European mercantilist trading systems broke down in practice, so that a great deal of inter-colony trading occurred. The scale of total commercial transactions was indicated by the fact that in 1787–88, some 627 *British* ships with 13,347 sailors engaged in the West Indian trade.[5] The economic boom sustaining this trade resulted, during the years 1781–90, in the British and French shipping an estimated 600,000 slaves from Africa into the region. These new arrivals added to the internal requirements for controlling the slaves and to existing social tensions. When the French revolutionaries emancipated their slaves, they opened the way to new forms of inter-racial and social conflict.

Even without these new challenges, geographical conditions in the region did not make warfare in Caribbean waters straightforward. Repeatedly in the 1790s the prevailing winds blowing from west to east across the Atlantic delayed and disrupted the sailing of expeditions from Britain in the winter months of November to February. Yet those months should have marked the beginning of Caribbean campaigns, following the hurricane season from late July to late October when sailing in the region was far too hazardous to permit naval operations. In practice during the 1790s, major amphibious operations occurred only in March to June, a very limited campaigning season which politicians in London repeatedly overlooked. Within the Caribbean, prevailing winds made naval operations far easier to mount from the south northwards than in the opposite direction. Finally, most islands were so small that campaigning concentrated on taking harbours and ports and relatively narrow, low-lying plantation belts. But those areas became death traps with rampant malaria and, later, yellow fever, especially damaging to men unseasoned to conditions in the region. Illness and disease necessitated the deployment of levels of force not justified by the territorial expanse of the islands themselves.

Operations in the Caribbean, 1793–97

The initial plan concocted in August 1793 called for over 16,000 troops to be despatched to the Caribbean during the autumn, in time to release a substantial part of the force to return for the reopening of Mediterranean campaigning in the spring of 1794. So ambitious and precise a plan proved wholly unrealistic.[6] Only 7,000 troops sailed in November, reaching Barbados during 6–10 January. The expedition's commanders – Vice Admiral Sir John Jervis and Lieutenant General Sir Charles Grey – opted to attack Martinique in order to secure Fort Royal Bay, the strongest harbour of the Caribbean, for the navy. The British had excellent troops and an overwhelming advantage in manpower and warships directed against fewer than 2,000 French defenders, mostly national guards, mulattos and blacks. They possessed detailed plans of the French defences. Careful thought was given to keeping the troops as healthy as possible; when at Barbados they exercised and trained on land from 3.00 a.m. to 8.00 a.m.

each day, returning to their ships for the rest of the day to avoid sickness. Finally, Grey and Jervis both possessed previous experience of combined operations, had worked together before and enjoyed an excellent professional relationship. Sailors and soldiers participated alike in mounting the final attacks, using cannon, mortars and howitzers, on Fort Bourbon. The bombardment had to be calibrated to avoid wrecking the plentifully-stocked arsenal which the British succeeded in capturing. Once Martinique fell on 25 March, Grey captured St Lucia on 4 April and Guadeloupe on 22 April.

Attention next turned to Saint Domingue. In August 1793 the French republic emancipated the slaves and, by September, mulattos loyal to the republic controlled the colony. Well before Grey's expeditionary force set sail, the British decided to exploit this political revolution and sent troops from the 3,000-strong Jamaican garrison to seize the port town of Jérémie, on Saint Domingue's south-western peninsula. Following this success, and the localized arousal of royalist support, a tiny British force captured Môle Saint Nicolas (and its capacious supplies) on 22 September. This position – one of the commanding naval stations in the western hemisphere – gave Britain control (if the harbour could be used) over access to the Caribbean between Saint Domingue and Cuba. Môle Saint Nicolas enjoyed such celebrity as a strategic strongpoint that its capitulation, a major blow against French maritime power, merited an artillery salute in London. During the European winter of 1793–94 the situation in Saint Domingue remained precarious for the 800 or so British troops, but the arrival of reinforcements from Ireland enabled the British to take Saint Domingue's capital, Port-au-Prince, on 4 June 1794, together with a huge stock of materiel, 131 guns and forty-five merchant vessels trapped there by British naval blockade and subject to distribution as prize-money.[7]

By mid-June 1794, therefore, Britain's fortunes soared. All four of France's main Caribbean colonies were under British control or, as in Saint Domingue's case, emasculated. Fort Bourbon on Martinique had been a major French defensive bastion, and *The Times* on 21 July proclaimed that the capture of merchant shipping at Port-au-Prince 'has given the finishing stroke to the trade of France'.[8] Elsewhere, the British were advancing on Corsica, while the Glorious First of June seemed to guarantee the safety of the western approaches to the Channel.

Yet, from this high point in mid-1794, the war turned against Britain. First, malaria and yellow fever began to afflict Grey's army, which, by 1 June 1794, was reduced to 4,761 effectives widely scattered among the conquered islands. Disease soon spread inland from coastal areas.[9] Worse followed when fresh troops arrived in Martinique and then proceeded, as disease carriers, to Saint Domingue. Second, local commanders further wasted their declining military assets by indulging in plundering and jobbery. Levies amounting to protection money were raised upon affluent merchants and planters, just the people who the British should have rallied to their side against revolutionary principles. This action led to a third shift, with disillusion with the British spreading among the white elite and rebellion erupting among the ex-slaves.

Fourth, the balance of power altered dramatically with the arrival at Guadeloupe on 2 June 1794 of 11,000 French reinforcements, to the surprise of the British in London and the Caribbean. By deploying naval guns on land and laying down some devastating fire from warships upon the British land advance, the French secured control of the agriculturally productive part of Guadeloupe, whereas the portion remaining in British hands was largely mountainous and of little agricultural value.[10] Moreover, the French return to Guadeloupe meant that Grey had no troops available for the further reinforcement of Saint Domingue. By the year's end conditions through disease both in Saint Domingue and Guadeloupe had become so bad that, from Grey's army of 9,750 officers and men in February 1794, a force of only 3,000 effectives remained in play. To the savage depletion in manpower were added the beginnings of revolutionary warfare during the summer of 1794, with the mobilization of newly emancipated slaves in Saint Domingue and the arousing of ex-slaves in Guadeloupe. The French had initiated emancipation in the years 1792–94 in order to raise troops among the former slaves.[11] The insurgency, by merely prolonging the time British troops remained in the West Indies, inflicted disproportionate losses by exposing those men to the ravages of illness and disease.

From the summer of 1794 to July 1795, the British were driven from their conquests of Guadaloupe and St Lucia, and pushed back in those parts of Saint Domingue which they held. Wider slave revolts challenged them in their own colonies of Grenada and St Vincent, as did a rising among free black Maroons in the interior of their main colony of Jamaica. Their capacity to respond was inhibited by various factors. First, the soaring death rate among white soldiers sapped energy and morale.[12] Second, Grey's conquest of islands had never been complete, with British forces taking towns, major roads and agricultural areas but failing to secure large tracts of islands' hilly and wooded interiors, so that hiding inland was relatively easy for those resisting British rule. Third, military reinforcements to the West Indies were slow to arrive. For example, the despatch of a force – eventually amounting to 145 warships, transport and specialist support vessels – originally planned for 15 September 1795, did not deliver troops to Barbados until 14–15 April because of delays in port and terrible gales.[13] Fourth the French eluding British naval blockading and conveyed reinforcements to the West Indies and evaded close British naval patrolling in the Caribbean. France sent nine ships in June 1794 and fifteen ships in January 1795 to take troops to Guadaloupe.[14]

The changing fortunes of these relatively minor campaigns demonstrated the difficulties involved in projecting British power in a theatre of operations where Britain enjoyed distinct advantages. Success in war depended not simply upon grand strategic dispositions, but also upon locally based forces' competence and determination, as well as the vagaries of wind and tide. Command of the oceans proved more difficult than is often implied.

Faced with high rates of attrition among its troops, the government in 1795 tried to strengthen its army by establishing new West Indian regiments recruited from among African slaves. Black soldiers were better at fighting, and surviving, in the jungles and along the low-lying coastal belts than were white troops. They also survived far longer. Even when white troops acclimatized and developed immunities, their death rates were usually twice as high as those of black troops when African enlistment eventually occurred. But in years when large numbers of white troops first arrived in the region, their death rates were eight to thirteen times higher than those of black soldiers.[15] Yet West Indian colonial legislatures staunchly resisted the extension of executive power which black recruitment to the army represented. They resented the army's interference in the regional labour market, the loss of their control over slaves which a transfer of slaves into the army entailed, and the freeing of slaves after five years of military service, as was initially proposed. With colonial resistance to raising black soldiers continuing long after 1797, Jamaica agreed to pay for 2,000 white troops to serve on the island, which eased British financial strains but hardly contributed significantly to recruitment.[16] The army therefore bought freshly arrived slaves off the slave ships, beginning with 1,366 for the Windward and Leeward Island command in 1795–97. For the years 1795–1808, until the abolition of the slave trade, the army was the leading single purchaser of slaves, acquiring in all some 13,400 men, with nearly 9,000 for the Windward and Leeward command, out of a possible total import of 195,000 slaves into the British Caribbean.[17]

Pitt intended that operations in the Caribbean would constitute Britain's main initiative for 1796. Turning planning into reality once more hit the perennial obstacle of severely adverse weather in the English Channel. Recurrent storms in late 1795 long prevented the transport fleet getting out into the Atlantic.[18] The objective was to seize key colonies belonging to France's new client state in Holland and to recoup recent losses. Local Dutch commanders agreed to surrender the Dutch settlements of Demerara, Essequibo, and Berbice on the north coast of South America into British protection. Those colonies (later grouped together as British Guiana) were sufficiently important to become the third largest slave-owning British colony by the 1830s. Elsewhere, the commander-in-chief, Sir Ralph Abercromby's main efforts were directed at retaking St Lucia from the French and restoring British control over St Vincent and Grenada. These minor expeditions posed their individual challenges and exacted a continuing toll. St Lucia, for instance, was taken quickly as the result of some hard fighting entailing the loss of 566 casualties. But Brigadier General John Moore, appointed governor and commandant, spent his first two months after the conquest almost perpetually on skirmishing operations against armed blacks who had been French troops, or who had escaped plantation servitude, or who had come as revolutionaries from Guadaloupe. The island was still not fully pacified by October, during which month alone the British lost 663 men from disease and illness.[19] Campaigning continued in Saint Domingue and an insurrection among the Trelawney Maroons in the interior of Jamaica was suppressed between November 1795 and January 1796 in operations which, if small in scale, required considerable adaptiveness, involving as they did the establishment and deployment of mulatto and slave militia companies in light infantry fighting, and the use of howitzers to shell rebels from hidden positions. By the end of 1796, some 28,000 troops had died, largely from disease, on their way to or while serving in the Caribbean since 1793. Having made colossal efforts to build up the army there in the winter of 1795/96 especially, the British government could not continue operating with a rate of loss of 70% through deaths, discharges for illness or disability, and desertions.[20]

Yet the sphere of operations expanded when Spain declared war on 8 October 1796. Trinidad became an immediate target because British merchants and planters viewed the island as a notable threat to their interests; its main town, Port-of-Spain, had been opened up as a free port during the 1780s and was flourishing in the 1790s, especially as a centre for privateering. Moreover, the Royal Navy was attracted by the presence of Spanish warships at anchor and the government saw the island as a useful asset in future peace negotiations. A force of 3,743 officers and men under Sir Ralph Abercromby reached Port-of-Spain on 17 February 1797 and readily took the surrender of a small, demoralized army garrison and a grossly undermanned naval squadron, capturing four line ships and a frigate, a major haul by any previous standards of naval conflict. British rule proved profitable by 1803, the slave population doubled, to 20,464, and sugar exports rose by about the same factor.[21]

Abercromby sent a further force of 4,100 officers and men to attack San Juan on the Spanish island of Puerto Rico, far to the north in the Caribbean. The British landing from 18 April 1797 proved ineffectual in the face of a superior defensive position about which, in sharp contrast to Trinidad, the British lacked detailed military intelligence. This action, though by no means a significant reversal, effectively ended major British offensive operations. Efforts to extend British control in Saint Domingue in 1797 proved fruitless while the costs of operations could no longer be justified once the internal, Afro-Caribbean revolution had wrecked the island's economy, destroying its value as a source of exports and its revenue base. A steady British withdrawal was negotiated in 1798 and completed by October. In Professor Duffy's words: 'The heyday of Caribbean warfare was over.'[22]

The Caribbean campaigns of 1793–97 have been pilloried over the years for their extraordinarily over-optimistic planning in London and their persistent waste of soldiers' lives through disease. How far those losses from yellow fever and malaria were exacerbated by a lack of acclimatization, excessive rum drinking, poor diet, or even lead poisoning from the equipment used in rum production, has been extensively debated. But the death of 38,000 troops (in 1793–98 inclusive) essentially from disease has been widely regarded as wantonly wasteful.[23] On the other hand, as Duffy concludes, the campaigns of 1793–97 strengthened British commerce and shipping, thereby boosting British government revenues, and in turn strengthening the government's capacity to borrow further funds.[24] By the standards of international power politics since the 1650s, these years proved spectacularly successful for Britain in destroying French power in the region and deprived Spain of the valuable sugar island of Trinidad. This achievement was little trumpeted at the time because the war in Europe went so badly wrong for Britain in 1797–98 that Caribbean success could not outweigh continental failure. Moreover, the severest blow against France – the destruction of the richest single colony in the world, Saint Domingue – was brought about by slave risings and slave assertiveness and not by British action. Britain's intervention failed to restore the former plantation order and secure an enormous economic prize. The revolutionary struggle by which mulattoes and former slaves ensured the destruction of the plantation economy and France's prime colonial asset could scarcely be celebrated by a rival colonial power.

The Cape of Good Hope, 1795–96

The attack on French interests in the Caribbean merely continued a saga of intermittent warfare in that region which had been recurrent since the seventeenth century. In contrast, the surge of French power in the Netherlands focused British geopolitical attention on key possessions of the Dutch empire. As the British front collapsed slowly in the Low Countries, the overriding ministerial objective was to prevent the French from taking over Dutch colonies. In the Caribbean, a small force was diverted from Barbados to secure the Dutch settlements on the northern coast of South America. The local commander and civil authorities accepted a British takeover in return for the British paying the wages of the Dutch troops in the settlements and maintaining the existing legal and administrative frameworks. Even more important was Cape Colony, described in January 1795 by Sir Francis Baring, a director and former chairman of the East India Company, as commanding 'the passage to and from India as effectually as Gibraltar doth the Mediterranean'. The naval commodore despatched with a squadron to watch the area defined the Cape's value in yet stronger strategic terms: 'what was a feather in the hands of Holland, will become a sword in the hands of France'. Apart from this strategic concern, Baring also emphasized the Cape's vital importance as a source of provisions, especially wheat, on the route to India. In French hands, not only would the East India Company fail to secure the supplies it needed, but the French islands in the Indian Ocean, themselves bases for privateering against British trade, would gain that source of foodstuffs. Once acquired, the colony was also seen as an excellent place for acculturating fresh army recruits on their passage eastwards, 'a seasoning station for European troops destined for India' as Charles Grant of the East India Company put it.[25] The British government therefore sent a naval and military force to the Cape after obtaining from the exiled Prince of Orange, as Stadtholder, written instructions directing the Dutch fleet at the Cape to cooperate with it.

Commanded by Vice Admiral Sir George Elphinstone, who had gained extensive experience in conjoint operations in the landing of troops and marines for the attack on Charleston in early 1780 and in the occupation and evacuation of Toulon in 1793, the force arrived at False Bay on 12 June 1795. Faced with the refusal of the governor and Council of Regency to adhere to the prince's instructions to surrender to the British, and short of fresh provisions, Elphinstone and Major General James Craig occupied Simonstown, and then on 7 August pushed along the coast of the bay to take control of the Dutch camp at Muizenberg, which commanded a 12-mile road northwards to Cape Town. Although their opponents deployed 1,000 regulars including infantrymen and perhaps 2,000 militiamen with artillery, the British assembled 1,600 soldiers and seamen and advanced along the coastal road very closely supported by off-shore naval gunnery. From their vantage point aboard ship, sailors followed the progress of the fighting and signalled information on Dutch movements to the forces on land.[26] Lack of transport and field guns made further progress impossible until the main expeditionary force of about 2,500 men under Major General Alured Clarke arrived in early September. The British resumed their advance and the colony surrendered on 16 September, progress having been badly impeded by lack of transport animals or indeed riding mounts. The campaign was marked by cautious efforts, initially at least while awaiting the arrival of Clarke's force, to conciliate the Dutch. Given the Dutch population's continuing opposition to the British, particularly inland where there had been growing disaffection from the exercise of any authority in Cape Town, the commanders decided to leave their entire force of 3,000 men as a garrison at the Cape. Further action followed the next year when a small Dutch squadron arrived at Saldanha Bay in early August. The Dutch, heavily outnumbered, surrendered their squadron of nine warships, including three ships of the line and two large frigates, to Elphinstone on 17 August, the result of successfully close collaboration between the services.[27] Although a large garrison had been built up in the Cape, much of the operational effort in taking the colony was the navy's.

Having taken Cape Colony as acting caretakers for the Orangeist government, the British had to settle upon an interim form of administration. It was widely recognized that the British had to win over the European population of 21,000, by respecting local laws and customs, by promoting, or claiming to promote, public works such as road and bridge building, and by fostering both internal and external trade. In considering forms of government, ministers were advised to hand the Cape over to the East India Company to administer, but this option won few backers. The second option, of continuing with military rule, was regarded as being incompatible with efforts to foster good relations with the Dutch population and counterproductive in intensifying local opposition to the British and thereby further increasing the demand for additional troops. Despite the fact that Britain had taken the Cape for strategic reasons, one expectation immediately arose that British rule might prove popular if the British authorities overthrew some of the monopolistic restrictions of Dutch official policy and broke the privileges and power of the local office-holders.

Allowing existing laws to remain in force, however, the British appointed a civilian governor, the widely experienced Lord Macartney, with Major General Craig, the military commander, as lieutenant-governor,[28] thereby entrenching a strong institutional voice for the army.

Naval warfare, 1796–97

Having secured the Cape and captured useful Dutch additions to her fleet, Britain faced a new naval challenge when Spain decided to forge an offensive alliance with France in August 1796, and declared war on Britain in October. Spain brought extra bases and a substantial fleet to the enemy camp and especially challenged the British in the Mediterranean. Britain's ability to hit the French hard at Toulon had depended upon the absence of any Spanish threat. The switch in Spain's alignment followed General Bonaparte's dramatic campaigning in northern Italy, which had forced the region's princes and then the papacy and the king of Naples to settle with the French. Those developments in turn forced the British to evacuate Corsica and attempt to anchor their position on Elba. As Nelson noted, 'when we quitted Toulon we endeavoured to reconcile ourselves to Corsica; now we are content with Elba'.[29] But the Mediterranean fleet was so weakened that Sir John Jervis, the commander-in-chief, could not prevent a massive Franco-Spanish fleet concentration at Toulon in late October, which obliged him to withdraw his remaining Mediterranean ships to Gibraltar by 1 December and abandon even Elba as a likely base. But the retreat to Gibraltar immediately proved insufficiently defensive. The possibility of a Franco-Spanish attack on Portugal led ministers to order Jervis to Lisbon, which he reached with his main fleet on 21 December 1796. Three years after the evacuation of Toulon came the humiliation of a withdrawal from the Mediterranean itself. French victories on land had thus in the relatively short space of 1795–96 closed the entire coast of Europe south of Bremen to British naval power. Given the extent and speed of this reversal of fortunes, the Royal Navy was under considerable pressure to demonstrate for the government's benefit its capacity to prevent the coalescence of enemy fleets and to deny Britain's opponents the benefits of this new naval alliance.

Retribution in fact came swiftly. The navy's opportunity arose from the movement of the Spanish fleet to at support a repositioning of the French fleet at Brest. The Spanish fleet, in making for Cadiz, was pushed by strong winds far to the west of its objective. Cruising on open, rather than close, blockade of Cadiz from his new base at Lisbon, Sir John Jervis came upon the Spanish fleet on 14 February. Although out-numbered by twenty-seven line ships to fifteen, Sir John attacked and, in one of the most daring engagements in the age of sail, his line passed across the path of the Spanish fleet making for Cadiz and caught it divided into two main flotillas. As the larger and rear flotilla sailed off course to avoid and escape the British line, so Jervis's ships tacked (turned) to pursue them. Commodore Horatio Nelson broke out of line early, followed by other ships' commanders, and attacked Spanish warships at very close quarters. Jervis captured four principal warships and disabled the largest battleship then afloat. The mauled Spanish fleet creaked back into Cadiz and the British returned to Lisbon.[30]

The battle of St Vincent was only the second major naval battle in nearly four years of war and was significant on three grounds. Jervis brushed aside reports of the sheer size of the enemy fleet with the exclamation that 'England badly needs a victory at present'. News of the victory reached London at the end of a winter of bruising setbacks. The victors themselves were showered with honours by a grateful government and some credibility at least was restored to the ministry's conduct of the war. Second, the battle demonstrated the professional skill, self-confidence and willingness to take initiatives which the Royal Navy had developed in its captains in four years of highly successful frigate and small squadron conflict. A great deal of debate has occurred over whether Nelson's action was initiated entirely by him, or was ordered by Jervis, or flowed from the broad encouragement Jervis gave to his subordinates to adopt flexible and opportunistic tactics. Nelson himself had earlier contemplated the probability of the British Mediterranean fleet encountering the far larger combined Franco-Spanish fleet, and prophecised the outcome: 'I will venture my life Sir John Jervis defeats them; I do not mean by a regular battle, but by the skill of our Admiral, and the activity and spirit of our officers and seamen.'[31] Third, the battle ensured that the Spanish fleet would not join the French fleet concentrated at Brest. Whether such a naval concentration in itself would have sufficed to provide the necessary cover for an invasion of Ireland is doubtful, for it would have induced a similarly massive British assemblage of warships and an extended blockade of north-west France. As it was, Jervis, now Lord St Vincent, cruised off Cadiz in April and early May and then established a close blockade of the flower of the Spanish fleet from May 1797 to May 1799 virtually uninterrupted.

Britain's ability to neutralize Spanish sea power and stave off invasion could not turn the war in her favour, but it yielded security and a firm position from which to negotiate peace. The need for peace negotiations grew more pressing as Bonaparte's army drew closer to Vienna. By March 1797 the French approached within 30 miles of the Habsburg capital, forcing the emperor to agree to a separate peace in April. Thus ended five years of Austrian war against France. The resulting international isolation of Britain, together with the severely worsening situation at home evinced in Irish troubles brewing, mainland rioting, and a localized naval mutiny in June, led Pitt and a majority of his cabinet to initiate peace negotiations. The radicalization of the French Directory in September, however cut off the prospects of peace.

Despite being isolated in Europe, Britain could readily defend itself against possible French attack. The Royal Navy's most powerful contribution to national security came in the period 1793 to 1797, before Nelson's rise to command and the supposed forging of a newly aggressive ethos of captaincy in 'Nelson's Navy'. During those years, the French lost 125 warships of 22 guns or more compared with Britain's loss of thirty-eight such warships. French losses included a staggering thirty-five ships of the line as a result of the fall of Toulon, engagements with the British, accidents and wreck. In the same period, British losses totalled eleven line ships plus one slightly smaller 55-gun warship and one of 50 guns. Yet only three of those thirteen major warships were taken by the French; the rest were lost to wreck, accident or fire. The British also lost a 44-gun warship and twenty-four frigates of 22 to 40 guns. Only six of those were taken or sunk by the French, and three of those were retaken by the Royal Navy.[32] Although Spain's switch from ally to neutral to enemy in 1796 forced the British from the Mediterranean and curtailed the reach of British naval power, retaliation followed with the seizure of Trinidad and the humbling of the Spanish navy at Cape St Vincent. The British had wrecked the French, Spanish and Dutch empires in the Caribbean, especially benefiting from the economic ruination of Saint Domingue, once a prime source of French colonial wealth, by revolution as well as war.

The final breakdown of peace talks with France on 18 September was followed by a stroke of naval luck. On 8 October, a large Dutch squadron left the main Dutch naval base at the Texel, probably with the intention of joining the French Brest fleet. This move was observed and Admiral Adam Duncan's squadron was summoned from Great Yarmouth. Duncan had been instructed by Lord Spencer, the First Lord of the Admiralty, in August 1795 to give the Dutch 'a hard blow' and spent 19 weeks cruising off the Texel in the summer of 1797 awaiting an opportunity to do just that. Determined to seize this long-awaited chance, Duncan caught his frightened and retreating opponent making for the coast near Kamperduin and decided to jettison procedure and break the Dutch line. The admiral initially commanded his ships into order of battle. But within 15 minutes of sending this signal, he instructed his captains to engage as they came upon their foes. This was a deliberate, if risky, decision, for it took his ships another three hours to come close to and begin firing on their enemy. With sixteen ships of the line, Duncan took on sixteen Dutch line ships, of which, after intense fighting, he captured no fewer than nine. Spencer described the battle to the king as 'one of the most complete and brilliant actions in the naval history of Great Britain'. Duncan stressed that the fighting proved fierce, with the carnage on the two British flag officers' ships being 'beyond all description'. His action provided a timely boost to naval and public morale and completed the emasculation of the Dutch navy, which had expanded in the 1780s and provided one of the assets which made the subjugation of the Netherlands so attractive to the French.[33] In the four years from 1793, the British had captured, destroyed or sunk thirty-one of their opponents' ships of the line. This total, excluding losses through accidents and wreck, represented the greatest shift in the balance of maritime power achieved by fighting to that date.[34]

Given this balance of advantage, with Britain dominant at sea and gaining an edge in the Caribbean, while failing to maintain allies on the continent, any peace settlement with France would have required a revolution in thinking about international relations. Some ministers and the chief diplomat charged with negotiations with France, Lord Malmesbury, offered the political ingredients to create a new relationship between Britain and France. During somewhat desultory peace negotiations from June to September, the British sought limited colonial gains. British desiderata included the retention of the Cape of Good Hope and Ceylon in the east, a minor French enclave in India and, in the Caribbean, one of Trinidad, Demerara in northern South America, Martinique, St Lucia, or Tobago. Significantly, these demands took more colonies from Holland than from France. In return for such relatively limited gains, Britain was prepared to recognize French sovereignty over the Austrian Netherlands and over Nice and Savoy. The first concession was scarcely contestable anyway in 1797 because Austria had accepted that loss in preliminary accords which were embodied in the Treaty of Campo Formio of October. But the negotiating position set out by Britain in fact represented a major shift in its global strategy in acknowledging French supremacy in a region from which Britain had traditionally sought to exclude France. Basic French demands included agreement that Britain drop its claims on the Austrian Netherlands' revenues, resulting from British financial subsidies to the emperor, and British restitution of the number of ships lost at Toulon, a clear indication of the damage inflicted by Hood on French naval power.[35] It has been argued that neither side was committed to finding a settlement and that the ministers responsible for the conduct of foreign affairs were opposed to recognizing French supremacy over the Low Countries. More powerfully, it seems clear that the rising men in the French Directory and the leading general, Napoleon Bonaparte, viewed any settlement as likely to be an interim pause in a continuing struggle to assert French supremacy over the German powers and in northern Italy.[36] Yet the French priorities in 1797 falsified the assertions of Tom Paine in *The Rights of Man* that the ending of monarchy and aristocracy would lead to the ending of colonial empires and the opening up of commercial relations. The Directory made the French republic's traditional Great Power ambitions abundantly clear when it denied itself any opportunity to reduce 'colonial' competition with Britain in return for British acquiescence in its control of the Low Countries.

Instead, and generalizing broadly, the wars of 1792–97 prefigured the emergence of the five Great Powers which dominated Europe after 1815. Russia (though a distant participant in these years) and Prussia gained greatly at the expense of Poland. Austria lost in some areas, but gained through the final dismemberment of Poland in 1795 and of the Venetian republic in 1797. France gained by pressing her Germanic opponents eastwards and by asserting her hegemony over the Low Countries. But Britain also gained by undermining all her opponents in the Caribbean, by taking over much of the Dutch empire, and by asserting crushing naval superiority over all three of her historic naval competitors. In the ledger-book of history it was the second-rank powers – Spain, Holland, Poland and Venice – and the Caribbean colonies of Britain's commercial and maritime rivals which paid the price of these wars. No wonder the British establishment, despite their country's isolation in Europe, felt content to carry on fighting.

Notes and references

1 William Laird Clowes, *The Royal Navy: A History From the Earliest Times to the Present*, 7 vols (London, 1897–1903), Vol. IV, p. 197.

2 Michael Duffy, *Soldiers, Sugar, and Seapower: The British Expeditions to the West Indies and the War against Revolutionary France* (Oxford, 1987), pp. 10–12.

3 Duffy, *Soldiers, Sugar, and Seapower*, p. 17, 26n.

4 Duffy, *Soldiers, Sugar, and Seapower*, p. 88; *The Times*, 2 May, 1774, p. 3.

5 Duffy, *Soldiers, Sugar, and Seapower*, p. 21.

6 Duffy, *Soldiers, Sugar, and Seapower*, pp. 42, 44–45, 54–55. Ministers anticipated allied successes on the continent until September 1793 and Dundas believed that his choice for British power projection lay between having troops available for a descent upon the French coast and the infinitely more important priority of an expedition to the West or East Indies. Cyril Matheson, *The Life of Henry Dundas* (London, 1933), pp. 180–84.

7 David P. Geggus, *Slavery, War, and Revolution: The British Occupation of Saint Domingue 1793–1798* (Oxford, 1982), pp. 108.

8 Duffy, *Soldiers, Sugar, and Seapower*, p. 105.

9 Duffy, *Soldiers, Sugar, and Seapower*, p. 100; *The Times*, 19 Sept. 1794, p. 3.

10 Duffy, *Soldiers, Sugar, and Seapower*, pp. 123–24.

11 Duffy, *Soldiers, Sugar, and Seapower*, pp. 117, 134–35; Geggus, *Slavery, War, and Revolution*, pp. 122, 131–32; Philippe R. Girard, 'Empire by collaboration: The first French colonial empire's rise and demise', *French History*, 19 (Dec. 2005), 482–90, esp. p. 489.

12 Buckley, Roger Norman, *Slaves in Red Coats: The British West India Regiments, 1795–1815* (New Haven, CT, 1979), pp. 34–35.

13 Paul David Nelson, *Sir Charles Grey, First Earl Grey* (Madison, NJ, 1996), p. 159; Duffy, *Soldiers, Sugar, and Seapower*, pp. 136–39, 159–60, 188–91, 196, 202–04, 206–09, 211, 214–15.

14 Duffy, *Soldiers, Sugar, and Seapower*, pp. 115, 141; *The Times*, 7 Aug. 1794, p. 2.

15 Duffy, *Soldiers, Sugar, and Seapower*, pp. 363, 366.

16 Buckley, *Slaves in Red Coats*, pp. 43–49.

17 Buckley, *Slaves in Red Coats*, pp. 55–56.

18 John Ehrman, *The Younger Pitt: The Reluctant Transition* (London, 1983), pp. 566–67; Duffy, *Soldiers, Sugar, and Seapower*, pp. 119–212.

19 Duffy, *Soldiers, Sugar, and Seapower*, pp. 220–21, 236–40; Carola Oman, *Sir John Moore* (London, 1953), pp. 141–50, 152, 157–58.

20 Duffy, *Soldiers, Sugar, and Seapower*, pp. 242–52, 332–33.

21 Duffy, *Soldiers, Sugar, and Seapower*, pp. 276–79; Lionel Mordaunt Fraser, *History of Trinidad*, 2 vols (Trinidad, 1891), Vol. I, pp. 149–51. The white population in 1797 was only 2,086.

22 Duffy, *Soldiers, Sugar, and Seapower*, pp. 267–91, 298–310; quote at 291.

23 Duffy, *Soldiers, Sugar, and Seapower*, pp. 332, 334–37, 355–62; Roger Norman Buckley, *The British Army in the West Indies: Society and the Military in the Revolutionary Age* (Gainesville, FL, 1998), pp. 279–93.

24 Duffy, *Soldiers, Sugar, and Seapower*, pp. 378–88.

25 Vincent Harlow and Frederick Madden (eds), *British Colonial Developments 1774–1834: Selected Documents* (Oxford, 1953), pp. 17–21; Maurice Boucher and Nigel Penn (eds), *Britain at the Cape 1795 to 1803* (Johannesburg, 1992), pp. 72, 84.

26 Boucher and Penn (eds), *Britain at the Cape*, pp. 22–23, 30, 43.

27 Clowes, *The Royal Navy*, Vol. IV, pp. 280–81, 294–96; Kevin D. McCranie, *Admiral Lord Keith and the Naval War against Napoleon* (Gainesville, FL, 2006), pp. 44–52.

28 Harlow and Madden (eds), *British Colonial Developments*, p. 90; Boucher and Penn (eds) *Britain at the Cape*, pp. 69, 89.

29 Nicholas Harris Nicholas (ed.), *The Dispatches and Letters of Vice Admiral Lord Viscount Nelson*, 7 vols (London, 1997 edn), Vol. II, p. 298.

30 Roger Knight, *The Pursuit of Victory: The Life and Achievement of Horatio Nelson* (London, 2005), pp. 219–33.

31 Nicholas (ed.), *Dispatches*, Vol. II, p. 6. The debate on the battle is led by Edgar Vincent, *Nelson. Love and Fame* (New Haven, CT, 2003), pp. 183–200.

32 Clowes, *The Royal Navy*, Vol. IV, pp. 548–58.

33 Clowes, *The Royal Navy*, Vol. IV, pp. 325–31; A. Aspinall (ed.), *The Later Correspondence of George III*, 5 vols (Cambridge, 1968), Vol. II, p. 627; John Ehrman, *The Younger Pitt: The Consuming Struggle* (London, 1996), pp. 98–99; J. David Davies, 'Adam, Viscount Duncan, 1731–1804' in Peter Le Fevre and Richard Harding (eds), *British Admirals of the Napoleonic Wars: The Contemporaries of Nelson* (London, 2005), pp. 45–65, esp. pp. 57–63; Earl of Camperdown, *Admiral Duncan* (London, 1898), pp. 49, 172, 206, 242–43, 255. There has been a long debate as to whether Duncan deliberately planned to break the Dutch line. He certainly studied tactics and took bold action at the decisive moment. T. Sturges Jackson (ed.), *Logs of the Great Sea Fights, 1794–1805*, 2 vols (London, 1899–1900), Vol. I, p. 299.

34 The figures are drawn from Clowes, *The Royal Navy*, Vol. IV, pp. 552–61.

35 Ehrman, *The Younger Pitt: The Consuming Struggle*, pp. 60–5.

36 Paul W. Schroeder, *The Transformation of European Politics 1763–1848* (Oxford, 1994), pp. 163–65, 173–76.

CHAPTER 5

The Irish rebellion, 1796–98

By 1798, the war with France had reached a curious stalemate. Britain had asserted her naval supremacy and greatly extended her overseas empire. France had become the hegemon in western continental Europe and controlled not only the Low Countries but much of northern and central Italy. Her political authority and military prowess exceeded anything achieved on the continent by the Bourbons. Despite its record of chronic internal political instability and repeated fratricidal bloodletting, the French government was absorbed in extensive administrative and political reorganization within the territories it had acquired or over which it asserted control. French power and the preoccupation Austria and Prussia felt for Poland meant that Britain by 1798 was as isolated and strategically threatened as she had been in 1779–80, confronting a continental European coastline in enemy hands from the southern North Sea to southern Italy and the three leading continental navies, of France, Spain and the Netherlands, combined – at least potentially – against her own. Yet France had few means with which to threaten Britain. The only, however distantly, viable option was to do in reverse what British strategists had urged in 1793–94: send small expeditionary forces to galvanize and strengthen internal discontent to the point of open rebellion. Those French generals and politicians who advocated direct intervention in the United Kingdom focused their attentions upon Ireland. No invasion of Ireland would, however, work unless it supplemented rebellion of the sort which had broken out in parts of France in 1793–94.

The safeguarding of Ireland for the British fell primarily to the navy. But the army was accountable for internal order and responsible for repelling any French invasion force if it succeeded in eluding the Royal Navy's blockade and patrols. Encouraged by the French and lulled by the parlous state Britain found itself in the European balance of power, disaffected groups chose this moment of Britain's geopolitical isolation to rebel. The army suddenly faced its gravest challenge after six years of war. It could be argued that the army's principal achievement in European actions before the Peninsular War was in reasserting British control over Ireland. Up to that point, it had achieved relatively little. Operations in the Low Countries were abjectly unsuccessful. Terrible losses and scant glory had been the reward of five years of campaigning in the Caribbean. Action in the Mediterranean had been limited. The navy tended to look down upon the army as lacking in proactive energy. Certainly, army officers had garnered precious little glory from the war. In contrast, the Irish rebellion called forth a substantial military effort and in particular engaged the services of the cream of the British officer corps. Yet, because the campaign conferred no military glory and involved the distinctly messy work of suppressing civil strife, the Irish rebellion has been glossed over as a military experience. John Fortescue, in his monumental history of the British army, regarded the rebellion as of limited relevance to his massive history and brushed aside the entire conflict as essentially one between rival fanatics.[1] In fact, the challenges raised were more demanding than that caricature suggests. Indeed, the rebellion and its suppression tells us a great deal about the nature and workings of an army frustrated by a lack of opportunities to fulfil its heroic role and smarting at its recent lack of success compared with the Royal Navy.

Irish discontent in an international context

Edmund Burke had warned of Ireland's potential significance in October 1794: 'It is no longer an obscure dependency of this Kingdom. What is done there vitally effects [sic] the whole System of Europe, whether you regard it offensively or defensively.'[2] In February 1797, Sir Lawrence Parsons, MP pressed for an even larger expansion of the yeomanry than the Irish government proposed, reminding the Irish House of Commons that Ireland was militarily weaker than Britain and more vulnerable to attack. He argued that British blockading of Brest was never absolutely secure. If a French expedition sailed from Brest, landed at Bantry, and forced the British into retreat, it would take Cork, the only fortified harbour in Ireland: 'when Cork is gone, Ireland is gone'. The Irish government, however, rejected the claim that France had earmarked an army for an invasion of Ireland and the Irish Commons overwhelmingly defeated a proposal to raise an additional 50,000 yeomanry troops.[3]

The threat seemed empty once three events from December 1796 to October 1797 demonstrated the risks of attempting to invade Ireland and of launching naval operations to support an invasion. First, the French Directory had indeed despatched 15,000 troops for Ireland in December 1796 only to have its fleet of warships and troop transports dispersed at sea. The French lost nine warships and thousands of men,[4] and no rising occurred inside Ireland to link up with the broken remnants of the expedition which eventually made it to dry land. The difficulty of coordinating expressions of internal political dissent with external military support provided a mirror image of Britain's typically frustrated efforts to back counter-revolution in western France. Yet, while much is made of British shortcomings in projecting power overseas, nothing compared with this French disaster. Moreover, British vulnerability to a possible allied naval concentration in the Channel was dramatically reduced during 1797 by two other events: the defeat of the Spanish off Cape St Vincent (February) and the Dutch at Camperdown (October). Yet despite the receding prospects of substantial French intervention in Ireland, the threat from internal discontent intensified.

French intervention was designed to galvanize the United Irishmen, a movement for political emancipation. Pressure to reverse the systematic exclusion of Catholics from the 1640s to the 1690s from landowning to civic participation mounted as the eighteenth century progressed. Many restrictions were eased, especially those upon Catholic recruitment into the army. Given the fact that about one-fifth of the entire population of the UK by the 1770s consisted of Irish Catholics, wartime manpower pressures encouraged governments to draw many poor Irish Catholics into the military labour market. But religious tensions remained strong. When ministers in London ruminated in 1798 on the possibility of providing money to improve the calibre of the Catholic clergy, one senior official dismissed any such intervention:

the whole body of the lower order of Roman Catholics of this country are totally inimical to the English Government . . . they are under the influence of the lowest and worst class of their priesthood . . . all the extravagant and horrid tenets of that religion are as deeply engraven in their hearts as they were a century ago, or three centuries ago, and . . . they are as barbarous, ignorant, and ferocious as they then were; and if Ministers imagine they can treat with such men just as would with the people of Yorkshire if they rebelled, they will find themselves mistaken.[5]

Legal discrimination was eased by eighteenth-century economic growth, which enabled many Catholic tenant farmers to prosper and save. Pressure therefore forced the lifting of restrictions on Catholic landownership. With an expanding Catholic middle class in the towns, where Protestants tended to predominate, as well as in the countryside, demands for political reform naturally followed. In 1793, again with a mind to continuing wartime political pressures, Catholics were allowed to vote in elections to the separate Irish parliament. But the franchise was extremely limited – confined to about 60,000 men in a population of 4.5 million – and only small numbers of affluent, landowning Catholics would qualify to join this tiny minority.

The demand for full Catholic emancipation was increased rather than deflected by these piecemeal political concessions. Catholic emancipation won support from some members of the British political establishment in the mid-1790s, but this provoked a furious reaction among conservatives in Ireland, manifested in the organization of militant Protestant Orange orders, boasting about 20,000 members by 1798. Catholic Defenders mobilized in response. But this tension was only one part of a dynamic political process. Formed in 1791, essentially from the urban middle classes in Ulster, the Society of United Irishmen pressed for parliamentary reform and Catholic emancipation. Having lost support by 1794, it regained ground against the conservative governing elite and by 1797 posed a significant threat to the establishment, especially among Presbyterians in Belfast and the north east. It faced, however, landowning gentry and their urban allies – with backing especially drawn from the island's 500,000 Anglicans – who rigidly rejected any proposed modification to the rights and privileges of the Anglican Church of Ireland and the established political order. The United Irishmen's new strength, in appealing across religious, class and urban–rural divides, proved ultimately to be a source of weakness. While some historians have seen the United Irishmen as offering a potentially powerful alternative future for the country, others have stressed the inherently self-destructive character of so broad an alliance of groups with strikingly divergent interests.[6] Political debate and political reaction were probably more intense in the economically diversified north-east counties and in Dublin than elsewhere in Ireland, but outside the cities much hinged on how the county elites – essentially made up of 5,000 major landowners – responded to demands for reform. Local magistrates reacted to incidents of dissent or disorder very differently across the country, guided by their varying political inclinations.

Given these considerations, the United Irishmen scarcely displayed political wisdom by advocating the creation of a republic and entering secret negotiations with the French in the midst of a major war. But Henry Grattan, a leading reformer, drew the opposite lesson in February 1795: 'if the Cabinet of Great Britain decides against the Catholic Bill, they decide also, that the first descent of ten thousand Frenchmen separates the two Countries for ever'.[7] This may have been true for Ulster, but Catholic opinion was very far from being universally anti-government and republican, even after the failure of Catholic Emancipation in 1795. There remained a threat from increasing, if still patchy, discontent, articulated by a republican organization which by 1798 asserted that it could field 40,000 armed men in the event of a rising.[8]

Military manpower

Whether Britain could meet such a challenge depended first on the availability of soldiers. In important respects, Ireland was a source of military strength to Britain. Its relative demographic and economic significance was radically different from that of present-day Ireland. Today Ireland as a whole has only 10% of the population of the rest of the British Isles and a population equivalent to less than 2% of that of the USA. But in the 1790s its population was nearly half that of England, Scotland and Wales and about the same as that of the USA. Yet the island required limited military control. In peacetime, from 1769 onwards, the Irish parliament paid for 15,325 British soldiers, mostly in battalions of about 500 men each (instead of the target size of 800–1,000) in order to provide organizational and command structures which could be expanded rapidly in wartime. With the extensive and excellent harbour facilities and barracks at Cork and relatively easy terrain to march across, the battalions stationed in Ireland were rapidly brought up to strength during wartime and despatched overseas.[9] Thus of 44 battalions serving in America in 1776, 16 went there from Ireland, and all 24 infantry battalions and half the cavalry regiments stationed in Ireland in 1793 were overseas by mid-1795.[10] The wider use of the forces recruited within and paid for by Ireland was well demonstrated in late 1799 when 29% of the active manpower of the Royal Irish Artillery were stationed in the West Indies.[11] In addition, Ireland supplied 50,000 recruits for the army and another 15,000 for the Royal Navy and marines from February 1793 to November 1796.[12]

Ireland scarcely seemed vulnerable to external threats in 1793–95. By 1796 there were only 1,900 line infantry and 3,700 regular cavalry on the island. To supplement the former, 9,141 fencible infantry, raised in Britain as regulars to be available for full-time service during war only in the UK, were sent to Ireland. The cavalry reinforcement consisted of only 664 fencibles. While, therefore, nearly 15,000 full-time troops were in place, no more than 5,600 of them belonged to regular regiments. To strengthen those forces some 18,152 Irish militia were embodied in 1796.[13] This level of military force seemed adequate as long as they were united in their desire to defend the country against the French. But the failure of Catholic emancipation and political reform in 1795 threw their loyalty into question. Lord Fitzwilliam as viceroy stressed that three-quarters of the militia were Catholics and the rest were religious dissenters and democrats from northern Ireland, men scarcely to be depended upon by the reactionary Dublin elite in times of civil disturbance.[14] Civil upheavals might, it was feared in the mid-1790s, readily destroy formal loyalties to the crown and degenerate into the widespread factional fighting which had characterized earlier Irish history.[15] This sense of vulnerability to political disaffection and politically inspired violence was reinforced by the fact that rural poverty in some areas drove many men to join the army and by the widespread dispersal of the armed forces into five regional districts with their separate commands and headquarters.[16]

The internal challenge increased. Massive recruitment to the United Irishmen – whose membership totalled 128,000 in spring 1797 – reflected the growing intensity of resentment against the lack of political reform. Although that society started from the basis of stoutly upholding individual and property rights, it also increasingly considered the prospect of cooperating with the Directory in France which, by 1797, no longer embodied revolutionary practices and had been recognized in international agreements by all the leading powers of Europe except the UK.

Faced with this political mobilization, the government in Ireland enhanced its military security. Because the militia was drawn from the whole population and reflected political divisions which themselves led to civil disturbance, the Irish administration decided in 1796 to raise a separate yeomanry force, totalling 30,000 men by early 1797. The men were provided with arms, uniforms and equipment – or the money to secure them – and were paid for two days' exercise per week. But they did not – as did the militia – reflect the composition of the population as a whole. Indeed as 1797 progressed and as the Orange order of Protestants and loyalists grew rapidly from a small original base in Ulster, so an increasingly notable overlap between Orangeism and the yeomanry occurred. Moreover, the yeomanry were not raised by the counties' governors (the equivalent of lord lieutenants) as were the militia. They were controlled directly by the government in Dublin because they were recruited by landowners and other leading worthies in cohorts commanded by junior officers. The government freed itself from over-dependence on county magnates who might prove politically unreliable. While the speed and scale of yeomanry recruitment varied considerably according to county politics and personal and factional rivalries, the yeomanry strengthened landowners' relations with their tenants and their own sense of status and power. For tenant farmers, the steady income from yeomanry service provided a major advantage, and joining a local yeomanry corps could secure for tenants benefits in tenancy transactions and business customarily associated with paternalistic landowner–tenant relationships. In the wider context of policing Ireland in 1797, the yeomanry strengthened the defence of people and property, both internally and as protection during invasion scares. They offered a more reliable counterweight than the militia ever could to the Society of United Irishmen.[17]

Accompanying this change in recruitment came changes in command and then in policy. Generals who had not performed well in the light of the threatened French invasion were replaced. The most important change came in October with the appointment of a new commander-in-chief, Sir Ralph Abercromby. An unusually well-educated, much respected general, Abercromby had the disadvantage of a political mind of his own which had led him to oppose the American war and decline to serve overseas during it. To counter the influence exerted by the United Irishmen and disgruntled Catholics over the militia,[18] the Irish government of Lord Camden (viceroy 1795–98) next decided to use its freshly acquired yeomanry muscle – for which the propertied and landowning classes were also paying in additional taxes – to disarm civilian dissidents. It began in northern counties where Presbyterian political reformism and Catholic disaffection gave powerful impetus to the United Irishmen. Severe punishments were inflicted, including some very well-publicised executions, on those convicted of disobedience. But the most immediately provocative initiative was the decision in March 1797 to throttle sedition in Ulster by finding and seizing arms.[19] The viceroy instructed the Northern District commander to achieve results without paying too much regard to legal niceties. Major General Gerard Lake had demonstrated dash and determination as a cavalry brigadier in Flanders at the battle of Lincelles. His energies were unleashed in a wholly repressive direction. One of his divisional generals, Thomas Knox, declared that 'I look upon Ulster to be a La Vendée', the region of counter-revolution subjugated only through gruesome devastation and massacre by the French republican regime. All manner of outrage committed by the troops met with the official justification that terror used by rebels could only be suppressed with yet greater terror.

This particular use of pre-emptive force raised problems for the new commander-in-chief. Abercromby, on arriving in Ireland, pressed for military action to be made conditional on the instructions of civil magistrates. He felt that the extent of rebelliousness had been grossly exaggerated, perhaps because, as Professor Bartlett has suggested, Camden's Irish advisers desired an open rebellion in order to flush out the disaffected and destroy them. Certainly, they wanted the army and militia to use vigorous force without obliging the civil authorities to shoulder responsibility for those actions. Their confidence in part flowed from their penetration of sections of the United Irishmen's organization through an extensive network of spies and informers. Abercromby, however, appalled by the atrocities and indiscipline displayed by the full-time soldiers, behaviour exacerbated by their widespread dispersal in small units to police the civilian population, wanted to concentrate the full-time soldiery at major garrisons and focus their attentions on proper training, firm discipline and the threat of French invasion.[20] Unfortunately, Abercromby's castigation (in February 1798) of his own soldiers' indiscipline and ferocity towards civilians was exploited by the government's political opponents in London. The commander-in-chief had alienated both the Irish administration and the London government. His decision to resign was rapidly followed by the appointment of Lake to acting command and the proclamation on 30 March, 1798, that all Ireland came under martial law, to enable the army to burn the property and flog and torture the persons of those suspected of plotting or intending rebellion through the possession of threatening weapons.

During April and May Lake drove forward a vigorous policy of punishing civilians in his quest to seize hidden supplies of weapons, extending to the midlands and south of Ireland the practices he had adopted the previous year in Ulster. The intensity of military action varied considerably from area to area. Operations in the Southern District, under Lieutenant General Sir James Stewart, were claimed later to have been tightly run with no arbitrary killing,[21] with free quartering on the civil population being organized by magistrates collecting provisions and supplying them to the army, and with the yeomanry converting their two days' paid exercise per week into two nights' patrolling per week to break up night-time meetings. Near Dublin, quantities of arms were surrendered

in Queen's and King's counties. But few were forthcoming in County
Kildare, leading Lake to authorize widespread house-burning and flogging.
And in mid-May, troops advanced into southern Wicklow to break what
was described as strong United Irish organization in that region.[22] The
Irish government made no effort to temper this extensive and ruthless
search for arms by offering any measures of conciliation.

The rising

The repression imposed from March 1797 to May 1798 helped provoke
rather than prevent a rising. On 23 May rumours, well grounded in
schemes developed by United Irishmen, were rife that rebels from outside
the city would march upon Dublin to reinforce United Irishmen within the
metropolis. The authorities moved quickly to round up suspected leaders
and confront rebels in the streets. It has been argued that mere hours
separated pre-emptive suppression and a rebel seizure of the capital.[23] But
fighting broke out on 23 May in County Kildare in a crescent-shaped area
around Dublin and began with attacks on small garrisons. By 26 May an
estimated 30,000 armed men had taken over most of County Kildare and
extended their sway to within twelve miles of Dublin. Open violence
spread to County Wexford. A dramatic local defeat for government forces
opened the way for anti-establishment leaders of long standing to seize the
political initiative in Wexford,[24] exploiting both fears that government
forces were intent on implementing a pogrom in the county and resentment locally at the uncompromising conservatism of the county's leading
landowner-politicians. One explanation for the outbreak thus emphasizes
the upward spiral of intense violence, provoking reactions which were
shaped decisively by local political conditions and calculations. Rural and
urban leadership and mobilization fused together under the influence of
increasingly republican political radicalism.[25]

Government success in the capital decisively shaped strategy by in-
advertently allowing the rebellion to spread. The viceroy's insistence that
troops be concentrated in Dublin to protect the capital with its 180,000
people, until reinforcements arrived from Britain, and the commander of
the Midland District, Ralph Dundas's concentration of his forces at the
town of Naas, meant that the countryside around the capital was stripped
of troops. This enabled the rebels in County Kildare and Dublin's environs
to cut communications between the capital and much of the west and
south of Ireland.[26] Even though the rebels failed to seize the capital, they
retained the option of holding the surrounding countryside until a French

force arrived to deliver the *coup de grâce*.[27] The Irish government's policy of suppression stemmed from fears of French intervention, since the French Directory included invading Ireland among its strategic options. During 1797 a debate between Generals Hoche and Bonaparte kept the advantages and (for the latter) disadvantages of such action under review. When news that an army under Bonaparte had sailed from Toulon on 19 May 1798 reached the British Isles, some in Britain and Ireland believed it was destined for Ireland. For their part, the United Irishmen continued to plot and plan on the basis that French forces would arrive to neutralize British regular troops. The government's concern to secure Dublin, one of the most populous capitals of Europe, comparable in size to Berlin and Madrid, was understandable, but it meant that senior officials could not coordinate their military dispositions in late May, while the lack of information from the military high command to the rest of the country simply added further confusion and uncertainty to an already feverish and alarmist situation.

Amidst this confusion, the scattered British commands had to react to widely dispersed threats. The most dramatic rising in late May led to the seizure of Wexford and the proclamation of a republic there. The rebellion owed more to prosperity and success in the surrounding farmlands and the market town of 10,000 people than to any economic distress or failure. Experienced and prominent anti-establishment leaders assumed political leadership when the opportunity, created by resentment against anti-Catholicism, arose.[28] But the rebellion in Wexford remained isolated, due to the town's position on the far south-east coast of Ireland. An attempt was, therefore, mounted in early June to break out of County Wexford and march rebel forces to the west. On 5 June rebels reached New Ross, a town commanding routes south to Waterford and north-west to Kilkenny as well as directly north towards Kildare. The garrison, strongly reinforced to 2,678 troops and six guns, repelled the insurgents after a ferocious day-long battle whose fortunes ebbed and flowed, and inflicted huge losses on them.[29] This reversal confined the Wexford republic to a narrow geographical area and boosted the government's standing.[30] Moreover, the dynamics of the rising in Wexford help explain the intensity of British repression. The local excesses of the rebels in Wexford, where the United Irishmen's organisation had never been strong, injected an avenging intensity into the conflict from its very beginning and thus served to justify systematic atrocities by government forces. Modern historiography emphasises the numerical strength of the insurgency, despite the lack of co-ordination within the United Irish movement, fractured as its organizational superstructure was by arrests based upon information from government spies and informants. The very scale of support for the rising in turn explains the ferocity of the repression.[31]

Thus leading United Irishmen in Ulster, impatient at their southern colleagues' failure to seize Dublin, which had always been the central objective of a rising, called out their followers, just as the battle for New Ross was being fought and lost. By 11 June the uprising gripped the whole of north-east Ulster. Government forces, relying on artillery, halted a large rebel army at Antrim town – at a vital strategic point commanding the road which crosses Ulster east-west from Londonderry to Belfast. The British commander of the Northern District, Major General George Nugent, did what his counterpart had done at Dublin and concentrated his forces and his efforts on the defence of Belfast. That decision denied the rebels their objective of securing Ulster's principal city, but gave them the opportunity to control much of the countryside, as they did in Kildare. Once Nugent felt confident enough to do so, he marched out of Belfast with 1,500 troops and eight pieces of light artillery, to attack an insurgent camp near Ballynahinch, a strategic focal point in County Down. A mixed force of Irish militia and yeomanry units, fencibles from Fife and York, regular cavalry, and a Royal Artillery detachment attacked the rebels on 12–13 June. Many rebels – often armed only with pikes – fell to grapeshot from the guns, to the dragoons as they fled, sometimes for many miles, and to the infantry after they were trapped in woods near Lord Moira's country seat.[32]

This victory was followed by a further decisive shift in the balance of power towards the British with the arrival of reinforcements from Britain at Dublin on 16 June. As soon as the rebellion broke out, the Secretary of State for War and the Colonies, Henry Dundas, agreed to send to Ireland virtually all the available battalions in Britain which were both fit for active service and not composed heavily of Irishmen. He did so in part because of 'the danger of the rebellion extending itself so far as to place the harbours of Cork and Waterford in the possession of the rebels, and consequently of France'.[33] But allocating substantial reinforcements proved challenging. Horse Guards insisted that only 3,197 men were suitable for immediate service. Since 1,344 of those were three battalions of Glengary, Nottingham and Cheshire Fencibles stationed in Guernsey and Jersey, regular regiments overwhelmingly Irish in composition currently in Britain were despatched to the Channel Islands to replace the fencibles there. Horse Guards insisted that, once reinforcements had sailed, only one battalion in Britain was fully prepared for immediate overseas service.[34]

Enough reinforcements arrived to enable Lake to leave the capital and mount an offensive of his own. Travelling 80 miles on the main road south he assailed a large camp of Wexford rebels at Vinegar Hill. Opening an artillery bombardment from twenty guns at 7.00 a.m. on 21 June, Lake failed to encircle and destroy the insurgents with his 10,000 troops, but forced them to flee southwards. Wexford, 15 miles south of the camp, was taken by Brigadier John Moore, heading a small force of regulars from New Ross, on the following day.[35] The recapture of Wexford was followed by the summary execution of the republic's leaders and savage retribution against the civilian population of Wexford county and neighbouring areas.

Within a month of its outbreak, the rebellion had failed to hold any significant town or to threaten Dublin. This was a body blow to a movement strong in urban support and rooted in urban social and political consciousness. Moreover, the British had reinforced their manpower and defeated the rebels in two open confrontations. On 21 June, a new viceroy arrived to replace Camden and to enforce a far higher level of military-political cooperation than had existed heretofore. Given the difficulties encountered in 1797 in finding a new commander-in-chief of the army in Ireland, and given the political circumstances of Sir Ralph Abercromby's departure, the solution to finding a suitable commanding general was to appoint Lord Cornwallis as both viceroy and head of the army. Having survived his surrender to the Franco-American forces at Yorktown (1781) with his reputation intact, Cornwallis had proceeded to win both administrative and military credit as governor-general and commander-in-chief in India in 1786–94, and then to serve from February 1795 in the military post of Master-General of the Ordnance, which carried a seat in the cabinet. Described in 1781 by Thomas Jefferson, one of the leading American revolutionaries and a wartime governor of Virginia, as 'the most active, enterprising and vindictive officer who has ever appeared in arms against us',[36] the general had defeated Mysore, the most modern military state in India, in 1793.

Cornwallis sought to impose military order as a preliminary to a political settlement. Greatly strengthened by reinforcements from the mainland, troops were dispersed widely across Ireland. Cornwallis thoroughly distrusted Irish forces as ill-disciplined and cowardly, and particularly deplored their officers' inadequacies. He noted of the newly formed corps: 'The yeomanry are in the style of the Loyalists in America, only much more numerous and powerful, and a thousand times more ferocious.' The Irish militia followed the volunteers closely 'in murder and every kind of atrocity' with the fencibles from the mainland adding, if less vigorously, to the violence. Owing to 'the ferocity of our troops who delight in murder', the viceroy sought to deploy well-disciplined regulars.[37]

Following the bloodletting of May–June, Cornwallis pressed for pacification through vigorous action tempered by restrained violence. Clearing insurgents who had taken refuge in the Wicklow mountains to the south-west of Dublin and north-west of County Wexford was given priority. Troops were ordered to treat the population with consideration, to pay for provisions secured, and to return horses captured from rebels to their rightful owners rather than treat them as booty. Step by step, the rebels were pressed into surrender until the last formally organized body of United Irishmen gave up their arms in Kildare on 26 July. At one camp at the Glen of Emall, the Gordon Highlanders invited the local inhabitants to visit their camp on a Sunday afternoon when it was set out like a fair. John Moore thought that the 'affable manners' of Lord Huntly, commanding the battalion, helped in reconciling the local population. The regimental history of the Gordon Highlanders, published in 1901, laid responsibility upon the yeomanry for horrible reprisals provoked by the rebels' own 'dreadful cruelties'. The excellent behaviour of the Gordon Highlanders 'has been a matter of honest pride to the regiment ever since', even though elsewhere in Ireland 'the peasantry were subjected to all the horrors of civil war'.[38] To mitigate this horror, Cornwallis, believing that the conflict concerned Jacobinism not Catholicism, insisted, somewhat late in the day, that no punishments should be inflicted without a court martial and approval by a general. While leading rebels were to face trial, pardons were to be extended to ordinary rebels if they surrendered their arms and swore allegiance to the crown.[39] This was a far cry from Lake's orders in May to take no prisoners.

Military events during 1797–98 demonstrated two enduring dilemmas created by the use of force for extensive internal policing operations. The pre-emptive strikes launched against those challenging, or suspected of planning to challenge, the government's authority were delivered by part-time volunteers and militia who indulged in blood feuds or random atrocities rather than implementing disarmament and peace-enforcement. The government did not have the kinds of soldiers – and regulars deployed in large numbers might well have behaved exactly as the irregulars did – to impose civil order with restraint. Yet most of the Irish political establishment felt that the only way to break the morale and potential fighting capability of the United Irishmen and other opponents of the regime was through savage repression. At least some generals ultimately, if tacitly, accepted the need to apply maximum force to crush their enemy.

Invasion

By July 1798 the rebellion had essentially been smashed. Only the eastern side of Ireland was seriously affected, with Kildare, Wicklow, and Wexford and, within Ulster, Down and Antrim counties, in the north-east and near Belfast, being prominent centres of disaffection. Limited disturbances affected the centre and (less) the west of the island. Ireland's second largest city, Cork, witnessed no more than skirmishing, while in the south-west province of Munster such disaffection as erupted was confined to the towns. Lord Cornwallis sought to build on this aspect of the rebellion in pursuing a policy of reconstruction. He wanted to adopt a more lenient approach in dealing with the rebels, and to stress the political causes of the rebellion rather than any deeper-rooted religious differences which might have been adduced as the origins of the rising.[40] He wanted to link the United Irishmen with radicalism, with the Whig party in Britain, and with the French republic. On the other hand, he deplored the repressive excesses of the governing elite in Dublin and intended to disband the Irish parliament and government, subsuming them within the governing arrangements of the United Kingdom, and complete Catholic emancipation.

Before this political process could be advanced, the French connection resurfaced. The central problem of the United Irish leadership was its failure to take either Britain and France or history and politics seriously. They willed an honourable end. They sought, in effect, to establish a republic on American lines, strong on middle-class values of property rights, equality and full protection before the law, and fair, but not necessarily democratic, political representation. They presumably desired, as the Americans effected at the federal level, a state detached from any particular religious denomination. Yet in 1798 they focused more on the composition of a new political convention than on the practicalities of managing a revolution. They somehow felt that centuries of British involvement could be swept away, that even the landed aristocracy and gentry would accept the logic of a secular republic, that an American system would flourish in a country where the vast mass of people were landless peasants and few belonged to the 'middling sort', and, perhaps worst of all, that French military aid could be enlisted painlessly and without political obligation while Britain was fighting a continuing war with France. From the worthy premise that the organization wished to avoid violence, the United Irish wanted French military intervention as the means of forcing the British and the Anglo-Irish landed establishment to recognize that their rule in Ireland was no longer acceptable. The idea was even put about that French military assistance would simply be paid for, with no political strings attached. While the expectation of French intervention buoyed United Irish morale in 1797,[41] the prospect of a French-sponsored and French-supported republic intensified loyalists' fears and activated their paranoia.

As far as the French Directory was concerned, Ireland receded in importance in the first half of 1798. Other military needs sapped manpower. Paris would have liked the Dutch, or Batavian Republic, to take a prominent role in providing an army for Ireland, but the naval losses inflicted by the British at Camperdown in October 1797 dampened Dutch interest in playing minor parts on the grand French global stage. Only the outbreak as to rebellion galvanized French advocates of an Irish strategy. Very ill-informed as to the current state of the insurgency and believing that any French presence would inject additional enthusiasm and energy into the uprising, General Humbert sailed on 5 August with a mere 1,000 troops and three field guns. His expedition was small enough to elude British naval surveillance, and he landed at Killala Bay in County Mayo in the far west. Although the expedition was under-resourced and under-staffed, Humbert started at least with a belief that a French presence virtually anywhere would make a huge impact.[42]

Since the likely eventual scale of French intervention was unknown, with Humbert's force being perhaps the first instalment of what would be a larger French invasion, Cornwallis decided to respond in overwhelming force. Convinced that he had no leeway for any failure against the French and that he needed to cow the population, the viceroy secured further reinforcements from Britain. The entire armed forces available to the British in Ireland rose from 77,589 in January 1798 to 102,181 a year later. But because it took some time to pull together battalions widely dispersed in Ireland for policing duties, the local commander in Galway, Major General John Hely-Hutchinson, the son of a prominent Irish MP, collected militia forces at Castlebar to hem Humbert in, and thereby prevent the French from inspiring more widespread resistance. On 26 August Lieutenant General Lake arrived to take charge of the 1,700 troops, and on the following day the French attacked their more numerous opponents, easily forcing them to break and run.[43] Cornwallis criticized Hely-Hutchinson for leading inexperienced militia commanded by local landowners against regulars. In 1801 when the major general was appointed to a senior command in Egypt, Cornwallis noted: 'I tremble for poor Hutchinson; he is a sensible man, but he is no General – at least he was not one in 1798.' The ominous defeat of militia, commanded by aristocratic amateurs, by numerically inferior French forces on 'home' territory led one cabinet minister, Lord Auckland, to describe Castlebar as the most disturbing military reversal in his 24 years' experience in politics, a span which covered the most humiliating reverses of the American war.[44]

Having drawn together regulars from throughout Ireland (leaving only 1,100 regulars in each of Dublin and Wexford) and dividing his army into two corps under Lake and himself, Cornwallis chased Humbert and forced his surrender. While Humbert's invasion lasted little more than two weeks, French threats spluttered on for another five weeks. The largest expeditionary force left Brest on 16 September, conveying 2,500 troops and Wolfe Tone, a prominent United Irish leader. A British squadron under Commodore Sir John Warren, highly experienced in pursuing, intercepting and fighting frigates, was patrolling for this purpose off Donegal and located the French on 11 October, immediately giving chase. In a series of engagements from 12 to 20 October, the British impressively captured one French ship of the line and six frigates; only three frigates of the French squadron returned home.[45] British actions thus largely discredited any case for the likely success of armed struggle and any lingering Irish hopes for French intervention.

The death toll from the rebellion may have been 20,000 – earlier estimates suggested 30,000 – men, women and children in 1798, the vast majority of them rebels or suspected rebels slaughtered some distance from any battlefield. After the battle of Vinegar Hill, Lieutenant General Lake observed: 'The troops behave excessively well in action, but their determination to destroy everyone they think a rebel is beyond description and wants much correction.' After Humbert's surrender at Ballinamuck, the militia set upon anyone suspected of being a rebel. One English sub-altern noted that provisions were taken by force, troops were billeted on civilians, and churches and chapels were used as barracks or stables. About a dozen towns were partially or wholly destroyed during the insurrection.[46]

Consequences

Ireland required far more military policing after 1798 than had been needed before 1797. Government continued with the embodiment of yeomanry, controlled from Dublin, organized by landowners, and not dependent upon the majority, Catholic population. Some 52,000 of them were engaged for two days a week as late as 1801, and 45,000 in December 1815.[47] Unsurprisingly, the military expenditure of the government of Ireland continued to soar, from £748,000 in 1793–94 to £2,032,000 in 1796–97, £3,865,000 in 1798–99 and £4,597,000 in 1799–1800. Civil expenditure was not much lower than military spending in 1793–94 but was equivalent to only 22% of it at the end of the decade. Expenditure was partly met by borrowing, with the funded debt, beginning from a low base, rising fourfold between 1792 and 1800.[48]

This heavily military government was clearly intended to provide short-term stabilization. Although Cornwallis made no concessions over sovereignty, he and other British officers had no illusions about the country's condition under the Anglo-Irish Ascendancy. Major General Moore had noted privately in July 1798 that the country would only become more orderly if the gentry and armed yeomanry behaved with restraint instead of in a spirit of revenge. The youthful Lieutenant-Colonel Lord William Bentinck, son of the Duke of Portland who was the British cabinet minister responsible for Ireland, served from 1795 in various garrison duties and as military governor of Armagh in 1797–98. Initially favourable towards the Irish, he gloomily concluded from the savagery of 1798 that the British might best withdraw from Ireland, leaving the Irish 'to fight it out among each other'.[49] The British connection would then be sought once more, as a positive blessing. Cornwallis took an equally gloomy view of the violence between Irish factions but reached the opposite conclusion. On arriving at the capital, the new viceroy found that, apart from the Lord Chancellor of Ireland, Lord Clare, most of 'the other principal political characters here are absurdly violent'. Cornwallis entertained virtually every night, only to find 'the conversation even at my table, where you will suppose I do all I can to prevent it, always turns on hanging, shooting, burning, etc, etc, and if a priest has been put to death the greatest joy is expressed by the whole company'. By mid-September, he told Portland that the leading politicians in Ireland had 'from their mode of governing' the country 'proved themselves totally ignorant' of it. On 17 November 1798, he confided to his brother: 'Ireland cannot change for the worse, but unless religious animosities and the violence of parties can be in some measure allayed, I do not think she can receive much benefit from any plan of Government.' By December, he described how everyone in 'this most corrupt country' viewed the great political questions of the day solely from the perspective of private 'ambition and avarice'.[50] By removing the Irish parliament, the British government would curb the excesses of the minority establishment in Dublin. While loathing the pettiness, selfishness and corruption that surrounded him, Cornwallis cajoled the Irish parliament to disband itself in 1800 and pass an act of union.

Cornwallis's conviction that a more tolerant, enlightened government could only flow from direct British rule was bound inextricably with Catholic Emancipation. In October 1798, Cornwallis urged emancipation upon the prime minister, Pitt, on the grounds that, since it would have to be extended from Britain eventually, the government should seize the present opportunity as the only occasion when Britain would obtain full credit for taking such action. But the settlement envisaged by Pitt and Cornwallis was never delivered in full. George III insisted that his coronation oath to uphold the Protestant faith prohibited him from condoning that reversal of policy towards Catholics. Pitt's ministry therefore resigned in early 1801.

Thus no side emerged victorious at that point. The insurgency had intensified Protestant–Catholic tensions and antagonisms which the United Irish had sought to transcend. In Britain the Irish rising encouraged popular anti-Papist rhetoric, which had long infused anti-French sentiment; the patriotic press used both Nelson's victory at the Nile and the rising's suppression to proclaim British success against the twin threats of Jacobinism and Catholicism.[51] The landowning Anglo-Irish Ascendancy lost their separate parliament and government. Cornwallis and Pitt failed to obtain Catholic Emancipation which they felt was essential to full political union. On the other hand, there was the unambiguous achievement of defeating French military and naval ambitions as an unalloyed benefit from the rebellion.

The military significance of the rebellion

This overwhelming sense of political failure and the sheer brutality of the repression inflicted in 1798 have deflected attention from the grim effectiveness of British military operations. John Fortescue, in his concentration upon the 'proper', fighting functions of the British army, dismissed the events of 1798 as an aberration. He blamed Pitt for ignoring Abercromby's warnings about the state of Irish militia and the government more generally for depending later in 1798 on under-trained reinforcements of British fencibles and some militia, whose actions were of limited relevance to the history of the British army. Indeed, Fortescue conveniently insisted that the regular army played little part in suppressing the rising: 'To all intents the rebellion was a savage fight between two factions of half-disciplined and undisciplined Irish.'[52] In fact, the campaigning in Ireland revealed a great deal about the British army's customary peace-enforcing and counter-insurgency role.

While the bulk of the forces deployed in Ireland were Irish militia and yeomanry, specialist forces and skills were vital to military success. Elite regular troops were significant in number and role. In January 1798 there were only 5,769 regulars in Ireland, over two-thirds of them cavalry. One year later the total had risen to 9,723. The number of semi-regular fencibles had also increased to 16,655. The regulars dominated the cavalry who were essential in providing mobility and pursuit. Specialist skills figured more prominently in the artillery, which played a decisive role in smashing the insurgents' morale and driving them into retreat at Tara Hill, north-west of Dublin on 26 May and notably at Vinegar Hill, as well as in retaking Antrim town and Ballynahinch. The defence of towns against direct rebel attack, as at Arklow, on the coastal road between Wexford and Dublin in early June, was boosted by artillery.[53] In November 1797, some 170 officers and men of the Royal Horse Artillery, with eight guns, constituting 15% of the manpower and guns of this elite force, were despatched from Woolwich to Ireland. But the artillery used was essentially from the separate Irish Artillery establishment. Guns of the Irish Artillery were distributed to regular infantry regiments who received more training in their use from mid-1795 onwards. In February 1797, guns were also distributed to eight militia battalions, with 300 militiamen being instructed to work them. In addition, an NCO and nine men from the Royal Artillery were attached to each of six regular army battalions operational in Ireland in 1798, to handle the battalion guns.[54] In an effort to improve the irregular troops' effectiveness, regular infantry were deployed, even in very small garrisons, to provide exemplars to local militia and yeomanry and stiffen their professional application and fighting skills, and regular battalions were brigaded with militia.

More striking, in reassessing the view of 1798 as a minor military sideshow, was the nature of the military command in Ireland. The suppression of the rebellion in Ireland in fact provided an extensive object lesson in imperial pacification for a long line of future senior generals. For an alleged sideshow, the campaign drew in a remarkably large number of talented or favoured senior officers. Six of the ten future commanders-in-chief in India in the period from 1801 to 1835 served in Ireland during the rebellion: Cornwallis, Lake, George Hewitt (Cornwallis's able Adjutant General), George Nugent (who succeeded Lake in the command in Ulster in 1798), the Earl of Dalhousie, and Lord William Bentinck. The estates of a seventh, Lord Moira (later Lord Hastings), were the scene of intense fighting. In addition, the Deputy Quartermaster General was Lt. Col. Robert Crawford, who had earlier served under Cornwallis in India and would later win renown as a fighting major general in the Iberian peninsula, dying of wounds at the storming of Cuidad Rodrigo in 1812. One of the rising stars of the British army was John Moore who was brought to Ireland by Abercromby in 1797 and distinguished himself, gaining promotion to major general in 1798–99. With so many talented and later successful officers commanding operations and with forces totalling up to 100,000 men by the end of the year, 1798 provided a sobering and toughening experience for Britain's military leadership.

The rebellion raised fundamental issues concerning Britain's conduct of counter-insurgency operations. Cornwallis and, for example, the young John Moore, found the Anglo-Irish ruling elite objectionably reactionary, the extent of the violence used against civilians disgusting, and the use of regular soldiers in warfare upon the population disagreeable in the extreme. But they accepted the obligation to uphold order as an end in itself and to maintain the British empire in Ireland. As divisional commander in Ulster, Lake oversaw vigorous search-and-destroy operations against the United Irish and their alleged supporters. In the year from September 1796, the government arrested about 500–600 people in Ulster for political reasons, and by July 1797 had seized 6,200 serviceable and 4,400 unserviceable guns. When the rising eventually exploded, its extent was severely curtailed by the practical effects and deterrent impact of this suppression, as well as by the destructive damage inflicted by government agents and activity on the United Irish system of command and communication. Another military technique was Abercromby's threat to quarter troops on the civilian population if people did not come forward to surrender arms. This sometimes worked as desired. In late April, for example, arms were given up in Queen's county in response to the threat of 'free quarters'. Under pressure from landowners who felt they were suffering from the application of this policy, Lord Camden in late April 1798 ended it, on the grounds that free quartering failed to distinguish between the loyal and the disloyal. That decision simply led to the army deploying even more violent means to secure weapons. In early May in County Kildare the army began to flog civilians tied to quickly erected wooden triangles to get individuals to admit to their disloyalty. In southern Wicklow, ten days of house-burning and flogging resulted in the seizure of 600–700 arms and 3,000 pikes.[55] Such practices sickened Brigadier John Moore who objected to the 'promiscuous and severe punishments' inflicted by flogging civilians and who bridled at soldiers being 'made instruments of oppression'.[56] His desire to resign from a divisional command made unacceptable by such widespread practices elsewhere in the country was overridden by the call of duty when open rebellion broke out. During the rebellion, some commanders made little effort to control – while some may even have encouraged – violence by the militia against rebels off and beyond the field of battle.[57] It is possible to attribute some of that brutality to the frustrations felt by militiamen who were not particularly effective in formal fighting and who were typically disparaged by regular officers and soldiers alike for their lack of military professionalism and perhaps competence. But the British military command in Ireland, whatever generals' personal distaste for non-regular warfare may have been, presided over a ruthless repression of the rebellion in 1798, just as the British commanders had done in the Scottish Highlands in 1746 and in South Carolina in 1780–81.

On the other hand, British generals' objective distrust of militia and, by easy extension, any citizens' army was strongly reinforced by the events of 1798. Although the Catholic militia had remained loyal during the rebellion, the British government maintained very large numbers of essentially volunteer Protestant yeomanry in post-rebellion Ireland. The yeomanry establishment – not normally matched by the effective numbers in uniform – totalled 50,000 in May 1798. It did not fall below that figure until 1815 and often stayed at 80,000 or more in the years 1803–10.[58] But the army remained adamant that regular forces were needed to police the country effectively. As of October 1799, units of the Royal Irish Artillery were stationed at twenty-nine different towns or points of observation. Although one-sixth of the regiment's manpower deployed in Ireland for active duty was concentrated at Cork and nearby Charles Fort,[59] as the island's vital naval base, the widespread distribution of artillery demonstrated the scale of the perceived need for guaranteeing order.

Following the fall of Pitt's ministry and his own departure from office, Cornwallis provided an assessment of the defence needs of Ireland for the Duke of York, in May 1802. The first requirement remained British supremacy at sea. When the French broke through Britain's maritime defences, it was usually in such bad weather as to produce no strategic advantages.[60] Even if the French did break through, the only points at which Ireland could be invaded were Bantry Bay or Lough Swilly or on the west coast in between. To cover that eventuality, Cornwallis therefore supported current proposals to construct new forts to the west of Cork (to protect that vital port city from its landward side), and, in the north, near Omagh. Another site he endorsed was the vital point at Tullamore, to cover the central route from the west across the Shannon River, towards Dublin.[61] Overall, the country needed 45,000 embodied troops if 20,000 line soldiers were among that number, the rest being militia and fencibles. That total far exceeded the late eighteenth-century peacetime establishment of 15,000 regulars and indicated the continuing official fear of violence during the precarious international peace of 1801–03. If such troop levels appear low for maintaining order over 4.5 million people, the vast majority of whom were at best passive subjects and at worst subjugated peasants,[62] those regular forces were supplemented by the yeomanry, established at 51,000 in June 1802, and designed as an essentially Protestant force to control the Catholic majority. The net effect of the turbulence of 1796–98 had been to increase the levels of military policing in Ireland to nearly 100,000 men.

The rebellion of 1798 has been described as being 'as stunning an event to contemporaries in Ireland as 1789 had been to French men and women in France'.[63] The increasing Catholic character of the protest and the subsequent depiction of the essential fissure as being a Catholic/ Protestant one went against the thrust of much late eighteenth-century, non-sectarian political development. By the 1820s, 1798 had gained notoriety as another instance of Britain's 700-year oppression of Ireland, as well as a year when Catholic exclusion was yet more deeply entrenched. At the time, in fact, the United Irishmen's main enemy was the Anglo-Irish Protestant establishment and not Irish Protestantism or even, in Wexford, the British connection as such. But out of the dual experience of 1798 and the act of Union in 1801 came an increasing rhetorical emphasis on the separate character and identity of Ireland, and on Britain's ruling the island by deliberately dividing its inhabitants and enlisting collaborators through the exploitation of religious differences.[64]

In military terms, the suppression of Ireland offers some instructive comparisons with the Americans' successful revolution. The British political establishment proved far more determined to hold Ireland than to hold America,[65] a reflection of the size of the 'British' population of the island, Ireland's importance in commercial and strategic terms, and the contribution Irishmen made to Britain's regular forces. The British started in 1797 and continued in 1798 to disarm the civilian population far more effectively than they did in America. Indeed, the army's initial efforts to seize stores of arms in villages outside Boston led to disaster for the regular troops. While the army in Ireland only partially achieved its objective, it reduced the amount of arms in circulation and operated with impunity for a long period in 1797–98, unlike Gage's troops in eastern Massachusetts in 1775. The savagery used in weapons seizure helped provoke the rising once an opportunity to rise occurred. But it may equally have deterred many from pushing resistance into informal modes of fighting for fear of reprisals. The pre-emptive violence of the militia seems to have ensured that the British forces enjoyed mobility unhindered by ambushes once they had the troop levels to go on the offensive. Moreover, before they went over to the counter-attack, the British secured the major cities by concentrating their forces in them. The government's defences ensured that no cities other than Wexford – a relatively minor one – fell to the rebels. There was no repeat of the humiliating defeat at and withdrawal from Boston in 1776, or of the wholesale failure to hold the other American towns in that year.

The authorities never lost control of the levers of power or of the militia and voluntary forces, and they were able to mobilize overwhelming manpower, far exceeding that available in America. Only in restricted parts of Ireland did the British have to engage in a reconquest. Once on the offensive, they intermingled regular and irregular units and used artillery very flexibly to break civilian resistance. The loss of perhaps 20,000–30,000 lives in 1798 compares with the total of 25,000 Americans estimated to have died for, or as a direct result of, the revolution over the entire course of seven years, even allowing for the fact that Ireland's population in 1798 was nearly double America's in the 1770s. It is often suggested that the British learned the political arts of conciliating colonial peoples from the experience of the American revolution. The absorption of a contrary lesson – to crush dissent with speedy, ruthless vigour – was demonstrated in Ireland.

Notes and references

1 John Fortescue, *A History of the British Army, 1763–1793*, 13 vols (London, 1899–1930), Vol. IV, p. 589.

2 Harvey C. Mansfield, Jr. (ed.), *Selected Letters of Edmund Burke* (Chicago, 1984), p. 429.

3 *Parliamentary Register: or History of the Proceedings and Debates of the House of Commons of Ireland*, Vol. XVII (Dublin, 1801), pp. 347–49, 352, 357.

4 William Laird Clowes, *The Royal Navy: A History From the Earliest Times to the Present*, 7 vols (London, 1897–1903), Vol. IV, p. 555.

5 Rt. Hon. William Beresford (ed.), *The Correspondence of the Right Hon. John Beresford*, 2 vols (London, 1854), Vol. II, p. 169.

6 Nancy J. Curtin, 'The transformation of the Society of United Irishmen into a mass-based revolutionary organization, 1794–6', *Irish Historical Studies*, XXIV (1985), pp. 463–92.

7 R.B. McDowell (ed.), *Correspondence of Edmund Burke*, 10 vols (Cambridge, 1958–78), Vol. VIII, p. 250.

8 Deirdre Lindsay, 'The Fitzwilliam episode revisited' in David Dickson, Daire Keogh and Kevin Whelan (eds), *The United Irishmen: Republicanism, Radicalism and Rebellion* (Dublin, 1993), pp. 197–208; Nancy J. Curtin, 'The United Irish organisation in Ulster: 1795–8' in *ibid.*, pp. 209–21, esp. p. 218.

9 Bartlett, T. and Jeffrey, K., (eds), *A Military History of Ireland* (Cambridge, 1996), p. 229.

10 Kenneth Ferguson, 'The army and the Irish rebellion of 1798' in Alan Guy (ed.), *The Road to Waterloo* (London, 1990), pp. 88–100.

11 Capt. Francis Duncan, *History of the Royal Regiment of Artillery*, 2 vols (London, 1872–73), Vol. II, pp. 80–81.

12 Ferguson, 'The army and the Irish rebellion', p. 88.

13 Ferguson, 'The army and the Irish rebellion', p. 93.

14 *Correspondence of Edmund Burke*, Vol. VIII, p. 171.

15 J.A. Houlding, *Fit for Service: The Training of the British Army, 1715–1795* (Oxford, 1981), p. 63. It has been argued that the British perception of high levels of Irish violence was accurate in relation to English levels of violence, but misleading if Ireland were compared with other eighteenth-century peasant societies or parts of North America. Neal Garnham, 'How violent was eighteenth-century Ireland?' *Irish Historical Studies*, XXX (1997), 377–92.

16 Ferguson 'The army and the Irish rebellion', p. 93.

17 Alan Blackstock, *An Ascendancy Army: The Irish Yeomanry 1796–1834* (Dublin, 1998), pp. 74, 92–93, 96, 212–25, 238, 243, 258.

18 Major General Sir J.F. Maurice (ed.), *The Diary of Sir John Moore*, 2 vols (London, 1904), Vol. I, pp. 273–75.

19 Bartlett and Jeffrey (eds), *A Military History of Ireland*, pp. 270–72.

20 Bartlett and Jeffrey (eds), *A Military History of Ireland*, pp. 273–77; Maurice (ed.), *Diary of Sir John Moore*, Vol. I, pp. 286–87.

21 *The Royal Military Calendar*, 5 vols (London, 1821), Vol. I, pp. 308–09.

22 Thomas Pakenham, *The Year of Liberty* (London, 1969), pp. 83–85, 96–98, 100–01.

23 Thomas Graham, ' "An Union of Power"? The United Irish Organisation: 1795–1798' in Dickson et al. (eds), *The United Irishmen*, pp. 244–55, esp. pp. 252–54.

24 Pakenham, *The Year of Liberty*, pp. 150, 169–76.

25 Fine overviews are: Ian McBride, 'Reclaiming the rebellion: 1798 in 1998', *Irish Historical Studies*, XXXI, (1999), 395–410; Jacqueline Hill, 'Convergence and conflict in eighteenth-century Ireland', *Historical Journal* 44 (2001), 1039–1063.

26 Pakenham, *The Year of Liberty*, pp. 95, 112, 115, 119, 125, 137–38, 143, 154.

27 Hill, 'Convergence and conflict', p. 1059.

28 K. Whelan, 'Politicisation in County Wexford and the origins of the 1798 rebellion' in H. Gough and D. Dickson, (eds), *Ireland and the French Revolution* (Dublin, 1990), pp. 156–78.

29 Pakenham, *The Year of Liberty*, pp. 229–34; 238.

30 Pakenham, *The Year of Liberty*, pp. 242–45.

31 Graham, 'An Union of Power', pp. 254–55.

32 *Royal Military Calendar*, Vol. I, pp. 395, 397–99; Pakenham, *The Year of Liberty*, pp. 259, 262–63; John Jones, *An Impartial Narrative of the Most Important Engagements . . . during the Irish Rebellion, 1798* (Dublin, 1799), pp. 55–56, 58, 61–63.

33 A. Aspinall (ed.), *The Later Correspondence of George III*, 5 vols (Cambridge, 1967), Vol. III, p. 70.

34 Aspinall (ed.), *The Later Correspondence*, Vol. III, pp. 70–1, and notes.

35 Pakenham, *The Year of Liberty*, pp. 284, 293–95.

36 Julian P. Boyd (ed.), *The Papers of Thomas Jefferson*, Vol. 6, *21 May 1781–1 March 1784* (Princeton, NJ, 1951), p. 24.

37 Charles Ross (ed.), *Correspondence of Charles, First Marquis Cornwallis*, 3 vols (London, 1859), Vol. II, pp. 357, 359, 371. Franklin and Mary Wickwire, *Cornwallis: The Imperial Years* (North Carolina, 1980), pp. 222–30 offer a brief summary of the rising; the account of British policy in Marianne Elliott, *Partners in Revolution*, (New Haven, CT, 1982), pp. 165–240, though British policy is not the central focus, is very acute.

38 Lt. Col. C. Greenhill Gardyne, *The Life of a Regiment: A History of the Gordon Highlanders*, 2 vols (Edinburgh, 1901–03), Vol. I, p. 42.

39 Gardyne, *The Life of a Regiment*, Vol. I, p. 43.

40 Elliott, *Partners in Revolution*, pp. 206–07.

41 Elliott, *Partners in Revolution*, pp. 212–13, 124–25.

42 Elliott, *Partners in Revolution*, pp. 214–18, 222, 224, 226–27.

43 Elliott, *Partners in Revolution*, p. 227; Bartlett and Jeffrey (eds), *A Military History of Ireland*, p. 249; R.B. McDowell, *Ireland in the Age of Imperialism and Revolution, 1760–1801* (Oxford, 1979), pp. 647–48.

44 Ross (ed.), *Correspondence of Charles, First Marquis Cornwallis*, Vol. II, pp. 413–14, Vol. III, p. 360; Pakenham, *The Year of Liberty*, p. 358.

45 Clowes, *The Royal Navy*, Vol. IV, pp. 344–51.

46 McDowell, *Ireland*, p. 632; Alethea Hayter (ed.), *The Backbone* (Bishop Auckland, 1993), p. 46; Pakenham, *The Year of Liberty*, pp. 392–93.

47 Blackstock, *An Ascendancy Army*, p. 114.

48 T.J. Kiernan, *History of the Financial Administration of Ireland to 1817* (London, 1930), pp. 216, 303.

49 John Rosselli, *Lord William Bentinck: The Making of a Liberal Imperialist, 1774–1839* (London, 1974), pp. 34, 112.

50 Ross (ed.), *Correspondence of Charles, First Marquis Cornwallis*, Vol. II, pp. 364, 371, 406, Vol. III, p. 8.

51 Stuart Andrews, *The British Periodical Press and the French Revolution, 1789–1799* (Basingstoke, 2000), pp. 152, 154, 187–91.

52 Fortescue, *History of the British Army*, Vol. IV, pp. 573–78, 589, 597.

53 Pakenham, *The Year of Liberty*, pp. 135, 182–83, 248, 262–3, 280–81, 293.

54 Duncan, *A History of the Royal . . . Artillery*, Vol. II, pp. 76, 78–9.

55 Pakenham, *The Year of Liberty*, pp. 77–85; 199–101.

56 Carola Oman, *Sir John Moore* (London, 1953), pp. 173–76.

57 Elliott, *Partners in Revolution*, pp. 192, 198, 202, 207.

58 Blackstock, *An Ascendancy Army*, p. 114.

59 Duncan, *A History of the Royal . . . Artillery*, pp. 80–81.

60 Ross (ed.), *Correspondence of Charles, First Marquis Cornwallis*, Vol. III, p. 490.

61 Ross (ed.), *Correspondence of Charles, First Marquis Cornwallis*, Vol. III, pp. 488–89.

62 Blackstock, *An Ascendancy Army*, p. 114.

63 Oliver MacDonagh, *States of Mind: A Study of Anglo-Irish Conflict 1780–1980* (London, 1983), p. 2.

64 MacDonagh, *States of Mind*, pp. 15–18, 75.

65 Thomas Bartlett, ' "This famous island set in a Virginian sea": Ireland in the British Empire, 1690–1801' in P.J. Marshall (ed.), *The Eighteenth Century* (Oxford, 1998), pp. 253–275, esp. pp. 270–71.

CHAPTER 6

Renewing alliances and positioning for peace, 1798–1801

The long struggle between Britain and France stretching from 1793 went through many phases. In 1798 British sea-power and the suppression of the Irish rebellion, drawing in more troops in relation to the population than Napoleon thought necessary in 1808 for the conquest of Spain, demonstrated the futility of any French dreams of invading the most politically vulnerable part of the British Isles. With the Caribbean virtually off-limits to French naval and military initiatives, there seemed to be a strategic stalemate in the Anglo-French war. Yet the French Directory, though at peace with the rest of Europe and involved in the political reconstruction of much of Italy, did not acquiesce in a strictly European role. Instead, it launched an ambitious offensive to seize control of Egypt, thereby amply vindicating British suspicions of French geopolitical expansionism. Through a sequence of events, the British turned the Egyptian adventure into the occasion for an extension of the European war. The extended participation of other Great Powers did not, however, endure beyond 1800. The fall of Pitt's government in the following year opened the way to a settlement which left Britain at peace for the first time since 1793 by accepting France's newly dominant role in western Europe and by returning nearly all the colonial conquests so dearly fought for over the previous eight years. How Britain came to acquiesce in the very international order which she so long and so determinedly struggled to thwart reveals much about the limitations of British overseas power projection and politicians' increasing frustration in trying to forge and sustain continental alliances. The British conduct of war in 1798–1801 demonstrated no lack of political will but rather the inability to deliver decisive blows with the forces available to the British.

Mediterranean initiatives, 1798–99

Unable to secure satisfactory terms with France herself, Britain in 1798 sought to construct a new Quadruple Alliance with Russia, Prussia and Austria. By the spring, it was clear that, while Prussia was not interested, Austria saw advantages in securing a British re-entry into the Mediterranean, from which they had departed at the end of 1796. This reflected a shift in Austria's geopolitical priorities since 1793. The settlement with France at Campo Formio (October 1797) confirmed the loss of the Austrian Netherlands to France (a loss largely unlamented in Vienna), the strengthening of Austria's territories on the south German borderlands, and the thorough reshaping of northern Italy following the Habsburg's acquisition of the Venetian republic and its capacious territories. A British fleet returning to the Mediterranean might provide regional support for Austria's new position in northern Italy and enhance the security of the Kingdom of the Two Sicilies or Naples, consisting of southern Italy and the island of Sicily. With the French setting up the Swiss Helvetic republic in January and a republic in the Papal states in February 1798, French advance upon Naples seemed distinctly possible. The British government therefore agreed to send a fleet into the Mediterranean on condition that the Two Sicilies gave them access to the harbour at Naples for the purposes of repairs and resupply, since they had no Mediterranean base. The agreement required Austria to support the Two Sicilies if the latter were attacked by the French from their position of recently increased strength in the neighbouring Papal states. Naval re-entry into the Mediterranean was thus driven by British eagerness to secure a continental ally and not by any pressing national interest in the region.

For its part, the Admiralty had no desire to re-enter the Mediterranean, feeling that its resources were already overstretched in guarding the English Channel and blockading the Spanish fleet at Cadiz. But political developments at Vienna hastened the cabinet in April 1798 into ordering a naval force through the Straits of Gibraltar. To enable Lord St Vincent at Cadiz to provide a squadron for this task, the Admiralty shifted eight line ships from the defence of Ireland which, given the state of rebellion there and the possibility of a French invasion, involved an element of risk. Any such risk was counterbalanced by the French decision in May to despatch an army under General Napoleon Bonaparte from Toulon to Egypt. Bonaparte, who came originally from Corsica, had distinguished himself as a junior officer at Toulon in 1793 and soared to fame with a brilliant campaign in northern Italy against the Austrians in 1796. He saw

Egypt as an alternative to the Cape route to India for the future, and as offering a more attainable objective for military action than any invasion of the British Isles did. The significance attached to Egypt by Bonaparte stiffened Henry Dundas's habitual concerns about French threats to the route to India. In April 1798, the war minister described Egypt to the First Lord of the Admiralty as 'the master key to all the commerce of the world'.[1]

The British intervention in the Mediterranean started badly. A British squadron proceeded to Toulon to watch over the French Mediterranean fleet but, scattered in bad weather, it failed to detect – let alone check – the departure from Toulon of a massive French flotilla of transports and warships on 19 May.[2] By early June, when a squadron under Rear Admiral Sir Horatio Nelson began searching for the French, Bonaparte's expeditionary force had taken Malta, an island commanding a strategic vantage point in the central Mediterranean. Bonaparte's enormous fleet evaded Nelson's pursuit and landed in Egypt without British intercession, thereby incensing Dundas and lowering Britain's standing with Austria.

From this low point, Nelson resiliently swept the Mediterranean in his quest of Bonaparte. Eventually, on 1 August, he returned to the Egyptian coast and found the French squadron – two and a half months after it had first eluded the British – at anchor in Aboukir Bay. Nelson, driven by a quite extraordinarily explicit and self-conscious hunger for annihilatory victory and spectacular glory, ordered an immediate attack, to the surprise of the French who expected no such action at dusk. Following the practice adopted by Jervis at St Vincent and Duncan at Camperdown, Nelson gave his captains considerable latitude in their conduct of the battle. The critical decision was taken by the lead ship's commander, Captain Thomas Foley, who also had the only available map of the bay, giving details of the depths of the seabed. Foley's tactical decision to sail between the French line and the coast enabled the British to attack their opponents from both sides simultaneously, with some British ships sailing between the French line and the shore and others advancing down the French line along its seaward side. The French ships were undermanned, their guns to the lee side were unprepared to receive an attack, and they were widely separated in their line, so that they failed to support each other. Thus, for example, the British directed four ships' broadsides at the first ship in the French line. When some French ships weighed anchor and attempted to manoeuvre out of line the following morning, they were mostly blown by onshore winds back into ever-shallower waters and the beach; in that way, three of the thirteen French line ships ran aground and another was burned as it made for the shore. The battle became a ferocious slugging match, marked by heroic French resistance. Of the sixteen most senior French officers, four, including the commander-in-chief, were killed and seven were wounded. Only two of the thirteen French line ships got away. With St Vincent bottling up the entrance to the Mediterranean from his position off Cadiz, thereby preventing French naval redeployment, this victory crippled the French Mediterranean fleet.[3] The battle boosted British morale and launched a new naval hero on to the international stage.

But Dundas remained concerned about the security of India: 'Fleets may be destroyed, and the armies who came in them be successful.'[4] The fate of the French army in Egypt – and the potential threats it posed – remained a major preoccupation of Dundas's until it was resolved in 1801. Across the Mediterranean region, the battle triggered immediate political reactions. At the beginning of September, there was a rising in Malta against the French which the British exploited during 1799–1800 to besiege the French garrison there. Turkey declared war upon France and so provided a counterweight to Bonaparte's army in Egypt. Russia, which had a special guardianship role over Malta, agreed to send a fleet through the Dardanelles. Nelson's victory opened the way to a British expedition using Major General Charles Stuart's forces based in Portugal to retake Menorca from Spain. When Nelson and his battered fleet arrived at Naples on 22 September, the Neapolitan prime minister told him, 'you have saved Italy, and especially the Two Sicilies'. In weakening the capacity of France to project power in the central Mediterranean, Nelson had met one of the objectives which Austria had set out earlier in the year. The wider strategic context was sketched to Lord Spencer by George III as soon as news of the victory reached London at the beginning of October:

The beating and destroying [sic] the Brest fleet would be highly glorious and advantageous to this kingdom, but the success of this brave Admiral is of more utility to the cause we are engaged in; if it electrifies Austria and Naples it may save Italy.[5]

Noting that the French fleet at Brest constituted the main naval threat to British interests, the king rightly stressed that the real value of the victory at Aboukir Bay lay in its potential to bring Austria into the war.

Enthused by his brilliant victory and, as ever, keen for aggressive action, Nelson encouraged the war party in Naples to attack the French in the Papal states. With British naval support – including transports for landing troops at Leghorn well north of Rome – the Neapolitans launched an offensive on 17 November which carried them to the eternal city. From there, the Anglo-Neapolitan position collapsed. The French regrouped, counter-attacked, swept southwards, and forced the court before Christmas to flee Naples aboard British warships, taking refuge in Sicily. In early 1799 the French established a client republic in the mainland kingdom of Naples, so rounding off a breathtaking conquest and the restructuring of most of Italy since 1797. French power had seldom been so dramatically exercised in the course of Europe's history.

Yet, by March 1799, the Mediterranean theatre had been transformed. The British had regained Menorca as a vital base, were besieging Malta, and were ready and able to defend Sicily. They had also isolated one French army, under the Directory's most dashing general, in Egypt. While mainland Naples had fallen under French control, its loss, coupled with a hugely expanded British naval presence and Russia's desire to assert itself, spurred Vienna to enter the war in March. In April and May the Austrians and Russians swept across northern Italy, forcing French retreats and eventual French withdrawal from mainland Naples and from the Papal states. Italy, virtually taken over by the French in 1797–99, was mostly freed from them by July.

This sudden counter-swing did not mean that British policy was vindicated. While the Austrians sought to make themselves the paramount power in Italy, Britain essentially wanted continental allies in order to force the French out of Holland and the former Austrian Netherlands, neither of which attracted much interest in Vienna. The Russians, who fought well in 1799, wanted to move upon France rather than support the Habsburgs in re-ordering northern Italy. More immediately difficult in the spring of 1799 was the definition of Britain's role in the Mediterranean. Nelson became mesmerized with the restoration of the Neapolitan monarchs to their possessions in mainland Naples and to their capital in the city of Naples, the third most populous city in Europe after London and Paris. Local republicans and a small residual French garrison continued to hold out at the city into June. Nelson therefore committed his naval squadron to supporting the Bourbon restoration and urged the use of naval power along the Italian coast to undermine the French. Apart from the naval facilities available in the port of Naples, there were no obvious assets in the southern kingdom in the circumstances of 1799. The Two Sicilies had the advantage of numbers, with five million living on the mainland and 1.5 million inhabiting the island of Sicily. (By comparison, the far richer northern provinces of Lombardy and Venetia supported about four million people in 1814, while Tuscany contained about one million people.) Yet British experience in 1793–96 indicated that the classic value of a large and impoverished population, as a recruiting ground for troops, did not apply to Naples, whose military capacity and performance were weak. In his official reporting to London, Sir William Hamilton, the British minister to Naples, stressed the regime's chronic corruption and inefficiency. The revolution within the kingdom in 1799 intensified such shortcomings by unleashing widespread anticlericalism and fuelling urban–rural tensions.[6] Avoiding such tumultuous complexities, Lord St Vincent, commanding the Mediterranean fleet, focused on defending and retaining Menorca and countering major French and Spanish fleet movements during April–August 1799. His drive to concentrate his fleet was weakened by Nelson's Italian strategy.

The Mediterranean fleet, particularly from December 1799, operated upon the coasts of northern Italy and southern France. Admiral Lord Keith, succeeding the ailing St Vincent, enforced a tight blockade of Genoa, in cooperation with the Austrian land forces, to squeeze Masséna into capitulating on 4 June 1800. But further progress ended when General Bonaparte's shock victory at Marengo against the Austrians on 14 June 1800 reversed the balance of military power in northern Italy and eventually pushed Vienna to settle with France. For Britain, there was little enduring to show for extensive and often challenging naval activity in the Mediterranean during 1798–1801. The principal gain was the surrender of the French garrison on Malta in September 1800, after a prolonged siege, and Britain's somewhat indirect takeover of the island.

The limitations of naval power, 1799–1801

Success in Italy in 1799 was meant to open the way for massive Austrian and Russian offensives into France. According to the assessment of Lord Grenville, the Foreign Secretary, the Austrians would invade France along the southern coastal route, while the Russians would push through Switzerland towards Lyon, with their northern flank protected by an Austrian advance between Basle and the Vosges. Britain would contribute to this mass attack by assisting with an Anglo-Russian invasion of Holland, for which Russian troops would arrive through the Baltic. This invasion was predicated upon the assumption that the Dutch would welcome the overthrow of a French puppet regime and that victory in the Low Countries would persuade Prussia to enter the war.[7] If the Anglo-Russian army could secure Belgium by the close of campaigning in late 1799, all would be set for a multi-pronged advance on Paris in the spring of 1800.

The British failed to meet their modest military obligations under this ambitious strategy. Projecting their power overseas, as distinct from blocking their enemies' naval projection of power, repeatedly proved difficult. As a first step, the Royal Navy blockaded Bruix's combined fleet, when it returned to Brest in August 1799, to ensure that it posed no threat to the expeditionary force against Holland. On 13 August the British expedition sailed from Margate Roads and the Downs but, dogged by bad weather, did not make its landing until 26 August. What appears on paper as a simple transfer of men and equipment across the southern stretch of the North Sea took nearly two weeks of hard sailing, even at the height of summer. The navy provided eleven line ships, eight frigates and many smaller craft to organize, keep together, and defend the transports conveying 17,000 troops. The landing itself met no resistance from the Dutch and transferred seven Dutch line ships, the remnants of a once proud navy, to British control. These naval achievements were not matched by the army. Despite some successes against French forces, the Duke of York's army had been pushed back to its original landing positions by October and withdrew at the end of the month. The French agreed to allow the British to re-embark without attacking them, in return for the restitution from Britain of 8,000 French prisoners of war.[8] The Dutch had not risen in rebellion against the French; the Prussians had not entered the war; and the Austrians displayed no inclination to invade France. Strategic options in 1800 proved difficult to reconcile with Austrian priorities. Vienna had no pressing need for increased British support in northern Italy and indeed distrusted the excessively pro-British leanings of the government of Naples.[9]

One possible strategic option was the hardy perennial of whether Britain should land expeditionary forces at some point on the French mainland to arouse and then sustain royalist insurgents. Earlier in the year the Austrians had argued for British assistance to counter-revolutionaries in western France. Following serious debate and assessment, a sizeable force was sent in June 1800 to Quiberon Bay, the scene of a dramatic British naval victory in 1759, to support royalists in the region. It proved inadequate to the task of challenging the powerful defences of Belle Isle and, after disembarking the troops for a time on one of the lesser islands, proceeded in force to the Mediterranean.[10] Further review led to attacks on Spain at Ferrol in August and Cadiz in October. The latter demonstration, involving twenty-two line ships, thirty-seven frigates and sloops, and eighty transports conveying 18,000 troops under Sir Ralph Abercromby, failed amid recriminations against the naval commander, Lord Keith, for

lack of commitment to the combined operation and inadequate preparation for landing the troops.

By late 1800 the renewed continental war had fizzled out. The elixir of
naval success, so galvanizing in the autumn of 1798, had lost its potency.
The expedition to Holland had exposed the uncertain timing inherent in
sea transport and the expedition along the Atlantic coast in 1800 had
revealed the limited influence which even sizeable forces could exert in
rallying resistance on land. Only at the third attempt did British power
projection prove successful in the long aftermath of the victory at the Nile.

Having secured Malta in September, the government decided at the
beginning of October to back Dundas's longstanding argument for a
major expedition to Egypt, using the forces assembled at Cadiz for this
new purpose. The logic of the British decision to send an expedition to
Egypt was reinforced by the collapse of the Austrian alliance. Following a
crushing defeat by the French at Hohenlinden, just south-east of Munich,
on 3 December 1800, Vienna sought a separate peace. If attacking the
French army left stranded in Egypt by Nelson's victory in August 1798
was one of few remaining options for the British, it also met various
objectives. It provided the symbolic opportunity for a strictly British
victory and a theatre of war in which Britain largely determined the scale
and timing of operations. It also built upon an alliance with the Ottoman
empire and held out the prospect of extending political influence and
commercial interests in the region. Finally, for advocates of an Egyptian
engagement, success would give Britain a bargaining chip in negotiations
for a global peace settlement with France and protect the overland route
to India from any French threat. Whereas re-entering the Mediterranean
in 1798 had been about securing a continental ally, the return to Egypt
agreed upon in October 1800 was about protecting imperial interests
and influencing the peace settlement.[11]

Before the Egyptian campaign was concluded another intervention
rounded off the military-strategic fallout from the collapse of the Second
Coalition. The French seizure of Malta provoked the entry of Russian
warships into the Mediterranean in 1799 because the sovereign order of
knights which ruled the island came under the broad protection of Russia.
But when the British forced the remaining French garrison out of Malta in
September 1800, they did not permit the Russians to return as the island's
protectors. In retaliation, Tsar Paul I in November banned British trade
with Russia and in December set up a League of Armed Neutrality, with
Denmark being forced to block the entrance of the Baltic Sea against
British shipping.[12] The Danes themselves were pressured into action by

their dependence upon a longstanding alliance with Russia to safeguard themselves against Sweden's acquisitive ambitions. But Denmark had its own running disputes with Britain over mercantile rights and an assertive use of neutrality for trading purposes from 1797 onwards.[13]

In order to break the League of Armed Neutrality, ministers in March 1801 despatched a major naval force, of twenty-one line, eleven frigates and twenty-three smaller ships, to break into the Baltic and halt Danish interference with the flow of British trade. The ensuing battle for Copenhagen in April 1801 offered sobering lessons. First, naval warfare remained very demanding. The eventual attack upon the harbour at Copenhagen, by a squadron under Nelson, followed a careful five-hour preparation of the ships and equipment deployed, full reconnaissance, and thorough assessment and extensive discussion of the options. Despite all the advantages the Royal Navy possessed, the battle proved intense and close fought, requiring Nelson's active and detailed management in a contest far more challenging than any other in which he had been involved. His squadron suffered nearly 950 killed and wounded, or 14% of those engaged,[14] more than fell at the Nile. Broader claims about the might of British sea-power need to be set against the sheer effort required to project that power effectively even against inexperienced and hastily prepared foes. Even Nelson was forced to recoup a desperate situation by negotiating a diplomatic settlement with the Danes. The death of the Tsar changed the dynamics of Russian foreign policy and led to an Anglo-Russian rapprochement. One consequence was the opening of trade routes and therefore of grain supplies from Russia and the Baltic more generally. By early May, grain prices, always a sensitive economic indicator for public opinion and government popularity, began to fall sharply, with imports from the Baltic, as well as from North America, expanding supply.[15]

The second implicit lesson of Copenhagen was that the projection of British naval power globally created two different kinds of warfare. By February 1801, the ships of the line available for active service were heavily concentrated – 49 of the 84 large ships – in the North Sea, the English Channel and the Irish Sea to meet the full range of continental European challenges. Only 17 such warships were assigned outside European waters to the defence of the empire or imperial trade routes. By contrast, 40 of the 160 frigates on active service operated in the Caribbean and 66 of them were detailed to the coast of Portugal, Gibraltar and the Mediterranean. Those smaller, faster craft watched enemy movements, protected British trade, and attacked enemy merchant shipping in a very different kind of warfare from that undertaken by the battle fleets. Only just over one-quarter of the frigate fleet was stationed in home waters. Naval strategy thus involved the dual-purpose allocation of resources across the Atlantic, from Newfoundland to the Cape, with some deployment into the Indian Ocean. Moreover, the demands of this service remained heavy. Despite all the successes since 1793 against the three principal naval powers of France, Spain and Holland, Britain deployed over 250 line ships, 50-gun ships, and frigates on active duty in early 1801, with another 74 such vessels in port for repairs and fitting.[16] Yet this formidable exercise in global power projection, while protecting and advancing a multiplicity of British interests, did not deliver easy or frequent battle victories or major continental gains.

The Egyptian campaign and the peace settlement

The expedition to Copenhagen, as a reaction to specific initiatives by the Tsar, exposed the wrenching problems posed by a continental strategy. Since even the strongest exponents of a continental alliance had distrusted Austria long before the debacle following June 1800, the break with the obvious ally, Russia, hit hard. The other option – of intervening in France to galvanize counter-revolution – had been exhausted by 1800. Debate in late 1800 over strategies for 1801, therefore, focused on three other possibilities. One was to concentrate forces at home to safeguard the country, once more isolated in Europe, from any invasion and to provide the field force necessary for action to support counter-revolutionaries in France if opportunities arose. A second was to provide an army for action on the continent, possibly protecting Portugal. The third, Dundas's persistent emphasis on the wider world, narrowly carried the cabinet in October 1800, when he secured approval for a major expedition to Egypt. Having consistently insisted on colonial acquisitions' value as bargaining chips in eventual peace negotiations, Dundas regarded success in Egypt as a major component in boosting the British government's morale and its negotiating position later in 1801. While geographically peripheral, Egypt was politically central to Britain's war policy in 1801.[17]

For military historians, British successes in landing, campaigning and fighting in Egypt from March to August 1801, dramatically lifted the army's morale and reputation. Indeed those victories were the first sustained, significant achievements of the army outside India since 1793. As soon as news of initial success in March reached London, ministers referred to 'consequences which cannot be too greatly appreciated' and 'important consequences to the interests of the British Empire and the additional lustre' acquired by British arms. George III anticipated a significant impact on France: 'No event could have been more providential than the defeat of the French in Egypt.'[18]

The British army's progress through the Mediterranean to Egypt was far slower than Bonaparte's had been in 1798. Leaving Gibraltar in late October, the army sailed to Malta before moving on to spend nearly two months at Marmaris in Turkey. Apart from acclimatizing to eastern Mediterranean conditions, trying to recover collective good health, and buying 850 horses, the army used this period to perfect the exceptionally difficult techniques of landing a large force on well-defended beaches from ships which would have to anchor miles from the shore. On 22 February, some 175 ships sailed from Turkey, sighting the Egyptian coast on 1 March, but the landing was delayed by adverse weather and sea conditions until 8 March.[19] The meticulously planned and organized landing succeeded in putting 5,500 troops on shore at agreed times in a coherent order of battle along a wide front. The men had to be transported in light craft from the sea-going ships across up to five or six miles of shallower open water and then aligned in fighting order beyond the reach of French shore guns. At the given signal, they made the final dash exposed to enemy artillery across open water to the beaches. The landing cost the British over 700 casualties – more than Nelson's squadron suffered at Aboukir Bay – in reaching its objectives. This was followed a few days later by victory at the battle of Mandara, which ensured that the British consolidated their position.

As was so often the case in 'limited wars', the fighting, if not extensive, often proved intense. At Mandara from among 300 men of the 92nd (later the Gordon Highlanders) committed to action, the commanding officer was killed and 18 officers and 150 other ranks were killed or wounded. One battalion, the 42nd, numbering 754 rank and file before the landing in Egypt, suffered 313 casualties on 21 March; after that battle Lord Dalhousie found most of the survivors of the 42nd 'officers as well as men, crying like children'.[20] By 18 March the British had about 14,000 troops ashore, but had suffered 2,000 casualties in the fighting. Another 3,500 men were sick, with 1,100 bad enough to be in hospital.[21] Casualties included the army's commander-in-chief, Sir Ralph Abercromby, who died on board ship before the end of March. Finally, the army's mobility was limited by its possession of only 219 cavalry horses for the tiny band of 625 cavalry; a lack of horses also contributed to British difficulties in moving their guns. Despite these disadvantages, they consolidated sufficiently well to send 5,000 troops up the Nile, cutting Alexandria off from the

French headquarters at Cairo and tightening their grip on the French position on the coast. Although the army was under orders to secure the coast, Major General John Hely-Hutchinson, who succeeded Abercromby in command, controversially decided to advance southwards, deep into the interior, upon Cairo, wholly against instructions.[22]

A number of developments justified that decision and ensured British success. The British had despatched an army from India to land on the Red Sea coast to the east of Cairo. This obliged the French to maintain a large garrison at the capital and prevented them from significantly reinforcing the coastal north to hit the British in superior strength there. The probe from the Red Sea lent extra weight to a British march on Cairo, because Hely-Hutchinson knew that the force from India would arrive shortly. Equally important, a Turkish army under the Grand Vizier reached Belbeis, 30 miles to the north-east of Cairo, on 11 May, just when Hely-Hutchinson's army was 40 miles north-west of the capital. Having failed to dislodge the Turks from their position at Belbeis on 16 May, the French were forced instead to consolidate at Cairo, where they faced the classic dilemmas of an occupying power. For a start, many French officers and men did not want to stay in Egypt and felt increasingly demoralized by their isolation from France; an attempt to reinforce them from Toulon failed in June because of the Royal Navy's deterrent power in the Mediterranean. French occupying troops also feared the resentment and revenge of the local population. After 16 May they came under an additional threat posed by the Turkish army, not from its military capability, which was limited, but from its vast preponderance of cavalry, able to range widely, eager to loot, and ruthless in dealing with enemy units which fell within their grasp. From 10 to 20 May some 1,600 French troops surrendered to the British in various posts and contingents, preferring the likelihood of a British safe passage back to France to a more uncertain fate at Turkish hands.[23] As French morale and outposts began to fall, so 1,200 Mamelukes in French pay deserted to the British on 29 May. Just over a week later the Turkish and Hely-Hutchinson's armies joined forces near Cairo. Once they brought their heavy guns into position, the British so threatened the vastly extended and vulnerable defensive walls of Cairo that the French surrendered.[24] In mid-July the British – with only 4,000 troops in that sector of Egypt – escorted 10,000 French soldiers from Cairo northwards for their return to France, with their arms, baggage and field artillery.[25] While the British deserved credit for their local strategic flexibility and boldness, much of their success resulted from the erosion of French will and French fear not of a 'modern' army but of the retribution they might suffer at the hands of Turkish tribal levies.

The final phase of the Egyptian campaign was as fully and imaginatively planned as its opening. Some 14,000 men attacked Alexandria from east and west simultaneously during 16–26 August 1801 and forced the French garrison of 10,524 officers and men to surrender on the same terms of repatriation which had been given to the army at Cairo.[26] Most of the British fleet and the reinforced army left on 9 September, although 6,000 troops remained at Alexandria under a rising young major general, John Moore.

British victory in Egypt dealt a blow to Bonaparte's Mediterranean ambitions. The successes in March and then in July lifted British ministers' morale and vindicated Dundas's argument that Britain should concentrate on initiatives in the wider world to bring pressure to bear upon France. The British continued to exert pressure where they could in 1801. For example, they took over five more West Indian islands – belonging to Denmark, France, Holland and Sweden – in early 1801, and despatched 1,000 troops supplemented by artillery in June to take Madeira, in case the French might have been tempted to seize it from Portugal.[27]

Under pressure to cut his losses, General Bonaparte, now First Consul of France, sought to complete negotiations with Britain before the capitulation of the last remaining French force in Egypt occurred or news of it arrived in London. The British government simply wanted to end the war and the strains it imposed on the economy and on government finances.[28] Not the least of the paradoxes of the wars of 1793–1801 was that a conflict which Britain entered with an eye to the free navigation of the Scheldt should have ended with a preoccupation with the route to India.

The peace settlement of 1801–02

Peace negotiations had been initiated by Henry Addington when he took over as prime minister in March 1801. They resulted in a settlement agreed in outline in October 1801 and finalized at Amiens in March 1802. Britain kept only Trinidad, a very rich sugar island possessing a fine harbour, which had been Spanish, and Ceylon, a relatively poor island with a magnificent harbour at Trincomalee, which had been Dutch; Lord Hawkesbury, the Foreign Secretary, described them to the king as 'the two most important naval stations in the two hemispheres and not less important when their value as colonies is consider'd'. Another strategic island,

Malta, was to be given up by the British, but the terms of handover were complex and the transfer was delayed.[29]

This settlement seemed to vindicate the case for engaging in colonial warfare in order to secure bargaining chips for settling with France in Europe. But in fact it discredited the advocates of *both* the continental commitment *and* the blue-water strategy. The end of eight years of war saw France considerably strengthened in Europe. Because Austria had already settled with France, Britain could not free the Low Countries from French domination. French influence was extended and consolidated in northern Italy. The only countervailing expectation was that the new Tsar Alexander I of Russia would prove cooperative to British policy in the Mediterranean and especially in the Baltic. Britain neither levered concessions on the continent from her system of alliances, nor traded off colonial gains for European concessions.

Peace was driven by political calculation. Most evidence for the state of public opinion in the summer and autumn of 1801 points to popular disillusion with the war. Pitt, who was effectively dismissed by George III earlier in the year over Catholic emancipation, was convinced that the Treasury could not finance the further prolongation of the conflict. Commodity prices hit exceptional highs during the summer of 1801. News of the preliminary peace in October produced a tide of popular endorsement which politicians sceptical of the terms were reluctant to swim against. When delays occurred in reaching a final settlement there were concerns about the possibility of naval mutinies in frustration at the failure to restore peace. But within this trend of popular anti-war sentiment were false expectations that peace would reopen the freer trade arrangements of 1786 with France. Such hopes were dashed by Napoleon's acceptance of tariff protectionism.[30]

Those responsible for the forward policy of the 1790s reluctantly bowed to public opinion. Most ministers responsible for the conduct of war until Pitt's resignation in March 1801 objected to the Peace of Amiens. Lord Grenville, the former Foreign Secretary, and Earl Spencer, the former First Lord of the Admiralty, were among those exasperated by the new ministry's geopolitical strategy. Spencer objected strongly to the new doctrine that 'the system of carrying on the war against France through her colonies', based upon 'so much good policy and wisdom', was 'at least as useless if not a criminal waste of war resources'. But most former ministers were hamstrung by their desire not to embarrass or criticize Pitt, who told the Commons on 3 November 1801: 'If we had retained all our conquests, it would not have made any difference to us in point of security . . . They would only give us a little more wealth; but a little more wealth would be badly purchased by a little more war.' He insisted, as ever, on the overriding need for financial strength as the basis of national greatness.[31] There were other factors. France had retained its empire, but without Saint Domingue, overwhelmingly its single most important colony and now an independent Afro-Caribbean republic. Britain had battered the French navy and demoralized its senior officer corps, while also humiliating the navies of France's allies. During the wars of the American Revolution, Britain faced severe challenges at sea in the Caribbean and in the Indian Ocean. Less than twenty years later, the likelihood of fresh challenges in those seas on any significant scale was negligible.

The peace settlement extended guarantees to Britain's remaining allies, Portugal, Naples and the Ottoman Empire. The strategic importance of Egypt was underscored by the French agreement to evacuate it; although their final exodus had already occurred. Britain returned twenty-four colonies she had taken during the previous eight years, retaining only two acquisitions. There were reservations about returning Cape Colony to Holland, but commercial interests were protected by the stipulation that Cape Town should become a free port.[32] The real test was whether Pitt's quest for security had been fulfilled. Critics of the settlement saw only French gains and little reason to trust Bonaparte. As Lord Spencer noted: 'If ever peace was precarious, this was that peace.'[33] And George III informed the Foreign Secretary (using the third person) that he 'cannot place any reliance' on the duration of peace:

He trusts therefore every attention will be given to put this country on the most respectable state of defence; for he can never think any Treaty with France can be depended upon till it has a settled and regular form of Government.[34]

The king proved to be prescient. But, before resuming the analysis of the long-running Anglo-French conflict, we need to consider how Britain reasserted its power in India during the 1790s and then, on the coat-tails of the European contest, vastly extended its empire in the east by 1805.

Notes and references

1 John Ehrman, *The Younger Pitt: The Consuming Struggle* (London, 1996), pp. 134–42, 146.

2 Ehrman, *The Younger Pitt: The Consuming Struggle*, p. 141.

3 Brian Lavery, *Nelson and the Nile* (London, 1997), pp. 169–71, 175–80.

4 Ehrman, *The Younger Pitt: The Consuming Struggle*, p. 149.

5 A. Aspinall (ed.), *The Later Correspondence of George III*, 5 vols (Cambridge, 1968), Vol. III, p. 134.

6 Harry Hearder, *Italy in the Age of the Risorgimento, 1790–1870* (Harlow, 1983), pp. 30, 125–26; John Rosselli, *Lord William Bentinck and the British Occupation of Sicily* (Cambridge, 1956), p. 172n; David Constantine, *Fields of Fire: A Life of Sir William Hamilton* (London, 2001), pp. 239, 243. For a review of some of the issues raised by the revolution, see Raffaella Buoso, 'Napoli 1799 fra Storico e Storiografia Convegno di Studi, 21–24 Gennaio 1999', *Rivista Storico Italiana*, CXII (2000), 404–16.

7 Piers Mackesy, *War Without Victory: The Downfall of Pitt, 1799–1802* (Oxford, 1984), pp. 3–6.

8 Mackesy, *War Without Victory*, p. 6.

9 T.C.W. Blanning, *The Origins of the French Revolutionary* (London, 1986), p. 237.

10 William Laird Clowes, *The Royal Navy: A History From the Earliest Times to the Present*, 7 vols (London, 1897–1903), Vol. IV, p. 415.

11 Cyril Matheson, *The Life of Henry Dundas*, (London, 1933), pp. 288–90.

12 Mackesy, *War Without Victory*, pp. 183–84.

13 Ole Feldbaek, *The Battle of Copenhagen* (London, 2004; orig. 1985), pp. 10, 16–17; 42.

14 Edgar Vincent, *Nelson: Love and Fame* (New Haven, CT, 2003), p. 427.

15 *The Times*, 4 May 1801, p. 2.

16 *Steel's Original and Correct List of the Royal Navy* (London, 1801), p. 21.

17 Mackesy, *War Without Victory*, pp. 151–59.

18 Aspinall (ed.), *The Later Correspondence of George III*, Vol. III, pp. 523, 524.

19 Piers Mackesy, *The British Victory in Egypt, 1801: The End of Napoleon's Conquest* (London, 1995), pp. 50–3.

20 Mackesy, *War Without Victory*, pp. 92, 20, 132, 138.

21 Mackesy, *British Victory*, pp. 99, 102, 109.

22 Mackesy, *British Victory*, pp. 109, 156–57, 166, 174–75.

23 Mackesy, *British Victory*, pp. 177–79, 181, 186, 196.

24 Captain Francis Duncan, *History of the Royal Regiment of Artillery*, 2 vols (London, 1872), Vol. II, pp. 123–30.

25 Mackesy, *British Victory*, pp. 190–91, 195, 202, 197, 207.

26 Mackesy, *British Victory*, pp. 157–58, 210, 213, 220, 230.

27 Aspinall (ed.), *The Later Correspondence of George III*, Vol. III,
    pp. 533; 560.

28 Charles John Fedorak, 'The French capitulation in Egypt and the preliminary
    Anglo-French Treaty of Peace in October 1801', *International History
    Review*, XV (1993), 525 ff.

29 Aspinall (ed.), *Later Correspondence*, Vol. III, p. 613.

30 Mackesy, *War Without Victory*, pp. 210, 212, 218–19.

31 Ehrman, *The Younger Pitt: The Consuming Struggle*, pp. 557–60;
    William Pitt, *Orations on the French War* (London, 1906), p. 428.

32 Mackesy, *War Without Victory*, pp. 203–210.

33 Mackesy, *War Without Victory*, p. 211.

34 Aspinall (ed.), *The Later Correspondence of George III*, Vol. III, p. 614.

PART THREE

Military imperialism in India

CHAPTER 7

India: Military efficiency and Mysore, 1790–92

British military challenges in India

A new phase of Indian warfare opened in 1790–92 with the British campaigns against Mysore, the most formidable power of the subcontinent. British military success was founded upon wide-ranging organization, for, if efficient government did not in itself guarantee military achievement, the effective maintenance and deployment of the East India Company's armies was an essential prerequisite to the expansion of British India.

The first measure which enhanced British military capability – though devised with political ends specifically in mind – was the India Act of 1784. Following lengthy and controversial debate and drafting, Pitt's new ministry imposed the government's direction upon the Company through a Board of Control in London, headed by a president who was a middle-ranking minister. Within India the supreme council acquired additional powers, including responsibility for controlling external relations with the 'country powers' of India, replacing the provision, under the act of 1773, that the presidencies conducted their own external relations with their neighbours. Further legislation allowed for the offices of governor-general and commander-in-chief in Bengal to be combined, to enable Pitt to entrust wide powers to Lieutenant General Lord Cornwallis. Such an arrangement proved to be not wholly *ad hominem*; during the 49 years from 1786 to 1835 those two offices were combined for a total of 19 years. More importantly, the governor-general after 1784 had the right to deal with the councils of Bombay and Madras as he did with that of Bengal. He could issue orders to officials without reference to the other two presidencies' governors or councils. Given the proconsular status of Cornwallis, who was not a Company official promoted from within, these measures together greatly enhanced the governor-generalship and reduced confusion over authority which had been widespread in the early 1780s. First tested under pressure in 1790–92, the restructured political authority in British India proved fundamental to the successful conduct of unprecedentedly military operations of unpecedented extent.[1] When in April 1791, the House of Lords overwhelmingly rejected a censure of the Board of Control for pushing for territorial expansion in order to increase the East India Company's revenues, much play was made of the outstanding and honourable leadership provided by Cornwallis.[2]

But a second civil reform not designed with any military requirements in mind also provided an essential underpinning to the management of war. Measures taken in Bengal during the 1780s altered the tax system to one based on a permanently fixed amount of revenue levied on landholders and farmers. Coupled with a drive to make the Company's bureaucracy more civil service-like in assumptions, attitudes and practices, this change gave the administration in Calcutta the financial capability for undertaking major military operations. Although Cornwallis contemplated the costs of the impending war in 1789 with gloom – 'I have the mortification of seeing the fruits of the labour of three years and a half likely to be destroyed in a few months by the increase of our debt, and the rise of the discount on our paper, etc.' – fiscal and administrative reforms enabled his administration to increase short-term spending with relative ease.[3]

The importance of these changes to the Company's war-making capacity was evident from the sheer scale of military expenditure. For example, a contemporary estimate gave the civil charges for the Madras presidency as £697,564 over the twelve years 1767 to 1779. The military charges were more than ten times that total, at £7,144,410. With the company raising only £5,785,349 in revenues, the difference was made up by the Nawab of Arcot who contributed £2,831,057 to costs, including the defence of his territories.[4] Since the main source of revenue remained land, territorial possessions and the security of rural land-tenures were vital to the financial viability of any state. This was a matter of great concern to Warren Hastings who, as governor of Bengal in the 1770s and 1780s, wanted the Company to conduct diplomacy as a great power would in Europe in order to dominate the new Indian states.[5] The conflicts of 1778–84 underscored the central importance of military power to the British position in India. In 1763, the armies of the three presidencies totalled 9,000 men in Madras, 6,700 in Bengal and 2,500 in Bombay. By 1782 the three armies had expanded from 18,000 men to 115,000, with the smallest of them, the 15,000 soldiers maintained by Bombay, almost rivalling the grand total in 1763. The presidency governments grew in tandem. In 1772 the net revenues of the Bengal presidency totalled £2,373,650 while civil and military expenses amounted to £1,705,278. By 1785 the receipts had soared to £5,315,197 while the civil and military charges stood at £4,312,519. By comparison, the British parliament voted £5,406,000 for 1783 to maintain the British army and marines of 110,000 men.[6] As Colonel William Fullarton, a politician who served in the army in southern India in 1781–84, stressed in 1787:

Whether it be for the interest of England . . . to retain her Indian possessions, is a question too intricate and important for me to determine; but it appears an irrefragable truth, that if we are to exist at all in India, it must be in the character of a great, warlike and territorial power – a power at all times able to exalt our allies, and depress our enemies . . . if any other system be adopted, it will in fact prove an absolute surrender of that country.[7]

The long wars of 1778–84 stretched the British to the point of vulnerability in Madras. But there were occasional triumphs. A particular source of pride was the capture of the fort of Gwalior in August 1780. This was significant because it had been regarded as virtually impregnable and commanded the key route into Hindustan. But it also symbolized the British ability to attack the most powerful of the innumerable fortress strongholds of the Maratha rulers. The fort was the principal embodiment of status and power at all levels of rulership in the vast Maratha confederacy and so the British made a strong point when they successfully assaulted fortified places in a type of warfare in which the Marathas did not excel.[8]

While such changes created an essential basis for the military successes of the years 1790–1805 and beyond, one paradox of this period of reform was the failure to reorganize the Bengal army itself. The problems undermining the army in India were its leadership, the size of its European contingents in wartime, and its potential sense of a distinctive identity. The Company appointed no generals and few field officers, so that its expanded, wartime armies required senior officers sent from the royal army and Company officers promoted to acting senior rank. In 1783 the Company's armies in India totalled 116,000 men but were commanded by a mere ten colonels and thirty lieutenant colonels, or about as many officers of those ranks who would command 24,000 troops in Europe. Moreover, in the militarily threatening years of 1780–82 the Company required reinforcements from Britain. One solution to these problems, favoured by Henry Dundas, was to integrate the Company army with the British army. Various imperial benefits would follow. British officers on half pay in peacetime in Europe could be offered postings to India, or an end to their British commissions, thereby saving public expenditure in Britain. British regiments could be kept intact at the Company's expense while serving in India. Since India would become involved in Britain's future global competition with European powers, it needed ample garrisoning and had to be seen as part of Britain's worldwide military capability. Finally, an Indian army integrated into the British army overall would be less vulnerable to separatist stirrings or actions.[9]

Given such thinking in government circles, Cornwallis arrived in India determined to tackle the 'most shocking state' of the Bengal army, particularly its six European battalions. But he soon gave up any idea of integrating the Company army with the British army, arguing that the officers commanding sepoys had developed skills that would be undermined and seniority that would be diluted if they were incorporated into the royal army. He promoted organizational reforms concerning costs, pay, career opportunities and military efficiency, but his efforts slackened with the mounting threat of conflict during the last months of 1789.[10] While the administrative and financial shape of British India had improved markedly from 1784 to 1789, it would be wrong to assume that British leaders in India were confident about the efficacy of the military instruments available to them.

The invasion of Mysore

Mysore's original aggression in 1789 was one of many border wars or predatory campaigns in the 1780s and 1790s between Indian princely rulers, of the type which in Europe would be described as cabinet wars, or short-term campaigns aimed at securing specific, limited objectives within a few months. The Maratha princes added predatory raiding to such an agenda and fought each other virtually every year in the 1790s. Buttressing itself against Maratha and British expansionism, Mysore was revived after 1761 by its new military ruler. The incisive political observer, William Fullarton, noted of Mysore in 1787: 'The recent growth and warlike advancement of that state exhibit a phenomenon unparalleled in history.'[11] The regime, however, was based on a combination of reform and periodic recourse to war. An obvious response to Mysorean army commanders' alleged disaffection in 1788, for example, was to indulge in external adventures, particularly when the rich lands of the Malabar coast to the west or the wealth of the Carnatic to the east (where the Mysoreans had done so well in the early 1780s) offered tempting opportunities for plunder. The extensive debate over the inadequacies of the British armies in India – publicly aired in the newspapers produced by British communities within the presidencies – presumably emboldened Tipu Sultan, ruler of Mysore. Moreover, British action was constrained by the continuing French presence at Pondicherry. Thus, when in 1787 the possibility of a European war between Britain and France arose from an uprising in the Dutch republic, the British in India expected that any such conflict would see Tipu joining the French by attacking the Carnatic. Although the sultan failed to secure a French alliance in 1788, the French presence remained a reassurance for Tipu.[12]

Having failed to expand against the Marathas on his northern borders in 1787, Tipu attacked the Raja of Travancore's army on his southern frontier on 29 December 1789, claiming feudal rights over two of Travancore's dependencies. Tipu's initial assaults on the lines of Travancore, a series of defensive fortifications, were repulsed and the British came to Travancore's aid. Although exasperated at the potential costs of war in the midst of his programme of fiscal retrenchment, the governor-general appreciated that defeating Tipu – in his eyes, that 'mad barbarian' – would bolster Britain's permanent position in India.[13]

Cornwallis's first priority in confronting this attack was to sort out the government of the Madras presidency. The acting governor, Edward John Holland, had failed to convey clear warnings to Tipu that the Company would aid its ally in Travancore and was alleged to have taken bribes from Tipu in return for clouding the Company's position on the border dispute and for holding back on preparations to support Travancore. Cornwallis privately described the government of Madras's conduct as 'very criminal'.[14] A new governor, Major General William Medows, arrived in Madras in January 1790. Demonstrating the significance of the organizational changes that Cornwallis was making, Medows, who had distinguished himself at the battle of Brandywine in 1777 when Cornwallis commanded a division, was also commander-in-chief of the Madras army.[15] With Medows' arrival, the governor-general concentrated on providing logistical support for operations to the south and in securing a triple alliance in June–July with the Marathas and with the Nizam of Hyderabad.

The campaign launched by Medows in May 1790 involved two quite widely separated forces operating from the east coast. Their aim was to draw Tipu away from Travancore by sending one army across the southern foot of India. The smaller force (eventually rising to 9,000 men) advanced from west and slightly south of Madras westwards into the hill district of Baramahal, with the task of putting pressure on Mysore and thus protecting the far northern flank of the main army. This main force of 15,000 troops assembled far south of Madras at Trichinopoly (or Tiruchirapalli). Established at least 2,000 years earlier, Trichinopoly formed a natural base for operations commanding routes to the north and the agriculturally rich delta lands of the Cauvery River to the east. From there the British planned to advance 150 miles upon Coimbatore, a town set in the hills and opening the way across those hills to the west coast. Tipu's forces had desecrated a major Hindu temple at Perur outside Coimbatore, adding yet further to the potential local support for a 'liberating' British force. Coimbatore, not in itself a military stronghold, was a major depot for food and military supplies and the leading town in the lower-lying southern region of Mysore. It commanded access to a good agricultural region, which generated ample revenues as well as foodstuffs and, during the four months of December to March inclusive, enjoyed an exceptionally fine climate.[16] An advance from Coimbatore was aimed at taking the strategic fort of Palghautcherry – established by Hyder Ali in 1766 – to the west. Gaining that point opened the river route to the western Malabar coast where troops from Bombay would add pressure on Mysore. These concerted advances were intended to force Tipu to retreat from the lines of Travancore back into Mysorean territory. The British, once established and reinforced at some point between Coimbatore and the Malabar coast, would be able to turn northwards into Mysore.

This proved an extremely ambitious plan. Starting on 26 May, Medows took eight weeks to cover 150 miles to Coimbatore. From there his force was diverted to securing neighbouring strategic points and sources of food, and capturing various towns. The slow rate of progress enabled Tipu to pull his army out of Travancore, replenish it within Mysore, and then, in September, raid into Coimbatore province, drive the British from some of their outposts, and deprive them of stores. In early November the Mysoreans radically switched their focus and threatened the smaller British army which had advanced into Baramahal. Medows had been completely wrong-footed by Tipu's mobility and use of interior lines. By August he was firmly lodged at Coimbatore but found resupply so challenging that in October, for example, he devoted much time to escorting a large convoy from the east to replenish his army. Coimbatore's value as a forward base receded once the British failed to box in Tipu's army, or force it back into Mysore. When Medows pursued the raja into southern Mysore, he failed to catch the Mysorean field force. Instead, Tipu pressed south towards Trichinopoly in early December, before swinging north and east, and ending in January 1791 well within British territories near the French base of Pondicherry, only some 80 miles south of Madras.[17]

Tipu's achievement was considerable. He had shifted his army right across the breadth of southern India from the lines of Travancore to the outlying areas of Pondicherry and evaded two British forces sent to bring him to battle and constrict him within Mysore respectively. By the end of 1790 he was plundering British possessions in the eastern coastal belt, living off British resources, and inducing his enemy to pull back from Mysore to protect their own domains. He had also positioned himself to seek French military assistance in his war against the British and he energetically pursued that objective in January. Contemporary criticism within the British camp, however, indicated that the Mysoreans benefited from the lack of British preparedness. Military stores and food supplies were concentrated at Madras, so that garrison towns such as Ambore, 130 miles inland from the coast and thus nearer Mysore, lacked sufficient stock for sustained defence, let alone attack. This decision recognized the vulnerability to sudden invasion which had sent the panic-stricken British reeling into Madras in 1780. But it did not offer any improvement on 1780. To overcome the absence of advanced magazines of supplies, the British needed to attain high levels of mobility. Yet they had no standing reserves of bullocks or oxen to provide immediately available transport, while the increased number of European troops, who were supported by far more baggage than that available for the sepoy soldiers, added appreciably to the demand for transport animals.[18]

Against this, the British had logged some successes. They had saved Travancore and, for part of 1790, thrown Tipu on to the defensive, while also probing into his southern lands. By strengthening their own cavalry, the British attempted during 1790 to counterbalance Tipu's advantage in that arm. At the end of the year they used forces brought south along the coast from Bombay to win victories at Calicut and Cannanore, thereby positioning themselves for a military probe from the Malabar or western coast into Mysore. Tipu's very success in striking first south to Trichino-poly and then north and east to Pondicherry – impressive testament to his mobility though it was – also provided eloquent testimony to his fear of battle against the British. His last act in this operation was to supplicate for French military assistance, a necessity if he were to meet the British upon a field of arms.

Cornwallis now intervened. As early as April 1790, he recorded his doubts about exposing the Carnatic to Tipu's raiding, but could not – from his position at Calcutta – alter Medows' strategy before its implementation began.[19] He had urged upon Medows the importance of bringing his allies into the overall campaign, writing in June 1790:

I know it is very easy to make all armies abuse the supineness and want of exertion of their Allies. But surely it can answer no wise purpose, nor tend to support our public credit or the confidence of our troops, to undervalue our confederates . . . We cannot deny that even their appearance in the field must distract and intimidate Tipu, and of course be productive of great advantage to our own operations.[20]

Cornwallis further noted severe defects in military intelligence and delays caused by the slow build-up of huge stores of provisions and the pack animals necessary to convey them. But the most telling criticism was that Medows had dispersed his army into too many small units, exposing them to the possibility of defeat in detail while failing to pin down Tipu with his main army. Cornwallis insisted that the appropriate strategy was to march westwards from Madras and invade the core of the Mysorean kingdom itself, proceeding through the mountain passes to advance upon the principal Mysorean cities of Bangalore and Seringapatam. Leaving Calcutta, the governor-general joined Medows's main army at Vellout, some 18 miles west of Madras, on 29 January 1791; the reinforced Madras army constituted, in John Fortescue's assessment, 'the finest army thitherto sent into the field by the British in India'.[21]

Cornwallis imposed rigorous objectives for a five-month campaign. He aimed to march upon Bangalore, some 200 miles west of Madras, and then proceed to Seringapatam, Mysore's capital, before the monsoons began in June. Bangalore was the country's second capital, possessing a major fort built in 1537 and modernized by Hyder Ali. Deceiving Tipu in the direction of his advance, Cornwallis pursued a circuitous route to the north and west before arriving outside the town on 5 March, having encountered only limited resistance and having neutralized Tipu's usual tactic of burning crops and destroying animals in the path of an approaching opponent's forces by taking an unanticipated route.

Maintaining the momentum of his advance, Cornwallis predictably decided to attack Bangalore as soon as he reached it. The capture of the town on 7 March provided the British with vital supplies of forage; they held under 40 days' worth by the time they reached Bangalore, and the area around Seringapatam itself was likely to be short of supplies. The longer they stayed in one place, the more vulnerable the British became to Tipu's superiority in fast-moving cavalry which could prevent the British from obtaining military intelligence, from establishing links with their allies from Hyderabad, and from securing fresh supplies of food from the neighbouring countryside. Cornwallis advanced upon Seringapatam, despite lacking knowledge of his allies' whereabouts and the cavalry cover they were to provide, and despite facing growing shortages of food for men and animals as Tipu enforced a scorched-earth policy. Heavy rains, following the unusually early onset of the monsoon season, made operations around Seringapatam extremely difficult. Having set out for Seringapatam with 20 days' supplies, the British suffered from famine among the camp followers, notably the bullock drivers, and an unexpectedly high death-rate among the bullocks, induced by food shortages and diseases preying on animals weakened by hunger.[22] Cornwallis's own cavalry, under Lieutenant Colonel John Floyd, was adequate for protection but too small for extended operations, and had lost an excessive number of horses in a poorly controlled foray outside Bangalore. In the absence of allies, Cornwallis decided to break off operations upon the capital and on 22 May destroyed his siege train because he lacked sufficient draught animals to convey numerous bulky weapons back to Bangalore. The British lost 40,000 draft and carriage bullocks in the campaign of 1791, equivalent to the total numbers accompanying the main army out of Madras in early February.[23] After withdrawing to fortified towns where he secured desperately needed food, Cornwallis reached Bangalore by 11 July and decided to await the ending of the monsoon season before launching another expedition against the Mysorean capital.[24]

Preparation for the new campaign consisted of six essential elements. First, much time and effort went into building up supplies for, as Cornwallis explained in September 1791:

The soil of all the parts of the Mysore country that I have seen is, in general dry and by nature unfruitful, and sustenance either for men or animals can only be raised upon it by a most persevering industry in its inhabitants; but the country adjoining to Seringapatam is peculiarly rugged and barren.[25]

The handicap of operating in the less fertile parts of Tipu's domains – parts of which were highly productive – was overcome because the army could afford by the beginning of 1792 to buy rice at three to four times the price paid in the Carnatic. This differential drew in large enough numbers of brinjarries – a caste of mobile retailers – to sustain 50,000 bullocks supplying the British camp through elaborate private trading networks. A second military development involved considerable improvements in transporting the siege train together with baggage and supplies. Elephants, rarely used by the British in their earlier wars, were enlisted to push heavy guns along the line of march if they got stuck. To improve the haulage of heavy guns, bullocks were yoked four, instead of two, abreast, the yoking chains were attached to the guns instead of to the timber limbers, the siege train left camp first in the early morning on the march, and the train used the main roads while the rest of the army marched along flanking roads.[26] Thirdly, although Tipu attempted to deflect the British from advancing on Seringapatam by besieging Coimbatore from 13 June until the garrison there surrendered on 3 November, Cornwallis concentrated on his principal objective and remained in Mysore itself.[27] Fourth, Cornwallis countered Tipu's capacity for launching raids upon British positions and lines of advance by besieging and taking the fort of Nundydroog, 36 miles north of Bangalore from 22 September to 18 October 1791, and the fort at Savandroog, 18 miles to the south and west of Bangalore, from 10 December to 22 December 1791. The brinjarries reportedly insisted that they could not supply the British at Seringapatam if Savangroog remained in Tipu's hands. Apart from reducing the threat to British convoys posed by forays from these forts, their capture served to project images of British power; Cornwallis made much of the seizing of Nundydroog, stressing that Hyder Ali had taken three years to take that hill fort.[28]

The fifth element in Cornwallis's preparations was to bring in substantial forces from the Bombay presidency. The groundwork for smooth coordination between the presidency armies had been laid with the appointment of Major General Robert Abercromby as both governor and commander-in-chief, thus providing a uniform system of military-political command and control under generals in all three presidencies. Abercromby, who, like Medows, had served under Cornwallis in America, returned to the Malabar coast from Bombay in November 1791 and in January marched into Mysore with 8,400 troops, sixteen siege pieces and twenty field guns. To this impressive additional force was added a sixth and final element. In January, the governor-general rendezvoused with the cavalry contingent from Hyderabad, which provided about 18,000 cavalry to keep open British supply lines exposed to what were described as Tipu's 'swarms of cavalry'[29] and to maintain the flow of political and military information to his headquarters, thereby compensating for Cornwallis's meagre complement of only 1,100 cavalry. Although it was later claimed that the Hyderabadi irregular horse proved highly troublesome to the expedition and that the Marathas supplied the critical cavalry support, the fact remained that, without substantial cavalry cover for the army's rear supply routes, the brinjarries refused to risk their merchandise by following the advancing forces.[30] To impress allies and opponents alike, the British staged a spectacular military inspection – including a mile-long battering train – near Outradroog, about 50 miles from Seringapatam, to greet the Hyderabadi contingent. Cornwallis's review provided the grandest military display staged by the British to that date in India.[31]

The Company's forces totalled 22,000 troops, supplemented by 6,000 available for service on the Mysore tablelands from the Bombay force. Allowing for inexact estimates of enemy numbers, the British and their allies probably deployed forces numerically equivalent to their opponents' forces in and around Seringapatam. (Suggestions that the invaders were heavily outnumbered at Seringapatam derive from vague estimates of Tipu's strength and ignore the vast Hyderabadi contingent assisting the British.)[32] The allied armies also achieved two decisive shifts in military capability. Tipu's cavalry, one of his most potent assets, was probably greatly weakened in 1792, whereas Cornwallis's strength in that arm was transformed. It is also likely that Tipu suffered food shortages for his troops and especially for his horses, because imports from the Maratha lands and Hyderabad were cut off and the region around Seringapatam had been laid waste in 1791.[33] Moreover, Cornwallis deliberately show-cased his artillery at the grand parade in January to signal that his army could break Seringapatam's fortifications, in which the sultan placed great faith. Nearly one-quarter of the 22,000 troops brought from Madras and Bengal belonged to the artillery, with its forty-six field guns, four howitzers, and thirty-six mortars and siege guns. The British thus fielded a larger and more threateningly constituted army than they had done the previous year and created an integrated command system managed by generals accustomed to working together in the past.

Success at Seringapatam

Arriving opposite Seringapatam on the north bank of the Cauvery River on the morning of 6 February, Cornwallis spent a day in reconnoitring before demonstrating his customary vigour by launching an attack that same night. Some 8,700 infantry advanced at night without field artillery in an operation described as 'bold beyond the expectation of our army', the troops being 'delighted to find themselves unincumbered [sic] with cannon'. Of the 533 total casualties in the fighting on 6–7 February a majority of 302 were Europeans, even though the latter provided only 6,000 of the Company's 22,000 men at Seringapatam. British success in storming the town owed much to intimidating military force, but the Mysorean army's will was also undermined. Tipu's reform programme alienated many jagirdars and lesser officials, while Seringaptam's defenders – perhaps disaffected – gave way to desertion after offering initial resistance.[34] Having achieved an immediate breakthrough, as he had done at Bangalore a year earlier, Cornwallis had no plans to assault the fortress at the western end of the four-mile-long island, reportedly objecting repeatedly to any suggestion that Seringapatam be taken with the repost, 'Good God! What shall I do with this place?'. The arrival of the Bombay contingent under Abercromby on 16 February added to the pressure on the Mysore ruler. But, probably worried at the rate of illness among his European troops, Cornwallis began negotiations on 26 February, leading to the conclusion of a treaty on 29 March.[35]

The settlement with Mysore represented a careful balancing of a range of military, territorial and financial factors. What had started as a defensive war for the British – Cornwallis genuinely opposed expansionist schemes – ended with a substantial extension of British territorial rule. This was designed to confine Tipu's realm and its capacity for regional disruption; Cornwallis predicted to Henry Dundas that Tipu was unlikely to disturb Britain's possessions in India 'for many years to come'.[36] The British acquisition of 20,000 square miles, many of them generating very high revenues, both reduced Tipu's fiscal resources and provided an annual revenue to the Company of £433,000, to offset the costs of the war.[37] George III approvingly noted to Dundas in August 1792 that private information from India 'contains a much more favourable account of the revenue of Madras than the most sanguine person would have dared to suppose'.[38] At the same time the allies were rewarded with lands which yielded the same amount of revenue as the Company's territorial acquisitions generated. Thus the Nizam and the Marathas each secured 'cultivated and fertile' areas worth £433,000 a year while Tipu lost, in total, half his revenue, with the core of his shrunken kingdom being dominated by 'rugged and unproductive' lands, although Mysore retained the rich agricultural district of Coimbatore. To counterbalance possible attacks from this region, the Company held on to an important line of forts from Dingigul, in the far south, to the Baramahal district. Dingigul, where Haidar Ali had served as governor before taking over the kingdom, possessed symbolic significance and offered protection, in British hands, to the southern parts of the Madras presidency. Cornwallis argued that the arc of forts he had secured to the north could not be taken by any power in India and thereby protected the Carnatic against any future thrust from Mysore. The settlement strengthened Bombay, the smallest and weakest British presidency, by securing possessions along the Malabar coast, including Cannanore and Calicut, which were important for pepper and other spices. Finally, Tipu had to pay £3,000,000 in compensation, split equally between the three principal allies. This sum represented the equivalent to substantially more than one year's revenue – computed at £2,597,259 – enjoyed before the war by Tipu. The settlement forced the regime to impose financial exactions and financial controls which alienated many of its subjects.[39]

Cornwallis's settlement both contained Mysore and balanced the gains granted to the Marathas and Hyderabad. The governor-general asserted of his allies in 1791: 'I have seen enough of the Military Chiefs of both states to be quite certain of the dread they have of Tipu's force and of their consciousness that they could not resist it without our assistance.' In September 1791, he noted that the Nizam entered the war because of 'his hatred and dread of Tipu'. But while the Nizam and the Marathas gained lands in northern Mysore as a result of the war, Cornwallis reassured Dundas in March 1792 that: 'We have effectually crippled our enemy without making our friends too formidable.' Cornwallis treated the Marathas and Hyderabad equally because he realized that Hyderabad's prompt and full assistance in 1792 was intended to secure the Company's commitment to the protection of their state against the Marathas' 'over-bearing and avaricious interference'.[40] His actions were designed to restrain his allies' future ambitions by impressing them with British military strength: 'The impression they have received of the power and superiority of our arms, will greatly over-balance any confidence with which their territorial acquisitions can possibly inspire them.'[41] Those responsible for the campaign therefore stressed both the magnificence of Seringapatam – 'the richest, most convenient, and beautiful spot possessed in the present age by any native Prince in India' – and the military distinction achieved by the attack on 6–7 February in fighting which 'will ever be contemplated with admiration in the annals of British transactions in India'.[42]

Cornwallis reversed the fortunes of the early 1780s by a combination of factors. He removed the politico-military impediments to effectively planning, organizing and supplying what became by far the biggest and most tightly coordinated campaign mounted by the British in India to date. Systems were modified in 1792 as a result of the previous year's experience and, after false starts, the allies were brought in to counter

Tipu's main advantage in light cavalry, an advantage which hindered Medows in 1790. But Cornwallis's strategic breakthrough came in his concentration on fixed objectives of prime importance within Mysore itself. He refused to be deflected by the movements of Tipu's marauding army and vain attempts to pursue it. By invading Tipu's realm he forced the ruler of Mysore to wage war on British terms and avoided the frustrating fate Medows suffered in 1790. All this organization and build-up culminated, however, in the aggressive, some might say impetuous, storming of Bangalore and Seringapatam. While their resilience and determination in war-fighting remained a vital ingredient in British success, the successful storming of Seringapatam depended upon the extensive attrition of Tipu's resources during two campaigns. British celebrations at their victory in 1792, and the acclaim Cornwallis won for it, still left untested their assumption that their military prowess would impress their Mysorean foes and their Maratha and Hyderabadi allies sufficiently to ensure the future stability and security of their possessions.

Notes and references

1 The key figures were Lord Cornwallis (1786–93), Lord Moira, later Hastings (1813–23), and Lord William Bentinck (1833–35 in both offices). The command system is not discussed in Franklin and Mary Wickwire, *Cornwallis: The Imperial Years* (Chapel Hill, NC, 1980), pp. 98–116, or Sir Penderel Moon, *The British Conquest and Dominion of India* (London, 1989), pp. 229–45.

2 *The Times*, 12 April 1791, p. 2.

3 Charles Ross (ed.), *Correspondence of Charles, First Marquis Cornwallis*, 3 vols (London, 1859), Vol. II, pp. 20–21.

4 *Fourth Report from the Committee of Secrecy*, appendix to the *Second Report from the Committee of Secrecy* (n.p., 1782), p. 164.

5 P.J. Marshall, 'The making of an imperial icon: the case of Warren Hastings', *Journal of Imperial and Commonwealth History*, 27 (1999), 1–16.

6 *The Annual Register for 1783* (London, 1800), pp. 304, 308.

7 William Fullarton, *A View of the English Interests in India* (London, 1787), p. 70.

8 Stewart Gordon, *The Marathas, 1600–1818* (Cambridge, 1993), p. 82.

9 Raymond Callahan, *The East India Company and Army Reform 1783–1798* (Cambridge, MA, 1972), pp. 22, 37, 45–49; Wickwires, *Cornwallis*, p. 99.

10 Wickwires, *Cornwallis*, pp. 100–14.

11 Fullarton, *A View of the English Interests*, pp. 57, 59–66. Recent revisionism in the history of Mysore includes the argument that Tipu made a serious effort to engage with the establishment of his rulership in the cultural context of southern India where religion, holders of local power, and the symbols and rituals of authority all raised significant challenges to him. Kate Brittlebank, *Tipu Sultan's Search for Legitimacy: Islam and Kingship in a Hindu Domain* (Delhi, 1997), pp. 7, 155. For the wider context, see Eugenia Vanina, *Ideas and Society in India from the Sixteenth to the Eighteenth Centuries* (Delhi, 1996), pp. 151, 154–57.

12 A positive, contemporary view of Tipu's improvements and of the years 1783–91 as a period of peace and prosperity is provided by *Michaud's History of Mysore under Hyder Ali and Tippoo Sultan*, trans. by V.K. Raman Menon (New Delhi, 1985 reprint), pp. 72–74. For a contrasting view of administrative instability and regular punitive expeditions against local rulers, see Mir Hussain Ali Khan Kirmani, *History of Tipu Sultan*, trans. by Col. W. Miles (New Delhi, 1986 reprint), pp. 60–65, 67–68, 72–74; Denys Forrest, *Tiger of Mysore: The Life and Death of Tipu Sultan* (London, 1970), pp. 93, 102–03, 120–21. The traditional view that his overthrow was welcomed to the vast majority of those with knowledge of India is in W.H. Hutton, 'Tipu Sultan, 1785–1802' in H.H. Dodwell (ed.), *British India 1497–1858* Vol. V of *The Cambridge History of India* (Cambridge, 1929), pp. 333–46.

13 Ross (ed.), *Correspondence*, Vol. II, pp. 20–21.

14 Ross (ed.), *Correspondence*, Vol. II, p. 8.

15 Entries in *Oxford Dictionary of National Biography*.

16 Fullarton, *A View of the English Interests*, pp. 171–72, 174, 176.

17 The basic details are in John Fortescue, *A History of the British Army*, 13 vols (London, 1899–1930), Vol. III, pp. 551–53; Wickwires, *Cornwallis*, pp. 133–36.

18 G.R. Gleig, *The Life of Sir Thomas Munro*, 3 vols (London, 1849 edn.), Vol. I, pp. 79–83.

19 Ross (ed.), *Correspondence*, Vol. II, p. 8.

20 Wickwires, *Cornwallis*, p. 136.

21 Fortescue, *History of the British Army*, Vol. III, p. 559; Wickwires, *Cornwallis*, p. 135.

22 Wickwires, *Cornwallis*, p. 147; Ross (ed.), *Correspondence*, Vol. II, p. 98.

23 Major Dirom, *A Narrative of the Campaign in India* (London, 1793), p. 17.

24 Wickwires, *Cornwallis*, pp. 151–53.

25 Sir George Forrest (ed.), *Selections from the State Papers of the Governors-General of India: Lord Cornwallis*, 2 vols (Oxford, 1926), Vol. II, p. 30.

26 Dirom, *A Narrative*, pp. 86–88, 113, 124.

27 Fortescue, *A History*, Vol. III, pp. 577–79.

28 Wickwires, *Cornwallis*, pp. 159–61; Dirom, *A Narrative*, pp. 66, 77.

29 Ross (ed.), *Correspondence*, Vol. II, p. 61.

30 Montgomery Martin (ed.), *The Despatches, Minutes, and Correspondence of the Marquess Wellesley, K.G.*, 5 vols (London, 1836), Vol. I, pp. 73–77.

31 Dirom, *A Narrative*, pp. 112, 119–23. The use of such military displays to exert political pressure has, of course, a long history. Xenophon, *The Persian Expedition*, trans. by Rex Warner (Harmondsworth, 1949), p. 23.

32 Wickwires, *Cornwallis*, p. 165 reports Cornwallis's estimate of Tipu's strength, accompanied by his disparagement of his allies' significance. A similar imbalance is indicated by Moon, *The British Conquest*, p. 256.

33 Gleig, *The Life of Sir Thomas Munro*, Vol. III, pp. 57–59, 76.

34 Dirom, *A Narrative*, pp. 141–42, 181–82; Kirmani, *History*, p. 103.

35 Gleig, *The Life of Sir Thoamas Munro*, Vol. I, pp. 128, 131.

36 Ross (ed.), *Correspondence*, Vol. II, p. 153.

37 Forrest (ed.), *Lord Cornwallis*, Vol. II, p. 178. I use figures in Dirom, *A Narrative*, p. 238n. The totals quoted depend on the exchange rate preferred and differ.

38 A. Aspinall (ed.), *The Later Correspondence of George III*, 5 vols (Cambridge, 1968), Vol. I, p. 610n.

39 Forrest (ed.), *Lord Cornwallis*, Vol. I, p. 177, Vol. II, pp. 66, 69; Kirmani, *History*, pp. 105–10.

40 Ross (ed.), *Correspondence*, Vol. II, pp. 102, 120, 155.

41 Ross (ed.), *Correspondence*, Vol. II, p. 155.

42 Dirom, *A Narrative*, pp. 180, 188.

CHAPTER 8

Imperial expansionism and Mysore, 1798–99

Mysore and the changed international context

Lord Cornwallis in 1792 reassuringly predicted that Tipu Sultan was unlikely to disturb the British in India 'for many years to come'. Yet the British in 1799 attacked the capital of Mysore a second time, killed its ruler and inserted a puppet regime in his place. Few episodes in the history of British expansionism in India have been as controversial in their origins or bloody in their impact. The fourth war against Mysore also contributed to an accumulating sense of disgust at unending conquests which William Cobbett expressed in 1808. Every war over the previous thirty years, he wrote, had been described as the last war. Instead, 'There is a constant, never-ceasing war in India'; indeed, 'the history of the whole world does not afford an instance of a series of aggressions so completely unjustifiable and inexcusable' as Britain's drive for gain in the subcontinent.[1]

The individual campaigns in India during 1790–1805 need to be seen in three contexts: the military, the geopolitical, and the historiographical. In analysing the war in Mysore in 1790–92, we have already stressed its importance in restoring, albeit neither speedily nor resoundingly, the East India Company's military reputation. The major campaigns of 1799 and 1802–05 not only laid to rest the haunting ghosts created by the reverses of the early 1780s; they demonstrated a high and rising level of military proficiency.

The second, geopolitical context, was more complex. The East India Company acted various roles, some of which encompassed ruthless commercial and financial self-seeking. But the transformation of the Company from the 1770s into a territorial power with rulership responsibilities made it a player in the Indian state-system. By the 1780s India included states of quite different types. Some important successor states were well-organized, territorially cohesive, and relatively politically stable: Mysore, Hyderabad, and Awadh stand out. Elsewhere there were states which had failed or were failing, often because British moneylenders had encouraged their rulers to mire themselves in debt or because the East India Company reduced them to a condition of more or less abject clientage. The Nawab of Arcot provided an example of such political-fiscal evisceration which provoked widespread and passionate political debate in Britain in the 1780s. The third type of state proved more nebulous and very frustrating for British policy-makers. Across west-central India stretched a number of princely houses whose revenue-generating lands were scattered rather than consolidated and whose claims to rights and possessions frequently over-lapped. Collectively known as the Marathas, these maharajahs developed their own form of principalities. One of the key issues for the British was the extent to which they should be treated, and indeed encouraged to organize, as a confederacy rather than as separate 'states'. The external relations of all these states were affected by conflicting internal interests and dynastic ambitions. All states were also affected by the flows of money and military manpower across India.

British policy-makers had to deal effectively with this variety of Indian states and to create a system of diplomacy or mutual obligation which guaranteed the overall inter-state stability which was essential to com-mercial relations and the protection of the East India Company's growing interests. A concern for the establishment of a stable inter-state system was not a constant priority in these years. But, whatever the vagaries of circumstances and politics, it was a recurrent and inescapable challenge. An additional spur to action came from exogenous pressure. Although France had a very limited presence in India after 1783, the threat of French diplomatic and military inference periodically swayed British assessments of political challenges in India and shaped British responses to those challenges.

One obstacle to understanding British war-making in the late eigh-teenth century is the absence of detailed modern studies of inter-state rivalries. Most of the literature on the competition between the ruling houses, their diplomatic relations and their persistent recourse to military campaigning is now dated or has a distinctly musty air to it. A leading mid-twentieth-century Indian historian of eighteenth-century India con-cluded that: 'The Mughal empire . . . fell because of the rottenness at the core of Indian society. This rottenness showed itself in the form of military and political helplessness.' Decline was followed by an historic renaissance, leading in turn to an independent Indian state: 'That political evolution has been made possible only by British imperialism.'[2] Such judgements obviously alienated later Indian scholars from the historiography which preceded them, with the result that recent trends in Indian historiography, running against the study of inter-state rivalries and court politics, tend to airbrush the *ancien régime* elite out of the Indian past and sideline a group whose authority and prominence waned after independence in 1947. The study of politics narrowly conceived has been assumed simply to underwrite the administrative and state-building preoccupations and value-system of the British Raj. Modern Indian historiography has been inspired by the ideological conviction that politics is an epiphenomenon arising from more fundamental economic and social realities. By emphasizing economic and social characteristics and changes in India, or cultural conflict in the subcontinent, historians implicitly or explicitly downgrade the significance of politics and government, stressing instead such long-term continuities that the impact of British rule is marginalized, or depicted as economic exploitation cloaked in the more high-minded imperatives of political improvement or the working out of assertive cultural imperialism.[3]

An alternative approach, linking socio-economic developments with political changes and the instability of international relationships, has been offered by Christopher Bayly. In arguing for the impact on India of resurgent Muslim powers and the breakout of major tribes in Afghanistan and the Middle East, Bayly depicts their expansionism as delivering the *coup de grâce* to the Mughal regime in India. While external Muslim powers and internal regional leaders broke the Mughal emperors militarily, the shift of strength was more fundamental than the loss of battles. Invigorated successor states within India galvanized religious commitment and political loyalty to their regimes and typically fostered increased goods production, money transactions and trade. Bengal and Mysore, for example, became highly dynastic economies under ambitious Muslim rulers. Meanwhile, the Maratha states, which had never been tied tightly to Mughal institutions and traditions, developed increasingly sophisticated and effective administrative and revenue-raising systems.[4] The Mughal Empire became an anachronistic political construct, increasingly irrelevant to its invigorated component parts. Although some of the rulers of central and southern states belonged to ancient lines of rulership, many in the 1760s headed new or relatively new houses or lineages seeking to secure or extend their influence.[5] The British constituted one emerging power in a remarkable surge of internal state formation in the eighteenth century.

The crumbling of Mughal power in the mid-eighteenth century coincided with a period of economic growth from which British commerce benefited and which in turn propelled the British into political interventionism. New commercially minded groups became less attached to traditional ruling elites than were established officials and village headmen, whose financial and social standing derived from tax-raising. Hindu merchants and bankers often suffered discrimination by Muslim rulers, encouraging their support for political rivals or conquerors. British traders and officials also seized lucrative opportunities to lend vast sums of money at high rates of interest to local rulers. The East India Company became increasingly involved in revenue collection rather than trade, in order to cover its defence costs.[6]

The dynamic nature of eighteenth-century Indian political and commercial life made British progress to paramountcy far from straightforward. Successor states either continued with existing forms of government and feudal organization – as in the cases of Awadh, Bengal, and Hyderabad – or pursued differing forms of westernization. Polities which adopted the latter course were especially open, in varying degrees, to European influences in administrative, economic and military affairs. Yet the more centralized administration and revenue-collection became in the late eighteenth century, the more vulnerable 'modernizing states' were to ready British takeover. If some Indian intellectuals saw benefits for India in utilizing European institutions and customs, Indians generally embraced the idea of human kind as grouped in communal entities, embedded in caste and loosed upon the world as individuals. Devolved, particularist, and 'traditional' governmental processes and taxation systems remained more difficult for the British to understand and to control, if they sought to do so.[7]

The decade or so from the period after the Mysore war of 1790–92 to the conclusion of the Maratha wars of 1802–05 was decisive in resolving the military and geopolitical challenges facing the British in India. War was central to the removal of the military challenge, but it was also essential to the creation of a new state-system in India. Whether the British might have achieved a political balance of power without recourse to such extensive war-fighting as occurred is open to discussion. But the need for such a state-system seems less debatable. And the speed and effectiveness of the British use of war as an instrument of policy more or less produced the result desired.

Cornwallis's settlement of 1792 sought to balance power and advantage between the Marathas and Hyderabad, while maintaining Mysore and Hyderabad as buffers against Maratha expansionism. By 1795 that balance – if so pseudoscientific a notion could be applied to so fluid a politico-military situation – had effectively broken down. The main catalyst for that breakdown came with the return in 1792 of Mahadji Sindhia to Pune, the Maratha capital, following an absence of eleven years defending, consolidating and expanding his domains in the north. By 1792 Sindhia – buttressed by the Mughal emperor's designating him in 1784 as regent of the empire's Delhi territories – had made himself the most powerful of the five great Maratha princes. But the Peshwa, the titular head of the confederacy, following the advice of Nana Fadnis, his principal minister, refused to recognize Sindhia's superior power and preferred instead to play off the claims of the Holkar house against those of the house of Sindhia. This continued internecine rivalry did not prevent the great Maratha princes from occasionally cooperating. Notably, they waged a brief campaign against Hyderabad in 1795, over rival claims to revenues. Disturbingly for British strategy, the Company's ally, the Nizam of Hyderabad, was readily defeated and forced to make extensive territorial and revenue-generating concessions, thereby thoroughly undermining the balance sought so carefully in 1792. One officer wondered 'whether any balance of power can long be maintained among purely military governments' where states were not differentiated by geography, history, religion or language.[8]

This weakening of Hyderabad in itself need not have strengthened Mysore, because military events from 1790 to 1795 enhanced the countervailing power of the Marathas. But succession disputes among the Marathas created extraordinary instability from late 1795 to late 1797. The death of the Peshwa, Madhav Rao, in October 1795 opened a prolonged and bitter struggle for the succession. Only in November 1796 was the formal proclamation of Baji Rao II settled, to the advantage of the veteran of Pune politics, Nana Fadnis, and of Hyderabad's interests. The house of Sindhia felt it had lost out in that power struggle. With the death of Tukoji Rao Holkar in August 1797 came an opportunity for Sindhia to compensate for such a setback by ensuring the succession of Tukoji's eldest and weakest son, who was amenable to Sindhia's influence. Daulat Rao Sindhia in 1797–98 pressed his claims to predominance within the Maratha confederacy, building on his father Mahadji Sindhia's efforts in 1784 and from 1792 until his death in 1794 to assert such predominance. But this interventionism provoked another of Tukoji Rao's sons, Jaswant

Rao Holkar, into offensive operations in 1798–99 in support of his claim to act as regent on behalf of yet another prince of his house.

All this made a mockery of any British drive to deal with the Marathas as a confederacy and to work with them collectively through the Peshwa at Pune. Worse, it deepened military competitiveness in south-central India, giving the edge to Sindhia with his well-trained infantry, under the command of French mercenaries. The example was not lost on the Nizam Ali Khan, who had ruled Hyderabad since 1761. He recruited French officers in the mid-1790s to establish an effective European-style infantry, and by 1798 was reputed to have 14,000 such troops. Such military competitiveness did not fit British military planning for the region, since Hyderabad's usefulness lay in its provision of cavalry to counter Mysore's undoubted superiority in that arm. Indeed, the British viewed Maratha divisions as corroding the confederacy's value as a counter to Mysore.[9]

The alleged existence of a French threat in south-central and southern India added a European dimension to this sense of crisis. In some ways the projection of French power into India seemed exceedingly unlikely, since the British had removed the most obvious staging points for any such attack. The remaining French colony and port of any significance in India, Pondicherry, was taken in 1793. When the Dutch Republic fell to the French, the British responded by seizing the Dutch colonies at the Cape and Ceylon (Sri Lanka). The Royal Navy effectively blocked any coastal access into India and the campaigns of 1790–92 had ensured that Tipu remained a landlocked potentate. On the other hand, the French possessed the island of Mauritius and Tipu Sultan had actively sought a French alliance in 1790–91.

Moreover, fears of French initiatives grew as the war in Europe continued. In March 1796, Henry Dundas confided his concerns to the First Lord of the Admiralty, Lord Spencer: 'A naval superiority of the enemy in the East Indies would be attended with incalculable mischief, in a military, political and commercial view.' Believing that France could never really damage Britain in home waters, Dundas added: 'I cannot help always entertaining an apprehension that if the enemy are in a condition to attempt anything, the Eastern World is their only rational object.'[10] Meanwhile, in late 1795 and late 1796, the Company's Resident at Hyderabad, William Kirkpatrick, expressed extreme concern at the build-up of French mercenary officers in the Nizam's army and at their influence over that army. In July 1797, Colonel Arthur Wellesley in Madras wrote to his brother, Lord Mornington, a junior minister under Dundas, arguing that the British would not be safe in India as long as the French held

Mauritius. He suggested that, once fighting ended in Europe, Frenchmen of all political stripes would go there to seek military employment in India. By introducing 'the new mode' of European warfare to India, they would force the Company to increase its military spending to a quite impossible extent.[11]

The notion of a French threat surfaced in various forms and from divergent sources by the end of 1797. Britain, isolated in Europe, was far more exposed to French attacks upon her overseas possessions than had been the case in 1793–96, at a time when continental allies campaigned against France. The possibility of a French invasion of Ireland – tried unsuccessfully in December 1796 – concentrated British naval resources on defence in home waters and obliged the Royal Navy to leave the Mediterranean Sea entirely to the French from December 1796 to May 1798. When Talleyrand became Foreign Minister in July 1797 he revived the idea of an invasion of Egypt, partly to take advantage of the anticipated collapse of the Ottoman Empire and partly to secure a route to India after the Dutch loss of Cape Colony. During 1797 Napoleon Bonaparte, the rising star among the republic's young generals, argued for the importance of extending French possessions in the eastern Mediterranean, to exploit Ottoman weakness and, by seizing Egypt, 'menacing the trade of India'. Against a background of discussions about a French attack upon India from Egypt, Bonaparte in 1798 invaded that Ottoman dependency, taking far more French troops than the total force of British, as distinct from sepoy, soldiers in India. With the Malabar coast, giving access to Mysore, about 20–30 days' sailing time from Suez, some members of the ruling Directory supported in early 1798 the extension of Napoleon's operations from Egypt to India.[12]

These various shifts in the fortunes of Indian states and the dramatic isolation of Britain in its war against France affected British evaluations of Tipu Sultan. A discontented player in southern India's geopolitics, Tipu responded to defeat in 1790–92 by narrowing his power base; administrative efficiency allegedly gave way to excluding non-Muslims from high civil and military offices, thereby alienating local rulers upon whose co-operation his regime depended. Revenues, already reduced by one-third through the territorial losses of 1792, fell. Perhaps only about one-eighth of the taxes stipulated reached the central treasury. The army was needed to enforce revenue collection, but its units were rotated between garrisons at least every two years and kept in the field rather than in garrisons if possible, to check against concentrated disaffection.[13] Every pressure existed for Tipu to seek to regain lost territories, and even sympathetic

British observers – and there were few of them – stressed how fundamental to Tipu's personal development and character were his upbringing and career as a warlord. While conceding that Tipu was used as a bogeyman to add spice to any threatened danger, Arthur Wellesley in July 1797 noted that Tipu was 'a constant object of fear to the English'. He also stressed that Tipu would have attacked British possessions in 1796 if circumstances had proved favourable and if the threat of an Afghan invasion of Hindustan to the far north, drawing off the main Maratha powers, had materialized. It was also said that Tipu merely awaited the death of Nizam Ali Khan before attempting to seize the lands lost to Hyderabad in 1792. A year later, in July 1798, Colonel Wellesley warned of the danger of Tipu's attacking the Carnatic if an opportunity to do so arose.[14]

Behind these concerns lay a sense of the vulnerability, not strength, of British military power. Sir James Craig, a divisional general in Bengal, asserted in 1798 that the army's enfeebled condition meant 'our Empire in India probably hung by a thread of the slightest texture' during the years 1794–98.[15] Fragility stemmed from the lapse of Cornwallis's firm system of central coordination, established in 1790 in an effort to link together the distinctive armies of the three presidencies, which were each in turn divided between sepoy and European battalions. Organizational fragmentation was intensified by efforts to overcome it. When Cornwallis returned to London in 1794 and entered the cabinet, he proposed reforms which he had put aside while serving in Calcutta. Vigorous opposition was expressed immediately by over 500 officers, which threw Cornwallis's successor as governor-general, Sir John Shore, and the emollient new commander-in-chief, Sir Robert Abercromby, on to the defensive in their protracted dealings with their disaffected officer corps.[16] After much delay and modification, proposals for reform reached India in April 1796. Shore and Abercromby headed off what they feared might become a mutiny by consolidating and increasing allowances at an annual cost of £350,000 or about 9% of total military spending in British India. They also 'suspended' contentious proposals for altering the system of promotion. Shore confessed to Cornwallis in June 1796: 'I cannot say I expect much credit for what we have done . . . I have submitted to circumstances which I could not control.' Although Cornwallis and Dundas persisted in pressing for a thorough reform of the army in India, the Court of Proprietors in London killed off proposals for radical change in May 1797.[17] This protracted and public dispute weakened both the command system and the external reputation of the Company's army in the period 1794–97, and encouraged Tipu to contemplate direct military action against the

British or their allies. One way of refocusing military minds and sweeping aside these acrimonious arguments over organization was for a new governor-general to pursue external confrontation rather than internal reform.

British strategy

The swirling cluster of ideas, developments, challenges and opportunities was pulled together by the new governor-general, Richard Wellesley, Lord Mornington and later Marquess Wellesley, who arrived at Calcutta in May 1798. En route to India, he had been well briefed by William Kirkpatrick, who had long and extensive official experience in India, and by correspondence with his brother, Colonel Arthur Wellesley, who was already stationed there.[18] Extremely ambitious, he believed he could make an impact consonant with his new status; on the journey out to India, he referred to being received as 'A Tutelary Deity', urging his former mistress, now belatedly his wife, to join him as the 'Queen of India'. His brother Arthur described the governor-general less grandiloquently, but still impressively as 'probably the most powerful subject in the world'.[19]

Mornington focused first on the establishment of 14,000 European-trained infantry under French officers at Hyderabad. Although he exaggerated those officers' ideological commitment to the Revolution – 'Frenchmen of the most virulent and notorious principles of Jacobinism' – he suggested expanding the existing British contingent at Hyderabad, broadening its role and utility to the Nizam, reducing the power of the French-led corps and, perhaps, removing the French officers altogether. He emphasized not only the military threat posed by this force, but also the way it undermined the Hyderabadi army's role in any future conflict with Tipu. He then proceeded to recommend the formation of a grand alliance of all Hindustan's powers (except 'perhaps' Tipu) 'against the expected invasion of Zemaun Shah', the Afghan ruler. The Marathas, he reasoned, would welcome such an alliance to protect their northern flank. But the most menacing aspects of the threat of an Afghan invasion were, first, that the Afghans intended to advance as far as Oudh, an extremely rich British semi-dependency and, second, that Tipu was trying to coordinate an attack of his own upon the Carnatic with Zemaun Shah's alleged plans for an assault on Oudh.

The scenario painted by Mornington has been rejected by Professor Ingram as a gross exaggeration of unconnected challenges designed to justify his real objective – the destruction of Mysore. The role of the

French at Hyderabad was, according to Ingram, largely fictitious. Contacts between Tipu and Zemaun Shah were minor and, in fact, Dundas from London had sound reasons for cultivating the Afghan ruler as a counter-weight to Persia to the west, rather than demonizing him as a threat to northern India, where in fact military advice indicated he would get bogged down well before reaching Oudh. Mornington, according to Ingram, pulled together shreds of evidence, ignored contrary information, and tied his selective thoughts together into a coherent strategy based upon the fiction of a French threat.[20]

The French threat took two forms. Much weight was given to the re-establishment of French power in India at 'the speedy conclusion' of a peace settlement in Europe. In February 1798, Mornington argued:

The best peace we can expect will restore to the French all, and to the Dutch (whom I consider as French under another name) a great part of their former possessions in India.

In addition, the return of Ceylon to Holland, the mere 'bondslave' to France, 'would enable the French interests in India to rise within a very short period to a degree of formidable strength, never before possessed by them'.[21] This restoration of French power would be aided by the resilience of France's most likely ally in India, Tipu Sultan. Josias Webbe, Secretary to the Government of Madras, cautioned in July 1798 against war on the grounds that the Nizam had been weakened by the campaign of 1795, the Marathas had been drained by their power struggles at Pune, and the British had been reduced by the pressures of the French war. Tipu had gained 'the vantage ground' and the British would be very hard pressed to defeat him without elaborate preparations and a vast infusion of military resources from the Bengal presidency; moreover, Tipu could undermine any British build-up, especially if the British lacked effective allies. Looking to the future, Major General George Harris, commander-in-chief in Madras, predicted that Tipu would grow stronger; 'the French, at the conclusion of a peace, will possess the desire they now feel of subverting our Indian Empire, and . . . the Sultan will at that period be fully prepared to assist their purposes if he should not be now arrested in his progress'.[22]

The need to break Mysore as part of a defence against a French return at the peace became a recurrent theme in British military analysis. On departing from his post as commander-in-chief, Bombay, in January 1800, Lieutenant General James Stuart informed Dundas in London:

The present interest, the ancient rivalship, and the fixed ambition of the French nation will perpetually incite them to drive us from this country.

Not only did the French possess an important base in Mauritius; 'the French character is more popular in India than ours'. They enjoyed a ready welcome at princely durbars, and through individual 'esteem and favour' gained influence at the Nizam's court. 'It was by the instrument of force and the agency of fear that we succeeded in expelling them from Hyderabad.' In Stuart's view the Marathas 'are secretly disposed to the French and will, whenever the occasion may offer, assist their schemes of commerce, or aggrandisement in opposition to us'.[23] One official, Thomas Munro, wrote to Arthur Wellesley in August 1800: 'I am for making ourselves as strong as possible before the French return to India.'[24] In November 1804, towards the end of his long stint in India, Major General Arthur Wellesley commented on a policy document sent by the President of the Board of Control, Lord Castlereagh:

the French have never ceased to look at the re-establishment of their power in India; and although they possess no territory themselves on the continent, they have at all times had some influence in the councils of the different native powers, and sometimes great power by means of the European adventurers introduced into native armies . . . the object of every French statesman must be to diminish the influence, the power, and the prosperity of the British Government in India. I therefore conclude that in the consideration of every question of Indian policy, or in an inquiry into the expediency of any political measure, it is absolutely necessary to view it not only as it will affect Indian power, but as it will affect the French.[25]

While generals had self-interested reasons to support Mornington's policies, they had no need to accentuate particular factors in internal and lengthy analyses of policy. Whether ultimately groundless or not, fear of French intervention flowed logically from the previous century of international rivalries in India and from French ambitions to profit from any weakening of the Ottoman Empire as demonstrated in 1797–1801.

The immediate trigger for action against Mysore was a proclamation issued in June 1798 by the French Governor of Mauritius and Bourbon Islands. This noted that discussions concerning an alliance were taking place between Tipu and the French. Although scant material assistance was likely to flow from Mauritius, Mornington, now arrived at Calcutta, immediately alerted the government of Madras to the possibility of war and started the elaborate process of military preparation. In August 1798, he made the general case for a pre-emptive strike against Tipu:

professing the most amicable disposition, bound by subsisting treaties
of peace and friendship, and unprovoked by any offence on our part,
he has manifested a design to effect our total destruction . . . he has
solicited and received the aid of our inveterate enemy for the declared
purpose of annihilating our Empire: and he only waits the arrival of
a more effectual succour [from the French] to strike a blow against
our existence.

Distrustful of Sindhia and fearing that Sindhia might be able to control the Peshwa, Mornington further argued that a combination of Tipu, Sindhia and the French officers in the Nizam's army 'might establish the power of France in India upon the ruins of the States of Poona and the Deccan'. Drawing lessons from his own reading of eighteenth-century history, Mornington demanded a 'comprehensive system of precaution and defence' in southern and central India.[26]

As a first step to this ambitious objective, the governor-general secured a new agreement with Hyderabad signed on 1 September. This entailed the Nizam's paying £242,710 a year to the Company for furnishing him with 6,000 sepoys. Although this subsidiary alliance was represented to London as a triumphant blow against the French, it gave the Nizam the right to deploy this sepoy force for his own internal security purposes. Further urgency was added to preparations for war against Tipu with the arrival on 12 October of news that Bonaparte had landed an army in Egypt. Although any immediate threat to British India was reduced a few weeks later by the news of Nelson's destruction of the French fleet at the Nile, the fact that one of the leading French generals had launched a major operation in the eastern Mediterranean vindicated Dundas's persistent concern for the fate of Britain's possessions overseas; the ministry had detailed 4,500 extra regular soldiers to India as soon as it learned of Bonaparte's departure for Egypt. Undeterred by the lessening of any immediate threat from the French in Egypt once he knew of the destruction of their naval squadron there, Mornington insisted that the arrival of any, as distinct from significant, French forces in Mysore should constitute a *casus belli*. With wide-ranging logistical preparations in train across India for a war against Mysore, Mornington demanded on 8 November that Tipu renounce all intentions of negotiating an alliance with France. When that demand met a firm rejection, the governor-general unleashed the campaign for which he had been planning since July.[27]

The war against Mysore fitted into a broader political context. If the French threat and Tipu's potential role as a French ally were exaggerated to justify a pre-emptive strike, concerns, which continued after 1799, over the vulnerability of British India to resurgent French influence following a peace settlement in Europe flowed from the geopolitical challenges which the British had faced since 1792. Mysore's peculiar status in Britain as an agressive power from the late 1760s and especially from the early 1780s gave Tipu an iconic prominence not lost on an ambitious politician like Wellesley. But fears of Tipu ran deep within the Indian establishment. One official, Thomas Munro, wrote privately in 1792 that balance-of-power ideas had little relevance in India, because the Company's regional allies were, individually, militarily ineffectual and highly volatile both as regimes and in their external alignments. In 1796 he repeated his initial insistence that the settlement had erred in leaving Tipu 'so strong at the close of the late war'. Major General Harris complained of Tipu in June 1798: 'His inveteracy to us will only end with his life, and he will always seize any opportunity that offers to annoy us.'[28]

The campaign against Mysore

The campaign launched against Tipu Sultan involved the entire British military establishment in India. In July–October 1798, the Bengal presidency worried about the danger of an Afghan advance and British defensive capabilities in the region to the north and east of Delhi, notably Oudh. Few had much confidence in the effectiveness of the army of the Nawab-Vizier of Oudh if Zemaum Shah probed towards that kingdom. The Company had no major garrison town beyond Allahabad and therefore gathered a field force of 20,000 troops under Sir James Craig at Kanpur to counter any Afghan threat, reinforcing this initiative with persistent diplomatic efforts to draw Sindhia away from Pune and to focus his political attention and military energies on the north. The Marathas, and especially Sindhia, were critical to defending the north-west frontier as it then was. Looking farther afield, Lord Mornington in late October 1798 sought to persuade the Ottoman government to get Persia to raise its level of military activity on Zemaun's western borders, thus compelling him to divert forces from eastern adventures. Mornington anticipated that the Bombay presidency would be brought into play in order to supply field guns and military stores to Persia, and to galvanize – and arm – tribesmen to the south of Punjab against any invading Afghan army.[29] Although Zemaun was reportedly ready to march on Lahore, the capital of the Sikh fiefdom in October, and although Mornington noted on 24 October that the Afghans were marching 'towards Hindustan', officials soon deemed

the danger to have passed; on 4 January 1799 Zemaun began his withdrawal from Lahore.[30]

By that time preparations for an attack on Seringapatam were well under
way. Mysore had been hemmed in by British alliances with Hyderabad
and Pune, by armies assembled on the west coast and in the Carnatic, and
by the navy covering the coast of Malabar. Very strong reservations about
the feasibility of successfully taking Seringapatam in one campaign had
been expressed in July by Josias Webbe, secretary to the Madras government. He objected politically that while war continued in Europe, 'peace
in India is indispensably necessary'; he was sceptical of securing a Maratha
alliance; and he viewed the Madras government as already financially
stretched. He especially emphasised the difficulties created in 1791–92
by problems of supply and the encumbrance to the army of the Nizam's
cavalry. Success had been achieved in 1791–92 by good fortune and
despite the depleted state of the armies deployed:

*I refer to the chance by which Bangalore fell, to the condition of Lord
Cornwallis's army before the junction of the Mahrattas, in May 1791,
to the difficulty with which the battering train was advanced to
Seringapatam in the second campaign, to the condition of the Bombay
army, and to the state in which our own army returned after the
conclusion of peace.*[31]

On 2 January 1799, Colonel Wellesley concluded that 'our war cannot
be successful in one campaign', and as late as 27 February he remained
'really apprehensive' that the best the British might achieve would be
to besiege Seringapatam in 1800.[32] These reservations were largely swept
aside. Having stripped Tipu of so much territory in 1792, the British faced
far fewer obstacles than had been presented to them in the earlier campaign. If Bangalore lay in too ruinous a condition to afford a source of
supply, at least there was no need to seize it. The way was open to entering Mysore from the south, reducing supply challenges, and the build-up
of supplies was likely to be more effective than it had been in 1791.[33] With
the start point of the invasion well forward of that in 1791 and 1792, the
British faced fewer problems from Mysorean cavalry raiding behind their
advancing army, partly because they controlled more Mysorean territory
and partly because of improvements in the British cavalry.

The military command system, however, remained far weaker than
it had been in 1790–92. Mornington arrived at Madras before the war
began to support or supervise his theatre commander, the commander-
in-chief of the Madras army, Lieutenant General George Harris. Harris

had served in America in 1775–78, including at the battle of Brandywine under Cornwallis, and later as ADC and secretary in 1788–92 to William Medows. His appointment represented clear continuity with Cornwallis's top officer corps. Given the presence of strong-willed subordinates vying for seniority, including Major General John Floyd, the cavalry commander, and Major General David Baird, who had served for nine years in India during the 1780s and returned to a new command in the following decade,[34] Colonel Wellesley felt that General Harris 'will require all the powers which can be given to him to keep in order the officers who will be in his army'.[35]

Formidable forces were assembled against Mysore. Harris's main army totalled 20,000 fighting men of whom 2,000 formed the artillery corps. Lieutenant General Stuart's contingent from the Bombay army consisted of 6,400 fighting men, while the Nizam's contingent provided about 21,000 soldiers, of whom 6,000 were sepoys from the East India Company's armies and nearly 800 men of the 33rd Regiment seconded to duties in Hyderabad and paid for by the Nizam. Mornington had made it plain in November 1798 that he wanted a Hyderabadi commander for the Nizam's contingent 'whose zeal for the common cause shall be accompanied by a due share of personal weight and authority' in preference to 'military knowledge and experience'.[36] Colonel Wellesley, commanding the subsidiary force, would supply the latter. In addition to these components of the invading armies, some 10,000 troops were detailed off to hold the southern lines through Baramahal and Coimbatore, areas important to resupplying the British. This force enabled the British to resist Tipu's attempt in February–March 1799, to distract British attention by launching a small raid towards Coimbatore. Overall, the main British invasion forces, including the Hyderabad contingent, amounted to about 47,000 troops, capable of matching the 22,000 troops available for the defence of Seringapatam supported by 13,000 Mysorean cavalry, available to delay the invading British army's movements and resupply.[37] The whole timetable of campaigning was limited by the closure which the advent of the monsoon in June would inevitably bring.

Apart from the advantages of higher troop numbers and wider control of territory than Cornwallis had possessed in 1791, the British effected a juncture with the Nizam's forces far earlier in the campaign, on 21 February 1799, than had occurred in 1792. The main army advanced to within 50 miles of Seringapatam by 2 March. During March the Mysoreans engaged detached British forces in two brief battles, both of which they lost. Having consolidated his position, by 5 April Harris was camped two miles from Seringapatam, where he was joined by the Bombay contingent on 19 April. The invaders focused on the fort at the west end of the island of Seringapatam, approaching their objective from a different direction from that used by Cornwallis seven years earlier. In late April, the British invested (surrounded) the town and set up an elaborate series of lines to enable them to fire upon the walls from a range of 400 yards. On 4 May, the British made a breach at one point in the walls, maintained their artillery fire to ensure that the defenders failed to make good the breach, and sent a column across a branch of the Cauvery River to storm the fort. After a two-hour battle and the loss of 389 casualties (343 of them Europeans), the British took the powerful fortress itself, with Tipu dying in the defence of one of the fortress's gateways. The whole campaign had taken Harris 257 miles from Vellore to Seringapatam and cost the British 1,384 casualties, 745 of them Europeans.[38]

Explanations for British success

Despite repeated warnings that 'our war cannot be successful in one campaign',[39] success was achieved, to a tight schedule, for three principal reasons. First, the demands of supplying food and forage were successfully met. On the march Harris's army at times covered 18 square miles – six miles long and three miles across – and needed to rest one day in every three to regroup and recuperate. To sustain this vast array of people – perhaps 100,000 of them including camp followers – and animals, the army built up large stocks of rice and grain at camps at and near border towns. The supply of food, and other materials, remained with Indian merchants who, backed by vast numbers of carriers, labourers and bullocks, accompanied the invading army.[40] Maintaining adequate supplies was assisted by a second factor – the effective neutralization of Tipu's light cavalry, described by Colonel Wellesley:

His light cavalry . . . are the best of the kind in the world. They have hung about us, night and day, from the moment we entered his country to this. Some of them have always had sight of us and have been prepared to cut off any persons venturing out of the reach of our camp-guards.[41]

Inadequate cavalry provision in 1791 was rectified in 1799 with a main British cavalry division of 2,635 men reinforced by 10,000 cavalrymen in the Nizam's contingent. Moreover, the rear of the British position, exposed in 1791, had become an 'iron frontier, the fortresses of which we never had in our possession in the last war'. Even the more exposed southerly border, which might have enabled Tipu to raid the southern Carnatic from Coimbatore, was blocked to him.[42]

The third factor in British success was the reduced military effectiveness of Tipu's regime. Internal and external campaigning meant that the longest period of peace in the period from 1765 to 1792 lasted no more than two years. Yet the cumulative impact of war and of the great loss of territory in 1792 led not to internal reform, but to intensified Muslimization and clannish favouritism in army promotions. The attack in 1792 on Seringapatam obliged the sultan to undertake costly repairs and extensions to its vast fortifications.[43] Internal repression, especially in northern Mysore, directed against local polygars or chiefs, meant that about 40% of Tipu's army had to be tied down in garrisoning 27 larger forts and 113 minor ones in 1799. On the eve of the campaign, Tipu had only 23,483 regular infantry. High-risk raiding was inhibited by the fact that three-quarters of his 13,000-strong cavalry supplied their own horses. The majority of his 70,000-strong army were militia or armed police or support forces. Mysore thus lacked the highly trained infantry to block the British advance in the forested region south of Bangalore or to launch a counter-assault into the Carnatic to throw the British campaign into disarray.[44] Worse still, the manpower available to Tipu in the defence of Seringapatam was probably allocated inappropriately, with far too many soldiers being bottled up in the cramped, overcrowded city itself, and not dispatched to harry British positions. Although the Mysoreans had plenty of firepower, the British brought up more artillery than in 1791 and the Nizam's field force contributed forty guns, easily outgunning anything Tipu put into the field to slow their advance and easily punching a breach in Seringapatam's over-extended defences.[45] The fact that so many Mysorean leaders fell in the final British assault suggests either that they recognized that the regime's fate – and their own – had been sealed or that ordinary soldiers needed exemplary acts of self-sacrificing leadership to inspire or shame them into fighting on.

Seringapatam on the night of 4 May received the full brunt of British revenge. Whatever his abilities as a ruler and commander, Tipu had a widespread reputation for cruelty and repression. It was said that British soldiers captured during the siege were murdered on Tipu's orders when the assault on Seringapatam opened.[46] Any siege followed by a breach under defensive fire almost inevitably raised the level of hatred and aggression among the attackers. Major General Baird, who led the storming of the fort, had endured 44 months of a harsh imprisonment by Tipu and was not notable for sensitivity to the feelings of Indian people. Once the fighting finished, the soldiers plundered virtually every house in the town. Colonel Wellesley entered Seringapatam the next morning: 'by the greatest exertion, by hanging, flogging etc. etc., in the course of the day I restored order among the troops, and I hope I have gained the confidence of the people'.[47] An official valuation put the total worth of all goods taken at £1,143,216 in prize-money, which represented only those seizures openly declared. For comparison, the whole annual revenue of British India was about £13 million.[48]

The political settlement creating a subsidiary regime in Mysore rested on three foundations. The legitimacy of the previously dethroned ruling family was upheld. Concluding that any independent authority would be far too vulnerable to the Marathas or the Nizam to provide regional stability, Mornington restored the dynasty of Hindu rulers which had been sidelined in 1761 and in whose name Haidar Ali had governed as regent. A five-year-old boy became the new raja, ceremonially installed at Seringapatam and controlled by a chief minister who had played a prominent role under Tipu. Secondly, British 'protection' was provided, with the Company's Resident guiding Mysore's external policy and the new state paying the Company to maintain a permanent contingent of six battalions within Mysore. Colonel Wellesley was appointed commander of the Company's forces in Mysore and during the following year and a half he headed a substantial force, usually including about 4,000 Europeans, to establish thirteen garrisons spread throughout Mysore and conduct punitive raids in 1799 and 1800 against local polygars who resented or rejected the new dispensation. One official reported in May 1800 that 'Colonel Montresor has been very successful in Bulum; has beat, burnt, plundered, and destroyed in all parts of the country'.[49] British success depended upon maintaining a substantial and active military presence in Mysore well into 1801. Yet a third prop was equally vital. Within days of entering Seringapatam, Arthur Wellesley insisted that prominent leaders be confirmed in their jagirs if they submitted promptly. Such accommodation of Tipu's leading sirdars worked particularly for those who had been powerful at the capital.[50]

The destruction of Mysore marked a dramatic reversal of the regional balance of power since the 1780s. While diplomatic alliances with Hyderabad and the Marathas contributed signally to this power shift, superior British war-making lay at its core. A French account of the campaign completed in 1800 described the British army collected by February 1799 as the best 'ever assembled in India and, relatively to its object, the most complete perhaps which has been assembled in any country'. It boasted strong artillery, excellent cavalry (including the Nizam's), plentiful supplies, and a vast array of non-combatants and carriage animals in support.[51] The combination of extensive logistical preparation, determined power projection into enemy territory, and intrepid attack at a decisive point had become by 1799, and was long to remain, a familiar British recipe for success. But not many of those leading the campaign in 1798–99 thought victory would be easy or achievable according to the governor-general's rigorous timetable. Once achieved, however, the destruction of Mysore's power simply took the British a step closer to the establishment of a wider balance of power in central India. As Henry Dundas forcefully reminded Lord Wellesley in March 1799: 'if you are able to consolidate in one defensive system the Nizam's power, the Mahratta power, and the power of Great Britain in India, we have nothing to fear in that quarter of the globe from any combinations that can be formed against us'.[52] This geopolitical summary scarcely indicated the self-assurance or self-reliance of a hegemonic power. Nor was its assumption of Maratha unity of purpose or diplomatic cohesion to prove well-founded.

Notes and references

1 Charles Ross (ed.), *Correspondence of Charles, First Marquis Cornwallis*, 3 vols (London, 1859), Vol. II, p. 153; George Bennett (ed.), *The Concept of Empire: Burke to Attlee 1774–1947* (1962 edn) p. 65.

2 Jadunath Sarkar, *The Fall of the Mughal Empire*, 4 vols, Vol. IV, *1789–1803* (New Delhi, 1992 reprint), pp. 289–90, 292–93, 295. A restatement of a traditional approach can be found in Sir Penderel Moon, *The British Conquest and Dominion of India* (London, 1989). A more innovative analysis is in Stewart Gordon *The Marathas, 1600–1818*, (Cambridge, 1993).

3 These issues are raised in: Burton Stein, *A History of India* (Oxford, 1998), pp. 209–10; Tapu Raychaudhuri, *Perceptions, Emotions, Sensibilities: Essays on India's Colonial and Post-Colonial Experiences* (Delhi, 1999), pp. ix–x, 155–57, 161; Barbara D. Metcalf and Thomas R. Metcalf, *A Concise History of India* (Cambridge, 2002), pp. 66–67. The most recent general history of the British armies in India concentrates on organizational issues – which were important – rather than on warfare. T.A. Heathcote, *The Military in British India* (Manchester, 1995), pp. 39–69. There is similarly little on warfare in the period 1780–1830 in Lawrence James, *Raj: The Making and Unmaking of British India* (London, 1997),

pp. 63–78. James sees the recurrent use of force as an indication of fears that British rule was 'precarious'. For perspectives on the wider structures of British influence and expansionism, see Karl de Schweinitz, Jr., *The Rise and Fall of British India: Imperialism as Inequality* (London, 1983), pp. 118–71; John Keay, *The Honourable Company: A History of the English East India Company* (London, 1991), is excellent on general policy, but has little on later eighteenth-century warfare.

4 Christopher Bayly, *Imperial Meridian: The British Empire and the World, 1780–1830* (London, 1989), pp. 22, 38–40, 44, 47, 54–55; Stewart Gordon, *Marathas, Marauders, and State Formation in Eighteenth-Century India* (Delhi, 1994), pp. ix–xi, 36–61, 79–81, 119–21; M. Athar Ali, 'The passing of empire: the Mughal case', *Modern Asian Studies* Vol. 9(3) (1975), pp. 385–96.

5 This process is well described for central India in Gordon, *The Marathas, 1600–1818*, pp. 103–20, 130, 138.

6 H.V. Bowen, *Revenue and reform: the Indian problem in British politics, 1757–1773* (Cambridge, 1991), pp. 12–13.

7 Richard B. Barnett, *North India Between Empires: Awadh, the Mughals, and the British 1720–1801* (Berkeley, CA, 1980), pp. 246–48, 251–52.

8 James Salmond, *A Review of the Origin, Progress, and Result of the Late Decisive War in Mysore* (London, 1800), p. 2.

9 Montgomery Martin (ed.), *The Despatches, Minutes and Correspondence of the Marquis Wellesley, KG, during his Administration in India*, 5 vols (London, 1836–37), Vol. I, pp. 1–15; Salmond, *A Review*, p. 3.

10 Julian S. Corbett (ed.), *Private Papers of George, Second Earl Spencer, First Lord of the Admiralty, 1794–1801* (Navy Records Society, 1913), Vol. I, pp. 239–40.

11 Duke of Wellington (ed.), *Supplementary Despatches and Memoranda of Arthur, Duke of Wellington, India, 1797–1805*, 15 vols (London, 1858–72), Vol. I, p. 13.

12 Steven Englund, *Napoleon: A Political Life* (Cambridge, MA, 2004), pp. 126–31; Robin Harris, *Talleyrand: Betrayer and Saviour of France* (London, 2007), pp. 99–102; Philip O'Dwyer, *Napoleon: The Path to Power 1769–1799* (London, 2007), pp. 336–43; Edward James Kolla, 'Not so criminal: new understandings of Napoleon's foreign policy in the East', *French Historical Studies*, Vol. 30 (2007), pp. 175–201, esp. pp. 181–84; Salmond, *A Review*, p. v. The evidence from French policy establishes the force of French ambitions towards the Ottoman empire and India.

13 Mir Hussein, *History of Tipu Sultan*, trans. by Col. W. Miles (New Delhi, 1986 reprint of 1864 edn), pp. 105–17; Martin (ed.), *Despatches*, Vol. I, p. 654.

14 Wellington (ed.), *Supplementary Despatches*, Vol. I, pp. 14, 8, 70, 113.

15 Martin (ed.), *Dispatches*, Vol. I, pp. 302–03.

16 Raymond A. Callahan, 'Cornwallis and the Indian Army, 1786–1797', *Military Affairs*, xxxiv (1970), pp. 93–7.

17 Raymond Callahan, *The East India Company and Army Reform 1783–1798* (Cambridge, MA, 1972), pp. 171–74, 186, 194–95, 202–04.

18 Iris Butler, *The Eldest Brother: The Marquess Wellesley, the Duke of Wellington's Eldest Brother* (London, 1973), p. 115; William Dalrymple, *White Mughals: Love and Betrayal in Eighteenth-Century India* (London, 2003), pp. 59–62.

19 Butler, *The Eldest Brother*, pp. 118–19.

20 Edward Ingram, *Commitment to Empire: Prophecies of the Great Game in Asia, 1797–1800* (Oxford, 1981), pp. 160–63. Ingram distinguishes between Dundas's focus on Napoleon's possible Indian aims from Egypt and Wellesley's concern for Mauritius, a French island base of long standing. My assessment differs from Ingram's overall analysis.

21 Martin (ed.), *The Despatches . . . Marquis Wellesley*, Vol. I, pp. 71–72, 77–79.

22 Martin (ed.), *The Despatches . . . Marquis Wellesley*, Vol. I, pp. 72, 75–9.

23 Edward Ingram (ed.), *Two Views of British India: The Private Correspondence of Mr Dundas and Lord Wellesley, 1798–1801* (Bath, 1970), p. 160; Martin (ed.), *Dispatches*, Vol. V, pp. 172–74, 318.

24 G.R. Gleig, *The Life of Major General Sir Thomas Munro, Late Governor of Madras*, 3 vols (London, 1849 edn), Vol. III, p. 144.

25 Martin (ed.), *The Despatches . . . Marquis Wellesley*, Vol. V, p. 319.

26 Butler, *The Eldest Brother*, pp. 144–46.

27 Denys Forrest, *Tiger of Mysore* (London, 1970), pp. 263–80; Ingram, *Commitment to Empire*, pp. 148–52.

28 On public attitudes to Tipu, see Peter Harrington, *British Artists and War: The Face of Paintings and Prints, 1700–1914* (London, 1993), pp. 55–64; P.J. Marshall, *Trade and Conquest: Studies on the Rise of British Dominance in India* (Aldershot, 1993), Ch. XIV; Franklin and Mary Wickwire, *Cornwallis: The Imperial Years* (Chapel Hill, NC, 1980), pp. 182–83. Gleig, *Life of . . . Munro*, Vol. I, pp. 122–24, Vol. III, p. 103; Martin (ed.), *The Despatches . . . Marquis Wellesley*, Vol. I, p. 65.

29 Martin (ed.), *The Despatches . . . Marquis Wellesley*, Vol. I, pp. 281–82, 307–08, 312–15, 610–11.

30 Martin (ed.), *The Despatches . . . Marquis Wellesley*, Vol. I, pp. 307, 323, 428.

31 Martin (ed.), *The Despatches . . . Marquis Wellesley*, Vol. I, pp. 73–79, 323–24.

32 Wellington (ed.), *Supplementary Despatches*, Vol. I, pp. 153–54, 194.

33 Forrest, *Tiger of Mysore*, p. 277.

34 *Oxford Dictionary of National Biography* entries; Jac Weller, *Wellington in India* (London, 1972), pp. 42–45.

35 Wellington (ed.), *Supplementary Despatches*, Vol. I, pp. 187, 189–92.

36 Martin (ed.), *The Despatches . . . Marquis Wellesley*, Vol. I, p. 333.

37 Weller, *Wellington in India*, pp. 82, 301–03; Wellington (ed.), *Supplementary Despatches*, Vol. I, p. 205.

38 Weller, *Wellington in India*, pp. 58–81, 85.

39 Wellington (ed.), *Supplementary Despatches*, Vol. I, pp. 153–56, 194.

40 Wellington (ed.), *Supplementary Despatches*, Vol. I, pp. 139–40, 143–49, 168, 172–73, 177–79.

41 Wellington (ed.), *Supplementary Despatches*, Vol. I, p. 208.

42 Wellington (ed.), *Supplementary Despatches*, Vol. I, p. 120; Weller, *Wellington in India*, pp. 301–03; Gleig, *Life of . . . Munro* (1849), Vol. I, p. 130.

43 Forrest, *Tiger of Mysore*, pp. 102–03, 203.

44 Wellington (ed.), *Supplementary Despatches*, Vol. I, p. 205; Martin (ed.), *Despatches*, Vol. I, p. 605.

45 Weller, *Wellington in India*, pp. 74, 76, 302–03; *Michaud's History of Mysore under Hyder Ali and Tippoo Sultan*, trans. by V.K. Raman Menon (New Delhi, 1985 reprint), p. 142.

46 T.E. Hook, *The Life of General the Rt. Hon. Sir David Baird, Bart.*, 2 vols (London, 1832), Vol. I, p. 211.

47 Wellington (ed.), *Supplementary Despatches*, Vol. I, p. 212.

48 Wellington (ed.), *Supplementary Despatches*, Vol. I, p. 223; Martin (ed.), *Despatches*, Vol. V, p. 314.

49 Weller, *Wellington in India*, pp. 86–7, 91; Wellington (ed.), *Supplementary Despatches*, Vol. I, pp. 214–17; *Michaud's History*, pp. 189–90; Gleig, *Life of . . . Munro*, Vol. III, p. 120.

50 Wellington (ed.), *Supplementary Despatches*, Vol. I, p. 214.

51 *Michaud's History*, pp. 129, 134.

52 Martin (ed.), *Despatches*, Vol. I, p. 611.

CHAPTER 9

Expansionism against the Marathas, 1802–05

Warfare against Mysore involved the curtailing and then removal of a regime founded in 1761 upon military power and dependent for its existence upon military expansionism. It concerned a particular state under a particular dynasty in a particular region. The next phase of British expansionism was far more wide-ranging. Intervention in the Maratha confederacy had little to do with British interest in securing lines of trade or potential investments or the protection of debt obligations undertaken by individual princes. It flowed instead from geopolitical concerns and the quest for a more stable inter-state order. Undertaking intervention was not simply politically and diplomatically ambitious – it also involved a military challenge which, when met, showed how British military capability had been transformed in India since the 1780s.

The drive to establish a new order hinged on an alliance with the symbolically leading Maratha prince, the peshwa, while thwarting the ambitions of three of the four other great houses within the confederacy. Through political pressures and because of the intense distrust felt by princes for each other, the British never faced a combination of all their Maratha opponents.

The Company and the Maratha princes

The defeat of Tipu should have created a regional balance of power acceptable to British interests. Admittedly, the post-war settlement left individually disaffected poligars or local chiefs in Mysore, against whom drawn-out border expeditions were conducted in 1800 and 1801. And in 1800 the Company absorbed Mysorean acquisitions transferred from the

Nizam of Hyderabad in 1800 in exchange for the annual charges he was required to pay the Company for Company troops maintained within his domains.[1] But the major strategic threats had been removed, and the responsible minister, Henry Dundas, stressed to the governor-general that 'my present creed with regard to India is, that nothing new is to be attempted without weighing well every rupee it will cost'.[2]

Lord Wellesley, however, insisted that the defeat of Mysore had lengthened the boundaries that required policing and stimulated Indian states' turbulent ambitions that would need restricting. In July 1800 he pressed for a massive increase in the numbers of European troops in India, arguing for a doubling of the European cavalry and an expansion of the European artillery which was 'everywhere extremely weak'. In October, he repeated to London 'the urgent and indispensable necessity of augmenting without an hour's delay our European force in India, to the extent demanded by the situation of this empire'. These proposals 'truly alarmed' the minister, who pointed out that the total number of troops in India had soared from 80,000 men in 1796 to 142,000 four years later. Conceding that the cavalry and first-class artillery might need strengthening as British territorial rule spread, Dundas insisted that about 20,000 European infantry would suffice, to be balanced by a reduction in the overall size of the Company's armies. To circumvent the government's refusal to provide additional King's troops, Wellesley greatly expanded the number of sepoy troops, in part by creating special units in the shape of 'revenue battalions' and 'volunteer battalions'. In February 1801, responding to this development, the Court of Directors in London instructed the government in India to cut the size of the sepoy forces. Wellesley simply 'suspended' those instructions for his remaining four years in office, insisting on his prerogative to make discretionary judgements on vital policy matters based on prevailing circumstances which might be unknown or unappreciated in London. Instead, and admittedly aided by the advent of new wars, he increased the number of sepoy battalions, already swollen in the late 1790s, by 25% between 1801 and 1805.[3]

This military expansionism was aided by Wellesley's loading the annual charges of additional sepoy regiments upon his allies. Subsidiary alliances with individual rulers typically included provision for Company troops to be stationed in the princes' territories and to be paid for by them. Some at least of the governor-general's officials deplored the high-handed way that subsidiary allies – notably at Hyderabad and Pune – were treated in 1800–02. The Resident at Pune, William Palmer, stressed in December 1802: 'Our weakness, arrogance and injustice cannot fail to draw upon us the vengeance of a united India.'[4] Dismissing such hesitations, Wellesley asserted that 'substantial security for durable peace in India is to be derived from a constant state of preparation for war'.[5]

Arguments over military spending occurred within the context of a continuing power struggle in the Maratha confederacy between the houses of Sindhia and Holkar. Although the Mughal emperor had raised Sindhia to the status of the peshwa's deputy, Nana Fadnis, the peshwa's long-serving prime minister, refused to recognize Sindhia as the paramount Maratha power and sought to maintain the peshwa's position by continuing to play Sindhia off against Holkar.[6] In June 1800–May 1801 two widows of Mahadji Sindhia fomented a rebellion against Daulat Rao Sindhia and secured Holkar's support. Sindhia defeated them in battle, then won a major victory outside Holkar's capital at Indore, which his troops proceeded to plunder. In response, Jaswant Rao Holkar – who in 1802 put himself forward as *de facto* head of his house instead of leading it as regent – resorted to wide-ranging plundering and fast-moving cavalry campaigning. In mid-1802 he advanced into the Deccan and the peshwa's territories and defeated the peshwa's ill-paid and demoralized forces. Pulling together infantry and artillery to complement his vast horde of cavalry, Holkar confronted Sindhia's still sizeable army outside Pune on 25 October 1802.[7] The two sides fought a prolonged battle of blow and counter-blow at Hadapsar involving an extended exchange of artillery fire and then various close manoeuvres. Sindhia's army lost all its guns and much of its camp and equipment and got no support from the local population. The peshwa, Baji Rao II, fled Pune which Holkar, careful not to plunder, took over as victor.[8]

The Maratha 'system' in which the British operated had collapsed and with it the idea entertained well into the 1780s, and which Wellesley tried to revive in 1799–1800, that the British could deal with a genuine confederacy through its head at Pune. With the defeat also of the peshwa's formally designated deputy, the possibility emerging in the late 1780s and early 1790s that Sindhia would emerge as the new dominant power now seemed equally unlikely.[9]

The East India Company became involved in this prolonged struggle for mastery in the Maratha confederacy because Baji Rao II sought its aid following his humiliation by Holkar. Bearing in mind the model which the Company had developed in its relationship with Hyderabad, Wellesley told the Court of Directors that the Maratha crisis offered a 'conjunction of affairs which appears to present the most advantageous opportunity that has ever occurred, of improving British interests in that quarter on

solid and durable foundations'.[10] British intervention was confirmed at
Bassein, near Bombay, in the treaty of 31 December 1802. It included the
standard ingredients for subsidiary alliances, with the peshwa agreeing
to pay the Company to maintain six battalions in his dominions and to
exclude all European countries other than Britain from dealings with
Pune. Baji Rao agreed to accept British arbitration on specified matters
and to make peace or war only in consultation with the Company. The
treaty recognized the Company's commitments to the Gaekwad of Baroda,
another of the leading Maratha princes, and to Surat. This settlement,
marking an extraordinary extension of British influence across south-
central and great swathes of north-central India, depended upon the
British ability to reinstate Baji Rao at Pune.

The imposition of a stable state system, if such a system could be
obtained through diplomacy, was hindered by more general economic and
social pressures. The entire region experienced an accelerating increase in
population, a long-term failure to lift agricultural productivity, a down-
ward pressure on producers from a governing elite rapacious for ever more
revenue, and a tradition, fomented by warlords especially among the
rajputs and Marathas, of raiding and tribalism rather than agricultural
improvement and commerce. The tighter the economic and fiscal circumstances became, the more traditional warfare fed on traditional warfare.
Rising populations supplied the increased manpower for extending
cavalry raiding which, to cope with growing populations, became more
aggressive.[11] When droughts occurred, as they did in 1802 in the Deccan,
village populations suffered yet more acutely. Raiding cavalry, often in
large numbers, sacked villages in order to discover hidden stores of grain,
leaving villagers to their fate. As competition for food and resources
intensified, so rulers recruited additional cavalry. To meet the accompanying need for extra pay, rulers squeezed more tax revenues from their
existing feudatories, or sought to take over others' territories for their
revenues, or resorted to yet more raiding and plundering. On the other
hand, soldiers themselves, if they were as ill-paid and ill-fed as Baji Rao's
were by 1802, became less willing to fight for their current overlord and
more willing to switch allegiances.[12]

These interlocking demographic, agricultural and fiscal pressures were
neither new nor independent variables. The struggle for resources and tax
revenues had been intense from the early eighteenth century. But the competition between ruling dynasties for revenue-yielding territories, and the
recourse they had to organizing and often leading vast raiding parties,
gave greater urgency to the pressures to provide a more formal structure

for ordering civil affairs throughout the Maratha confederacy. The system of power brokerage which British officials had operated, or attempted to operate, from 1762 to 1800 had failed to entrench the peshwa as the linchpin of a fluid and often dynamic set of rival dynasties. Nor had the house of Sindhia imposed itself as the predominant power and therefore arbiter following its military successes in 1788–93. Whatever the economic and social dynamics behind the warlordism of the late eighteenth century, some form of political solution was needed to control it. The intensity of rivalries within the confederacy, the ejection of the peshwa from his capital, and Holkar's ascendancy over both Sindhia and the peshwa underscored the extent of political disorder flowing from rulers' struggle for ascendancy in a period of social and economic disruption. One option might have been for the British to back Holkar to the hilt and promote a new hegemony among the Marathas; but Jasvant Rao was feared and loathed by the British. Another might have been to leave the Marathas to fight for their own solutions; but Wellesley was determined to extend the subsidiary alliance system as a catch-all framework to stabilize political relations between Indian powers. Instead, then, Wellesley decided to restore the peshwa and, through him, make the Company an active participant in the Maratha system for the first time. Neither Cornwallis, as an influential former governor-general, nor the Court of Directors supported this option. But it flowed from Wellesley's eagerness to create inter-state stability through a political order which reflected the longstanding assertion that the affairs of central India would best be regularized through a confederacy controlled from Pune. Back in 1791, a young official, Thomas Munro, reflected on over a decade of Indian service:

Those who prefer the security of treaties, know little indeed of India.
In Europe, where every people is nearly on a level with respect to the arts
of peace and war, and where the boundaries of most of the great
kingdoms have been long fixed, alliances are sometimes successful.

But in India rampant instability meant that the British should trust to 'the terror of our arms' rather than 'idle dreams of policy and balance of power'.[13]

The war against the Marathas

Responsibility for returning Baji Rao II to Pune lay with the forces of the Madras presidency, ironically in the light of that presidency's distinct lack of enthusiasm for expansionism back in the late 1790s. But Major

General Arthur Wellesley more than compensated for earlier official scepticism. From late 1802 he made extensive and detailed preparations for war, stockpiling supplies of food and transport animals on the Mysore–Maratha border, and building a hospital to support the campaign. He depended upon close cooperation with merchants who ran the bazaars which accompanied the army, upon local leaders who supplied him with light cavalry, upon jagirdars among the Marathas who supported his invasion, and upon cooperation from villagers in sustaining the flow of grains to his army. Above all, he grasped the need for speed of movement in order to pin down Holkar's army: 'the intentions of the British government regarding the affairs of the Mahratta empire cannot be carried into execution unless Holkar's army is either defeated or dissipated. The object of the campaign must therefore be to bring him to a general action at as early a period as possible'. Holkar enjoyed all the advantages in trying to avoid such an outcome, since his essentially cavalry army travelled light. Wellesley therefore made arrangements, including the forward storage of, or provision for, supplies, in order to improve his army's mobility. He collected a contingent of 14,700 troops and crossed into Maratha territory on 12 March 1803. He was joined there by 8,900 troops from the Company's force in Hyderabad, which thus provided an immediate dividend, in terms of power projection, from the settlements of 1798–1800 with the nizam. Fearing that Holkar's forces would set fire to Pune on the British army's approach, General Wellesley led an advance party in a dash for the capital, covering nearly 60 miles in 32 hours, and thereby forcing his opponents to evacuate the city speedily as he entered it on the 20 March. Wellesley's initiative enabled Baji Rao II to return to Pune in May.[14] Holkar now pulled back from intervention in the southern part of the confederacy and instead led an expedition to Gujerat, north of Bombay. Lord Wellesley's principal objective had been achieved.

Reviewing his position from September 1803, the governor-general claimed his swift measures had thwarted Jaswant Rao Holkar's attempt to acquire 'the whole military power, and civil authority of the state'. Since a victorious Holkar – so Lord Wellesley argued – would not have been able to maintain his army in the countryside around Pune, given the army's roving depredations and the desolation of those lands, the maharajah would have pursued yet further territorial gains, at the expense of the Company's ally, the Nizam of Hyderabad, or of the Company itself. Baji Rao's restoration was thus justified as ensuring a regional balance of power, while ejecting Holkar from the southern lands of the Maratha confederacy was justified as an act of self-defence.[15]

The peshwa's restoration still, however, lacked political efficacy as long as Sindhia and Holkar declined to acknowledge it. The British, in negotiations during May and June, repeatedly demanded that Sindhia recognize Baji Rao's restoration and disavow any aggressive intentions. But Daulat Rao Sindhia and his ministers prevaricated and held lengthy discussions with another of the five great Maratha princes, the Bhonsle, raja of Berar. Sindhia was repeatedly warned to withdraw his forces well away from the frontier lands bordering on the peshwa's and the nizam's domains and lodge them north of the Narbudda River. The British insisted to Sindhia and Berar that maintaining two large manoeuvrable armies so near British allies' possessions would be interpreted as an act of war. The local commander, Major General Wellesley, was given authority to respond as he deemed appropriate. It seems likely that local conditions favoured an early campaign by the British. Food prices rose sharply in June, creating a scarcity of food for the Maratha armies – and those armies were already behind in pay – while the local bankers refused to lend Sindhia additional money.[16] An early British advance in the south would exploit the demoralization felt by armies already short of food and pay.

Lord Wellesley urged a different political case for action against Sindhia in the north. He emphasized the dangers of French influence being extended through Sindhia's employment of mercenaries under General Perron in the Doab. Invoking an international threat echoed the governor-general's arguments of 1798–99 and resonated with the arrival on 11 September 1803 of news of the resumption of war against France. But privately the British treated Perron and his colleagues as mercenaries who might be induced either to quit India, with guarantees that they could take their accumulated fortunes with them, or to join the East India Company's pay-roll.[17] The governor-general assured the commander-in-chief in India, Lieutenant General Gerard Lake, 'I shall cheerfully sanction any obligations or expence [sic] incurred for the purpose of conciliating the officers or ministers of the confederates'. Despite the prospective use of financial inducements, Lake's detailed planning in July placed overwhelming priority on the defeat of Perron's army because he believed that the regional rajas would not support the British while Sindhia could use that mercenary force to retaliate against them.[18]

Why a campaign against Holkar in March–May 1803 led to a war against Sindhia in August is most plausibly explained by Lord Wellesley's drive to impose the system created by Bassein upon the Maratha princes. Even though they regarded Baji Rao as weak and unreliable, British officials in 1803 refused to treat the other Maratha princes as the peshwa's equals, insisting instead that they should accept his position as leader of the confederacy. As they had recognized in 1800, 'Scindiah has as many irons in the fire as we have, without the same exertion to get them out'. Sindhia mobilized and manoeuvred his armies in mid-1803 because he, or factions at his durbar or court, distrusted British involvement at Pune, refused to accept the Treaty of Bassein, reasoned that the Company would inevitably challenge other Maratha leaders' power, and concluded that he needed to prepare himself against such eventualities. Sindhia may have felt the pressures suggested by the socio-economic explanation for war. The internecine conflict of 1802 had depleted much of the Maratha country-side and the lure of plunder – always a motive – may have been reinforced by a more urgent and basic need to secure food supplies. He was probably swayed by Berar, who may himself have sought paramountcy at Pune. For whatever reasons, Sindhia assembled a large army on the frontiers of Hyderabad during the period when Major General Wellesley was advancing upon and taking Pune. By July 1803 the maharaja and Berar had over 54,000 men and 87 guns available for their operations in the Deccan, with a concentration near Ajanta, a fortress-town held by the Nizam of Hyderabad at the farthest edge of his territories and commanding an important pass some 170 miles north-east of Pune. The immediate trigger for war was Sindhia's refusal, despite repeated warnings and diplomatic pressure from the British, to pull back from the Hyderabadi frontier in the south and return to his customary garrisons.[19] General Wellesley determined in early August to go on the offensive once weather conditions permitted. Lake in the north attacked Sindhia's armies, under the command of French mercenaries, at the same time.

The southern campaign, 1803

The war began in the first week of August 1803 with Arthur Wellesley attacking and swiftly seizing the town and fort of Ahmadnagar, defended by only about 2,000 of Sindhia's trained soldiers. Controlled directly by the Mughal imperial house in the seventeenth century, it had been the place of the great emperor Aurangzeb's death in 1707. By taking the city ('full of everything we want') situated in a rich flood plain, Wellesley supplied his own army, denied Sindhia major assets, and established a major base for his campaign.[20]

During the latter part of August and into September, Major General Wellesley attempted to pin down Sindhia's and Berar's main armies in the borderlands between Hyderabad and the central region of the Maratha

confederacy. Wellesley's campaign hinged on three critical factors. Geographically, the key line was the road linking Ahmednagar to Aurangabad and
then running north-eastwards to the vital banking and supply town of
Burhampur. Beyond that, the road led much farther north to Agra, which
also came under Sindhia's control. To the west of this strategic through-
fare at Burhampur lay the agriculturally rich area of Khandesh whose
produce gave Burhampur its importance as a source of supply. Wellesley
had to keep to the west of Sindhia's army and drive his adversary ever
eastwards, away from the main north–south road. By 16 October, British
forces had taken or neutralized three (Aurangabad, Daulatabad, and
Burhampur) of the five banking centres in the region of campaigning, and
a fourth, Nagpur, was both distant and the raja of Berar's capital. Apart
from pushing Sindhia away from his critical sources of food, munitions
and money, Wellesley's strategy also reduced any distant possibility of
cooperation between the Maratha armies operating in the central area of
India and those fighting Lake in the north. Finally, having got his enemy in
the place where he wanted him, Wellesley needed to bring the Marathas to
battle and inflict a dramatic and demoralizing defeat upon them. As he
wrote towards the end of August 1803: 'dash at the first fellows that make
their appearance and the campaign will be our own. A long defensive war
will ruin us.' Gaining the initiative through battle was also vital because
the widely armed peasantry attacked whichever side fell into disarray.[21]

Following some weeks of marching and counter-marching around the
borderlands of the Marathas confederacy and Hyderabad, Wellesley on
23 September came upon Sindhia's main army dispersed in camp over a
distance of six miles along the river Kaitna. It was early in the afternoon.
What followed became legendary:

*India has been won for us by the boldness of our generals, who from the
days of Lord Clive to those of Lord Roberts have ever seized opportunity
by the forelock, no matter what the peril or how great the responsibility.
But seldom has such a daring decision been arrived at as that which led
to the battle of Assaye. [sic]*[22]

The battle of Assye has spawned much debate. It is not clear whether
Sindhia chose the position behind the Kaitna River in order to lure the
British into battle. One assessment holds that the Marathas were moving
off to avoid action and that they were stretched over six miles because
their army was in motion, except where Wellesley's sudden arrival obliged
the regular infantry to concentrate in defence of the precious and suddenly
vulnerable artillery. Yet analysis at the time by British political officers –

Barry Close, the Resident at Pune, and Edward Strachey – argued that the Marathas had indeed intended to draw Wellesley into battle. By sending his irregular cavalry to threaten the routes towards Pune and Hyderabad, Sindhia had diverted attention from his artillery and regular infantry so as to enable him to advance through the hill country to a position of his own choosing.[23] Related to the debate over whether the Marathas intended to give battle was the extent of their commitment to the fight. At the point of contact, even recent accounts describe 5,000 British troops 'attacking' at least 50,000 or even 60,000 Marathas.[24] The real odds were more like 5,800 taking on about 10,500 regular infantry. Most accounts of the battle ignore the fact that Wellesley, in addition to his battle force, had enough Indian light cavalrymen – about 5,000 of them – to protect his camp and rear when he pushed his regular army across the Kaitna, while the bulk of the Maratha cavalry simply declined to engage in the battle itself. Again, the general's greatest modern biographer asserts that it was Wellesley's 'genius' that detected the surest way of launching an attack by spotting the possibility of crossing the River Kaitna by a ford near the junction of two rivers.[25] In fact, the river was readily crossable, while the specific point chosen offered the best available cover for the advancing army against Maratha artillery. Although pursuing his chosen line of attack involved considerable courage, Wellesley greatly reduced the advantage in regular infantry numbers which the Marathas enjoyed by positioning his army on the selected narrow strip of land between the two rivers, thus preventing the deployment into line of Sindhia's full force.[26]

Surprised by Wellesley's decision to attack, the Maratha infantry switched their front to face Wellesley's advance with more speed and completeness than Wellesley probably anticipated. They anchored the left side of their new line on the village of Assye. Coming under heavy artillery fire, and having to attack their opponents' guns in order to survive, the British advanced upon the Maratha infantry and artillery at an uneven rate, with the British far right moving too far ahead and becoming overexposed. Only the supreme courage of the 74 Highlanders and the swift intervention of the cavalry under Lieutenant Colonel Patrick Maxwell (who was killed) saved that front and turned resistance into flight. Out of 5,800 'British' soldiers engaged in the battle, some 1,594 became casualties, a high proportion (27%). The casualty rate among the European troops climbed to 32% among 2,000 present. In addition, some 325 horses were killed and 111 were wounded, a significant blow to mobility in an army of only 1,200 regular cavalry.[27] Reorganizing after the loss of one-third of the elite European troops and one-third of the elite cavalry, and making arrangements to secure and move ninety-eight captured guns ruled out any pursuit of Sindhia's retreating army.

Following the battle, Sindhia moved upon his crucial base at Burhampur and the British advanced north-eastwards to that city. Wellesley's subsequent march eastwards towards Berar's capital at Nagpur obliged the Marathas to shift southwards and eastwards once more, exposing Burhampur to British capture on 16 October. But the balance of military advantage did not tip entirely away from Sindhia, for Wellesley's own military intelligence remained patchy and the British had to counter – at the cost of 'some terrible marches' – Maratha light cavalry probes to the south and threats to supply trains in the Godavari valley. Wellesley acted to redress these factors by launching offensives against Sindhia's fortress towns and by offering European officers and NCOs in the maharaja's service equivalent rank and pay if they deserted to the East India Company; some sixteen did so.[28]

During October and November, British forces operated over a wide area, partly to deter Maratha bands from sweeping southwards to raid and plunder the lands of the peshwa and the nizam, partly to seize Asirgarh, a strategically vital hill fortress, cutting Sindhia off from an area in which he might have been able to regroup and re-equip his infantry, and partly to press the main Maratha armies eastwards.[29] Eventually, after advancing only about 160 miles since 1 November, Wellesley, towards the end of the day on 29 November, came upon the Maratha army, drawn up prepared for battle, at Argaum.

Argaum was a set-piece tactical triumph. Wellesley commanded perhaps 10,000 regular infantry against, at most, 15,000 Maratha infantry with their main artillery. The Marathas' numerical advantage was counterbalanced because they were drawn up in two parallel lines, with one substantial force placed well behind the other and therefore unable to fire at the advancing British. Wellesley's line was formed to bring considerable firepower to bear, and marched forward under good cover, with the infantry at some points lying down to avoid incoming artillery fire, a technique successfully continued in the Peninsular War. The Maratha artillery gunners tired themselves and overheated their guns by starting to fire too early when the British were still at a considerable distance. Once the British line punched its way through the first line of Maratha infantry, the Marathas' second line simply broke and fled, much as the Maratha cavalry had done earlier in the battle when pummelled by British guns and cavalry on Wellesley's flank. As at Assye, the psychological blow inflicted by the British capture of the Marathas' guns – in this case thirty-eight of them – proved decisive, and once again Maratha casualties were relatively light. Wellesley estimated only 1,200 at Assye – fewer than the total he sustained – and contemporary estimates suggested 2,000 at Argaum. Reports of 5,000–10,000 Marathas killed or wounded in the pursuit should be treated with extreme scepticism.[30]

The loss of their modern artillery and their inability to halt Wellesley's advance piled pressure upon Sindhia and especially Berar, who had been particularly aggressive in earlier discussions about going to war. A small British force from Calcutta invaded and took over his coastal province of Cuttack. Wellesley continued his own operations by attacking the Bhonsle's important fortress town of Gawilghur, sited at 3,595 feet above sea level and celebrated as a hill fort from its foundation in the 1420s. Wellesley had prepared a very detailed memorandum on the defensive gates and approach roads of Gawilghur in mid-August, stressing that the main difficulty lay in approaching the town.[31] Considerable exertion, sound engineering skills, and a sure eye for the appropriate route to take were required to make good a road suitable for hauling artillery up to the town's defences. Once five heavy guns were dragged to within about 250 yards of the wall, they were used from 12 December to pound a section of the six-mile-long perimeter. On 15 December about 4,600 troops stormed the walls, and the garrison's morale simply broke, with the British losing only 126 casualties. Many defenders probably escaped, but possibly thousands were slaughtered in the crush within the fortress to which they retreated when the town's extensive defensive walls could no longer be held. Berar lost a large stock of weapons, yet more artillery, and his brother, who had commanded at Argaum and had died fighting – like Tipu Sultan – inside the fort. This victory occurred only 80 miles from Berar's capital of Nagpur, and created enough pressure, buttressed by the threat of further British operations within Berar's territories, to persuade the raja to conclude a peace treaty on 17 December 1803.[32]

The northern campaigns, 1803

Despite the historiographical attention paid to the future Duke of Wellington's offensive in central India, the more important campaigning of these wars occurred in the north, where Lake took on Sindhia's European-officered armies. The general argued in July that he would probably need to fight Sindhia's forces before financial inducements could be used to win over the maharaja's European mercenaries: 'the early defeat of Perron in the field . . . would in all probability be decisive of the success of the campaign'. Reducing Sindhia's military power would also encourage local rulers – especially among the rajputs and the Jat rajas and notably the raja of Baratpur (Bhurtpore) – to conclude alliances with the British. However much they resented Sindhia, they would not oppose him until his military power had been curtailed.[33] Lake's operations were designed also to tighten British ties with the raja of Jaipur, and to insert British power between Sindhia's domains and the borderlands towards the Punjab. To reduce Sindhia's prestige still further and to symbolize the strengthening of British authority in India, Lord Wellesley wanted the emperor at Delhi taken from Sindhia's protection and secured under British control.[34]

Leading a strike force of about 10,000 troops, Lake left Kanpur (Cawnpore) on 7 August and entered Sindhia's possessions on 29 August. His initial sphere of operations lay in the rich agricultural lands between the Ganges and Jumna (Yumana) Rivers, where he sought to drive Sindhia's forces from their maharaja's fortified possessions while pushing towards Delhi.[35] Lake's first obstacle on the road from Kanpur to the Mughal capital was the formidable Aligarh (meaning 'high fort') which had served as a stronghold for at least 600 years and which had fallen to Sindhia in 1784. The general estimated that a siege would take one month, time he could not afford. When negotiations to 'get the troops out of the fort by bribery' failed, Lake – whose largest guns were only four 12-pounders and three $5^1/_2$ inch howitzers, far short of the artillery required to assault Aligarh's well-constructed defences – decided to storm the fort's main gate as the only way to maintain his campaign's momentum. At dawn on 4 September, he launched a rush at the entrance. When this, and an attempt to escalade the main gateway walls, both failed, close-range artillery was dragged in to break the main gates, after which three inner gates had to be rushed and stormed before the fort was won and its defenders fled, many being hunted down and slaughtered by the cavalry. A large quantity of munitions was seized, together with 281 artillery weapons, of which 99 were usefully mobile, rather than being emplaced to defend the walls. The attack cost about 270 casualties, including Lieutenant Colonel William Monson who commanded the assault, and the other battalion commander engaged in it. Lake felt that this speedy success against a fort 'hitherto deemed impregnable, and defended on all sides with the utmost obstinacy'[36] demonstrated British troops' irresistible determination and courage. The victory owed nothing to scientific thinking or technological superiority.

From Aligarh the British marched to Delhi some 84 miles to the north-west. On 11 September, Sindhia's forces left the city and crossed the

Jumna to attack Lake. The British army had already covered 18 miles that morning – a rapid rate of advance – and had encamped when its outposts were attacked. Discovering the whole Maratha force ahead of him, Lake reacted characteristically by leading his cavalry to reconnoitre the enemy's lines. The cavalry rode into an ambush when they came upon their opponents' massed artillery and infantry. With the British cavalry retreating, the Marathas pursued in the belief that the British had been repulsed. By then, the main British army was drawn up, and the retiring British cavalry dispersed to left and right to expose the lines of British infantry. Counterattacking, the British infantry line pressed through an intense artillery barrage to within 100 yards of the Maratha line, discharged one volley from their firelocks, and then charged with the bayonet. They seized sixty-eight guns of good quality, a total exceeding their own field army's artillery. A rapid cavalry manoeuvre then cut off many Maratha troops before they reached the Jumna River, inflicting apparently substantial casualties, though these probably included women, children, and camp followers. Although Lake's losses – 485 casualties – were relatively heavy for a battlefield army of about 4,500 men, this victory opened the way to the British entry into Delhi on 16 September and secured the political momentum in alliance-building which this high-profile success was intended to achieve.[37]

Lake's next objectives were Agra, some 139 miles from Delhi, and Perron himself. Some British officers felt it was a mistake to become involved beyond the rich agricultural region on the Doab and even to extend British influence or interests to the west of the Jumna. On the other hand, Agra was a centre of immense prestige built up by the Mughals from the 1520s. Sacked by forces led by the raja of Baratpur in 1761, it had then been seized by the Marathas. Its huge fort, built originally in the sixteenth century, had walls running for 1.5 miles. Lake reached it on 4 October and, concerned lest Maratha reinforcements might arrive, took the town on 10 October. Assailing the fort within the town began with the breaching batteries opening fire from 350 yards on 17 October. Progress became so rapid that the garrison decided by nightfall to surrender, in return for safe-conduct for themselves and their property. Lake was relieved to avoid a costly assault, and anticipated a major psychological impact upon the local population and local rulers on taking what was regarded as 'the key to Hindustan' after so little fighting: 'the fall of Agra has completely astonished the natives and convinced them we are most superior to them.'[38] More prosaically, three factors explain British success. The period between Lake's arrival at Agra on 4 October and his attack on the fort itself on the 17th allowed the Maratha jagirdars and their men to

consider their options carefully and decide to cut their material and political losses by settling their differences with the British. Lake had predicted
in July that the rajput and Jat chiefs west of the Jumna would join the
British against the Marathas once Perron's army met defeat. Sindhia's
most senior foreign officers – mostly French but some British mercenaries
– steadily absconded to the British, many getting safe conduct to Calcutta.
Second, Lake deployed thirty guns, howitzers and mortars, including
much artillery captured at Delhi, in the final assault on the fort. This concentration depended upon a third factor; the besieged were hemmed in
with the assistance of 5,000 cavalry contributed by the raja of Baratpur
who agreed an alliance in early October. Victory at Agra gave the British
more munitions and weapons, a well-organized revenue-raising bureaucracy, and vital command of the river route to Delhi, enabling them to
send materiel and supplies more quickly by river than by road.[39]

Maintaining his strategic focus on Sindhia's manpower, Lake left Agra
on 27 October in pursuit of a Maratha army composed of some battalions
which had escaped from Delhi, together with troops sent northwards from
the Deccan to strengthen the northern effort. Delayed by rain, Lake dispensed with his own heavy artillery and closed upon the Marathas by
forced marches. His cavalry pressed a night march, covering 40 miles in
the last 24 hours, to catch Sindhia's army at Laswari at 6:00 a.m. and
daybreak on 1 November. In order to pin the Marathas down before they
completed their dispositions and to seize their artillery, Lake attacked
with cavalry and mounted artillery. Although, unsurprisingly, he was
forced to pull back out of range of the Maratha cannon, he held the
Maratha army in place, awaiting the arrival of his own infantry. About an
hour after it arrived at midday, he attacked across the whole front. Lake
fought a tactically daring battle, forcing his opponents to shift their position once and their line a second time, concentrating his manpower on one
stretch of his opponents' lines and using his cavalry to hold the rest of the
Marathas in place away from the point of his keenest attack. Only when
the Marathas' seventy-one guns were seized did their fierce resistance
break. The savage fighting cost Lake 824 killed and wounded. One of
Lake's ADCs was killed, he had two horses killed under him, and his son
was wounded in front of him. He commented to Lord Wellesley: 'I never
was in so severe a business in my life or any thing like it, and pray to God
I never may be in such a situation again.' (Lake, it might be noted, had
fought bravely against the French revolutionaries in Flanders in 1794.)
Although the general was depressed for days after the battle, he had
achieved his principal strategic objectives by seizing Aligarh, Delhi, and
Agra, taking the Mughal emperor under British protection, forging an

alliance with Baratpur and, most important, destroying Sindhia's French-trained or French-officered forces. The only remaining objective in the north, urged again by the governor-general in October, was to take Gwalior to the south of Agra, because it commanded the main roads leading south, and the main passes from Hindustan into the Deccan.[40]

But the speed and scale of these successes sufficed to lead Sindhia to settle by the end of December. His biggest territorial losses occurred in the north where the feudal rights which he had granted to Perron and Perron's associates were transferred to the British, who gained lands in the Doab which, with other revenue rights in the north, yielded an annual revenue of £1,500,000. He yielded the port of Broach, which the British from Bombay had taken in order to deny him external access to French assistance and which commanded the trade of a very rich cotton-growing region. The British returned some possessions to Sindhia or his allies and feudatories but, in the south, handed Ahmadnagar to the peshwa and extensive areas around Ajanta to the nizam. Unlike Berar, the maharaja was obliged to accept an East India Company subsidiary force, based on his borders. He was also required to refer all future disagreements between himself and the peshwa and the nizam to the British for decision. The treaty of 30 December 1803, following the settlement with Berar, achieved what Wellesley wanted in June–July.[41] The British had backed Baji Rao II as peshwa, and Sindhia and Berar had been forced to accept both that decision and a diplomatic framework in which they could deal with the Maratha leader only through British official intermediaries. The house of Sindhia was stripped of the impressive artillery and European-trained and -officered infantry which it had built up over a generation. Since the British controlled the lands bordering on the Sikhs' territories, they denied the Marathas ready access to external allies; they also reduced Sindhia's southern territories so as to remove him farther from Pune. Yet one element in the shifting balance of Maratha power remained outside British political intervention at the end of 1803 and that was the ruthless but enigmatic head of the house of Holkar. Although Lord Wellesley suggested that he be treated as a friend in negotiations with Sindhia and Berar, his 'extremely suspicious' conduct was a further spur to a rapid conclusion of peace.[42]

British military effectiveness

The reasons for British military success have been vigorously debated. Randolph Cooper has argued for the fundamental importance of British control of the South Asian labour market. Exploiting their financial power, the British recruited excellent sepoy soldiers and destabilized the command structures of the Maratha armies once campaigns began, by offering financial and other inducements to the Marathas' European mercenaries with and subordinate jagirdars to change sides. Kaushik Roy stresses instead the Marathas' difficulties in integrating differing developments in the use of artillery, cavalry and infantry, and the weapons available to them, into a rapidly changing practice of warfare. The Marathas were handicapped by complex legacies of their own military culture, political leadership, and organizational effectiveness.[43]

It is probably fruitless to seek one decisive factor to explain the signal military achievement over time, space and numbers which the British secured in the campaigns of 1803. The most obvious explanation – that the British possessed technically superior weapons – seems erroneous. Maratha artillery was better and more numerous than British artillery; as Lord Wellesley asserted in June 1799 that 'Our artillery throughout India is very deficient'.[44] Yet it has long been argued that this proved a mixed blessing for the Marathas. The adoption of such weapons and new tactics placed the Marathas in a quandary, since they were adapting to European technology and techniques while also retaining huge numbers of light cavalrymen in their midst who were ineffectively integrated into dispositions for battle. The failure to utilize their large numerical superiority in light cavalry goes to the heart of Kanshik Roy's argument. Their light cavalry, for example, might have been used more systematically throughout their wars with the British to disrupt British supplies and to raid British territories. The British made strenuous efforts in key battles in 1803 to take the Maratha guns, which were heroically defended, in the knowledge that once the guns were taken, Maratha resistance tended to fade away, especially since the Marathas did not fight independently in battalions as the British were trained to do. In addition, jealousies between the better paid infantry and the 'feudal' tribal levies, and the fact that the levies owned their horses and had no desire to see them endangered unnecessarily, often made the cavalry indifferent to the infantry's needs. In 1793, one British officer commented on the Maratha cavalrymen's treatment of their infantry: 'they ride through them without any ceremony on the march, and on all occasions evidently consider them as foreigners, and a very inferior class of people and troops'. Maratha infantry campoos (or battalions) were formed essentially of mercenaries, from Oudh, Rohilkhand and the Doab, and were often officered by Europeans. Cavalry and infantry thus differed in ethnic background, pay, status, leadership and attitudes to war.[45] If the British could seize Maratha artillery and in doing so weaken and reduce the Marathas' European-style infantry, then the cavalry had little motivation to exert themselves to reverse the outcome of the conflict. But this still leaves the need to explain British success against those parts of the main Maratha armies which consisted of well-trained infantry and artillery.

A clear British advantage was their more effective integration of their forces. During 1802–03 Lake prepared for war by thoroughly training his cavalry at Kannauj, a large plain some 50 miles from his headquarters at Kanpur (Cawnpore). In his planning before the campaign, the general, following innovations within the Company's army, also stipulated that field artillery be widely dispersed, with each cavalry regiment having two light galloper guns and each of his infantry battalions being accompanied by two six-pounders. These field guns were distinct from the line artillery of heavier guns and his battering train.[46] The commander-in-chief approved in 1801 a proposal developed by the Bengal staff to train ten men in each sepoy company as light infantry and marksmen; they could be grouped as separate companies in each battalion as needed, and serve especially as flankers on the march. In contrast, Maratha officers did not make up for their generally rudimentary education by reading about warfare, and demonstrated little commitment to the detailed management of battles, particularly failing to integrate traditional cavalry with modern infantry and artillery.[47] The inescapable conclusion is that British commanders managed their campaigns and battles with greater insight and application than their opponents did. They also drew on greater manpower than Sindhia, who had 26,000 regulars of all branches and perhaps 43,000 irregular cavalry.[48]

Contemporary British leaders exaggerated the margin of victory both privately and for its impact at home. When he learned of the fall of Agra – 'the key of Hindustan' – Lord Wellesley told Lake on 29 October that his successes alone 'would astonish all Asia'. Combined with victories in the south, 'it is impossible to convey to you an adequate idea of the splendour of your fame in this part of the world'. The speed of these achievements exceeded even the governor-general's optimistic hopes. His formal despatch to the Secret Committee on 31 October went further:

The glory of this uninterrupted success is not surpassed by any recorded triumph of the British arms in India, and has been attended by every circumstance calculated to elevate the fame of British valour, to illustrate the character of British humanity, and to secure the stability of the British empire in the east.[49]

Lake attributed his success at Delhi to the intrepid courage of his infantry:

the business was one of the most gallant actions possible; such a fire of cannon has seldom been seen if ever, against which our men marched up within one hundred yards without taking a firelock from off their shoulders, when they gave one volley, charged instantly and drove the enemy.[50]

Lake's secret report to the governor-general on Laswari emphasized the high calibre of Sindhia's army:

battalions are most uncommonly well appointed, have a most numerous artillery, as well served as they can possibly be, the gunners standing to their guns until killed by the bayonet, all the sepoys of the enemy behaved exceedingly well, and if they had been commanded by French officers, the event would have been, I fear, extremely doubtful.[51]

Against such an opponent, Lake pressed for an increase in the numbers of British troops assigned to Indian service. After Laswari he again stressed 'how impossible it is to do anything without British troops, and of them there ought to be a very great proportion'.[52]

Despite this repeated emphasis on British soldiers' special fighting qualities, British success resulted from the interplay of various factors, which were pulled together by planning and an efficient system of command. Speed in the conduct of operations was essential because the logistical requirements of campaigning were so onerous. In planning in late 1802 for an invasion of the Maratha lands from the south, Arthur Wellesley emphasized the problems of supplying food to his army. The country into which he was advancing produced grain rather than rice, so that he had to take rice with him for sepoys accustomed to that diet. He needed 20,000 sheep a month for meat. His cavalry horses fed upon gram, not available in the Maratha territory, with the result that every cavalry horse had to be supported by a bullock carrying that feed. In order to protect his army and its vast supply train and to forage for fodder for the oxen, he estimated that he would need to raise about 20,000 light cavalrymen within the Maratha territories or furnished by the nizam. Their horses, unlike his own, would be able to feed on crops grown in the invaded lands. Turning to artillery, the general decided to take guns no stronger than twelve-pounders, partly because he did not envisage encountering the most modern types of fortifications, but mainly because he foresaw the need for long marches, which would be impeded if his guns had to be conveyed by carts rather than being strapped to carriage cattle.[53] One critical difference between the two sides was that the British planned for specific offensive campaigns, intending them to be relatively short-lived, whereas, for example in 1803, three of the Maratha princes kept large armies in being, mainly it would seem to put diplomatic pressure on each other. That practice added greatly to their costs and to political uncertainty and disagreement within their darbars.

Sheer numbers as well as logistical support played a key role in British success. We have already noted the tendency to distort the record of British victories in combat by comparing what were grand total estimates of Maratha levies with the core fighting cadres of regular, British-trained soldiers, when, in fact, the differences in numbers of troops drilled in European-style battlefield manoeuvring did not vastly advantage the Marathas. More generally, the British campaigns of 1803 depended upon the deployment of large regular forces to box Sindhia's and Berar's armies into an ever more confined geographical area. In the southern campaign of 1803, the British fielded 58,483 regular troops, supported by 6,946 military camp-auxiliaries and sizeable levies of indigenous and untrained cavalry. From the regular forces, some 10,000 troops were stationed along the Malabar coast and in Goa to prevent enemy movements in that direction and cut off any assistance for Britain's opponents from that quarter. Another 6,500 officers and men garrisoned Mysore to ensure no defections from the jagirdars in the north of that territory. A further 2,163 held the position at Pune, while 2,425 were based at Hyderabad. The field forces were distributed in four distinctive groups. The army directly under Major General Wellesley totalled 12,000 men while the Hyderabadi Subsidiary Force, operating to its south, came in at just under 10,000. In addition, 8,668 men in Guzerat, to the west, protected agriculturally rich lands and threatened Sindhia's northern possessions and capital. A further 5,876 troops on the eastern coastal belt in Cuttack added pressure to Berar's frontier from that direction.[54] Sindhia and Berar thus faced constant pressure and uncertain challenges from British forces so distributed as to threaten widely separated parts of their domains.

Having boxed their opponents in, Lake and Major General Wellesley both then actively downgraded the Marathas' war-making capacity by seizing key towns, which were vital sources of food, munitions, treasure and prestige, and by inducing European officers to desert to the Company's army. A traditional feature of Indian warfare had long been the political negotiation of a fortified town's surrender to a besieging opponent.[55]

British generals typically expected that such practices, lubricated with bribes and inducements to change sides, would continue. A wider extension of this approach was the application of British financial power to the task of controlling northern and central India's military labour market. The East India Company paid its soldiers regularly and well, thereby inducing defections and inhibiting opponents' capacity to build and maintain modern armies. In 1803 the British positively suborned European officers in Sindhia's army, making it easy for them to leave their employer (retaining their fortunes while receiving payments from the Company) and even to join the British. This systematic policy not only gave the British military intelligence; it also undermined Sindhia's command and control system in the midst of the campaign. The British then pursued their enemy's main armies with tenacity, keeping them on the move, hemming them in, limiting their initiative, and preventing them from breaking out to plunder. Although the idea that British success in the subjugation of India in the 1800s and 1810s flowed from cumulative military momentum alone has been criticized, the British management of operations in 1803 focused on the overriding need to create and maintain the momentum of the particular campaign. Finally, they sought battle – even more aggressively in Lake's case than Wellesley's – in order to break the Marathas' regular infantry and seize their guns.[56] Sindhia's numerous irregular cavalry proved of little use in battle, while his infantry now suffered from the long-term shift from traditional obedience under semi-feudal rulers to regimental loyalties. The system in which regimental commanders enjoyed considerable autonomy in recruitment and operations was suddenly corroded by European senior officers' treachery. With Sindhia's infantry disadvantaged by the defection of European mercenary officers, his artillery became more important to his army's battlefield performance because the use of the guns depended on small-group cohesion and effectiveness rather than large-group manoeuvre and thus officers' detailed leadership.[57] The British seized an estimated 429 guns from Sindhia in two months at Assye, Agra, Delhi and Laswari,[58] an extraordinary performance. On the battlefield, the British had to take their opponents' guns in order to destroy an arm in which the Marathas enjoyed superiority. British commanders achieved victory through persistent efforts to undermine the Marathas' military structures, the organization of sustainable and well-distributed armies, and strong coordination of aggressive campaigns in order to bring their opponents to battle. The ensuing clashes of arms repeatedly entailed determined fighting and the plentiful sacrifice of infantry lives to break the Maratha armies thus engaged.

The war against Holkar

When British officials pressed Sindhia to come to terms in June–July 1803 he and his ministers had persistently delayed and prevaricated. One reason was their own lack of agreement over policy; another was the need to coordinate responses with Berar. There remained also the possibility that Holkar might be drawn into the confederacy. His reluctance to do so puzzled the British, even though he remained Sindhia's intense rival for supremacy among the Marathas and cannot have regretted the reduction of the maharaja's army. Lake in late November informed Lord Wellesley that Holkar 'talks of oversetting the British' even after failing in September to help Sindhia and Perron halt the British advance on Agra:

I can scarcely believe it possible such an idea could have entered into his head, for by all accounts he is a shrewd, sensible man, with an extraordinary firm mind, and supposed to be ever watchful, and ready to seize a good opportunity for carrying his plans into effect . . . he surely cannot have any intention to attack us when we have the entire possession of Hindustan, the strong fortress of Agra, and very many chieftains on this side India [sic; in Rajasthan] with us.

While the threat from Holkar receded in December, the governor-general in January 1804 reviewed the situation and considered one option which exploited the constitutional semi-fiction maintained for over a decade by the British that the peshwa, now subjected to British control, held ultimate authority over the Maratha confederacy. The British might use the peshwa to remove Jaswant Rao by upholding the claims of another member of the Holkar family to rule the dynasty. That option would be deployed only if Jaswant Rao opposed the British or intervened in neighbouring principalities. But its plausibility may be gauged by Arthur Wellesley's private depiction of the rival claimant as 'an infamous blackguard, despised by everybody . . . and without one adherent or even a follower'. No wonder the governor-general preferred in early 1804 to believe that an active resident and British subsidiary force at Sindhia's court would give him enough deterrent leverage to restrain Jaswant Rao, by hemming him in with British possessions and British allies. He maintained this line in March in informing Lord Castlereagh – the responsible minister in London – of his expectation that Holkar would settle with the British.[59]

 Yet the commander-in-chief did not agree with this optimistic assessment. In early February, he urged that unless Holkar were 'annihilated', he could not foresee a general peace. By early April Lake was depicting

Holkar as irreconcilable to British suzerainty, acting in a way 'hostile' to British interests, and running an army 'composed of the restless and disaffected from all quarters of India' who could only be satisfied by plundering raids against neighbouring feudatories or states. Lake defined two threats in the north. Many chiefs in the Doab – between the Ganges and Jumna east of Delhi – were reluctant to accept British rule and offered potential alliances and support to Holkar. Lake responded by planning to stay in the Doab well into 1805 and ensure that judges, collectors and soldiers worked hard to enforce British authority and raise the revenues required. Beyond this region, Holkar seemed poised to interfere in Rajasthan to the west. Lake believed that Holkar's army might advance on Jaipur to extract money from the raja and proceed farther west to threaten Ajmer. Ajmer commanded important roads to the south and was a fortified town of enormous significance as a Muslim place of pilgrimage – second to Mecca at the time – in an area where Sindhia held feudal rights.[60] Lake proposed that Holkar's forces should be pushed away from Jaipur and Ajmer, and kept well out of Rajasthan.

By 16 April 1804, Lord Wellesley agreed that Lake should prepare for operations against Holkar, and in July ordered that the general should launch 'an early and vigorous attack' in order to bring him into the system of subsidiary alliances which the British were establishing across the Maratha confederacy. Wellesley was probably influenced by Sindhia's continuing delays in settling the terms of the peace settlement. Moreover, British officials argued strongly over the best policy to adopt towards Sindhia. Major General Wellesley believed the British were wrong on key issues. John Malcolm, representing the Company at Sindhia's durbar, urged the pursuit of 'a liberal and conciliating policy' towards the maharajah and recommended the return to him of his celebrated fortress of Gwalior. Yet Lord Wellesley, knowing that opposition to his own continuation in office was mounting in London, believed that concessions would open his earlier policies to challenge at home. He probably felt that another war would prolong his indispensability and justify his conduct in 1803.[61]

It was easy enough for Lake and Wellesley to agree that a decisive battle would shatter Holkar's army. Their difficulty was to assemble a force of sufficient firepower and mobility to achieve this objective while also protecting Hindustan from Holkar's possible incursions. With this danger in mind and expecting Holkar to become 'extremely troublesome' once the heavy rains of July, August and September were over, Lake moved his army back to Kanpur in late May and June. But he despatched a field force to ward Holkar away from Jaipur and Ajmer and to move south in June and July. The idea was to block the westerly road into Rajasthan by marching down it and, eventually, to squeeze Holkar's westerly flank by linking this force with one probing out northwards from Gujarat. A possible junction was Ujain, Sindhia's main seat, itself not far to the north and west of Holkar's capital at Indore, partly to ward off the possibility of an attack by Holkar and partly to secure cavalry from Sindhia.[62]

The force moving southwards had reached a point about 70 miles north of Ujain far earlier than Lake had planned, when its commander, Colonel William Monson, learned that Holkar was advancing with his main army. Monson was forced to begin a long retreat on 8 July. Short of food supplies and unable to find a fortified town with sufficient food stocks in which to take refuge, Monson had to keep retreating. During 24–29 August this small army broke down under repeated attacks and fragmented into smaller units which staggered separately back to Agra on 30–31 August and into September. Monson's failed expedition had destroyed the operational value of about 4,000 troops; Arthur Wellesley privately asserted that 'Monson's disasters are really the greatest and the most disgraceful to our military character of any that have ever occurred'.[63]

Monson's humiliating retreat stiffened Lake's resolve to crush Holkar. Leaving Kanpur on 3 September, the commander-in-chief began preparations to pursue his enemy. Lord Wellesley wrote on 11 September agreeing that 'the first object must be the defeat of Holkar's infantry in the field and to take his guns'.[64] But this clarity of aim immediately became clouded by the political consequences of Monson's failure. The raja of Bharatpur decided to back Holkar. Lake in November confidently assured the governor-general that 'we shall have no more trouble except the taking of the forts of the Bhurtpore Rajah, which will fall immediately, and terminate the war in a very short time'.[65]

Lake spent October and November trying to break Holkar's forces, insisting for that purpose on heading an army more lightly equipped 'than I believe any army in India ever was before'. In mid-October he relieved Delhi from a brief siege by Holkar. In mid-November his subordinate, Major General Frazer, captured the bulk of Holkar's 160 guns (including thiteen earlier taken from Monson) in a battle at Deig which Lake described as likely 'to have been the hardest fought battle on this side of India' and 'to surpass any thing that has hitherto been done in India'. After chasing Holkar's cavalry for sixteen days, covering 23–24 miles each day, Lake's own force rode 58 miles in one full day and additional night to surprise Holkar before dawn under the defensive walls of Furrackabad.[66] There, on 17 November, Lake seized his adversary's baggage train and destroyed his cavalry force, pursuing its fleeing remnants for up to 12 miles:

The rapidity of my march has astonished all the natives beyond imagination, and made them think there is nothing we are not equal to . . . the country has been saved by this pursuit . . . if I had remained on the other side of the Jumna nothing would have prevented the country from being up in arms.[67]

Yet the immediate effect of this newly achieved mobility was counter-balanced by the withdrawal of the successful army at Deig, back towards the army's supply base at Agra. Despite all the British pressure mounting in the region, and warnings earlier that communications with Holkar should cease, the raja of Bharatpur – or his ministers and advisers – continued to provide vital succour to Holkar's cause, enabling the Maratha prince to garner reinforcements. In an attempt to weaken Holkar among his allies and dependencies, Wellesley in December 1804 authorized Lake to attack Bharatpur, 'to serve as an example to other petty states'.[68] The general case for punitive and exemplary strikes had been made by Major General Wellesley in late 1803 when commenting on the borderlands of Berar: 'there is no established authority, or even an acknowledged boundary, on any part of the frontier, and the killadars and other officers on both sides have been in the habit of carrying on private wars against each other'.[69] Border turbulence became unavoidable because 'these people cannot manage their troops'.[70]

The punitive expedition against Bharatpur, so lightly and self-confidently undertaken, turned into one of the signal disasters of British campaigning in India. The British stormed the fortifications of Bharatpur on four occasions, on 9 and 21 January and 20 and 21 February 1805, without success and at the cost (together with operations at Deig) of 3,099 casualties during January and February. Concerns for British prestige mounted. One lieutenant noted that, during the fourth assault, the 76th regiment apparently refused to enter a bombarded breach: 'to think that Countrymen, whose very name and appearance, used to strike a panic in Hindustan, hang back and are afraid! – is more than scandalous or disgraceful – It is alarming – It threatens the very existence of British India!' Upbraided by Lake, the battalion returned to the attack to regain that reputation which seemed so vital to governing India: 'We should prefer enduring any hardships of Climate, any losses of war – to sinking in the Minutest degree, in that *opinion* of the Natives, by which alone, we may be said to rule in India.'[71] Yet the continuing diversion of so many British troops allowed Holkar time to regroup and encouraged Sindhia to consider resuming his own campaign against the British, resulting in much diplomatic energy in March and April being devoted to constraining the latter prince. This risk of a break with Sindhia, as well as the impending arrival of the hot and then the rainy seasons, spurred Lake to settle with the raja of Bharatpur in April. The raja – unable while besieged to raise revenues from his territories to meet mounting defence costs – agreed to pay a large sum in compensation to the Company in instalments ending in April 1809.[72]

By May 1805, Lord Wellesley believed that another war with Sindhia was as unlikely as it was undesirable but, with Holkar still undefeated, he ordered Lake to station his troops in such summer cantonments as would enable him to move readily and rapidly against Sindhia should the need arise. Despite attaining high levels of mobility and sacrificing manpower profusely at Bharatpur, Lake had still not delivered the swift settlement with Holkar which Wellesley had anticipated in September 1804.[73] A British official in 1805 reported the peshwa Baji Rao II's view of Jaswant: 'Holkar is a bad man from his heart; he loves disorder – he hates repose. Whatever he does proceeds from himself: he is a monster who must be destroyed.'[74] Holkar's campaigning demonstrated that, given the high level of Maratha mobility, it was impossible to secure reliably enduring frontier alliances with minor rajas, who were exposed to rapidly changing local balances of power brought on by Maratha raiding or campaigning. The only solution in the general's view was 'subjection on their part and government on ours'.[75]

Problems of British overstretch

The prospect of such further prolongation of conflict and conquest destroyed political confidence in the governor-general. In December 1803, Wellesley informed George III, with typical hyperbole: 'the result of a glorious and uninterrupted course of victories has extinguished the last remnant of French influence in India, and has confirmed the stability of the British empire in the East'.[76] Eighteen months later the subsidiary system and relations with the Maratha princes remained uncertain. By October 1804, Cornwallis argued privately that Wellesley had acted 'wantonly and criminally' against directives and regulations in going to war against Holkar. By December the prime minister, Pitt, wanted Wellesley out of India. Lord Castlereagh, the minister responsible, spent a day at Cornwallis's country house talking over the defects of Wellesley's subsidiary alliance system and Cornwallis's own return to the governor-generalship.[77] The general's strategic analysis had been clearly stated in December 1803:

Whatever ideas Lord Wellesley may entertain of the extension of our territories, or of those under our influence and protection, we must at least fix some boundary, and I think he could not easily have found a more convenient neighbour on his northern frontier than the Maratha State, which would tend very much to secure our possessions against any other northern invader, and which by good management we might easily keep in order, by making a prudent use of their intestine jealousies and quarrels.[78]

The Secret Committee of the East India Company's Court of Directors had made it plain to Lord Wellesley in 1804 that they did not seek a deep engagement in the Maratha confederacy and saw no objection to 'an entire restoration of all our conquests' to the Marathas to end the conflict.[79] As one senior official in India informed Major General Wellesley, 'the action which is to decide the destiny of our Indian Empire must be fought ... upon the banks of the Thames, not on the banks of the Ganges'.[80]

Given this deep division over priorities, the ailing Lord Cornwallis was sent to India to replace the discredited Wellesley. Once in India, in July 1805, Cornwallis told General Lake of his desire to end 'this most unprofitable and ruinous warfare'. Over-extending the alliance system had dragged the Company into pointless commitments and irrelevant power struggles. Cornwallis adhered to a prudential, cosmopolitan view that Britain's standing as a power depended upon her fiscal strength. Where Wellesley pointed to increasing revenues matching rising debts, Cornwallis saw only financial obligations. He therefore proposed to pay off large bodies of irregular troops whom he dismissed as costly and unnecessary. He was prepared to run the risk that they might join the Company's enemies, from whom many had deserted in the first place.[81] Although Cornwallis died in October 1805, his policy was implemented. Holkar, eventually driven into the Punjab, agreed relatively generous terms in January 1806, thereby regaining some Rajput districts and retaining his freedom of manoeuvre over the Rajput rajas. In line with Cornwallis's belief that the Company's territorial boundaries in the north should stop at the Jumna, exceptions being allowed only for local security, Sindhia regained some territories, most notably the important and prestigious fortress at Gwalior.

If the Maratha princes were exhausted by 1805, so was the Company. During Wellesley's governor-generalship, the India debt had risen from

£17 million to £31 million and both Company and government in London would stomach no more Wellesley wars. The governor-general's public defence was that the permanent revenue had soared from £8.06 million in 1797–98, when its total outgoings slightly exceeded that sum, to nearly £13.50 million by 1803–04 when, despite the rise in annual debt charges from £604,000 to £1,457,000, the Company was in overall surplus. Its officials ensured that acquisitions included richly productive lands on the Malabar coast and in Gujerat.[82] In 1813, *The Times* stressed that Wellesley had added three times as many people and three times as much territory to the British Empire, without losing any British possessions to the enemy, as Napoleon had acquired for France. By then, Wellesley's annexations had doubled the Indian Empire's receipts in an age when inflation was very limited.

Annual receipts of the three presidencies in £million (rounded)

	1797–98	1806–07	1812–13
Bengal	5.78	9.16	10.39
Madras	1.94	4.00	5.26
Bombay	0.34	0.77	0.69
Total	*8.06*	*13.93*	*16.34*

Despite Bombay officials' efforts in the late 1790s to secure additional territory, that presidency remained the junior partner. But the wars of 1798–1805 greatly strengthened the importance of Madras in relation to Bengal; having secured an income equivalent to one-third of Bengal's in 1797–98, Madras generated the equivalent of half by 1812–13.[83]

While halting further expansion and questioning the strategic necessity of Wellesley's system of alliances, Cornwallis maintained the subsidiary network. Sindhia held his own as a prominent participant in inter-state relations. Although recent allies were dropped, they received land rights within the elaborate feudal structure of revenue-holding and military-political obligations. These adjustments were made in 1805 without triumphalism and against a background of financial deficits in every year since 1798–99. In August 1805 Cornwallis explained to General Lake why the forward policy should be reversed:

it is not the opinion only of the Ministers, or of a party, but of all reflecting men of every description that it is physically impracticable for Great Britain, in addition to all other embarrassments, to maintain so vast and so unwieldy an empire in India, which annually calls for reinforcements of men and for remittances of money, and which yields little other profit except brilliant Gazettes. It is in vain for us to conceal from ourselves that our finances are at the lowest ebb, and that we literally have not the means of carrying on the ordinary business of Government.[84]

Yet the conclusion of the Maratha wars did not mark the cessation of the application of military force so vigorously desired. Although standard histories give the impression that little happened militarily over the next nine years, except for internal tensions within the Madras army, military interventionism did not follow the course which Cornwallis preferred. The Bengal army alone launched periodic punitive expeditions: two in Bundelkund and the Doab in 1807, each involving an assault upon a fortress; another in Bundelkund in 1809, again ending with an attack on a fort; one in 1809 into Hurriana, a province ceded by the Marathas in 1804; yet another one in Bundelkund in 1812, against the province's capital; and a small one in 1813. Border tensions led to the dispatch of troops to Sirhind on the Punjab frontier in 1809 and to the establishment of a new base at Ludhiana. In addition, volunteers were dispatched overseas; a small force to Macao in China in 1808–09; two battalions to the Île-de-France (Mauritius) in 1810–11; and a much larger force to Java in 1811, when some 7,000 Bengal sepoys served overseas.[85] If the titan appeared weary to some official eyes, its military obligations, interests and expanding influence rendered it far from inert.

The transformation in Britain's military position in the period 1790–1805 has been variously explained. It would be fair to conclude that a range of developments contributed to British success. Access to manpower and the suborning of opponents greatly assisted. But just as the *levée en masse* and the fragility of the anti-French alliance were necessary but not sufficient causes of French victory in 1793–95, so the sheer scale of operations in 1803 required more of the British than numbers and vulnerable enemies. The military achievement was impressive in terms of logistics, the attainment of stunning levels of mobility, courage and driving, aggressive leadership. The British carried off the Marathas' artillery, at great human cost, and stripped them of their mercenaries. At the expense of very considerable effort, the British in 1803 forced the Marathas into battle and fought four major engagements within three months, an unprecedented intensity of formal conflict. This dynamic military effort was matched by determined diplomatic activity. The geopolitical vision was Napoleonic in scope and scale while relying far more intensely than Napoleon did on cooperation with the existing structures of power and systems of rule. By 1805, the British in India possessed the experienced personnel and the appropriate system of residents at the princely courts to operate the newly expanded subsidiary alliances. The British politico-military elite in India had created a new empire.

Notes and references

1 Duke of Wellington (ed.), *Supplementary Despatches and Memoranda of Arthur, Duke of Wellington, KG*, 15 vols (London, 1858–72), Vol. II, pp. 29, 41–42, 47, 85–87; Iris Butler, *The Eldest Brother: The Marquess Wellesley, the Duke of Wellington's Eldest Brother* (London, 1973), p. 209.

2 Edward Ingram (ed.), *Two Views of British India: The Private Correspondence of Mr Dundas and Lord Wellesley, 1798–1801* (Bath, 1970), p. 322.

3 Ingram (ed.), *Two Views of British India*, pp. 163, 273–76, 308–09, 315, 318–19, 341, 358–59, 368n.

4 William Dalrymple, *White Mughals* (London, 2003), pp. 230, 263, 275.

5 Ingram (ed.), *Two Views of British India*, p. 355.

6 Jadunath Sarkar, *Fall of the Mughal Empire*, Vol. IV, *1789–1803* (New Delhi, 1992 ed.), pp. 1–5, 16–29, 41–42; Andre Wink, *Land and Sovereignty in India: Agrarian Society and Politics under the Eighteenth-Century Maratha Svarajya* (Cambridge, 1986), pp. 150–51.

7 Sarkar, *Fall of the Mughal Empire*, Vol. IV, *1789–1803*, pp. 156, 161, 164–69.

8 Sarkar, *Fall of the Mughal Empire*, Vol. IV, *1789–1803*, pp. 171–78.

9 Edward Ingram, *Commitment to Empire: Prophecies of the Great Game in Asia, 1797–1800* (New York, 1981), p. 187.

10 Butler, *The Eldest Brother*, p. 302.

11 C.A. Bayly, *Imperial Meridian: The British Empire and the World 1780–1830* (London, 1989), pp. 46–48, 184–86.

12 Evidence for this is in Sarkar, *Fall of the Mughal Empire* Vol. III (New Delhi, 1992 edn), pp. 157, 164–66, 176–77.

13 Rev. G.R. Gleig, *The Life of Major General Sir Thomas Munro, Bart.*, 3 vols (London, 1830), Vol. III, p. 65.

14 Wellington (ed.), *Supplementary Despatches*, Vol. III, pp. 422–24, 429–36, 445–46, 449, 453, 482–83, 488; Jac Weller, *Wellington in India* (London, 1972), pp. 140–45.

15 Montgomery Martin (ed.), *The Despatches, Minutes and Correspondence of the Marquess Wellesley, KG, during his Administration in India,* 5 vols (London, 1836–37), Vol. III, 361–65.

16 Martin (ed.), *Despatches . . . Marquess Wellesley,* Vol. III, p. 171.

17 Martin (ed.), *Despatches . . . Marquess Wellesley,* Vol. III, pp. 183, 300, 382.

18 Martin (ed.), *Despatches . . . Marquess Wellesley,* Vol. III, pp. 167–70, 188–93.

19 Ingram, *Commitment to Empire,* p. 187; Martin (ed.), *Despatches . . . Marquess Wellesley,* Vol. III, pp. 138, 140–41, 146; Wellington (ed.), *Supplementary Despatches,* Vol. II, p. 267; Anthony S. Bennell, *The Making of Arthur Wellesley* (London, 1997), pp. 58–66, 69.

20 Weller, *Wellington in India,* pp. 154–60; Bennell, pp. 55–58, 67; Philip Davis, *Monuments of India,* Vol. II *Islamic, Rajput, European* (London, 1989), pp. 418–19.

21 Lakshim Subramanian, 'Banias and the British: the role of indigenous credit in the process of imperial expansion in Western India in the second half of the eighteenth century' *Modern Asian Studies* 21(3) (1987), 473–510, esp. p. 481; Weller, *Wellington in India,* pp. 164–65, 197–98; Dirk H.A. Kolff, *Naukar, Rajput and Sepoy: The Ethnohistory of the Military Labour Market in Hindustan, 1450–1850* (Cambridge, 1990), pp. 8–9.

22 Herbert Compton, 'Laswaree and Assaye' in Archibald Forbes, G.A. Henty, Major Arthur Griffiths *et al., Battles of the Nineteenth Century,* 2 vols (London, 1896), Vol. II, pp. 376–77.

23 Elizabeth Longford, *Wellington: The Years of the Sword* (London, 1972) pp. 103–07; Lawrence James, *The Iron Duke: A Military Biography of Wellington* (London, 1992), p. 91; Bennell, *The Making,* pp. 82, 84–85.

24 Paddy Griffiths, 'The myth of the Thin Red Line: Wellington's tactic', in Paddy Griffiths (ed.), *Wellington Commander: The Iron Duke's Generalship* (Strettington, Chichester, n.d.), p.144.

25 Longford, *Wellington,* p. 104.

26 Longford, *Wellington,* p. 103; Major Basil Jackson and Captain C. Rochfort Scott, *The Military Life of Field Marshal the Duke of Wellington,* 2 vols (London, 1840), Vol. I, pp. 178–81, 184.

27 Martin (ed.), *Despatches . . . Marquess Wellesley,* Vol. III, p. 669; Randolph G.S. Cooper, *The Anglo-Maratha Campaigns and the Contest for India: The Struggle for Control of the South Asian Military Economy* (Cambridge, 2003), pp. 96–116 provides an excellent analysis.

28 Wellington (ed.), *Supplementary Despatches,* Vol. IV, p. 153; Bennell, *The Making,* pp. 87–92.

29 Wellington (ed.), *Supplementary Despatches*, Vol. IV, pp. 199–200.

30 Weller, *Wellington in India*, p. 210; Jackson and Scott, *Military Life*, Vol. I, p. 193.

31 Wellington (ed.), *Supplementary Despatches*, Vol. IV, pp. 155–56.

32 Weller, *Wellington in India*, pp. 216–27.

33 Martin (ed.), *Despatches . . . Marquess Wellesley*, Vol. III, pp. 190–93.

34 Martin (ed.), *Despatches . . . Marquess Wellesley*, Vol. III, pp. 167–70.

35 Colonel Hugh Pearse, *Memoir of the Life and Services of Viscount Lake* (Edinburgh, 1908), pp. 143, 147–49; Martin (ed.), *Despatches . . . Marquess Wellesley*, Vol. III, p. 167.

36 Martin (ed.), *Despatches . . . Marquess Wellesley*, Vol. III, pp. 287, 291–94; Cooper, *The Anglo-Maratha Campaigns*, pp. 166–67.

37 Martin (ed.), *Despatches . . . Marquess Wellesley*, Vol. III, pp. 307–09, 313, 667; Cooper, *The Anglo-Maratha Campaigns*, pp. 172–82.

38 Martin (ed.), *Despatches . . . Marquess Wellesley*, Vol. III, pp. 393–96, 407–09, 414.

39 Martin (ed.), *Despatches . . . Marquess Wellesley*, Vol. III, p. 192; Cooper, *The Anglo-Maratha Campaigns*, pp. 198–99.

40 Martin (ed.), *Despatches . . . Marquess Wellesley*, Vol. III, pp. 439–45, 494–96, 666, 672; Cooper, *The Anglo-Maratha Campaigns*, pp. 148, 201–09. Cooper provides an excellent account of the battle.

41 Butler, *The Eldest Brother*, pp. 312–21.

42 Martin (ed.), *Despatches . . . Marquess Wellesley*, Vol. III, pp. 499–500.

43 Cooper, *The Anglo-Maratha Campaigns*, pp. 310–12; Kaushik Roy, 'Military synthesis in South Asia: armies, warfare, and Indian society, *c.*1740–1849', *Journal of Military History*, 69 (2005), 651–90, esp. pp. 660–76.

44 Ingram (ed.), *Two Views of British India*, pp. 81, 163; Cooper, *The Anglo-Maratha Campaigns,* pp. 295–99.

45 Sarkar, *Fall of the Mughal Empire* Vol. IV, *1789–1803*, pp. 87–88, 259; Major Dirom, *A Narrative of the Campaign in India* (London, 1793), p. 11; John Pemble, 'Resources and techniques in the Second Maratha War', *Historical Journal*, 19 (1976), 375–404; Roy, 'Military synthesis', pp. 651–90.

46 Pearse, *Memoir of . . . Lord Lake*, pp. 151–54; Martin (ed.), *Despatches . . . Marquess Wellesley*, Vol. III, p. 189; Cooper, *The Anglo-Maratha Campaigns*, pp. 144–45.

47 Captain Williams, *An Historical Account of the Rise and Progress of the Bengal Native Infantry* (London, 1817), pp. 275–76; Sarkar, *Fall of the*

Mughal Empire Vol. IV, *1789–1803,* pp. 91–92, 225, 259; Randolph G.S. Cooper, 'Wellington and the Marathas', *International History Review,* 11 (1989), 31–38; review by Kaushik Roy in *Indian Historical Review,* Vol. XXIV (1997–98), pp. 192–94; Roy, 'Military synthesis', p. 685.

48 Seema Alavi, *The Sepoys and the Company: Tradition and Transition in Northern India 1770–1830* (New Delhi, 1995), p. 216n.

49 Martin (ed.), *Despatches . . . Marquess Wellesley,* Vol. III, pp. 420, 433.

50 Martin (ed.), *Despatches . . . Marquess Wellesley,* Vol. III, p. 310.

51 Martin (ed.), *Despatches . . . Marquess Wellesley,* Vol. III, p. 445.

52 Martin (ed.), *Despatches . . . Marquess Wellesley,* Vol. III, pp. 312, 320, 396, 446.

53 Wellington (ed.), *Supplementary Despatches,* Vol. III, pp. 389, 433, 435–36, 443, 495.

54 Wellington (ed.), *Supplementary Despatches,* Vol. IV, pp. 308–09.

55 Jos Gommans, 'Warhorse and gunpowder in India *c.*1000–1850' in Jeremy Black (ed.), *War in the Early Modern World* (London, 1999), pp. 105–27, esp. pp. 114–15.

56 Cooper, *The Anglo-Maratha Campaigns,* pp. 213–83, 286–87, 299–307, 310; Wellington (ed.), *Supplementary Despatches,* Vol. III, p. 432; Vol. IV, p. 105.

57 Alavi, *The Sepoys and the Company,* pp. 217–20; Cooper, *The Anglo-Maratha Campaigns,* pp. 293–95, 299, 305–06.

58 Weller, *Wellington in India,* p. 190; Cooper, *The Anglo-Maratha Campaigns,* pp. 185, 196, 198, 208.

59 Martin (ed.), *Despatches . . . Marquess Wellesley,* Vol. III, pp. 361, 471; Vol. IV, pp. 3–11, 45.

60 Martin (ed.), *Despatches . . . Marquess Wellesley,* Vol. IV, 19, 46–47, 49–50.

61 Martin (ed.), *Despatches . . . Marquess Wellesley,* Vol. IV, pp. 18, 27, 57, 60–61, 180–81; Wellington, (ed.), *Supplementary Despatches,* Vol. IV, pp. 333–38, 347–49, 355–60, 376, 384; John William Kaye, *The Life and Correspondence of Major General Sir John Malcolm,* 2 vols (London, 1856), Vol. I, pp. 268, 271, 274–75, 279.

62 Pearse, *Memoir,* pp. 270–76; Martin (ed.), *Despatches . . . Marquess Wellesley,* Vol. IV, pp. 176–82, 190–91, 197.

63 Wellington (ed.), *Supplementary Despatches,* Vol. IV, pp. 198–201, 464–66.

64 Martin (ed.), *Despatches . . . Marquess Wellesley,* Vol. IV, p. 205.

65 Martin (ed.), *Despatches . . . Marquess Wellesley,* Vol. IV, pp. 193, 222, 242.

66 Martin (ed.), *Despatches . . . Marquess Wellesley*, Vol. IV, pp. 220, 235–36, 241, 243.

67 Martin (ed.), *Despatches . . . Marquess Wellesley*, Vol. IV, p. 245.

68 Martin (ed.), *Despatches . . . Marquess Wellesley*, Vol. IV, pp. 250, 262.

69 Wellington (ed.), *Supplementary Despatches*, Vol. IV, p. 199.

70 Wellington (ed.), *Supplementary Despatches*, Vol. IV, pp. 303–05, 311.

71 D.D. Khanna (ed.), *The Second Maratha Campaign, 1804–1805: Diary of James Young, Officer, Bengal Horse Artillery and twice Sheriff of Calcutta* (Bombay, 1990), pp. 121, 142, 145.

72 Martin (ed.), *Despatches . . . Marquess Wellesley*, Vol. IV, pp. 302, 309, 523, 636.

73 Martin (ed.), *Despatches . . . Marquess Wellesley*, Vol. IV, pp. 207, 535–36.

74 Martin (ed.), *Despatches . . . Marquess Wellesley*, Vol. V, pp. 47, 58, 205, 262, 577.

75 Wellington (ed.), *Supplementary Despatches*, Vol. IV, pp. 480–81.

76 A. Aspinall (ed.), *The Later Correspondence of George III*, 5 vols (Cambridge, 1968), Vol. IV, p. 146.

77 Charles Ross (ed.), *Correspondence of Charles, First Marquis Cornwallis*, 3 vols (London, 1859), Vol. III, pp. 519, 523.

78 Ross (ed.), *Correspondence*, Vol. III, p. 509.

79 Martin (ed.), *Despatches . . . Marquess Wellesley*, Vol. IV, pp. 227–29, 230.

80 Kaye, *Life and Correspondence of . . . Malcolm*, Vol. I, p. 290.

81 Ross (ed.), *Correspondence*, Vol. III, pp. 533–35, 537–39, 541–42, 545. Cornwallis insisted that Britain's status as a European power depended upon her financial prudence (p. 489).

82 Butler, *The Eldest Brother*, pp. 323, 340; *Parliamentary Debates*, T.C. Hansard, Vol. II, 5 April–31 July 1804 (London, 1812), col. 1165.

83 *The Times*, 15 March 1813, p. 3; House of Commons, *Parliamentary Papers*, 1854–55 (336), pp. 2–7.

84 Ross (ed.), *Correspondence*, Vol. III, p. 545; *Parliamentary Papers, idem.*; P.J. Marshall, *Problems of Empire* (London, 1968), pp. 74–77.

85 Williams, *An Historical Account*, pp. 325–42.

PART FOUR

The war against Napoleon

CHAPTER 10

The quest for objectives, 1803–08

The renewal of war

Nothing illustrates better the tensions and contradictions faced by Britain in conducting foreign policy and in projecting power than the search for a viable strategy following Trafalgar. When Napoleon extended the continental war in 1805–06, it was not obvious how Britain could encourage continental allies to adhere to a settled politico-military strategy of containment or how Britain could best maximize her own naval power to contribute militarily to the formation of any such alliance. Between Trafalgar and the continental expeditions to the Iberian peninsula and to Walcheren (in the Netherlands) in 1809, strategic initiatives were launched in Cape Colony, South America, Egypt, Sweden and Italy. The government also projected British power in Europe in opportunistic bursts. Yet British interventions failed to stimulate or secure continental alliances.

War resumed in 1803 because Britain and France disputed the possession of the tiny Mediterranean island of Malta. Britain's refusal to cede it to France stood proxy, of course, for more deep-seated suspicions and antagonisms aroused by Napoleon's refusal to accept a new balance of power. An essential division of power would have left Britain pre-eminent at sea and in her colonies, France predominant in western Europe, Austria and Prussia competing for position in central Europe, and Russia the master of eastern Europe. Any such balance proved unworkable because Napoleon's own position as ruler of France depended upon expansionism and, certainly in his own thinking, upon regaining that extensive French overseas influence which had been secured under the Bourbons and so recently jettisoned by the Revolution of the 1790s. With few British politicians regarding the settlement of 1802 as permanent, adherence to both the spirit and letter of its requirements soon proved impossible.[1]

When Britain's war resumed, it unfolded in circumstances wholly different from those ten years earlier. Then there had been plausible grounds for believing that the French republican regime would soon collapse; now it was palpably the ascendant continental power. Then there were powerful potential allies already at war who enjoyed proud military reputations; now Prussia and Austria were discredited in British eyes and Britain needed Bonaparte to attack the continental powers, or their vital interests, in order to provoke them into joining her in the renewed struggle against France. Then Britain confidently began the conflict with a major expedition to assail French territory, at Toulon, and planned for other assaults to galvanize the regime's opponents; in 1803–05 the British laid out serious and extensive preparations to thwart a French invasion of south-eastern England.

The first five years of the resumed war witnessed the central contradictions of British war-making. The British state and its armed forces successfully met key challenges: blocking the French battle fleet, securing strategically important enemy colonies, defending Ireland, mobilizing substantial forces for home defence, and negotiating continental alliances. These challenges had similarly been addressed in 1793–98. But the first five years of renewed war witnessed only one major battle involving British forces. Despite the spectacular character of Trafalgar, that victory yielded a relatively small dividend compared with the impact on the naval balance of power exerted by the naval victories of 1793–98, when France and her allies were still competitive on the high seas. In fact, British success in 1803–08 lay within the global reach of her naval power and in the Royal Navy's destruction of French naval forces wherever they operated and upon whatever scale. The war for trade required and secured extensive and effective operations by frigates and smaller warships against the threat from French commerce raiding. The struggle to secure commercial sea routes and the failure to establish an enduring continental alliance led to a compromise effort to project British power in European waters. In 1803–08, the British secured a firmly-held base in the Mediterranean, starting with Malta and then supplementing it with a dominant presence in Sicily from 1806 to 1814. There was no repetition of the banishment from base to base suffered in 1796 and the retreat from the Mediterranean endured from late 1796 to mid-1798. The Mediterranean commitment flowed from a stake in the region's trade. But it was also aimed at shaping continental diplomacy. The resumption of war thus raised questions about how Britain would organize its defences and protect its interests and project its power.

The challenges of war

The renewal of war raised five immediate challenges. First, the navy was rapidly mobilized for extensive blockading. Given Bonaparte's ambitious plans for invasion, great pains were taken to prevent the concentration of the French fleet. By September 1804, Lord Keith commanded an extraordinary concentration of 218 warships and support vessels at the Downs, directly opposing the main concentrations of French troops at Calais, Ostend, Dunkirk, Boulogne, and Le Havre. The Channel fleet, under Lord Cornwallis's younger brother, William, had forty-four line ships with which to patrol the Atlantic approaches, bottle up the main French fleet at Brest, prevent a smaller French squadron from operating out of Rochefort, and watch over the Spanish Atlantic port of Ferrol.[2] These prolonged blockading operations, often in difficult conditions, demanded considerable organization, seamanship and application. To cope with these tasks and with the larger requirements of warring upon French trade, the navy grew from 388 vessels of all kinds in 1803 to 534 such craft by 1805. Most of this expansion – 118 out of 146 extra commissioned ships – comprised small warships, such as sloops, brigs, cutters, and so forth, while, for example, the number of ships of the line increased by only five, to 116 in 1805. Extensive activity at sea resulted in forty-seven ships being lost in the 19 months of war from May 1803 to the end of 1804, the overwhelming majority to storms, accidents and wreck. By contrast, Britain's French, Dutch and, from late 1804, Spanish opponents lost a total of 103 ships in that same period, the majority of them captured by the British. Of those, some thirty-three were in a suitable condition to be added to the Royal Navy, including twelve frigates to replace the eleven British frigates lost in those years. Although French ships seized were mostly very small warships, the damage inflicted on the French was extensive and extremely helpful to sustaining British morale. One notable confrontation occurred on 5 October 1804 when four frigates under the 32-year-old Captain John Gore (who had distinguished himself at Toulon in 1793 and as a frigate commander in the late 1790s) captured or destroyed four Spanish frigates returning home from Montevideo and seized about £1 million in treasure. The fact that Britain was not at that time yet at war with Spain did not deter the ministry from rewarding Gore with a knighthood for providing a particularly dramatic instalment in the long-running saga of successful frigate warfare.[3]

A second challenge was to strike blows against French colonial power. As soon as conflict started, George III urged that the army in the Leeward Islands conquer French West Indian islands. St Lucia, twice taken by the British in the 1790s, fell almost immediately. The next targets, however, were the Dutch possessions on the northern coast of South America. Demerara, Essequito and, a little later, Berbice were once again taken, their seizure being eased by the presence there of British property-holders and the fear among all property-holders of subordination to the French, since retaliatory British blockading would cripple their economies.[4] With news of such successes, the king particularly commended the local army and naval commanders 'for their preserving that unanimity in the two Services, on which principally depends the success of every enterprise'.[5] These gains were further extended by the British capture of the last Dutch South American colony, Surinam. By September 1804, the first cargo of coffee and cotton from Surinam reached England.[6]

The other main action taken against French colonies in 1803–04 involved Saint Domingue. The turmoil of the 1790s had left the island in the hands of Afro-Caribbean revolutionaries and the plantation economy in ruins. In 1801, Bonaparte took advantage of the peace to despatch a major expeditionary force to reassert French control of the western part of the island. Arriving there in February 1802, the French attempted to reconquer what had been, ten years earlier, a prize colonial possession. Once Britain went to war against France, she deployed warships from Jamaica to harry the French in and about Saint Domingue. Of the fifty-four French ships lost in 1803 alone, eighteen were lost at, or near, the island, including one line ship and five frigates.[7] By the beginning of 1804, the French were driven out, opening the way for the ex-slave revolutionaries to declare the formation of the empire of Haiti. *The Times* proclaimed the expulsion of the French as a significant triumph against Bonapartism:

Possessed as we are of such incontrovertible proofs of the union of the blackest perfidy with the most unbounded ambition in the mind of the French usurper, we cannot doubt but that a part of his plan was, by throwing in a number of troops sufficient to overwhelm all opposition, to obtain such a preponderance in the West Indies, as might enable him to seize our colonies, and those perhaps of every other European power.[8]

Altogether, the British declared French losses of some 50,000–60,000 men, almost entirely to disease, in their humiliation in Saint Domingue, thus adding to British success in Egypt (1801) in thwarting Bonapartist imperialism.[9]

In the south Atlantic, the reconquest of Cape Colony was readily achieved in January 1806. Part of the expeditionary force proceeded in June 1806, well beyond instructions, to Buenos Aires. This latter apparent sideshow boosted morale at home, leading *The Times* to praise the troops' impressive bravery and resolution and to predict that 'nothing but a speedy peace can prevent the whole of Spanish America from being . . . placed for ever under the protection of the British Empire'. The Spanish colonists would quickly embrace British rule, won over by the generous spirit of the British army, which eschewed the rampant plundering adopted by the French, and would in turn provide 'a never-failing market for our commodities'. Such ardour was dampened by the expedition's humiliating military failure in 1807.[10] Apart from targeting the Cape, ministers did not resume the Dundas strategy of seizing island colonies until 1809–10 when they took Martinique, Guadaloupe and Mauritius. The logistical effort involved 12,000 troops being despatched to Martinique, and 7,800 men being collected in 1810 from Halifax, Barbados, other Caribbean islands, and Portsmouth for the attack on Guadaloupe.[11]

A third challenge emerged in Ireland. Following the failure of the rebellion in 1798, the United Irishmen continued to work for the overthrow of British rule. No major build-up of discontent occurred in 1801–03, but exiles monitored the international situation and conditions within Ireland very closely. A number of key exiles returned to Ireland by January 1803 and planned a rising in the event of renewed war with France. During March–July about 30–40 men bought buildings in Dublin and acquired ammunition and the materials to make pikes, but secured no muskets or other guns. Their rising on 23 July focused on seizing Dublin Castle, the seat of government, but its organization proved abysmal. Despite the rising's failure, resulting in its leaders' arrest and execution, United Irishmen in exile continued to hope that a French invasion would trigger a widespread and effective popular rebellion against alien rule.[12] Bonaparte's ambitious plans for a cross-Channel invasion of southern England, elaborated from June 1803, were indeed supplemented by preparations for an invasion force to be shipped from Brest to Ireland. By September 1804, this planned force had grown to 18,000, with 25,000 men from the Texel in Holland somewhat fancifully added. But French ambitions to send reinforcements to the West Indies diluted the manpower available, while British naval pressure led in 1805 to French fleet activity being concentrated on protecting the forces assigned to the planned invasion of southern England.[13] By the spring of 1805, the prospects of any French invasion of Ireland had disappeared, and Trafalgar confirmed the improbability of any significant maritime expedition against Ireland being launched. From July 1803 to early 1805, however, the British government faced at least some concerns over the security of Ireland.

The resumption of war created a fourth challenge, that of mobilizing forces. In January 1803, the effective strength of the British army was 95,375 men, of whom 45,071 were stationed in the UK. The demands of home defence led to the immediate recall of the militia, with 58,559 men in place by July 1803. Troop numbers were steadily expanded during the rest of the year to bring the total army to 220,418 men by January 1804, of whom 174,380 were available to protect the British Isles. These forces were so widely dispersed that uncertainty remained as to their ability to combat a large French invading army, possibly of 120,000–150,000 troops. To meet the pressure on troop numbers, the ministry called for volunteers, raising some 380,000 men in Great Britain and a further 83,000 in Ireland by the end of 1803. This vast force certainly provided the numerical basis for counteracting any French invasion. Over time, however, volunteering could not be sustained on such a scale. When the returns on inspections of volunteers were completed in early 1806, most corps were deemed fit for military service but were below strength. For example, the Home District, covering Middlesex and surrounding areas, had 24,213 men present under arms against an establishment of 50,804. The recruitment drive raised some central issues about mobilization. Many argued that the different demands upon manpower – from the navy, the army, the militia, and the volunteers – created administrative misunderstanding and uncertainty. Others noted that the dependence upon parish officers for raising men for the militia exploited the voluntary work of local 'worthies' belonging to groups of employers – for example, farmers – who did not want to see workers leave for military service. Many rural officials asserted that recruitment was easier in manufacturing towns, where labour markets were far more fluid, workers were replaceable, and public office-holders had fewer qualms about enlisting men who might be their fellow-employers' workers. So while mobilization succeeded in 1803, strong doubts remained about labourers' and workers' willingness to join the army or meet the militia quotas in times when wages were high and labour was relatively scarce.[14]

The whole process of volunteering remained controversial. Experience in Ireland aroused scepticism about the political reliability of volunteer recruits and the extent to which they could be so trained as to acquire military values. Two key ministers, Lord Hobart, the Secretary of State for War and the Colonies, and a former senior army officer, and Charles Yorke, the Secretary at War, who was an active colonel of the

Cambridgeshire Regiment of Militia in 1803, remained doubtful about the military capability of volunteers.[15] Since volunteering, in reformers' eyes, promised to encourage wider political participation and representation, which would in turn further foster volunteering, conservative reservations arose from the political as well as military implications of this process.[16] Despite such reservations, men had to be found quickly when full-time and longer-term service in the militia sparked limited enthusiasm. The political case long made by Henry Dundas and William Pitt for the importance of volunteering as a way of fostering, channelling and demonstrating popular loyalty and nationalism remained compelling, despite contrary doubts about volunteers' potential radicalism. Pitt exploited the volunteer issue to revive his personal political fortunes in 1803. He threw himself enthusiastically into soldiering as commander of three battalions, totalling nearly 3,200 officers and men, raised in the Cinque Ports. At the same time, Dundas, now Lord Melville, commanded the three regiments of the East India Company volunteers, totalling 2,100 officers and men, in London. These were exceptionally large and highly visible commands for those ex-ministers to take.[17]

Despite continuing doubts about the military effectiveness of mass volunteering, the numbers raised were impressive and patriotic sentiment vigorous. While volunteering was rooted in the localities and linked to the leadership of the landed gentry and aristocracy, who disproportionately furnished volunteer units' commanding officers, participation in leadership involved about 16,600 men serving in 1803 as volunteer officers – in addition to officers in the army and militia – and nearly 15,000 men enrolling as sergeants in the task of making this vast organization operational.[18] This involvement demonstrated an unprecedented identification with the institutions of the state.

The final challenge of 1803 arose from the continent. Because the French enjoyed access to their client Batavian republic, or Holland, they forced their way readily into Germany and took over George III's electorate of Hanover. Britain remained helpless to counter that blow because French aggression in Germany failed to provoke either of the greater German powers – Austria and Prussia – to intervene in the war.[19] As Lord Cornwallis recognized in November 1802, a naval war unsupported by a continental ally would do nothing to advance Britain's aim 'to counteract the ambitious designs of France on the Continent, to play the game against Bonaparte which our ancestors did against Louis XIV'.[20] Rivalry between the two 'German' powers even encouraged the Prussians to see themselves as potential sharers in French spoils.[21]

As usual, it was Napoleon's geopolitical restlessness and inability to settle upon any form of international condominium which opened the way to a new coalition. Instead of abiding by the principle, which shaped the peace settlement of 1797, of giving Austria a leading role in Italy, the Emperor of the French decided in May 1805 to proclaim himself king of Italy. This was followed by an attack on Genoa, pushing Austria into an alliance which Russia had been seeking for some time and opening the continental front which Britain needed. Napoleon switched his invasion army from the Channel coast to an advance against Austria, thus changing the nature of the war. Although Austria was quickly defeated, Napoleon faced continental foes until July 1807.[22] But continental alliances, even when in place, left Britain semi-isolated because Austria, Prussia, and Russia had no interest whatsoever in assisting Britain or thwarting France in their naval and colonial ambitions and intensely distrusted each others' eastern European intentions.

The difficulty in building a viable coalition against Napoleon in 1805 resulted from a profound difference of objectives. Russia and Britain actively sought a coalition, but their plans hinged on Austria's supplying the majority of any grand coalition's troops. Pitt's ministry saw a potential reshaping of central Europe through the territorial strengthening of Prussia against France in north Germany and, possibly, in the former Austrian Netherlands. Austria would be compensated by gaining additional territories in Italy, thereby blocking Napoleonic expansionism in that direction. But such thinking did not appeal to Russia, which wanted to weaken Prussia, contain Austria, and create a federation of the other, minor, German states under its own protection. When the war of the Third Coalition began in 1805, Austria, supposedly about to bear the brunt of fighting against France, instead invaded Bavaria in order to extend its domains into southern Germany. Russia, wanting France contained in western Europe, intended also to extend its influence and interests against the Ottoman Empire in the east. Such divergent interests unsurprisingly weakened and then broke the Third Coalition. Austria's defeat in turn enabled Napoleon to create, in July 1806, a Confederation of the Rhine as a subservient organization of sixteen western and southern German states, including Bavaria, Württemberg and Baden, from which Austria and Prussia were excluded.[23] Once he won a short war against Prussia and forced Russia to peace settlement in 1807, Napoleon held a continental position far stronger than it had been in 1803–05, and Britain's quest for objectives seemed ever more hopeless. Grinding survival and peripheral pinpricks seemed the only options.

The Trafalgar campaign

There was, however, one major beacon in this environment of uncertainty, provided by the most celebrated naval victory in British history at Trafalgar. Given its significance in naval warfare and the importance attached to it in British geopolitical strategy, the battle and its impact require some assessment.

Trafalgar's most important consequence was the destruction of French ambitions to invade southern England. Against the continuing backdrop of mobilization and counter-mobilization, Bonaparte drew up four different invasion schemes in 1805, all of which required control of the Channel for at least a number of weeks. To that end, French naval strength, including the Mediterranean fleet based at Toulon, needed to be consolidated at the Channel. Once Spain entered the war in December 1804–January 1805, plans were drawn up for the Toulon fleet and French and Spanish squadrons from Ferrol to sail with the prevailing currents and winds to Martinique and then return across the Atlantic to cover the invasion of England from Boulogne. On 30 March Vice Admiral Pierre Villeneuve, an aristocrat who entered the navy in 1778 and escaped as a captain at Aboukir Bay, sailed from Toulon. Having collected a Spanish squadron under Admiral Don Federico Gravina at Cadiz, he reached Martinique on 16 May. When Villeneuve learned that Nelson, commanding the small British Mediterranean fleet, had arrived, in pursuit of him, at Barbados on 4 June, he sailed back to Europe. Nelson eventually gave chase, but made for southern Spain, whereas the Combined Fleet made for Spain's northern coast and Ferrol/La Corunna, which it reached on 2 August.

The Combined Fleet's return to Europe included an engagement which decisively shaped Villeneuve's and Nelson's thinking in the build-up to Trafalgar. On 22 July, some 117 miles from Ferrol, Villeneuve's fleet encountered a British fleet under Sir Robert Calder. The two fleets came upon each other during the late afternoon and evening, in fog which hung heavy in a light breeze, with the smoke of gunfire adding to the confusion. The six Spanish line ships in the combined fleet bore the brunt of the fighting and Villeneuve, having counter-manoeuvred effectively to nullify Calder's skilful dispositions, subsequently covered up the limited role taken by his twenty French ships of the line. Neither commander pressed for action the next day, when the two fleets drifted in light wind some 12–18 miles apart. On 24 July the fleets broke off, following their different courses. Although Calder captured two Spanish line ships, their advanced age and poor condition only underscored his failure to engage his opponents more energetically on the 24th. Despite the fact that Calder was heavily outnumbered, commanding only fifteen line ships, the British admiral later received a formal reprimand.[24] His 'failure' further fuelled the public appetite for the 'Nelson touch', which Nelson himself found burdensome as well as flattering. Having sailed 6,686 miles between 12 May and 18 July in the vain pursuit of Villeneuve, Nelson noted on the latter day, 'no French fleet, nor any information about them: how sorrowful this makes me'.[25] While Calder's limited action raised the public and private stakes for Nelson to achieve decisive results, it also prevented Villeneuve from sailing north to rendezvous with other French fleets, forcing him instead, after a brief sojourn on the northwest Spanish coast, to Cadiz and towards Nelson's and Vice Admiral Cuthbert Collingwood's squadrons.[26] On the other side, Villeneuve's lack of frankness in his brief and vague despatches on the engagement with Calder aroused Napoleon's distrust and disapproval, while his behaviour both during and after the engagement corroded such trust and confidence which the Spanish admirals had in the commander of the Combined Fleet.

By 14–15 August the relevant British forces – the Channel and Mediterranean fleets and Calder's squadron – concentrated off Ushant, commanding the sea approaches to France's principal naval port, Brest. But on 11 August Villeneuve sailed from northern Spain not towards the Channel but southwards to Cadiz, which he reached on 21 August. The British now covered a non-existent Franco-Spanish fleet concentration. Once the conclusion of an Anglo-Austrian alliance on 9 August confronted Napoleon with a major continental enemy for the first time in four years, Napoleon quit Boulogne on 26 August in order to attack Austria. To stiffen the pressure on Austria's position in northern Italy, Villeneuve was ordered in mid-September to prepare to return to the Mediterranean and blockade Genoa. At the end of September, following brief leave in England, Nelson resumed command of the Mediterranean fleet, now heavily reinforced, to prevent Villeneuve from sailing from Cadiz for the northern Mediterranean. Over the course of nine months, Nelson had thus worked through a full array of strategic scenarios, thinking that the French Mediterranean fleet had been directed against Egypt, chasing it to the Caribbean, pursuing it back to Spain, and now, off Cadiz, deploying to stop it operating upon the northern Italian coast.

Nelson conducted an extremely skilful blockade off Cadiz. He had consistently avoided close blockading, as practised by British fleets containing the French in Brest, in favour of looser, more distant surveillance

of enemy ports with the overriding aim of luring his opponent out to sea
and battle.[27] This entailed the risk that an opposing fleet would elude him
entirely, as happened at Toulon on a number of occasions. But only by
allowing the enemy out of safe harbours would Nelson have any chance of
destroying him. On 6 October, hoping for a major battle, he stressed that
'it is . . . annihilation that the Country wants, and not merely a splendid
Victory'. *The Times* had predicted in August that, if Villeneuve's twenty-
six line ships met Nelson and Collingwood en route to Cadiz, 'we see but
little chance that a single line-of-battle ship belonging to the Combined
Squadron shall be able to effect her escape'. Under such a weight of expectation that he would inevitably achieve a 'decisive' victory, Nelson craved
a crushing blow 'to bring Bonaparte to his marrow-bones'.[28] Concerned
at their Combined Fleet's deficiencies in armaments and manpower, the
senior French and Spanish naval commanders declined to sail for Italy
except under Napoleon's explicit orders. Yet, on 18 October, after learning that he was to be replaced, Villeneuve ordered his fleet to put to sea
and on 21 October, failing to make the Straits of Cadiz and the entrance
to the Mediterranean, placed his 33-strong fleet on a course directly
exposed to the approaching British fleet. The French commander-in-chief
understood Nelson's probable battle plan and his own instructions –
'The Captain who is not in action is not at his post' – mirrored Nelson's
celebrated order, 'No captain can do very wrong if he places his ship
alongside that of the enemy'.[29]

The British battle plan owed much to the pattern established informally at The Saintes in 1782 and attempted at the Glorious First of June
(1794) and St Vincent (1797). The Combined Fleet was stretched out from
north to south. Nelson and his deputy Collingwood each led a column of
line ships towards their enemy's line, with the deliberate intention of dis-
guising until the last moment the exact points which they would attack.[30]
Nelson hit the enemy line at the point where the twelfth and thirteenth
ships from the van, or head of the line, were positioned. Collingwood and
two more of his column hit a little earlier not far from Nelson's point of
attack and confronted only three enemy ships there. Most of the other
ships in Collingwood's column panned out to the south to attack ships in
the rear of the Combined Fleet. Thus, although the two British columns
advanced separately at right angles to the enemy line, they attacked so
close together that the Combined Fleet lost its numerical advantage.
Meanwhile, ten Franco-Spanish ships were sailing northwards away from
the fighting. Some of them were able to double back and enter the fray,
but only later in the battle. At the end of the day five of those line ships

reported slight, trivial or no casualties, as did another four allied ships, indicating that 27% of the allied fleet was scarcely engaged.

What followed was a mêlée battle lasting about five hours. Some British ships were incapacitated within two hours or so of the start of firing, but four others did not even become engaged in ship-to-ship duels until then. By 6.00 p.m. about half the British line were unable to continue any further action. The experience of battle varied widely. The two leading British flagships were among the four ships sustaining the heaviest British losses. Nelson himself was severely wounded very early in the action, dying below deck about three hours later. In contrast, eleven of the twenty-seven British line ships suffered little, with no more than 26 casualties in any one of them. But most warships at some time entered a fray where perhaps 2,500 to 3,000 naval guns were used in an area of about two or three square miles creating an unprecedented concentration of heavy gunnery.[31] (By comparison, a Napoleonic land battle brought together 400 guns from both sides.) Although the usual explanation for British success centres on their better guns and their rapidity and direction of fire, success flowed more precisely from intense spasms of concentrated gunnery at close range. For example, Villeneuve's flagship, *Bucentaure*, suffered its first broadside in the stern over three hours before it finally surrendered, following three more stern broadsides and attacks by five British ships resulting in nearly 450 casualties, or over half its men. Determined, close fighting led to the death or wounding of five of the seven admirals leading the Combined Fleet. At the end of the day, the British had captured seventeen enemy ships of the line and destroyed another, an unprecedented triumph in naval warfare.[32]

The impact of Trafalgar was immediate and considerable. A national day of thanksgiving occurred on 5 December and Nelson's burial in St Paul's Cathedral on 9 January provided one of the greatest pageants of nineteenth-century Britain, rivalled only by Wellington's funeral in 1852 and by Queen Victoria's Diamond Jubilee of 1897. Many other forms of commemoration followed, including public monuments and statues, although it was not until the late 1820s that Trafalgar Square was cleared and created, and in the late 1830s Nelson's column was erected at its centre. In 1806 the President of the Royal Academy, Benjamin West, painted a vast tableau of the death, in an imposing scene of fifty-eight figures variously depicted on *Victory*'s main deck. Some 30,000 people paid to view this spectacle at West's studio in the space of six months in 1806. The image of heroic self-sacrifice and a death experienced with dignity and in unison with God's will – however distant from the reality –

completely captured public attention. West reportedly stated, 'No Boy . . . wd. be animated by a representation of Nelson dying like an ordinary man, His feelings must be roused & His mind inflamed by a scene great & extraordinary'.[33] Coming at a time when the worst threat of possible invasion had lifted and Britain's isolation in fighting France had ended, Nelson's death acted as tragic catharsis for many people while also providing a potent boost to patriotic fervour.

Yet the battle's impact at the time and over the next decade or so was not clear-cut. First, British performance in battle was flawed by significant variations in gunnery and capacity to engage the enemy closely.[34] Second, on the night of 21 October a hurricane struck the scene of the battle and the accompanying storm, lasting seven days, forced Vice Admiral Collingwood to let go fourteen of his seventeen captured ships, most of which ran aground and were destroyed rather than being added to the Royal Navy. Moreover, the final tally of French, as distinct from Spanish, battle ships lost at Trafalgar was nine, two fewer than France lost at Aboukir Bay. Such losses were replaceable and a considerable French naval challenge remained.

Trafalgar's impact on the composition of the French battle fleet needs to be kept in context. The British took out more French line ships after Trafalgar than they did at the great battle; from 3 November 1805 to June 1808, the French lost another seventeen line ships in five different engagements or incidents.[35] Even so, Napoleon possessed eighty line ships in 1813 and had thirty-five more under construction. Meanwhile, the threat from French small warships and privateers increased substantially after Trafalgar, with British merchant ship losses rising from 387 in 1804 to 619 in 1810.[36] While Trafalgar ensured that no invasion could be mounted – a distant prospect anyway – and destroyed any likelihood that the French would ever again collect together a battle fleet to challenge a British fleet, the victory did not guarantee Britain command of the high seas. Many ordinary Britons engaged in the daily workings of commerce did not see Britannia readily ruling the waves after 1805. The struggle for such mastery was continuing and strenuous.

Moreover, Trafalgar capped a process, well under way in 1779–82, whereby the British imposed their superiority in great fleet battle. But it also closed a chapter in naval warfare since Britain never again fought a destructive sea battle; the only subsequent major battle at sea, Jutland in 1916, though its strategic consequences were important, was more of a manoeuvre encounter. The only two major naval engagements fought in the age of sail after 1805 were in-shore: the bombardment of Algiers in

1816 (when the British suffered heavy casualties in relation to the number of ships involved) and the battle against the Turks in Navarino Bay in 1827. If Trafalgar, as Professor Rodger stresses, confirmed British naval supremacy, it was a conditional supremacy which had constantly to be upheld.[37]

The truly significant follow-up to Trafalgar came through the widely diffused application of naval power and a reinvigorated British role in the Mediterranean. In January 1805 Nelson's Mediterranean command contained twelve line ships, deployed in small groups, and twenty-eight other warships. In July 1808 the Mediterranean fleet under Lord Collingwood included twenty-nine line ships and fifty-five other vessels. It worked constantly in promoting British interests and blockading the numerous ports controlled by France and its puppet states. It fought very little, however, for in his five years as commander-in-chief before his death in 1810, Collingwood engaged in only one action involving more than one ship. Yet, despite this lack of dramatic battles, the British continued to reduce the power and size of the French navy. Between November 1805 (after Trafalgar) and 1809 the French lost twenty-three line ships and thirty frigates in various actions and incidents across the world, more, that is, than they lost in Nelson's two annihilatory battles of Aboukir Bay and Trafalgar.[38] This activity merely maintained the existing pattern of naval warfare. Some 206 enemy frigates were captured by the British during 1793–1815. (That total nearly equalled the 217 new British frigates built in those years, although many captures were unfit for further service.) Trafalgar may have boosted fighting spirits, with the British seizing twenty-eight frigates in 1806 and 1807, but the peak years of frigate warfare had been in 1793–99 inclusive, when 106 enemy frigates, or fifteen a year on average, were added to the Royal Navy.[39] This broad-based and widely diffused patrolling and fighting efficiency – not the legacy or lessons of Trafalgar – constituted British naval power.

The Mediterranean

Trafalgar opened the way to British domination of the Mediterranean Sea if not its littoral. But the expectation was that a British presence in the Mediterranean would smooth the way to new coalition-building. Austria's entry into the war increased the strategic importance of the Mediterranean and the position accorded to Italy and especially Naples. From mid-1804 the diplomatic prospects for an Anglo-Russian alliance had improved. Both countries saw themselves as the arbiters of Europe's fate while recognizing that the bulk of any fighting to be done against France would be Austria's responsibility. Russia urged Britain to join it against the French in Naples in order to lever Austria into an alliance, as had happened, without Russian involvement, in so dramatically an ill-planned way in 1798–99. Eventually in July–August 1805, Russia and Britain settled upon an alliance, and Austria – with great reluctance and after an intense internal debate – agreed to join it. Britain and Russia would relieve pressure on Austria by sending forces to Naples where their presence would deter French troops based in central Italy from marching off to reinforce the army preparing to confront the Austrians in northern Italy.[40] In mid-September Napoleon decided to retain a military presence in central Italy and ordered Villeneuve, then at Cadiz, to re-enter the Mediterranean. But the Neapolitan government countered this threat by agreeing with France to stay neutral during the war. The neutrality sought by Queen Maria Carolina was privately not endorsed by her ministers and served only to stimulate the intervention of Russia and Britain in Neapolitan affairs. From their bases on Corfu and Malta respectively, the Russians and British landed over 18,000 troops in mainland Naples by November. But, as was so often the case when trying to counterbalance the Napoleonic juggernaut with thoughtfully deployed penny-packets of force, these interventions were rendered futile by the emperor's whirlwind attack on Austria. Defeated at Ulm, pushed from northern Italy by Masséna, and crushed at Austerlitz (2 December 1805), Austria settled with Napoleon without paying the slightest regard to Neapolitan concerns. Confronted by Austrian collapse, the commanders of the Anglo-Russian forces regret-fully concluded that 'their purpose in coming to Naples, which was to create a diversion in favour of the operations in North Italy, could no longer be fulfilled'. They evacuated mainland Naples in January 1806, followed by Ferdinand IV who returned to Palermo. As in 1799, the French pushed south, entered the city of Naples on 14 February, and remained there until the peace settlement of 1815. French rule drew many Neapolitans into policy-making and administration, ended feudalism, brought about land reforms which improved agriculture and strengthened land-owning aristocrats' and *bourgeois* interests. The peasantry, urban lazzaroni, and lower clergy did not, as they had in 1799, rise up to restore Bourbon reaction. The mainland population's great reluctance to respond to a call to arms provided another, compelling reason for a British with-drawal to Sicily.[41]

   The collapse of Naples meant that, within months of the destruction of the Combined Fleet at Trafalgar, the British position in the Mediterranean looked fragile, indeed worse than it had in 1799. The island of Menorca, well situated to enable naval blockading of Toulon and boasting an extremely secure harbour in Mahon, had been returned to Spain under the peace settlement of 1802. Malta was very distant for sustaining operations off the French coast; for that reason Nelson had impressed upon the prime minister in August 1805 that 'I cannot rest until the importance of Sardinia, in every point of view, is taken into consideration'.[42] Moreover, Malta depended for food supplies and other products on Sicily. With the French advancing southwards through mainland Naples, the Bourbon government allowed Lieutenant General Sir James Craig, insistent on Sicily's importance, to evacuate his army to the island.[43] When General Reynier reached the Straits of Messina on 25 March 1806, Craig's army of 8,000 men, together with a naval squadron, prevented a French invasion of the island.

These events led to Britain's domination over Sicily until the final settlement of 1815. Various diplomatic initiatives in 1806 showed that Sicily was by no means the Mediterranean base of first choice. If the British could have secured territorial compensation for Ferdinand in the Adriatic and naval bases on Sardinia and Menorca, they would have been content to give up the island. But no such deals were available. So, Sicily with its 1.5 million people, its poverty, its large feudal aristocracy, and its feeble armed forces, became, through sheer force of circumstances, the pivot of Britain's Mediterranean power. Although Palermo was too exposed to northerly onshore winds and too weakly fortified to serve as an effective naval base, the city, one of Europe's most populous, eventually prospered as a commercial centre for circumventing Napoleon's later Continental System, and the island supplied food for the naval base at Malta. Under Major Generals John Moore and John Sherbrooke, the British established an inland base in a strategically central and healthy position and built roads and forts to make it more accessible and defensible.[44] Its military significance grew rapidly. By January 1807 some 20,000 British troops were stationed on the island, compared with fewer than 7,000 at Gibraltar and 5,700 at Malta. Although the garrison's size fell after early 1807, a treaty in 1808 between Ferdinand and Britain stipulated it would be maintained at a minimum strength of 10,000 supplemented by a subsidy; the force rose again to 20,000 during 1810.[45]

The British did not rest entirely content with simply holding Sicily as a base. During the French takeover of mainland Naples in 1806, the British military commander, Major General Sir John Stuart, decided to cross from Sicily to the mainland in order to disrupt French operations in

Calabria. He tried to rouse the population to rise against the French, promising to respect their religious and civil laws and customs, to pay for all provisions, to provide arms and ammunition, and to protect the women from Gallic lechery. He also offered monetary rewards for all French prisoners brought to the British.[46] On 4 July the British marched upon a French force of over 6,000 men near the Maida River and, although outnumbered, took the initiative before General Reynier received reinforcements. For his part, the French general felt that his opponents offered an easy target and feared that they might withdraw unless he advanced upon them immediately. He therefore quit a good defensive position to assail a British force of 4,800 men. Partly as a result of timely reinforcement from the coast, the British eventually prevailed, gaining in reputation and capturing materiel for the loss of only 326 casualties.[47]

The battle has been cited as having greater significance than its small scale suggests was likely, for it foreshadowed the success of the British line and its volley-firing over the French column. But one officer present, Colonel Bunbury, does not describe anything approaching that level of coherence. The fighting almost took three different forms, with the classic ingredients of concentrated volley-firing and ferocious bayonet charging being more characteristic of the fighting on the French left than of the battle as a whole. At the centre, the British resorted to defensive squares and on the French right the British only seized the initiative through a vigorous flanking movement by a freshly arrived battalion.[48] What stood out from this engagement was the flexibility and variety of approaches adopted by brigade and battalion commanders who adapted to unfolding developments rather than enacted a master-plan. Ten 4-pounder field guns were distributed among four corps so as to be usable by the separate small brigades. The artillery reserve consisted of only six guns and howitzers. There was no cavalry for pursuit. Given such limited resources, officers conducted the fight rather as British naval officers engaged in mêlée battles, though without the scenario-planning provided by Nelson. For example, Lieutenant Colonel Robert Ross marched the 20th from the beach-head to stage a decisive flanking move, thereby demonstrating the value of the intensive training, involving exercises in the countryside of eight hours a day, which he had insisted on in Malta. Stuart in his despatch also specifically thanked the medical department for coping with so many French as well as British wounded, an indication of British humanity as well as effectiveness in inflicting such extensive injury upon their opponent.[49] This brief campaign demonstrated all those qualities of initiative, improvisation, daring and determination under fire which the

British informally nurtured in their peculiar brand of warfare by raids and incursions. The Secretary of State for War and the Colonies, William Windham, who had witnessed the campaign of 1793, told the House of Commons:

There never was an instance of a British army brought more fairly into contact with the enemy. There never was an action . . . that captured fairly the military character of the respective armies . . . If a set of philosophers had contrived the business, so as to set aside everything extraneous, and to place it on a fair trial of courage and prowess, they could not have contrived it better . . . at the moment of the trial, the resolution of our troops held out, while that of the enemy failed.

This dramatic example of British military capability, and the fear which advancing British soldiers instilled in the French, provided a wider lesson:

our enemies had worked themselves up to believe, and had endeavoured to persuade the world, that our military power was confined to operations by sea; that we were indeed great and powerful by sea, but by no means equally so by land . . . Glory is the only acquisition which nothing can ever take away. Ships, colonies, and increase of territory, which may be won in war, may on some other occasion be lost, but the recollection of glorious exploits can never be lost; it will be recollected in the history of the empire, it will live in the memories of future ages, and its effect will not be temporary but eternal.[50]

Sadly for Stuart, the Maida yielded little more substantial than glory when, unsupported by any popular rising, he was obliged to retire to Sicily. Two Sicilian garrisons were left in Calabria to help sustain the increased local guerrilla activity which Stuart's incursion had assisted. By the end of 1806, the French may have lost about 11,000–12,000 dead and wounded in the course of their operations in the kingdom of Naples. That was a sizeable depletion of manpower in relation to the scale of the British war effort; but, if it made the Neapolitan commitment demoralizing for French soldiers posted to Naples, it did not constitute a severe drain on Napoleon's vast manpower resources. The fundamental problem with Naples remained as it had been in 1793, when Britain sought troops from that kingdom to assist in the occupation of Toulon, and in 1798–99 when the Neapolitan army fell apart under a French counter-attack. For a country with the largest population of any single Italian state, there was no military tradition or capability worth tapping into. Napoleon warned that any Neapolitan troops raised by the French would prove worthless in war.[51] The British found no better prospects of recruitment in Sicily. During the summer of 1806 the Sicilian army fielded only about 6,000 men in serviceable condition (from a population of 1.5 million) and they were dismissed as of poor fighting calibre. No doubt morale was sapped by pay being customarily in arrears. More fundamentally, Sicily's nobility offered no social leadership to the army, having little interest in it as an institution or source of social or professional pride.

Yet, in the absence of alternatives, Sicily remained a vital asset. Its central position in the Mediterranean became even more important when Russia made peace with France in July 1807. Britain again stood alone against France and needed Sicily as a base to complement Malta in watching the French navy, blockading the Italian ports if necessary, and checking Russian ambitions in the eastern Mediterranean against the Ottoman Empire. As Napoleon tightened his Continental System in 1807 to exclude British trade from mainland Europe, so Sicily also proved useful as a centre for commercial activities beyond French control. The island was irritating enough for Napoleon to instruct Murat on taking power in Naples in August 1808: 'Threaten Sicily by all sorts of operations.'

By this time, Britain had committed 57,000 soldiers, sailors and marines to the Mediterranean. In the summer of 1808 the Mediterranean fleet accounted for eighty-four ships, including twenty-nine of the line, and nearly 28,000 seamen. The Mediterranean also absorbed nearly 30,000 troops, with Gibraltar and Malta each being garrisoned by about 5,000 men and 20,000 being based in Sicily. During 1808 some Whigs, inspired by ideas of Italian risings, pressed for military intervention to foster Italian unity. But Lieutenant General Sir John Stuart in Sicily insisted in August and September 1808 that any rising against the French in Italy depended on Spain's capacity to tie down French forces, and on Austria's resumption of war against France.[52] Collingwood, as naval commander-in-chief in the Mediterranean, dismissed any notion of an Italian rising: 'there is no stuff to work upon there – the people are licentious, the nobles unprincipled . . . It is a superior army alone that can effect any change, or maintain it . . . They have not the Spanish spirit.' The French in fact tightened their grip when Marshal Murat took over in Naples in September as Napoleon's new king, dampening any British enthusiasm for Italian landings and obliging the British to maintain a vigilant defence of Sicily.[53] If new prospects opened briefly in 1809, when Austria went to war and mounted diversions in Italy, Austria's defeat at Wagram and the possibility that the French Toulon fleet would become proactive, confined General Stuart to Sicily. The main British success in the Mediterranean theatre during 1809 was the capture in October of most of the Ionian Islands, which, since they 'covered' the entrance to the Adriatic Sea, gave the British a maritime counterweight to French control of the central Adriatic littoral of Dalmatia and Illyria. Possession of those islands also helped Britain block French moves towards Greece and later encouraged moves against the French in the region.[54] Yet this was a small return on the deployment of nearly 60,000 sailors and soldiers in the Mediterranean in 1808.

Conclusion

Nearer home, various options were tried in the Baltic Sea. Following the French victory at Austerlitz in December 1805 and Austria's subsequent withdrawal from the war, alliances with Prussia and Russia offered the prospect of denting Napoleon's efforts to control European trade, protecting an important source of naval supplies, and fostering Britain's trading interests in the Baltic. The aspiration was realized in 1806–07 when Prussia and Russia were again at war with France. In June–July 1807 Britain despatched troops to the Baltic to work with Sweden in league with the two greater powers. But Tsar Alexander's sudden settlement with Napoleon at Tilsit, on 25 June, weakened the potential alliance and Prussia's defeat and the subsequent evisceration of Prussian territory by the French destroyed it. France now controlled, or sought to control, much of the Baltic trade; Russia had to adhere to Napoleon's suppression of commercial ties with Britain, while the French took over the port of Danzig, the leading commercial conduit into former Poland and under Prussian control since the 1790s. To counter this new accession of French power, in July–August the government sent a fleet to Copenhagen to stop Denmark cooperating with France. With troops sent earlier to the Baltic joining the fleet at Copenhagen, the British bombarded the city on 2–5 September, forcing the Danes to surrender their fleet of fifteen ships of the line and minor vessels together with naval stores. This action yielded the Royal Navy more direct gains at lower cost than Trafalgar did: a supplement of four ships of the line, with the other eleven captured not being worth preparing for wartime service at sea.[55] Yet many – including George III – objected to the morality of the intervention, which had been pressed by the highly dynamic and ambitious Foreign Secretary, George Canning. The king reportedly told Canning, 'It is a very immoral act. So immoral that I won't ask who originated it' and argued that it would throw Denmark into a firm alliance with France.[56] Only the army and navy commanders on the spot persuaded the cabinet against establishing a permanent base in Zealand to shield Sweden against a possible French invasion. Instead, protection for Sweden was provided by a British financial subsidy and later, in 1808, when Russia invaded Swedish-ruled Finland, by 12,000 troops under Sir John Moore intended to free the Swedish army from responsibility for defending its southern region.[57]

Assessing the results of five years of war-making is complicated by the insistence of analysts of grand strategy that governments should have formulated clearer models of military and naval planning. Theoretical lines have been drawn from the late nineteenth century to stipulate that different approaches to strategic planning offered absolute alternatives. Should Britain have adhered rigorously to a continental commitment? Should naval strength have been directed more fully to dominating the Western Approaches to the English Channel and to the destruction of the French battle fleet? Should priority have been given to seizing and retaining the colonial possessions of Britain's enemies? The failure of successive governments to choose between such strategic alternatives is often seen as evidence of the intellectual flaccidity or political cowardice of the ruling establishment. The record from five years of war in 1803-08 appears to justify such criticism. Even the brutal splendour of Trafalgar scarcely compared with the varied achievements at St Vincent, Camperdown, Aboukir Bay, and Copenhagen in 1797-1801. Few long stretches of Great Power conflict have been waged with so limited an overarching offensive strategy and with such limited results as Britain manifested in 1803-08. Although the capture of islands often necessitated hard if limited fighting, the only unambiguous military successes achieved against France in 15 years of war, from early 1793 to 1808 (allowing two years of peace), were in small-scale engagements in Egypt in March 1801 and in Calabria, at the Maida in July 1806. The first, as we have seen, was won against a French army, led by a despised commander, which was demoralized, yearning for a return home and fearful of being exposed to the revenge of the local population. The second could not halt the French takeover of southern Naples, even though it prevented a French invasion of Sicily. Lord Castlereagh, on returning to office as Secretary of State for War and the Colonies in March 1807, opposed sending forces to assist continental allies because the army, in his view, was in poor condition, overstretched and under strength. If the cabinet decided to work with European allies, it did so in distinctly limited ways.[58] But, as this chapter has shown, Britain met a range of real challenges in those years and resisted France at the apogee of its continental power. The application of British power has to be seen in relation to the sheer might of Napoleon's France. Only when all three of the continental European powers had coalesced against France, only after Napoleon had lost about 600,000 men in the Russian campaign of 1812, and only when the continental powers' military muscle was supplemented by British, Portuguese and Spanish troops pressing the French hard in and from northern Spain, was Napoleonic France brought to its knees. There was little the British could do before a continental coalition emerged. Yet, despite Castlereagh's misgivings, Britain applied itself sedulously to the organization as well as the practice of war in these years. The number of muskets, carbines, rifles, and pistols supplied annually to the Ordnance rose from 181,000 in 1805 to 270,000 in 1809. In the two years to July 1810, Birmingham manufacturers supplied 1,045,000 barrels and locks for gun-making to the department. Contemporaries were impressed by the massive rise in annual expenditure by the Ordnance between the mid-1790s and 1806–10.[59] This represented a significant surge of military activity. That in turn reflected pressure to defend Britain's widely dispersed economic and political interests which, given the relative openness of the government system and of the public sphere in Britain, ministers in London had to meet. The profusion of objectives flowed from the diversity and wealth of the British economy and empire. To protect and advance those interests, the armed forces steadily built up an impressive record of achievement in naval actions across the world and in minor, but demanding, engagements on land. Those years demonstrated a widely diffused competence in military and naval operations as the British became indefatigable practitioners of small-scale warfare.

Notes and references

1 Paul W. Schroeder, *The Transformation of European Politics, 1763–1848* (Oxford, 1994), pp. 231–45.

2 N.A.M. Rodger, *The Command of the Ocean* (London, 2004), pp. 529–31; William Laird Clowes, *The Royal Navy: A History from the Earliest Times to the Present*, 7 vols (London, 1897–1903), Vol. V, p. 85.

3 Clowes, *The Royal Navy*, Vol. V, pp. 10, 350–51, 549–50, 555–56, 562, 564.

4 A. Aspinall (ed.), *The Later Correspondence of George III*, 5 vols (Cambridge, 1968), Vol. IV, pp. 94, 104, 116, 140–41.

5 Ibid, Vol. IV, p. 143.

6 *The Times*, 23 June 1804, p. 4, 22 September 1804, p. 3.

7 Clowes, *The Royal Navy*, Vol. V, pp. 555–56.

8 *The Times*, 28 January 1804, p. 2.

9 *The Times*, 28, 30 January 1804.

10 *The Times*, 15 September 1806, p. 2; Rory Muir, *Britain and the Defeat of Napoleon* (New Haven, CT, 1996), pp. 6–7.

11 *The Times*, 17 February 1809, p. 4, 5 February 1810, p. 3.

12 Marianne Elliott, *Partners in Revolution: The United Irishmen and France* (New Haven, CT, 1982), pp. 302–21.

13 *Ibid*, pp. 331, 338, 339–40.

14 *Further Papers . . . relating to the Additional Force Act* (House of Commons, London, 24 March 1806), pp. 17, 33–6, 70–1; *Returns . . . of the Volunteer Corps of Cavalry, Infantry and Artillery in Great Britain*, 26 March 1806; *Volunteers of the United Kingdom, 1803* (House of Commons, London, 9 and 13 December, 1803), pp. 65, 100–01.

15 J.E. Cookson, *The British Armed Nation, 1793–1815* (Oxford, 1997), p. 75; Aspinall (ed.), *The Later Correspondence of George III*, Vol. IV, p. 114.

16 Brendan Simms, 'Reform in Britain and Prussia, 1797–1815: (confessional) fiscal-military state and military-agrarian complex' in T.C.W. Blanning and Peter Wende (eds), *Reform in Great Britain and Germany 1750–1850* (Oxford, 1999), pp. 79–100.

17 For an excellent analysis, see Cookson, *The British Armed Nation*, pp. 68–71; *Volunteers of the United Kingdom, 1803* (House of Commons, London, 9 and 13 December 1803), pp. 7, 36–7.

18 *Volunteers of the United Kingdom, 1803* (House of Commons, London, 9 and 13 December 1803), p. 65.

19 Christopher Hall, *British Strategy in the Napoleonic War, 1803–15* (Manchester, 1992), p. 107.

20 Charles Ross (ed.), *Correspondence of Charles, First Marquis Cornwallis*, 3 vols (London, 1859), Vol. III, p. 496.

21 Schroeder, *The Transformation of European Politics*, p. 255.

22 Hall, *British Strategy*, pp. 107, 115; Schroeder, *The Transformation of European Politics*, pp. 253–55.

23 Schroeder, *The Transformation of European Politics*, pp. 260–64, 273–5, 291.

24 Nicholas Tracy, 'Sir Robert Calder's action', *Mariner's Mirror*, Vol. 77 (1991), 259–70; Nicholas Tracy, 'Sir Robert Calder, 1745–1810' in Peter Le Fevre and Richard Harding (eds), *British Admirals of the Napoleonic Wars: The Contemporaries of Nelson* (London, 2005), pp. 197–218; Alan Schom, *Trafalgar: Countdown to Battle 1803–05* (London, 1990 edn), pp. 229–37, 240–41.

25 Edgar Vincent, *Nelson: Love and Fame* (New Haven, CT, 2003), pp. 547–51.

26 *The Times*, 5 August 1805, p. 2; 8 August 1805, p. 2.

27 Colin White, 'The Mediterranean Command 1803–05', *Mariner's Mirror*, Vol. 91 (2005).

28 Nicholas Harris Nicholas (ed.), *The Dispatches and Letters of Vice Admiral Lord Viscount Nelson*, 7 vols (London, 1997 edn), Vol. VII, p. 80; *The Times*, 5 August 1805, p. 2; 10 August 1805, p. 2.

29 Schom, *Trafalgar*, pp. 302–05, 308–10, 313–14, 348, 354.

30 There is a good, succinct analysis in Marianne Czisnik, *Horatio Nelson: A Controversial Hero* (London, 2005), pp. 33–41.

31 Available guns totalled 2,568 in the Combined Fleet and 2,148 in Nelson's fleet. Schom, *Trafalgar*, p. 315.

32 Schom, *Trafalgar*, pp. 334, 378–89.

33 Helmut von Erffa and Allen Staley, *The Paintings of Benjamin West* (New Haven, CT, 1986), pp. 221–22.

34 Michael Duffy, ' "All was hushed up": The hidden Trafalgar', *Mariners' Mirror*, Vol. 91 (2005), 216–40.

35 Lists are in Clowes, *The Royal Navy*, Vol. V, p. 555–56.

36 Jan S. Breemer, 'The burden of Trafalgar: Decisive battle and naval strategic expectations on the eve of World War I' in Geoffrey Till (ed.), *Seapower: Theory and Practice* (London, 1994), pp. 33–62. Rodger stresses that the rebuilding programme produced only poor quality warships. Rodger, *Command of the Ocean*, p. 562. For further assessments, see David Cannadine (ed.), *Trafalgar in History: A Battle and Its Afterlife* (Basingstoke, 2006).

37 Rodger, *Command of the Ocean*, p. 543.

38 Piers Mackesy, *The War in the Mediterranean, 1803–1810* (London, 1957), p. 398; Clowes, *The Royal Navy*, Vol. V, p. 555.

39 Paul Webb, 'The frigate situation of the Royal Navy 1793–1815', *Mariner's Mirror*, 82 (1996), 28–40.

40 Schroeder, *The Transformation of European Politics*, pp. 256, 262–67, 272–75.

41 Sir Henry Bunbury, *Narratives of Some Passages in the Great War with France (1799–1810)* (London, 1927), p. 280.

42 Nicholas (ed.), *Nelson Letters*, Vol. VII, p. 20.

43 Bunbury, *Narratives*, pp. 287–91.

44 Bunbury, *Narratives*, pp. 212–14, 218.

45 Mackesy, *War in the Mediterranean*, p. 16, Appendix; Harold Acton, *The Bourbons of Naples (1734–1825)* (London, 1956), p. 561.

46 *The Times*, 6 September 1806, p. 2.

47 Mackesy, *War in the Mediterranean*, pp. 131–39. The numbers present are from Stuart's despatch. *The Times*, 5 September 1806, p. 3.

48 Bunbury, *Narratives*, pp. 162–70.

49 B. Smyth, *History of the XX Regiment, 1688–1888* (London, 1889), p. 114; *The Times*, 5 September 1806, p. 3. Wellington after Badajoz in April 1812 is usually credited with the first ever mention of the medical service in despatches. Lieutenant General Sir Neil Cantlie, *A History of the Army Medical Department*, 2 vols (Edinburgh, 1974), Vol. I, p. 343.

50 *The Times*, 23 December 1806, p. 4.

51 Acton, *The Bourbons of Naples*, p. 561.

52 Mackesy, *War in the Mediterranean*, pp. 398–99.

53 *Ibid*, pp. 288–89, 291–93.

54 Muir, *Britain and the Defeat of Napoleon*, pp. 163–64, 170–71.

55 Muir, *Britain and the Defeat of Napoleon*, pp. 22–4; Clowes, *The Royal Navy*, Vol. V, pp. 209–16.

56 Aspinall (ed.), *The Later Correspondence of George III*, Vol. IV: 607 (n.): King to Castlereagh, 18 July 1807.

57 Muir, *Britain and the Defeat of Napoleon*, pp. 25–6.

58 Muir, *Britain and the Defeat of Napoleon*, pp. 15, 42.

59 'The Fifteenth Report of the Commissioners of Military Enquiry: Ordnance', *Reports from Commissioners*, Session 1 November–24 July 1810–11 (London, 1811), Vol. IV, p. 383; 'The Thirteenth report' *ibid.*, p. 5.

CHAPTER 11

The Iberian peninsula commitment 1808–12

The most important shift of focus in Britain's long wars against France came about by stages and remained subject to regular review. The British first sent forces to Portugal in the summer of 1808, drawing them from Sweden and Ireland with some personnel going from Gibraltar. A substantial re-engagement occurred in spring 1809. But ministers continued into 1811 to offer the local commander, if hard-pressed, the option of evacuation. Although one of the most important mainstays of the British intervention remained government commitment to it, that commitment was always measured rather than absolute. The key principles behind the British presence were a combination of optimism that the Portuguese would actively support a British army in their midst, that the Spanish would fight the occupying French, and that the French forces in Spain were at the end of their lines of communication, reinforcement, and supply and were far more vulnerable to British intervention than they would be elsewhere in continental Europe. Initially at least, it was unclear whether operations in the Iberian peninsula would have precedence over the British commitment to Sicily and draw men from that island into Portugal and especially Spain. Nor was it clear whether the British in Iberia would play a significant fighting role in defeating the French, as distinct from a supporting role in assisting the Spanish to exhaust and reduce the French invading army. For some British commentators, British troops would add peripheral pressure to a widespread Spanish uprising against Napoleonic despotism. Very few, if any, observers or policy-makers envisaged in 1808 or 1809 that Britain would fulfil a prominent military part in the war for the peninsula or that the peninsular campaign would later take on mythic status in the history of British warfare. The war, therefore, needs to be examined in relation to the nature and scale of the British commitment, and in relation to what effect British intervention had and how well the British developed their military capability.

The defence of Portugal

Britain's military commitment to the Iberian peninsula started as another relatively minor and reactive sideshow. Nothing in its beginnings indicated that the involvement would lead to a war which became from the 1820s more commemorated and celebrated in writing than any previous British conflict and which remains probably the 'British' pre-twentieth-century war most familiar to British military history aficionados. Britain's priority from November 1807 until April 1811 was to defend Portugal. The salvation of Spain became a spin-off, albeit a largely welcome one, from that primary objective. Despite the image developed of British involvement in a prolonged military struggle in Spain, the British conducted an extensive war within that country only from January 1812 to September 1813.

Portugal suddenly loomed large in late 1807 when Napoleon insisted on drawing it into his Continental System of trade restrictions against British commerce. He also wished to use a Franco-Spanish invasion of Portugal as a means of extending his control over Spain which, in his eyes, was proving an increasingly unreliable ally. In October 1807, French troops crossed Spain and marched into Portugal, while Charles IV of Spain pledged 27,000 Spanish troops to join that attack, providing slightly more men than the French themselves. Additional French troops proceeded into northern Spain as reinforcements for the army occupying Portugal, and these took over key towns in northern Spain in February–March 1808. French leverage grew further when Marshal Joachim Murat entered Madrid with 20,000 troops in late March.[1]

The British responded actively, if at the periphery, to the French conquest of Portugal and incursion into Spain between October 1807 and March 1808. They initiated four measures. The Royal Navy assisted the escape of the Portuguese king and his court, together with 8,000–15,000 people, vast treasure, and half the country's money in circulation, on 25 November 1807. This massive armada sailed to Brazil just ahead of the French army's entry into Lisbon. Once ensconced in Brazil, the Portuguese government opened the colony's overseas trade, previously channelled solely through the home country, to British merchants. Whereas British exports to Portugal totalled £811,000 in 1808, they exceeded £2 million to Brazil in 1812.[2] Further to protect their trade, the British in December 1807 took over the Atlantic island of Madeira to hold it as long as France threatened the island's Portuguese rulers. The government simply diverted reinforcements intended for Halifax (Nova Scotia) and India to furnish a small invasion force.[3] Thirdly, in late February 1808, some 5,000 British troops sailed for Gibraltar. Attempts to deploy this force on active operations by landing it at, for example occupied Lisbon or Port Mahon in Menorca failed. Finally, in late April 1808, as French interference in Spain burgeoned, the cabinet decided to send a small army to South America to support anti-Spanish risings there and to prevent a French takeover of the Spanish Empire. These piecemeal initiatives offered no strategy for the liberation of Portugal, but they showed how widely distributed projections of power were coordinated in order to counteract Napoleon's seizure of that country.

A political transformation in Spain in May 1808 stimulated British hopes that the peninsula might offer the occasion for a blow against French ambitions. A combination of rioting in Madrid and Napoleon's political machinations at Bayonne led to French military suppression of the city and the emperor's despatching his brother Joseph to replace the Bourbons as king of Spain. Yet the rising which triggered the French seizure of power spread rapidly. British delight at this turn of events flowed from the gloom widely felt in Britain at the extent of Napoleon's achievements in 1805–07. The emperor had forced the Austrians to come to terms for the third time in ten years and then in 1807 had spectacularly crushed Prussia, a state whose military power and territorial extent had expanded beyond recognition from the 1740s to 1795. That expansion was reversed, with Prussia being reduced to lands containing 4.9 million people instead of a kingdom of 9.7 million to which it had grown. Its army and revenues were slashed, and it was forced to maintain a large French army on its remaining soil.[4] Compared to these apparently craven capitulations, the resistance in Spain, a country not considered in remotely the same military light as late-eighteenth-century Prussia had been, offered sudden and welcome relief to those in Britain who despaired at the oppressive scale of French military and political power.

The British response was immediate but uncertainly directed. British representatives in Spain were instructed in May to encourage Spanish resistance without committing Britain to aiding it. Reinforcements joined the mobile force of 5,000 troops sent in February to Gibraltar. The cabinet focused British influence on Cadiz, as a rallying point for Spanish patriots or as an exit point for their escape to South America. If resistance in southern Spain collapsed, this British force would proceed to South America to ensure the exclusion of the French from that colonial cornucopia, for Cadiz accounted for over 75% of Spain's trade with South America.[5] Yet commercial motives did not dominate the cabinet's strategic assessments. For example, when delegates from the Asturias and Galicia eventually reached London in June, the cabinet exploited popular enthusiasm for the Spanish cause by proposing that the British intervene in northern Spain. Yet both delegations opposed such a move. The Galicians in response pressed the option of a British expedition to Portugal, an option made more attractive by the recent reduction in the size of the French army there. The government decided on 30 June to despatch a force to Lisbon. This, the most heavily populated city in the peninsula, with about 180,000 people, was splendidly placed on a broad basin of the Tagus River, which provided a substantial expanse of anchorage protected from the open sea. It was the world's leading port directly on the Atlantic Ocean.

Recapturing Lisbon was fundamental to the entire subsequent conflict in the peninsula. The Tagus basin and Lisbon became the principal entry point for the British war effort in the peninsula well into 1813. The city provided the food markets and mercantile and financial infrastructure to support the complex needs of the British military forces sent through it and furnished an ample base for the naval squadron stationed there. In effect, though not self-consciously, the British replicated their set-up in North America when in 1776 they captured New York City and then used it as their command and logistical base for the rest of the war.

While the decision to recover Portugal was to shape the entire strategy and much of the character of the operations undertaken by the British in 1808-11, the Portuguese commitment was made possible by an explosion of successful Spanish resistance to the French putsch. Ministers persistently saw this new commitment to the peninsula as a means of fostering risings elsewhere on the continent.[6] Meanwhile, on 14 June, the Spanish gained their first victory when a French fleet, blockaded by the British in the bay of Cadiz, surrendered with 3,566 men and 442 guns after being bombarded by Spanish naval and shore artillery. In late June, French soldiers failed to take Gerona, on the north-eastern road from France into Catalonia, and were forced to retire to an enclave in and around Barcelona. On 28 June, Marshal Moncey was forced to withdraw from besieging Valencia, a leading Mediterranean port and one of Spain's three principal cities after Madrid. In the south, General Dupont, having taken and sacked Cordova, returned northwards, leaving the large, heavily populated and agriculturally wealthy province of Andalucia untouched by the French. Pursued and hemmed in by Andalucian forces, Dupont surrendered his army of 17,635 men at Bailen on 23 July.[7] And on 14 August, the army which thought it could overwhelm Zaragoza, the capital of Aragon, withdrew, having lost 3,350 casualties in the first siege of that city lasting two months and being obliged to leave behind fifty-four guns.[8] Five French reverses in two months may not have been unprecedented; but they were dramatic, unexpected and threw the French conquest of Spain into doubt.

While exciting if ill-coordinated events were proceeding in Spain, the British rapidly put together a new expeditionary force for the liberation of Portugal. Some 11,000 men sailed from Cork on 12 July. Another 5,000 were to join from the force sent to Gibraltar earlier in the year, while a further 10,000 men were to be transferred, under Sir John Moore's command, from southern Sweden. Assembling an army from such widely dispersed forces was itself something of a logistical triumph. The acting commander, in charge of the troops from Cork, was Sir Arthur Wellesley. He landed his force, joined temporarily by the 5,000 men from Gibraltar, at Mondego Bay, on the Atlantic coast between Oporto and Lisbon, about as far west of the Spanish rising as he could be. It took eight days to get the total of 16,400 men ashore and, once there, the British obtained limited assistance from the Portuguese. The last occasions when the British had so landed on distant shores in close vicinity to the enemy had been at Aboukir Bay in March 1801 and at the Maida in July 1806. Wellesley followed these precedents and pressed straight into action. He proved lucky in that, after a very hard fought if small-scale engagement at Rolica, he was attacked by a French division of only about 13,000 against his own force of 17,000 at Vimiero on 21 August. Wellesley already knew of the defeat inflicted on an isolated French division at Bailen in southern Spain, and his eagerness to advance from his beachhead may have been influenced by this news.

The victory at Vimiero led to the negotiation of a highly controversial French withdrawal. Following the battle, Wellesley was superseded in active command by his senior commanders who refused to authorize any pursuit of the retreating French, preferring instead to allow the evacuation of a French army of 25,000 troops in Portugal under terms agreed in the Convention of Cintra. Critics of this settlement, which enabled the French to extract substantial booty and plunder as personal effects from Portugal, correctly stressed the depth of distrust of the British which this action implanted in the Portuguese. But critics erred in exaggerating the ease of driving the French from that country. Men and horses needed time to acclimatize to new conditions, especially after the confinement of a long sea journey, which in this case took three to four weeks. The first contingent of reinforcements spent five days on board ship in Mondego Bay because the surf rose too high to enable them to land.[9] The severe difficulties horses encountered when they landed – in terms of acclimatization and in getting accustomed to new forage – were noted of the Corunna campaign later in the year.[10] At home, ministers responded to public anger at the generous terms accorded the French by instigating a Court of Inquiry. A public row ensued between the three generals involved, with Arthur Wellesley blaming his seniors for their failure to grasp the opportunities for a swift, complete victory which his actions up to Vimiero had allegedly created. The decision at Cintra and its vindication in turn by the court of inquiry fuelled radical attacks on the alleged incompetence of British generals and their dependence for place upon a corrupt oligarchy. Popular support for Spanish freedom committed British radicals to the Peninsular War but called into question the effectiveness of the military instrument being used to attain British objectives.[11] Thus the first victory against a major French army soon degenerated into ritual disparagement of British military incompetence.

With the three principal generals in Portugal summoned back to Britain to defend themselves over Cintra, the command fell upon Lieutenant General Sir John Moore. Probably the most celebrated of contemporary generals, with a fighting career spanning America, Corsica, the West Indies, Ireland, Holland and Egypt, Moore was distrusted and disliked by the cabinet. But with Spanish resistance proving vigorous and successful, Moore had a golden opportunity to assist the Spanish rising and to restore the reputation of the British army at home. The British poured war materiel into Spain, with 155 artillery pieces and 200,227 muskets being sent between May 1808 and May 1809.[12] This aid was followed by an attempted concentration of forces at a suitable port on the north-west Spanish coast. Sir David Baird, a highly experienced fighter, sailed with 10,000 men from Falmouth but, ominously for future allied cooperation, had to wait ten days after arriving on 13 October at La Coruña before the Spanish even gave him permission to land. Moore decided, against his instructions from London, not to sail from Portugal to Coruña but, in a classic failure to maintain close coordination, to march across Portugal, enter Spain and wait at Salamanca for Baird. Instead of conducting operations in Galicia, inland from Coruña, as ministers intended, Moore plunged deep into the interior and expected Baird to complete a long march in order to join him. He proceeded on this highly risky course with very few cavalry, to act as his army's eyes and ears and to protect its flanks. Worse, his army fell far short of the 60,000 men which, for example, the Duke of York, as commander-in-chief, had asserted was the minimum required for a viable force.

Strategically flawed, Moore's plans fell further into disarray when Napoleon, reacting to the surrender of over 50,000 men in six weeks at Bailen and by the Convention of Cintra, completed a truly massive deployment of 279,000 troops into Spain, and entered the country to take personal charge of operations. With French pressure mounting, Moore decided to move northwards from Salamanca on 11 December and draw parts of Napoleon's striking force far to the north-west and well away from the southerly line of advance either into Portugal, or towards south-central Spain. Within weeks, the French had committed some 52,000 men to a counteroffensive which forced Moore into a withdrawal to La Coruña. Although the weather was often bad, the road system of Galicia was sound and the British came under fire from the French for only part of the 270 miles of their retreat. Moore's army made good progress, but the pursuing French marched much faster. One criticism was that Moore lost his composure and self-confidence in high command and failed to take a grip on his army. He failed to rally his men by staging defensive stands or even counterblows against the advancing French, as Soult by contrast was to do in withdrawing before Wellington in 1813–14. Once retreat became headlong, discipline broke and much of the army degenerated into a rabble.[13] Yet, on reaching La Coruña, Moore gave battle to cover his army's embarkation, at last restoring cohesion to his force, and held off Soult for long enough for the army to board their transports home. Moore was killed by round shot and brought forth an encomium that has resonated through the folklore of military heroism. Moore's admirer William Napier, both a Peninsula War officer and the author of a six-volume history of the war wrote of 'a man whose uncommon capacity was sustained by the purest virtue, and governed by a disinterested patriotism more in keeping with the primitive than the luxurious age of a great nation'.[14]

After this desperate, dramatic retreat, the British evacuated 28,732 officers, men and support staff from La Coruña. A tense touch-and-go retreat, a theatrical death, and a back-to-the-sea withdrawal seemed to provide a model for one significant mode in the British conduct of war. But of the force as organized in October, an estimated 3,800 men died in action, or on the march, or in hospital, and another 2,200 fell prisoner to the French by the time the evacuation occurred. Since horses and mules could not be evacuated, thousands were shot or had their throats cut, reducing the town to a 'vast slaughter-house' and bringing the total of such animals lost in the retreat to about 5,000.[15] When the tattered and often emaciated soldiers returned to southern England, their condition and plight dented popular enthusiasm for the war. Moore, possibly the most overtly 'professional' British general, had singularly failed to restore public confidence in the army's efficiency and fighting capacity.

The British intervention from August 1808 to January 1809 had a disputable impact on the conflict in Spain. The Coruña campaign has fared less badly in hindsight than might have been expected. According to David Chandler, it 'in effect, earned a full year's respite for southern Spain and Portugal' and, in David Gates' view, 'irretrievably shattered Napoleon's reconquest of Portugal'.[16] These claims hinge on Moore's impact in distracting a large French striking force, which might otherwise have entered Portugal, into marching into north-west Spain from 21 December. Yet Napoleon grossly minimized the difficulties of controlling this heavily populated region anyway. Nor did the 'diversion' of French forces – which might have been required without Moore's campaign – prevent the French from returning to northern Portugal within six weeks of Corunna. Only the reappearance of Wellesley, with a new army, drove Soult from northern Portugal in May 1809. Moreover, the vital role assigned to Moore underplays the continuing range of Spanish military resistance to the French. Seven Spanish armies, marshalling 161,000 men, were operational in the autumn of 1808 and posed an immediate threat to the French until defeated at Ucles on 13 January 1809 and at Medellin on 28 March. In addition, a French army of 44,500 with 144 guns was pinned down at the ferociously contested second siege of Zaragosa from 20 December 1808 to 20 February 1809 in the most extraordinary urban resistance to French invasion that Europe had witnessed.[17] It is a little hard on the Spanish to insist that Moore's 30,000 men and sixty-six guns saved southern Spain and Portugal while they staged such extensive resistance.

Renewed commitment in 1809

Just as the initial decision in 1808 to send troops to the peninsula emerged from a sense of British relief that France was at last taking a severe blow in its continental expansionism, so the decision in March 1809 to re-enter Portugal in force was made when the British government hoped that the war was to become far more widespread. The war party's return to the ascendancy in Vienna revived prospects of Austria's again taking up arms against France. From early April to early July 1809, the British pumped nearly £1.2 million in subsidies into Austria, while Vienna in turn pressed for British action in the peninsula and in north Germany. Initially the British rejected a plan to attack Antwerp and the Scheldt. The cabinet only agreed to an expedition to the Low Countries after Austria defeated the French at Aspern-Essling. As for the peninsula, the British preferred Cadiz as their centre of operations in Spain. The Spanish authorities declined British military reinforcement, since Cadiz and Andalucia faced no French threat in early 1809, and since the British were suspected of wanting to expand their influence from Gibraltar across southern Spain and to expand their trade with Spanish America. This response, together with the reversal at La Coruña and general disappointment with Spanish military competence, stiffened British scepticism in early 1809 about the Spanish entanglement. But the cabinet eventually, after much debate, decided to reinforce Britain's position in Portugal, where about 5,000–7,000 troops had remained when Moore led his army into Galicia.

The renewed involvement in the peninsula looked in retrospect more permanent than was initially intended. Greater permanence occurred partly because the British took over important functions of the Portuguese state. Continuity was provided because responsibility for the campaign was assigned in February and March 1809 to two British generals who retained their positions until the end of the war. William Carr Beresford took over command of the Portuguese army and Arthur Wellesley was appointed to command British forces in Portugal. The semi-colonial relationship these commanders proceeded to establish with the Portuguese government sat easily with their status and worldview as sons of Anglo-Irish landowning peers. The two appointments were closely linked, since the British sought to shape Portuguese policy and rebuild the Portuguese army to such a point as would enable them to forge a major Anglo-Portuguese fighting force for deployment, if occasion arose, in Spain. The application of such force was left very much to Wellesley's discretion. Lord Liverpool, as Secretary of War and the Colonies, laid out the position for Arthur Wellesley in 1809, at the time when the general's elder brother served as diplomatic representative to the junta:

I trust you will be satisfied with the large discretionary powers which have been recently sent to Lord Wellesley and yourself. You on the spot can alone only estimate the ultimate chances of success in Spain; we know you will estimate them dispassionately; and it is therefore properly left to your discretion to follow up your advantages or to extricate yourself from your difficulties, as the aspect of affairs in the Peninsula may appear to render most prudent and advisable.[18]

Because the Spanish opposed a British garrison being stationed at Cadiz, the ministry placed its whole disposable force in Portugal. Lieutenant General Wellesley had first to decide whether the manpower available to him would enable the British to advance into Spain and even to drive the French from Spain, or whether it was only sufficient to defend Portugal. If Wellesley concluded that he could indeed mount offensive operations in Spain, he was asked next to consider his requirements for cooperation with the Spanish.[19] London in 1809 remained intent on establishing a British garrison at Cadiz, partly to ensure that captured Spanish and French warships there would not fall into the hands of any invading French army, and partly to provide a base if the British were driven south-wards in that direction by a future French counter offensive.

Given this local accretion of manpower, and given Austria's entry into the war, the cabinet in June authorized Wellesley to advance into Spain if conditions justified such a movement. The general believed that he would advance up the Tagus valley and, in combination with the Spanish armies, clear the French from the central region around Madrid. This highly ambitious strategy failed completely. In 1809 Wellesley's first expedition into Spain – admittedly in the face of far more numerous French forces that were present the previous year – lasted, in effect, for one month from his army's departure from Abrantes on 28 June to the battle of Talavera, 75 miles from Madrid, on 28 July. Wellesley hoped to descend rapidly upon Marshal Victor's army stationed on the Tagus River and defeat him in detail, relying on the cooperation and agility of General Cuesta and his substantial army of Estremadura. The campaign foundered because Cuesta, distrusting Wellesley, hesitated to act decisively at critical moments and because the Spanish government refused to endanger its army of La Mancha by committing it to operations to keep French armies apart. The Spanish authorities wanted to preserve that army to check Cuesta's power and ambition. Thus, Wellesley, with nearly 21,000 British and German troops and Cuesta's 32,000, did not enjoy the decisive superiority of num-bers at Talavera which he had anticipated.

Talavera, where over 100,000 troops gathered for combat, was the greatest battle the British had been involved in since the long wars with France began in 1793. Fought over two days, the British defended their position from repeated French assaults, but at the cost of very heavy casualties in key sectors of the British line. The British force, mauled by massive casualties and debilitated on 29 July by lack of food and medical supplies, was obliged to withdraw in the face of mounting threats from large-scale French troop movements. During August, the British retired

200 miles to the south-west and a position inside the Spanish border, from where, in December 1809, after months of inactivity, they slipped back to Portugal.

Although Talavera was hailed as a major victory, with Wellesley becoming Viscount Wellington, its aftermath was dire. Half the 4,000 British wounded were eventually captured by the French or died in the British retreat, in which the victorious British general was reduced to despair at his inability to secure transport carts. Wellesley's losses could not be readily replaced. The withdrawal to the frontier, compounding Austria's capitulation to France in July, led to a critical strategic evaluation in September 1809. When ministers in London asked what a British army of 30,000 men could achieve in the peninsula, Wellington insisted that, while the Portuguese border could not be defended, the enclave around Lisbon could be. If local political pressure delayed his pulling out of borderland Spain in the autumn of 1809, Wellington concentrated essentially on defending Portugal and indeed hardly played any significant aggressive role in the war for the next two years.

Wellington's withdrawal to the Spanish borderlands coincided with the last major Spanish campaigns for many years. The French repelled Spanish attempts to free Madrid. The army of La Mancha, of 54,000 men, was broken on 18–19 November at Ocaña, while the army under the Duque Del Parque, advancing into the area south of Salamanca, met a severe rebuff at Alba de Tormes ten days later. Having defeated the Spanish so frequently, the French secured 90,000 reinforcements in December, since troops were more freely available at the end of Napoleon's Austrian war. Thus strengthened, the French invaded and partially subjugated Andalucia in January–March 1810.

The autumn of 1809 shifted the character of the war. It ended the phase of the war in which Spanish armies operated on an extensive scale, and did so with no systematic Spanish effort to secure British military co-operation. Despite the collapse of both Andalucia and large-scale Spanish military resistance to the French, the new ministry in London, suitably buttressed by Lord Wellesley's appointment as Foreign Secretary, increased rather than reduced its commitment to defending Portugal, subsidizing it financially, and maintaining a sizeable army there. Although opposition politicians objected to this policy, the government in 1810 entrenched the British presence at Lisbon and its hinterland and its involvement at Cadiz. The paradox that the ministerial commitment to a peninsular strategy became firmer just when the Spanish ability to wage war against the French declined, is perhaps explained by the government's desire to retain a role on the continent following Austria's settlement with France in 1809, and by its realization that the French military occupation of Andalucia, challenged by Spanish forces operating to the north, east and south, absorbed about as many French troops as Napoleon in 1810 added to the legions in Spain. By reorganizing and expanding the Portuguese army, exploiting the country's geography, and carefully preparing defensive positions, Wellington ensured that he had a good chance of securing Portugal with a relatively small British force. Given the restriction on British troop numbers typically assigned to overseas interventions, Wellington systematically used Portuguese resources to provide himself with the force-multiplier so desperately needed for success.

The strategic purpose of Britain's peninsula commitment changed radically between 1808 and 1810. When first undertaken, the commitment entailed assisting the Spanish rising. In 1809, the re-engagement formed part of more general mobilization involving Austria. By 1810, the objective was to preserve the newly constructed Anglo-Portuguese army as a player and to secure the Lisbon enclave. When the campaigning season for 1810 approached in April, Wellington, based about 80 miles from Ciudad Rodrigo, learned that the French were preparing for a spring offensive. As he wrote in early June: 'I am convinced that the French now see the necessity of getting us out of the Peninsula as the first object of their attention, and that they will risk every thing for that object, and the trial will be made in a short time.'[20] Wellington not unreasonably in May expected that the French were preparing for a vigorous attack upon his army. He laid preparations for a military evacuation from the Tagus basin at Lisbon, and considered the possible points at which he might later reinsert his army into the theatre of war.

French strategy in 1810 proved to be unusually cautious and gave Wellington ample time to build the defences needed at Lisbon. Instead of pursuing the Anglo-Portuguese army with all possible speed, Masséna decided in June 1810 to besiege the heavily fortified border towns of Ciudad Rodrigo and Almeida. The French first took up position at Ciudad Rodrigo on 26 April and only captured it on 9 July. Their leisurely movement upon Almeida again surprised Wellington, who believed as of 27 July, that the French would 'dash at us as soon as they shall be prepared, and make our retreat as difficult as possible'. Admittedly, the French suffered from the effects of poor roads and heavy, persistent rain in May and from inadequate planning and provision for the siege until well into June. Moreover, Napoleon's own directions from Paris insisted on a methodical approach, the capture of both forts, and delay in invading Portugal until the summer heats had receded and the harvest was forthcoming.[21] Surprised by such delays, Wellington confided to his brother Henry: 'This is not the way in which they have conquered Europe!'[22] The British had ample time to complete the elaborate lines of Torres Vedras, defending Lisbon, so that by 11 October, when the French eventually reached them, some 126 of the 152 redoubts were ready,[23] providing an unassailable position which rendered superfluous Wellington's planning in May and June for a British evacuation of Portugal.

When the French moved deeper into Portugal on 2 September 1810, their progress proved slow and difficult, a tough terrain made worse by poor choices of route, ignorance of the roads (again reflecting inadequate French military intelligence), the evacuation of the local people with their animals, and the destruction of crops. Frustrated by these various obstacles, and having chosen to advance towards Lisbon by the more westerly of two roads running south and taking the important inland city of Coimbra on the way, Masséna then displayed extraordinary impetuosity when, on 27 September, he attacked what he assumed were isolated units of the British army at Busaco blocking his advance on Coimbra. Wellington had in fact positioned his army to make a stand at that well-defended point.

For all the importance attached to the British military effort in the peninsula in pinning down French troops and for all the marching and countermarching undertaken by Wellington, the army under his personal command fought only two battles, at Busaco and the double engagement at Fuentes de Onoro (3 and 5 May 1811) during the 29 months between Talavera (28 July 1809) and the opening of the British siege of Ciudad Rodrigo (8 January 1812). Busaco was one of Wellington's trademark battles, fought on excellent defensive ground very much of the general's choosing. He stretched his own army of 52,000 men with sixty guns along a ridge 9 miles in length which was impossible to flank and which offered a high, rough, much overgrown front to the approaching French. Masséna simply could not see where precisely, and in what strength, his opponents were and could not use his artillery to soften up the British lines because the trajectory was too high; Napoleon later expressed astonishment that a frontal assault had been launched without artillery support. The main French attack was halted by British firing at 50 yards, followed by bayonet charges that sent French infantry, tired by their uphill climb, reeling into retreat.

Wellington's success meant that, since his return to the peninsula in April 1809, he had outfought five marshals: Soult at Oporto, Victor and Jourdan at Talavera, and now Masséna and Ney, one of the corps commanders, at Busaco. To have thwarted Masséna, one of the most determined and hard-hitting of Napoleon's subordinates who had been a general since 1793, was no mean achievement, since the Prince de Essling had been sent especially to the peninsula to roll the main British army into the sea.

After Busaco, Wellington withdrew steadily to the assiduously prepared Torres Vedras line. When Masséna discovered those lines on 14 October, he realized that they formed an impenetrable block. To Wellington's amazement and admiration, the French, after pulling back from the lines, held out all winter until shortages of food and the ravages of disease obliged them to begin a phased withdrawal from Portugal in late February 1811. The campaign finally closed when Masséna returned to Salamanca on 11 April, having lost 25,000 men, including 2,000 killed in action, and 8,000 taken prisoner, together with 60% of his army's horses.[24] It says little for the French commissariat or planning arrangements that resupply from or across a secure and extensive hinterland failed so thoroughly in early 1811, whatever the difficulties created by weather and terrain. Moreover, Masséna had devoted an entire year to his campaign, in which he had captured one significant and one minor border town, lost a battle, and returned to where he had begun. Wellington's prediction that his deep defence of Portugal would exhaust French manpower was vindicated even if the process took longer than he had anticipated.

Wellington's survival depended in part on the dispersed nature of the conflict. The war from December 1809 to May 1813 became a fragmented series of regional struggles accentuated by Spain's customary particularism and by the breakdown of effective national government. The peninsula's size and the geographical challenges it posed meant that the war fought by the British in 1810 and 1811 was largely divorced from the war fought by Spaniards. For the latter, four centres of highly organized resistance stood out. On the east coast, Catalonia, bordering on France, remained contested territory throughout the war, while farther south, in Valencia and Murcia provinces, French control was never more than patchy and sporadic. Although the French took over the heavily populated and agriculturally wealthy province of Andalucia in January 1810, they failed to capture Cadiz – described by Oman as 'one of the strongest places in the world'[25] – and fruitlessly deployed a substantial army to besiege that city until they withdrew in September 1812. During 1810 the allies stationed 26,000 troops in Cadiz, about one-fifth of them British. At the opposite end of the country, Galicia, Spain's most heavily populated province, eluded French conquest and control.

Given the fragmentary nature of the war, ministers in London continued to think in terms of a relatively limited commitment of troops and continued to juggle with various strategic alternatives in the conduct of the war. Once Masséna's invasion of Portugal had been repelled in 1810–11, ministers suggested in April 1811 that the army in Portugal might be pruned back to its earlier maximum of 30,000 men, with reserves of 10,000–15,000 men in Ireland and western England being available for despatch to counter any new threat. At the same time, they asked if small forces might be deployed on the coasts of Catalonia, the Bay of Biscay, and Galicia in order to reinforce and galvanize Spanish resistance.[26] None of this suggested a clear ministerial commitment to a strategy of overthrowing – as distinct from containing and corroding – French rule in Spain. Moreover, when the war's costs were challenged at home, Wellington claimed that the specific *additional* charges incurred by the peninsular commitment totalled a relatively small £1 million to £1.5 million:

If we are able to carry on war at all . . . I believe it will be found that it cannot be done at a much cheaper rate; and I can only assure the government that if they don't give Boney employment here or elsewhere on the Continent, he will give them employment at home; and they will find it not quite so easy to husband our resources as is imagined.[27]

Wellington argued in December 1811 that there was nowhere else where a force of the size he commanded could tie down as many French troops as in Spain, or where the British would secure the same degree of command over allied forces.[28]

Yet the second phase of the peninsular conflict for the British, stretching from autumn 1809 to the end of 1811, proved to be a war of two enclaves, not a war to free Spain from the French. The more important of the enclaves was Portugal and, in the winter of 1810–11, essentially the region immediately around Lisbon. The second enclave, Cadiz, became especially important in 1810 after Soult drove the Spanish central junta from Seville as he swept through Andalucia. The French besieged Cadiz and its peninsula from February 1810 until they were forced to withdraw in August 1812. Fearing that Andalucia would soon be conquered by the French, ministers in February 1810 pressed Wellington to choose between that city and Portugal. In their view, Portugal would not be defensible if Andalucia and Cadiz both fell, but the possession of Cadiz would enable the British to continue the struggle effectively, especially with their own colony of Gibraltar close by. In March, Lord Liverpool not only gave Wellington the option of evacuating Portugal, but emphasized that 'the chances of successful defence are considered here by all persons, military as well as civil, so improbably that I could not recommend any attempt at what may be called desperate resistance'. However, from this low point of ministerial gloom at the fate of Portugal, the allies' fortunes improved. Liverpool reassured Wellington in September 1810 of the government's determination to defend Portugal, consistently with the safety of the British army there. Meanwhile, a British force of about 5,000 troops continued to contribute to Cadiz's defence. Wellington insisted on the strategic importance of sustaining both enclaves, since the two together weakened the French ability to undermine or destroy either in turn and forced the enemy to divide his own, much larger forces, thereby denying him the fruits of his superiority in manpower.[29]

British commitment to a war for the enclaves was scarcely altruistic, since they provided considerable economic advantages to Britain. Britain's relationship with the transposed Portuguese regime resulted in the grant of free access by British merchants to the Brazilian market, with its two million people and long connections with British merchants.[30] In turn, Cadiz was Spain's principal port for trade with her Latin American colonies. Moreover, with Lisbon and Cadiz now dependent on British protection and with the Royal Navy constraining any renewed French naval threat, commercial interests undermined the Continental System and revived trading with parts of southern Europe, through Lisbon, Cadiz and those Spanish south-eastern ports which successfully resisted French takeover. In 1806, British exports and re-exports to, first, South America and the West Indies and, secondly, Gibraltar, Malta and the Ionian islands (these often serving as entrepôts for goods breaking into Napoleon's closed system) totalled £2.6 million and reached £2.8 million the following year. But after 1808, with new access to Latin America and Spain, the total soared: £9.1 million in 1808; £12.15 million in 1809; £10 million in 1810; £8.45 million in 1811; and £12.8 million in 1812. These 'official' figures, probably under-representing the real scale of the trade, compared impressively with the total average annual value of British exports and re-exports together of £42.5 million during 1808–12.[31] However, there was a downside, since this lucrative trade reduced the Portuguese government's customs revenues. As Wellington confided in August 1810 to his brother Henry, who was Britain's diplomatic representative in Cadiz from late 1809: 'Great Britain has ruined Portugal by her free trade with the Brazils: not only the customs of Portugal, to the amount of a million sterling per annum, are lost, but the fortunes of numerous individuals, who lived by this trade, are ruined.'[32]

The main attraction of the Portuguese enclave for Wellington, however, was military manpower not trade. The need for troops led to an
increasingly intrusive role played by the British in the government of
Portugal. According to one of the French generals, Maximilien Foy, even
the rudiments of the Portuguese army left in July–August 1808 assisted
the British by putting pressure on the French; the reaction against the
invaders ensured a daily 'increase of numbers, of moral energy, and of
physical strength'.[33] In May 1809, soon after Wellington's return to
Portugal, locally raised soldiers constituted 14,000 of the 35,000 troops
under his overall command. By September 1809 the British had organized
44,000 Portuguese regulars, including 6,000 cavalry, an arm in which the
British were then numerically weak, and 4,500 artillerymen, based on
the main cities. In addition, the militia was reorganized in 1809, depending
on conscripted service for short periods from within each of forty-eight
regions.[34] It demonstrated its value for defence in 1810 by supplying
nearly 40,000 militiamen to guard the lines of Torres Vedras. Only if the
French broke through the fortifications would they have confronted
the regular Anglo-Portuguese army, which was positioned to move along
newly improved and constructed roads behind the lines to hit the enemy
wherever required to do so.[35] Portuguese regular battalions, however,
were integrated into Wellington's field army. The allied army at Albuera,
under General William Beresford, consisted of 14,600 Spaniards, 10,200
Portuguese, 9,000 British and 1,100 men of the King's German Legion.
By September 1811, for example, the 47,000 troops of the 'British' army
assembled for campaigning under Wellington included 17,349 Portuguese
and at least 3,500 Germans.[36] At the battle of Vitoria, Wellington's
greatest peninsular victory, less than half his army was made up of British
soldiers. Among the infantry there were 27,600 Portuguese and 6,800
Spaniards to 27,400 British troops.[37] By 1810–11, British manpower
planning presupposed Portuguese military capability, secured through
the secondment of British officers to the Portuguese army. For all the
disparagement periodically heaped upon the British officer corps, British
officers' detailed control of the Portuguese forces gave Wellington the
confidence to use them side by side with British troops in all his demanding campaigns from early 1812 onwards. Indeed, when Napoleon returned
to France in 1815, Wellington wanted 12,000–14,000 Portuguese troops
for the Netherlands, because 'we can mix them with ours and do what we
please with them, and they become very nearly as good as our own'.[38] This
was a far cry from the feeble Portuguese resistance to the French in 1807
which led Oman to conclude: 'There is certainly no example in history of

a kingdom conquered in so few days and with such small trouble as was Portugal in 1807.'[39]

On paper at least, the general mobilization of Portugal's population of fewer than three million seemed impressive. In April 1810, Wellington informed his older brother that 'Portugal has done as much, and will do more, in the contest than any province in Spain of the same extent and population'.[40] In May 1810 the country reportedly provided a grand total of 51,000 regular troops (the British paying for 30,000 of them), 54,000 militiamen and 329,000 lightly armed ordenanza or local levies.[41] Moreover, the construction of the celebrated Torres Vedras Line across 29 miles between the Atlantic and the River Tagus would have been impossible without about 7,000 local labourers being engaged in the project during much of 1810. Yet mobilizing the Portuguese war effort proved challenging. Wellington stated that in July only 25,000 militiamen were actually armed and that 7,000 of those were absent without leave. Even among the regulars, he complained, there was a high rate of sickness in winter quarters, especially since being sent to hospital amounted to a virtual discharge.[42] Managing the Portuguese army in tandem with the Portuguese authorities, responsible to the Prince Regent in Brazil, led to running disagreements as to whether the agreed numbers of troops were being recruited by the Portuguese, over who had the final say on the promotion of officers, and over responsibility for the provisioning of the Portuguese army. In May 1810, before the scorched-earth policy that accompanied the retreat upon the lines of Torres Vedras, Wellington acknowledged that 'War is a terrible evil', especially in the theatre of operations, but insisted that the British inflicted less suffering on local populations than others did.[43] Yet, by October 1810, the movements of troops even in the area under British control left villages depleted of people, with many failing to return when it became possible to do so. Roofs were stripped from houses, which then fell into decay. Livestock were removed. Villagers had no incentive to grow crops only to see British forces simply seize them. While senior officers abided by instructions to pay for food and fodder, junior officers and commissariat officials were far more flexible in their approach.[44]

By January 1811, when the exigencies created by the retreat to Torres Vedras began to bite, the Portuguese government's finances felt increasing strains and, although the population and the army in Lisbon had enough food, supplies ran short farther afield. Inland food supplies proved so much more uncertain that there were distinct benefits to moving troops into Spain, where cattle were more plentiful and cheaper than in Portugal. For winter quarters, particularly in the Beira region of north-central

Portugal on the route to the Spanish border town of Ciudad Rodrigo, the army had to be widely dispersed in order to secure accommodation and supplies in an upland and barren countryside.[45] This worsening situation led Wellington to confide in Lord Liverpool that the British should have made Portugal 'the basis of all the military operations of the Peninsula' and carried the state through the war by 'actively' controlling all the departments of government, developing the country's resources through official action, and applying those resources to the conduct of war. Having failed to do so, and faced with declining political influence, a lack of cooperation from magistrates to ensure the free flow of supplies, and the growth of an anti-British party, Wellington argued that the British government should increase the subsidy paid to the Portuguese. He further suggested that the British Commissariat should take over responsibility for supplying the Portuguese army, with the Portuguese government reimbursing the British for this.[46] Wellington stressed to the British minister in Lisbon in 1810 that the Portuguese people in general remained insufficiently dedicated to their public duties as distinct from their private interests; in particular, 'the higher classes of society . . . must be forced to perform their duty'. In February 1811 he complained of the need to ensure that the 'inferior magistrates' did their duty more thoroughly.[47]

Thus the process by which the political and administrative requirements for the recruitment, provisioning, payment, command and leadership of an army led inexorably to demands upon the state were well illustrated by the chain of events in Portugal. A similar process went a stage or so further in Sicily where Lord William Bentinck undertook political and economic reforms in 1812 aimed at making the island a usable base and a constitutional exemplar. When Bentinck found that his ideal of providing constitutional government and political liberty failed, he concluded by December 1813 that British rule was necessary in order to cut through the intricacies and resistances endemic in Sicilian society and politics. He insisted that the introduction of British rule would make Sicily 'after Ireland, the brightest jewel in the British crown'.[48] Although this alternative to Wellington's narrower approach in Portugal failed to win ministerial approval, it suggested the extent of the administrative and political dilemma created for British commanders in establishing large base areas overseas. By 1812, the British had created dependencies in Portugal and Sicily and linked them with smaller colonial bases at Gibraltar, Malta, and the Ionian Islands. The French Empire in Spain, Italy and along the Dalmatian or eastern Adriatic coast was girdled by a chain of British bases. This successful containment of French power in the

Mediterranean proved repeatedly difficult, however, to translate into actions which might overthrow French rule in Spain or Italy separately.

British offensives, 1812

If the British wished to push inland from their Portuguese base, they needed to break open the Spanish–Portuguese border and especially the key land routes between the two countries commanded by Ciudad Rodrigo in the centre and Badajoz in the south. Yet this need conflicted with Spanish indifference to a region which was lightly peopled and devoid of resources. Spanish economic and military interests were concentrated elsewhere, leaving Wellington dependent essentially upon his own efforts to seize the border towns.

The one area where the British shared a more immediate strategic concern with the Spanish was the main road into Spain from Bayonne passing through Vitoria, Burgos, Valladolid, and Salamanca and from there commanding roads to Madrid and to the fortified town of Ciudad Rodrigo, which in turn dominated one of the principal routes into Portugal. This line was contested both by the regular forces opposed to the French and by prominent guerilla bands which controlled some of the region through which it passed. The strategic importance of the road had led Moore in December 1808 to advance upon Salamanca, and two of Wellington's most brilliant battles were fought at Salamanca in July 1812 and Vitoria in June 1813 on that vital artery. But before he could contest control of that great land route connecting France to northern and central Spain, Wellington had to secure his chosen base in Portugal. Only in the first four months of 1812 did he finally deny the French control of the Spanish border towns and thereby secure the strategic routes into and out of Spain from that base. To Wellington these two theatres formed by the main Bayonne–Salamanca road and by the Spanish–Portuguese border were of overwhelming strategic importance, whereas to most Spanish opponents of French rule they remained of secondary significance in the struggle to expel the invader from their towns and provinces or to prevent his entry into them.

Towards the end of 1811, however, conditions tempted Wellington to try a fresh advance into Spain. Spanish resistance ensured the continued fragmentation of the French war effort and King Joseph at Madrid lacked the psychological will and practical means to coordinate the disparate armies that in early 1812 were thrown back under his apparent overall control. When in early 1812 units from Marmont's Army of Portugal were despatched to the east to stiffen the campaign against Valencia, Wellington moved from his winter quarters on the Portuguese border and invested Ciudad Rodrigo, storming and taking the fortress on 19 January. The whole operation, despite bad weather and tough fighting, went smoothly to timetable. Ciudad Rodrigo offered a relatively simple target, since its garrison was small for the size of the town and guerrilla activity in the neighbouring region made supplying the fortress extremely difficult for the French. The fortifications proved vulnerable because British artillery battered parts of the walls filled in after the French attack in 1810. Yet Cuidad Rodrigo's capture inflicted a psychological blow on the French commanders, who neither expected it nor believed it could be done so quickly.

Wellington next turned his attention to the far greater fortress of Badajoz, steadily shifting his forces southwards from 19 February 1812. Badajoz, commanding the southern road into Portugal, had only been taken by Soult, from his command in Andalucia, after a siege lasting from 27 January to 10 March 1811. Its capture had been intended to support Masséna's failing invasion of Portugal. Moving faster than Soult a year earlier, the British completed the investment of Badajoz by 16 March and assaulted and took the town on the night of 6 April. This was successful only because French manpower had been deployed away from the Portuguese border, to Valencia and then Alicante in the east, and to the north, to replace in part the units being assembled for the invasion of Russia. Wellington deployed at and around Badajoz an army of about 55,000 men, using large portions of it to support the efforts of Spanish guerrillas and some regular divisions to disrupt the region and to prevent any possibility of the army of Andalucia under Soult being brought to bear against the British. To avoid being delayed in a prolonged siege, Wellington stormed Badajoz, suffering 3,700 killed, wounded or missing in the process. Despite such heavy losses of manpower, the successful seizure of the two strategically most important frontier fortresses opened the way at last for the British to fight within Spain.

Wellington hoped that his presence in Badajoz would draw Soult into Estremadura, enabling the British to fight him there, and thereby reduce or end the French occupation of the southern province of Andalucia. But Soult, pressed by Spanish resistance and made wary by mobile British divisions, had the good sense not to lead his army into any such trap. Meanwhile, the French again blockaded Ciudad Rodrigo and became active in neighbouring northern Portugal. On 11 April, Wellington decided, as a second-best strategy, to return northwards and try to lure into battle

Marshal Marmont and his Army of Portugal, based on Salamanca. Before commencing his offensive on 13 June, Wellington safeguarded his main army through various diversionary attacks launched by Spanish forces, with some British assistance, in Andalucia, by the Spanish army of Galicia (whose strength totalled 24,000 men, with about 6,000 of them in garrisons), by British naval forays, beginning on 17 June, along the coast of the Bay of Biscay, and by a planned descent on the eastern coast by British forces from Sicily.

Before the Sicilian diversionary force had arrived, Wellington and Marmont had fought one of the most dramatic battles of the Peninsular War, at Salamanca on 22 July. Wellington and Marmont had been operating against each other for five weeks when Marmont initiated a long flanking movement which greatly overstretched his army along an exposed front of 6 miles. Suddenly noticing the error which Marmont, an able commander who erred through a lapse in concentration, had made, Wellington ordered an attack starting at the west. General Foy, who was present, noted in his diary shortly after the engagement:

It raises Lord Wellington almost to the level of Marlborough. Hitherto we had been aware of his prudence, his eye for choosing a position, and his skill in utilising it. At Salamanca he has shown himself a great and able master of manoeuvres. He kept his dispositions concealed for almost the whole day: he waited till we were committed to our movement before he developed his own: he played a safe game[49]

In an extended battle over open terrain British cavalry proved unusually effective and the French suffered heavy losses.[50] The fact that one allied general was killed and three were wounded indicates the complexity and closeness of the manoeuvring under fire. Having expelled one major opponent from central Spain, and after agonizing over the options and their dangers, Wellington decided on 5 August to move upon Madrid, in order to induce King Joseph to insist on Soult's and Suchet's evacuating their viceroyalties in order to recover his capital and its surroundings. On 12 August 1812 the British marched into Madrid to a rapturous welcome. This success provoked a French strategic regrouping, as desired by Wellington. Soult evacuated Andalucia, the country's second most populous province and a wealthy one as well, beginning modestly on 12 August and finishing with his arrival near Valencia by 1 October. Although this north-easterly movement of 55,000 troops enabled the French to enter Madrid on 2 November 1812, the recapture of the capital offered meagre compensation for the permanent withdrawal from Andalucia, whose loss appreciably reduced the occupying power's revenue-raising capacity.

While the extensive movement of French forces progressed during the autumn, Wellington decided to strike along the great northern route to the French frontier and secure Burgos, a prosperous commercial centre at a vital crossroads which had been designated by the French as a principal depot and fort between Bayonne and Madrid. The allies readily took the town, but spent from 19 September to 22 October waiting for the garrison of 2,000 men to give up the castle. New defences added to the natural strength of the fortress's dominant geographical position above the ancient city. Under pressure, Wellington failed to take Burgos castle by frontal assault. With the weather worsening, he withdrew, beginning a movement which degenerated into a shambles, dogged by illness, desertion, and drunkenness, and ended when Wellington's army ensconced itself in winter quarters in the borderlands around Ciudad Rodrigo. The balance of advantage by December 1812 had still not tipped decisively in Wellington's favour. If the commanding border fortresses of Ciudad Rodrigo and Badajoz were firmly in British hands, after long years under contention, Wellington's field army of 45,000 men languished in a condition of indignity rather than triumph. To the 2,100 men killed, wounded and missing during the month-long siege of Burgos were added the 5,700 British and Portuguese troops who fell casualty (mostly prisoners or missing) in the month-long retreat from the city.[51] By the end of 1812, Wellington had expanded the Portuguese enclave, but had not yet broken out of it.

This reversal of fortunes should not disguise the British achievements after four years of war in the peninsula. The British had created a new army, developed, as so often was the case, as a hybrid force drawing heavily upon the local population. Whether the Anglo-Portuguese army would be of value beyond the confines of the peninsula remained to be seen. But it had defeated and outmanoeuvred a succession of leading French marshals and their armies. The British had held Lisbon, the greatest Atlantic seaboard port, and secured lucrative commercial advantages in Latin America. They had contributed to the destabilization of French rule in Spain, taking hold of the border with Portugal and playing a role in forcing the French evacuation of Andalucia. What remained to be seen was whether the Portuguese enclave and its extension to the Spanish borderlands could be translated into more than temporary incursions into the Spanish heartland. Moreover, while the chain of British bases from Portugal to the Ionian islands formed a British crescent of power, setting the limits to the southern rim of the French Empire, it was still not clear whether the British could project power against France from that rim. Only the Portuguese enclave had served the purpose by 1812 of providing a successful springboard for the projection of force against the distended French Empire. Although the French had failed to conquer all of Spain, the British remained on the periphery of southern Europe.

Notes and references

1 David Gates, *The Spanish Ulcer: A History of the Peninsular War* (London, 1986), pp. 8–11.

2 David Francis, *Portugal 1715–1808* (London,1985), pp. 282, 284.

3 A. Aspinall (ed.), *The Later Correspondence of George III*, 5 vols (Cambridge, 1968), Vol. IV, p. 623.

4 Adam Zamoyski, *1812* (London, 2004), pp. 43–44.

5 John Fisher, *Commercial Relations Between Spain and Spanish America in the Era of Free Trade, 1778–1796* (Liverpool, 1985), pp. 93–101, 107.

6 Denis Gray, *Spencer Perceval 1762–1812: the Evangelical Prime Minister* (London, 1963), pp. 178, 182–83, 420–21.

7 Sir Charles Oman, *A History of the Peninsular War*, 7 vols (Oxford, 1902–30), Vol. I, p. 145.

8 Oman, *A History of the Peninsular War*, Vol. I, pp. 133–37, 145–46, 161.

9 W.S. Moorsom, *Historical Record of the Fifty-Second Regiment, 1775–1858* (London, 1860), p. 83.

10 Captain Alexander Gordon, *A Cavalry Officer in the Corunna Campaign, 1808–09: The Journal of Captain Gordon of the 15th Hussars* (Worley, 1990; first published 1913), pp. 17, 41.

11 Peter Spence, *The Birth of Romantic Radicalism* (Aldershot, 1996), pp. 87–93.

12 Charles J. Esdaile, *The Spanish Army in the Peninsular War* (Manchester, 1988), p. 140.

13 D.W. Davies, *Sir John Moore's Peninsular Campaign 1808–1809* (The Hague, 1974), pp. 56–61, 64, 77, 110, 196, 268–69; R.J.B. Muir and C.J. Esdaile, 'Strategic planning in a time of small government: the wars against revolutionary and Napoleonic France, 1793–1815' in C.M. Woolgar (ed.) *Wellington Studies I* (Southampton, 1996), pp. 1–90, esp. 71–80; Gordon, *A Cavalry Officer*, pp. 167–70, 177–78, 182–83, 209.

14 Oman, *A History of the Peninsular War*, Vol. I, pp. 593, 602.

15 Oman, *A History of the Peninsular War*, Vol. I, pp. 646–48; Gordon, *A Cavalry Officer*, pp. 199–200, 208.

16 David Chandler, *The Campaigns of Napoleon* (London, 1966), p. 653; Gates, *The Spanish Ulcer*, p. 115.

17 Oman, *A History of the Peninsular War*, Vol. II, pp. 5–7, 11–13, 90, 104, 157–58, 168; Gates, *The Spanish Ulcer*, pp. 483–85.

18 Duke of Wellington (ed.), *Supplementary Dispatches of the Duke of Wellington*, 12 vols (London, 1858–72), Vol. VI, pp. 331–32.

19 Wellington (ed.), *Supplementary Dispatches*, Vol. VI, pp. 350–51.

20 Lieutenant Colonel Gurwood (ed.), *The Dispatches of Field Marshal The Duke of Wellington, 1799–1815*, 12 vols (London, 1838), Vol. VI, pp. 52–53, 172, 177, 228.

21 Gurwood (ed.), *Dispatches*, Vol. VI, pp. 187, 257, 266, 276, 281, 300, 304, 306, 316; Donald Horward, *Napoleon and Iberia: The Twin Sieges of Ciudad Rodrigo and Almeida, 1810* (London, 1994 edn), pp. 59–62, 112–16, 155, 185.

22 Gurwood (ed.), *Dispatches*, Vol. VI, pp. 94, 120, 169, 172, 187, 193, 233, 257–58.

23 Horward, *Napoleon and Iberia*, pp. 318–22.

24 Gates, *The Spanish Ulcer*, p. 241.

25 Oman, *A History of the Peninsular War*, Vol. III, p. 145.

26 Wellington (ed.), *Supplementary Dispatches*, Vol. VII, pp. 104–05, 116–17.

27 Wellington (ed.), *Supplementary Dispatches*, Vol. VII, pp. 93–94.

28 Wellington (ed.), *Supplementary Dispatches*, Vol. VII, pp. 246, 259.

29 Wellington (ed.), *Supplementary Dispatches*, Vol. VI, pp. 483–84, 491, 493, 498, 511, 591–93.

30 Francis, *Portugal 1715–1808*, pp. 202, 284.

31 A.D. Harvey, *Britain In The Early Nineteenth Century* (New York, 1976), p. 331.

32 Gurwood (ed.), *Dispatches*, Vol. VI, pp. 174, 340, 349–50.

33 General Foy, *History of the War in the Peninsula under Napoleon* (trans.), 4 vols (London, 1827), Vol. II, part 1, pp. 471–72, 483, 495.

34 Oman, *A History of the Peninsular War*, Vol. II, pp. 629–31. The British were involved in detailed defence arrangements with the Portuguese in 1801 and 1803. Francis, *Portugal 1715–1808*, pp. 243–44, 253.

35 Horward, *Napoleon and Iberia*, p. 29; Muir, *Britain and the Defeat of Napoleon*, pp. 126–28.

36 Oman, *A History of the Peninsular War*, Vol. IV, pp. 644–47.

37 Jac Weller, *Wellington in the Peninsula, 1808–14* (London, 1967), pp. 83–84, 267–69.

38 Gurwood (ed.), *Dispatches*, Vol. XII, pp. 281, 302.

39 Oman, *A History of the Peninsular War*, Vol. I, p. 26.

40 Gurwood (ed.), *Dispatches*, Vol. VI, p. 68.

41 Horward, *Napoleon and Iberia*, p. 78.

42 Gurwood (ed.), *Dispatches*, Vol. VII, pp. 403, 408, 419.

43 Gurwood (ed.), *Dispatches*, Vol. VI, pp. 114, 271–73, 357; Vol. VII, pp. 435, 437–39.

44 *The Royal Military Panorama or Officer's Companion*, Vol. III (1813–14), pp. 226–27.

45 Gurwood (ed.), *Dispatches*, Vol. VI, p. 272; Vol. VII, pp. 379–80; Oman, *A History of the Peninsular War*, Vol. VI, p. 182.

46 Gurwood (ed.), *Dispatches*, Vol. VII, pp. 63–64, 98, 102, 107,122, 192–93, 276, 340, 342.

47 Gurwood (ed.), *Dispatches*, Vol. VI, p. 103; Vol. VII, p. 276.

48 John Rosselli, *Lord William Bentinck: The Making of a Liberal Imperialist 1774–1839* (Berkeley, CA, 1974), p. 164.

49 Oman, *A History of the Peninsular War*, Vol. V, pp. 472–73.

50 Weller, *Wellington in the Peninsula*, pp. 227–30.

51 Oman, *A History of the Peninsular War*, Vol. VI, pp. 747–48.

CHAPTER 12

Victory in Spain and France, 1813–14

Victory in Spain seemed a very distant prospect in December 1812. Nine months later the French were largely forced from that country. What proved to be the final phase of the fighting in Spain then carried over into a successful British invasion of south-western France. In an unremitting sequence of often very hard fighting from May 1813 to April 1814, the British army fought the toughest and longest campaign against a strong enemy army in its history to that date. Victory depended upon a number of developments: the depletion of French forces, Napoleon's relative lack of interest in the peninsula, the Spanish contribution to France's defeat, the role of British sea power, the effectiveness of the British army, the development of British generalship and wider military leadership, the geopolitical strategies pursued by Britain. It also hinged on the military balance of power in all its dimensions, including the dynamic and unstable relationship between the British concentration on the military efficiency of the Anglo-Portuguese army and the wider interaction between the British and Spanish authorities.

Before considering the various factors which explain British success, it is worth noting the importance of the peninsula commitment to the French. Napoleon fought in Spain only for a few months in 1808. As supreme warlord, he focused on the three Great Powers of central and eastern Europe. As imperial predator, his ambitions lay more in Italy than in Iberia. As a global strategist, his animus against Britain led him into a protracted struggle to control or channel the flow of commerce rather than to crush every peripheral effervescence of British land forces around the world. Yet, despite these qualifications, Spain was important to France and substantial forces were assigned to that theatre of war even in 1813. This was partly a matter of prestige once the initial drive to conquer Spain had occurred; the French had invested considerable reputational capital and blood-sacrifice in trying to take over the country. But the determination to control Europe's commerce in order to exclude the British and thereby break their financial power had led Napoleon into the peninsula in the first place. The French fought very hard indeed to hold on to Spain. It is essential therefore to conclude this assessment of the conclusion to Britain's long continental campaign by evaluating Britain's war-fighting capability, for it was fighting alone which finally ended the Napoleonic regime. While recognizing that nations' political fates were in the melting pot in 1813–14, it is also essential to emphasize that the British conduct of war remained incremental, hesitant, and conditional upon central European alliances and fighting. The British contribution to the grand finale remained localized and spasmodic.

The Vitoria campaign, 1813

Napoleon's invasion of Russia opened a new phase of the war. The transfer of French forces out of Spain and the channelling of recruits conscripted in 1812 to the east facilitated the allies' advances in 1812 while the disasters of late 1812 on the Russian front provided new opportunities in the peninsula. As Dr Muir has stressed, if Napoleon had defeated Russia, he would have been in a powerful position in 1813 to reverse all the previous year's defeats in Spain. Lord Liverpool, the prime minister, wrote to Wellington on 22 December, 1812:

There has been no example within the last twenty years, among all the extraordinary events of the French Revolution, of such a change of fortune as Bonaparte has experienced during the last five months.[1]

Liverpool reasoned that Napoleon would concentrate during 1813 on defending French interests in Germany against a probable Russian counter-offensive, which would oblige him either to transfer yet further troops from Spain or to raise a new army by May 1813. As shown in the table below, the beginning of the campaigning season in May 1813 in fact saw the French outnumbered in Spain for the first time since the summer of 1808, and numbers, as Wellington's every calculation in his operational planning recognized, were usually decisive. While a smaller army might defeat a larger one, outnumbered forces could rarely shape campaigns. In mid-1811, the Spanish and Anglo-Portuguese armies had fielded about 160,000 troops in total, no match for 291,000 men deployed by their enemy. By mid-1813, the allies sustained about 201,000 men actively under arms: 105,000 in the Spanish armies, 80,000 mainly British and Portuguese under Wellington's direct command, including the cavalry for which he had long pleaded, and 16,000 Anglo-Sicilian troops under Sir John Murray available on the eastern seaboard. By then the French had only 176,000 effectives left in Spain. The shift in numerical strength was the decisive factor in opening the door to victory. Even so, many regarded the retreat from Burgos in late 1812 as a worse reverse than the flight to La Coruña nearly four years earlier, and substantial pressures and problems remained for the allies to resolve before they could exploit the new balance of military power. For his part, Napoleon, retaining six armies and about 200,000 men in Spain, planned to secure central and most of northern Spain. This meant that French dispositions were fluid from February to May, with many north-western towns in particular being evacuated and local concentrations being formed,[2] while other troops were withdrawn to France. But, if the sick and detached were excluded, French forces outside Catalonia had fallen from 268,000 effectives in July 1811 to 185,000 in October 1812, and then to 151,000 by June 1813. This was the dramatic collapse in French numerical strength which opened the way to allied victory.

French forces in Spain[3]

	Effectives (excluding sick and detached troops, to nearest 1,000)	*Troops in Catalonia (included in the effectives, to nearest 500)*
February 1809	194,000	39,000
January 1810	297,000	34,500
July 1811	291,000	23,500
October 1812	214,000	29,500
June/July 1813	176,000	25,000

The British advance from 24 May to 2 August 1813 was one of the most striking achievements in the operational history of the British army. Wellington's force moved across miles of often difficult terrain in the summer heat and defeated and then pursued soldiers from the most battle-hardened armies in the world. From the battle of Vitoria to the halt called on 2 August, the allies under Wellington lost 12,000 casualties. But the punishment they inflicted on the French changed the balance of military power. In launching the campaign of 1813, Wellington radically changed his own dispositions. Whereas in 1812, he and his subordinate,

Sir Rowland Hill, had operated separately, Wellington during May 1813 gathered his main forces into one army of 81,000 men, which included 29,000 Portuguese and 4,300 Germans, mostly in the King's German Legion.[4] Exploiting their numerical advantage, and quitting their winter positions on 24 May, the Anglo-Portuguese troops marched to the north-west of the main French army, covering its own moves by a strong cavalry screen, and forced the French to retire step by step. When Wellington entered Salamanca in June 1813, he was, although no farther forward than Moore had been in November 1808, at last strong enough to overwhelm the French forces immediately opposing him. Once Wellington left his winter quarters, the French finally evacuated Madrid altogether on 27 May 1813. Retreating initially to Burgos, King Joseph concluded that the city was incapable of supporting such a large French army and ordered the city's evacuation and the destruction of its works on 13 June. An objective that had so humiliatingly eluded Wellington the previous year was thus obtained without a fight. For the next stage of his own advance, Wellington split his army into contingents, pushing them forward along separate routes which made it possible for them to concentrate at a decisive point, following the best Napoleonic premises. As the French retreated towards the lush Ebro Valley, Wellington's army maintained its momentum, push-ing with daring and energy through difficult mountain routes to come upon the French from both north and west simultaneously. Having sur-rendered control of so much of one of the two main strategic highways in Spain, Joseph halted at Vitoria to await the arrival of subsidiary forces under General Clausel, engaged in fighting guerrillas to the south-west, and to gain time for an orderly withdrawal back to France.

Wellington attacked Joseph's army at rest at Vitoria on 21 June. He brought his superior numbers to bear across four different approach routes, some of which involved crossing difficult mountain terrain. The French army of 57,000 troops had not expected an advance of such rapidity or on such a scale; strung out over 12 miles, they were only patchily prepared for consistent and effective defence. The allied divisions, scattered over ground far more extensive than in any previous engagement and forming by far the largest Anglo-Portuguese army (of 75,000 men) Wellington had so far deployed, depended upon good timing and the coordination of widely separated attacks. For their part, French commanders, both at the army level and at lower levels responsible for making detailed defensive arrangements, failed to anticipate even such basic needs as securing or destroying the eleven bridges over the River Zadorra which commanded access to the French positions. Attacking those positions at different vulnerable points, the allies broke their opponents' spirit. The two sides lost similar numbers of killed and wounded in the fighting: 4,880 on the allied side and 5,170 on the French. But whereas Wellington reported only 268 men missing, the extent of French panic and flight was evidenced in the 2,829 French troops who went missing or were taken prisoner.[5]

The immediate impact of Vitoria upon the French seemed decisive. Writing on 3 July that 'This awful catastrophe takes from me by a single blow all that has been won by five years of hard work and devoted service', Marshal Suchet withdrew from the south and brought his main field army to the Ebro by mid-July. As soon as he heard of Vitoria, Napoleon dismissed his brother from command and appointed Marshal Soult to consolidate and reinvigorate all the five French armies of Spain, other than Suchet's forces in Catalonia and the south-east. Lord William Bentinck, from his base in Sicily, meanwhile transported an army of 16,000 troops drawn from five countries and including 5,000 British soldiers, along the Spanish east coast, reaching Tarragona during July and August.[6] Back home, public celebration of the victory reached such proportions that one leading Whig complained that the third night of illuminations in the capital manifested that 'feverish ignorance which John Bull is so apt to display'; 'the drunken and inflamed enthusiasm of London is at this moment ready for eternal war'.[7] Farther afield, Beethoven composed a celebratory piece performed in Vienna in December.

Yet, within a week, victory created its own problems for Wellington. The farther he advanced from his supply bases, the more difficult he found it to obtain replenishments of money and munitions. He depended for a time on plentiful French artillery and ammunition seized at Vitoria to maintain his operations. Success in battle after an intense and demanding campaign released tensions and relaxed discipline in the British army, which became incapable of further rapid pursuit of the retreating French and Clausel's dispersed forces. Moreover, French withdrawal eased the pressure on both Portuguese and Spanish politicians opposed to British dominance, opening the way to a greater assertion of their demands in dealing with the British.[8] The terrain east from Vitoria, being far more constricted than the open, rolling high plains from Ciudad Rodrigo to Burgos, inhibited further easy advances.

In the face of such difficulties and Soult's ability to launch stern counter-offensives, Wellington pushed the French back to the Pyrenean frontier, deciding then to halt and consolidate the British hold on north-eastern Spain. The fighting on the Pyrenees front from 25 July to 2 August accounted for 7,096 British, Portuguese and Spanish casualties – compared with 5,180 losses at Vitoria – and about 12,500 French casualties, with perhaps 3,000 of them being taken as prisoners.[9] Better still for the British, the French army retreating from Spain was 8,000 depleted by 10,000 stragglers falling behind, demonstrating that Soult's appointment did not reverse the declining morale of the French army. Despite these advantages, Wellington repeatedly stressed that his operations would 'depend a good deal on what passes in the North of Europe'; recent battles fought by Napoleon against Prussia and Russia were 'more important' than his own campaign.[10] Until he learned on 7 September of Austria's declaration of war on France, Wellington saw no possibility of advancing into France, remaining sceptical about allies whose objectives diverged:

The object of each should be to diminish the power and influence of France, by which alone the peace of the world can be restored and maintained: and although the aggrandizement and security of the power of one's own country is the duty of every man, all nations may depend upon it that the best security . . . is to be found in the reduction of the power and influence of the grand disturber.[11]

Given the overriding importance of coordinating national efforts and resources against Napoleon, Wellington's own ability to place his achievements modestly within the grander geopolitical context raises the question of how effectively the British utilized a range of components to gain the victory in Spain which was virtually assured by September 1813. Even with Napoleon's shift of military resources to Russia in 1812, the British faced considerable difficulties in exploiting the opportunities available to them in 1813.

The Spanish military contribution

In considering the various factors which contributed to victory, the British were probably least even-handed in their assessment of the Spanish war effort. The British interest in Spain centred on mercantile pressures to open up Spanish America to British trade and Wellington's concentration on building an army. Admittedly, interest in the Spanish cause soared among British radicals with the risings of May 1808, but more because of their wider implications than because of deep fascination with Spanish affairs. Radicals claimed that Spanish opposition to the French would only be sustained if the Spanish people embraced revolution. Perhaps more importantly, William Cobbett argued that if the Spanish succeeded in overthrowing the French through a popular uprising, they would set a welcome precedent for a more general, Europe-wide, disbanding of standing armies and volunteer forces with all their attendant privileges and costs.[12] Such radical hopes for a people's contest rapidly receded in 1809, to be superseded by traditionalists' insistence that wars were won only by regular armies.

Meanwhile, commercial interest in trading with the Spanish empire grew. As individual British subjects supported Latin American independence and as the independence movements of the Spanish colonies gained strength from 1810 onwards, so Spaniards dependent on the old colonial monopoly objected to Britain's role in the New World. The liberal constitution of 1812 stipulated that the Latin American colonies would remain part of Spain. While the British government did not object to such a position, British ministers wanted freer trade with the Latin American colonies. By mid-1813, the Spanish authorities complained of increasing British trade with Latin America and a growing number of independent Britons serving as volunteers with revolutionary levies. The Spanish government also conducted its own military policy in Latin America, sending out troops to the Spanish colonies without informing the British. These tensions were exacerbated by the growing interdependence between the British and Cadiz, because the city – being blockaded by the French on its landward side – needed to communicate with the rest of the nation by sea. Cadiz's large and prosperous mercantile community had been heavily dependent on commerce with Latin America. In February 1813, Henry Wellesley noted in Cadiz 'a violent spirit against us here; and it is to be attributed entirely to our conduct in South America'. British ministers thus faced Spanish politicians who resented their wartime financial dependence on Britain, pressed for constitutional reform of limited interest to British conservatives, and sought to retain a colonial empire whose trade regulations the British wanted to dismantle.

While reformers at Cadiz had little reason to trust British liberalism, Wellington's concentration on building an army intensified mutual distrust between him and the liberals of the Cortes who, isolated from the rest of Spain for most of the period 1810–13, loathed militarism and sought the overthrow of pre-1808 Spain, its feudal privileges and its aristocratic order. They tried to restrict the generals' power because they feared Caesarism, hoping instead to forge a citizens' army whose *élan* and effectiveness would flow from its dedication to a national and enlightened political ideal embraced in the constitution of 1812. One leading liberal newspaper illustrated this leapfrogging logic when it asserted that the constitution 'has been the most formidable army that the French have had to face, for it has transformed what they regarded as a horde of savages into a nation of free men'. Wellington in January 1813 dismissed the Cortes as devoid of influence beyond Cadiz:

The Cortes have formed a constitution very much on the principle that a painter paints a picture, viz, to be looked at, and I have not met . . . any person of any description . . . who considers the constitution as the embodying of a system by which Spain is, or can be, governed.[13]

When the Cortes on 16 June relieved General Castaños of his command of a Spanish army in the north because of his political unreliability, it infuriated Wellington, who respected the general and who expected to control military appointments:

We and the Powers of Europe are interested in the success of the war in the Peninsula, but the creatures who govern Cadiz . . . feel no such interest. All that they care about really is to hear the praise of their foolish Constitution.[14]

Finally, relations between soldiers and civilians provoked yet further Anglo-Spanish antagonism. Wellington conceded that discipline broke down after Vitoria. Vivid images remained of British soldiers by turns fraternizing with Spaniards and despising and plundering them. The destruction of San Sebastian in September 1813 even occasioned public demands for a popular rising to expel the British from Spain.

Once Wellington had the main French peninsular army on the run after Vitoria, he displayed relatively limited interest in the political fate of Spain. The final phase of the war – the invasion of France from September 1813 to Napoleon's abdication – saw the British concentrating on manoeuvring their Anglo-Portuguese army with modest assistance from Spanish forces. British ministers and generals never believed that Napoleon would be defeated through war in the Iberian peninsula. As with so many other, smaller and briefer interventions, their intention was to chisel away at the formidable French military machine and to encourage other powers to make sustained war upon an over-mighty France. Wellington himself did not entirely discount the long-term, debilitating effects which civil disaffection, as well as military resistance, would have on his opponent. In April 1810 he wrote to one of his generals:

I do not despair of seeing at some time or other a check to the Bonaparte system. Recent transactions in Holland show that it is all hollow within, and that it is so inconsistent with the wishes, the interests, and even the existence of civilized society, that he cannot trust even his brothers to carry it into execution.[15]

But, despite such threats of civil disruption, the key element in the military-political contest against Bonapartist expansionism remained for Wellington the regular army.

While Wellington's insistence on the primacy of regular armies was wholly intelligible, his frustrations with the battlefield performance and lack of strategic coordination of the Spanish armies, later reinforced by military historians' preoccupation with battles rather than campaign processes, has led to a systematic devaluation of the Spanish armies' resilience. Since the Spanish had engaged in little fighting in the previous forty-five years, senior officers had acquired limited experience of managing small armies of 5,000 to 15,000, unlike senior British commanders who had participated in almost continuous campaigning since 1775. This exposure helped Horse Guards develop able senior officers, appropriately deploy the less effective, and weed out the incompetent. Imperfections remained in the British army's command, but filters existed and competent commanders practised their skills. Frustrations with Spanish generals were inevitable in a system which lacked clear political and military control and coordination in the absence of an authoritative central government. The fragmented nature of Spanish political leadership encouraged the appointment of territorial magnates who were not full-time officers, such as the Dukes of Albuquerque, Del Parque, and Infantado, to high military command. By contrast, while local landowners commanded militia battalions in Britain, senior home commands went to professionally committed generals. By mid-1809 the dispersed and poorly coordinated Spanish armies had expended huge efforts and resources only to meet repeated reversals.

Yet despite their lack of fighting experience and their endemic particularism, Spanish armies engaged the French extensively over a long period. The most intensive period of engagement occurred in 1808–09. From the defence of Zaragoza against the first French siege beginning on 15 June 1808 to the surrender of Gerona on 11 December 1809, Spanish regular forces fought the French in thirty significant engagements, either battles or sieges. The overall level of commitment to fighting may be demonstrated by the casualties suffered in twelve of the principal engagements undertaken by the Spanish alone, excluding Talavera, where the Spanish fought alongside the British, and also Bailen and operations around Barcelona. In those twelve engagements, Spanish military losses totalled an estimated 108,000 men (see table below). These figures are broad contemporary estimates, not based on detailed battalion returns, and are almost certainly exaggerated. However, they do not include all of the engagements involving the Spanish and French or the losses from the normal wear and tear of protracted military campaigning. Given the fact that Spain's population was only 10–11 million, or about 35–40% of that of France plus the former Austrian Netherlands incorporated into France by 1808, this was a proportionate loss of manpower equivalent to at least 270,000 troops for France. Such losses would have stretched and weakened even the brutal Napoleonic war machine. Despite their massive losses, however, Spanish armies continued to mount formal resistance in the first six months of 1810, with the invader being held up for about a month in besieging each of Astorga, Lerida and Ciudad Rodrigo.

Levels of resistance may be gauged by reference to the eight Spanish towns whose populations exceeded 50,000.[16] All four towns of over 100,000 were contested. Madrid rose against the French in May 1808 and was briefly freed by Wellington in August 1812. By May 1810 there were 26,000 troops, mostly Spanish, defending Cadiz, which never fell to the French.[17] Some 16,000 Spanish troops in the city of Valencia held out from 25 December 1811 to 8 January 1812 before being overwhelmed by their attackers. The region around Barcelona, if not the city itself, remained strongly contested throughout the French occupation. The smaller town of Tarragona, on the strategic road south of Barcelona, held out for three years until June 1811, tying down 22,000 French troops who at one time or another participated in the siege, and inflicting 4,300 casualties (excluding the sick) upon them.[18] Among the towns of 50,000–100,000 people, Seville was not taken until February 1810, while Cartagena, Granada, and Malaga played a limited role in French strategy. Moreover, the Spanish continued, if only occasionally, to raise small armies with which to challenge the French in the field, as Joaquim Blake did, although unsuccessfully, with 28,000 troops at Sarguntum in October 1811.[19] If Spanish regional armies were mostly reduced by 1810 to relatively small corps based in remote areas, they continued to interfere with French lines of supply, communication and movement, and to tie down French field armies. The Spanish also suffered crucially after February 1810 from the French seizure at Seville of the country's main military arsenal and centre of arms production; those resources sustained the French army in the south for the three years it remained in the region.[20]

Spanish military resistance, 1808–09[21]

		Engagement/battle undertaken by Spanish	Spanish casualties	Spanish prisoners taken/deserters
1808	14 July	Medina de Río Seco	3,000	
	10 November	Gamonal	2,500	1,000
	10–11 November	Espinosa de los Monteros		11,000
	23 November	Tudela	4,000	
1809	13 January	Uclés	1,000	6,000
	20 December–19 February	2nd siege of Zaragoza	10,000	8,000
	29 March	Medellin	8,000	2,000
	15 June	Mariá Belchite	5,000	3,000
	11 August	Almonacid de Toledo	3,500	2,000
	19 November	Ocaña	12,000	14,000
	28 November	Alba de Tormes	3,000	
	24 May–11 December	Siege of Gerona	6,200	3,000
Totals			58,200	50,000

No nation kept so many regulars in direct fighting contact with the French for as long as the Spanish did from May 1808 to April 1814. In the summer of 1811, despite their losses and their battlefield defeats, the Spanish had 98,405 effectives in the field,[22] compared with the 63,000 troops in the Anglo-Portuguese army that autumn. Two years later, in June–July 1813, the Spanish assigned 46,000 men to serve in Wellington's general theatre of operations, to be coordinated with the movements of the 81,000-strong Anglo-Portuguese army. In addition, 59,000 Spanish regulars served in three dispersed armies along the eastern coast of the country.[23] Yet the 160,000 regulars in arms were so enfeebled by political divisions as to punch below their weight. The Cortes in Cadiz distrusted the regional captains-general, who in turn found it difficult to work together. Administrative procedures had so broken down that supplying the munitions of war and food proved unreliable, forcing Spanish armies to rely on local suppliers and even plunder, thereby undermining morale and restricting their mobility.[24] The closer the full liberation of Spain approached, the more damaging became the potential political divisions among the generals, between supporters of the Cadiz constitution, local, self-made political adventurers, and those preferring an absolutist or lightly constrained monarchy.[25]

The juntas and the generals tried to strengthen resistance through the establishment of local partidas, loosely linked initially to the militia and formally organized from December 1808. Partidas, responsible to regional generals, were intended to engage in guerrilla or small war to assist the movements and actions of the regular armies. Most guerrillas were peasants, typically forced to join partidas because they were deserters or in trouble with the French or suffering from wartime privation or keen on plunder. The number of guerrillas is impossible to ascertain, but in 1812 widely dispersed bands were claimed to have 38,500 members. Those bands, rarely composed of freedom fighters, probably inflicted as much damage upon the indigenous population as they did upon the French. Although guerrilla raiding added to French difficulties in securing fodder, food and revenue, disrupted the French lines of communication, and provided intelligence to the British, Wellington remained correct in his strategic insistence that victory depended upon the operations of large armies and the holding of major towns, not upon any alleged upsurge of populist resistance.[26] National opposition to the French, as Lord Liverpool insisted in December 1812, remained vital to sustaining war, but no single campaign would destroy Napoleon. Britain was committed to the careful husbanding of its military resources for the long haul, while acting as a military entrepreneur.

The British view remained as it had been since 1808 that Spain was a pawn in the struggle with Napoleon and a useful means by which to thwart the extension of the Continental System, and extend trade. Wellington revealed scant devotion to the cause of Spanish liberation, focusing instead on the unremitting tasks of raising, arming, feeding, paying, organizing, disciplining, marching and directing the regular armies he wanted for battle with the French.

Sea power and British victory

While the British underplayed the Spanish military contribution to the defeat of France, they have probably overplayed the significance of sea power in eventual victory. A recent study of the period contends that sea power failed to give Britain a decisive edge in acting as a continental power.[27] The most important contribution of sea power was obviously the British capacity to convey armies, both to the Iberian peninsula and from place to place within the theatre of war. Sea power guaranteed an escape route from disaster and logistical support for success. The campaign ending with La Coruña in January 1809 depended entirely on close naval support. During the winter of 1810–11 the navy kept more than 250 transports, backed up by eleven ships of the line in November, at the Tagus basin at Lisbon in case the defensive works of Torres Vedras failed and another sudden evacuation was required.[28] Sea power also underpinned resupply. For example, Portugal and Spain historically imported a great deal of fish from Newfoundland and the volumes of such imports rose greatly in the 1810s. Munitions flowed in, including 336,000 muskets in 1808–11 alone. From 1808 to 1814 some 404 convoys, involving 13,427 ship voyages, went from Britain to Spain, under Royal Naval escort.[29]

Throughout the war, operations within the peninsula could be shaped by major troop movements. When the French thrust into Andalucía threatened Cadiz in February 1810, the navy was able to convey 2,500 Anglo-Portuguese to the city – achieving an insertion of British forces long desired by the British government – and brought some 3,000 Spanish troops along the southern Atlantic coast to escape the French and reinforce Cadiz. During the French siege of another port, Tarragona, in 1811, the Royal Navy arranged and ensured the transportation of 6,300 Spanish troops to buttress the town's defences. In June–July 1812, some 7,000 Anglo-Sicilian troops from Sicily and 4,000 Spanish troops from the Balearics were shipped to the coast of Catalonia to replenish the anti-French rebellion there. In 1813, 2,000 Spanish soldiers at La Coruña were transported to the east coast where they strengthened the army under Lieutenant General Sir John Murray at Alicante. The general exploited sea power to ship 17,000 British, Spanish and Sicilian troops, and 1,600 horses and mules to a point south of Tarragona by 2 June.[30] The numbers being transported were relatively significant but mainly local in impact.

Close cooperation between the army and navy depended partly on the personalities involved and partly on expectations of what naval power might achieve. Vice Admiral George Berkeley, commanding the fleet at Lisbon in 1808–12, was particularly effective in cooperating with Wellington and providing the naval support which the land operations required. Yet, although by August 1813 the squadron operated twenty-three warships, Wellington's demands upon it rose steeply after Vitoria. By the summer, exchanges between the Admiralty and Wellington had reached a high level of acrimony.[31] Problems mounted as the British land forces neared the northern Spanish coast, with one commander noting 'all armies look to H M ships for assistance of every description'. Through professional rivalry or just plain oversight, the army provided little co-ordination of its demands on the other service. Even in September, before winter set in, ships of the line found difficulties operating in the Bay of Biscay where the seas were described as 'prodigious' in early autumn, and coastal blockading northwards from Bayonne, to include the route to and from Bordeaux, proved impossible for square-rigged vessels except when the wind was offshore. Despite such challenges, during the winter months the squadron maintained sixteen effective vessels on the coast from the River Adour – on which Bayonne stands – to Cape Ortegal, to the north-east of Ferrol. The local naval commander complained that, even though Wellington knew that 'it was the *Navy only* that could have made the movement of the left of the army' in the advance to and across the River Adour, Wellington's scant recognition of this contribution in his despatches contrasted strongly with 'the volumes published of every walk his Lordship takes from village to village'.[32]

The contribution of sea power to theatre strategy was thus ambiguous. British command of the oceans clearly underpinned the entire peninsular commitment. But in 1813 the squadron attached for specific peninsula service, other than along the Mediterranean coast, contained a total of twenty-three, mostly small, warships from over 630 warships in Britain's service. The enjoyment of naval supremacy on the high seas led to the over-sanguine exploration of too many options, with ministers attempting to shape strategy within the peninsula by reference to where seaborne landings could be effected, sometimes at the cost of ignoring the over-riding need to break French military power. So, too, Wellington in 1813 based his theatre strategy on ill-informed ideas of what, locally, naval power might achieve; by September, the First Lord of the Admiralty told Wellington that the general did not understand the nature and constraints of sea power. Even after twenty years of naval expeditions across the globe in all their assorted successes and failures, the projection of power remained complex and contentious.

The balance of British difficulties and advantages

British success at the operational level depended on the strong manage-ment of a host of working arrangements. A perennial issue, therefore, was whether the British possessed an officer corps capable of organizing and managing an army deployed in extensive operations in a prolonged con-tinental war. One of the most frustrating aspects of any command was the coordination of immediate subordinates. Wellington did not control senior appointments to his army but instead depended on Horse Guards for the assignment of suitable officers. He made many complaints about the calibre of senior officers, with the steps from battalion command to divisional command and, among generals, from senior command within the main army to independent operational command being especially challenging transitions. Very few of his senior subordinates combined the full range of abilities required for high command. That was scarcely surprising given the need to plan and organize logistics, manage increasingly numerous and diversely specialist staffs, manipulate the political agenda, understand theatre strategy, control multiples of numerous battalions (each of about 500–760 men) in battle, and provide inspiring, possibly heroic, and preferably charismatic, leadership under prolonged fire. William Beresford, who commanded the Portuguese army, proved outstanding at organization and overall management but was far less competent on the battlefield. Other generals brought extraordinary determination and drive to their conduct of operations and their engagement on the field of arms, some sacrificing limbs and life in demonstrating such prowess. By 1812–13, Wellington had acquired a reasonably accomplished team of senior subordinates, whatever their individual vagaries and deficiencies.

Equally importantly, by then his army was benefiting from dramatic improvements in the training of junior officers. The establishment of the Royal Military College, pressed forward by the Duke of York, yielded far better trained staff officers by the 1810s. The effective running of the army in the peninsula, including the discharge of such easily overlooked tasks as surveying, sketching and mapping the terrain, benefited from the skills inculcated into cadets at the college. Many officers who completed this training were assigned to the Adjutant General's department to handle a wide array of administrative, managerial and technical functions. One aspect of operational effectiveness which received much attention from Wellington was the gathering of constant, wide-ranging and accurate information about French troop strengths and movements across Spain. Wellington built up a formidable network of civilian agents and correspondents to supply him with such information. In addition, he developed both the capacity of intelligence officers and cavalry patrols to acquire and feed back military intelligence and the procedures to evaluate the steady flow of data thus acquired. Throughout his operations, Wellington's decisions depended upon an understanding of exactly where the French were, where they might intend to proceed, where they had the capability of proceeding and, always, in what precise numbers all these movements would occur. Staff work and intelligence operations and assessment marked significant advances in the army's professionalization.[33]

The army's commissariat became increasingly reliable and efficient. The dramatic occasions when the commissariat failed, leading to severe food shortages, occurred when the army was in retreat and encountering very bad weather. It was rarely the failure of the commissariat which hamstrung military strategy, but rather the failure of military strategy which created conditions in which the commissariat could not operate within reasonable margins of mission stretch and human error. The failures of the supply of artillery and munitions at Burgos and at the first attack on San Sebastian resulted more from over-optimistic estimates of likely enemy resistance than from inherent inadequacies in the administration of the ordnance department within the theatre of operations.

Improvements in leadership and staff work would have had limited effect without the guarantee of an adequate supply of military manpower. When challenged in parliament after the dismal retreat from Burgos, the prime minister claimed that shortfalls in troop numbers were not to blame; he stressed that the total British military commitment to the peninsula, Sicily and the Mediterranean in June 1812 amounted to 127,000 men, including Germans and 36,000 Portuguese.[34] From among these, the total British force designated for service in the peninsula at the end of 1812 consisted of sixty-seven infantry battalions and seventeen cavalry regiments. Their full establishment of rank and file totalled 65,887 infantry and 7,980 cavalry. The establishment of 65,887 infantry turned out, however, to be only 31,163 effectives in late 1812. Some of the established battalions did not have all their companies with them when they were despatched to the peninsula. Others were simply understrength through steady attrition. The supply chain for replenishing the army proved to be long and complicated. The manpower for the sixty-seven infantry battalions assigned to the peninsula came from over thirty UK battalion depots, while the seventeen cavalry regiments drew their recruits from another six. Scottish battalions recruited their men throughout Scotland from Inverness to Ayr and Glasgow to Edinburgh. There were a few recruiting bases in northern England for battalions designated for the peninsula, at Carlisle and Hull. A whole array of such bases, however, spread across southern England from Barnstaple and Taunton to Colchester and Chelmsford with many dotted along the south coast and just inland from it. Finally, there were two recruiting bases in Ireland, at Omagh and Dundalk, and one in the Channel Islands. Maintaining the steady flow of recruits required activity over a very wide area.[35]

In addition to the problems of recruiting was the impact of illness. No fewer than 19,263 men, or one-third of the army, were sick in mid-December 1812. This level of sickness partly reflected the annual rhythms of campaigning. With the heavy campaigning against the border fortresses of Ciudad Rodrigo and Badajoz in January–April 1812, the sickness rate rose by May to 30%, requiring the services of eleven hospitals, often placed in convents, monasteries and churches, to meet the army's needs. With continued and demanding military exertions over the summer, levels of sickness remained high, reaching 35% in September, though spells in hospital tended to be brief, the consequence of malaria, diarrhoea, and dysentery. The long period in winter quarters from November 1812 ensured that a reasonable level of overall health was attained by the beginning of the campaign season in late May 1813, when the sickness rate dropped to 16%. By July 1813, with the dramatic shift of the campaign to the north, new hospitals were established at Vitoria and in towns on the Bay of Biscay, with Bilbao providing 2,500 beds in a convent and a rope factory, and Santander providing 4,000. Overall, some 352,000 cases were treated in all regimental and general hospitals in the peninsula and south-western France in the years 1812, 1813 and 1814. Of those cases, 82,000 were serious enough to be transferred to other hospitals and 17,000 resulted in deaths, mainly from dysentery, malaria and typhus rather than enemy action; wounds treated in hospitals resulted in only 2,700 deaths.[36]

The continuing supply of manpower and the enlarged and enhanced provision of medical services depended upon political commitment at home. One of the more fully documented revisions to earlier interpretations of the long wars against France has been the weight given to ministers' support for the peninsular strategy, certainly by 1811. Napoleonic France was more efficient than Britain at delivering conscripted soldiers and, probably, as efficient in furnishing the material needed to support armies, even though the forced extraction of revenues, food and other supplies from conquered countries provoked longer-term resentment and hostility among subject peoples. But the British government ensured that Wellington had under his command in 1813 three times the number of troops assigned in 1809 to the peninsula. This was achieved by various means. The total numbers of troops available from Britain for the peninsula was fixed, while the British paid for 30,000 Portuguese troops from 1809 onwards. The British in 1812 also provided a £1 million military subsidy to the Spanish authorities, with comparable sums in the following years. The widespread deployment of British officers to senior commands in the Portuguese army meant that, as in India, control of wholly non-British forces was kept in British hands, while, as a career incentive and reward, additional opportunities for promotion and advancement were made available to the relatively small British officer corps in the peninsula.

No assessment of British military effectiveness in the peninsula would be complete without at least some mention of the tactical level of military performance. When Wellington sailed home from India in 1805, he attributed British achievement in the subcontinent to the fighting prowess of the British soldier, a prowess unsurpassed, in his view, by any but Frenchmen. The battles won in the peninsula from 1808 displayed both tactical acumen and fighting ability. The resilience at La Coruña and Talavera, the savage determination at Badajoz, the speed of manoeuvre and initiative at Salamanca and Vitoria all showed how far the British army had come in tactical accomplishments since its more confined days of 1793–95. Even at less celebrated engagements as the defence of the line of the Pyrenees in July–August 1813, this raw tactical effectiveness seemed to Wellington to be his army's ultimate achievement. As the general reported privately:

We have some desperate fighting in these mountains, and I have never known the troops behave so well. In the battle of the 28th we had hard fighting, and in my life I never saw such an attack as was made by General Barnes's brigade . . . the loss of the French is immense.

To the prime minister, he reiterated, 'I never saw such fighting as on the 27th and 28th of July . . . nor such determination as the troops showed'. He described that fighting to Lieutenant General Lord William Bentinck as 'fair *bludgeon* work'. Vital to such effectiveness were discipline, instruction, and organization. As Wellington informed the prime minister, 'Our own troops always fight, but the influence of regular pay is seriously felt on their conduct, their health, and their efficiency'.[37]

Assessment

The impact of the British war effort in the peninsula is difficult to assess. The extent to which Spanish resistance depended upon the British presence remains ambiguous. Financial and direct military assistance provided important underpinnings throughout the war. But the mobilization of Spanish manpower had a more telling effect than those contributions. For example, in January 1811, in the middle of the period when total French effectives assigned to the peninsula peaked at over 290,000 men, the forces deployed under Masséna against Wellington's Anglo-Portuguese army amounted to 64,000 men, leaving 230,000 French soldiers present for duty in early 1811 not deployed against the British. Moreover, British victories were usually qualified. Masséna's losses in 1810–11 were inflicted by food shortages and disease; even so the marshal fielded a full-scale army within weeks of returning to his base at Salamanca. Only once, at Salamanca, did British forces break a French army and by themselves open the way to a significant British advance. Although the encouragement Wellington's operations gave to the Spanish and the threat posed by the British to the French probably exceeded a straightforward headcount of troops, when all such allowances are made, the Spanish armies, although discredited and dispersed, continued to occupy the bulk of the French army's attention.

The difficulty in evaluating the Spanish role flows from three factors. First, British interest in the war has focused on Wellington's achievements in building an army and using it effectively for five years from the spring of 1809. The entire war is often subconsciously treated by British military historians – who dominate the historiography of this particular theatre of war – simply as the setting in which the British created an army capable of challenging the best soldiers in Europe. Offering an alternative to this focus is made extremely difficult by the second factor, which is the lack of concentrated documentation on the Spanish forces. That defect in turn reflects the third, the particularist realities of resistance in Spain.

The Peninsular War was part of a more complex revolutionary situation than any other conflict which the British engaged in during the long years of war from 1775 to 1830. The American Revolution and even the upheavals in contemporary India were less multilayered than the impact of revolution in Spain. The French invasion triggered widely divergent political and social movements. Many middle-class townspeople welcomed the advent of reform, particularly as it enshrined a range of constitutional and civil rights and was accompanied by the loosening up of land markets, through the suppression of Spain's 3,000 monasteries and nunneries and the confiscation of some proscribed nobles' estates. Many of the humbler parish clergy accepted the abolition of the closed orders and of the Inquisition. The church hierarchy, led by Cardinal Don Luis de Borbon, cousin of Charles IV, Archbishop of Toledo, and primate of Spain, accepted the Bonapartist regime. But efforts to create a new system of government encountered immense obstacles from the country's diffused system of power. Because local authority was as much in the hands of landowners and the church as it was in royal hands, varying by province and within the provinces, there was no straightforward mechanism by which power could be transferred and there was enormous vested interest in the defence of local autonomy. For example, Galicia in the north-west was the most heavily populated province, but a majority of the towns and villages there came under church jurisdiction. This may have explained why the British – representing a most insistently Protestant power – were so unwelcome there in 1808. It certainly fuelled persistent and vigorous opposition to French rule. To the south of the River Tagus, the great estates had long dominated, three-quarters of men were labourers, and the great landowners exerted considerable power. Many leading grandees initially cooperated with the new order, but by December 1808 some of the greatest landowners in the country were branded as traitors by Napoleon. Some areas came under the leadership of new men, who started as rebels forming guerrilla bands and acquired formal military rank from the anti-French juntas. The leading two guerrilla leaders were Francisco Espoz y Mina and Juan Martin Diez – 'El Empecinado'. Mina was appointed by the regional junta to command all partidas in Navarre; leading 3,500 men by 1810, when the Regency at Cadiz appointed him a colonel, he controlled much of that province. Subsequently promoted further by the Regency, he commanded 13,500 men as part of the Spanish Seventh army in 1813. El Empecinado operated to the north-east of Madrid in the region between the capital and Zaragosa. His forces grew from about 1,000 men in 1810 – when he was promoted by the Regency to brigadier general – to about 5,000 in 1814. These two generals controlled territory and attacked and pinned down French forces. Yet they were no friends to Bourbon absolutism, gaining in heroic mystique from their opposition to the restored Ferdinand VII in the 1820s. During the war, both the Spanish opposition to the French and the Bonapartist regime in Madrid thus drew support from the heady mix of clerics, liberal reformers, landed aristocrats, and adventurers, while localists fought off any centralizing bureaucratic moves emanating from Madrid.[38] A modern view of the Peninsular War emphasizes the intensity of the internal conflict rather than depicting an inspiring national rising betrayed after 1814 in sustained outbreaks of treachery and reprisals. The vicious fighting within Spain rather than the British army operating in Portugal tied down massive French forces, especially in 1810–12.

How far the French commitment in Spain prevented Napoleon from succeeding in his invasion of Russia in 1812 and therefore contributed decisively to Napoleon's defeat there remains doubtful. Even with his dispositions in Spain, Napoleon placed between 550,000 and 600,000 troops east of the Nieman River at some time in the period June–December 1812. Much of that manpower was raised specifically for the Russian campaign and half came from allied and subjugated countries. About 300,000 Frenchmen were dispatched to Russia, while about 240,000 Frenchmen (and about 60,000 French allies' troops) served in Spain. The demands of the Russian campaign created their own supply, notably in the shape of 96,000 soldiers from Poland and 125,000 from Austria and the principal German states of Bavaria, Saxony, Prussia and Westphalia.[39] Subsidiary rulers, commanders, units, and individuals all had stronger reasons for agreeing to serve in this venture than in Spain. As for the disintegration of Napoleon's army, heavy losses from food shortages and ferocious heat began as soon as the invasion started and before a battle was fought. By mid-July 1812, the emperor lost about one-third of his initial army, or at least 100,000 men. Under these conditions desertions rapidly mounted, accounting at the end of the campaign for 50,000 men. Once winter set in and fighting commenced, about 100,000 troops were taken prisoner.[40] It could be argued that Napoleon's peninsular commitment saved France from even bigger losses of French troops, for the weather would have sapped whatever manpower, however numerous, that was sent east.

Even the appalling losses from the Russian campaign did not prevent Napoleon from raising replacement divisions with which to confront a new continental alliance in central Europe in 1813. He called 400,000 fresh conscripts to the colours from September 1812 to January 1813, by accelerating the date of enlistment for many (including 150,000 due to serve in 1814) and summoning 100,000 men not called upon in 1809–12; in addition, he mobilized 100,000 National Guardsmen for military service within France.[41] Given France's average annual births of over one million in 1787–99,[42] and allowing for infant mortality, there were 350,000 to 400,000 young men reaching the age of military service each year. The annual average conscription was just over 100,000 men from May 1802 to February 1812. Napoleon was able in 1812–13 to lift conscription above that level because he commanded the bureaucratic machinery and reserves of population to do so. While he could not sustain another prolonged Spanish war, his peninsular commitment did not prevent him from summoning the resources for what he anticipated would be yet another of his customarily short and politically conclusive campaigns.

Finally, the Spanish role was overshadowed by Wellington's focus on the military organization under his own control and the superior calibre of the army he created in comparison with the far more diffuse and weakly integrated Spanish forces. Wellington ceaselessly complained of the incompetence of Spanish army officers and political leaders and thus, without analysing the competing challenges they faced, created an enduring impression that the Spanish elite impeded the war effort rather than organized extensive and often complex operations.[43] On the other hand, Wellington overcame substantial obstacles to forge an effective army and sustain the pressure for steady improvement within it. By 1813–14 the army in the peninsula had become proficient in most of its branches and even the cavalry was said by some to have achieved parity with the French, which it did not enjoy in the 1800s.

Equally important, although the military dimension has dominated the historiography of the war, Wellington developed striking advantages over the French in political organization and intelligence. He worked closely with ministers in London, and largely shared their assumptions and priorities. There was an intellectual and analytical transparency about his relationship with the home government which few historians detect in the transactions between Napoleon's military and political subordinates in the peninsula and the emperor. Moreover, Wellington controlled much of the diplomatic relationship between Britain and Portugal and independent Spain, essentially through the diplomatic work of Charles Stuart and Henry Wellesley, able young emissaries to the Portuguese and Spanish governments respectively who enjoyed long and successful careers as ambassadors. His clear, unwavering, and hard-headed focus on managing an army within the complex and turbulent political world of the peninsula, without seeking to interfere radically with the political order created by the Portuguese and Spaniards, differed sharply from Napoleon's and Joseph's reformist, if often inconsistent and incoherent, plans and dreams for their conquered domains. More credit is now being given to the means by which the British established and operated civilian and military networks for gathering intelligence and how Wellington himself created a system for managing and evaluating the resultant information and linking strategic and operational intelligence. In this he built on improvements in intelligence gathering and storing developed at Horse Guards in London.[44] Finally, in operational matters Wellington brought to his command rigorous planning, sound judgement, quick understanding, and excellent assessment of terrain. Stern application to the routine business of running complex operations was reinforced by 'firmness and decision' in the conduct of affairs.[45]

While his foresight, insight and range of understanding of military and political affairs, within a sharply delineated sphere, and his sheer energy and drive in mastering a daunting array of planning, organizational, and

operational challenges, distinguished Wellington as an exceptional commander, his understated bravery and charisma in action made a powerful
contemporary and longer-term historical impact in exemplifying a specifically 'British' military culture. It is misleading to suggest that the Peninsular
War 'made' the British army, since its performance elsewhere before 1809
and its condition in the retreat from Burgos in November 1812 puncture
easy generalizations. But Wellington managed and led the forces in the
special conditions of the peninsula to unusual and excellent effect.

The final campaign

Wellington's invasion of France and the campaign that ended with the
armistice in April 1814 are typically treated as an almost inevitable and
uncontroversial sequel to the drama and vicissitudes of the previous five
years of war in the peninsula. One modern account even suggests that the
French lost their fighting edge after September 1813, adding to this sense
of inevitable British victory.[46] In fact, from the Bidassoa River crossing on
7 October 1813 to the attack on Toulouse on 10 April 1814, Wellington
fought more battles than in any comparable period of the Peninsular War.
Those five major engagements cost the French 19,000 casualties, while
the British and Portuguese lost 16,500 casualties. The armies fought and
manoeuvred continuously, except for their recourse to winter quarters in
the latter part of December and during January. Of the battles, three (the
Nivelle on 10 November, Orthez on 27 February, and Toulouse on 10
April) involved concentrated British onslaughts upon well-defended and
well-entrenched hill positions. The battle of Nive, actually two engagements on 9 and 13 December, saw the British resisting two separate
and imaginative counter-attacks. These battles revealed Wellington's full
range of accomplishments against one of Napoleon's ablest commanders,
Marshal Soult.[47] The marshal was a gifted master of manoeuvre and a
tenacious mover of men, conducting his retreats with skill and vigour,
as Wellington had found in pursuing him from Oporto in May 1809.
Displaying great caution in giving battle, Soult only lost his touch (and
here lay the decisive difference between Wellington and his French adversary) in his lack of adroitness, flexibility and insight once fighting began.
As Napoleon famously insisted, Soult would win 'if only he will exhibit
pluck and place himself at the head of the troops'.[48]

The war's final campaign also tested the sustainability of the wartime
alliances with the Portuguese and Spanish and the capacity to manage
an invasion of France. Progress proved initially tentative because doubts

multiplied over holding the advancing allied army together and because French military intentions and capabilities remained unclear. The Portuguese provided the most reliable component of the allied army. But this success led to the Portuguese government's increasing dissatisfaction at the lack of recognition given to its army's military prowess. As the end of the war in the peninsula seemed to approach, such recognition became an increasingly important factor in building the prestige of the post-war Portuguese regime. Wellington agreed that greater attention should be given in the existing media – through his and Marshal Beresford's dispatches back home and through ministerial speeches in Parliament, both extensively reported in the press – to the separate efforts and achievements of the Portuguese army. A second 'ally', in the form of German troops, was far less numerically important than the Portuguese, but raised more problems. Wellington claimed that he lost 1,200 soldiers through desertion, especially from the King's German Legion, during July–October 1813. Such a level of desertion threatened to become so dangerously corrosive that Wellington suggested that all the Germans should be transferred to Hanover if and when the French retreated from Germany, to be replaced by 8,000–10,000 British militia if they could be properly trained by experienced British regular officers. Few Germans remained with the field army into 1814.[49]

Far more complex and wide-ranging were local, national, strategic, and behavioural problems with the Spanish. Close cooperation with diverse local authorities did not become any easier with the French withdrawal from much of Spain. A particularly irksome example of tension arose when the authorities in Santander, the main port on the Spanish north coast, placed the British military hospital under quarantine in early 1814. The British felt this decision owed more to animosity against their presence than any medical danger posed by the hospital. It was also galling since portable buildings to house 40–50 men each had been shipped from Britain to ensure suitable accommodation at Santander and because the only alternative was to prepare hospitals at Falmouth and Plymouth to receive men currently using the facilities in northern Spain. At the national level, the British found themselves in late 1813 and 1814 at the receiving end of a campaign in some leading liberal newspapers which publicized any lapses in British behaviour. Especially biting were accusations of atrocities in the storming of San Sebastian in early September, accompanied by a call for the people of Spain to rise against the British. The national government failed to disclaim such inflammatory rhetoric and Wellington suspected that officials in the Spanish ministry of war, and possibly the minister himself, planted those stories in order to undermine his own ill-defined position as commander-in-chief of the Spanish armies. The removal of the minister, Don Juan Donoju, at the end of January at least eased this tension.[50]

Larger difficulties remained as to the most appropriate strategic deployment of the Spanish armies. The Mediterranean seaboard posed challenges for effective cooperation between the Anglo-Sicilian force operating on and along the coast, supported by British naval power, and local Spanish armies whose natural lines of operation stretched not along the coasts but inland. For the winter of 1813–14, Wellington saw little value in continued action by the Anglo-Sicilian force, condoning instead its withdrawal. The task of holding down Suchet in eastern Spain and taking over the fortresses on the coast was assigned wholly to Spanish forces. For his own invasion of France, Wellington allocated, at the end of November, only a small number of Spanish troops. Added to his longstanding disquiet about Spanish armies' performance in battle was his distrust of the Spaniards' likely behaviour in France. A substantial force, comprising 20,000 men, instead provided a reserve within Spain, just across the frontier from France.[51]

Wellington's invasion strategy depended upon conciliating the French. Believing that support for Napoleon was confined to senior army officers and civilian officials, Wellington still remained extremely cautious about associating the allied army with regime change or dynastic politics. This caution stemmed both from the lack of any overt support to be found in south-western France for a Bourbon restoration and from British distrust of Austria and indeed the other continental allies. There was no point pressing hard or fast into southern France if the major continental powers concluded their own peace settlement with Napoleon. Following the crushing defeat inflicted upon Napoleon at the battle of Leipzig on 16–18 October, Russia, Prussia, and Austria opened negotiations at Frankfurt. On 9 November the central European allies, with the Austrian chancellor Metternich viewing the war, according to Castlereagh, as a 'game of statesmen', offered Napoleon the natural frontiers of France. British concern focused on the need to guarantee British maritime rights, which won the allies' acknowledgment, and Holland. One cabinet minister later stressed, 'Antwerp and Flushing out of the hands of France are worth 20 Martiniques in our own hands'.[52] Although Napoleon declined the Frankfurt terms, the possibility of negotiations remained open. Wellington, who did not learn of Leipzig until after the Nivelle (10 November), recommended on 21 November that Britain make peace with France. If Britain could secure its objectives and if Napoleon moderated his policies, 'he is probably as good a Sovereign as we can desire in France'. If he were to resume his aggressive ways, then all France and indeed all Europe would oppose him.[53] Castlereagh in January 1814 repeated Britain's position that she would discuss terms with Napoleon if he remained ruler of France.

While the international situation remained fluid, Wellington faced pressure to push forward a Bourbon restoration in France. He saw an opportunity for the Bourbons to make an effective personal bid for their throne, but he offered no overt aid to royalist activists and, when victory over Napoleon became increasingly likely, simply responded to local declarations in favour of the Bourbon king, avoiding the risk of returning the king to France at the point of foreign bayonets. When the third in line to the Bourbon succession, the Duc d'Angoulême, arrived at the front in early February 1814, he had to remain under cover. Wellington clashed with the prince over claims made by Bourbon sympathizers that they had British backing and would be guaranteed British protection. On 29 March, the general reminded the duke: 'I will not give the assistance of the troops under my command to support any system of taxation or of civil government which your Royal Highness may attempt to establish.'[54]

Given such continuing political uncertainties, Wellington also insisted that British success in France depended upon 'our moderation and justice, and upon the good conduct and discipline of our troops'. In March 1814, he stressed that his army was

not sufficiently strong to make any progress if the inhabitants should take part in the war against us. What has occurred in the last six years in the Peninsula should be an example to all military men on this point, and should induce them to take especial care to endeavor to conciliate the country which is the seat of war.

Soldiers had to remain under 'the most strict discipline' and officers had to demonstrate to the civilian population that they neither encouraged soldiers' misbehaviour nor allowed it to pass unpunished.[55]

The allied advance into southern France, therefore, was not so straightforward an affair as it might at first appear to have been. If Leipzig inflicted massive losses on the French army, thereby easing Wellington's fears of Soult's receiving reinforcements, doubts continued over Russian and Prussian intentions and further uncertainty arose nearer the Franco-Spanish border from the fate of Suchet's army in Catalonia, because any evacuation of that province would have shifted 40,000 troops in Soult's direction. Far from being reinforced from Catalonia, however, Soult lost men heavily during December and January. His total army, standing at 87,000 men on 1 December 1813, fell to 60,000 men by 21 January 1814; 14,000 of those troops were dispatched to Orléans or Lyon, in the expectation in mid-January that Napoleon would pull off a new political settlement in Spain.

For his part, Napoleon tried to escape from his remaining Spanish entanglement and cut Wellington's army off from Spanish support. The emperor offered Ferdinand VII, whom he had imprisoned since 1808, a wide-ranging settlement embodied in the Treaty of Valençay on 10 December by which the Spanish Bourbons would be restored to their throne if, among many other matters, Ferdinand established close links with Napoleon's regime, reinstated the Spanish *afrancesados*, and expelled the British from his realm. The emperor hoped thus to isolate Wellington's army and force it into an evacuation, if not defeat and capture, and to free French soldiers for use in central Europe. Throughout January, Wellington feared that Napoleon would indeed find some means of withdrawing from Spain and inducing the Spaniards to end their war.[56] The Council of Regency, headed by a member of the royal family, Cardinal Archbishop Don Luis de Borbon, recommended rejection of the treaty, a move virtually unanimously accepted by the Cortes on 4 February 1814. Although Ferdinand, ready to sign anything in order to escape his captivity, had never intended to abide by the treaty, this decision finally cleared the way for a full advance into France.[57]

The fact that the allied army had done little more than push into the south-western French borderlands by February reflected the constraints created by these diplomatic manoeuvres. But it also resulted from bad weather and stiff French military resistance. The first great Wellingtonian battle in France occurred at the forcing of the Nivelle River, where Soult had tried to deny his enemy access to the port of St-Jean-de-Luz, on 10 November. Soult had established a thoroughly defended position because the British seizure of St-Jean-de-Luz would enable them to shorten their lines of supply, stretching at that time back to Santander, the main Spanish port much farther west on the Bay of Biscay. After being pushed across the Nivelle, Soult still tried to contain Wellington, by holding the line of the River Nive, hinging his defence on the well-stocked and thoroughly buttressed city of Bayonne. Again, defeat at the battles of the Nive led Soult to focus on protecting the Adour River, which formed his principal supply route, flowing from the interior. Wellington concentrated on investing Bayonne rather than breaking Soult's internal communications, since he aimed to push Soult ever farther eastwards and to expand his own seaward supply lines. This approach held the additional advantage, seen already at San Sebastian and Pamplona and at various places in Catalonia, of leaving sizeable residual French garrisons in towns isolated by British advances. Only in early January 1814 did Wellington learn that the Russians, Prussians and Austrians had crossed the Rhine on 22 December.[58] As campaigning shifted into France itself, Russia and Prussia became less eager to settle for peace, while Napoleon's continued ability and willingness to counterpunch also reduced Austria's readiness to accept his long-term pacific intentions.

Reassured by this more settled diplomatic context, Wellington resumed his campaign on 12 February. By pushing units of the allied army eastwards on the Adour River, he obliged Soult to shuffle eastwards himself, leaving Bayonne increasingly exposed. By feints, manoeuvring, pontoon bridge-building, and using a flotilla of small boats, Lieutenant General Sir John Hope completed the investment of Bayonne by 27 February, deploying 18,000 Anglo-Portuguese troops and 16,000 Spaniards, who Wellington had agreed to add to the allied armies in order to secure his lines of communication and supply and free his field army for further advances. Crossing the Adour River, Wellington forced the French to increase the pace of their main army's withdrawal inland away from the Bayonne River and the allies' coastal lines of communication. On 27 February, the British attacked and defeated Soult in a very good defensive position on high ground at Orthez. Only then did the campaign for southern France open up, for Orthez lies a mere 50 miles in a direct line across the Pyrenees from Sorauren, where the two sides had battled each other seven months earlier in the last days of July. Pushed from his chosen defensive line, Soult steered his retreat far eastwards upon Toulouse, hoping that his continued presence in the field would deter Wellington from despatching a substantial corps northwards to the great city-port of Bordeaux. Wellington, however, pressed Soult's main force sufficiently to the east to enable the allies, after summoning sufficient reserves, both to check the marshal and to take Bordeaux on 12 March. The British advanced farther in the early months of 1814 than they had between Vitoria and the end of 1813. This success and evidence of royalist support in Bordeaux, as well as elsewhere, persuaded the British government to concur with increasing demands at home for the overthrow of Napoleon.[59]

Meanwhile, Soult sought to establish himself at Toulouse, which offered the considerable advantage of being the French army's principal supply base in southern France. Determined to push him out of this major city, the British with difficulty crossed the Garonne River, doing so in small units on 4 April and then *en masse* from 7 April. Only on 10 April did Wellington attack a narrow front of Toulouse's strong fortifications. Although artillery played its role, the British breakthrough hinged on fierce, close fighting, with the British sixth division of about 5,000 men suffering 30% in casualties.[60] After sustaining 3,236 losses, Soult evacuated on 11 April, and Wellington on the following day entered a city renowned for royalist sympathies. It was then that everyone learned of Napoleon's abdication, declared on 6 April, following the allies' entry into Paris on 30 March.

The last phase of the peninsular army's war had been hard fought. Persistent and determined French military resistance inflicted 7,000 casualties on Wellington's army in the last two major engagements (Orthez and Toulouse) during the six weeks from 27 February to 10 April; and further losses occurred in minor clashes on the way.[61] In return, the British took Bordeaux and Toulouse, two of the six French cities, other than Paris, of over 50,000 inhabitants. A land invasion of south-western France resulting in such gains had never formed any part of the strategic options for Britain's contribution to the wars against either the Revolution or Napoleon. Strategic incrementalism had thus yielded gratifying but unanticipated results.

The post-war settlement in Spain

The political settlement with France showed the limitations of Britain's influence in the Iberian peninsula. For all the expenditure of men and treasure over six years of military intervention, the British enjoyed limited influence over the new regime. They wanted moderate constitutional monarchy, continued access to Spain's Latin American markets, an end to the slave trade, and support in the diplomatic containment of France in the future. The restored Bourbon monarchy acceded to none of these desires. Much depended on Ferdinand VII who had agreed to abide by conditions stipulated by the Regency in order to secure his release from Napoleonic captivity. Cheered by popular responses to his return on 24 March 1814 to Catalonia, where the captain general was a conservative, Ferdinand gained further political support from regional leaders of the struggle against the French and from stage-managed street agitation in Madrid. Army generals, of whom there had been 327 in 1792, 422 in 1808, and 690 by 1814, devoted as much attention to jockeying for power as they did to fighting the fast-fading French threat. Ferdinand's absolutism was proclaimed on 11 May. The Cortes, which had moved to

Madrid in September 1813 and the cause of liberal reform survived the last engagement of the Peninsular War, the sortie from Barcelona on 16 April, for less than four weeks.[62]

Following the restoration, Wellington visited Madrid from 24 May to 5 June 1814. He sought to prevent any military reaction against Ferdinand and, upon arrival at the capital, to moderate royal policy. The likelihood of the former was debatable. General Freire, commander of the most heavily engaged division in south-western France, opposed any reaction against the restoration. The other leading army commander of Spanish forces in France, the Prince of Anglona (formerly the Duque del Parque), though disliked by the ultra-conservatives, appears not to have leaned towards the liberals. The fragmentation of the Spanish army into regional entities, its wide dispersal, and the feebleness of the Cortes's control over it, all made the counter-revolution more straightforward than it would probably have been if the army had been unified, concentrated and more completely answerable to the politicians. Oman pointed out that Freire and Anglona might have sympathized with the Cortes, but their commands were far from Madrid. Other possible sympathetic commanders were in Galicia, again distant from central Spain.[63] On the political front, Wellington had urged in June 1813 that the widest possible amnesty be extended to Spaniards who had, under difficult circumstances, cooperated with the French.[64] He regarded the restoration of absolutism in May 1814 as ominous, for the government seemed more intent on revenge against liberalism than on administering the country, and seemed oblivious to the dangers and difficulties it faced.[65] Wellington continued to urge the establishment of a workable constitution.

British priorities, however, concentrated on international and commercial policies in relation to Spain. A particular concern was Spain's relationship with its Latin American colonies. In April 1812 Lord Castlereagh, as Foreign Secretary, pointed out that unless the Spanish government, whatever its prejudices, placed its American colonies on an equal commercial standing with Spain itself, those colonies' 'separation from the parent state is inevitable and at hand'. Such a separation need not, in Castlereagh's view, be disadvantageous to Spain. The minister stressed the desirability of reminding the Spanish regency and Cortes that 'Great Britain has derived more real commercial advantage from North America since the separation than she did when that country was subjected to her dominion and part of her colonial system'. Yet even the argument that Spain might raise money from duties on British trade with Latin America failed to dampen Cadiz's commitment to suppressing Spanish American revolutions and imposing the tightest restrictions on trade. During 1813 Castlereagh gave up pressing for the opening of trade with the Latin American colonies, and duties on British manufactured goods exported to Spain remained extremely high.[66]

When the Cortes moved to Madrid it did not change its position on Latin America. Its principal foreign policy request to Britain consisted of British assistance in recovering Louisiana from the USA and the offer of an alliance which would stipulate that Spain would not renew the Family Compact with Bourbon France. In the peace settlement of July 1814, Castlereagh persuaded France to cede the Spanish portion of San Domingo back to Spain, but Lord Liverpool described the Spanish quest for Louisiana as 'ridiculous'. Ferdinand VII's claims to the throne of Naples and the Grand Duchy of Parma, as well as his attempt to be included among the principal powers of the emerging Vienna system, added to British frustration with Spanish hubris.[67] The Treaty of Alliance on 5 July 1814 offered two significant concessions: Britain would be accorded most favoured nation treatment if Spain threw open her Latin American trade and, in a secret article, Spain promised not to revive a Family Compact with France. This last provided a useful antidote to fears about a double Bourbon restoration during the spring of 1814. At the Congress of Vienna later in the year, however, Spain refused to abolish the slave trade throughout its Latin American possessions, despite British offers of a substantial payment and British approval for Spain to raise a loan in Britain itself. In the end Spain refused to sign the Treaty of Vienna, unyielding on the declarations (and more concrete steps) for the abolition of the slave trade and disaffected by its failure to secure Louisiana. Britain also suffered from Portuguese petulance when Portugal declined to join allied forces against Napoleon in 1815. This was despite the fact that Lord Beresford continued to command the Portuguese army until the liberal revolution of 1820; indeed in 1819, some ninety-six British officers, including fifteen lieutenant colonels, were seconded to that army.[68]

The long peninsular engagement eventually yielded Britain what she wanted, in the expulsion of France from Spain and in assisting the overthrow of Napoleon's European expansionism. The British overcame daunting challenges of terrain, climate, logistics and manpower requirements. They had to control Portugal and cooperate with the Spanish authorities. Yet military experience in the peninsula did not provide transferable knowledge, for the British never fought there again and indeed ceased to maintain garrisons on continental Europe after 1818. The Peninsular War reinforced British claims to join the Great Powers in

shaping the peace after 1814, but her naval might, commercial preponderance, and ability to subsidize the continental allies would probably have
guaranteed that anyway. Moreover, as the post-war years revealed, British
military prowess in the peninsula did not later translate into continuing
political leverage there. As Lord Castlereagh crossly wrote in August
1815: 'the only two Courts with which we find it difficult to do business
are those of the Peninsula . . . It seems as if the recollection of our services
made it impossible to them to do anything without endeavouring most
unnecessarily and ungratefully to display their own independence.'[69] This
complaint was repeated over the following twenty years as Britain continued to seek tangible commercial and diplomatic rewards from her protracted peninsular commitment.

Notes and references

1 Rory Muir, *Britain and the Defeat of Napoleon 1807–1815* (New Haven,
   CT, 1996), p. 216; Sir Charles Oman, *A History of the Peninsular War*,
   7 vols (Oxford, 1902–30), Vol. VI, p. 215.

2 *The Times*, 2 March 1813, p. 4; 5 May 1813, p. 2.

3 The figures are from: Oman, *A History of the Peninsular War*, Vol. II,
   pp. 624–27, Vol. III, pp. 532–39, Vol. IV, pp. 638–42, Vol. VI,
   pp. 741–45, 768.

4 Oman, *A History of the Peninsular War*, Vol. VI, pp. 750–52.

5 Oman, *A History of the Peninsular War*, Vol. VI, pp. 367–68, 377, 388,
   391–92, 395; Jac Weller, *Wellington in the Peninsula* (London, 1967),
   p. 269.

6 Oman, *A History of the Peninsular War*, Vol. VI, pp. 490–95, 500, 513–15,
   768, Vol. VII, pp. 69–70.

7 Historical Manuscripts Commission, *Report on the Manuscripts of J.B.
   Fortescue, Esq., Preserved at Dropmore*, Vol. X (London, 1927), p. 348.

8 Lieutenant Colonel Gurwood (ed.), *The Dispatches of Field Marshal The
   Duke of Wellington, 1799–1815*, 12 vols (London, 1838), Vol. X,
   pp. 458–62, 471–75.

9 Oman, *A History of the Peninsular War*, Vol. VI, pp. 738–40.

10 Gurwood (ed.), *Dispatches . . . Duke of Wellington*, Vol. XI, p. 3.

11 Gurwood (ed.), *Dispatches . . . Duke of Wellington*, Vol. X, p. 640.

12 *Cobbett's Political Register* (London, 1808), Vol. XIV, *July to December
   1808*, cols. 65–67, 932.

13 Gurwood (ed.), *Dispatches . . . Duke of Wellington*, Vol. X, pp. 53–54.

14 Gurwood (ed.), *Dispatches . . . Duke of Wellington*, Vol. X, p. 474.

15 Gurwood (ed.), *Dispatches . . . Duke of Wellington*, Vol. VI, p. 12.

16 The population figures, from 1787, are given in Richard Herr, *Eighteenth-Century Revolution in Spain* (Princeton, NJ, 1958), p. 87.

17 David Gates, *The Spanish Ulcer: a History of the Peninsular War* (London, 1986), pp. 242, 249.

18 Oman, *A History of the Peninsular War*, Vol. IV, pp. 525–26.

19 Oman, *A History of the Peninsular War*, Vol. V, pp. 584–85.

20 Oman, *A History of the Peninsular War*, Vol. III, p, 144.

21 I have taken the engagements, excluding those in which the British played a significant role, from Charles Esdaile, *The Wars of Napoleon* (London, 1995), pp. 325–30, and the casualty figures from Gates, *The Spanish Ulcer*, pp. 80, 97–99, 103, 117–18, 123, 127, 164, 172, 190, 201, 203–04.

22 Gates, *The Spanish Ulcer*, pp. 507–10.

23 Gurwood (ed.), *Dispatches . . . Duke of Wellington*, Vol. X, pp. 568–69.

24 Gurwood (ed.), *Dispatches . . . Duke of Wellington*, Vol. X, pp. 441, 568–69, 618–20; Vol. XII, p. 44.

25 Gurwood (ed.), *Dispatches . . . Duke of Wellington*, Vol. XII, pp. 17–18; Oman, *A History of the Peninsular War*, Vol. VII, pp. 521–22.

26 Charles Esdaile, *Fighting Napoleon: Guerrillas, Bandits and Adventurers in Spain, 1808–14* (New Haven, CT, 2004), pp. 105–09, 113–18, 159, 183–86, 198–200; David French, *The British Way in Warfare 1688–2000* (London, 1990), p. 118; Capt. Hon. D.A. Bingham (ed.), *A Selection from the Letters and Despatches of the First Napoleon*, 3 vols (London, 1884), Vol. III, p. 222.

27 Russell, F. Weigley, *The Age of Battles: The Quest for Decisive Warfare From Breitenfeld to Waterloo* (London, 1991), pp. 352–53.

28 Christopher D. Hall, *Wellington's Navy: Sea power and the Peninsular War 1807–1814* (London, 2004), pp. 95–8.

29 Hall, *Wellington's Navy*, pp. 112, 117–18, 137.

30 Hall, *Wellington's Navy*, pp. 63–5, 148–9, 172–4, 184, 187–8, 203–04.

31 Hall, *Wellington's Navy*, pp. 210–12; Gurwood (ed.), *Dispatches . . . The Duke of Wellington*, Vol. VIII, pp. 144–7.

32 Christopher Lloyd (ed.), *The Keith Papers*, 3 vols (London, 1927–55), Vol. III, pp. 252, 262–63, 286; Hall, *Wellington's Navy*, pp. 78–80, 215.

33 Anthony Clayton, *The British Officer* (London, 2006), pp. 55–71 gives great weight to Wellington's role in creating the British officer corps. John Peaty has reviewed the arguments for crediting reforms at home for British success overseas. John Peaty 'Architect of victory: the reforms of the Duke of York' in Jose Maria Blanco Nunez *et al.* (eds), *Actas*, XXXI International Congress of Military History (Madrid, 2006), pp. 193–204.

34 *The Times*, December 1, 1812, pp. 1–2.

35 Duke of Wellington (ed.), *Supplementary Despatches of Field Marshal the Duke of Wellington, 1799–1815*, 12 vols (London, 1858), Vol. VII, pp. 522–24.

36 Lieutenant General Sir Neil Cantlie, *A History of the Army Medical Department*, 2 vols (Edinburgh, 1973), Vol. I, pp. 346, 349, 351, 361, 508–09.

37 Gurwood (ed.), *Dispatches . . . Duke of Wellington*, Vol. X: 569, 591, 597–98, 602.

38 Herr, *Eighteenth-Century Revolution*, pp. 89, 95–96; Richard Herr, *Rural Change and Royal Finances in Spain at the End of the Old Regime* (Berkeley, CA, 1989), pp. 714–15, 760; James Simpson, *Spanish Agriculture: The Long Siesta, 1765–1965* (Cambridge, 1995), pp. 59–61; Raymond Carr, *Spain 1808–1975* (Oxford, 1966), pp. 39, 45–47; Emiliano Fernandez de Pinedo, Alberto Gil Novales, Albert Derozier, *Centralismo, Ilustracion y Agoria del Antiguo Regimen* (Barcelona, 1981 edn), pp. 268–69, 273–76; Juan Mercader Riba, *Jose Bonaparte Rey de Espana (1808–1813)* (Madrid, 1983), pp. 236–49, 316, 318–19, 322; G. Lovett, *Napoleon and the Birth of Modern Spain*, 2 vols (New York, 1965), Vol. I, pp. 701–20.

39 Figures are in Adam Zamoyski, *1812* (London, 2004), pp. 86–87, 536–40; Gunther E. Rothenberg, *The Art of Warfare in the Age of Napoleon* (Bloomington, IN, 1980), p. 158. Oman, *A History of the Peninsular War*, Vol. VII, pp. 515–18, 521 argued for the uplifting nature of Spanish resistance and for the critical role the war played in tying down veterans who might otherwise have fought against Russia in 1812 and into Germany in 1813.

40 Rothenburg, *The Art of Warfare*, p. 237; Zamoyski, *1812*, pp. 143, 184–85, 190.

41 Figures for conscription and its administrative implications are in Isser Woloch, 'Napoleonic conscription: state power and civil society', *Past and Present*, 111 (May, 1986), 101–29.

42 Colin Jones, *The Longman Companion to the French Revolution* (London, 1988), p. 287.

43 Wellington (ed.), *Supplementary Dispatches*, Vol. VI, pp. 372–73, 388, 491, Vol. VII, pp. 52, 80, 420 provide instances of such failure to do anything but

disparage the Spanish on the part of Wellington and his two brothers who served as successive ministers to the Spanish supreme junta and regency. Bingham, *A Selection from the Letters*, Vol. III, p. 273.

44 Paul Kennedy, *The Rise and Fall of the Great Powers* (New York, 1987), p. 134; French, *The British Way in War*, p. 118; Huw Davies, 'Integration of strategic and operational intelligence during the Peninsular War', *Intelligence and National Security*, Vol. 21 (2006), 202–23; Huw Davies, 'Wellington's use of deception tactics in the Peninsular War', *Journal of Strategic Studies*, Vol. 29 (2006), 723–50.

45 J. Blakiston, *Twelve Years' Military Adventure*, 2 vols (London, 1829), Vol. II, pp. 368–74.

46 Gates, *The Spanish Ulcer*, pp. 428–29.

47 Oman, *A History of the Peninsular War*, Vol. VII, pp. ix–x. Muir, *Britain and the Defeat of Napoleon*, pp. 299–305 provides a concise analysis of the final campaign and points out that the troops committed to defending southern France would have greatly boosted Napoleon's army in the north in early 1814.

48 Paddy Griffith, ' "King Nicholas"-Soult' in David Chandler (ed.), *Napoleon's Marshals* (New York, 1987), pp. 456–77, esp. p. 466; Bingham (ed.), *A Selection*, Vol. III, p. 329.

49 Gurwood (ed.), *Dispatches . . . Duke of Wellington*, Vol. XI, 257, 259–60, 272–73.

50 Gurwood (ed.), *Dispatches . . . Duke of Wellington*, Vol. XI, pp. 298, 301, 313, 446–47, 457, 478.

51 Gurwood (ed.), *Dispatches . . . Duke of Wellington*, Vol. XI, pp. 275–77, 315–16.

52 C.J. Bartlett, *Castlereagh* (London, 1966), pp. 120–21, 123; Muir, *Britain and the Defeat of Napoleon*, p. 309.

53 Gurwood (ed.), *Dispatches . . . Duke of Wellington*, Vol. XI, pp. 305–06.

54 Gurwood (ed.), *Dispatches . . . Duke of Wellington*, Vol. XI, pp. 495, 607, 608–11. At the same time, the British government waited for guidance on negotiations with the allies before deciding to land arms for the royalists along the French coast, south from Jersey in the Channel Islands, or from ships of the Channel fleet south of Ushant. Lloyd, *The Keith Papers*, Vol. III, p. 251.

55 Gurwood (ed.), *Dispatches . . . Duke of Wellington*, Vol. XI, pp. 303–07, 551–53.

56 Gurwood, (ed.), *Dispatches . . . Duke of Wellington*, Vol. XI, pp. 445, 480–81.

57 Oman, *A History of the Peninsular War*, Vol. VII, pp. 298–313.

58 Oman, *A History of the Peninsular War*, Vol. VII, p. 295.

59 C.K. Webster, *The Foreign Policy of Castlereagh, 1812–1815* (London, 1931), pp. 521, 530.

60 Oman, *A History of the Peninsular War*, Vol. VII, pp. 487–88; Ian C. Robertson, *Wellington Invades France: The Final Phase of the Peninsular War, 1813–1814* (London, 2003), pp. 228, 237–38.

61 Oman, *A History of the Peninsular War*, Vol. VII, pp. 555, 559–61.

62 Charles Esdaile, *The Spanish Army in the Peninsular War* (Manchester, 1988), pp. 15, 167, 182–84; Oman, *A History of the Peninsular War*, Vol. VII, p. 409; Lovett, *Napoleon and the Birth of Modern Spain*, Vol. II, pp. 824–33.

63 Lovett, *Napoleon and the Birth of Modern Spain*, Vol. II, pp. 802–04; Esdaile, *The Spanish Army in the Peninsular War*, p. 184; Oman, *A History of the Peninsular War*, Vol. VII, p. 427.

64 Gurwood (ed.), *Dispatches . . . Duke of Wellington*, Vol. X, pp. 430–33.

65 Gurwood (ed.), *Dispatches . . . Duke of Wellington*, Vol. XII, pp. 17, 26–7.

66 Webster, *The Foreign Policy of Castlereagh*, pp. 70–72; Henry D. Inglis, *Spain in 1830*, 2 vols (London 1831), Vol. II, pp. 134–35.

67 Gurwood (ed.), *Dispatches . . . Duke of Wellington*, Vol. XII, pp. 38–40.

68 Parliamentary Papers, *Estimates and Accounts*. Session 21 January–13 July 1819, Vol. XV, pp. 149–51.

69 Webster, *The Foreign Policy of Castlereagh*, pp. 310–13, 411, 412, 416–23.

Britain's global reach

CHAPTER 13

The war of 1812

By 1812 Britain had worked to limit the Continental System by opening up particular lines of trade. Engaging with the French directly in the Iberian peninsula and creating a network of bases in the central Mediterranean secured some useful markets. From 1809, the British retook a number of French island colonies in the Caribbean, thereby denying their opponents regional commercial advantages. The new order in Portugal and Spain after 1808 had also enabled Britain to break into those countries' colonial markets. But economic conditions remained tough and the struggle for international trade landed the British in 1812 in a tense diplomatic dispute with the USA. The disagreement in itself was resolvable but the distance between London and Washington led to a delay in diplomatic exchanges which in turn degenerated into war. This outcome was almost the last thing desired by the British government and by significant sections of American public opinion. But enough enthusiasm prevailed in parts of the USA to energize the war in the west and threaten an invasion of Upper Canada.

The war of 1812 showed how difficult it was for the British to project power inland in North America. The particular circumstances of controlling the rivers and lakes defied ready solution. More generally, the British struggled to raise manpower quickly enough to deter American advances. They found it necessary to forge Indian alliances. Using naval power proved difficult because the Americans did not operate a battle fleet and so the Royal Navy had to concentrate on frigate warfare on a small scale. On land, the British had to avoid provoking more wholehearted American commitment to the war and so they refrained from any invasion campaign. The strategic challenge for the British was to find points against which to apply sufficient force to persuade the Americans to negotiate.

While, however, the war remained a limited conflict, it was intensely fought at those places where fighting occurred. When British pressure failed to bring the Americans to a negotiated settlement, but only after the cessation of the war in Europe, the British government despatched large forces to North America in order to force the USA to come to terms.

Origins of the war

The war of 1812 seemed an accidental and quixotic affair. It began with an American declaration of war in Washington DC on 18 June, just two days after the Foreign Office in London made concessions which, if they had been known across the Atlantic, would have delayed if not forestalled hostilities. The speech from the throne on 30 November 1812 expressed the government's 'sincere regret' at the outbreak of war. Lord Liverpool, the prime minister, stressed in February 1813 that 'The war was not one of interest, but of passion and inflamed feelings'. President James Madison and his party were repeatedly blamed for destroying the customarily friendly and financially fruitful relationship between the two countries through what *The Times* described as 'a train of the grossest impostures'.[1] The conflict ended with the war's most celebrated battle – the stunning American victory at New Orleans, on 8 January 1815 – being fought after the two countries had officially settled their differences and concluded peace at Ghent on 24 December 1814. Aside from one or two incidents, the war is scarcely even noted in British historiography. It has been variously described as 'a sideshow', 'an expensive sideshow' and 'a tiresome irritant'. In American consciousness, however, the war was celebrated as an American triumph over the might and military experience of Britain, while the victory at New Orleans boosted Major General Andrew Jackson as the conqueror of seasoned Peninsular War veterans and a supreme American patriot. Jackson went on to run for the presidency for the first time in 1824, and won it in 1828. The party he shaped, the Democrats, incorporated Anglophobia into their rhetoric and commemorated 8 January as their party's special anniversary for formal dinners and party political celebrations. Many other American political leaders who served in the wartime congress or as senior military officers subsequently glossed over defects or failures in the American conduct of the war and insisted instead on the nationalistic implications of victory.[2] For the British, the conflict arose from efforts to regulate neutral trade with France, so that the end of war in Europe in April 1814 had already removed the war's underlying cause. By the autumn, the continuing campaigning became a diplomatic embarrassment to the British in their negotiations at Vienna to reconstruct post-Napoleonic Europe, as well as a political embarrassment to the British government in its efforts to slash spending after the war against Napoleon ended.[3]

Although the war with the USA was a sideshow compared with campaigning in Europe, Britain's conduct of the war raised serious questions about the British management of joint operations, handling of multi-ethnic armies, capacity to define strategic objectives, and military efficiency. One contemporary analyst in 1813 implied comparisons with the British conduct of operations in North America in 1776–81: 'there is not now a boy of fourteen, who has been at a regimental drill, or seen a regiment change its front, who would be guilty of such errors'. Strategic objectives had been insufficiently defined and civilian and military officials had suffered from an overwhelming 'contempt of an enemy'.[4] In fact, the war of 1812 involved difficult strategic challenges. The land frontier was open to attack at four points: in the far west at Fort Detroit, an outpost of about 800 inhabitants in 1812;[5] between Lakes Erie and Ontario where Niagara was situated; at the eastern end of Lake Ontario, where Kingston was a British base and near which lay York, later Toronto; and stretches of the St Lawrence River giving access to the larger towns of Montreal and Québec City. This was a very long frontier with no water communication possible along the St Lawrence to the Great Lakes, although ships afforded the best means of transport along the shores of the Great Lakes. This region thus raised the challenges of both a land war, fragmented into widely separated campaigns, and a naval contest to control lakes which could not be reached by British warships from the sea. A wholly different naval struggle arose from attacks on British merchant ships on the high seas by American warships and thousands of armed privateers. The Royal Navy had to blockade and counter-attack in a contest between small craft. In addition, whether Britain should take the war to other parts of America was debated from the autumn of 1812.

The disparity of objectives flowed from the dispute's origins in Napoleon's effort in 1806 to exclude British goods from Europe under the Continental System. Britain retaliated from 1807 onwards with a series of Orders in Council to restrict neutrals' trade with Britain's enemies. Reacting to those measures, President Thomas Jefferson imposed an embargo on American ships and goods leaving America for British or French ports. Instead of forcing the leading European trading countries to climb down, the embargo, lasting from December 1807 to March 1809, devastated America's export trade, which crashed from $108 million in 1807 to $22

million the following year. Trade continued thereafter to be subject
to American schemes of non-importation of British or French goods. Yet
goods were increasingly traded through neutrals and through the West
Indies. For example, American exports of flour to Portugal and Spain
increased nearly ninefold from 1809 to 1812; although the trading partners were neutrals, the produce ended up supplying the British army in
the peninsula. A further tension arose from the Royal Navy's practice of
stopping and searching American vessels on the high seas on the grounds
that British sailors working on American vessels remained subject to
impressment. Searches of American commercial ships by British warships
allegedly resulted in thousands of Americans being dragged off into
British service. By 1812 these disputes had created enough resentment for
President James Madison's Republican party to push for war. Voting in the
House of Representatives and Senate indicated that Republican members
of the two houses favoured war by 98 votes to 23, whereas all 39
Federalists who voted opposed the declaration of war.[6]

The Republicans' enthusiasm for war owed a good deal to western
expansionist interests little connected with maritime disputes. In 1811,
local expansionists in the north-western region, which is today Indiana
and Illinois but which was then sparsely penetrated by whites, attacked
and defeated a powerful Native American leader, Tecumseh, at the battle
of Tippecanoe. Their appetite whetted for further action, they portrayed
the British, across the frontier, as allies to 'savage' Indian tribes; removing
British support for those tribes would clear the way for further white
settlement in the region. Congressman Henry Clay, a leading war hawk,
explained in December 1812 the rationale for an invasion of Britain's
western territories in North America: 'Canada was not the end but the
means, the object of the war being the redress of injuries and Canada
being the instrument by which that redress was to be obtained.' Some
Republicans even envisaged an American citizen militia, fired up by
national feelings, assisting Canadians to liberate themselves from British
rule. Former President Jefferson wrote privately in August 1812 that
taking most of Canada would amount to 'a mere matter of marching'.[7]

The war at sea

The first challenge the British faced was to assert their superiority at sea.
By late 1812, press criticism mounted in Britain over the navy's ineffectiveness in the western Atlantic. The tiny American navy ranged
widely, capturing fifty British merchantmen during 1812, while American

privateers took about 450 more. These were significant losses since the British merchant marine in the 1810s totalled about 4,500–5,000 ships. The Royal Navy seized about 150 American privateers in retaliation in 1812 and in the early months of 1813, but failed to prevent the bulk of American merchant shipping from returning safely to harbour.[8] The British government insisted that an immediate and tighter blockade in 1812 was impossible. It was in British interests to keep American ports open, so that American grain could reach the Iberian peninsula, the West Indies could adjust to wartime commercial conditions, and British manufactures could enter American markets. The government emphasized the regional divisions in America over going to war and its reluctance to punish the eastern states unduly in a contest which they opposed. Indeed, *The Times*, supporting the government, urged that Britain should try as far as possible 'to spare the inhabitants of New-York and New England, who are reluctantly dragged into the war'. Moreover, the ministry responded to its critics by reminding them of the challenges posed by blockading; the French fleet in Toulon had escaped even Nelson's blockades in 1798 and 1805.[9] A blockade of the Chesapeake and Delaware ports was not implemented until February 1813 and was not extended more widely until well into 1813.[10] By then, Napoleon's humiliating defeat in Russia loosened his grip over eastern Europe, undermined the Continental System in the region, and led to grain exporting from the Baltic being reopened for the British.

The American war immediately stretched the Royal Navy's resources. In 1812, the stations nearest America's eastern ports, at Halifax (principally) and in Newfoundland, possessed only one ship of the line, nine frigates and twenty-seven other vessels. Although the United States navy counted only seventeen seaworthy warships against those thirty-seven, the Americans enjoyed the advantage that their seven frigates were well armed, very fast and easily a match for the nine frigates the British stationed outside the Caribbean in 1812.[11] Their officers were young and skilful, unlike their senior army officers, and their navy drew on a large and impressive supply of ordinary seamen. The near parity in numbers of frigates constricted British naval strategy. Only by concentrating their squadron could the British hope to challenge American warships, yet concentration exposed British merchantmen to seizure by privateers and made it easy for American merchant vessels to return to home ports. The British feared that by dispersing their own frigates they risked being picked off singly, as occurred in American victories in three engagements between single American and single British frigates from August to

December 1812. The American frigates were far larger than the British frigates they engaged, carrying more and heavier calibre guns and 66%–80% more sailors.[12] Moreover, Napoleon's invasion of Russia in 1812 threatened to tighten the Continental System, a prospect which Madison reasoned would enhance the importance of Canadian exports yet further to Britain's economy. French efforts to constrict European timber supplies to Britain had already led to a 500% increase in Canadian timber exports from 1807 to 1811, with the volume taken from Canada in 1811 exceeding total British timber imports from the Baltic in any year before 1807.[13] The disruption of that trade offered a major strategic gain for the Americans, but it proved a short-term objective, since the Baltic timber trade was resumed from autumn 1813.

It is often argued that Britain suffered discomfort or humiliation in the war at sea. Yet the British boosted the North America fleet by early 1813 to ten ships of the line, thirty-eight frigates and fifty-two other warships. One of the most successful frigate and small-squadron commanders of the 1790s and 1800s, Sir John Borlase Warren, was appointed to command the station, and one of the most daring young inshore captains of the 1800s, Sir James Yeo, who had already, by the age of 30, served twice in the West Indies, along the coast of Brazil, in action off north-west Spain, and in the capture of French Guyana in 1809, was given the Great Lakes command. Subsequent success during the summer offensive of 1813 in Spain eased pressures on the Royal Navy still further in Europe. The British were therefore able to extend their blockade by November 1813 from the southern end of New England to Spanish Florida. American warships found it difficult to get to sea. For example, the USS *United States* returned to New York in December 1812 with a captured British frigate; the two vessels sailed from that city in June 1813, but proceeded only a short way up the New England coast before being blockaded again, for the rest of the war. Of the seven American frigates in existence when war began, four had been rendered *hors de combat* by war's end.[14] Overall, the British captured (as distinct from destroyed) twelve American warships during the conflict. For their part, the Americans made an impressive net gain of sixteen British warships, adding about 3,000 tons of Royal Navy shipping to their own navy, and sinking one British warship. Yet such losses were trivial compared with British wartime achievements in naval fighting. The main British losses were three 38-gun frigates; the rest were smaller ships of 22 guns or fewer. For comparison, the Royal Navy captured or destroyed nine French 40-gun ships and captured one ship of 74 guns during 1814–15 alone. The British seizure of 450,000 tons of enemy naval shipping during the period 1793–1815 dwarfed the Americans' haul against the Royal Navy.[15]

Admittedly, some American privateers continued to raid with success, even in British waters, during 1813 and 1814, but British losses fell as the blockade of American ports tightened and as the British strengthened their system of convoys already in operation at the beginning of the war. While 1,504 British merchantmen were taken by the Americans during the war, mainly by privateers, about half were recaptured.[16] According to returns available before reports from the New Orleans campaign, the British captured or destroyed forty-two US warships during the war; but only nine of them carried 22 or more guns and nineteen were tiny craft bearing 2 guns each. They also seized or destroyed 228 privateers or other armed vessels commissioned for war; again, these were mainly small vessels, with 117 of them carrying 6 or fewer guns. Finally, the Admiralty received official notice by February 1815 of the capture, destruction or detention in port of 1,407 merchant vessels, contributing to a grand tally of at least 1,677 American ships of all types taken out by the British. Nearly 21,000 American sailors were captured or detained in port.[17] These losses indicate the extent of British success at sea.

The British blockade from 1813 onwards constrained the southern states' overseas trade, but did not impede the continued export of grain to Portugal, where local merchants sold it on to the British army, while commodities needed in the West Indies also escaped interception. Congress tightened up on American shipping sailing on British licences in July 1813, but by this time Britain had little need for American grain for its army in the peninsula. The extension of the blockade to New England in April 1814 slashed America's official exports from $61.3 million in 1811 to $6.9 million by 1814.[18] Falling imports halved America's customs revenues just when federal government expenditure soared. By 1814, Boston harbour was full of idle ships; Newburyport, Massachusetts, suffered escalating poverty and sagging property prices; and Southern export commodities could not be sold. John Randolph, a prominent Virginian, described the region surrounding the Chesapeake as being 'in a state of paralysis'.[19] America went to war to protect her trading rights and within two years her officially registered overseas trade was devastated.

The Royal Navy's successful retaliation against the Americans formed a small but effective part of its global policing operations. The extent and growth of this activity can be demonstrated by reference to five significant years (see table below): 1803, when war against France was renewed; 1805, the year of Trafalgar; 1809, the year when the Continental System

Size of the Royal Navy, 1803–1814

	Seamen and marines	Captains, commanders and lieutenants	Active ships in the Royal Navy (of which line ships)	Total naval supplies granted (£m)
1803	100,000	3,561	388 (111)	10.2
1805	120,000	3,533	534 (116)	15.0
1809	130,000	4,268	728 (127)	19.6
1811	145,000	4,382	657 (124)	19.8
1814	117,400	4,711	637 (118)	19.3

threatened to be most effective; 1811, the year before the conflict with America broke out; and 1814, the last full year of war.

Despite the conflicts of the surrounding years, the effects of the Continental System produced the highest level of naval activity of the war. The year in which the navy kept afloat its largest number of warships was 1809 when over 20% more ships were in active service than at the height of the British scare about invasion and the danger posed by the Franco-Spanish fleets in 1805. The largest expansion of naval activity came through the deployment of small warships – especially sloops but also brigs and cutters – armed with fewer than 20 guns each. But throughout the years 1806–14 inclusive the number of ships of the line on active service exceeded those available in 1805. The number of sailors and marines provided for in the naval budget peaked at 145,000, again over 20% more than in 1805, in the consecutive years of 1810, 1811 and 1812. The resulting financial burden in the years 1809–1815 inclusive ranged between a low of just short of £19 million in 1810 and a high of £20.1 million in 1813. This level of spending was over 25% more than the total voted by parliament in 1805. Such expenditure resulted from delivery in 1813 of the largest amount of naval shipping built in any one year of the long wars. Indeed, the three years from 1812 to 1814 inclusive saw the completion of 23% of all British naval tonnage launched in the entire period 1793 to 1815. So, too, the years 1811–14 witnessed the peak in the demand for naval officers, whose junior and middle ranks increased by nearly one-third in the nine years of war after Nelson's last victory.[20]

Such a large naval effort imposed costs which could be unpredictable. The normal hazards of keeping so many ships on duty meant that the navy lost vessels to accident, shipwreck and, occasionally, capture throughout the world. The North American war increased those hazards while adding the humiliating experience of warships falling to enemy action. In 1812, the British lost forty-two warships, mostly through accident and misadventure. None of them was a ship of the line or fourth-rate. But the loss among the remaining, smaller 498 warships in service reached 9%. The number of guns mounted by those forty-two ships lost totalled at least 653, or the numerically equivalent armament of nine 74-gun ships of the line, or the French losses at Trafalgar.[21] Losses suffered by the Royal Navy to the Americans were thus a relatively small part of the relentless and appreciable wear and tear sustained by the senior service in its global patrolling.

Limited campaigning

The British position within North America was more difficult than their position on the high seas. The first line of defence stretched from the naval port of Halifax over 800 miles by sea and river to Quebec. The capital of the old French colony of Canada provided the only permanent fortress in Canada itself, excluding the maritime colonies and was regarded by the commander-in-chief in North America, Sir George Prevost, as, in May 1812, 'the key to the whole'.[22] It lay at about midpoint on the arc of British possessions. Beyond Quebec, the St Lawrence River was not navigable even by small warships let alone ships of the line, and transporting supplies and soldiers depended also on smaller vessels. The colonies stretched another 800 miles from Quebec to the effective outer limit of British possessions, across the border from Fort Detroit. But much of the western border with the USA was marked by Lake Ontario and Lake Erie, with relatively narrow strips of territory, as at Niagara and around Detroit, offering the only land frontiers between the British colonies and the USA west of northern New England. Those stretches were, therefore, hotly contested. This attenuated set of British colonies was protected in the spring of 1812 by only 11,500 regular troops supplemented by Canadian fencibles. Some 4,300 of them were stationed in Nova Scotia, New Brunswick and Newfoundland to protect those maritime colonies and especially their port facilities against the French. A further 5,500 defended Lower Canada (later the colony and the province of Quebec) and only 1,700 were allocated to Upper Canada (later Ontario) and dispersed across over 1,000 miles. The concentration of forces in Lower Canada reflected the central importance of Quebec City and the agricultural areas along the St Lawrence River. Although the Americans in fact never launched an invasion into French-speaking Lower Canada, as they had done in 1776, British concern that they might anchored Prevost's troops to that central point. British commanders also wanted to prevent the defection of the French-speaking majority. Thus, by the end of 1812, immediate reinforcements greatly expanded the regulars and fencibles available in Upper Canada to 2,692, while further strengthening the central position along the border by increasing the garrisons in Lower Canada to 6,320.[23]

At first glance, the British faced a dramatically different scenario inland from that at sea, where they summoned overwhelmingly superior naval resources to bottle up the American fleet. The total population of British North America was about half a million whites compared to the United States' estimated 7.5 million people in 1812, excluding Native Americans. The mobilization of hardy, patriotic citizens – many of whom were accustomed to handling guns – against the hated imperial foe, from whose alleged tyranny the Americans had freed themselves only a generation earlier, led to some 528,000 military enrolments during the war, with 458,000 of them being in the militia.[24] Yet this stupendous advantage in manpower was more apparent than real. Since the British recognized the folly of invading America as distinct from raiding into it, American patriotism was not widely ignited. Most militiamen enrolled in short-term enlistments for service only within their home states or within the United States. There was no question of a nationalist crusade to liberate Canada from the Hanoverian yoke, and militia units customarily refused to cross into Canada even for local border operations. The totals for militia service were inflated by re-enlistments and by the offer of cash rewards. Moreover, one region closest to the scene of fighting on land and most directly affected by the blockade – New England – increasingly opposed the war. The Federalist party, which voted against war in 1812, controlled all six New England states during 1813 and 1814, and in 1814 tried to dissociate the region from the entire conflict.[25]

Although America enlisted 57,000 men into its regular army during the course of the war, the number of regulars at any one time fell far short of the authorized totals, with some estimates suggesting that the army never had more than 30,000 men in arms and that desertion rates remained high. At best, the American army may have risen to 40,000 men during 1814. When the war began the British had nearly as many regulars in North America – some 11,500 troops – as belonged to the US regular army, which consisted of not quite 12,000 men. By September 1814, the British had 30,000 regulars in North America and in December 1814 they had 40,000, about as many the Americans may have had,[26] and both armies were concentrated in widely scattered areas. Moreover, hurriedly raised American recruits were not integrated effectively into the regular army until 1814. Mobilization succeeded only through the offer of very sizeable bounties of cash and land – 'probably the highest bounty ever paid by any army in the world', according to one very careful historian.[27] The morale of men going off to combat, while leaving ample material rewards behind, must have differed sharply from the spirit enthusing the French revolutionary citizens' armies as they advanced in 1793–95 with the prospect of loot and plunder in enemy country dangling before them. The massive advantage the Americans enjoyed in manpower therefore proved difficult to translate into military effectiveness. There were dramatic occasions when militia troops served decisively, as in the short campaign in Upper Canada in autumn 1813, the organization of the defence of Baltimore in 1814, and at the battle of New Orleans in 1815, but such troops were unreliable for prolonged operations.

The British faced similar problems in mobilizing colonial forces in Upper Canada. The Assembly in early 1812 resisted government efforts to strengthen militia service. Former Americans among the colonists had little appetite for confrontation; there was hostility to the dissemination of 'military habits'; and concern about the harvest led to a stipulation that men liable for militia service should be balloted to serve for three months over two successive summers. Given the almost entire absence of outdoor training opportunities during the long seven-month Canadian winters, the constricted use of summer time obviously impeded even basic military preparation for regular soldiers. Another worry for British commanders was the shortage of experienced officers, with one consequence being the emergence of the Glengarry Volunteers as a prominent fencible regiment because the area from which they were raised in 1812 had a scattering of half-pay officers in residence; the local Scottish settlers had long enjoyed a reputation for martial reliability.[28] When war broke out, General Prevost stressed to the government in London that any British advances into America would unite US public opinion in support of the war, whereas a defensive strategy might foster political disunity in the USA.[29] The British decided, however, to initiate local incursions across the borders from Upper Canada, despite the disadvantages that the colony possessed a white population of only 70,000 (of whom perhaps one-third were Americans) and a colonial assembly reluctant to vote for early preparations for war.[30] The British offensive exploited one significant countervailing factor. Native American nations in the region responded positively to offers of a British alliance, seeking revenge for the defeat they suffered in 1811, and encouraging the commander in Upper Canada, Major General Isaac Brock, to begin operations promptly despite the significant drawbacks the British faced. An American invasion force from Fort Detroit was pushed into retreat and thrown back into the fort on 16 August. The American commander, William Hull, surrendered the same day, even though his army outnumbered its adversary. Significantly, the British force of 350 regulars and 450 militia men was supplemented by 600 Native Americans, secured through Tecumseh's enthusiastic alliance.[31] Although the newly appointed American commander in the north-west, William H. Harrison, in collaboration with political leaders in Kentucky, raised large numbers of regulars, volunteers and militiamen by December,[32] the British advanced well into Michigan Territory and easily defeated their opponents at Frenchtown on 21 January 1813.

While the British gained the initiative in the far west, the Americans attacked across the 36-mile strip of land where the Niagara River links the long lakes of Ontario and Erie. Gathering some 6,000 men together, with a possible further 2,000 troops nearby at Buffalo, the Americans crossed the Niagara River on 13 October and assailed the British front at Queenstown. The defenders had only 800 regulars, 400 militia and 200–300 Native Americans to cover the entire 36-mile front. But the American advance soon petered out, the militia men simply refusing to cross the Niagara to reinforce the beachhead on the Canadian side. Whatever the obvious dangers of crossing under the range of British artillery during daytime, the militia claimed that their service, limited to the defence of American soil, did not encompass offensive operations beyond America's boundaries. Once reinforced, the British rolled back the Americans, forcing 925 of them to surrender, adding to the Americans' loss of 300 men killed, wounded or drowned. British casualties totalled only 100 men. If the small size of the British force precluded any counterthrust, the victory at Queenstown quashed any possibility of an immediate American invasion of Upper Canada. The British defensive line on the Niagara River front held for the rest of the war.[33]

During 1813, campaigning in sectors around Lakes Ontario and Erie tipped more in the Americans' favour, but without any sustained success. The American Secretary of War, John Armstrong, believed that powerful blows delivered on the shores of Lake Ontario would compel the British to withdraw from Kingston (the principal town, of about 1,000 people, in Upper Canada) and fall back upon Montreal. Armstrong also wanted a military success before late April in order to assist the Republican party in New York's state elections at the end of that month, since the Federalists, who opposed or criticized the war, had carried New York in the presidential contest of 1812. As soon as the ice in Sackett's Harbor, the American naval base on Lake Ontario, melted on 19 April, the Americans launched a flotilla to attack York, Upper Canada's tiny capital of 600 people, and captured the town on 27 April. By land they took Fort George, opposite Fort Niagara, in May. The British counter-attacked with a raid on Sackett's Harbor and in December crossed the Niagara River, thereby gaining the upper hand against American militia men demoralized by lack of pay and the prospect of increasing British numbers on their front.[34]

The campaign went far more the Americans' way to the west around Lake Erie. The British took the offensive in April 1813, once the spring thaw permitted, with a raid against Fort Meigs in Ohio. While the incursion was relatively brief, some of their 1,200 Native American allies massacred Kentucky militia prisoners, thereby intensifying anti-British feeling. Another British–Native American advance occurred in July, only to be repelled at Fort Stevenson on 2 August. Meanwhile, the conflict acquired a new dimension with a naval struggle on Lake Erie. An American flotilla blockaded their British counterparts at Amherstburg, south of Fort Detroit. With food running low, the six British ships left harbour in an attempt to break the American blockade. When they encountered Commodore Oliver H. Perry's squadron of nine ships on 10 September, a ferocious three-hour battle followed, ending with the surrender of the entire British flotilla. This humiliation had several causes. The wind changed direction shortly before fighting began, denying the British the chance to select gunnery ranges. The matches and tubes from store in Amherstburg proved of such poor quality that pistols had to be fired into the vents to ignite the guns. The flotilla was inadequately manned: of the 440 men aboard the six small British warships, 250 were soldiers, 140 were French Canadians, who allegedly had problems in understanding English, and only 50 were sailors. Even so, British resistance was stubborn enough to cost them 135 men killed or wounded, including all the naval officers present.[35]

This dramatic, if minor, defeat on Lake Erie deprived the land forces of supplies and obliged them to retreat. Major General Procter conducted the withdrawal at a relatively leisurely pace, allowing himself to be caught by Major General Harrison's army at Moraviantown on the River Thames on 5 October. The Americans' 3,000 men included 1,200 mounted Kentucky volunteers who, in an extremely unusual manoeuvre, rode through the thin, attenuated British line, dismounted, and peppered the 800 British regulars and their 500 Indian allies with a crossfire from the rear and flank. Some 350 troops surrendered on the spot, and another 250 were captured during the pursuit and from among the sick. Tecumseh was

killed and Procter was court-martialled for misconduct and publicly
reprimanded. Yet, despite the heavy blow inflicted by the battle of the
River Thames, Harrison could not maintain the momentum of his campaign, because the Kentucky volunteers, satisfied that their victory had
ensured security for their own state and the territories between it and Upper
Canada, and eager to return home for the harvest and hog-butchering, left
the front from mid-October.[36]

The widening conflict, 1814

British strategy in 1814 was to wear the Americans down in order to force
a negotiated settlement. The blockade by sea remained extremely effective
and American exporting and America's trading ports suffered heavily.
Northern areas of New York, Vermont and Maine traded extensively and
illegally with the British in Lower Canada during 1814, supplying beef,
grain and timber, the first on a massive scale by the summer; the enlarged
army of 1814 could not have been fed without such American supplies.
Lord Bathurst, Secretary of State for War and the Colonies, ruled out the
risky option of sending a large army into American territory, insisting
instead on the priority of dismantling American naval installations on
the lakes, starting with Sackett's Harbor on Lake Ontario and including
American ports on Erie and Champlain. He also wanted to improve
British security by occupying Detroit and Michigan Territory and areas
around Fort Niagara. Because these objectives required the application of
naval force on the lakes, and because no ships could reach the lakes from
the sea, the British in 1814 had to build more warships on the lakes than
the Americans could complete on their side, and then use them effectively.
At the same time, the British army needed to forestall possible American
military threats to Upper Canada.[37]

British reluctance to mount large-scale assaults on America's coastline receded when the European war ended in April 1814, thus releasing
troops from south-west France. There was little activity in Canadian campaigning before April anyway, since only then did ice and snow begin to
melt, shipbuilding accelerate, and troop movements become possible. By
June, the first reinforcements released by peace in Europe reached Canada,
putting pressure on the Americans to strengthen their own regular forces
because, as William H. Harrison informed the Secretary of War in March
1813, 'Militia can only be employed with effect to accomplish a single
distinct object, which will require little time and not much delay on the
way.'[38] British efficiency and resolve were demonstrated by the fact that,

at the end of 1814, British regular forces in North America totalled perhaps 40,000 men compared with the approximately 40,000 regulars in
the US army, embodied only with considerable difficulty.[39]

Before British reinforcements flowed from Europe, the Americans
launched what turned out to be their main attack of the year. They moved
on to the Canadian side of the Niagara River and seized the lightly
defended Fort Erie at the southern end of that area, opposite Buffalo.
But their subsequent advance was held at Lundy's Lane, in a minor but
intensely fought battle on 25 July. The British in turn took the offensive,
recapturing Fort Erie, after the Americans first defended and then destroyed
it, on 5 November. The British, though suffering 2,875 casualties in four
engagements from 5 July to 17 September, denied the Americans any gains
on what their Secretary of War had expected to be the leading front.[40]

In considering offensive options for 1814, Prevost, the British commander-in-chief in North America, was torn by two conflicting possibilities. One was to attack Sackett's Harbor, as his army commander in
Upper Canada and the naval commander, Sir James Yeo, argued.[41] The
other was to switch to an offensive campaign against upstate New York.
Given his own strategic concentration on safeguarding Quebec and the
line from Montreal to Kingston,[42] and given the publicly expressed notion
that commanding the lakes and the Hudson River were central to controlling the USA,[43] Prevost decided to advance along the western shore
of Lake Champlain in order to dominate that stretch of water and to
threaten the American position on the upper reaches of the Hudson. This
line of advance was justified also by the existence of widespread anti-war
sentiment in Vermont, to the east of Champlain, and indeed in much of
New England beyond.

Having enough men to hold the Niagara line, protect the St Lawrence
River and launch an advance of his own, Prevost set out with 11,000
troops on 6 September to take Plattsburg on Lake Champlain. He proceeded cautiously because the narrow lakeside road was strewn with
obstacles left by the Americans – as had been done to delay Burgoyne in
1777 – and was vulnerable to attack by the American flotilla on the lake.
Needing to destroy the American squadron and establish a lake-borne line
of supply, Prevost impatiently insisted on naval action. On 11 September
British vessels attacked the American flotilla in the bay at Plattsburg. As
they entered the bay, the wind fell, making it impossible for the warships
to gain their intended stations. The British longer-range cannon were
neutralized by the American warships which closed and anchored in such
a way as to swing from fixed positions and maximize the use of their guns.

The British lost their four main warships, accounting for 75 of the 92 guns in their lake flotilla. Stripped of protection for his lines of supply by a naval encounter lasting no more than an hour or two, and exposed at the end of a road traversing rough terrain, Prevost had no option but to retreat.[44] Some twenty months earlier Wellington had written privately that success in Canada would follow 'if we could take one or two of their dread frigates'. In mid-November 1814 the key to a settlement lay not with generalship, but, he insisted, with 'naval superiority on the lakes'.[45]

Attempts to control the lakes led to a naval arms race which in itself created tensions between the Royal Navy and Prevost. Captain Yeo in August–October resented Prevost's tendency to see the navy as a transport service or mere tactical support for military operations. For his part, the army commander-in-chief complained to Lord Bathurst that the increase in naval strength and autonomy had made the navy less cooperative and more inclined to believe that it alone would decide the war's outcome. To dominate Lake Ontario, the Admiralty built the massive 102-gun *St Lawrence*, launched in September 1814 as the only freshwater, flat-hulled ship of the line ever constructed for the Royal Navy. Prevost groaned that this vast warship absorbed naval resources and warped strategic thinking, and blamed the navy for his failure on Lake Champlain and lack of success at Niagara. The dispute became so corrosive that both Prevost and Yeo were recalled to London in December 1814 and neither returned to North America.[46]

After the war, Lord Wellesley criticized the 'system of predatory incursion' upon which it was fought, reflecting instead on the desirability of massing Britain's naval and military strength at a single point. This line of argument conveniently ignored the impossibility of defining any such single point in so diffuse a society as America's. Early in the conflict, however, some emphasis had been given to attacking particular centres in the south, notable among them Baltimore and, because its slave population was allegedly disaffected, New Orleans.[47] Because the Americans' plans to invade Canada forced the British to commit large numbers of troops to the northern fronts, only the end of fighting in Europe released from May–June 1814 the additional manpower needed for wider campaigning. During 1814, stocks of small arms, powder and cartridges were accumulated at Bermuda to make it the third largest British repository of munitions in the new world, after the garrison towns of Quebec and Halifax.[48] The principal object of any British attack on the Atlantic seaboard was Baltimore. This port, with 36,000 people in 1810, was the third most populous city in the United States. It had expanded its interior trade networks rapidly and had developed the speedy 'clipper' ships which could out-sail British merchantmen and naval vessels alike. The British had raided America's Atlantic coast at various points in 1813–1814, and Rear Admiral George Cockburn had already familiarized himself with the shorelines of the Chesapeake Bay, acquiring substantial military intelligence concerning American defences and preparations in that region of extremely important commercial agriculture. Since a direct assault upon Baltimore seemed daunting, Cockburn argued instead for an attack upon Washington DC as a positive step in itself – the fall of the capital was 'always so great a blow to the government of a country' – and as a means of advancing upon Baltimore by road from Washington rather than approaching the port by water. Washington in 1810 had only 8,200 people, limited military manpower, and no defences. The British chose to land at a point where food and horses (for hauling British equipment and munitions) were in plentiful supply.[49]

The British attack on Washington DC resulted from Rear Admiral Cockburn's redefinition of the strategic targeting of America's important Chesapeake trading interests.[50] The naval commander-in-chief, Vice Admiral Sir Alexander Cochrane, and his captain of the fleet, Rear Admiral Edward Codrington, preferred instead to conserve their naval forces for a projected attack on New Orleans. But Cockburn secured military support, derived from a build-up of troops in Bermuda and, once landed, Major General Robert Ross pushed ahead with about 1,200 of his 4,500 force and defeated the Americans at Bladensburg. There has been some debate as to whether the 5,000 American defenders – overwhelmingly militia and volunteers – were overcome by the precision, discipline and attacking spirit of the British regulars, were disconcerted by the use of Congreve rockets, or were undone by confusing and defective orders on their own side. The Secretary of State, James Monroe, had deployed the Americans in a way that meant their second line could not readily support their front ranks. The battlefield commander, Brigadier General William Winder, a lawyer who owed his appointment to political influence, focused on retreating and then reforming his lines. Once outflanked, the American lines withdrew too readily.[51] Yet the British attack was impetuous, with no time spent on carefully reconnoitring the enemy's position or even waiting for the complete British force to reach the scene. The battle had, therefore, to be managed in detail by Ross, who had a horse shot under him, and Rear Admiral Cockburn, who only just missed being severely wounded in the thick of the fighting.[52]

From this victorious encounter the British proceeded to Washington, where they burned public buildings and destroyed the dockyards and munitions of war. In an expedition farther up the Potomac River, which lasted twenty-three days, they also spent some time at Alexandria, and carried off much looted cargo. The propaganda coup was considerable; the smoke from burning buildings at the capital could be seen 45 miles away at Baltimore. Cockburn wanted to exploit the high morale of the British forces and press on to attack the port-city. By September, seven ships of the line operated in the Chesapeake and on the Potomac, and the British created a base on Tangier Island, 150 miles south of Baltimore, where a barracks and hospital were established and stores accumulated. By 12 September, they had landed 4,500 men 14 miles south-east of Baltimore, but now encountered major problems. The Americans deployed rapidly embodied militia about three times more numerous than the British forces, and had prepared effective defensive positions. Secondly, when the invaders disrupted defensive American positions, they lacked the cavalry to turn American withdrawals into retreat or flight. Thirdly, the naval squadron of seventeen frigates, sloops, bomb boats and a rocket ship brought up to bombard Fort McHenry, which commanded the river approach to Baltimore, failed to destroy the fort or force its surrender. In the meantime, Major General Ross had been killed by sharpshooters in an ambush. His successor, Colonel Arthur Brooke was not prepared to incur heavy casualties in an extremely risky assault, especially when he needed to consolidate manpower for the planned campaign against New Orleans. The British therefore withdrew on 14 September, leaving Fort McHenry intact, and regrouped their forces at Jamaica in preparation for their main campaign against New Orleans.[53]

With success at Washington counterbalanced by defeat on Lake Champlain and stalemate on the Niagara front, the British had failed to force the Americans into a peace settlement. Scope thus existed for a dramatic further incursion to hit American exporting and to undermine support for the war where it was strongest – in the south – by attacking New Orleans, America's sixth most populous city and one where vast amounts of sugar, tobacco, cotton and hemp had been stockpiled during the naval blockade. The Gulf coast offered other attractions for a British attack. Campaigning was possible during the mild southern winter. The invasion could be launched from Bermuda, with back-up at large British military and naval bases in Jamaica, relatively near the southern coast. Since slaves outnumbered whites along the coast, the need to police the plantations and provide against the threat of slave rebellion reduced the manpower available to fight the British, as did tensions with Native American nations in the interior.[54] Two naval commanders – Sir John Borlase Warren and Alexander Cochrane – went so far as to claim in 1812 that the British would not need many troops against New Orleans, and could rely instead on southern Native Americans and rebellious slaves, while planning to garrison the captured city from the black regiment which Britain maintained in the Bahamas. By 1814, however, Jackson had destroyed Creek power in the region to the far north-east of the city, thus reducing the potential support for the British from Native Americans.[55] Even so, for most of 1814 the people and politicians in and around New Orleans felt demoralized by and disaffected from the war effort, which was by then costing the city dear.[56]

The British approached the American coast on 5 December and, with New Orleans being 105 miles from the sea, reached a point 80 miles from their objective on 13 December. Crossing Lake Borgne and progressing slowly via various bayous, they arrived 8 miles south of the city. Meanwhile, Andrew Jackson's arrival on 1 December lifted morale and led to a thorough reorganization of the city's defences. On 23 December, Jackson attacked a British advance party and determined to halt the invasion well before it reached the city. By 28 December the Americans had lodged themselves in an excellent defensive position, much strengthened by the labour of 900 slaves, between a swamp to their east and the Mississippi River to their west.[57] It was argued that the British expedition should have landed behind the city and attacked on 24 December or 1 January when the Americans were outnumbered and not well prepared.[58] The British were hampered by their troops' lack of battle-readiness, impaired by their prolonged journeyings by sea and inland waterway, and by delays in the arrival and emplacement of heavy naval guns, which were hauled into position only with great exertion on 1 January.[59]

British commanders devised an imaginative plan to defeat their opponents, which depended upon precise movements requiring coordination between naval units and soldiers, the exact achievement of designated objectives, and excellent timing during a night-time operation. It involved sending part of the army across the Mississippi River to seize American artillery on the river's west bank, and training those captured guns upon the main American army so effectively dug in on the river's east bank. Unhappily for the British, the boats necessary for the nocturnal river crossing got stuck, a dam constructed by the British across a canal gave way so that fewer troops could be conveyed to the west bank, and the American guns on the west bank were not seized in time to use in the battle. Nevertheless, the dawn attack by Sir Edward Pakenham's main army went ahead on 8 January. Advancing in three columns, the British infantry were exposed on flat, open ground to devastating artillery fire. Massed as they were in columns, the British both offered a dense target, and could not return sustained or concentrated fire. The generals leading the attack believed their best option was to press the advance upon the American lines, negating the impact of American artillery fire, and put their opponents to the bayonet. The soldiers, caught in the open and lacerated by the cannonade, halted in column to return fire close to the American line and suffered even worse losses. Pakenham, who already had had a horse shot under him, was killed trying to rally the attack. Of the commanders of the three advancing columns, two were killed and Major General John Keane was very seriously wounded.[60] After sustaining nearly 2,000 casualties out of 6,000 troops, the British retreated. American losses in the main battle totalled only 13, with another 67 falling casualty on the west bank of the Mississippi. The entire campaign from 23 December to 8 January had humiliatingly drained the British of 2,450 casualties against Jackson's losses of 350. Yet, despite this defeat, the British did not withdraw from Louisiana until 4 February and Jackson continued to regard them as a potential threat.[61]

British performance at New Orleans was criticized from within the army. Wellington observed that it was curious that the army had chosen to land at the lakes where regular trade was not plied, for, if the system of navigation was not good enough for normal trading vessels, it would scarcely take boats conveying significant numbers of troops.[62] A Peninsular War veteran, John Surtees, argued that the most battle-hardened battalions present would have fought their way to the American lines, but were held in reserve, while the advance fell to units with limited experience of fighting. He also noted that British officers typically exuded 'apathy and fatal security arising from our too much despising our enemy'. On the eve of battle, he claimed, only one battalion commander inspected the terrain over which the battalion would march the following morning, a precaution which would have been standard practice in Spain. Instead, the British believed that they would simply sweep aside 'an army of un-disciplined and unmanageable peasants, however numerous'. On the other hand, American claims that triumph resulted because 'every soldier was a patriot' fighting for his country were misleading.[63] Jackson vigorously galvanized the defences and drew militia and volunteers, including a contingent from his own state of Tennessee, into the defence. Yet his victory was effected not by patriotic fervour, but by the artillery skills of

1,000 Baratarian pirates who joined Jackson's army on 18 December, in return for federal pardons and immunity from federal prosecution.[64] Nor did Jackson possess either the cavalry or the confidence in his soldiers' discipline or power to launch any counteroffensive, so that the British held their position for a few days before continuing operations against lesser coastal positions. They then focused their campaign, on a more modest scale, along the Gulf coast until news arrived of the Treaty of Ghent. In England, the response to the defeat was muted. When information about the battle reached London, it was overshadowed by the tumult aroused by the government's proposals for duties on imported corn – one of the most controversial pieces of class legislation of the age – and, two days later, by news of Napoleon's landing in France.[65] For its impact in Britain at least, the disaster was perfectly timed.

British military performance

The defeat at New Orleans raises the question of whether British military performance in the Iberian peninsula was transferable elsewhere. In assessing the Americans' military performance in 1812, Donald Hickey argued that the 'principal reason for America's failure was poor leadership'. The obvious exception, provided by Jackson's experienced and energetic command at New Orleans, was a necessary if not sufficient cause of American success. For their part, British generals have been criticized for their poor planning and lack of commitment to battle. With rare exceptions they are described as providing efficient responses to the Americans rather than developing a strategy.[66]

British leadership was far from discreditable. The army's command set-up was acutely sensitive to the significant challenges of managing civil–military relations and appointments reflected this. The governor and commander-in-chief in British North America from 1811 was Lieutenant General Sir George Prevost. The son of a Swiss officer in the British army, Prevost was bilingual in French, and had extensive military experience in the West Indian island colonies taken from France, before his posting to Nova Scotia as lieutenant-governor and commander-in-chief in 1808–11. At Quebec, he cooperated with the Roman Catholic bishop and the French politicians who dominated Lower Canada's assembly, securing the financial settlement and the changes he wanted in the militia law passed in 1812 and 1815; but he proved less successful in 1813 and 1814, especially in failing to secure the authority to declare martial law.[67] His cautious strategy in 1812 flowed from constrictions on British military manpower and from a well-reasoned determination to avoid measures that would unite the Americans. Because the US government, 'resting on public opinion for all its measures, is liable to sudden and violent changes', he opted for measures which would intensify disagreements within the USA over the war.[68] But by late 1814 his pro-French leanings were attracting intense criticism from the British minority population of Lower Canada.[69]

Other commanders chosen with an eye to local experience included Isaac Brock, Roger Sheaffe, Major General Baron Francis de Rottenburg, a Pole who had served in the French army in 1782–91 and spoke fluent French, and Lieutenant General Sir Gordon Drummond. These generals possessed first-hand knowledge of Canada and a great deal of experience of operations involving close cooperation with the Royal Navy. Some of them also had the linguistic ability to bridge the white ethnic divide in Lower Canada.[70] The army at New Orleans was similarly commanded by generals with extensive relevant experience, in this case in joint operations. Sir Edward Pakenham had served as a lieutenant colonel in four separate campaigns (including three in the West Indies) by 1809. Already experienced in joint operations with the navy, he held senior posts in the peninsular army before going to America. Major General Samuel Gibbs, also killed at New Orleans, had long experience of joint operations, having served as a lieutenant colonel in the West Indies, at the Cape, in south-western India and, with distinction, on the expedition to Java in 1811. Major General Keane, who led a column in the battle, had been an ADC in Egypt in 1801, when close cooperation with the navy was essential, and had participated in the capture of Martinique in 1809 (where Pakenham was also engaged). He led a brigade at the battle of Vitoria where coordinated movement and attacking spirit, as well as imaginative planning, were central to British victory.[71] Despite their experience and professional dedication, the generals devised an excessively ambitious and complex plan and then failed to instil a sense of urgency, and sufficient respect for American fighting ability, into their battalion commanders. The decision to proceed with the frontal assault at dawn on 8 January, despite failing to take the American guns on the west bank of the Mississippi,[72] showed Pakenham's determination but also his frustration after having called off two earlier attacks. At the point of battle, recently promoted and relatively young generals failed from an excess of dedication to completing their mission stiffened by professional over-confidence.

On the Canadian front, in contrast, British generals have been criticized for the opposite failing – excessive caution. British military performance, needs to be set in context. In much of Upper Canada the militia was far too small to provide any effective defence if the British regulars went on the offensive. The Colonial Assembly defeated a number of measures proposed by the colonial authorities in February in preparation for war. Uncertainty about political support and the availability and effectiveness of militia forces within the colonies acted as major constraints on military planning. During the crisis of 1812, Brock estimated that Upper Canada needed about 4,000 militiamen constantly in arms; from a population of 70,000, that requirement equated, roughly, with 25% of men of military age. While he felt optimistic about embodying that number, Brock had to agree to let militiamen return to their farms at harvest times, to forestall heavier desertions. As for Lower Canada, there were uncertainties about the political reliability of the French population, who vastly outnumbered the British and were reportedly inclined to believe that Napoleon would win the global war. Brock had concluded in late 1809 that a French army of 4,000–5,000 would easily conquer Lower Canada, since 'The Canadians will join them almost to a man'.[73] The dramatic shift in the emperor's fortunes by early 1813 eased British concerns for that part of the home front.

These various factors helped shape the cautious military strategy adopted by British generals. Whereas Theodore Roosevelt argued that British naval officers' overconfidence, flowing from their gross underestimate of American naval capacity and fighting edge, brought its nemesis in naval defeats, Turner faults British generalship for its extreme caution in the face of American numbers and its lack of enthusiasm for decisive battle. In fact, military commanders' caution resulted from the ethnic mix in the Canadas, the small size of the population compared with America's, and the absence of unified colonial support for the war effort. Moreover, even if a dazzlingly successful offensive had been undertaken, the political impact on America of a British victory inside US territory would have been counterproductive, stimulating American unity and retaliation at a time, in 1812–13, when Britain had few troops in Canada. Finally, British army commanders in fact well understood the Americans' fighting capability. As Brock emphasized to Prevost in December 1811, American volunteers proved expert on horseback as riflemen,[74] with precisely those technical skills which the British lacked, thereby constraining their ability to launch deep-probing campaigns into US territory. Caution on the Canadian front could be said to flow from judgement and experience, not from inadequacy.

The war of 1812, despite its reverses, underscored Britain's ability to project power and to counter America's substantial advantages in controlling interior lines of communication, commanding large reserves of manpower, and calling forth a patriotic response from its population. The British ran an effective sea blockade from Halifax, used Bermuda and Jamaica as jumping-off points to attack the American mainland, and set up beach-heads on American territory. Even after the apparently decisive defeat at New Orleans they set out the timetable for their own withdrawal, and indeed maintained military pressure by transporting the army to Mobile, where it took an outlying fort in February; only the news of the peace prevented the planned advance on the port of Mobile itself. The long frontier with Canada proved defensible, despite the difficulties encountered with supply lines in under-populated Upper Canada and the attenuated lukewarm response of the colonial assemblies to gubernatorial requests for manpower and money. Perhaps most significantly, even this war of small engagements produced intense combat, inflicting severe casualties in relation to the numbers of troops engaged. Harry Smith, an officer widely experienced in major campaigns, later described the firing at New Orleans as 'the most murderous I ever beheld before or since'.[75] Such war-fighting amply demonstrated the heavy demands of upholding British imperial power. Economic might, commercial influence, financial clout, and seaborne supremacy of themselves were necessary but far from sufficient factors in successfully defending territory or repelling invaders. Wars had to be fought to be won, and even the war of 1812, discounted as a sideshow by British contemporaries and historians since, required from both the army and navy high levels of sustained professional commitment and expertise to conduct exceptionally widely dispersed campaigns. Their leaders, in managing battles that were often ferociously fought, went to lengths that often resulted in the sacrifice of their own lives to affirm the values and honour of the services in which they so thoroughly believed.

Notes and references

1 *The Times*, 1 December 1812, p. 1; 19 February 1813, p. 2; 28 September 1814, p. 3; 14 April 1815, p. 2.

2 C.J. Bartlett, *Castlereagh* (London, 1966), p. 108; Clive Emsley, *British Society and the French Wars, 1793–1815* (London, 1979), p. 167; N.A.M. Rodger, *The Command of the Ocean: A Naval History of Britain, 1649–1815* (London, 2004), p. 571; Donald R. Hickey, *The War of 1812: A Forgotten Conflict* (Urbana, IL, 1989), p. 2.

3 Rory Muir, *Britain and the Defeat of Napoleon 1807–1815* (New Haven, CT, 1996), p. 334.

4 *Military Panorama or Officers' Companion*, July 1813 (London, 1813), pp. 325–26.

5 Alec R. Gilpin, *The War of 1812 in the Old Northwest* (East Lancing, 1958), p. 63.

6 Hickey, *The War of 1812*, pp. 46, 117.

7 Hickey, *The War of 1812*, pp. 72–3.

8 Hickey, *The War of 1812*, pp. 96–7; Geoffrey J. Marcus, *The Age of Nelson* (London, 1971), p. 423.

9 *The Times*, 29 October 1812, p. 2; 19 February 1813, p. 2.

10 Robert Gardiner (ed.), *The Naval War of 1812* (London, 1998), p. 25.

11 Marcus, *The Age of Nelson*, p. 455; Hickey, *The War of 1812*, p. 92.

12 Jon Latimer, *1812: War for America* (Cambridge, MA, 2007), pp. 85–87, 96, 102–06.

13 J.C.A. Stagg, *Mr Madison's War: Politics, Diplomacy and Warfare in the Early American Republic, 1783–1830* (Princeton, NJ, 1983), pp. 39–40.

14 Hickey, *The War of 1812*, p. 151.

15 William Laird Clowes, *The Royal Navy: A History From the Earliest Times to the Present*, 7 vols (London, 1897–1903), Vol. V, pp. 567, 554–55, 562; Jan Glete, *Navies and Nations: Warships, Navies and State Building in Europe and America 1500–1860*, 2 vols (Stockholm, 1993), Vol. II, p. 384.

16 Gardiner (ed.), *The Naval War*, p. 28.

17 'Papers relating to the war with America', *House of Commons Sessional Papers*, Nov. 1814–July 1815 (London, 1815), Vol. 9, pp. 489–90, (BOPCRIS).

18 Latimer, *1812*, pp. 100–01, 162; Hickey, *The War of 1812*, pp. 215, 217–18.

19 Hickey, *The War of 1812*, pp. 229–31.

20 Clowes, *The Royal Navy*, Vol. V, pp. 9–10; Roger Morriss, *The Royal Dockyards during the Revolutionary and Napoleonic Wars* (Leicester, 1983), p. 28. The totals for enlisted men in 1803 and 1814 give the peak enlistment for each year.

21 From the individual ship entries provided in W.P. Gosset, *The Lost Ships of the Royal Navy 1793–1900* (London, 1986), pp. 82–7.

22 Wesley B. Turner, *British Generals in the War of 1812: High Command in the Canadas* (Montreal, 1999), p. 29.

23 Robert Malcolmson, *Lords of the Lake: The Naval War on Lake Ontario, 1812–1814* (London, 1998), pp. 27–8, 61, 115; Turner, *British Generals*, p. 27; Ferdinand Brock Tupper (ed.), *The Life and Correspondence of Major General Sir Isaac Brock, KB* (London, 1845), p. 168.

24 Hickey, *The War of 1812*, pp. 72, 302.

25 Hickey, *The War of 1812*, p. 232.

26 Hickey, *The War of 1812*, pp. 73, 222–21; Stagg, *Mr Madison's War*, pp. 162, 456; Latimer, *1812*, p. 259.

27 Hickey, *The War of 1812*, p. 76.

28 Tupper (ed.), *The Life and Correspondence . . . Sir Isaac Brock*, pp. 32, 35, 107, 111, 130–31, 135–37.

29 Turner, *British Generals*, p. 30.

30 Malcolmson, *Lords of the Lake*, pp. 4–6; Turner, *British Generals*, pp. 63, 68, 71.

31 Hickey, *The War of 1812*, pp. 80–84; John Fortescue, *A History of the British Army, 1763–1793*, 13 vols (London and New York, 1899–1930), Vol. VIII, pp. 530–32.

32 Stagg, *Mr Madison's War*, pp. 217–19.

33 Fortescue, *A History of the British Army*, Vol. VIII, pp. 533, 537, 541–44.

34 Stagg, *Mr Madison's War*, pp. 286–88; Hickey, *The War of 1812*, pp. 130, 140–43; Fortescue, *A History of the British Army*, Vol. IX, p. 345.

35 Hickey, *The War of 1812*, p. 135; Fortescue, *A History of the British Army*, Vol. IX, pp. 331–32.

36 Hickey, *The War of 1812*, pp. 137–39; Fortescue, *A History of the British Army*, Vol. IX, pp. 333–36; Stagg, *Mr Madison's War*, p. 330.

37 Latimer, *1812*, pp. 263–65.

38 C. Edward Skeen, *Citizen Soldiers in the War of 1812* (Lexington, KY, 1999), p. 87.

39 Hickey, *The War of 1812*, pp. 225–27.

40 Fortescue, *A History of the British Army*, Vol. X, pp. 115–16, 122–24; Hickey, *The War of 1812*, pp. 183–89.

41 Malcolmson, *Lords of the Lake*, pp. 274–75, 301.

42 Turner, *British Generals*, pp. 41–42.

43 *The Royal Military Panorama or Officer's Companion*, July 1813, p. 332.

44 Fortescue, *A History of the British Army*, Vol. X, pp. 120, 125–34; Hickey, *The War of 1812*, pp. 190–93.

45 Fortescue, *A History of the British Army*, Vol. VIII, p. 549; Vol. X, p. 136.

46 Malcolmson, *Lords of the Lake*, pp. 301, 306, 314, 317, 322.

47 *The Times*, 29 October 1812, p. 2; 14 April 1815, p. 2.

48 'Estimate of the charge of the Office of Ordnance for Great Britain, for the year 1814', *House of Commons Sessional Papers*, November 1813–July 1814 (London, 1814) Vol. 11, pp. 112–13, (BOPCRIS).

49 Anthony S. Pitch, *The Burning of Washington: The British Invasion of 1812* (Annapolis, 1998), pp. 19–21, 24, 36; George Rogers Taylor, *The Transportation Revolution* (New York, 1951), pp. 7–8.

50 Cockburn secured post rank in 1794 at the age of only 22. He had been involved, as captain of a 74-gun ship, in the complex landing of the expeditionary force on the island of Walcheren in 1809 and in the bombardment of Flushing. Earlier in the year he had served under Sir Alexander Cochrane as second-in-command of the naval force which escorted 10,000 troops to Martinique. He had thus played a proactive part in leading seamen on land to capture an important position. Clowes, *The Royal Navy*, Vol. V, pp. 42, 272, 275, 283, 284.

51 Skeen, *Citizen Soldiers*, pp. 133, 136–39; Pitch, *The Burning of Washington*, pp. 75–82.

52 Sir Harry Smith, *The Autobiography of Sir Harry Smith, 1787–1819*, G.C. Moore Smith (ed.) (London, 1910), pp. 198–200, 81, 83.

53 Smith, *The Autobiography of Sir Harry Smith*, p. 206; Pitch, *The Burning of Washington*, pp. 126, 148, 173–4, 179, 185, 189–90, 193–4, 202, 210–12.

54 Stagg, *Mr Madison's War*, pp. 485, 492–95; Latimer, *War of 1812*, p. 252.

55 J. Leitch Wright Jnr., *Britain and the American Frontier, 1783–1815* (Athens, GA, 1975), pp. 122, 125, 131, 132–33, 160–65; Latimer, *1812*, pp. 220–21.

56 Hickey, *The War of 1812*, pp. 206–07.

57 Hickey, *The War of 1812*, pp. 208–09, 210–11; Latimer, *1812*, p. 380.

58 William Surtees, *Twenty-Five Years in the Rifle Brigade* (London, 1973), p. 389.

59 Smith, *The Autobiography of Sir Harry Smith*, p. 232.

60 Smith, *The Autobiography of Sir Harry Smith*, pp. 247, 304, 237; Surtees, *Twenty-Five Years in the Rifle Brigade*, pp. 390, 374, 376.

61 Fortescue, *A History of the British Army*, Vol. X, pp. 160–74; Hickey, *The War of 1812*, p. 212; Latimer, *1812*, p. 388.

62 Smith, *The Autobiography of Sir Harry Smith*, pp. 304–05.

63 Surtees, *Twenty-Five Years in the Rifle Brigade*, pp. 372, 388.

64 Hickey, *The War of 1812*, p. 207; Latimer, *1812*, p. 377.

65 *The Times*, 9 March 1815, p. 3; 11 March 1815, p. 3.

66 Turner, *British Generals*, pp. 143, 148; Hickey, *The War of 1812*, p. 90.

67 Turner, *British Generals*, pp. 25–27, 150.

68 Tupper (ed.), *The Life and Correspondence . . . Sir Isaac Brock*, pp. 178–79.

69 Malcolmson, *Lords of the Lake*, p. 27.

70 Turner, *British Generals*, pp. 59–62, 80, 84–88, 102–03,115–116.

71 *ODNB* entries.

72 Smith, *The Autobiography of Sir Harry Smith*, pp. 231, 236.

73 Tupper (ed.), *The Life and Correspondence . . . Sir Isaac Brock*, pp. 103–04, 182, 172, 180–81, 192, 54, 175, 130–31.

74 Tupper (ed.), *The Life and Correspondence . . . Sir Isaac Brock*, p. 103.

75 Smith, *The Autobiography of Sir Harry Smith*, p. 247.

CHAPTER 14

The Waterloo campaign: lessons learned?

The battle's significance

Just when the allied powers were immersed in reordering the post-war political order in negotiations at Vienna, Napoleon escaped from exile on the island of Elba and seized control in Paris. The allies promptly organized massive armies to halt the emperor's restoration and it fell to the British and Prussians to bear the brunt of his military advance. The resulting confrontation at Waterloo has been described by one military historian as 'the most decisive battle of the age'.[1] A leading American military historian has seen it as the final episode in what he describes as the 'age of battle'. Opinions diverge widely as to its significance and impact in the final overthrow of Napoleon.

Two contrasting assessments, however, suggest the battle's relatively limited impact. From the allies' perspective, ministers in London behaved during the crisis of March–June 1815, as if Napoleon's defeat was inevitable. The size and military resources of the coalition against him – and the availability of their forces for immediate deployment – seemed sufficient to deny the emperor any chance of maintaining himself in power.[2] As long as Britain pumped generous financial subsidies into the allies' war-chests, as she did immediately upon Napoleon's return to Paris, and as long as Britain worked the diplomatic levers to keep the coalition intact, Napoleon could not survive. Waterloo merely accelerated a process of inexorable overthrow. An alternative analysis minimizes the battle's impact on the balance of power while stressing instead its political impact. As David Hamilton-Williams has stressed, Napoleon after the battle still possessed significant military assets. He had engaged only a part of the army available to him in the Low Countries' border region. A successful corps under

Grouchy held the field; units from the main force at Waterloo itself could be regrouped; other divisions were nearby. More important, there were sizeable armies in north-eastern France and at Paris, while recruitment had only just begun. Alienation from the restored Bourbons and disaffection among soldiers and officers suddenly discharged in 1814 offered prospects for raising new armies. What destroyed Napoleon, in this view, was not military defeat, but the machinations of his political opponents in Paris.

Against such assessments, it could be argued that Napoleon might have transformed international affairs if he had beaten Wellington at Waterloo and if Marshal Grouchy had kept the Prussian army out of play. Napoleon – as always – sought to use battle to force diplomatic initiatives, his immediate objective being to detach the new kingdom of Holland from the allies. Napoleon hoped to exploit popular reaction within the former Austrian Netherlands (largely Belgium from 1830) and the former United Provinces of the Netherlands against the House of Orange, whose head secured the crown of Holland under the restoration. If Napoleon could overthrow the new order in Holland, he would turn a buffer against France into a populous and economically wealthy base from which to put pressure on Prussia. Napoleon's first objective at Charleroi placed him on a good road system designed to speed the transport of coal and iron to the Brussels area, necessary because that southern region was the hub of Belgium's coal and iron production. From Charleroi he could also move along the Sambre to the other coal and iron centre of Liège, commanding the iron-producing Ardennes. The southern region of Belgium thus offered a rich industrial prize where the Walloon people spoke French. If he could capture Brussels then he would be able to fan out to the north-west and take the leading textile production area centred on Ghent and ultimately cut the British off from access to vital sea lanes. If he had been able to defeat, as distinct from just pushing back, the Prussians as well, then thwarting or agreeing terms with Austria and Russia might, according to some historians, have been attainable.[3] In this analysis, therefore, Waterloo was vital in denying Napoleon major economic assets and the use of his re-energized military juggernaut in punching a hole through the coalition's political as well as military flank.

From the British military perspective, the main challenges posed by Napoleon's advance into the United Netherlands concerned the coordination of the allied armies and the fighting capability of Wellington's hastily assembled army. The allied commanders had to ensure that Napoleon did not push them apart upon divergent trajectories, and it became Wellington's responsibility, particularly difficult as a general unaccustomed to co-operating with equals, to cement an effective working relationship with Prussians who had already fought Napoleon in major battles in central Europe. Once contact was made with the enemy, the British had to manage an army drawn recently from many states using commanders who were unaccustomed to working together. Indeed the entire command structure of Wellington's army was almost *ad hoc*. The troops' bravery and the resilience of the regimental system were to be tested virtually to destruction. They had to overcome the disadvantages of fighting on the defensive, of operating as a highly polyglot force, and of confronting an opponent with such fame, skill and self-confidence. Waterloo has thus rightly been regarded as the supreme test of British military capability and as an extreme exemplification of how far the British had come since their somewhat humbling experience of the campaigns of 1793–95.

The campaign and battle

The events of March–June 1815 represented a remarkable final outburst of Napoleonic war-making. The former emperor landed in southern France on 1 March. Initially leading about 1000 men, he was joined within weeks by garrison after garrison of the restored regime's army. Such defections may not have surprised the allies, who had long understood how peace had left the army and especially former officers and soldiers intensely dis-satisfied.[4] On 20 March Napoleon entered Paris without firing a single shot and proceeded by early May to create a field army of 284,000 men and mobilize 220,000 National Guardsmen.

Napoleon's return was immediately condemned and rejected by the great European powers – Austria, Britain, Prussia and Russia – whose representatives were involved in an extended conference at Vienna deliberating on the shape of post-1814 Europe. Wellington pressed for the speediest possible entry – initially hoping with stunning optimism for late April – into France of three large allied armies, in order to overwhelm the *revanchistes* and to throw the burden of supplying those armies upon an invaded France. By mid-April, the usual delays over mobilization, the continental allies' demands for financial subsidies from Britain, and Napoleon's own dynamic resuscitation of the French army injected more caution into such planning.[5] The emperor positioned his newly formed army corps at various points along France's frontiers and decided to take Brussels, where the Dutch king was in residence, in order to break up the United Netherlands or force the king to change sides, as the Dutch republic had done in 1795. On 12 June he left Paris, and on 15 June his 128,000-strong army on the Belgian frontier, spread over an arc of 20 miles, began its movements converging on Charleroi, across the border in the United Netherlands.

Being in extended conference at Vienna, the allies drew up a strategic plan within weeks of Napoleon's landing and before he had reached Paris. Austria fielded an army of 150,000 in Italy to defend its extensive interests there as well as the southern route to Vienna. In May, this army delivered the first, largely ignored, blow against Napoleon's restoration by defeating Marshal Murat, the French emperor's brother-in-law and client King of Naples, who had retained his throne – if precariously – in 1814–15, and whose value to Napoleon's plans had been given considerable weight by Wellington.[6] The southern stretch of the Rhine was to be held by 200,000 troops drawn from various German states under Karl Philip, Prince Schwarzenberg, a cautious, conservative general who had headed the mighty allied army at Leipzig – the greatest battle of the age – in October 1813. The northern Rhine was assigned to 120,000 Prussians, with additional Prussians farther south. 200,000 Russians were to advance across central Europe to reinforce the central and southern Rhine fronts, although the Tsar felt no urgency for this movement and had no particular enthusiasm for the restored Bourbons.[7] Wellington was given command over two small forces to guard the United Netherlands.[8] While the actual numbers increased by June, especially in Wellington's sector, the fundamental fact remained that the Netherlands offered a tempting target to Napoleon because such large numbers of allied troops were committed to the southern Rhine and Italy.

Napoleon's immediate objective was to divide the two northern armies under Wellington and Blücher, and defeat one of them or both in turn while driving his own force as fast as possible to Brussels. He expected the British to fall back to protect the coast, which guaranteed their escape route to England, while the Prussians would withdraw towards their possessions in the Rhineland. With Austria essentially preoccupied with Italy and with Russia concerned with securing the largest possible share in Poland from any peace settlement – and having already paid a huge blood sacrifice in 1812 and 1813 – Napoleon hoped that surprise, speed, decisiveness and the capitulation or realignment of the Netherlands would overthrow the alliance and ensure his restoration.

Pursuing his primary objective of dividing the British from the Prussians, Napoleon, to his opponents' surprise, advanced on 16 June with separate forces up the two roads going northwards from Charleroi towards

Brussels. The more direct road led to Quatre Bras, a crossroads – as its name records – defended by a collection of allied units within Wellington's army. To the east, two of his three corps pressed past Fleurus (site of a major French victory in 1794) and advanced upon the Prussian position at Ligny. The emperor attacked the Ligny position from 3.00 p.m. onwards, concentrating on the Prussian's westerly flank, the one nearest Quatre Bras, in an effort to force the Prussians to retreat eastwards and thereby enable the French army to insert itself between its two opponents. At Quatre Bras, Wellington succeeded just in time in bringing enough reinforcements southwards to block Ney and prevent the marshal either from gaining ground or from reinforcing the main French army to the east. German and Dutch units played a particularly prominent part in the early stages of that battle, but the position was held by British battalions arriving at the scene from the north. By the evening Wellington had got 36,000 men in place, easily enough to ensure that Ney, commanding half that number, withdrew at around 9.00 p.m., having failed to insert his corps between Wellington's force and the Prussians.

Ligny, often brushed aside in British accounts of the Waterloo campaign, saw a full-blown confrontation between 84,000 Prussians with 224 guns and 58,000 Frenchmen supported by 210 guns. Tactically, Napoleon won because the Prussians pulled back from their chosen position and withdrew northwards, remaining separated from Wellington's army. Moreover, Wellington's failure to come to the assistance of the Prussians' threatened west flank incensed the Prussian Chief of Staff, Graf von Gneisenau. The Prussians did not bother to inform their ally that they had withdrawn from Ligny, leaving Wellington to find out for himself only at 10.00 a.m. on the following day. Such a lack of coordination seemed to vindicate Napoleon's dominant strategy of dividing, pushing apart and defeating in detail the ill-assorted coalition that opposed him.

Yet Napoleon suffered two severe setbacks on 16 June. Both battles inflicted heavy casualties on the advancing French. Although the emperor replenished his field army to 72,000 men the next day, he was grappling with two armies each about the same size as the field force under his own command. The second reverse on 16 June was the failure to throw the Prussians into a hurried retreat pursued and harried by the French. Gneisenau, disgusted at Wellington's apparent failure to relieve the Prussian westerly flank, wanted to march eastwards and regroup with Prussian forces in Luxembourg, just as Napoleon would have wished. Blücher, and others, argued for maintaining contact with Wellington. Only when his staff persuaded him that proceeding on the easterly road among the routes going to Brussels would still keep his options open, did Gneisenau accept Blücher's preferred operational strategy. Napoleon, despite gaining tactical and indeed strategic surprise, had thus failed to drive the allied armies apart. They were instead both moving northwards in the direction of Brussels along broadly parallel roads, one, to the east, through Wavre and the other through Waterloo.

All three armies were on the move on 17 June. Napoleon decided to switch his point of concentration and pursue Wellington, despatching a force of 33,000 troops under the Marquis de Grouchy (a pre-Revolutionary officer and *Ancien Régime* aristocrat) to tie down the Prussians as Ney had held the allied force at Quatre Bras on the previous day. Wellington decided to stand at an excellent defensive position at Waterloo, where his front stretched over about 2.5 miles and took advantage of a ridge. Critical defensive positions were held in strength at the heavily walled and wooded Chateau Hougoumont and at the far smaller La Haye Sainte farmhouse, to the west and centre of the allied front respectively, and in the lower-lying ground which separated the opposing armies. The allies assembled 68,000 men and 156 guns to block Napoleon's 72,000 troops and 246 guns. The French suffered from the twin disadvantages of needing to attack – and to attack against a general who had repeatedly shown an ability in the Iberian peninsula to hold his ground successfully against French assaults – and of having to advance over wet ground already churned up by the allied army's march to their own positions at Waterloo. Wellington planned to withstand whatever French attacks were flung at him and await the arrival of two Prussian corps, which were about 8 miles to the east, across difficult terrain. Only at 2.00 a.m. on 18 June, just hours before fighting was likely to begin, did he secure assurances from Gneisenau and Blücher that he would indeed receive such assistance. The battle's decisive moment came at that nocturnal meeting just before fighting commenced.

The ebb and flow of the battle of Waterloo have been recounted frequently and in immense detail. By Napoleon's standards it was not a big battle, nor did it involve intricate military manoeuvring. It became instead a terrible slogging match of fierce and close intensity. Wellington did not expect the seven hours of French artillery pounding which accompanied the contest. Napoleon did not anticipate the tenacious opposition that greeted his repeated efforts to break through the allied front. One battalion, the 27th Foot (the Inniskillings), in defending a critical road behind La Haye Sainte lost 480 casualties out of 698 combatants, an extraordinary loss for one day, the bulk being sustained from artillery fire.[9] By about

7.00 p.m. the Prussian approach from the east had begun to be felt. Napoleon could not reinforce the centre of his front because he had to send troops to ward off or at least slow down the Prussians' arrival. This delay at the main battlefield enabled Wellington to strengthen his central lines, exploiting his advantageous position on the ridge to do so. Then the climax of the battle arrived. The Imperial Guard, customarily held back in order to deliver the crushing final blow, marched past the emperor 600 yards from the allied line and advanced in spectacular style up the slope towards Wellington's army. Canister from thirty guns poured into them; volley after volley followed. As the Guard fell back, the decisive allied attack occurred not on Wellington's front, but on the French right, where the Prussian 1st Corps plunged into the flank and rear of the divisions attacking Wellington. Only then did the British commander order his first advance of the day and only then did the French break and flee in retreat. Although some 40,000 French soldiers escaped, their army had lost virtually all its guns as well as its cohesion. The Prussians pushed French forces about 25 miles to Charleroi.

Fighting continued, however, on the Wavre front. Marshal Grouchy stuck firmly to his orders to follow and pressurize the Prussians on the Wavre road. He continued fighting the Prussians until about 11.00 p.m. and resumed his advance the next morning (19 June), capturing Wavre and pursuing Prussian units. Only at 10.30 a.m. that day did Grouchy learn of the emperor's defeat some 8 miles away, and even then he believed Napoleon remained in command of a withdrawing, not a retreating, army. At 11.00 a.m. he began his own withdrawal through Namur, Dinants, and beyond. This was a quixotic final paragraph in the epic history of Napoleonic warfare, which had been renowned for speedy communications and the rapid movements of its interdependent corps.

The decisive verdict on Waterloo was delivered by the administrative and political elite in Paris. The emperor sped back to his capital with the intention of repositioning over 400,000 men under arms available to him while raising new forces. But Napoleon had staked his domestic credibility and political future on overcoming international opposition to his regime. Amidst the political upheavals of 1814–15, many leaders in Paris unsurprisingly kept their options open, some by maintaining direct contact with the Bourbons. In such a political environment the emperor, who had chosen to put his return to a trial by battle, could scarcely complain – nor did he – that he had failed that test. Fouché, the minister of Police, and Talleyrand, a politician and diplomat who had survived numerous changes of regime, immediately orchestrated opposition in the Chamber of Deputies which called Napoleon's resumption of power into question. Marshal Ney then delivered the *coup de grâce* when, in a tense debate in the Chamber of Peers, he depicted a complete débâcle after Waterloo, probably in order to avoid blame for French defeat. Because the emperor felt constrained to maintain his rule through the Chambers instead of imposing a political dictatorship, Napoleon decided to abdicate in favour of his four-year-old son. His opponents, including Marshal Davout, who commanded the army in and around Paris, then opened negotiations with the allies. In this analysis, Waterloo triggered Napoleon's downfall, but did not cause or necessitate it.[10]

Before learning of the abdication, Wellington privately offered his own verdict on 23 June:

I may be wrong, but my opinion is, that we have given Napoleon his death blow; from all that I hear his army is totally destroyed, the men are deserting in parties, even the Generals are withdrawing from him. The infantry throw away their arms, and the cavalry and artillery sell their horses to the people of the country and desert to their homes.[11]

The destruction of the French army's morale was vital because, in Wellington's analysis in March, it was 'the desire for war, particularly in the army, which has brought Buonaparte back, and has formed for him any party, and has given him any success'.[12]

British military efficiency and the Waterloo campaign

The whys, wherefores and what-ifs of the Waterloo campaign have been analysed and disputed since 1815 and will continue to be so. What is more appropriate here is to consider how the campaign concluding the long wars against France compared with the British army's initial experience of revolutionary warfare, how the British learned from the wars of 1793–1814, and how effectively the British performed in arguably the most important and most successful European campaign they engaged in during this period.

One of the main British complaints in the 1790s was that their small expeditionary forces suffered from the inept decisions and weak leadership of the allied high command. At Tourcoing on 17–18 May 1794 six allied columns were to advance in a concerted plan. Only two – including the Duke of York's – met their objectives, with the British furious at being ordered by the Habsburg Emperor to move forward without adequate cover for their flanks.[13] There was an element of such frustration in June 1815 because the commander of the largest allied army, Prince Swarzenberg, did not intend to begin offensive operations until the end of June. Wellington and Blücher were not therefore prepared for major French advances when Napoleon came crashing up the roads from Charleroi. But both the British and Prussian commanders had independent authority to react to the French attack. They were not constrained by a cautious or unenergetic supreme commander. In his own sector, Wellington had gone to some lengths to secure the command-in-chief (subject to reference to the King and Crown Prince) of the Dutch forces. The British army's new standing reflected the successful British military record in the Iberian peninsula, Wellington's prestige and ability to secure allies' agreement to his command in the Netherlands, and the increased – though still not large – scale of the British military contribution. In May 1794 the British contingent in Flanders totalled 10,750 men. In June 1815 the contingent in the field approached 25,000. The British had sent nearly 22,000 troops to Belgium from 25 March to 25 May in a quick, effective transfer, despite Wellington's complaints in early April that he was not receiving good quality troops quickly enough,[14] and despite objections that this swift despatch would expose the British in Ireland to danger there.

Such a prompt response owed more to the example of previous experience and the thrust of political need than to any radical change in personnel. York had commanded British forces in Flanders in 1793–94; in 1815 he headed the army as a whole. The second highest military figure in London, the Master-General of the Ordnance, Lord Mulgrave, furnished munitions and artillery as promptly as possible. In 1793 he had served as lieutenant-governor of Toulon during the brief British occupation of the principal French Mediterranean port. The army's Adjutant General in London was Henry Calvert, who had been a lieutenant at Yorktown and an ADC to the Duke of York in Flanders in 1793–94. Troops sent to Belgium belonged to fifteen battalions (plus some rifle units) which had been kept well below strength during the peace. The rapid deployment of such battalions and their effectiveness in fighting disproved the official doubts – notably from the Duke of York as commander-in-chief – about the viability of under-strength battalions. Reinforcing this sizeable and speedy injection of troops was the massive financial underwriting of other allies' armies which the British immediately provided on Napoleon's return.

The extensive military experience that the British had gained since 1793 may have made some difference to their performance in this campaign.

The senior officers generally had more recent and relevant wartime experience in 1815 than had been the case in 1793. Among Wellington's total staff of thirty-three officers, no fewer than thirty-one had some Peninsular War experience. In contrast, relatively few ordinary soldiers were veterans of earlier conflicts. The battalions present in 1815 which had served in the peninsula contributed only 11,500 of the British force; and many individual soldiers within those battalions had not been with them when they had been in Portugal and/or Spain.[15] The French army almost certainly contained far more veteran troops than Wellington commanded. On the other hand, military service was not universally popular in France, especially after the invasion of Russia and the terrible loss of troops in 1812; those who could afford to do so customarily bought substitutes if conscripted. Across the battlefield of Waterloo the rallying call to French troops and the cry of the wounded for assistance was '*Vive l'Empéreur!*' – an affirmation of personal and professional loyalty, not a declaration of national identity.[16]

An important contrast between 1815 and 1793–95 was the improvement in relations with the Dutch. As early as September 1793, the Duke of York complained that the Dutch army behaved in a manner which was 'more shameful than can be conceived', adding: 'It is impossible almost to have an idea of the horror and detestation in which the Dutch troops are held in this country for their cowardice.'[17] This relationship was worsened by November 1794 by the 'jealousy and misunderstanding' that developed between York and the Stadtholder. Once the allies retreated in 1794–95, the Dutch population treated the British army as the enemy, the *Annual Register* noting: 'No direct hostilities were committed; but every species of injury and disservice was done that inveterate malice would suggest.'[18] The Hanoverian and British commanders in January 1795 saw no point in trying to hold the line of the Waal River owing to 'the shameful conduct of the Dutch'.[19] In contrast, Wellington acted vigorously to prevent a resurgence of such chronic mistrust in 1815, and the youthful Prince of Orange, an ADC in the peninsula, commanded one of Wellington's corps. But the image of Dutch cowardice and military inefficiency, however unfairly, was carried over into public lambasting of the Belgians and Hanoverians for their military inadequacy at Waterloo, for example by Walter Scott, Britain's bestselling poet, who visited the battlefield only six weeks after the engagement.[20]

Although Wellington was famously disparaging about the campaign of 1794–95, in which he served as a lieutenant colonel, the British army's conduct in 1793–95 was far from uniformly defective. David Dundas's common system of drill was used in operations for the first time. The British developed the use of the two-deep line. Light companies, one attached to each battalion, were developed to combat the heavy French use of skirmishers. Cavalry operated well, including in small formations and over rolling countryside. Discipline was good.[21] Problems arose because logistical support became increasingly difficult in the winter of 1794–95 and health care became problematic as sickness mounted.[22] But the main challenge arose from the new capacity of the French to maintain the vigour of the offensive, even after sustaining heavy casualties. This provided a vital link to the events at Waterloo. Wellington's long experience in the peninsula made him fully aware of the determination of the French army. He prepared a defensive position of sufficient depth to withstand the anticipated force and length of the French onslaught. Wherever possible, he chose 'dead ground' in which his men could lie down during artillery assaults, and he moved battalions into squares to ward off cavalry attacks, which were launched on twelve main occasions in efforts to smash the infantry. The courage and stubbornness of British leadership at every level proved impressive, as it had to be against so formidable a foe.[23]

Whether that characteristic was as new as those who argue for Wellington's transformative influence upon the British army is more difficult to determine. Soldiers have always regarded battle as the culminating test of their professional ability. The battles the British participated in during 1794 posed the ultimate challenge at the time. On 18 May 1794, York's force of 10,750 men extricated itself from an enveloping movement at Tourcoing only with great difficulty. A reduced brigade of 1,120 men at the most exposed point of the battle lost 590 casualties. At Tournai on 22 May 1794, the battle stretched from 5.00 a.m. to 10.00 p.m. Harry Calvert asserted that the fighting in one sector involved the heaviest musketry and artillery fire which the oldest soldiers present had ever witnessed.[24] Prince Adolphus reported from the front to George III, his father, that the small-arms firing, lasting six hours, was 'so strong that, according to the opinion of those who have served in the Seven Years War, there was not so heavy a one during the whole last war'. The British artillery inflicted terrible casualties on the French, while the infantry, he noted, 'stormed with their accustomed bravery'.[25] In that sense little changed by 1815. Perhaps the single difference lay in Napoleon's trust in mass column advances which offered deep targets to lines of infantry if those defenders had not been reduced in spirit or numbers by preparatory cannonading. When deep columns were halted by British firing in line, as they were at two critical points in the battle, men at the rear and centre of those columns, who were too boxed-in to fire back, began panicking and fleeing, thereby breaking the columns.[26]

Although the significance of regimental attachments in this period has been questioned and, from the other end of the analytical spectrum, the myopic tendency of regimental self-regard criticized,[27] the development of regimental pride probably gained from Waterloo. Of the seventy-seven battalions in the Germano-British army (excluding the Dutch-Belgian, Orange-Nassau and Dutch 'Indian' forces), only eighteen had more than 650 men each present. Some thirty-three battalions each brought 400 to 600 soldiers to the battle.[28] Being relatively small, these battalions were highly visible and manoeuvrable. Micro-managing the battle by Wellington became easier with discernible and small units, each with its own colours (flag) and commanding officer and tiny staff. Regimental effectiveness depended in part at least on leadership. There are no particular reasons for suggesting either that the experience of the long wars made any difference to the commitment or non-commitment of British officers to fighting or that the French army in 1815 was better led than the British. In 1794 leaders such as Sir Ralph Abercromby and Major General Henry Fox were notable for their calmness under fire. Despite his severe limitations as a field commander, the Duke of York was active and courageous in battle. At Waterloo, British generals were as committed as Marshal Ney to securing victory. Overall, 34% of all British officers in Wellington's army were casualties compared with 30% of all British rank and file and 22% of the rank and file of all nationalities under Wellington's command.[29] What distinguished the two main protagonists at Waterloo was Wellington's detailed management of the battle. Almost all the duke's staff were killed or wounded in the action, being wholly engaged as their commander's messengers and assistants. It was claimed that none of Napoleon's large personal staff suffered a similar fate.[30]

Wellington's own energy and mobility as a commander helped to improve communications, which had been poor in mid-1794. Even so, British military intelligence provided no warnings, or any that were heeded, of the French attack at Quatre Bras. At his meeting with Blücher and Gneisenau on 17 June, Wellington did not know the full position of his own army,[31] while the duke's staff could not cope by then with the sheer volume of messages and new, thoroughly revised sets of orders.[32] Yet Napoleon's command system ran scarcely any better and probably worse than Wellington's. The rationale that the death of Napoleon's long-time chief of staff, Marshal Berthier, earlier in 1815 deprived the French of necessary coordination in this field severely undermines claims to superior French professionalism in a vital field.

Wellington's leadership extended to overcoming two major disadvantages. First, he drew together extremely diverse forces. Of the
68,000 troops he commanded at Waterloo, only 24,000 on the battlefield
were British; and, of those, 5,800 in the cavalry and 3,000 in the Royal
Ordnance belonged to specialist arms. The German contingents included
3,300 regulars of the King's German Legion, 14,500 Hanoverians other
than the KGL, 6,000 Brunswickers and 2,900 from Nassau. The contribution from the United Netherlands totalled 17,200. Wellington's long
experience of campaigning in India and the Iberian peninsula equipped him
exceptionally well to lead so diverse an army. During April he organized
all but one of the army's divisions to intermingle the nationally distinctive
battalions. Among the regulars, veteran battalions were mixed with
battalions possessing more limited or less recent exposure to battle.[33] This
method of organization, standard British practice in India, represented an
important organizational response to a difficult challenge. As one regimental history pointed out in 1860, Napoleon enjoyed the advantage of
commanding 'an army of one nation only, well combined and organized,
and with its *morale* in the highest state of enthusiasm'. In contrast,
Wellington needed all his prestige and determined sense of authority to
pull the allied army into shape: 'the leaders of its component parts acted
under the direction of six different Governments, each independent of
the other'.[34]

A second disadvantage suffered by Wellington was being on the defensive. This appears less clearly a disadvantage to later analysts than it did
to practitioners of eighteenth- and early nineteenth-century warfare.[35]
The range of effective musket-fire before the advent of the Lee–Enfield
rifle from the 1850s was only about 80–100 yards. The killing zone on a
battlefield was thus spatially limited, although it was extended through
the damage inflicted by artillery. But defending armies were easier targets
for sustained artillery fire – because they were not moving – than were
advancing columns. Equally important, eighteenth-century doctrine urged
the advantages of the attack because momentum and seizing the initiative
lifted enthusiasm and morale. Defenders suffered the disadvantage of
being increasingly encumbered by the demoralizing presence of wounded
and dead fellow-soldiers, whereas advancing forces left their casualties
behind. Flanking movements and manoeuvre and selecting weaker – or
apparently weaker – points in an opponent's line to assail added to the
advantages which the offensive offered. Against this, the British had the
advantage of possessing in their 6-pounder guns far lighter artillery than
Napoleon deployed; the British guns proved more manoeuvrable in the
heavy, rain-soaked soils and required fewer horses to draw them. Although

Napoleon's army lacked light or field artillery to enable it to smash home its attacks on Wellington's very hard-pressed squares, the initiative lay with the French against a largely inexperienced, coalitional army resting on the defensive. It took determination, courage, confidence and skill to manage the allied army until the Prussians' arrival ensured victory.[36]

The tactics adopted did not escape criticism. Sir Harry Smith, then a dashing lieutenant colonel, complained of Waterloo: 'It was no Salamanca or Vittoria, where science was so beautifully exemplified: it was a stand-up fight between two pugilists' which 'has destroyed the field movement of the British Army'. Heavy manoeuvres, squares, centre formations, and massed movements dominated the mode of fighting by 1815 because, in Smith's view, the Prussians and Russians could not move more quickly on the battlefield.[37] Yet Waterloo substantially boosted the army's self-image and pride. Wellington himself described the battle to Lord Beresford as the triumph of British military determination:

Never did I see such a pounding match . . . Napoleon did not
manoeuvre at all. He just moved forward in the old style in column,
and was driven off in the old style. The only difference was that he
mixed cavalry with his infantry and supported both with an immense
quality of artillery . . . I never saw the British infantry behave
so well.[38]

For Walter Scott, who was one of the first visitors to the battlefield, the battle would become England's/Britain's most renowned engagement with the French:

> *Yes, Agincourt may be forgot*
> *And Cressy be an unknown spot*
> *   And Blenheim's name be new;*
> *But still in story and in song,*
> *For many an age remember'd long,*
> *Shall live the towers of Hougomont,*
> *   And field of Waterloo.*[39]

An authority on Britain's long wars against France, Rory Muir, con-cluded: 'The war as a whole, and Waterloo in particular, gave Britain a sense of uniqueness, an inner confidence, which lasted a full century until it was shattered on the Somme.'[40] Jeremy Bentham saw the battle as no less decisive, though for reasons wholly dissociated from the greater glory of Britain. In his *Plan of Parliamentary Reform* (1817) he saw the victory as an entrenchment of the Tory establishment:

The plains, or heights, or whatsoever they are, of Waterloo, will one day be pointed to by the historian as the grave – not only of French but of English liberties.[41]

This suggested outcome of the most celebrated land battle in British history thus raised questions about the impact of eventual victory in the long wars against France upon the British establishment and its conduct of overseas policy. Waterloo's more fundamental impact was encapsulated in Tennyson's description of Wellington, after the duke's death, as 'the great World-victor's victor'.[42] Although Napoleon was capable of stimulating and initiating political, administrative and legal reform, his unbridled restlessness and uncontrollable appetite for conquest and territory infused his very being and underpinned his legitimacy. As Mussolini was later to describe Fascism, Bonapartism at root was about action. Without territorial expansionism based on military victories, Napoleon's political *persona* and claims to rulership simply palled. Waterloo smashed his credibility as a warrior and as a man of destiny. Confirming the cumulative impact of the disastrous retreat from Moscow in late 1812, the pulverizing the French received at Leipzig in October 1813, and the long drawn-out corrosion of French rule in Spain, it was a defeat too far which turned political opinion in Paris against a supreme warlord who could no longer deliver speedy and politically catalytic victories. In so far as the political impact of the battle ended Napoleon's rule, the fighting at Waterloo was indeed decisive.

Notes and references

1 Philip J. Haythornthwaite, *The Armies of Wellington* (London, 1994), p. 263.

2 Paul W. Schroeder, *The Transformation of European Politics, 1763–1848* (Oxford, 1996), pp. 551–53.

3 Jan Dhondt and Marinette Bruwier, 'The Low Countries 1700–1914' in Carlo M. Cipolla (ed.), *The Fontana History of Europe: The Emergence of Industrial Societies Part One* (London, 1973), pp. 330–50; Rory Muir, *Britain and the Defeat of Napoleon, 1807–1815* (New Haven, CT, 1996), p. 374. Austrian fears of encirclement and an annihilatory battle with Napoleon if the allies plunged deep into France had permeated strategic discussion in early 1814. Michael V. Leggiere, *The Fall of Napoleon*, Vol. I, *The Allied Invasion of France 1813–14* (Cambridge, 2007), pp. 546–54.

4 Lieutenant Colonel Gurwood (ed.), *The Dispatches of Field Marshal the Duke of Wellington*, 12 vols (London, 1838), Vol. XII, pp. 205, 210.

5 Gurwood (ed.), *Dispatches*, Vol. XII, pp. 296–97, 303–05.

6 Gurwood (ed.), *Dispatches*, Vol. XII, pp. 236–38, 285, 288.

7 David Hamilton-Williams, *Waterloo: New Perspectives* (London, 1993), p. 69.

8 Hamilton-Williams, *Waterloo*, pp. 37, 68, 99–101.

9 Charles Dalton, *The Waterloo Roll Call* (London, 1978), p. 133.

10 Hamilton-Williams, *Waterloo*, pp. 357–61; David Chandler, *The Campaigns of Napoleon* (New York, 1974), pp. 1093–94. Isser Woloch, *Napoleon and His Collaborators: The Making of a Dictatorship* (New York, 2001), pp. 226–34 argues that the emperor's return depended upon his conceding greater power to parliament and that defeat at Waterloo destroyed any chance that Napoleon had of using military success to force the allies to recognize the new order. The political basis of his return was that he ceased being a warlord. Steven Englund, *Napoleon: A Political Life* (Cambridge, MA, 2004), pp. 442–45 also stresses Napoleon's initial hope of regrouping and his attempt through the legislative process to abdicate in favour of his son.

11 Gurwood (ed.), *Dispatches*, Vol. XII, pp. 499–500. Soult reported on the infantry's total demoralization by 22 June. Alessandro Barbero, *The Battle: A New History of Waterloo*, trans. by John Cullen (London, 2005 edn), p. 421.

12 Gurwood (ed.), *Dispatches*, Vol. XII, p. 280.

13 Colonel Ramsay Weston Phipps, *The Armies of the First French Republic and the Rise of the Marshals of Napoleon*, ed. by C.F. Phipps, 5 vols (Oxford, 1926–39), Vol. I, pp. 296–9.

14 Gurwood (ed.), *Dispatches*, Vol. XII, pp. 281, 291–92.

15 Jac Weller, *Wellington at Waterloo* (London, 1967), pp. 39, 237–43.

16 John Keegan, *The Mask of Command* (London, 1987), pp. 126–27; Maj. Gen. H.T. Siborne (ed.), *Waterloo Letters* (London, 1891), pp. 158; 198–200; 255–383; 406–7.

17 A. Aspinall (ed.), *The Later Correspondence of George III*, 5 vols (Cambridge, 1968), Vol. II, p. 96.

18 *The Annual Register 1795*, pp. 49, 55.

19 Aspinall (ed.), *The Later Correspondence of George III*, Vol. II, p. 291.

20 John Sutherland, *The Life of Walter Scott* (Oxford, 1995), p. 186.

21 G.J. Evelyn, ' "I learned what one ought not to do": The British Army in Flanders and Holland, 1793–95' in Alan Guy (ed.), *The Road to Waterloo* (London, 1990), pp.16–22.

22 Paddy Griffith, *The Art of War of Revolutionary France 1789–1802* (London, 1998), p. 21.

23 John Keegan, *The Face of Battle* (London, 1978 edn), pp. 156, 159–61, 163, 185–94. Keegan's chapter on Waterloo remains one of the most enlightening analyses of the battle: pp. 117–206.

24 Phipps, *Armies of the First French Republic*, Vol. I, pp. 309–11.

25 Aspinall (ed.), *The Later Correspondence of George III*, Vol. II, p. 214.

26 Keegan, *The Face of Battle*, pp. 170–74.

27 Keegan, *The Face of Battle*, p. 193.

28 Weller, *Wellington at Waterloo*, pp. 237–43.

29 Rory Muir, *Tactics and the Experience of Battle in the Age of Napoleon* (New Haven, CT and London, 1998), p. 190.

30 Siborne (ed.), *Waterloo Letters*, p. 279.

31 Hamilton-Williams, *Waterloo*, p. 238.

32 Hamilton-Williams, *Waterloo*, p. 185.

33 Weller, *Wellington at Waterloo*, pp. 33–4.

34 W.S. Moorsom, *Historical Record of the Fifty-Second Regiment, 1775–1858* (London, 1860), pp. 236–37.

35 Christopher Duffy, *The Military Experience in the Age of Reason* (London, 1987), p. 190.

36 John Fortescue, *A History of the British Army, 1763–1793*, 13 vols (London and New York, 1899–1930), Vol. X, pp. 409–20; Weller, *Wellington at Waterloo*, pp. 176–78; Keegan, *The Face of Battle*, pp. 154–94.

37 *The Autobiography of Sir Harry Smith 1787–1819*, intro. by Philip Haythornthwaite (London, 1999 edn), pp. 277–78.

38 Gurwood (ed.), *Dispatches*, Vol. XII, p. 529.

39 J. Logie Robertson (ed.), *The Poetical Works of Sir Walter Scott* (London, 1904), p. 626.

40 Muir, *Britain and the Defeat of Napoleon*, p. 374.

41 Peter Spence, *The Birth of Romantic Radicalism* (Aldershot,1996), p. 208.

42 Alfred, Lord Tennyson, *Ode on the Death of the Duke of Wellington* (1856), stanza 4.

CHAPTER 15

Completing British paramountcy in India, 1814–19

Most general accounts of British history treat 1815 as closing a peculiar era of British military and naval activism. After 1815, the armed services were massively reduced in size, much of the officer class went into suspended military animation on half-pay, government spending fell, and little overseas projection of British power occurred. Such a description needs to be modified. It will be suggested instead that the military expertise developed over twenty-five years of campaigning was not dissipated after 1815, that the officer corps and the aristocratic and gentry values which dominated it remained prominent and significant, and that Britain was far from being an inactive global power in the years following Waterloo.

'Achieving' paramountcy in India

The end of the Napoleonic wars was marked in India by a renewal of campaigning, which asserted British paramountcy in a sequence of largely forgotten wars from early 1815 to June 1818. After initial setbacks, the British defeated the Gurkhas and emasculated the Maratha princes' military power. Yet the final reduction of those often warring rival Maratha states scarcely produced any fanfare or even calculated political relief at home. When George Canning, as the cabinet minister responsible for the East India Company's affairs, introduced resolutions formally thanking the governor-general and army in India, he told the House of Commons that the vote he recommended was 'intended merely as a tribute to the military conduct of the campaign and not in any wise as a sanction of the policy of the war'.[1] This declaration, made in March 1819, suggests that the completion of British paramountcy in the subcontinent seemed of little importance at the time and indeed was explicitly underplayed by the government.

The lack of interest even in London, let alone the rest of the country, gave weight to Seeley's later insistence that India was not conquered by Britain but by rulers within India who were British; the British state rarely made war in India and hardly ever upon Indians, as distinct from European, especially French, rivals for imperial possessions or influence in southern Asia.[2] One participant offered a variant on this line in 1824 when he stressed that the British, in establishing a liberal imperium, proved themselves 'Unambitious of empire, yet forced by the ambition of their enemies to become sovereigns'.[3] Yet this depiction of reluctance squares ill with the campaigns against the Pindaris and Marathas in 1816-19, which involved, in 1817, the deployment of 113,000 government soldiers – regulars and irregulars – buttressed with 304 guns.[4] By mid-1818 three of the five principal Maratha potentates were removed or reduced to subordination. Subsidiary alliances were imposed on a number of Rajput chiefs, further extending British dominance in the region south of Delhi and west of the upper reaches of the Maratha territories. One of the mainstays of the Marathas' economy and military effectiveness, the wide-ranging seasonal raiding by parties of up to about 10,000 armed horsemen, was ended. The politics and military culture of central India were transformed. Yet the refrain of reluctance recurred. Canning in March 1819 regretted, as Cornwallis had done in 1805, repeated expansionism to achieve political-military security:

> Would to God that we could find, or rather that we could long ago have found, the point – the resting place – at which it was possible to stand. But the finding of that point has not depended upon ourselves alone.[5]

The war against Nepal

The war of 1814-16 between Nepal and the British began as an elaborate and extensive policing operation and ended with a large-scale military campaign. Its interest lies in what it revealed about the British ability to plan and mount complex operations requiring coordination across a wide front, their capacity to apply military pressure speedily and effectively at the appropriate points, their competence in providing consistent military leadership to sustain dispersed but coordinated advances, and their expertise in linking military measures to achievable political ends.

The conflict arose from the systemic tensions created by porous borders. Nepal had been created during the eighteenth century, much of its apparently cohesive shape arising from the dynamic aggressions of a raja of Gurkha in the 1760s and early 1770s. Although by the 1810s Nepal was about as long east to west as Britain is from south to north, its western extremities were very recent acquisitions and its core had been assembled from separate rulerships mostly within the previous sixty years. To the west, both the Sikhs and the British wanted to block further Gurkha expansionism. While the British in 1809 extended a protectorate over the Sirhind Sikhs, the Gurkhas claimed rights over some of the villages in this region, with such claims fuelling a full-blown dispute over the sovereignty of six villages in 1813. To the east, the porous border created even graver differences. Many local rulers within Nepal held rights, largely as tenants to the nawabs of Bengal and Oudh, to areas of land in the lowlands now ruled by the Company. Such rights or claims came increasingly into conflict with British policies directed at regularizing patterns of land tenure. The build-up of tension over a number of years led the Court of Directors in February 1814 to authorize a war to protect British interests. The Council in Calcutta decided in June to fight the Gurkhas.[6]

The decision to confront, rather than compromise, with Nepal, came from the new governor-general, General Lord Moira, later Lord Hastings. Moira arrived in India in October 1813 and, like Cornwallis, combined the positions of governor-general and commander-in-chief. The general had first seen active service in 1775 at Bunker's Hill and, as Lieutenant Colonel Rawdon, had been a notoriously aggressive, fast-moving, and hard-fighting pursuer of American troops in South Carolina. As the 2nd Earl of Moira he had been tasked to lead a major raiding force against the French coast in 1794. Long distrusted by Pittites for his close personal and political connections with the Prince of Wales, Moira was a leader unlikely to be swayed by cautious counsels or constrained by counting-house calculations. He rejected the advice of David Ochterlony, who had negotiated with local rajas and the Nepalese from 1809 to 1814, that the British create a buffer line of minor states between Nepal and the Company's possessions.[7]

The governor-general sought to put maximum pressure on the Nepalese court by despatching a small expeditionary force to the east to keep the ruler of Sikkim on the British side and by invading the Gurkha kingdom at four, widely separated points. From the far west, Major General David

Ochterlony would lead about 6,000 troops – all Indians – from Ludhiana, a post only established in 1808–09, into western Nepal's hill country. Ochterlony was expected to confront the main enemy army in the west, probably finding that it would withdraw to mountain fastnesses where the primitive roads would not even accommodate beasts of burden. The second line of advance would proceed from the longer-established British garrison of Meerut (north of Delhi); Major General Rollo Gillespie would lead 3,500 troops into the fertile agricultural valley of Dehra Dun, occupy it and then fan out to the west to capture a key fort. Speed was of the essence in this sector because the overall strategy was to ensure that the Gurkha army in the north-west would not be able to escape from Ochterlony by moving south-east. Once he had blocked off a significant escape route, Gillespie was to turn eastwards and invade Kamaun, a rich and fertile country capable of providing supplies and an area which, having been conquered by the Gurkhas only in 1790, was deemed likely to support the British challenge to Gurkha power. Both probes were to start as soon in the second half of October 1814 as possible and were intended to yield significant territorial and political gains quickly without absorbing large forces.

The third advance again involved a relatively small force, of under 4,000 troops, assembled at Banaras and Gorakpur. Major General John Sullivan Wood was to start on 15 November for Butwal (from where a British force had withdrawn in April, and where a bloody, if small-scale confrontation had broken out in May) and then push into Palpa. The biggest, and fourth, thrust was aimed in the direction of the Gurkha capital of Kathmandu. Nearly 8,000 troops were assembled for an advance under Major General Bennett Marley from 15 November through mountain passes towards Kathmandu. Additional troops would follow their advance to secure depots and lines of communication. This force was accompanied by far more artillery than other single corps, although the total artillery even for Marley's force amounted to only twenty-six guns, mortars and howitzers.[8]

First off the mark on 22 October was the column from Meerut under Gillespie, an officer of fiercesome reputation for personal daring.[9] He quickly advanced upon the fort of Kalanga, which stood on a hill about 5 miles beyond the strategic town of Dehra. On 31 October he launched two frontal attacks which failed at the cost of 260 casualties among a relatively small force. Furious at the stalled advance, Gillespie and his ADC were killed and the brigade-major was wounded in pressing the attack. Although much has been made in recent histories of the British in

India of the extent and value of their intelligence-gathering activities, Gillespie clearly underestimated the strength of the defences devised by his opponents before his approach. Indeed, the Gurkhas' command of the passes into their country and the absence of local collaborators prevented the British, despite much effort, from determining their opponents' detailed military dispositions. British officers' preoccupation with lines of communication and potential Gurkha ambushes led to an over-reliance on attacking concentrations of Gurkha troops and overconfidence in assailing a visible and immobile enemy.[10] Gillespie had been asked on 19 September whether he wanted artillery, but had been content to advance without such armaments. He was presumably satisfied with the preparatory information he received on routes to Kalanga and with a plan of the fort provided him. While his impetuosity and pig-headedness may have been personal traits, he was also under intense pressure to achieve results. The Adjutant General repeatedly instructed him on the need to occupy Dehra Dun and the surrounding passes – 'a measure of peculiar and immediate urgency' – by 15 October or soon thereafter. As the conflict began, the *Calcutta Monthly Journal* reflected senior officials' optimism in declaring that 'the war will be speedily brought to a satisfactory and bloodless conclusion, by the entire submission of the Raja of Nepal to all the stipulations demanded of him'.[11] Denied such painless victories, the corps formerly led by Gillespie awaited the arrival of more guns, shelled the fort, and captured it on 30 November. The two separate attacks on a garrison estimated at about 600 and further operations against a nearby hill-top position, at Jaithak, lifted the casualty list in this one sector to 1,200 men by the year's end.[12]

To the west, Ochterlony proceeded with great caution. He is credited with understanding from the beginning that warfare in Nepal would not provide any opportunities for pursuing a fast-moving foe, but would instead involve a close contest to secure enemy posts, well-stockaded in secure defensive positions.[13] He therefore constructed a road – the existing ones were minor tracks – into the hills and brought up heavier guns to use against fortresses. He used elephants to help roll the iron barrels of two 18-pounder guns (weighing over one ton each) along paths believed to be impassable to elephants as carriage animals. In emphasizing the role of artillery, Ochterlony realized that his sepoys would not relish close bayonet fighting against Gurkhas armed with their notorious special knives or khukuris.[14] British planning was also premised on the resentment of local people against the Gurkhas who ruled with a 'rod of iron', keeping the population in 'a state of the most servile subjection'. Some years later, while touring the region in 1824, Bishop Heber noted that people 'in every village lent their help not only as guides, but in dragging our guns up the hills, and giving every other assistance which they could supply'.[15] Yet political progress in enlisting such aid was very slow until Kalanga fell to the British. Handicapped by the initial reverse at Kalanga, Ochterlony worked during November and December to manoeuvre his troops through valleys and hills, carefully overcoming skilfully defended positions.[16]

The two corps advancing in the east faced a different set of problems from those which challenged Gillespie and Ochterlony. The towns where the British gathered their forces lay along the Ganges at some distance from the border. Major General J.S. Wood delayed his start from Gorakpur for over five weeks because of difficulties in getting hill porters for his baggage and supplies. When he then pushed forward, Wood insisted – wrongly – that he was opposed by a very large Gurkha army and that he needed additional cavalry and irregular horse to scour the country and provide his eyes and ears in the face of this numerically superior opponent.[17] Once again, British intelligence – hindered by the daunting terrain – proved insufficient for operational purposes.

In order to probe the mountain foothills leading into Nepal, Major General Bennet Marley was tasked to lead the largest single corps into three major mountain passes: 'The maintenance of the established renown of our country in Asia, the future security of a vast proportion of our dominions, and the prevention of future wars of a similar character, will greatly depend on a speedy and successful issue to the approaching contest.' The Adjutant General provided Marley with detailed instructions and plans, amounting to fifty-three paragraphs setting specific objectives and operational advice. In addition, details of routes and distances were provided.[18] But the general did not begin operations until mid-December and then spent the rest of that month acquiring detailed knowledge of the country and watching flank movements and defiles. In response to the general's growing belief that he lacked sufficient manpower, Hastings provided troop reinforcements, but concluded that it was 'not so easy to restore confidence to the mind of the commander'. Marley snapped under pressure, and quit his command on 10 February, even though his force had been expanded to 13,400 regulars.[19] Thus two of the four original divisional commanders fell victim to the pressures of leading an invasion of Nepal's mountainous domain.

By March 1815, the number of troops, deployed in four divisions, had risen from 24,600 to 49,000, more men under British colours than fought at Waterloo a few months later. In addition, just over 56,000 camp followers accompanied these divisions. Expanding the war effort was matched by tangible successes in the west. The ridge-top fortress of Jaithak surrendered in May 1815, five months after it had first been attacked. To the south-east of that point, the British recruited levies of Putans or Rohillas to compensate for troop shortages and to gain agility in hill-fighting. In early April Colonel Jasper Nicolls, a rising officer who had served in the West Indies, at Argaum and Gwalighur in 1803–04, Buenos Aires, Coruña, Walcheren, and in Ireland, led 3,000 irregulars, with a small body of regulars and ten pieces of artillery, into Kamaun, whose surrender he forced in early May. Bowing also to the pressures created by Ochterlony's advance, rajas to the west of the Kali or Gogra River agreed on 15 May 1815 to reject Gurkha rule.[20]

The settlement had two outstanding features. First, Kamaun, with a population in the 1820s estimated at about 300,000,[21] was incorporated into British India. Seven local rajas and ranas were confirmed in power and their annual tribute set. This accord flowed from Hastings' earlier insistence that the invading British were to pay 'the utmost regard . . . to the persons, property, temples, and religious prejudices of the inhabitants', and to ensure that the people 'soon feeling the contrast between the galling yoke of their present rulers, and the benevolent hand that is raised to free them from it, may be expected to range themselves on the side of their deliverers, with whatever they can command of aid or exertion'.[22] Second, efforts to win over the population included inducements to the ordinary soldiers. In January, Ochterlony had offered cash rewards and well-paid service with the British to troops deserting from the Nepalese army. In finalizing a peace settlement in the west, Ochterlony formed three special battalions and a provincial corps for civil duties in Kamaun, embodying 4,650 Nepalese soldiers in such units.[23]

There followed a long lull in campaigning farther east as the rainy season from June to October precluded operations. A preliminary settlement agreed at the end of November 1815 aroused strong and successful opposition from the war party at Kathmandu, on the grounds that it would open the way to yet deeper British interference and that Baratpur (in 1804–05) provided an example of how British power could be resisted. With delays threatening to consume the entire campaigning season for 1815–16, Hastings ordered a resumption of operations.[24]

The sheer scale of the British war effort enabled Ochterlony, having been transferred to the east, to bring about 20,000 effectives, from the total force of 33,000 under his command, to foothills of the Himalayas. In very difficult conditions and by single-file marching, the British outflanked the Gurkhas, forcing them to evacuate their strong defensive positions to cover the near approach to Kathmandu. After sharp if localized fighting, Ochterlony built up enough pressure to persuade the Gurkha court to accept Hastings' peace terms in early March 1816. Partly because British territorial advances were constricted by the difficulties of securing supply routes and defending them, Hastings settled for the removal of the western territories from the Gurkhas' control and retaining selected strategic points on the border of Oudh.[25] It has been suggested, not unreasonably, that the unexpected stoutness of Nepalese resistance dissuaded British officials locally from annexing the entire kingdom. But the most difficult fighting occurred in the west, which the British annexed. As events later were to prove, there was little need to impose direct British rule on the rest of Nepal.

One lesson, however, seemed clear to Colonel Nicolls, as he confided to his diary in May 1817: 'To hope that the Natives of India will attend to promises is in vain. The first argument they quote is that of Power and in fact it is the only one.' And Sir David Ochterlony in 1825 explained to the Court of Directors that government by 'consent' in India meant 'a belief in the governed that the Wisdom, Resources, but above all, the Military strength of the Rulers, remains unexhausted and invincible'.[26]

The Pindari threat

Despite claims that military success maintained British prestige in India, the campaign against Nepal did not deter further challenges to the British imperium. The decision in 1816 to engage once more with the Maratha princes illustrated three strategic pressures. The first was the need to establish a boundary to British India. Cornwallis, in calling a halt to Lord Wellesley's expansionism in 1805, argued that the Maratha boundaries should mark the interior limits of British India. To proceed farther would prove dangerous and expensive, as well as remain unnecessary. Yet the difficulty of achieving such security had been pointed out by Arthur Wellesley before Cornwallis had returned to India. Once the Marathas were no longer organized in regular armies, the general noted, they would exercise their need to acquire resources and maintain their militarized lifestyle by forming vast raiding parties operating beyond, and indifferent to, political boundaries.[27]

A second strategic challenge thus flowed from this. Lord Hastings in 1815 asserted that no reductions in the military establishment could be achieved 'until the foundations of lasting Peace and tranquillity be laid in the suppression of the Predatory Powers, the revision of our relations with the remaining Military States, and the general settlement of Central India'.[28] Of the four military powers identified by the governor-general, three were the Maratha princes, Sindhia, Berar, and Holkar. The Pindari raiding parties and the military adventurer Mir Khan – who, according to the British, controlled Holkar's government – were only constrained by British power: 'we owe our security to the dread of our power alone'.[29] If the existing frontiers failed to restrict the Marathas and the Pindari raiders and if only an enlarged army could guarantee British security in central India, Hastings urged the desirability of further constricting the Marathas' power.[30]

The Pindaris had grown in strength after the wars of 1803–05. Dismissing large numbers of cavalry auxiliaries, Sindhia had granted them lands for their basic subsistence. They staged plundering raids to supplement their income and came to prefer raiding to military operations because they could choose when and where to raid and because their expeditions proved more profitable than military service.[31] It is possible to characterize them in different ways: as demilitarized irregular support cavalry who were adapting to conditions in which their services were no longer required by the great Maratha princes; as victims of tightened financial circumstances who needed to supplement their income with periodic raiding; or as opportunistic freebooters who were carrying out economic gangsterism by less formal means than had been the case within the framework of eighteenth-century Maratha warfare. At times they comprised all three groups. At their core were Pathan warriors who had earlier contributed to the military labour market of northern and central India, and who depended on raiding for part of their livelihood. But distant raiding attracted opportunists seeking quick plunder.[32] The British government insisted on the third definition, the prime minister in 1819 ascribing the origins of the war to 'the aggressions of the Pindarees, a body consisting of about 30,000 men, subject to no regular discipline, and having, in fact, no national existence'. Their raiding had impinged upon territories neighbouring British possessions and would have justified much earlier British action if it had not been for 'the peace policy adopted by this country'. According to Lord Liverpool, only when these depredations reached the British presidency of Madras in 1816 did it become 'absolutely necessary to resort to measures of self-defence'.[33] Dealing with the Pindaris became entangled with their relationship with the princes, for they needed the Maratha rulers' tacit if not positive approval to ride across their territories, and the possible protection of Sindhia and Holkar in periods of danger.[34]

The third strategic issue concerned the larger significance of Pindari/ Maratha power. Some younger officials in the Company's service urged the case for pre-emptive action. Charles Metcalfe, the Resident at Delhi, depicted the Pindaris as challenging the British in the same way that the Marathas had undermined the Mughal empire in the eighteenth century. Powerful indigenous rivals to the British would exploit any openings offered by conflict between the British and the Pindaris in order to weaken the Company and fragment its rule. Such strategic danger was exacerbated by the Company's allies' defects. The government of Hyderabad was allegedly undermined by the subordination of ministers to British interests and a sullen acceptance of British predominance. In Oudh otherwise good relations with the court had been poisoned by the officiousness of an over-bearing Resident.[35] The death of the Nawab of Bhopal in March 1816 opened up uncertainties over the strength of a recently formed alliance. And in Jaipur, the raja – who sought British protection against Mir Khan and Pindari raiders – was at odds with many nobles who preferred the opportunities created by continuing uncertainty over territorial boundaries and rights to the constrictions imposed by peace.[36] Given this uncertain context, Hastings by December 1816 believed that the Pindari leaders were strong enough to press Sindhia into 'a Community of Interest' with them. While Sindhia was normally hesitant, he faced growing pressure to become, in effect, 'their Instrument', with Holkar likely to follow Sindhia's lead. Hastings argued for a vigorous pursuit of the Pindaris into and across Sindhia's territories, demanding the maharaja's support and co-operation in this campaigning. Action was thus required both to punish recent and unusually damaging Pindari raids and to quash the Pindaris before their successes spawned a new and threatening alliance against British rule.[37]

This decision flowed also from British diplomatic concerns about the power politics of the Holkar and Sindhia states. The death in 1811 of Jaswant Rao Holkar and the succession of his son, a minor, sparked a struggle within the durbar between two of Jaswant's widows and the adherents of the independent warlord, Mir Khan. The regime's capacity to maintain order among its feudatories and with its neighbours was severely tested in 1812–17. Daulat Rao Sindhia lacked the power to intervene, but he could not resist the temptation to dabble in the affairs of his rival state. He also allowed the Pindari bands regular access to and through his territories.[38]

The immediate trigger for war was the failure of a recent alliance with one of the five leading Maratha princes, Berar, to restrict renewed Pindari raiding. The death of the raja of Berar (the Bhonsle) in March 1816 led to tension between the new Bhonsle's followers and a faction led by Apa Sahib, his cousin and heir who initially sided with the British. Once British troops reached the capital, Nagpur, on 9 June, a military agreement was struck. Two British battalions were assigned to a cantonment 3 miles outside Nagpur and the other four battalions of the British subsidiary force were posted on the Narbudda River guarding the southern route used by the Pindaris from the Maratha lands down towards the Nizam's territories. A Nagpur contingent of about 5,000 soldiers was formed, with the British Resident having the right to advise on discipline and internal management.[39] Yet in October 1816, when Pindari raiding was to be blocked, none of the Nagpur contingent moved to the front stretching 120 miles on the southern bank of the Narbudda to assist the British subsidiary force, demonstrating the failure of the new alliance with Berar to impede the Pindaris' customary incursions.[40]

In these circumstances, Hastings proposed to pursue the Pindaris into Sindhia's territories without seeking the maharaja's prior agreement. But the Court of Directors had prohibited any attack on the Pindaris which might give offence to Sindhia. Hastings' case for an immediate and vigorous pre-emptive attack was initially rejected by N.B. Edmonstone, the senior member of the Supreme Council in Calcutta who had served under Lord Wellesley and long been sceptical about territorial aggrandizement and expanded alliance-building. He queried the strategic claim that Pindari mobilization, reinforced by Sindhia's and possibly Nagpur's support, might threaten British security, arguing instead that Pindari actions were shaped by planning for the following season's raiding rather than by broader geopolitical visions. Edmonstone suggested approaching Sindhia when British preparations were well advanced to seek his neutrality, if not his cooperation.[41] Hastings dismissed such diplomatic half-measures and asserted that the Pindaris posed an impending threat which enabled the Council to set aside the Court of Directors' earlier instructions. He brushed aside caveats about the timing of the campaign by ensuring that, as commander-in-chief, he had positioned plentiful forces between the Narbudda and Kishna Rivers, buttressed by January 1817 with infantry and cavalry from the Nizam's and Peshwa's brigades.[42] Sweeps against the raiders began in December.

The extent of the Pindari threat has never been conclusively assessed. An official estimate in 1812 gave a total of 33,900 horsemen within ten different Pindari bands, but at least one prominent official privately scoffed at the numbers being publicly promulgated by his colleagues.

Thomas Munro suggested that their real strength was closer to 7,000–8,000 horsemen of all kinds; he dismissed higher figures as implausible given the fact that Tipu Sultan, commanding very significantly higher revenues, had maintained 20,000–25,000 cavalry.[43] On any comparison Hastings' preparations were overwhelmingly powerful.

The Pindari/Maratha war: opening phase

The governor-general's careful preparations were soon confounded by an unanticipated extension of the conflict. This was triggered by a confrontation with Baji Rao II, the peshwa or titular chief functionary of the Maratha confederacy, who had used his alliance with the Company from 1802 to tighten his authority within his own territories. Tensions with the British, however, led the Resident at Pune, Mountstuart Elphinstone, to take forcible action at the peshwa's capital in September 1815.[44] Baji Rao, or some of his advisers, saw the Pindari crisis as an opportunity to use the peshwa's increased territorial control to wrest back the overlordship of the Maratha confederacy which Baji had been forced to disclaim at Bassein in 1802. The court at Pune attempted to do this when, in February 1817, the new raja of Berar – already gravely incapacitated – died, or was probably murdered. Although his successor, Apa Sahib, had worked with the British in May–June 1816, he was now receptive to overtures from Pune, perhaps as a response to the hostility aroused by his pro-British stance among Nagpur's nobles.

The entire character of the planned war changed. Instead of mounting operations against the Pindaris in which the peshwa was a subordinate ally and Apa Sahib in Berar was a client, the British faced an emerging alliance to the rear and across their intended line of operations. They therefore diverted forces to march upon Pune, took the surrender of three key forts in May 1817, and forced Baji Rao to sign a new treaty, updating the settlement he had concluded at Bassein in 1802. In June 1817, he renounced his title as chief official of the Maratha confederacy, a status acknowledged at least ceremonially by the other princes, and pledged not to negotiate with other Indian powers except through the British Resident. He gave up the fort of Ahmadnagar, yielded his rights in Hindustan and, among other concessions, engaged to pay the British to maintain a contingent of 5,000 cavalry and 3,000 infantry instead of raising and paying such a military force himself.[45] Thus, within six months of embarking on a campaign provoked by geopolitical concerns about Sindhia and the Pindaris, the British had forced the peshwa into becoming a subsidiary ally and recorded their first territorial gains against the Marathas since 1805, but at the peshwa's not Sindhia's or the Pindaris' expense.

The government justified this sideways lurch in operations by alleging the existence of a conspiracy among the Marathas. *The Times* in London concluded in May 1818 that the Marathas 'have been seldom remiss in seizing whatever appeared to them a plausible opportunity for striking a blow at the British empire; and it was perhaps to be inferred, that where anyone of their confederated chieftains faced us openly, he was secure of the cooperation of his brethren'. When reviewing the war's origins in 1819, Lord Liverpool went further in claiming 'that a very deep-laid conspiracy existed for striking a blow' to 'overthrow the British power' within the Maratha territories.[46] What appears to have happened is that the Maratha chiefs, in the style of European 'cabinet wars' of the eighteenth century, formed, dissolved, and reformed alliances to wage short campaigns according to tactical circumstances.

Following such a pattern of behaviour, a new scenario for the peshwa emerged when the British concentrated against the Pindaris late in 1817, after the intense summer heat had receded. Deciding to strike out against the terms imposed in June 1817, Baji Rao gathered his own feudatories, amassed troops and forced the British Resident to leave his capital. One of the five army divisions deployed in the southern sector to advance upon the Pindaris was thereupon diverted to Pune. Entering the Peshwa's capital on 17 November, this division forced Baji (whose men had burned the British Residency and killed a party of travelling officers unaware that hostilities had broken out) to flee.[47]

It remains difficult to understand Baji Rao's actions, although the official insistence on the existence of a conspiracy was never substantiated. Perhaps international conflict theory offers a more plausible, if hypothetical, explanation. It has been suggested that rulers whose position is uncertain, or exposed to threatening opposition at home, may respond assertively or aggressively to external pressure or coercion lest any policy based on compromise or conciliation serves to strengthen their domestic opponents. Such an analysis squares with Baji's predicament from virtually the beginning of his rulership in 1796 and certainly from 1803. The propensity to take risks is then increased by the political dynamics of decision-making. The shifting interplay of influence and power within a cabinet or, in this case, a court, may well lead to the choice of what turns out to be a high-risk policy if the ruler is not already determined on the direction in which he intends to proceed. The peshwa, under pressure from key advisers, may have seized an apparent opportunity to reverse years of declining power and the humiliation of May 1817, having rather than have been engaged in a Maratha conspiracy. The terms of the treaty of 1817 proved the final provocation.[48] Whatever the cause, however, Baji's rejection of the British alliance and his subsequent flight necessitated a reappraisal of the entire plan of operations in the south.

The governor-general had insisted in May 1817 that he sought to extend British influence rather than territory and to promote the security of Sindhia's and Holkar's regimes. If, however, they aided the Pindaris either openly or covertly he would treat them as 'predatory aggressors'.[49] To mount a vast hammer and anvil operation against the Pindaris from north and south, he assembled forces totalling about 80,000 regular troops (of whom 10,000 were Europeans) and 34,000 irregulars, supported by 303 guns. They were organized into nine divisions, capable of acting independently, together with two corps of observation, and one reserve division. Four divisions were assigned to the north, on the Jumna River line from Delhi to south of Allahabad. Five divisions and the reserve went south of Hindustan and essentially started on the line of the Narbudda River sweeping from Nagpur to Gujerat, with an eye also to defending Hyderabad against Pindari raiding. The area between the lines of the Narbudda and the Jumna Rivers and the line of the Aravelli hills to the west covered about 150,000 square miles – over 50% larger than Britain – and offered starkly contrasting terrain, from dense jungle to arid, open country. Hastings intended his southern divisions to advance northwards across Hindustan breaking down Pindari bands, seizing forts and towns, and obliging great rulers and petty chiefs alike to join the British. The governor-general had set out a thorough, bold plan of systematic subjugation.[50]

On 17 November 1817 the advance from the south – the key to the whole strategy – stopped. The field commander, Lieutenant General Sir Thomas Hislop, made this decision on learning of fighting outside Pune because he feared that Baji Rao's offensive might stimulate others' disaffection.[51] Suspecting that the raja of Berar, Apa Sahib, might join Baji Rao, Hislop despatched troops to Nagpur. In these newly uncertain political circumstances, Hislop also suspected that Sindhia would not hand over Asirgarh fortress, as he had agreed to do, for British use during the campaign. The general assigned another force to move in that direction. The vast southern field army of five divisions assembled to crush the Pindaris shrank to half its planned strength on 17 November. Hastings disagreed with these fresh dispositions, insisting that Hislop concentrate on the planned offensive against the Pindaris.

Just as Hislop began his advance, on 26 November, Apa Sahib threatened the Residency outside Nagpur. On the following day, he tried to seize the British cantonment from which, eighteen months earlier, he had drawn support for his power struggle against the cousin whom he had now succeeded as raja. Defending themselves on the Sitabaldi hills outside Nagpur, a Company contingent of 1,600 men held their position against repeated onslaughts which left nearly one quarter of them, or 364 men, killed or wounded; fifteen of the thirty-four British officers present were casualties. While this savagely fought defence broke the raja's momentum, events at Nagpur further redefined the war. One of the army's five southern divisions was diverted to the city to ensure that the British reasserted a military presence there by 12 December. About 3,000 of Apa Sahib's Arab mercenaries continued to hold out in Nagpur fort which the British failed to take by storm on 24 December; five days later the mercenaries agreed to evacuate the fort in return for concessions including a money payment. Various mopping-up operations forced Apa Sahib to submit in February 1818. Nagpur ceded fertile districts along the Narbudda to direct British rule, opened all the raja's forts to British garrisons if and when the British required such access and occupation, strengthened the British cantonment outside Nagpur city, and fortified the Sitabaldi hills there. The ceded districts were expected to generate more than enough revenue to pay the British military costs involved in their expanded presence in Berar. Again, the Berar campaign, a diversion from the Pindaris, had resulted in the extension of formal British control in an area where Hastings had sought not territory but an ally to free him for offensives elsewhere.[52]

The offensive against the Pindaris encountered yet a further obstacle. Perhaps encouraged by the peshwa's moves against the Company, some of Holkar's chieftains brought troops together at the end of November at Mehidpur, to link up with Pindari bands. British forces scattered those bands but, on 19–21 December, the chiefs in Holkar's camp, divided in their opinions, decided not to come to terms with Lieutenant General Hislop. After advancing 8 miles before and after dawn, Hislop sighted Holkar's army at 9.00 a.m. and, despite his opponent's excellent defensive position across a river, attacked the Marathas. The battle of Mehidpur proved to be the only substantial battle of the whole war. Hislop led 4,500 regular infantry, nearly 1,500 regular cavalry, and about 3,000 irregular cavalry in an advance which was daring to the point of rashness. The cavalry especially suffered from the Marathas' superior weight of artillery and the intensity of their artillery fire. Disorganized by a hard-fought battle following a lengthy early morning march, depleted by many wounded

COMPLETING BRITISH PARAMOUNTCY IN INDIA, 1814-19   379

soldiers dying from the lack of proper medical supplies, deflected by the prospects of booty offered by Holkar's camp, and delayed until the arrival of the Bombay army's division from Gujerat, Hislop's army failed to pursue Holkar's retreating men until 27 December.[53]

This pursuit, together with the subjugation and submission of the peshwa and Berar, created enough political pressure on Holkar's durbar to induce Holkar to agree terms on 6 January 1818. The maharaja ceded various territories, some of which the Company retained and some of which it awarded to an ally as a reward for his support. Holkar made an important political concession in giving up any right to receive tribute from the Rajput chiefs,[54] thereby opening the way to a British alliance, buttressed by a financial settlement highly advantageous to the Company, with Jaipur, the wealthiest and most important of the Rajput states.[55] Wide-ranging operations followed Holkar's submission. By February 1818, the three main Pindari bands, having been driven hard, had broken up, allowing large parts of the four divisions which Hastings had assembled in the north to return to their garrisons.

The prolonged campaign of 1818–19

A major operation was still required to crush Baji Rao. He fled Pune in late November 1817 and moved south, succeeding in taking into his camp the raja of Satara, the titular head of the Maratha confederacy. Boxed in by British divisions moving both north and south of Pune, the peshwa failed to re-enter his capital and was pursued throughout January by one or other of the two divisions operating against him. Frustrated in his efforts to bring the peshwa to battle, Brigadier General Lionel Smith decided to refocus his strategy and deploy his division for an attack on Satara. The town surrendered on 10 February, on the day when the mortar battery arrived and began firing on the fortifications.[56]

The capture of Satara enabled Mountstuart Elphinstone, the Resident at Pune, to launch a political initiative to win over the Marathas by publicly pledging to restore the representative of the titular founding dynasty of the Marathas, whose flag and not the Company's was flown over the surrendered town, and to exclude Baji in perpetuity. As one senior British official stressed, 'though the natives would understand perfectly well the relation between the Raja and the British Government, and the motives which dictated this proclamation', local feudatories felt the need to secure the raja's formal authority for rebelling against Baji.[57] Elphinstone next linked the announcement that the British would take over Baji's possessions with a declaration that existing jagirdars – territorial and tax-raising rights given to local officials or leaders in return for agreed revenues, services or troops – would be upheld for those accepting British authority within two months, but denied to any who delayed longer in submitting to the Company.[58] The legal right to appoint to or confirm jagirdars – even though the peshwa had long ceased to control the holders in practice – remained a central attribute of power.[59] Accompanying this political initiative, Elphinstone, rather than the generals, developed a new military strategy. Instead of fielding two mixed divisions, the British from February concentrated their light forces, including all the cavalry, in a division under Brigadier Smith, and the heavy artillery and forces sufficient for sieges and similar operations, under Theophilus Pritzler.

Setting off on 13 February, Smith came upon Baji's army at Ashti on 20 February and freed the raja of Satara and his family. While Baji escaped, his fleeing army was increasingly prone to desertion since Ashti decisively shifted political and public support away from the deposed peshwa. Applications to confirm jagirdars flowed in, while landowners and farmers declined to pay taxes and financial dues to Baji's officials or revenue jagirdar-holders. Elphinstone exploited the victory at Ashti by assuring religious leaders that the British would maintain all their existing establishments and endowments. The re-establishment of the raja of Satara reassured older Maratha elites and allowed them to accommodate to the new political order by depicting Baji's as a personal not a national cause.[60]

But some of the elite remained loyal to Baji and many in the military class who held no lands had little inducement to switch sides. So the British maintained the existing pressure by taking fortress after fortress, selecting forts to attack with an eye to the impact their capture would have on other rulers' or chiefs' morale and willingness to submit. British forces also successfully restricted the supply of gunpowder in the region they controlled.[61] In late January and during February a reported eighteen forts surrendered to Pritzler's division, which enjoyed the powerful addition to the British armoury of accurate and sustained shelling, against which the Maratha forts had no defence.[62] Taking forts and fortified villages enabled the British to tap the support of village headmen and traders who were frustrated with Maratha rule, and to deny the peshwa's cavalry sources of resupply. The British brought in revenue police from Mysore and the ceded provinces to protect captured villages, to free up their field forces for continuing operations.[63]

The direct pursuit of Baji's forces was resumed on 10 March, conducted through independent initiative by dispersed, autonomous forces which, by capturing key fortified towns in mid-May, drove the peshwa to surrender his hereditary lordship and withdraw into internal exile. Sir John Malcolm defended a controversially generous settlement of £100,000 a year for life because it ended a war which Baji, commanding 10,000 troops, might have prolonged, and 'on the score of policy: our own dignity; considerations for the feelings of Baji Row's adherents, and for the prejudices of the natives of India. We exist on impressions; and on occasions like this, where all are anxious spectators, we must play our part well, or we should be hissed'.[64] One official later reflected with satisfaction on the peshwa's journey into exile:

The effect produced on the minds of the native population by his progress in the character of an exile and a prisoner through Malwa, was considerable; but the knowledge of his present abject situation must necessarily have made even a greater impression on his late subjects in the Dukhun [Deccan], and have contributed, in no small degree, to their rapid submission.[65]

In addition, local leaders in the southern region of the peshwa's domains were encouraged to defect from Baji, and over 9,000 revenue-collecting troops or peons were recruited by June 1818, and deployed in contingents ranging from 30 to 400 men to support those leaders and 'to protect the revenue and cultivation, by giving confidence to the inhabitants'.[66]

Just as the campaigns against Baji came to what proved their climax in May, a final front in these vast operations suddenly opened up. The British Resident at Nagpur had arrested Apa Sahib in March 1818 and sent the raja from the city under escort. The Bhonsle escaped his captors on 13 May and spent the rest of the year trying to raise support, while cooperating with one of the leading Pindari chiefs. Eventually he fled in early 1819 to Asirgarh, an extremely well-fortified position on one of the two main roads running from Pune north to Indore and eventually to Agra and Delhi. Nominally under Sindhia's feudal overlordship, the town and fort should have surrendered immediately. Following convoluted local negotiations, however, the British broke off diplomatic exchanges on 17 March. They then deployed more guns than were used at any other confrontation in this conflict, even though nearly all the forty-six principal guns, including mortars and howitzers, were of medium calibre by the standards of European siege operations:

the eyes of the whole population of India being on the issue, it was desirable to strike the blow with an eclât that would redound to our perpetual credit and advantage.[67]

Even so, the garrison in the fort, amounting to only 1,200 men, surrendered on 9 April 1819, less because the British had inflicted much damage than because the defenders were fast running out of powder. The reduction of Asirgarh, which Hastings had foreseen, in October 1817, as a potential danger spot, together with Sindhia's other forts, was the last act of the war.[68] Ironically, it had held out against the British through the duplicity of Sindhia, whose potential collaboration or neutrality in a campaign against the Pindaris had been one of the trickier diplomatic issues at the conflict's beginning.

Reasons for British success

The British enjoyed a number of advantages in these extensive campaigns. They had the financial, administrative and military capacity to raise, organize and deploy 116,000 regular and irregular troops under arms by 1817. These forces were supplemented by unknown numbers of men under local officials within the Indian states who undertook excise or policing duties. For example, in December 1817, Brigadier General Thomas Munro appointed military aumildars, or revenue collectors, for the Marathas' 'central' authorities under the peshwa, in the district where he operated. He authorized them over the coming months to raise local policing forces or peons in occupied territory or to deny the enemy resources there. How such forces were used depended on the state of political and military conciliation and reconciliation. At one end of the spectrum of options was the approach pressed by Munro, who had administered the ceded territories of Mysore in 1801–08 and who directed British operations in the region from the Mysore border into the peshwa's southern domains in 1817–18. Munro argued for an early declaration of the Company's intent to occupy all the peshwa's territories while linking British authority to sources of sovereignty going back further than the raja of Satara. He believed that many jagirdars in the south would welcome any means of escaping from war.[69] On the other hand, Munro's argument, that the positive example of effective British administration in the neighbouring ceded provinces would lead Maratha landowners and officials to embrace British rule, did not translate readily to Maratha territories outside the south where no such proximate examples of British rule could be invoked as immediate role models.

At the other end of the range of options was severe repression. An unintentional instance of this arose at Talnar, covering a ford across the Tapti River. Lieutenant General Hislop arrived there in late February

1818. He had Holkar's orders that the fort surrender to the British, but the killedar refused to comply with them until British troops occupied the open town, fired upon the fort's gateway, and entered the fort. Deep within the fort, however, an argument flared with a group of soldiers including Arab mercenaries who then fired on a small British advance party, killing two officers and wounding three in what seemed like an act of treachery. The British responded in force, slaughtering all 300 men in the inner garrison. Hislop noted: 'a severe example, indeed, but absolutely necessary, and one which I have no doubt will produce the most salutary effect on the future operations in this province'. The general's official dispatch added: 'The killedar I ordered to be hanged on one of the bastions immediately after the place fell. Whether he was accessory or not to the subsequent treachery of his men, his execution was a punishment justly due to his rebellion in the first instance, particularly after the warning he had received in the morning.'[70] Although one senior official in India noted that this severity 'was probably useful' in inducing much stronger forts to surrender, the reaction in Britain proved less supportive. Hislop himself was excluded from the formal vote of thanks passed by the House of Commons at the end of the war and Wellington felt obliged in the House of Lords to defend the general on the basis of his previous good character.[71]

Between these possible approaches of winning over the Marathas by promoting an exemplary model of British rule to which they would be attracted or by summarily executing diehard opponents, the British more customarily combined force with an appeal to the self-interest of those seeking to maintain structures of landownership, power and authority. Considerable efforts were made to manage the breakdown of opponents' armies. Prinsep claimed that the British dealt with the dissolution of Baji's 'tumultuous host' far better than the sudden reduction of a European army would have been arranged. Many fugitive levies were rapidly recruited to the Company's local contingents, established 'to furnish the means of livelihood to many that must else have been left wholly destitute'. Such troops served important local functions:

the regular army was unequal even to furnish garrisons for the forts reduced, much less was it in a condition to provide detachments for the duties of internal administration.[72]

This approach had been adopted in Nepal and went back at least to 1782 when a district collector in Bihar, Augustus Cleveland, was credited with suppressing local hill tribesmen by turning them into uniformed locally based soldiers.[73]

Among British advantages were extensive networks and sources of intelligence. Elphinstone was certainly assiduous in gathering information at Pune. On operational matters, the importance of assiduous reconnaissance was stressed by the Adjutant General, who urged a divisional commander to deploy 'intelligent officers, accompanied by the best guides' to examine routes, to take the heights before entering defiles, and to use diversionary false attacks and mountain tracks in order to turn enemy positions.[74] But in large matters and small this was at best a limited asset. The biggest lapse of political intelligence was the failure to anticipate Baji's intentions in 1817. Sindhia's duplicity over Aligarh in 1819 also seems to have escaped the attention of the British intelligence networks. On tactical matters, leading Pindari raiding parties repeatedly eluded British detection and the pursuit of Baji in 1818 and Apa Sahib in 1819 demonstrated how difficult it was to determine the whereabouts of a fast-moving foe. Probably the clue lies in the observation of one sepoy soldier who served during this war and who, extremely unusually, wrote up his memoirs. He surmised that the agents the British used and rewarded during these campaigns probably told the Pindaris what information they passed to the British. The key to British success for this sepoy was less their military intelligence-gathering than the character of their army. He was impressed by the fact that the British 'do not worry about defeat' but would renew attacks even after being driven back repeatedly. British armies' command systems meant that, if leaders were killed or badly wounded, they were, without con-fusion, replaced by other officers. Moreover, the ordinary soldier in the Company's forces enjoyed regular pay, medical attention if wounded, and financial support if disabled or pensions to families if killed.[75] By contrast, the intense political instability afflicting the Holkar and Sindhia states in the 1810s arose partly from the maharajas' inability to control or regularly pay their armies.[76]

Conclusion

Sir Thomas Munro, a sceptical analyst of Indian affairs, saw the war as a significant turning point in the history of Maratha society. Dismissing the Marathas as 'little better than a horde of imperial thieves', preferring plundering to other forms of labour, he argued that the new settlement of central India would boost its economy and wealth, as had occurred south of Pune. Farther afield, British intervention ensured that raiders could no longer return safely from raiding to their home villages in Malwa, thereby destroying a vital underpinning of the Pindari system.[77] Equally important, many wealthy men, senior officials, 'hereditary senior officers' in the villages, and more substantial farmers had contributed to the military economy by breeding horses for military use, often hiring them to jagir-dars and government under the charge of their servants and labourers. Such prominent men were 'horse-dealers rather than soldiers; and when they find that there is no longer the same demand for horses as formerly, they will breed fewer, and seek employment for their funds in some other branch of trade'.[78] Expanding upon this theme, the conservative *Quarterly Review* in January 1818 insisted that the Company's superior administration of justice and the 'permanence of its civil institutions' freely elicited the 'decided preference which a great proportion of the inhabitants of India have shown towards the rule of the British government'. British India 'contains fewer of those elements, which produce acts of violence and injustice, than any other state in the universe'.[79] Despite the grandiloquence of such claims, the suppression of the Pindaris was indeed accompanied by the extensive demilitarization of the countryside and a significant break with India's military past.[80] John Fortescue saw this outcome as the product of Moira's courageous decision to act upon his political analysis backed up by excellent organization and sound generalship in a theatre of operations extending over 150,000 square miles. An official history written ninety years later stressed how effectively freestanding divisions had been widely dispersed in order to contain their opponents and how 'the necessity for attacking as soon as possible a Native force, wherever met with and however numerous' had been demonstrated.[81] Munro in 1817 detected a military revolution since the late 1790s, with the British achieving overwhelming superiority in the numbers and calibre of their troops and, especially important, no longer suffering from deficiencies in cavalry.[82]

Yet contemporaries recognized two major political-military flaws in the British system of rule. First, the reliability of the subsidiary alliance system was contested. Lord Wellesley had developed the system as a means of extending British political influence – he hoped control – without arousing the East India Company's hostility to even more territorial aggrandizement. He had also used it as a means of maintaining far more troops than the Company, or the government, desired by charging them to subsidiary allies. But he also extended the system to create a favourable balance of power in key regions of India by using allies as pawns in complicated games of regional geopolitics. His critics, however, charged him with overlooking the internal political implications of subsidiary alliances upon the allies themselves. In 1805, Cornwallis objected 'that the States who are most intimately connected with us, such as the Peshwa and the Nizam, are reduced to the most forlorn condition', with neither reliable troops nor secure funds to draw on. Without the involvement of British residents well beyond their remits, those governments 'would be immediately dissolved'.[83] Munro, who had advocated vigorous measures against Tipu Sultan in the early 1790s, objected to any extension of the use of subsidiary forces in 1817. Such use might have been justified in the more uncertain geopolitical circumstances of the 1790s and 1800s, but

It has a natural tendency to render the government of every country in which it exists, weak and oppressive; to extinguish all honourable spirit among the higher classes of society, and to degrade and impoverish the whole people. The usual remedy of bad government in India is a quiet revolution in the palace, or a violent one by rebellion, or foreign conquests. But the presence of a British force cuts off every chance of remedy, by supporting the prince on the throne against every foreign and domestic enemy.

Regimes underpinned in that way soon slid into economic and social decay. Worse, as British rule itself spread, so Indians would no longer 'look forward to any share in the legislation, or civil or military government of their country'. National demoralization ensued.[84]

Analysing India in 1829, Lieutenant Colonel James Tod argued that the alliances were 'pregnant with evil from their origin'. British officials were almost certain to pry into the subsidiary allies' revenue accounts, from which the British had a vested interest in drawing tribute, in ways that would provoke political conflicts from 'the general laxity of their governments coming in contact with our regular system'. The regulation of military contingents would prove difficult under pressure because the traditional feudal leaders – whose powers were entrenched by conservative administrators such as Elphinstone – remained masters of their own retainers.[85] Within the princely states, the British presence added a further element to existing tensions between princes and their feudatories, with those chiefs seeking ways to undermine their sovereigns' commands while rulers' ministers might need British support to extract tributary revenues. However well-intentioned, British alliances would corrode interdependence and obligations within the native states, thus depriving them of national status or popular respect: 'Can we suppose such denationalized allies are to be depended upon in emergencies?' In an obvious echo of Gibbons's concluding reflections on Rome's decline and fall, Tod questioned whether British India could defend its frontiers against 'barbarians' without by employing 'barbarians' within, and whether such men would remain loyal for £10 a month.[86]

The second defect, partly flowing from this unreliability of allies, lay in the system's inherent dynamic for expansionism:

the local government of India, throughout all its branches, is impelled, by its very nature, to promote change and the aggrandizement of the state. Public officers, from the governor-general to the lowest of those who hold stations of any consequence, must, from the ephemeral character of their power, have an anxiety to recommend themselves, during the short hour of their authority, to their superiors; and men of the most distinguished virtue and talent often desire action with an ardour that makes them more ready to combat than to attend to the cold dictates of moderation and prudence.[87]

Charles Metcalfe, a prominent younger official, argued in 1814 that 'it is only by an extension of territory that we can obtain an increase of revenue for the support of our necessary expenses'. Hastings' wars had the predicted impact. Receipts in 1813–14 and the following two years totalled just over £17 million. By 1818–19, they had risen to £19.4 million and by 1821–22 they reached £21.8 million. While the immediate consequence of war was to deliver deficits in 1818–19 and 1819–20, the annual accounts returned to surplus for four years in the early 1820s.[88] Despite much mulling over natural frontiers and well-structured alliances, viceroys responded to challenges within the Indian state system because it was their specific sphere of responsibility, expanded through Wellesley's subsidiary alliances, and their preferred sphere of political initiative: 'deeds in arms and acquisition of territory outweigh the meek *éclat* of civil virtue'. Britain's position in the east was 'one in which conquest forces herself upon us'.[89] Whether the 'Pax Britannica', on whose benefits for India so many Britons who worked in or thought about the subcontinent reflected with increasing satisfaction and pride, did indeed depend upon the periodic continuance of war remained a deeply troubling question for the senior servitors of the Raj.

If the completion of paramountcy in 1819 did not settle debates about the extent and durability of the British military presence in India or the desirability and stability of the subsidiary alliance system, it did demonstrate major achievements of British power projection. The campaigns were thoroughly planned and very well resourced. They hinged on the coordination of geographically separated forces in concerted drives against the enemy across considerable distances. They were conducted while political alliances and military collaboration were negotiated with local rulers. In more strictly military terms, they depended upon the maintenance of military morale without receiving sustenance from victorious battles or from the seizure of numerous defended towns open to plunder by successful British attackers. Indeed, progress and morale were often punctured by small-scale reverses suffered through efforts to adhere to over-ambitious timetables and over-optimistic assaults upon minor but expertly defended enemy positions. Commanders were often challenged by the weight of expectation of speedy and relatively painless victories, and sometimes numbed by uncertainties about their enemies' precise whereabouts and military strength. Despite such problems, these campaigns took British military achievement to new levels, typically unappreciated because there were no crowning victories in major battles. Instead, the British managed campaigns over areas far larger than any they had mastered in land warfare in the past. They finally broke the Marathas' light cavalry, the trademark arm which had traditionally given the Marathas a distinctive military capability. They conducted a relentless campaign to capture the small forts which provided status and local domination to the feudatories of the Maratha princes. British campaigning went beyond the methods of 1799, when the massed strength of Seringapatam fell to formal siege. It went beyond the achievements of 1803, when Sindhia and Berar were subdued in formal battle. It destroyed the very taproots of Maratha military strength, the cavalry and forts from which Maratha success had sprung and upon which the Marathas had come once again to rely after the removal in 1803 of their recent accretions of modern artillery and western-style regular infantry. The campaigns of 1817–19, conducted by unprecedented numbers in wide sweeps and with tenacious pursuits, afforded ruthless confirmation of the insistence that British rule in India depended directly and irrevocably upon military force.

Notes and references

1 Wendy Hinde, *George Canning* (Oxford, 1989), p. 291.

2 J.R. Seeley, *The Expansion of England* (London, 1895 edn), pp. 240–41, 246, 248.

3 R.G. Wallace, *Memoirs of India* (London, 1824), pp. 402, 479, 481.

4 John Fortescue, *A History of the British Army*, 13 vols (London and New York, 1899–1930), Vol. XI, pp. 174–75.

5 Hinde, *George Canning*, p. 291.

6 John Pemble, *The Invasion of Nepal: John Company at Work* (Oxford, 1971), pp. 10–15, 19–20, 24–25, 39–51.

7 *Oxford Dictionary of National Biography*, Marquess of Hastings entry; B.D. Sanwal, *Nepal and the East India Company* (London, 1965), pp. 119–26, 129–30.

8 Court of Proprietors of East-India Stock, *Papers Relating to the Nepaul War* (London, 1824), pp. 145–46, 160, 163, 179–81. (This source is used with caution; Pemble, *Invasion of Nepal*, p. 208.); H.T. Prinsep, *History of the Political and Military Transactions in India during the Administration of the Marquess of Hastings, 1813–1823*, 2 vols (London, 1825), Vol. I, pp. 82–86.

9 *ODNB*, Sir Rollo Gillespie entry; Pemble, *Invasion of Nepal*, pp. 134–39.

10 Prinsep, *History . . . Marquess of Hastings*, Vol. I, pp. 87–90; *Papers Relating to the Nepaul War*, pp. 162–63; C.A. Bayly, *Empire and Information: Intelligence Gathering and Social Communication in India, 1780–1870* (Cambridge, 1996), pp. 100–13.

11 *Papers Relating to the Nepaul War*, pp. 157, 160–63; Pemble, *Invasion of Nepal*, pp. 133, 208.

12 For the entire episode see Pemble, *Invasion of Nepal*, pp. 139–60; Prinsep, *History . . . Marquess of Hastings*, Vol. I, pp. 91–93, 99–103.

13 Pemble, *Invasion of Nepal*, pp. 251–54.

14 Pemble, *Invasion of Nepal*, pp. 287–88; Prinsep, *History . . . Marquess of Hastings*, Vol. I, pp. 104–05; *Papers Relating to the Nepaul War*, p. 160.

15 *Papers Relating to the Nepaul War*, p. 147; Reginald Heber, *Narrative of a Journey through the Upper Provinces of India, 1824–1825*, 2 vols (London, 1828), Vol. I, p. 270.

16 Prinsep, *History . . . Marquess of Hastings*, Vol. I, pp. 106–14.

17 Prinsep, *History . . . Marquess of Hastings*, Vol. I, pp. 60–61, 116.

18 *Papers Relating to the Nepaul War*, pp. 214–24 (quote on p. 221).

19 Prinsep, *History . . . Marquess of Hastings*, Vol. I, pp. 121–28, 140; *Papers Relating to the Nepaul War*, pp. 214–24.

20 *Papers Relating to the Nepaul War*, p. 980; *Royal Military Calendar*, 5 vols (London, 1821), Vol. IV, pp. 184–86; Prinsep, *History . . . Marquess of Hastings*, Vol. I, pp. 142–3, 150–58, 172–74.

21 Heber, *Narrative of a Journey*, Vol. I, p. 274.

22 *Papers Relating to the Nepaul War*, p. 183.

23 Prinsep, *History . . . Marquess of Hastings*, Vol. I, pp. 175–77; Pemble, *Invasion of Nepal*, p. 348; *ODNB* Sir David Octerlony entry.

24 Prinsep, *History . . . Marquess of Hastings*, Vol. I, pp. 183–92; Pemble, *Invasion of Nepal*, pp. 312–14, 317–20.

25 Prinsep, *History . . . Marquess of Hastings*, Vol. I, pp. 194–206; Pemble, *Invasion of Nepal*, pp. 345, 350.

26 Douglas Peers, *Between Mars and Mammon: Colonial Armies and the Garrison State in Early Nineteenth-century India* (London, 1995), pp. 9, 56.

27 Charles Ross (ed.), *The Correspondence of Charles, First Marquis Cornwallis*, 3 vols (London, 1859), Vol. III, p. 509; Duke of Wellington (ed.), *Supplementary Despatches of the Duke of Wellington*, 15 vols (London, 1858–72), Vol. IV, p. 481.

28 Moira to Secret Committee, 21 August 1815, India Office Library, L/P & S/5/84, p. 3.

29 Moira to Secret Committee, 21 August 1815, pp. 9, 12.

30 Moira memorandum, 6 December 1816, L/P & S/5/94, pp. 2, 4–5.

31 Edmonstone memorandum, 13 December 1816, L/P & S/5/94, pp. 34–36.

32 Jadunath Sarkar (ed.), *Daulat Rao Sindhia and North Indian Affairs (1810–1818)*, Vol. 14, *Poona Residency Correspondence* (Bombay, 1951), p. 370.

33 *The Times*, 3 March 1819.

34 Prinsep, *History . . . Marquess of Hastings*, Vol. I, pp. 330, 333–34.

35 Sir Penderel Moon, *The British Conquest and Dominion of India* (London, 1989), pp. 384–88.

36 Prinsep, *History . . . Marquess of Hastings*, Vol. I, pp. 337–39, 371–72.

37 Moira memorandum, 6 December 1816, L/P & S/5/94, pp. 2, 5.

38 Sarkar (ed.), *Daulat Rao Sindhia*, pp. 96–100, 292–95, 313–15, 371–72.

39 Prinsep, *History . . . Marquess of Hastings*, Vol. I, pp. 230, 339–41, 344–48, 352–57, 366–68.

40 Prinsep, *History . . . Marquess of Hastings*, Vol. I, pp. 395–97.

41 L/P & S/5/94, pp. 4–5, 7–10, 14–16, 24, 27.

42 L/P & S/5/94, pp. 29–32, 47–50.

43 Sarkar (ed.), *Daulat Rao Sindhia*, pp. 154–57, 195, 379; Rev. G.R. Gleig, *The Life of Major General Sir Thomas Munro, Bart.*, 3 vols (London, 1830), Vol. III, pp. 243–45.

44 Prinsep, *History . . . Marquess of Hastings*, Vol. I, pp. 274–76, 314–17, 440–43; Moon, *The British Conquest and Dominion of India*, pp. 395–98.

45 Prinsep, *History . . . Marquess of Hastings*, Vol. I, pp. 437, 440, 445–46, 451–54.

46 *The Times*, 5 May 1818; 3 March 1819.

47 Prinsep, *History . . . Marquess of Hastings*, Vol. II, pp. 47–52, 55–57, 64–66.

48 Daniel Byman and Matthew Waxman, *The Dynamics of Coercion: American Foreign Policy and the Limits of Military Might* (Cambridge, 2002), pp. 63–64; Gleig, *The Life of Major General Sir Thomas Munro*, Vol. III, pp. 242–43, 301.

49 John William Kaye, *The Life and Correspondence of Major General Sir John Malcolm*, 2 vols (London, 1856), Vol. II, p. 155.

50 Fortescue, *A History of the British Army*, Vol. XI, pp. 173–76.

51 Prinsep, *History . . . Marquess of Hastings*, Vol. I, p. 430.

52 Prinsep, *History . . . Marquess of Hastings*, Vol. II, pp. 95–102; Fortescue, *History of the British Army*, Vol. XI, pp. 190–92.

53 Fortescue, *A History of the British Army*, Vol. XI, pp. 207–14.

54 Prinsep, *History . . . Marquess of Hastings*, Vol. II, pp. 135–38.

55 Prinsep, *History . . . Marquess of Hastings*, Vol. II, pp. 371–74.

56 Prinsep, *History . . . Marquess of Hastings*, Vol. II, pp. 155–61, 164, 167–72.

57 Gleig, *The Life of Major General Sir Thomas Munro*, Vol. III, pp. 237–38.

58 Prinsep, *History . . . Marquess of Hastings*, Vol. II, pp. 172, 294.

59 Wellington (ed.), *Supplementary Despatches*, Vol. III, p. 435.

60 Prinsep, *History . . . Marquess of Hastings*, Vol. II, pp. 289–95.

61 Gleig, *The Life of Major General Sir Thomas Munro*, Vol. III, pp. 226–32, 235–37.

62 Prinsep, *History . . . Marquess of Hastings*, Vol. II, pp. 183–85.

63 Gleig, *The Life of Sir Thomas Munro*, Vol. I, p. 473.

64 Prinsep, *History . . . Marquess of Hastings*, Vol. II, pp. 235–36, 277–83; Gleig, *The Life of Major General Sir Thomas Munro*, Vol. III, 272.

65 Prinsep, *History . . . Marquess of Hastings*, Vol. II, p. 281.

66 Gleig, *The Life of Major General Sir Thomas Munro*, Vol. II, p. 271; Vol. III, pp. 224, 294.

67 Prinsep, *History . . . Marquess of Hastings*, Vol. II, p. 326. A comparison with the artillery provided, e.g., at Badajoz, can be gained from Lieutenant Colonel Harry Jones (ed.), *Journal of the Sieges Carried on by the Army under the Duke of Wellington, in Spain . . .* 3 vols (London, 1846), Vol. I, p. 157.

68 Prinsep, *History . . . Marques of Hastings*, Vol. II, pp. 31, 322–32; Fortescue, *A History of the British Army*, Vol. XI, pp. 248–49.

69 Gleig, *The Life of Major General Sir Thomas Munro*, Vol. III, pp. 247–48, 301.

70 *The Times*, 29 August 1818.

71 Prinsep, *History . . . Marquess of Hastings*, Vol. II, pp. 297, 215–18, 287; *ODNB*, Sir Thomas Hislop entry.

72 Prinsep, *History . . . Marquess of Hastings*, Vol. II, pp. 296–97.

73 Geoff Quilley and John Bonehill (eds), *William Hodges 1744–1797: The Art of Exploration* (London, 2004), pp. 171–72.

74 Sanwal, *Nepal and the East India Company*, p. 146.

75 James Lunt (ed.), *From Sepoy to Subedar: Being the Life and Adventures of Subedar Sita Ram* (Basingstoke, 1988), pp. 37–38, 42.

76 Sarkar (ed.), *Daulat Rao Sindhia*, pp. 100, 195–97, 330, 339, 359, 376, 401.

77 Gleig, *The Life of Major General Sir Thomas Munro*, Vol. III, pp. 276–80.

78 Gleig, *The Life of Major General Sir Thomas Munro*, Vol. II, pp. 269–70.

79 *Quarterly Review*, Vol. XVIII (1818), pp. 386–87.

80 Dirk H.A. Kolff, *Naukar, Rajput and Sepoy: The Ethnohistory of the Military Labour Market in Hindustan, 1450–1850* (Cambridge, 1990), pp. 8–9, 187.

81 Fortescue, *A History of the British Army*, Vol. XI, pp. 250–54; General Staff, India, *The Mahratta and Pindari War 1817* (n.p., 1910; Uckfield, 2004 reprint), p. 109.

82 Gleig, *The Life of Sir Thomas Munro*, Vol. I, p. 462.

83 Ross (ed.), *Correspondence*, Vol. III, p. 546.

84 Gleig, *The Life of Sir Thomas Munro*, Vol. I, pp. 462–66.

85 Lieutenant Colonel James Tod, *Annals and Antiquities of Rajasthan or the Central and Western Rajput States of India*, ed. with intro. by William Crooke, 3 vols (London, 1920), Vol. I, p. 146.

86 Tod, *Annals and Antiquities*, Vol. I, pp. 149–51.

87 *Quarterly Review*, Vol. XVIII (London, 1818), p. 387.

88 S.J. Owen (ed.), *A Selection from the Despatches . . . of the Marquess Wellesley during his Government of India* (Oxford, 1877), pp. 811–12; House of Commons, *Parliamentary Papers*, 1854–55 (336), pp. 6–9; *Parliamentary Papers*, 1823 (536), pp. 4–5. I have used the more optimistic version of the accounts, which depended on the attribution of charges paid in Britain. Even using the more constricted version, revenues returned to surplus in 1820–21, after six years of deficits. Total debt for India rose from £30.7 to £37.8 million between 1814 and 1822.

89 Tod, *Annals and Antiquities*, p. 147.

PART SIX

The impact of war

CHAPTER 16

Instruments of power

British military and naval expansionism required two fundamental developments: the state's commitment to military
and naval spending and the creation of an infrastructure through which
power was projected across the globe. John Brewer, in showing how the
eighteenth-century and early nineteenth-century state was shaped by war,
depicted a military-fiscal state whose navy accounted for the country's
largest fixed-capital assets, in the shape of the battle fleet, its largest industrial enterprises, in the shape of the naval dockyards, and its leading units
employing skilled labour, in the shape of the 900-man first-rate warships.
Military and naval expenditure consumed high proportions of national
income while the armed services were the state's and the nation's largest
organizations.[1] This depiction needs, however, to be extended to include
a description of how a global infrastructure was established to provide
for the projection of power, for Britain's war-making capability depended
not only upon robust finances and long-term borrowing but also upon
complex military and naval support facilities.

The baseline for British power projection was relatively weak in 1790.
Given the general absence of barracks in England and their small size
elsewhere in most of the United Kingdom, the acculturation of civilians
drawn into the armed forces was itself a challenging process. When facilities
for the development of regimental organization were later built up, much
of the initiative came from defensive needs rather than from expansionist
ambitions. From enlarged bases at home, the British confidently spread
their forces throughout the world. The insertion of forces into so many
countries overseas required a major effort of will and expenditure. The
physical infrastructure was essential to the morale and mindset as well
as the operational viability of the soldiers and sailors posted overseas.

It created a familiar environment in which soldiers and sailors could move from Britain to the wide variety of overseas postings to which they were assigned with a reasonable assurance of regularity in conditions and circumstances. Sea lanes and roads connected ports and garrisons so as to ensure that the transitions involved as little disruption to customary procedures as possible. It provided regularity and standardization for the soldiers and sailors in their working and private lives. It both integrated them into the armed services and segregated them from local populations. A growing and often impressive infrastructure served also to instil into servicemen a sense of awe at the power of the British state. The way the men were organized – soldiers into rigorously differentiated regiments and sailors into ships' companies, rather than into the 'army' or the 'navy' respectively – helped to articulate with the system of barracks and bases to reinforce regiments' and ships' cohesiveness and pride. These divergent feelings of distinctive group identity, discipline, fear of authority, and fighting pride were intensified by differing rituals and ceremonies replicated wherever the soldiers and sailors were posted across the globe. The built environment of imperial power animated the spirit as well as channelled the efficiency of the armed services despatched overseas. How this process worked was an important aspect of the projection of British imperial power. But the structures which the British built also defined British power as the capacity to create and control enclaves in every corner of the globe.

Military and naval infrastructures at home

Britain was more lightly militarized than some heavily populated and much-fought-over parts of continental Europe, notably north-east France and the Austrian Netherlands and northern Italy. By the 1780s few towns boasted, or needed, modern fortifications, the most heavily fortified British town being Berwick-on-Tweed, made thoroughly defensible in the sixteenth century against the Scots. The Jacobite rising of 1715 encouraged the construction of the first purpose-built barracks in England there in 1719. Forts were built in Scotland after the rebellion of 1745, but had limited military value by the 1770s; the most impressive, and remote, fortification in eighteenth-century Britain, Fort George, near Inverness, provided barracks for 1,600 troops but was obsolete when completed in 1769. In Ireland, barracks were more amply provided by the 1740s, certainly for the larger towns, although they were not necessarily well maintained. While infantry regiments were concentrated in Dublin, Limerick, Galway,

Cork and nearby Kinsale, and Waterford, the troops spent much of their time detached and quartered in surrounding villages.[2]

The invasion scares of the 1790s and 1800s transformed the armed services' physical presence within Great Britain. Travelling in 1821, William Cobbett, the radical journalist, described the poorer lands from Deptford to Dartford as covered with 'barracks, magazines, martello towers, catamarans, and the excuses for lavish expenditure, which the War for the Bourbons gave rise to'.[3] Across the country, total barrack accommodation soared from provision for 20,847 men in 43 forts and garrison towns in 1793 to provision for 155,000 troops in 155 barracks in Britain by 1815. This transformation provided evidence for E.P. Thompson's celebrated conclusion: 'England, in 1792, had been governed by consent and deference, supplemented by the gallows and the "Church-and-King" mob. By 1816 the English people were held down by force.'[4] In fact, barrack-building was a response to practical and political difficulties created by the huge wartime expansion in the army and militia, which put intolerable strains on normal peacetime billeting, very often in inns. The need for greater discipline and more frequent drill, and the desirability of keeping troops, with their sometimes drunken and raucous behaviour, away from civilians added further weight to the case for housing soldiers in greater numbers together. But, whatever the arguments, most construction occurred in direct response to threats of invasion. About 37% of all money spent on barrack-building in the UK during 1793–1819 was allocated in just three years, 1796 and especially 1804 and 1805, precisely the years when French invasion was most feared.[5] By 1815, with no invasion threats looming, each of the thirty-four official garrisons in Britain and twelve in Ireland rarely accommodated more than a battalion and typically far fewer men than that.[6]

In 1832 there were ninety-seven permanent and eighteen temporary barracks in Britain. Only seventeen of those had the capacity to take 1,000 or more soldiers. Nine of those were on the south coast of England and on Jersey and Guernsey. Only two of these large barracks were in major industrial cities (Glasgow and Manchester), the object of the establishment's gravest fears about public order. Few housed anywhere near the numbers they were designed to contain. Even among the thirteen barracks with a capacity for 500–1,000 soldiers, no fewer than seven were at coastal towns or at militarily obsolete strategic positions in Scotland, and only six were at manufacturing towns and commercial ports, and even then only two of them actually accommodated over 350 troops. Repeatedly, the story was one of small scale and wide dispersal. Similarly in Ireland, soldiers were very widely distributed in small towns across the country, apart from a large concentration of men in eight different barracks in Dublin. The six barracks in Cork, the second Irish city in military and naval importance, and at Cork harbour could take 2,845 men but in 1832 held only 554. The dispersal into small towns reflected demands placed upon the army for domestic policing. In the years after 1815, Peel, the minister responsible for Ireland, landowners who objected to the constitutional restriction upon the use of military forces except when accompanied by and authorized by a magistrate. Peel claimed that troops in Ireland were too often used for private ends by the Protestant landowning minority to control the disenfranchized and mainly landless Catholic majority.[7] The 1820s saw increased threats of possible disorder. One of Wellington's correspondents in 1824 warned that Ireland 'is in a far worse state of disaffection than immediately prior to the Rebellion of 1798'.[8] The Irish militia and yeomanry could not be called out 'unless its composition should be rendered solely *Protestant*', but any such purging would not be politically feasible or advisable. Since only regular troops were regarded as being reliable, Wellington agreed that the situation in Ireland merited extra forces, and unsuccessfully argued in December 1824 for an increase in the army's overall strength of 14,000 men or in excess of 10%.[9] The duke bemoaned the fact that throughout the kingdom:

every demand, even of a battalion to put an end to a riot in a colliery or a manufacturing town, much more for a reinforcement abroad, puts us to the most miserable shifts to comply with it; shifts which are not only disgraceful to a country like this, but injurious to the service, and expose the public service to risk.[10]

This prognostication proved particularly pertinent just as, and just after, Wellington left office as prime minister in 1830. Domestic policing needs and the imperial network overseas ensured that the fragmented character of the British army of the eighteenth century remained a firm feature of the mid-nineteenth century service.

The wars of 1775–83 and 1793–1815 spurred the construction of prominent military and naval buildings other than barracks. The Royal Hospital, Chelsea, built in 1682–91, following the example of Kilmainham outside Dublin, provided a retirement home for invalided soldiers. Its numbers greatly expanded during the years 1793–1815. The Royal Military Asylum, on King's Road, Chelsea, was built in 1801–03 for soldiers' orphaned children; some 4,266 boys passed through it from 1803 to 1826. At Woolwich, installations were massively expanded. Beginning during the wars of 1775–82, additional facilities for the Royal Artillery and Royal Engineers were provided from 1793, so that by the time the Royal Arsenal was designated in 1805 it encompassed 114 acres. The Grand Store built there in 1806–13 took the form of a large quadrangle open to the River Thames, adorned with corner pilasters and elegant capitals; its main block stretched twenty-one bays across. According to Lord Chatham, the Master General of the Ordnance, in January 1811, the new facility, designed in part to meet 'the sudden demands frequently made for Foreign Expeditions', seemed likely to be overstretched even before it was completed.[11] In 1775–82 half the Royal Artillery Barracks was completed at Woolwich Common; by 1802 the rest was finished. It included a 1,000-foot-long façade and was laid out in Roman style with crossing roads all ending in triumphal arches. Facing the barracks, a new Royal Military Academy was completed in 1808; the building's north front was 720 feet long.[12] At Plymouth, there was steady improvement on a vast scale. The Royal Naval Hospital, built in 1758–62, became a model of European significance. The Ropery of 1763–72 consisted of two buildings each 1,200 yards long. Large Royal Marine Barracks were added in 1779–85. Plymouth itself enjoyed a wartime boom and its town centre was rebuilt in 1812–20. Finally came new naval yards constructed in 1825–33 on a 14-acre, partially reclaimed site. Entered through a grand gateway topped by a 13-foot statue of William IV, the Royal William Yard was 'among the most remarkable examples of an early nineteenth-century planned layout of industrial buildings anywhere in England'.[13]

When soldiers left the country or returned to it, Portsmouth and Chatham were major ports of embarkation and arrival. Portsmouth boasted probably the best harbour in Britain. Soldiers stationed in and around Portsmouth, or moving through it, witnessed the full panoply of the state. From the 1770s onwards governments spent lavishly on fortifying the defences of Portsmouth, Gosport and Portsea. In 1797–1802 a large new basin and accompanying docks were constructed. One of George III's sons informed the king from Portsmouth in December 1800: 'The new dock will be finished in a very few months, and from its solidity bids fair to be as lasting a monument of our naval grandeur as any Roman edifice I recollect to have seen in my travels abroad.'[14] At the end of the wars, the naval dockyards at Portsmouth employed 4,257 people, setting them among the largest single industrial enterprises in the country. At Gosport, when the Haslar Naval Hospital, to accommodate 1,800 patients, was completed in 1761 it became the largest purpose-built medical establishment in Britain; in 1779 it was expanded to provide for 2,100 patients.[15]

Chatham was smaller but underwent a major expansion of its defences and barracks in the late eighteenth and early nineteenth centuries. The school for engineers was established in 1812, its barracks being described by a visiting Frenchman as 'a model of their kind', impressing him 'by the grandeur and regularity of their construction, by the majestic beauty and simplicity of the architecture'.[16] Even in peacetime after 1815, it was busy with battalions arriving from and departing for overseas duties. It received all those invalided home and despatched all the East India Company's British recruits.[17] Built on the north banks of the River Medway – described as one of Europe's deepest rivers for all its short length – the dockyard facilities were viewed in 1841 as 'the finest naval arsenal in the world'.[18] Overall, by March 1814, the royal dockyards employed 15,600 people. But the impact of naval construction spread far wider, since 78% of the naval tonnage built in 1793–1815 was completed in private yards. Moreover, the wartime impressment of sailors into the Royal Navy affected more than the naval ports, since commercial shipping and therefore sailors engaged in foreign trade were concentrated in ports which did not have a strong royal naval presence: London, Liverpool, and then Hull, Whitehaven, and Newcastle.[19]

If the eighteenth century witnessed the forging of a military-fiscal state, the wars from the 1770s stimulated the creation of a military–naval infrastructure of far greater physical extent and impressiveness than anything preceding it. War connected far more men and, less directly, women to state institutions than ever before. Even the demobilization after 1815 left substantial numbers of people dependent upon the state through pensions, invalid support, and orphanages, as well as through work in military and naval installations.

Military and naval infrastructures overseas

For all Britain's global expansionism from the late 1780s, contemporaries faced various impediments to viewing Britain as a global power. First, the Royal Navy typically concentrated its largest warships and fought nearly all its greatest battles in the seas around Britain or across vital European sea lanes. The naval achievements which most thrilled contemporary opinion tended to be those that played up emotional relief at the lifting of threats of invasion or coastal raiding upon the British Isles. *The Times* greeted news of the Glorious First of June, 1794, by noting 'We never recollect to have witnessed more general joy, than was manifested on every countenance throughout yesterday' at 'a victory, which we may say with confidence, has so crippled the navy of France, that it will be impossible for the French to send another grand fleet to sea, at least during the present campaign. To the commerce of this country, the advantages of this victory are inestimable'.[20] Second, there was no notion of formal strategic analysis or planning in either the armed forces or government departments. Staff work at the strategic level remained minimal, and planning usually took the form of prioritizing responses to challenges as they arose.[21] This inhibited the development of a systematic picture of British global interests. Third, the army often gained little kudos from its extra-European campaigning. Henry Wellesley, an admittedly biased official, noted that 'military successes, and indeed proceedings of all kinds in India, however important and advantageous, produce but little effect in England . . . All Sir Arthur Wellesley's and Lord Lake's victories over the Mahrattahs, with all the important consequences which resulted from them, were less considered than the battle of Maida', a minor battle in southern Italy in 1806.[22]

Yet the long wars of 1790–1815 greatly enlarged Britain's global network of naval and military bases, enabling soldiers and sailors to move across the world to and from enclaves of British authority. An initial base of operations was Cork in southern Ireland, which possessed by the late eighteenth century a very well-protected port upriver from the sea; its harbour, the Cobh, was said to be capable of accommodating the entire British fleet. Extensively rebuilt, the city, at least in part, boasted a prosperous, modern character, its middle and upper classes being heavily Protestant and its Grand Parade containing a statue of George II.[23] Cork served as a vital transit point, necessitating the building of vast barracks just to the north of the city. In addition, Kinsale, some 24 miles from Cork, had the only naval dockyard in Ireland, and was well guarded by Fort Charles. Across the Atlantic, after 1776 the main British bases were Halifax, for entry into Canada, and the ports of the West Indies. Halifax had been established only in 1749, with its crucial asset being the 6-mile-long and generally one-mile wide harbour providing excellent year-round protection to shipping. A dockyard covering over 16 acres was established in 1758. Enjoying a short-term boom, growing rapidly to about 12,000 people, during the American war, the town was later dominated by the citadel which was essentially built up in the 1790s. In the Caribbean, Port Royal (Jamaica) and, after 1805, English Harbour (Antigua) were, with Halifax, among the four Royal Navy dockyards overseas. Port Royal's dockyard was nearly half a mile long by 1799. Jamaica was Britain's leading single West Indian colony and its legislature paid for barracks built from the 1760s to 1774 to house 2,572 troops.[24] From the 1770s the British stationed about 3,000 troops on the island, whose population in 1820 exceeded 400,000 (mostly slaves and apprentices). Tensions persisted between the plantation owners, who wanted troops to be dispersed across the island to control the slaves, and the army authorities, who wanted to house troops in large, residentially segregated barracks out of Kingston and on higher ground surrounding the bay.[25] The defence of the West Indies absorbed 18,000 troops as late as October 1815, after the end of the war of 1812 and the struggle against Napoleon. While the peacetime establishment fell, a substantial garrison – 7,500 men in 1832 – remained, and the island assemblies contributed to costs; Jamaica paid on average over £52,000 a year towards defence costs in 1825–28 inclusive.[26]

In their global drive for strategic enclaves, the British became kleptomaniacs for harbours. Kingston, Jamaica, has been described as the world's 'seventh largest' natural harbour. Port of Spain, Trinidad, commanded a big, safe bay for a harbour. Grenada, finally ceded to the British in 1783, possessed a fine harbour at St George's, commanded by two forts built by the French. Bridgetown, established on the only natural harbour on the important sugar-producing island of Barbados, acquired, in the early nineteenth century, a major parade ground and barracks.[27] When General Sir Charles Grey seized Martinique he described Fort Royal as 'the finest harbour in the universe'.[28]

The British took over Cape Town from the Dutch in 1796 in order to prevent the French from gaining access to such a useful staging point for troops and warships going to India. The Royal Navy and British East India Company ships had used the port and town in the eighteenth century under agreement with the Dutch. But wartime seizure dramatically increased British involvement. In 1797 the estimated population of the Cape district totalled 6,261 free people and 11,891 slaves. Free adult males totalled only 1,566. British forces, which by July of that year consisted of 4,000–5,000 British troops plus sailors on eighteen to twenty warships, had a dominant impact. The army and navy consumed over half the beef cattle, a fifth of the sheep and two-thirds of the wheat supplied to Cape Town in 1797. Despite such increases in economic activity, Cape Town remained small and the image of it from the sea, as a tiny settlement clinging to the shore in the open sweep of the spacious bay and monumentally overshadowed by Table Mountain behind it, gave it the feel of a refuge and comforting way-station rather than an awe-inspiring military base.[29]

An equally vital pre-emptive strike brought the Dutch colony of Ceylon (Sri Lanka) into the British net. During 1746–95 the British East

Indies squadron often wintered in Trincomalee – described in 1819 by one midshipman as 'the first and most important naval station in the Indian Seas' – by agreement with the Dutch. With no natural harbours existing on the south-east or south-west coasts of India, Trincomalee's large, deep, safe harbour offered effective refuge from both the main monsoons.[30] Farther east, Captain Arthur Phillip, leading the earliest British settlement near Sydney in 1788, described it as commanding one of the finest harbours in the world, capable of shielding a thousand sail of the line, or about nine times the total complement of Britain's battle fleet. In 1828 an officer advocated annexing the Swan River estuary in Western Australia because, apart from the potential use of the surrounding country for European settlement, the river afforded safe anchorage 'which may easily be converted into one of the finest Harbours in the world'. Its position – enabling warships stationed there to attack shipping in the Malay archipelago destined for either India or China – meant, in his view, that Britain needed to prevent the French, who were showing interest in the region, from seizing the area. Late in 1828 the ministry ordered a warship from the Cape to take possession and in 1829 the settlement which grew into Perth was founded.[31]

The safe anchorages and ports thus acquired enabled the British to create a global military infrastructure. Their sailors and soldiers serving around the world depended on settling into a reasonably familiar environment virtually wherever they went. One pressure in the 1820s was to ensure that barracks were sited in healthier positions outside towns, to help check 'in some degree' soldiers' heavy drinking. In 1828, in a step towards greater standardization, and financial control, the Ordnance Board took over responsibility for all strictly military buildings in the colonies.[32] The harbours and their official buildings, the forts which overlooked and protected them, and the spaces in which the British drank, debauched, drilled, prayed and slumbered all reinforced the global projection of British power.

Not only were the elements that made up the infrastructure of British power replicated across the globe, so too were the rituals that animated it. Troops stationed anywhere near naval ports – in England as well as overseas – heard the warships' morning and evening guns and occasional signal guns. When a warship entered port it fired a salute to the commanding officer according to his rank and in turn received a salute in acknowledgement, calibrated to the rank of the most senior office-holder or officer on board; a captain going ashore and returning to his ship received the acknowledgement of an eleven-gun salute. Lists of who and what occasions should be so honoured were widely published by 1800 with local annual almanacs enumerating an imposing hierarchy of salutation by gunfire.[33]

In India, the three great entry points into British territories – Calcutta, Madras, and Bombay – all expanded in the late eighteenth and early nineteenth centuries from their humbler origins as trading centres founded by the East India Company. By 1800 Calcutta was second only to London as the most heavily populated city under British rule and one of the world's most populous cities; according to Lord William Bentinck in 1805, it exceeded in riches the grandest cities he had visited – Paris, Vienna and Constantinople.[34] Bombay had more people than any city in the British Isles except for London and Dublin. All three Indian centres recreated some of the physical ambience of British cities, or at least the very modern parts of them. Calcutta's riverside quays, merchant houses, imposing official buildings, wide avenues, and spacious and stylish up-to-dateness were European in purpose, architectural design and taste. The road from Calcutta upriver to Barrackpur, where troops to defend the capital of British Bengal were stationed, was, by the early nineteenth century, a broad avenue shaded by trees along its entire length. The military quarters at Barrackpur were carefully segregated from the indigenous population. A large arsenal had been started at Fort William by 1769 and before the end of the century was linked, far upcountry, to Kanpur and its military facilities by seven depots, at Midnapur, Monghir, Berhampur, Futtyghur, Buxar, Chunar, and Dinapur.[35]

From the core bases in Bengal, the British stamped their authority on a long line of territory north-westwards to the Punjabi border. Some garrison towns, like Allahabad and Farrukhabad, experienced new growth after stagnating as former Mughal fortress towns, attaining populations of 50,000 and 30,000 people respectively by 1815. The British established others, notably Kanpur and Meerut. The former, founded in 1778, reached a population of about 34,000 in 1803 entirely as an army bazaar town. The military provided the second most important spur to early eighteenth-century urban growth in India after the supply and transfer of cotton. British garrisons acquired well-laid-out barracks and offices with parade grounds for exercises and drill, as well as racecourses and churches, although the latter were far from common by the 1820s. The approach road to Dinapur was dotted with bungalows and bazaars among gardens and mango groves and businesses catering to British needs; to Walter Heber, the first Bishop of Calcutta, the town's cantonment was 'the largest and handsomest which I have seen, with a very fine quay, looking like a battery, to the river, and . . . three extensive squares of barracks uniformly built, of one lofty ground-storey well raised, stuccoed, and ornamented with arcaded windows, and pillars between each.'[36] This increasingly extensive, elaborate, and imposing infrastructure enabled the British to move readily around the world within their professional military and naval networks. Organizations as hierarchical and reliant upon obedience as the armed services sought overseas to separate soldiers and sailors from local populations and to maintain their sense of distinctiveness as fighting men, as well as to provide facilities which eased those men's relatively smooth transition from posting to posting.

The army and regimentalism

The wars of 1793–1815 deepened the sense of history for many regiments by enhancing the importance both of their long periods of service overseas and of individual regiments' reputations for endurance and courage. Campaigning from 1793 increased the frequency of battles, with the Peninsular War especially breaking the traditional mould of wartime experience for the British army. To record and parade such achievements, the regimental colours, or flags, had the names of engagements at which a regiment received battle honours sewn on to them. The colours, acting as a collective row of battle medals, were raised in battle to direct the movements of troops and to indicate where the regimental surgeon, supported by one of his assistants, would be located.[37] When in 1801 Sir Ralph Abercromby led his army ashore in Egypt, he knew all the units. At La Coruña in 1809, Sir John Moore exhorted the 71st, which had served under Abercromby, to 'Remember Egypt!'[38] Regimental identity, reinforced by traditions, became increasingly systematized and memorialized in India and during the Peninsular War. Such a sense of identity was vital in an army with no structure of brigades or permanently formed divisions, but, as in all large institutions, the efficiency and cohesiveness of critical units was an essential safeguard against the vagaries of strategy and transient organization.

Entrenching a strong regimental system was not achieved without difficulty. One problem was securing recruitment. From the late 1790s locally raised militia battalions were used increasingly explicitly to feed men into the regular regiments. This often created problems of training, to ensure that such recruits were well enough drilled to be committed with confidence to the rigours of wartime campaigning. Once in a regiment, soldiers did not necessarily remain wedded to their units. In 1815, for instance, 4,721 men deserted. Many soldiers also developed ties –

presumably often emotional ties – to the country, or people within the country, where they served overseas. When the 65th returned to England after being evacuated from Boston via Nova Scotia in 1776, it consisted of nineteen officers, twenty-eight sergeants, twenty-one drummers and fifty-three rank and file, the majority of the ordinary soldiers having joined other regiments and stayed in North America. It was common in India for soldiers to secure transfers to regiments that remained in the country when a battalion was sent home after a tour of duty. In 1801, the Duke of York bemoaned the fact that two battalions returning from the West Indies 'are perfect skeletons having, as usual, allowed such men as chose to turn out volunteers to inlist [sic] into the Regiments remaining in the West Indies'.[39]

Officers displayed a similarly ambiguous set of attitudes towards their regiments. Wealthy young men purchased their commissions and then bought promotions in other regiments whenever vacancies arose for sale. For instance, by the time Arthur Wellesley sailed for India in June 1796 he had belonged to six different regiments in a career which was still not ten years long. Young officers of more limited means who served during wartime and took on distant or unpopular duties moved equally often. Alexander Dirom, for example, became a talented staff officer after serving in six different regiments in the first eight years of his career, with five years' service in the West Indies and a posting to India accelerating his regimental transfers.[40] Regimental attachment was qualified in India, where purchase was not permitted in the East India Company's army, but where better pay and promotion lay in administrative and staff posts or on attachment to an allied ruler's forces. During the 1820s, varying by year, only 35% to 49% of regimental officers in the Bengal army were with their regiments, the rest being on leave or on secondment.[41]

Counterbalancing such tendencies were powerful tugs of regimental loyalty. The backbone of the system came from those officers who could not purchase promotions – or more than one of them – and who depended on wartime promotion without purchase to provide some degree of career movement. For example, the average prior service for lieutenant colonels in both cavalry and infantry in selected years from 1775 to 1792 inclusive was twenty or more years. The wide disparities in career advancement are well illustrated by the fate of the twenty-five officers (other than staff and surgeons) of the Gordon Highlanders in 1794. By 1815 nine had been killed or had died in campaigning, thereby creating wartime vacancies normally filled without purchase. Of the twenty-two officers below the rank of major in 1794, ten attained the rank of at least lieutenant colonel before or by 1815, four more were killed or died by 1806 before reaching that rank, and three retired as majors. The remaining five officers remained in junior rank before retiring.[42] War aided promotion but regiments continued, as was common in the eighteenth century, to be officered by men whose long service provided continuity and stability.

Regimental self-respect and pride clearly grew with achievement on campaign. That achievement came at a considerable blood sacrifice. The 76th furnished an extreme example in the Maratha campaign of 1803–05 when 170 officers and men were killed and 675 battlefield woundings were sustained.[43] During the year 25 December 1811 to 25 December 1812, for example, the British army (including its colonial, West Indian and foreign battalions, but excluding the Company's sepoy forces) lost 26,700 men who died, deserted, received discharges, or were taken prisoner or went missing. Among the 187 HM infantry battalions, thirty-six lost 100–199 men and twenty-eight lost over 200, against a typical strength of 600–800 officers and men in each battalion.[44] Specific examples of officer casualties in the Gordon Highlanders demonstrate the high incidence of losses over relatively short periods. The 95th sustained ninety-five officer casualties during 1808–14, including thirty-two dead. In January 1813 the 92nd, the Gordon Highlanders had fifty-seven officers on its rolls other than the colonel and the ensigns. Of those, five died on active service in 1813–14, four were killed at Quatre Bras in 1815, and four died while serving in Jamaica in 1819. Within seven years nearly 23% of those officers had died on active service. Among the twelve young ensigns of January 1813, four died in action during that year.[45] Although battlefield casualties were not necessarily high, the cumulative loss on campaign could be. An individual soldier, of any rank, who survived fifteen or twenty years during the long wars of 1793–1815 would have witnessed the demise of many fellow-soldiers. The 19th regiment, the Green Howards, spent from 1797–1819 in Ceylon, mainly at Trincomalee. Maintaining an average strength of 870 men entailed the death of 1,478 soldiers during those twenty-three years, or over 7.5% each year.[46] Regimental pride developed out of shared suffering and in order to provide intellectual and moral purpose or justification to such levels of sacrifice.

Regiments also enabled ministers to manage the numbers within the army. In peacetime the overall size of the army fell, but middle-ranking officers and senior NCOs were retained by keeping regiments intact while severely reducing each regiment's size. For example, from 1769 until its demise in 1801, the Irish parliament paid for 15,000 British troops to be stationed in Ireland. In 1772 each battalion in Ireland had 477 men, plus a company of light infantry, falling short of the total which a wartime battalion would contain. The peacetime total manpower supported a larger number of senior regimental officers than the Irish parliament would have provided if this total had been composed of 800-man battalions. When war came – and sixteen of the forty-four British battalions assembled in America in 1776 went from Ireland – the existing battalions could be readily expanded and new battalions, and their command systems, could be recruited at a reasonable pace.[47] This approach was repeated in India. During the mid-1820s a series of wars increased the number of HM troops deployed to the subcontinent. With the return of peace, the East India Company sought to cut back the HM force it paid for to the stipulated total of 20,000, whereas the army command in India and the government in London sought to keep a larger number on the Company's payroll. The solution was to maintain a substantial number of HM regiments of reduced size in India, supporting an overlarge senior officer corps which would be available for future contingencies requiring the speedy expansion of forces.[48]

Ritual and ceremony

To animate this structure and the troops within it, ritual and ceremony played a growing role in the military experience. From the early eighteenth century, the army's system of annual inspections of all regiments stationed in the UK involved formal parading as well as close examination of battalions' state of recruitment, equipment and training, their mix of recent volunteers from the militia and seasoned veterans, and their officers' knowledge of their men.[49] Harsh discipline and the showy emphasis upon uniforms and drills, many of which were designed specifically as spectacles, attracted often satirical criticism. But smart martial appearance and ritual helped to bolster recruitment and morale and developed patriotism and pride in the army. Ritual occasions on which to parade and demonstrate military cohesiveness drew more participants than any civil events attracted.[50] In 1799 William Surtees first experienced a military assembly at a ceremony on Barham Downs to celebrate the successful landing and victory of British forces in Holland: 'Nothing would be more brilliant than our display upon this occasion appeared to me – we were nearly 20,000 strong, I imagine, and, being formed in one extensive line, the firing of the *feu de joie* produced a fine effect.'[51] On 18 July 1800 the king reviewed 32,000 troops on Winkfield Plain near Bagshot Heath in a three-hour ceremony attended by a vast crowd, some of the more affluent of whom slept overnight in their carriages to secure a vantage point. Smaller demonstrations periodically occurred. For example, undergraduate volunteers, the Cambridge Rangers, with Viscount Palmerston (the future Foreign Secretary and Prime Minister) as their enthusiastic captain, gathered in the market square on news of Trafalgar and fired three *feux de joie*.[52]

Celebratory rituals were carefully staged overseas. Royal anniversaries were routinely marked by gun salutes, formal dinners, and energetic drinking. In August 1795 the recently arrived warships and troops at Simon's Bay, preparing to attack the Dutch Cape Colony, fired a salute to mark the Prince of Wales's birthday.[53] Success in arms was noisily announced. In India, when Major General Arthur Wellesley took the fort of Admadnuggar to open his dramatic campaign of 1803 against Maharajah Sindhia, he ordered all garrisons and detachments under his extensive command across southern India to fire royal salutes. To mark the general's victory at Assye, his elder brother, the governor-general, ordered formal salutes throughout British India's garrisons, describing the battle as 'equal in skill and fortitude to any of which the account exists in history'.[54] The sense of historic power created by the regular movements of British forces from station to station and duty to duty in India struck Bishop Heber when he met the elderly veteran Major General Sir David Ochterlony 'on a desert plain in the heart of Rajpootana'. The bishop, having been reading a life of Marlborough, felt an extraordinary sense of the historical implausibility – one hundred years from the great duke's heyday – of a British general and bishop meeting there. Ochterlony, who had won a legendary reputation in the Nepal war of 1814–16, was accompanied by a princely personal military escort, demonstrating how the Rajput princes and nobles were, according to Heber 'kept in awe by British residents and British garrisons'. On the road towards Kanpur (Cawnpore), Heber came across about 2,300 infantry on the march with 'a long train of baggage, elephants, camels, bullocks, and camp-followers':

The groups afforded by the line of march, the little parties halting under trees, the loaded animals, the native women conveyed in 'dhoolies', or litters, and hackeries, the naked limbs of the baggage-drivers and camp-followers, the different gradations of horse . . . with the uniforms and arms, were some of them beyond description beautiful.[55]

Across the globe, British soldiers and sailors were in constant motion, projecting their military and naval capabilities, imposing their presence, and proclaiming their pride.

More sobering, but equally designed to impress, were rituals of military punishment. In June 1795 the Oxfordshire regiment was marched out of Seaford, near Brighton, to arrive at a 'spacious valley' by dawn. On the higher ground overlooking the valley an estimated 3,000 cavalry, with horse artillery, took position while the infantry regiment formed in line below. Corporal punishments were inflicted on various convicted soldiers followed by the execution of two men for riotous and disorderly conduct. According to the *Annual Register*: 'From the disposition of the ground, and from the arrangement of the troops, a more magnificent and a more awful spectacle was never exhibited in this country.'[56] Rifleman Harris recalled being among 15,000 soldiers assembled at Portsdown Hill from all the garrisons in the area around Portsmouth, to witness the execution of a deserter. The regiments marched slowly past the body: 'The sight was very imposing and appeared to make a deep impression on all there.'[57]

More positive impressions may have been gathered from the sight of an army at sea. When Sir Charles Grey's great expeditionary force sailed out of Barbados in 100 ships in February 1794, one junior officer was deeply impressed: 'The morning was brilliant beyond conception, the sight grand above description. The bands of music, the sounds of trumpets, drums and fifes, the high panting ardour, zeal and discipline of the soldiers and sailors' all encapsulated the sense of confidence and commitment. On another occasion, Rifleman Harris noted:

I wish I could picture the splendid sight of the shipping in the Downs at the time we embarked with about 20,000 men. Those were times which the soldiers of our own more peaceable days have little conception of.[58]

Military landings also attracted suitably uplifting sentiments. In 1813, one essayist noted of the expedition to Egypt in 1801: 'Language does not describe, nor history record, a military operation of more dignity and interest, or conducted with greater skill and intrepidity, than this memorable descent on the Egyptian coast'. Those present, it was noted later, described the landing as:

the most beautiful, solemn and imposing spectacle, that man could witness or imagine, a scene that filled the reflecting mind with the most sublime and lofty ideas, which carried it back to those ages hidden behind the veils of fable, or to those more heroic times when the shores of Egypt were trodden by the kings of the world, the heroes of Homer, the patriots of Greece.[59]

Finally, of course, there was the ritual of battle itself. Rifleman Harris commented on his feelings as Vimiero (August 1808) was about to begin:

As I looked about me, whilst standing enranked, and just before the commencement of the battle, I thought it the most imposing sight the world could produce. Our lines glittering with bright arms; the stern features of the men . . . the proud colours of England floating over the heads of the different battalions, and the dark cannon on the rising ground, and all in readiness to commence the awful work of death, with a noise that would deafen the whole multitude. Altogether, the sight had a singular and terrible effect upon the feelings of a youth who, a few short months before, had been a solitary shepherd upon the Downs of Dorsetshire.[60]

William Surtees observed that, following the grim, hard marches of the retreat to La Coruña, the prospect of battle made 'every pulse beat high'; 'All was life and animation' in preparing for battle. Over four years later this campaign-hardened veteran could still say of the assemblage of opposing armies at Vitoria: 'never did I witness a more interesting and magnificent sight'. A cavalry officer in 1811 was in a position to watch a British move upon French forces near Redinha in Portugal: 'The advance over the plain in line was one of the finest things I ever saw.'[61] One officer present at Fuentes de Oñores in May 1811 commented: 'The execution of our movement presented a magnificent military spectacle.' Another officer observed of the build-up to the battle at Salamanca in July 1812: 'The movements which followed presented the most beautiful military spectacle imaginable.'[62] Sailors experienced similar sensations. One said of the manoeuvring of warships at Copenhagen in April 1801:

A more beautiful and solemn spectacle I never witnessed . . . A man-of-war under sail is at all times a beautiful object, but at such a time the scene is heightened beyond the powers of description . . . our minds were deeply impressed with awe.[63]

Military service was typically spartan, often harsh, and sometimes horrendous. But the wars from the early 1790s demonstrated also that the regimental system fostered reputational pride, while collective rituals periodically engendered awe, stimulated morale, and emphasized the distinctive and manly nature of soldiering. It also created models and myths of individual and collective courage and self-sacrifice. These complemented the support provide by an expanded network of bases to sustain Britain's global projection of power.

Conclusion

One of the strongest deterrents against the development of British militarism and yet one of the principal aids in making Britain the first global military power was the fragmented character of the British armed forces. The British army was operationally divided into four different clusters, stationed in Britain, Ireland, the colonies and India, with its regiments transferred periodically between and within them. The specialist arms of the Royal Artillery and Royal Engineers were financed and organized separately from the army. HM regiments were posted to India to reinforce the East India Company's army, which was independent of Horse Guards in London and managed as three distinct armies for Bengal, Madras, and Bombay.

Individual regiments enabled such a diverse army to be deployed across the globe. The regiment itself – not 'the army' – recruited soldiers, and most promotion for officers up to and including the rank of lieutenant colonel was within a regiment. Many regiments expanded in wartime to contain two or even three or four battalions, each consisting of some 600–800 men, commanded by lieutenant colonels. The operational requirements of the empire and the demands for troops to be available for policing duties within the UK both fostered regimentalism.[64] The battalion within the regiment was a convenient size for deployment overseas and at home. Great professional care and attention were devoted to the training, disciplining, and posting of individual battalions, underpinned by regimental inspections, typically annual, by one of a number of generals attached to the staff for that purpose. Their reports, emphasizing the state of health, fitness, acculturation to military values, and discipline of each battalion in the army, provided the basis for assessing the suitability of regiments for particular forms of domestic or overseas service, depending on the men's physical fitness, their ability to drill properly, their riding abilities and the condition of their horses.[65] Such analyses demonstrated an appropriate understanding of the dynamics of organizational groups and the limits of men's endurance, matched by concern for training and ensuring troops' battle-readiness, and touched by a sense of humanity that men should not be committed to the rigours and trials of campaigning without suitable and extended preparation.[66] While most eighteenth-century peacetime armies were dispersed into small units and garrisons – the Prussian army's largest peacetime concentration of the 1770s, for example, was at the strength of two battalions – British regiments differed in the extent to which they served overseas, especially in wartime. Frequent movement overseas heightened regimental cohesiveness.

The organizational structure for British power projection was insufficient by itself to account for success. Morale – developed through unit emulation and pride, savage discipline, and ritual consciousness-building – was also vital to military and naval effectiveness. A willingness to fight and collective resilience on campaign in the face of scourging privation and suffering were also essential characteristics attributed to the British by Wellington as early as 1805. But the description of the instruments of British power points to another fundamental aspect of the British way in war. Almost all the campaigns of this period flowed from the initial securing of enclaves from which to project power. Where the British did not hold a substantial land base from which to march into the interior, they customarily used a fleet as the platform for a land advance, as at the Cape in 1796 and Egypt in 1801, or as the bridge from another base to their objective, as from Sicily to the Maida in 1806 or from Bermuda and Jamaica to New Orleans in 1814–15. Only in India, with the Maratha wars of 1803–05, did the British operate far inland from their enclaves. In Spain, they were anchored to their lines of communication and base towns in Portugal until May 1813, nearly five years after they had first landed in the peninsula. The British acted as a global power by creating enclaves, some permanent, others temporary, throughout the world and then building victories from these enclaves of power, by acting not as a hegemon but as the impresario of numerous and widely dispersed contacts and conflicts with local neighbouring states. Because Britain was an enclave power and involved herself in so many local political relationships, success depended upon a military-naval-political leadership managing forces which were widely distributed geographically but rarely large, except in occasional emergencies, at any one place.

Notes and references

1 John Brewer, *The Sinews of Power: War, Money and the English State 1688–1783* (London, 1989), pp. 34–37, 41–42, 57–60. Brewer does not deal with the projection of power.

2 Nikolaus Pevsner, Ian Richmond *et al.*, *Northumberland* (London, 1992 edn), pp. 175–79; John Giffard, *Highlands and Islands* (London, 1992), pp. 174–75; J.A. Houlding, *Fit for Service: The Training of the British Army, 1715–1795* (Oxford, 1981), pp. 52–55.

3 William Cobbett, *Rural Rides*, 2 vols (London, 1912 edn), Vol. I, p. 41.

4 Elie Halevy, *England in 1815*, trans. by E.I. Watkin and D.A. Barker (London, 1961 edn), p. 73; E.P. Thompson, *The Making of the English Working Class* (London, 1968 edn), p. 663.

5 *Journal of the House of Commons*, Vol. 75.

6 *Army List 1815* (London, 1815), pp. 513–16.

7 Norman Gash, *Mr Secretary Peel* (London, 1961), pp. 186–87.

8 Duke of Wellington (ed.), *Despatches, Correspondence and Memoranda of Arthur, Duke of Wellington, KG . . . from 1818 to 1831*, 8 vols (London, 1867–80), Vol. II, pp. 290–91.

9 Wellington (ed.), *Despatches*, Vol. II, pp. 378–80.

10 Wellington (ed.), *Despatches*, Vol. II, p. 379.

11 'The thirteenth report of the Commissioners of Military Enquiry: the Master General and Board of Ordnance', *Reports from Commissioners*, Session 1 November–24 July, 1810–1811, (1811) Vol. IV, p. 237.

12 Bridget Cherry and Nikolaus Pevsner, *London*, Vol. II, *The South* (London, 1983), pp. 240–41, 286–90; A.W. Cockerill, 'The Royal Military Asylum, (1803–15)', *Journal of the Society for Army Historical Research*, 79 (2001), pp. 25–44; House of Commons, *Reports from Commissioners: Accounts and Papers*, (1811) Vol. IV, p. 237.

13 *Parliamentary Gazetteer for 1841* (London, 1841), Part III, p. 464; John Newman, *North Kent and East Kent* (London, 1983 edn), p. 361; Bridget Cherry and Nikolaus Pevsner, *Devon* (London, 1989 edn), pp. 638, 651–55.

14 A. Aspinall (ed.), *The Later Correspondence of George III*, 5 vols (Cambridge, 1968), Vol. III, p. 459.

15 Nikolaus Pevsner and David Lloyd, *Hampshire and the Isle of Wight* (London, 1967), pp. 410, 415, 421; Robert Gardiner (ed.), *Fleet, Battle and Blockade: the French Revolutionary War, 1793–1797* (London, 1996), p. 163. In 1809–11 the naval hospital was built at Great Yarmouth, constituting a massive monument of four individual blocks each twenty-nine bays wide. Nikolaus Pevsner and Bill Wilson, *Norfolk. Vol. I Norwich and the North-East* (London, 1997), p. 148.

16 Charles Dupin, *A Tour through the Naval and Military Establishments of Great Britain* (translated, London, 1822), p. 115.

17 Major M.L. Ferrar, *A History of the Services of the 19th Regiment* (London, 1911), p. 179.

18 John Newman, *West Kent and the Weald* (London, 1976); *Parliamentary Gazetteer for 1841*, Part III, p. 403.

19 Brian Lavery, *Nelson's Navy: The Ships, Men, and Organization 1793–1815* (London, 1989), pp. 221, 228–29; Roger Morriss, *The Royal Dockyards during the Revolutionary and Napoleonic Wars* (Leicester, 1983), pp. 28, 97–98, 109; Gordon Jackson, 'Ports 1700–1840' in Peter Clark (ed.), *The Cambridge Urban History of Britain*, Vol. II, *1540–1840* (Cambridge, 2000), pp. 705–31.

20 *The Times*, 12 June 1794, p. 2.

21 N.A.M. Rodger, 'Sea-power and empire 1688–1793' in P.J. Marshall (ed.), *The Eighteenth Century* (Oxford, 1998), pp. 169–83.

22 Colonel the Hon. F.A. Wellesley (ed.), *The Diary and Correspondence of Henry Wellesley, First Lord Cowley 1790–1846* (London, n.d.), p. 35.

23 Carola Oman, *Sir John Moore* (London, 1953), pp. 65, 77.

24 Michael Pawson and David Buisseret, *Port Royal, Jamaica* (Oxford, 1975), p. 136; Andrew Jackson O'Shaughnessy, *An Empire Divided: The American Revolution and the British Caribbean* (Philadelphia, 2000), p. 46.

25 Braithwaite, Edward, *The Development of Creole Society in Jamaica, 1770–1820* (Oxford, 1971), pp. 28, 30, 105, 135, 151; Buckley, Roger N., *Slaves in Red Coats: The British West India Regiments, 1795–1815* (New Haven, CT, 1979), p. 104; Lieutenant Colonel C. Greenhill Gardyne, *The Life of a Regiment: The History of the Gordon Highlanders*, 2 vols (Edinburgh, 1901), Vol. II, p. 418.

26 'A return of the effective strength of the land forces stationed in the West India Islands, in the year 1815', House of Commons, *Sessional Papers: Accounts and Papers* 1816 (42), p. 395; 'An account of all sums of money voted by the House of Assembly in the island of Jamaica', House of Commons *Sessional Papers: Accounts and Papers* 1830 (349), pp. 179–81.

27 *Jamica: The Rough Guide* (London, 1997) p. 55; *Lonely Planet: Eastern Caribbean* (Melbourne, 2001 edition), pp. 26, 129, 133–34, 160, 162–64, 216, 229.

28 Michael Duffy, *Soldiers, Sugar and Seapower: The British Expeditions to the West Indies and the War Against Revolutionary France* (Oxford, 1987), p. 88.

29 Maurice Boucher and Nigel Penn (eds), *Britain at the Cape 1795–1803* (Johannesburg, 1992), pp. 113–14, 173, 185. The scale of the town is well brought out in contemporary drawings and sketches (*idem*, pp. 32–33, 36–37, 144–45).

30 Gerald S. Graham, *Great Britain in the Indian Ocean: A Study in Maritime Enterprise, 1810–1850* (Oxford, 1968), pp. 316–28; Eric Poole (ed.), 'The letters of Midshipman Noel, 1818–1822' in N.A.M. Rodger (ed.), *Naval Miscellany*, Vol. V, Navy Records Society (London, 1984), p. 341.

31 *ODNB* entry; C.M.H. Clark with L.J. Pryor (eds), *Select Documents in Australian History 1788–1850* (Sydney, 1977 edn), pp. 79–80, 88. Friends and family of ministers in London and half-pay officers were keenly involved in land speculation. Jan Kociumbas, *The Oxford History of Australia*, Vol. 2, *1770–1860. Possessions* (Oxford, 1995 edn), pp. 120–23.

32 War and Colonial Office to Ordnance Office, 25 February 1824, Sierra Leone file, Ordnance Correspondence; 'Relative to the Conditions of the Transfer to the Ordnance of Works and Buildings by the Colonies', 1828, Ordnance Correspondence, WO 44/503, The National Archives, London.

33 *The Madras Almanac for the Year of our Lord 1800* (Madras, 1799).

34 John Rosselli, *Lord William Bentinck: The Making of a Liberal Imperialist 1774–1839* (Berkeley, CA, 1974), p. 46.

35 Reginald Heber, Bishop of Calcutta, *Narrative of a Journey Through the Upper Provinces of India, 1824–1825* 2 vols (London, 1828), Vol. I, pp. 33–34, 36; H.A. Young, *The East India Company's Arsenals and Manufactories* (Oxford, 1937), p. 44.

36 C.A. Bayly, 'Town building in North India, 1790–1830', *Modern Asian Studies*, Vol. 9(4) (1975), 483–504; Heber, *Narrative of a Journey Through the Upper Provinces of India*, Vol. I, p. 143.

37 Lieutenant General Sir Neil Cantlie, *A History of the Army Medical Department*, 2 vols (Edinburgh, 1974), Vol. I, p. 299.

38 Major General Sir Frederick Maurice, *British Strategy* (London, 1929), p. 131; Christopher Hibbert (ed.), *A Soldier of the Seventy-First* (n.p., 1975), p. 36.

39 'Return of the number of discharges and desertions from the Regular Army', House of Commons, *Sessional Papers: Accounts and Papers* 1817 (209), p. 199; Aspinall (ed.), *The Later Correspondence of George III*, Vol. III, p. 570.

40 *Royal Military Calendar*, 5 vols (London, 1821), Vol. II, pp. 341–42.

41 Douglas Peers, *Between Mars and Mammon: Colonial Armies and the Garrison State in Early Nineteenth-century India* (London, 1995), pp. 76–79.

42 Gardyne, *The Life of a Regiment*, Vol. I, pp. 117–18.

43 Colonel Hugh Pearse, *Memoir of the Life and Military Services of Viscount Lake, Baron Lake of Delhi and Laswaree, 1744–1808* (Edinburgh, 1908), p. 385.

44 'Return of the casualties of the different regiments of the British Army', *House of Commons Sessional Papers, 1801–1834: 24 November 1812–22 July 1813*, Vol. XIII, pp. 24–28 (BOPCRIS).

45 John A. Hall, *A History of the Peninsular War: The Biographical Dictionary of British Officers Killed and Wounded 1808–1814* Vol. VIII, Charles Oman,

A History of the Peninsular War (London, 1998), p. 638; Gardyne, *The Life of a Regiment*, Vol. I, pp. 421–23. For a general discussion, see Rory Muir, *Tactics and the Experience of Battle in the Age of Napoleon* (New Haven, CT, 1998), pp. 223–31.

46 Ferrar, *A History of the Services of the 19th Regiment*, pp. 172–73.

47 Thomas Bartlett and Keith Jeffrey (eds), *A Military History of Ireland* (Cambridge, 1996), pp. 228–29.

48 Peers, *Between Mars and Mammon*, pp. 220–21.

49 Aspinall (ed.), *The Later Correspondence of George III*, Vol. III, pp. 318–21.

50 Scott Hughes Myerly, *British Military Spectacle from the Napoleonic Wars through the Crimea* (Cambridge, MA, 1996), pp. 11–19, 41–42, 49, 53, 67, 103, 139–41, 169.

51 Surtees, William, *Twenty-Five Years in the Rifle Brigade* (London, 1973), pp. 4–5.

52 Bartlett (ed.), *85th King's Light Infantry*, pp. 44–45; Kenneth Bourne, *Palmerston: The Early Years 1784–1841* (London, 1982), p. 41.

53 Brian Lavery, *Nelson and the Nile: The Naval War Against Bonaparte 1798* (London, 1998), p. 284; Boucher and Penn (eds), *Britain at the Cape*, p. 45; Oman, *Sir John Moore*, pp. 332–33.

54 Duke of Wellington (ed.), *Supplementary Despatches and Memoranda of Arthur, Duke of Wellington, India, 1797–1805*, 15 vols (London, 1858–1872), Vol. IV, pp. 152, 187n.

55 Heber, *Narrative of a Journey Through the Upper Provinces of India*, Vol. II, pp. 13, 29–30; Vol. I, p. 198.

56 *The Annual Register . . . for 1795* (London, 1800), pp. 23–24.

57 Christopher Hibbert (ed.), *Recollections of Rifleman Harris* (Hamden, CT, 1970), pp. 2–3.

58 Duffy, *Soldiers, Sugar, and Seapower*, p. 67.

59 *The Royal Military Panorama or Officer's Companion*, Vol. III (1813–14), p. 11.

60 Hibbert (ed.), *Rifleman Harris*, p. 26.

61 William Surtees, *Twenty-Five Years*, pp. 79, 206; Lieutenant Colonel Tomkinson, *The Diary of a Cavalry Officer in the Peninsular War and Waterloo Campaign, 1809–15*, edited by his son James Tomkinson (London, 1895; first published 1894), p. 82.

62 Captain Sir John Kincaid, *Adventures in the Rifle Brigade* (London, 1929), pp. 55, 117.

63 Ole Feldbaek, *The Battle of Copenhagen* (London, 2002 trans.), p. 141.

64 There is relatively little systematic study of this phenomenon, though a new standard has been set for a later period by David French, *Military Identities: The Regimental System, the British Army, and the British People, c.1870–2000* (Oxford, 2005). The regiment continues to be the army's foundation-stone. Anthony Sampson, *Who Runs This Place?* (London, 2004), p. 167.

65 Aspinall (ed.), *The Later Correspondence of George III*, Vol. II, pp. 614–15, 396–97.

66 Aspinall (ed.), *The Later Correspondence of George III*, Vol. II, pp. 614–15; Vol. III, pp. 318–23.

CHAPTER 17

Aristocracy and British military culture

Recent studies of British expansionism have demonstrated the multifaceted ways in which individuals and groups engaged with and tried to dominate the wider world. Experts, explorers, evangelists and entrepreneurs mixed with convicts, craftsmen and community-builders in a tumultuous process driven by curiosity, conscience, careerism and greed.[1] All classes and most areas of the United Kingdom were affected by the enhanced pace and range of such diverse interactions. Yet this inclusive approach to imperial historiography has tended to obscure the centrality of warfare to British empire-building, the consolidation of the position and power of the elite most closely identified with leadership in war – the landed aristocracy and gentry – and the development of a distinctive British military culture resulting from the interaction between the traditional elite and military efficacy.[2] This chapter explores some of the most important ways in which aristocracy – in terms of caste and the more general aspiration to high social status – was central to British militarism. There were different possible models for the interaction between politics and the military, with the situation in Britain offering its own peculiar ambiguities and contradictions. But despite political and ideological limitations on aristocratic influence, the armed services' command systems were dominated by those of aristocratic and gentry background or aspirations. Members of the aristocracy served in the armed forces in disproportionately high numbers during the long wars. This widespread involvement had three impacts which will be assessed here. Leadership in war, and the discipline and professionalism which infused that leadership, offered a behavioural exemplar from which to defend semi-feudal ideas and a model of elite values with which to rebut critics' castigation of the upper classes' dilettante or sybaritic lifestyles. Of more practical application were the infusion of military skills into the landowning elite and that elite's use of those skills to organize the militia and to face down domestic challenges or threats to the prevailing political and social order. Finally, the landowning elite's deep involvement with the armed services during the long wars increased the interlocking links between the country's political and military leadership networks.

The consolidation of aristocratic power

Much British historiography implies that the long wars exerted a negative impact. Admittedly, Britain secured enhanced standing as a European power. But diplomacy as practised by Castlereagh when Foreign Secretary from 1812 to 1822 has won admiration from *aficionados* of the craft of conducting foreign relations and from proponents of conservative, balance-of-power precepts rather than excited the interest of scholars concerned to see foreign policy advance more dynamic ideas than those of dynastic legitimacy. Where there was movement in overseas affairs – and we will return to this in the next chapter – it often involved imperial extensions of limited appeal or salience to the 'public' at home. Even more negative has been the standard historiographical assessment of the impact of the long wars on Britain itself. The immediate post-war years witnessed dislocation, deprivation and suffering, as technological change undermined traditional craft skills and as high unemployment resulted from demobilization and massive cuts in government war-related spending after 1815. The landed interest, while protecting itself from foreign competition in foodstuffs through the Corn Laws, which artificially prevented the price of grains from falling in line with world supplies, supported savage cuts in government expenditure without consideration for the consequent decline in living standards inflicted upon hundreds of thousands of people.[3] It is, however, often overlooked that all political groups pressed for retrenchment in public spending as soon as the war ended. Opponents to the government persistently portrayed spending on large peacetime armies and navies and the accumulation of public debt as characteristic features of monarchical and aristocratic regimes.[4] Politicians in general and ministers, not just sought to rein in the national debt and uphold sound finance.

The end of the long wars has generally been seen as the occasion for resuming public pressure for political reform. Such pressure can be viewed as evidence for an increasingly acceptable challenge to aristocratic rule and for the Tory government's inability to conciliate rising middle-class self-confidence and assertiveness. Yet it has been argued that the reforms of the early 1830s helped consolidate the aristocracy's social and political position. The Whigs, by accepting limited reform and social responsibilities, and by using central government power to initiate reforms involving social welfare, vindicated their own aristocratic rule and, by bringing sections of the middle class into the 'political nation', reconciled the middle classes to the aristocratic order.[5] This view implies that successful leadership in war – the quintessential activity associated with aristocratic status – and the expansion of the empire – the supreme act of an assertive state – did not pay significant political dividends for the British establishment in the years immediately after 1815.

An alternative perspective is worth considering. Instead of prioritizing the roots of middle-class political mobilization and working-class consciousness in the post-war period, it should be emphasized that the long wars and imperial expansion enhanced the standing of the aristocracy and gentry and increased the importance of empire to the British state. The formation of elites, developing coterminously with the expansion of the state, occurred in different ways in the eighteenth and nineteenth centuries as particular states expanded their territory or transformed their power structures. How this happened was related to the role of military force and imperial acquisitions, as may be shown by three examples of the different ways in which military power interacted with the growth of states.

In Prussia, the army itself became a central organ of state power and territorial expansionism. The Hohenzollern rulers of Prussia brought the landowning elite into the newly expanded army as a means of attaching it to the dynasty and its government; Frederick the Great declared that the nobility's relationship to an absolute monarch was 'the first ornament of his crown and the lustre of his army'. The landowning class welcomed military academies as a source of education and military careers as a source of income for their sons. By 1806 less than 10% of the 7,000 Prussian army officers were non-noble. The army in turn became the instrument by which Prussia massively extended its possessions from 1740 to 1795. This success entrenched the Prussian landowning class within the government and army, so that at least 60% of landowning Junkers by 1800 were or had been army officers. Even the later expansion of the Prussian army into the vast German army did not undermine aristocratic dominance. In 1860, 65% of Prussian officers were aristocrats, while even as late as 1913, when 53% of German colonels and generals were from that caste, aristocrats controlled the elite corps, notably the cavalry, and the General Staff.[6]

In revolutionary France, a different model developed. Although the revolutionaries did not destroy the aristocracy, they considerably reduced it by the generous use of the guillotine and the stimulus this practice gave to leading aristocrats' flight from France. The grand court nobility lost their position in the armed forces, but the minor nobility, far less wealthy, far less cosmopolitan, and far less socially overbearing, survived.[7] Relatively open promotion meant, however, that the army by the mid- and certainly late 1790s had become an autonomous source of power and status. Senior officers had, for the most part, no inherited standing in civil society and no independent sources of wealth. With the country constantly engaged in foreign wars, the vastly expanded army became in effect a standing army, despite the rhetoric about its constituting a citizens' levy. The army as a result took control of the state, as eighteenth-century critics of standing armies predicted would happen. Having made himself First Consul, General Bonaparte soon grasped the need to broaden his appeal and base of authority and in 1804 proclaimed himself emperor. Continuing to replicate traditional princely rulership, in 1810 he married the Habsburg emperor's daughter, describing her as 'the daughter of the Caesars', and extended the historic connection by designating the son and heir born to his new bride as the 'King of Rome'.[8] Consistent with this process, Napoleon created a new aristocracy to support his imperial regime. Within ten years the emperor bestowed 8,000 titles corresponding to British knighthoods and peerages, with 3,263 of the recipients becoming nobles. About one-third of these titles went to existing *Ancien Régime* aristocrats. Although this new aristocracy vastly exceeded the British aristocracy in size, the very top ranks of the new elite were restricted as in Britain, with only thirty-four princes and dukes being created. Of that top group, twenty were soldiers, while of the entire Napoleonic aristocracy, 59% were army officers. The peers among them were granted estates or revenues, typically in conquered lands, to sustain their new status.[9] Napoleon exploited and controlled the army by giving its leaders social status buttressed by wealth on an unprecedented scale.

In the United States of America very different efforts were made to forge a new political order stripped of monarchy, aristocracy and a standing army of any size. Although America was forged by success in war, the new country emerged in the 1780s in a geopolitical context in which there were no external threats requiring more than a tiny army. Only in 1812–15 and, to a lesser extent, 1846–48 were large-scale military mobilizations needed. But recurrent campaigns against Native American nations were undertaken with devastating effect by state militias on short-term service with occasional supplementary activity involving regular units. This meant that very short-term military service became widespread, despite the smallness of the US army. Predatory frontier wars and military service substantially assisted many aspirants to political leadership. Of the first fifteen men *elected* as presidents of the USA, five were regular army generals and one was a wartime brigadier. The war of 1812 produced a generation of future political leaders in the northern trans-Appalachian states who had commanded militia in the extensive operations affecting their region. For example, at the Battle of the Thames in 1813, the 7,000 troops, including militia and volunteers, involved in that remote frontier campaign counted among their number a future president, a future vice-president, three future state governors and four future US senators, as well as other office-holders.[10] In this model, military leadership was civilianized and militia leadership became an important means by which those seeking high office developed their public profile, personal authority and political credibility.

Some elements of these different models were reflected in Britain. The taming of the territorial aristocracy through military service was less systematic than in Prussia, but had a similar effect, for example, in drawing Scottish Highland clan chiefs and their prominent kinsmen into the British state. Secondly, those who achieved military and naval success were accorded titles and peerages incorporating them into a socio-economic establishment, as Napoleon did far more lavishly in France. And, as in the United States, the British gentry and aristocracy asserted themselves and ensured their local and national political leadership through military and especially militia service. A distinctive characteristic of the British establishment, however, was the exploitation of overseas imperial opportunities, through both military and political service, to bolster its fortunes and power at home. It developed extensive interconnections between its imperial and military roles and its claims to rule in the metropolis, despite the implication, flowing from a customary historiographical separation of domestic political history from the history of the colonies and of war, that events in the empire had limited impact on the elite at home. As a small sample illustrates, nearly all the seventeen prime ministers who served between 1762 and 1830, as well as the Whig reformist politicians who came to power in 1830, had a close relative who held imperial office or overseas military or naval command.[11] Christopher Bayly has argued more generally that the period 1783–1830s saw a global shift from notions of universal kingship to notions of legitimacy more closely aligned with territory and ethnicity or nationhood. Just as the Mughal Empire collapsed in India, so did the Holy Roman Empire collapse in Europe. Bayly sees the forging of closer alignments between states, commercial classes, and the controllers of land.[12] The British establishment embodied that alignment, but used military and naval service to enhance its status and power.

Military service and aristocratic legitimation

Overseas expansion vastly extended the sphere in which to pursue the traditional aristocratic concerns of rulership, command, dynastic aggrandizement, status and precedence, and in which to exercise authority in deciding issues of land ownership and property-holding, rent-rolls and debt management. The establishment constantly sought financially well-rewarded high offices where its personal, political and military networks could be exploited and where habits of command were an essential transferable skill. War remade the empire, and both warfare and empire-building strengthened the position of the aristocracy and gentry in British political life. These were central and continuing activities of the British state, and were often vital determinants of careers and lives for those who directed the state, with effects transmitted through family connections far beyond the officials themselves.

This extended role for the aristocratic establishment did not go unchallenged in the 1790s. Debates sparked by the attack on aristocratic status and privilege in France were expressed for the first time in the eighteenth century as direct and fundamental critiques of the House of Lords and hereditary place, with the publication in 1791 of Tom Paine's *The Rights of Man* and William Godwin's *Enquiry Concerning Political Justice* in 1793. The aristocracy, under pressure to defend its own claims to privilege and status, broadened the public display of qualities of civic wisdom, virtue and benevolence that implicitly and sometimes overtly had been used to justify their position. Paul Langford has explored the complexities of aristocratic behaviour designed to offer models of restraint and accessibility, and involving leadership of local communities and service as patrons of organized societies. In the 1790s the aristocracy was expected to work within a middle-class society, cultivate the mind and good manners, and participate seriously in all manner of voluntary and public affairs.[13]

Yet paralleling such developments, the long wars of 1793–1815 allowed, for the first time, opportunities on a large stage for displaying the heroic values classically associated with aristocracies, and for the further legitimation of aristocratic and gentry status by rewarding successful commanders with peerages and knighthoods. In 1797–98, three admirals were promoted to the peerage for their leadership in battle: Sir John Jervis, Adam Duncan and Sir Horatio Nelson. Earl Spencer, the minister responsible for the navy, recommended to George III that Duncan be made a viscount, a high honour which 'from the very great sensation which the victory has excited, will not be considered by the publick as too great for the occasion'. The only public objection to Nelson's ennoblement was that the rank of baron, the lowest rank in the peerage, amounted to an insufficient reward for his services.[14] Mainstream newspaper opinion accepted rather than questioned the appropriateness of titled rank, even though twenty-two of the thirty-five peerages given under George III for military and naval services went to members of noble or socially high-ranking families. Nine of the remaining thirteen were naval officers, and only one of the ennobled admirals' fathers was not at least a clergyman, an army officer, or a barrister.[15] The award of the highest honours thus tended to confirm the social position and martial skills of the social elite, but there was nevertheless enough provision of peerages and especially knighthoods for officers of non-landed backgrounds to add legitimacy to the system. An illustration of the interaction of inherited and acquired status on the officer elite was afforded by the first major naval battle of the wars of 1793–1815, the Glorious First of June 1794. Of the forty senior officers in the rank of captain or above present at the battle, seven were the sons of peers and five others later received peerages for their naval services, meaning that nearly one-third of this group of officers enjoyed or acquired direct aristocratic status.[16] The public acceptance of the traditional link between martial attributes and social rank helps explain why, by 1800, even William Godwin conceded that reformist critiques of the establishment had waned.[17]

It has been said of the late seventeenth century that 'Alone among the European aristocracies, the English nobility and more substantial gentry did not form a militarised class devoted to the profession of arms'.[18] Prolonged warfare and empire-building from 1793 did not transform that position but did create a continuing strand of aristocratic militarism. The aristocracy and landed gentry were not primarily a military caste, but they were far more militaristic than any other class and they provided nineteenth-century Britain with a distinctive warrior elite. The growth of this role can be seen in: the presence of aristocrats in the army's higher command, the relationship between that aristocratic presence and military professionalism, and the interaction between the aristocratic army and politics.

The disproportionate number of aristocrats in the army's higher ranks can readily be demonstrated. For example, the army lists of 1812, when wartime demands had led to increased numbers of promotions, show that, of eighty-three full generals, twenty-three were peers or younger sons of peers, and three others were royal dukes. Of 178 lieutenant generals, the next rank down, twenty-three were peers or sons or heirs of peers. This definition excludes, of course, most grandsons of peers, men related to peers by marriage, and all members of families holding baronetcies and knighthoods or enjoying gentry status unadorned by titles. Spreading the net further to include the entire officer corps, one enumeration for 1800 shows that about 250 adult peers or sons of peers were among 12,000 army officers then commissioned. Those 250 represented a high proportion (17%) of the 1,500 total number of adult peers or sons of peers then living.[19] One reason for the aristocracy's high military profile was their prominence in the elite Guards regiments, permanently headquartered in London. These regiments recruited their officers from among 'young men of high rank and fortune' specifically because they did not serve overseas for long periods in peacetime, thereby enabling officers to maintain their family and other commitments. As the Duke of York emphasized: 'To these therefore the Guards offer an opportunity of honorably pursuing the military profession without subjecting themselves to those inconveniences which would otherwise preclude their belonging to the service.' In wartime, however, the elite regiments were immediately available for campaigning in the near continent.[20] Thus, for example, the aristocracy was extremely well represented at the battle of Waterloo. Again defining aristocrats extremely narrowly as those bearing a title or a designation as a son of a peer – and thus excluding grandsons or sons-in-law – some forty-seven aristocratic families, out of 500 or so in the English, Irish and Scottish peerages, were represented there. As only about 28,000 British troops fought at the battle, a Waterloo veteran could be claimed by very few British households, but by a high proportion of aristocratic families.[21] The prestige accruing to participants in battle, and especially Waterloo (and Trafalgar) remained considerable, for, as Clausewitz stressed: 'Fighting is the central military act; all other activities merely support it.'[22] The legacy of the long wars endured. In 1830, a large sample of the peerage shows that very nearly half of all aristocratic households contained a peer, brother or son of a peer with military or naval experience. That proportion rises to three-quarters if militia rank is included and the definition is extended to include fathers, uncles, and, occasionally, grandfathers and great-uncles of peers.[23]

The disproportionate presence of aristocrats in the high command partly reflected the use they made of their local power and prestige to raise battalions for wartime service. In 1793–95, for example, a small number of Scottish peers who were very active in raising new fencible regiments for use within the UK secured political credit or advantages from those efforts and dispensed considerable patronage through their distribution of commissions.[24] Some themselves became lieutenant colonels of fencible regiments.

War meant that the aristocratic link with the volunteers, militia and army involved active participation in defensive arrangements, not merely totemic status. For example, if Napoleon had invaded southern England in 1803–04, he would have confronted volunteers commanded by a combination of local grandees. In Kent some 10,295 volunteers were embodied. Twelve units each totalled 400 or more men, five of which were commanded by peers, one by a baronet and one by a privy councillor. One peer was the former prime minister Lord North's son and heir and another, Earl Camden, had been and was again to be a cabinet minister. From the Cinque Ports on the Kent–Sussex coast came 3,505 volunteers. Three big battalions together totalled 2,705 men, under the overall command of the former prime minister, Colonel William Pitt. The individual battalions were commanded by Lord Mahon, heir to an earldom; Lord Carrington, a former MP and banker (one of whose clients was Pitt); and a Lieutenant Colonel Lamb.[25] In late 1803, Pitt noted that 'I shall be so constantly occupied all next week in going round to my different battalions' that he would not be able to attend parliament. A close friend observed him going 'through the fatigue of a *drill-sergeant*. It is parade after parade, at fifteen or twenty miles distant from each other'.[26]

Any defensive action on British soil would self-evidently involve local landowners, because they were the group most fully engaged in raising and commanding the militia and the volunteers. But service overseas could give equal prominence to the aristocracy. The army operating in Spain in December 1808 offers an interesting example. Its commander, Sir John Moore, came from a middle-class professional family, although his rise had benefited from the active assistance and patronage of the Duke of Hamilton. The high command of his army contained eleven other generals, including brigadiers. Of those, seven had aristocratic connections, including a German Baron commanding forces from the King's German Legion. Even more strikingly, this small group included Lord William Bentinck, son of the prime minister, Charles Stewart, half-brother of Castlereagh, the Secretary for War and the Colonies, and Henry Fane, nephew of another cabinet minister, the Earl of Westmoreland.[27]Although the army's commander had no establishment credentials, his senior command was replete with aristocrats enjoying the closest links to the political decision-makers at home. Since he was at odds with the government, and especially Castlereagh, over strategy, this presence may have intensified his problems as army commander.[28]

An enduring legacy

The period from the 1780s to the 1820s, coinciding with the Industrial Revolution and sporadic wartime radicalization of political opinion, has often been depicted as the decisive moment in producing a pronounced, capitalist class structure in Britain manifested in growing middle- and working-class consciousness and cohesion. Much debate has raged over whether such an entity as 'the working class' was or was not made in this period. But it can equally well be argued that this long period of external challenge, war and empire-building increased the importance, salience and viability of the aristocracy and associated social groups and their values.[29] An aristocratic order, whose influence remained powerful down to the 1960s, and perhaps even to the 1980s, was reinvigorated in those years. This phenomenon was partly explicable by the aristocracy's great wealth; public acceptance of rank was associated with deference to financial and economic power and position. Another explanation was aristocrats' increasing visibility in public spheres other than politics, notably as patrons of community, cultural and benevolent organizations. But the increasing influence of the aristocracy was also due to the enhancement of its traditional roles as rulers and soldiers. The long wars' remembered heroes were not national political leaders but Nelson and Wellington, the pre-eminent sailor and soldier of their age, and Nelson eagerly aspired to join the caste into which Wellington was born. By raising regiments and rallying defenders, the establishment reinforced its local power. By serving in battle and securing commands vastly beyond their proportionate numbers among army officers, aristocrats and landed gentry asserted their authority as leaders in war redolent of the feudal origins of aristocratic and knightly status. By endorsing and engineering the expansion of empire, the landowning elite extended its experience of occasionally coercive rulership over the Scottish Highlands and Ireland across the globe, to India and a wider imperium. Buttressing its military capability and political power at home and overseas with wealth and economic influence, the British establishment created a military-political culture which suffered from neither Prussian rigidity nor Napoleonic excess.

Descriptions of the elite during the long wars underscored the connection between rank, lineage and service. The *Annual Register . . . for the Year 1783* included, unusually, a lengthy appreciation of Captain Lord Robert Manners who died at the age of twenty-four from multiple wounds received at the battle of The Saints in April 1782. Since both his paternal and maternal grandfathers were dukes, it could reasonably be said that he had pursued a tough naval career by 'sacrificing the ease of his former situation, the indulgences of a splendid fortune, and the pleasures of private society, to the dangers of a perilous element, and the honourable hazards of a military life'. He served in eleven general actions, and was extolled for his humane firmness as a disciplinarian; concern for the welfare of his sailors; modesty; reserve; lack of ostentation, good humour and high professional skill and bravery.[30] Other examples were provided in 1812–14 by a substantial monthly publication, *The Royal Military Panorama or Officer's Companion*, which regularly featured prominent biographies of leading generals. In sketching those officers' family backgrounds, great efforts were made to remind readers that their social status was reassuringly high. Of the twenty British generals accorded biographical articles in 1812–14, some fourteen were directly related to peers or baronets. One who lacked noble birth or close connections was described as belonging to a 'family of great antiquity and celebrity', while another sprang 'from a very ancient family' and two had ancestors who had received knighthoods.[31] These accounts were intended to stimulate emulation. Lord William Bentinck's career was described in the hope that

the young nobility of these islands may seek to emulate the illustrious example displayed by his Lordship, and, discarding the frivolous pursuits of fashion, and the baneful influence of the gaming table, endeavour to acquire by a similar mode of conduct the love, the admiration, and the lasting gratitude of their country.[32]

Aristocratic status was reinforced by professional attainment. When Captain Lord Robert Manners was eulogized by the *Annual Register*, his professional dedication won prominent mention: 'His chief study was that of his profession, in which he read and perfectly understood the most approved authors' and had he lived beyond his twenty-four years he would have become 'one of the greatest and ablest officers, this or any other country has produced'.[33] The *Royal Military Panorama* repeatedly accentuated – whether accurately or not is less important than the fact of such emphasis – the aristocratic elite's professional approach to its duties. In 1812 a journalistic biographer noted the Duke of York's careful preparation for 'the profession of war' and his 'unremitting attention to his official duties' as commander-in-chief. The future Marquess of Anglesey was described as assiduous in performing his regimental duties and committed to making the cavalry regiment he later commanded into one of the best such regiments in the British army. Another aristocratic general, Lord Cathcart, was described as an excellent regimental officer in his thirties and an excellent trainer of his regiment in the 1790s. As a commander-in-chief, he was notable for 'promptitude and discernment'; 'his activity of body and mind cannot be exceeded'. In commending the courage and initiative of Charles Stewart (the second son of the Earl of Londonderry), the journal not only noted that he had been wounded in action as a young officer and as a lieutenant colonel, but also stressed 'his general professional merits and services'. Other generals were held up as exemplifying similar qualities. One had visited Berlin 'for the purpose of acquiring a perfect knowledge of the profession'. Another serving as a lieutenant colonel in the West Indies in 1793–95 showed 'the greatest gallantry, singular presence of mind, and professional knowledge'. Such dedication and leadership meant that in October 1812 'the British army at this moment presents a model of perfection to every other military nation in the world' and in May 1814 'the British army has become the best of any that can be brought into the field'.[34] The message to the wider public was that the leaders who produced and maintained this instrument of power and glory formed a professional, as well as a social, elite.

It could be objected that the significance of military and naval service receded rapidly after 1815. With the return of peace, the active leadership of aristocratic or gentry generals and colonels became irrelevant and such patriotic demonstrations as occurred rarely took the form of military celebration. Some have suggested that imperial expansionism was an upper-class displacement activity which showed how peripheral rather than how central the aristocracy and gentry had become.[35] In fact, the strong links between aristocratic and gentry status, military service and civil rulership remained robust. The post-war period saw some acts of aristocratic paternalism in relation to the navy and army. Government retrenchment, demanded by all political parties and radicals opposed to the establishment, threw hundreds of thousands of men on to the job market and the treatment of most ex-servicemen was typically callous. But the government's navy yards were sustained on the much reduced business of ship maintenance and repair, and the major burden of financial cutbacks in shipbuilding fell on private contractors. Some 75,000 ex-soldiers and an additional number of men formerly belonging to the Royal Artillery and Royal Engineers received pensions in recognition of disability or long service.[36] The officer corps was far better treated, with half-pay available for officers who were surplus to the requirements for active service and pensions and allowances provided for some officers' widows. Awards may not have been lavish or particularly generous, but officers in particular were tied into the military establishment. More generally, even the age of increasing political mobilization against the old political order witnessed significant manifestations of conservative loyalism. Demonstrations against Catholic Emancipation in 1828 drew vast crowds while also reaffirming military values.[37]

It was widespread disaffection in 1830–31 which provoked the sternest manifestation of loyalism. A poor harvest in 1829 and high food prices had provoked arson attacks on farmers who were selling food dear while underpaying and underfeeding their labourers, while the pressures of high prices upon incomes and rising unemployment drove urban workers to form associations and destroy machinery. Popular discontent – exacerbated by wheat prices kept artificially high in the landowners' interests – led to widespread establishment fears of revolution. Charles Greville, a senior government official, recorded at the end of 1830 that 'I never remember times like these, nor read of such – the terror and lively expectation which prevail'. A month later Colonel William Napier – the historian of the Peninsular War – in discussing the state of manufacturing districts in Manchester and rural discontent in Wiltshire believed 'a revolution inevitable'.[38] Widespread rick-burning spread rapidly across southern England. In Hampshire, Wellington, as Lord Lieutenant, was informed that rebels controlled part of the county, intimidating magistrates and outnumbering the available two troops of dragoons and the 42nd regiment. The duke, however, believed that the magistrates would deal with the situation by raising constables, if aided by specially formed yeomanry and volunteers.[39] In West Sussex, the Duke of Richmond, who had served in the peninsula for nearly four years, been severely wounded in early 1814, and acted as an ADC to Wellington at both Quatre Bras and Waterloo, raised a constabulary of shopkeepers, yeomen and 'respectable' labourers under local commanders to police the countryside.[40] In November 1830 he overwhelmed 200 labourers with fifty of his own farmers and tenants. He then 'harangued' the labourers and 'sent them away in good humour'. He was described as immensely hospitable, 'a sportsman, a farmer, a magistrate, and good, simple, unaffected country gentleman with great personal influence'.[41] His 'Sussex Plan' was commended for adoption elsewhere by the Whig Home Secretary, and the new ministry, of which Richmond was a junior member, offered rewards for bringing offenders to justice while instructing magistrates to act more vigorously. A combination of improving economic conditions and robust repression – including nineteen executions and 481 transportations – contained the protest in 1831.[42] One of the most important factors working against any threat of revolution in the UK was the social and political cohesiveness of the British army's officer corps, compared with the divisions which rent the French officer corps in 1789–92 and in 1830.[43]

Landowners' military experience, suitably maintained in part by regular hunting, came into its own. At Woburn in Bedfordshire – the seat of the family to which Lord John Russell, one of rising Whig reform-minded ministers, belonged – a hunt with the King's hounds was returning to London, but responded to a call to help suppress a riot; 'the gentlemen charged and broke the people and took some of them' before troops arrived to secure the prisoners.[44] At Radborne, outside Derby, Captain Edward Sacheverell Chandos-Pole, who had served in the peninsula, barricaded his imposing country house, and set a small cannon at the top of the entrance steps, training his daughters, among others, to fire it. He also raised a corps of ninety Yeomanry Cavalry to deter aggrieved local workers. More generally, by January 1832, the yeomanry cavalry of England and Wales embodied some 19,047 men, divided into ninety-five local corps. No fewer than fifteen of the twenty-three larger corps (of 300 or more men each) were commanded by peers, or heirs to peers, or baronets, men most conspicuously at the top of the landed social ladder. Heading up this local 'policing' activity were the forty-one lords lieutenant in England and Wales, all of them aristocrats and thirty-eight of them possessors of the higher titles of duke, marquess, and earl.[45]

The post-war period thus witnessed the continuing importance of the link between military experience and capability and political and governmental leadership, while the expanded empire offered new opportunities and status to military leaders operating in the political world. By 1831 there were 6,768 officers in the British army and another 9,404 on half-pay, still eligible for promotion and for a return to active service.[46] Although the officer corps is often disparaged as being so small, it constituted one of the largest single definable professions in Britain, rivalling in size the most numerous 'respectable' profession of the early nineteenth century, the clergy of the Church of England. It also enjoyed high prestige.

Among the governors of the thirty-two British colonies in late 1830, only four were civilians. All 180 holders of the prestigious KCB were army or navy officers, while fifty-six holders of the higher knighthood, the GCB, were senior officers, compared with just sixteen civilians, of whom eight were peers.[47] Given its size and its status after the success of the long wars and Waterloo, the officer caste had acquired a sufficient level of professionalism and developed a sufficient degree of self-confidence to sustain Britain's global military role.

This prominent role, however, entailed continuing blood sacrifice. For example, four of General Lord Cornwallis's great grandsons were killed or died of wounds during the Crimean War, and of General Lord Lake's sixteen sons and grandsons, twelve served in the army or navy, of whom four were killed in action, while a fifth was severely wounded in India.[48] Curiously, the last duke to be killed in action was Captain the 6th Duke of Wellington, in 1943. Maintaining its presence in regiments likely to attract public notice, and preserving the linkage, by inheritance or ennoblement, between aristocratic status and higher command, the aristocracy reaffirmed its traditional, semi-feudal role as a warrior caste which had been elaborated and consolidated in the long period of warfare from 1775 into the 1820s.

The interlocking of social rank and service experience was seen also in the Royal Navy's high command at the end of our period. During 1827–30, three of the top four naval commands were held by aristocrats. Portsmouth came under Sir Robert Stopford, a younger son of the 2nd Earl of Courtown. His services included the command of the naval force in the expedition to, and invasion of, Java in 1811. Devonport was in the hands of Admiral the 7th Earl of Northesk. His eldest son, Lord Rosehill, had been lost at sea aged 16 in February 1807 when the *Blenheim*, 74 guns, had sunk in the Indian Ocean under the command of Rear Admiral Sir Thomas Trowbridge, one of the most highly rated naval captains of the 1790s. At the Nore, the commander-in-chief was Sir Henry Blackwood, a younger son of the second baronet and of the first Baroness Dufferin. Only the Mediterranean fleet, where Vice Admiral Sir Pulteney Thomas (who had first been placed as a midshipman in 1778 at the age of 10) was in command, did not, among the four principal stations, have an aristocratic head. All four of these principal commanders-in-chief had been involved in the Trafalgar campaign. Active service and status were intertwined among the next generation. At the battle of Navarino in 1827, four of the twelve officers present in the rank of commander or above were sons of peers, including a future Earl Spencer, and a fifth, Captain

Edward Curzon, was the illegitimate son of a peer.[49] During the three years 1831–33 inclusive twenty-four of the navy's 3,218 lieutenants were promoted to commander. But whereas seventeen of them had been lieutenants since 1825 or earlier (with six of them serving thus since 1815 or earlier), the fast-track promotions went almost entirely to the social elite. Of the six men promoted after being commissioned as lieutenants only since 1829, three were sons of peers and one was Vice Admiral Sir Edward Codrington's son. The lucky aristocratic few included the 'reform' prime minister's grandson, George Grey.[50]

Networking among the elite was advanced by various means. Senior army, later joined by naval, officers determined in 1815 to establish a club in London where 'acquaintance formed on service' could be maintained. Although initially looked upon with suspicion by ministers and MPs, the United Services Club won government approval and by 1833 had a membership limited to 1,500 senior officers and a prestigious building in central London. In the light of the physical presence of so palpable a lobby, Wellington discouraged officers on leave or on half-pay from wearing uniform when in London, in order to deflect criticism of military spending provoked by such military display.[51] The aristocracy's and gentry's leadership of the armed forces helped to civilianize British military culture in other ways. The army and navy did not stand apart as distinctive institutions led by men with interests and loyalties centred solely or even principally upon their particular service. Instead, service leadership blended smoothly into social and political leadership. This phenomenon was clear in 1830 when political power changed hands in the most dramatic way for nearly fifty years. The Tory government was led by Wellington, the only British general whose military fame helped him secure the prime ministership. Among his senior colleagues were Lord Aberdeen, the Foreign Secretary, whose brother was killed at Waterloo, and Robert Peel, whose father-in-law was a general. The new Whig ministry was headed by Lord Grey, whose father had commanded the forces in the West Indies in 1793–94 and one of whose sons, a lieutenant colonel, acted as the new prime minister's private secretary. His more prominent colleagues included Lord Palmerston, who had won a school prize for a Latin verse on Nelson's victory at the Nile and later served enthusiastically as a volunteer officer, Lord Althorp, whose brother had commanded a ship at the battle of Navarino in 1827, and Lord John Russell, whose brother had fought in the peninsula. Among the fourteen members of Grey's cabinet, three were the sons and one was the grandson of generals. The British establishment was neither besotted by military and naval institutions and power nor alienated from them. Those institutions were simply part of the fabric of customary family and public life.

The widespread concern in the late eighteenth century that prolonged engagement in war would strengthen the traditional landowning elite was proved correct. Warfare and the expansion of empire helped, together with rising income from landed estates, to remake the ruling landowning class. Its numbers were replenished, its values were reburnished, its leadership role was reinstated, and its self-confidence was reinforced. By giving due weight in any account of 1790–1830 to war and the expansion of empire, we are better able to understand why a period when so much attention has been directed at the making of the working class and the politicization of the middle class also witnessed the resilience and durability of the aristocratic and gentry elite. War cast a long shadow on nineteenth-century Britain.

Notes and references

1 A fine introduction to a wide variety of approaches is Kathleen Wilson (ed.), *A New Imperial History: Culture, Identity and Modernity in Britain and the Empire 1660–1840* (Cambridge, 2004).

2 Boyd Hilton, *A Mad, Bad, and Dangerous People? England 1783–1848* (Oxford, 2006), pp. 133–41 reviews the arguments for aristocratic revival while recording scepticism about them. The military element, as C.A. Bayly hinted (*Imperial Meridian: the British Empire and the World 1780–1830*, London, 1989, pp. 126–29, 133–36, 253), was too central to be as systematically overlooked as it customarily remains. The conventional view, that the wars of 1793–1815 had limited direct impact at home and little affected the affluent classes, is stated by Asa Briggs, *The Age of Improvement, 1783–1867* (London, 1959), p. 167.

3 Norman Gash, *Aristocracy and People: Britain 1815–1865* (London, 1979), pp. 73–81.

4 E.A. Smith, *Lord Grey 1764–1845* (Oxford, 1990), pp. 208–09.

5 Peter Mandler, *Aristocratic Government in the Age of Reform: Whigs and Liberals, 1830–1852* (Oxford, 1990), pp. 1–8.

6 T.C.W. Blanning, *Reform and Revolution in Mainz 1743–1803* (Cambridge, 1974), p. 309; Edgar Melton, 'The Prussian Junkers, 1600–1786' in H.M. Scott (ed.), *The European Nobilities in the Seventeenth and Eighteenth Centuries*, 2 vols (London, 1995), Vol. II, pp. 71–109, esp. pp. 95–100; Dennis E. Showalter, 'The Prussian military state' in Geoff Mortimer (ed.), *Early Modern Military History, 1450–1815* (Basingstoke, 2004), pp. 118–34;

Christopher Clark, *Iron Kingdom* (London, 2006), pp. 157–58; Martin Kitchen, *The German Officer Corps 1890–1914* (Oxford, 1968), pp. 22–24.

7 Samuel F. Scott, *The Response of the Royal Army to the French Revolution* (Oxford, 1978), p. 203.

8 Adam Zamoyski, *1812* (London, 2004), p. 4.

9 Philip G. Dwyer, (ed.), *Napoleon and Europe* (Harlow, 2001), pp. 71–73.

10 J.C.A. Stagg, *Mr Madison's War: Politics, Diplomacy, and Warfare in the Early American Republic, 1783–1830* (Princeton, NJ, 1983), p. 330. An introduction to these issues is provided by Marcus Cunliffe, *Soldiers and Civilians: The Martial Spirit in America, 1775–1865* (London, 1968).

11 The families of prime ministers may be traced in *Sharpe's Genealogical Peerage of the British Empire*, 2 vols (London, n.d., but 1833 edn.) and the *ODNB*.

12 Bayly, *Imperial Meridian*, p. 255–56.

13 Paul Langford, *A Polite and Commercial People: England 1727–1783* (Oxford, 1989), pp. 595–600, 690–92; Paul Langford, *Public Life and Propertied Englishman 1689–1798* (Oxford, 1991), pp. 548–58, 561–69, 579–81. For a different emphasis on civic leadership, on generalized British patriotism in 1793–1815, and on the decline of militaristic patriotism after 1815, see J.E. Cookson, *The British Armed Nation 1793–1815* (Oxford, 1997), pp. 239–44, 253–54. He also stresses the importance of philanthropic associations to the post-1815 monarchy.

14 A. Aspinall (ed.), *The Later Correspondence of George III*, 5 vols (Cambridge, 1968), Vol. II, p. 627, Vol. III, p. 135.

15 Elie Halevy, *England in 1815*, translated by E.I. Watkin and D.A. Barker (London, 1961 edn), pp. 61–62, 82.

16 William Laird Clowes, *The Royal Navy: A History From the Earliest Times to the Present*, 7 vols (London, 1897–1903), Vol. IV, p. 226.

17 William St Clair, *The Godwins and the Shelleys: The Biography of a Family* (London, 1989), pp. 196–97, 215, 219–20.

18 J.R. Jones, *Britain and the World 1649–1815* (London, 1980), p. 145.

19 A.D. Harvey, *Britain in the Early Nineteenth Century* (London, 1978), pp. 21–22. Harvey (p. 6) points out that there were 9,458 armigerous families in England in 1800 and about 4,000 in Scotland. A comparison of 'aristocratic' participation in the army with Prussia or France would probably be most accurately based on a study of all those who possessed such coats of arms.

20 Aspinall (ed.), *Later Correspondence of George III*, Vol. III, pp. 622–23.

21 I have come to the figures by working through the index to Charles Dalton, *The Waterloo Roll Call* (London, 1971 edn), pp. 279–96.

22 Carl von Clausewitz, *On War*, edited and translated by Michael Howard and Peter Paret (Princeton, NJ, 1976), p. 227.

23 I sampled peers whose titles went from A to G, providing 247 peerages out of the total of 560. *Sharpe's Genealogical Peerage of the British Empire*, Vol. I.

24 For an excellent discussion, see Cookson, *The British Armed Nation*, pp. 130–44.

25 *Volunteers' Additional Act: Returns from April 1803: Parliamentary Papers 1803–06*, pp. 7–8, 27–28.

26 William Hague, *William Pitt the Younger* (London, 2004), pp. 520–21.

27 They are listed in W.S. Moorsom, *Historical Record of the Fifty-Second Regiment . . . 1775–1858* (London, 1860), pp. 91–92.

28 R.J.B. Muir and C.J. Esdaile, 'Strategic planning in a time of small government: The wars against revolutionary and Napoleonic France, 1793–1815' in C.M. Woolgar (ed.), *Wellington Studies I* (Southampton, 1996), pp. 1–90, esp. pp. 71–79.

29 Bayly, *Imperial Meridian*, pp. 133–36, 160, 194–95.

30 *The Annual Register . . . for 1783*, 2nd edn (London, 1800), pp. 36, 38–40.

31 *The Royal Military Panorama or Officer's Companion* Vol. III (1813–14), p. 101; Vol. II (1813), pp. 396, 297; Vol. III (1813–14), pp. 216, 4, 411; Vol. IV (1814), pp. 3, 12.

32 *The Royal Military Panorama*, Vol. I (1812–13), p. 406.

33 *The Annual Register . . . for 1783*, p. 40.

34 *The Military Panorama*, Vol. I (1812–13), pp. 8, 15, 17, 497–98; Vol. II (1813), pp. 102, 200, 202, 205, 207, 396; Vol. IV (1814), pp. 4, 6, 9, 12, 101.

35 Cookson, *The British Nation Armed*, pp. 242–45, 250–52; Hilton, *A Mad, Bad, and Dangerous People?*, p. 137.

36 'Estimates of army services for the year 1819', *Estimates and Accounts . . . Session 21 January–13 July, 1819*, Vol. XV, pp. 40–41; 'Estimates on the charge of the Office of Ordnance . . . 1819', *ibid.*, p. 137.

37 Kathryn Beresford, 'The "Men of Kent" and the Penenden Heath meeting, 1828', *Archaeologia Cantiana*, CXXV (2005), pp. 151–71; ' "Men of Kent": Militarism and masculinities, 1815–1837', unpublished paper.

38 E.J. Hobsbawm and George Rude, *Captain Swing* (London, 1973 edn), pp. 59, 62; Charles C.F. Greville, *The Greville Memoirs: A Journal of the Reigns of King George IV and King William IV*, ed. by Henry Reeve, 3 vols (London, 1874), Vol. II, pp. 68, 77, 99, 108.

39 WP4/2/2/9 and WP4/2/2/21, Wellington Papers, University of Southampton.

40 Hobsbawm and Rude, *Captain Swing*, p. 218.

41 Greville, *Memoirs*, pp. 67–68, 183.

42 Hobsbawm and Rude, *Captain Swing*, pp. 224–25.

43 Thomas Bartlett, 'Indiscipline and disaffection in the French and Irish armies during the revolutionary period' in H. Gough and D. Dickson, *Ireland and the French Revolution* (Dublin, 1990), pp. 179–201, esp. pp. 195–96. Bartlett makes the point for the 1790s, but it can be extended to 1830.

44 Greville, *The Greville Memoirs*, p. 77.

45 J.L. Randall, *A History of the Meynell Hounds and Country 1780 to 1901* (London, 1901), pp. 61–62; 'Returns of the various Corps of Yeomanry Cavalry in England and Wales', *Estimates and Accounts*, Session 6 December 1831–16 August 1832, Vol. XXVII (1831–1832), pp. 455–57; *The British Imperial Calendar for . . . 1831* (London, 1830), p. 144.

46 Hew Strachan, 'The British Army's legacy from the Revolutionary and Napoleonic Wars' in Alan Guy (ed.), *The Road to Waterloo* (London, 1990), pp. 197–205, esp. p. 198.

47 *The British Imperial Calendar for . . . 1831*, pp. 73–75, 159–76.

48 Colonel Hugh Pearse, *Memoir of the Life and Military Services of Viscount Lake* (Edinburgh, 1908), pp. 421–27; Charles Ross (ed.), *Correspondence of Charles, First Marquis Cornwallis*, 3 vols (London, 1859), Vol. I, table opposite p. 1.

49 Clowes, *The Royal Navy*, Vol. V, pp. 128, 163; Vol. VI, p. 256; *ODNB* entries.

50 'Returns of the number of Midshipmen promoted to be Lieutenants', House of Commons *Sessional Papers: Accounts and Papers* 1833 (57), pp. 280–81. Other samples would be less dramatically skewed, but this shows how establishment influence periodically worked.

51 Louis C. Jackson, *History of the United Services Club* (London, 1937), pp. 1, 3, 6, 9, 25, 30, 37.

CHAPTER 18

Interventions overseas, 1820–30

Great Power status after 1815

Let us consider two propositions concerning the international order after 1815. First, the long wars have been depicted as decisive for Britain's geopolitical position. J.R. Jones concluded that 'Britain emerged in the years 1810–14 as the first authentic world power'. According to Michael Duffy, 'Britain's long wars against Revolutionary France and against Napoleon . . . resulted in the most complete triumph in the great age of European imperial warfare and left her as the predominant maritime and imperial power', while Jeremy Black claimed that 'In 1815 Britain was the strongest state in the world' and Peter Padfield, reflecting a navalist position, saw Britain in 1815 as 'the supreme world power'.[1] The period 1815–48 has been characterized as one of opportunity 'when Britain was almost without competitors in what proved to be key areas of expansion'.[2]

Second, this great increase in British power occurred within a context where the conduct of international relations was transformed. According to Paul Schroeder, international disputes were resolved for the first time through concerted negotiation by countries treating each other as equals. The system made manifest at the congress of Vienna in 1814–15 did not depend upon a competitive balance of power between militarized rivals. Nor did it flow from the assertion of priorities by an overwhelmingly potent 'hegemon' capable of securing adherence or obedience from other powers through the threat of force, implicit or overt, or through its superior resources or political and 'cultural' influence – the 'soft' power emphasized by the American political scientist, Joseph Nye. The system relied instead upon a genuine determination by Austria, Britain, France, Prussia and Russia to reach consensual decisions and to avoid the recurrent warfare of 1792–1815. Underpinned by a conservative determination to maintain the prevailing social order and, when necessary, to repress liberal political dissent, it rejected the competitive approach to eighteenth-century international relations in which recourse to war was an acceptable and inevitable part of the conduct of foreign policy.[3]

Both these propositions need strong qualification. First, Britain's position was strengthened but not revolutionized after 1815. A review of British overseas policy demonstrates that British power was peculiarly fragmented. Instead of being a superpower, Britain deployed naval and military strength throughout the world, but rarely in locally overwhelming strength outside its generally confined possessions. Even in India, the paramountcy achieved by 1819 was not easily transferable into a military predominance capable of meeting all the geopolitical challenges which the British faced without additional and considerable effort.

Nor was Britain, in pursuing or defending its interests in disparate regions across the globe, constrained by the Congress system. The Schroeder model of consensual Great Power diplomacy was compatible with British militarism because the two major powers strengthened by the long wars of 1792–1815, Britain and Russia, enjoyed wide spheres of influence outside continental Europe. Potential for conflict between them existed outside Europe as Russia expanded its empire rapidly into central Asia and began, by the late 1820s, to threaten British interests in the Middle East and India, yet, even if tensions deepened in the 1830s, they did not trigger direct confrontation. More important, in the argument advanced by Schroeder, 'most European states considered Britain's use of its naval power tolerable, even beneficial', while 'the way the British after 1815 ran their formal and informal overseas empire clearly contributed to stability, at least in Europe'.[4] The British emphasis after 1815 on spreading free trade and limiting its armed forces in Europe underscored this impression of a state devoted to peacekeeping and even international altruism.

Yet the stress upon European consensus-building plays down two elements in the post-1815 Great Power system. France continued to be widely viewed as the potential destabilizer of the continental order. Lord Palmerston, who directed British foreign policy-making for much of the period from 1830 until his death in 1865, noted in 1830: 'The policy of France is like an infection clinging to the walls of the dwelling, and breaking out in every successive occupant who comes within their influence.'[5] Nor was this perception merely a Palmerstonian prejudice. When Clausewitz in the early 1830s reflected extensively on the long wars, he did not suggest that Europe had entered a new era of stability brought about by the overwhelming and successful use of force against Napoleon. Instead, he recommended the strategy which an alliance of Austria, Britain, the Netherlands, the North German states and Prussia should adopt in a future war against France. With two massive thrusts towards Paris and the Loire and decisive battle as the objectives, 'France can be brought to her knees and taught a lesson any time she chooses to resume that insolent behavior with which she has burdened Europe for a hundred and fifty years'. His only concern was that political moves to develop a German federal state would weaken the natural centres of German power, Austria and Prussia: 'Theirs is the genuine striking-power, theirs is the strong blade. Each is a monarchy, experienced in war.'[6] The greatest contemporary student of the age of revolutionary warfare thus predicted the continuation of international rivalries by the usual means and insisted that the surest guarantor of international peace remained the conservative social and political order.

The second qualification is that war remained an instrument of policy resorted to by the powers individually in their colonial spheres while being almost too dangerous to employ between the Great Powers in Europe. Britain did not condone French and Russian expansionism, but concluded both that it occurred where such expansion did not threaten British interests and that Britain could do nothing to prevent it.

This cautious position qualifies the claim that Britain emerged in 1815 as a dominant world power. The very idea of domination and acting as a world power in fact exaggerates the extent of British intentions for the post-war world. The foreign policy shaped by Lord Castlereagh, a northern Irish landowner who had experienced the horrors of rebellion as Chief Secretary for Ireland during 1798, preserved an aristocratic and monarchical order throughout Europe. Although popular movements directed towards Napoleon's overthrow had been acceptable, legitimacy took precedence over liberalization after 1815. Britain supported constitutional reform where it was compatible with monarchical restoration, as in France, Holland and Sweden. Yet when confronted with obstacles to liberal reform – as in Spain and Italy – the British government accepted the political realities created by legitimist authority.[7] Such conservatism did not escape criticism. From his position of command in Sicily, Lieutenant General Lord William Bentinck, son of a former prime minister, most notably wanted in 1814 to promote the creation of a united Italy. But the initiatives he took in recognizing the restored Genoese republic after his troops secured Genoa from the French, and the policies he proposed for Italy, were rejected by ministers in London.

Britain sought to contain French ambitions in the Low Countries and to restore the Bourbons, albeit with constitutional trappings. Abiding war aims were achieved by neutralizing the arsenals at Antwerp and creating in the United Netherlands a buffer against French expansionism. To compensate for retaining the Dutch colony at the Cape of Good Hope, Britain paid Holland £2 million and earmarked that sum for strengthening the newly expanded country's border fortresses against France. To balance such cautionary measures, the settlement deprived the restored Bourbon monarchy of little territory, merely confining France to its boundaries of 1790. But France had to pay a vast indemnity and meet the costs of a huge army of occupation for three to five years.[8] The allies' acceptance of French territorial integrity was partly an inducement to the French to accept the return of Louis XVIII, the uninspiring but politically accommodating brother of the guillotined Louis XVI, who in 1813 had been the favoured candidate for the crown only of the British government. Seeing himself in a paternalistic and politically healing role, Louis readily granted a constitution, on condition that it emanated from him as monarch and not from any political group. Since Louis had no sons, the succession would go (in 1824) to his younger brother, the Comte d'Artois, an energetic and vengeful reactionary who believed passionately in the melding of religious and national ideals. Charles X's objections to the constitutionalism accepted by his brother inspired a favourite remark that he would rather saw wood than govern England.[9] Despite efforts to purge the army command in favour of Bourbon legitimists in 1814–17, Bonapartism remained strong among the soldiery, while pay and conditions engendered boredom, demoralization and disaffection from the regime by the late 1820s. Wellington in 1823 asserted that the military 'are the real government' who 'could overthrow the Bourbons' if they wished to, but instead underpinned the monarchy's more autocratic tendencies.[10]

Although Britain promoted a relatively weak but stable regime in Paris, it did not covet France's colonies. A cabinet memorandum of early 1814 indicated Britain's willingness 'with certain exceptions to sacrifice these conquests for the welfare of the continent, being desirous of providing for her own security by a common arrangement rather than by an exclusive accumulation of strength and power'. Colonies taken during the previous two decades were returned in 1814, except for Mauritius, Tobago, and St Lucia. The first was an island in the Indian Ocean which could, in French hands, threaten the sea route to India. The only French colony kept in 1815 for commercial reasons was the Caribbean island of Tobago, where the British had placed large wartime investments and which had been British before the 1780s anyway.[11] St Lucia, lying south of Martinique (the rich sugar island returned to France), had been disputed for many decades by the British and French. Its main asset was the long bay and yet another fine harbour, desired by the Admiralty, where the main port of Castries was sited. But the British government was not un-animous even on the extensions of the empire which occurred in 1815; the prime minister, Lord Liverpool, in his quest for immediate and massive post-war financial savings, expressed serious reservations about the costs of additional garrisons which Britain was acquiring worldwide.[12]

Despite such relative moderation in its treatment of post-war France, Britain ended the long European wars in 1815 with forty-three colonies, a striking advance on the twenty-six of 1793. The Dutch, having been so easily taken over by France during the wars, lost heavily; three small sugar-producing settlements in northern South America – Demerara, Essequibo, and Berbice – were kept by Britain, as were Ceylon (Sri Lanka) for its capacious harbour at Trincomalee, and Cape Colony for its posi-tion on the route to India and for its capacity to supply suitable foodstuffs to ships travelling that route. Other acquisitions were added to the defence of strategic sea routes, notably Malta and the Ionian Islands in the Mediterranean and Ascension Island in the Atlantic. Perhaps because the British had controlled most of these new possessions for a number of years, their retention in 1815 made little political or public impact. More-over, most of them were geographically small and contained few people; even Cape Colony's population was only 75,000 (including merely 25,757 Europeans) in 1806.[13] When compared with the riches and populations of northern Italy, where the Habsburgs made substantial gains in 1814–15, or the territorial scale and population of Poland whose dismemberment was so important to Prussia and Russia, as well as Austria, Britain's expansionism resulting from two decades of war against France seemed insignificant indeed.

Perhaps it was because political and 'public' opinion was generally so indifferent to India, and because the British took so long to defeat the 'real' enemy, Napoleon, and even then had to fight and beat him again when he made his dramatic return to power in 1815, that they made so little, in rhetoric or in ideological terms, of the new empire they had gained. Moreover, British governments' focus on the continental balance of power and the containment of France disguised rather than reflected the realities of British global power.

These contradictions British concerning imperial gains do not suggest the strength normally associated with a world superpower. It is important therefore to consider Britain's conduct of overseas policy in the post-war period because what happened and, in striking instances, what did not happen in the 1820s revealed Britain's limitations as well as strengths as a state operating on a global scale.

Relations with Spain and Portugal in the 1820s

Britain's closest wartime partner, Spain, suffered more than any other European power from the consequences of resisting France for a continuous period unmatched elsewhere. The restored royal government's failure to find a political accommodation with its Latin American colonies opened major economic advantages to Britain, even though it also exposed Spain itself to expanded French influence. A variety of possible ways of preserving the link between the Latin America colonies, including colonial representation in Madrid, were aired in the early 1810s and during the liberal revolution in Spain in 1820–23, but Ferdinand VII refused to accept either power-sharing or, for example, an independent Mexico under himself or his brother as emperor. By 1818–20 Spanish ministers leaned towards military suppression. The navy, possessing only twenty-four seaworthy line ships and frigates in 1814, complained that it lacked the resources to coerce the colonies. Small army contingents fought bitter campaigns against insurgents from 1815, but Spain sent only 27,342 troops from the mother country to Latin America from 1814 to 1821. Service in the New World bred discontent and when, eventually, an army of 14,000 was assembled at Cadiz to sail to Buenos Aires, units within it rose in revolt in January 1820. Rebel officers forced the king to accede to the liberal constitution of 1812 which he had so summarily rejected on being restored to the throne in 1814. By 1823, when Ferdinand reasserted his autocracy, Mexico, Colombia and Buenos Aires province were already independent in practice, and the king realized that the empire in America was lost.

Although the movement to Latin American independence, confirmed *de facto* by 1825, was delayed by royalist counter-attacks within Latin America and by spasms of extreme violence, the colonial crisis demonstrated the restoration army's weakness. The army was riddled with tensions between royalist returnees, liberals who wanted to advance French-inspired reforms, and former guerrilla leaders who resented the restored authority of regular army officers and the denial of their local autonomy and influence.[14] Spanish military capability became by the 1820s as enfeebled as Spanish naval power had been after 1805. Given such weakness, and following three years of acute political uncertainty and spasmodic and localized army revolts, the conservative French ministry, with a recently installed quixotic Romantic, the Comte de Chateaubriand, as Foreign Minister, decided to intervene in 1823 with 100,000 troops, in order to overturn the liberal constitution.[15] The resulting assertion of French influence over Spain, which Napoleon had failed to establish, encouraged the French government to consider intervening on the side of absolutism in Portugal as well.

The British government's position was conditioned by various factors. First, the British consistently rejected the doctrine that the Great Powers could and should intervene to overthrow revolutionary governments by force, as reasserted by Russia, Prussia and Austria at Troppau in October 1820. If there were to be interventions, British ministers worked to restrict the numbers of Great Powers involved in them, so that in late 1822 Wellington, a member of the cabinet, prevented the Congress of Verona authorizing a general expedition against Spain.[16] Second, in considering intervening in Spain or in neighbouring Portugal to prop up a friendly government there, the British weighed the extent and limitations of their own power. As early as December 1814, Wellington noted of Portugal, 'Nations are never so grateful as their benefactors expect'.[17] In February 1823, when considering British responses to the French intervention in Spain, he observed to Canning, by now Foreign Secretary, that although 'the sober-minded and reasonable people' in Britain wanted peace, 'it does not appear that it would be very difficult to rouse the country to war if war should be necessary'. At the same time, he insisted that a limited intervention based on sea power alone would not deliver British objectives:

It is the greatest mistake to suppose that if we enter into this or any war we can do it by halves, or confine our operations to one branch of our military power and resource. We must deploy our whole force by land as well as by sea . . .[18]

Ships alone would not force the French to raise their sieges of Barcelona and other ports on the coasts of Catalonia and Valencia. On the other hand, if the Spanish liberals fortified and defended the Isla De Leon at Cadiz in the same way as the British had done during the Peninsular War, then the French siege of Cadiz would fail even without British intervention. Worse, limited intervention might provoke other European powers into war against Britain, in which case sea power would only enable the

British to take French colonies, none of which were of any value to Britain.[19]

A more immediate concern to Wellington was that French intervention in Spain might enable French troops to support the absolutist faction in Portugal. The duke argued in July 1823 that 6,000 British troops should be despatched to Portugal to act against troops or militia rebelling against the king, since a naval squadron sent to the Tagus River would not suffice to deter French intervention against the constitutionalist government in Lisbon. The prime minister, Lord Liverpool, objected that Britain could not become involved on the grounds of a potential – as distinct from an actual – internal danger. Nor did he see an imminent threat from the overstretched French. He also doubted that 6,000 men would suffice, challenging Wellington instead to consider the likely requirement to be 12,000 to 20,000 troops. Yet Liverpool also felt constrained by military and political pressures from even a modest intervention. The British army was fully committed, acute problems were pressing in Ireland, and Parliament would have to be recalled to approve any significant despatch of troops. The clear implication was that the prime minister did not see that parliamentary approval would be readily forthcoming. Wellington had earlier conceded the general principle that naval interventions seemed politically more attractive for the non-military reason that parliament and the press made less fuss about naval deployments than about the despatch of troops overseas.[20]

Thwarted by the apparent lack of political will to intervene in Portugal, Wellington came up with alternative proposals in July 1824. Demonstrating how a Great Power might use its disparate assets flexibly, the duke suggested sending 6,200 Hanoverian troops, paid for by the Portuguese government, to operate on strict guidelines within a specific geographical area in and around Lisbon. The British would contribute royal marines sent to garrison the forts on the Tagus River, thus providing security for British ships in the harbour, and safeguarding the Hanoverians' disembarkation. News of this scheme unsurprisingly provoked opposition when it reached Portugal. Wellington lamely conceded that, despite all his earlier insistence on substantial land forces being needed, a naval squadron with royal marines might indeed prevent all 'mischief'.[21]

Mounting tensions between constitutionalists and absolutists in Portugal led eventually, after three years' discussion, to British intervention. Throughout that period, ministers, whatever their own inclination to think globally, clearly believed that Parliament required them to exercise geopolitical restraint. When intervention was proposed in response to an intensified power struggle in late 1826, Canning as Foreign Secretary popularized its contribution to the advance of European constitutionalism. Countering criticisms of the ministry's inability to remove the French from Spain, where they remained until 1828, Canning boasted in December 1826 that he had denied France the most threatening gains that might have been derived from her peninsular intervention by positively fostering the independence of Spain's Latin American empire. He memorably inflated his accomplishment:

Contemplating Spain, such as our ancestors had known her, I resolved that if France had Spain, it should not be Spain 'with the Indies'. I called the New World into existence to redress the balance of the old.[22]

A modest intervention in Portugal was thus justified by reference to possible French Latin American ambitions and, more broadly, to the commercial benefits for Britain which a liberal foreign policy towards the former Spanish colonies had produced. Parliament agreed to intervention to enable the Portuguese government to defeat absolutists who, having earlier fled to Spain, moved back across the border in armed strength during November 1826. Canning had already insisted that Portugal 'has been, and always *must* be English so long as Europe and the world remain in anything like their present state'.[23] In despatching 5,000 troops to back the constitutionalist order, Canning told the Commons:

We go to Portugal, not to rule, not to dictate, not to prescribe constitutions, but to defend and to preserve the independence of an ally. We go to plant the standard of England on the well-known heights of Lisbon. Where that standard is planted, foreign dominion shall not come.[24]

This pressure produced the desired result in the short term. The end of 1827 witnessed Ferdinand of Spain's recognition of the Regency in Lisbon and the Portuguese expulsion of absolutist forces.[25] By April 1828 British troops had returned home.

Yet this withdrawal demonstrated the transience of British influence, since it opened the way to resurgent absolutist activity when the infant Queen Maria II's uncle, Dom Miguel, seized power in 1828 after British forces left Lisbon. Having cooperated with the French in Greece in 1827–28 and having seen a French withdrawal from Spain, a new ministry discerned no grounds for further British intervention. Wellington pointed out that his earlier advocacy of intervention flowed from the desire to thwart external interference, whereas any decision to install Miguel as king became a matter for the Portuguese.[26] The cause of Canningite liberal interventionism found a new champion in Lord Palmerston, a former minister who had defected from the Tories. In 1829 he denounced neutrality for succouring the self-proclaimed King Miguel:

this destroyer of constitutional freedom, this breaker of solemn oaths, this faithless usurper, this enslaver of his country, this trampler upon public law, this violator of private rights . . .

Faced with such an ogre, Palmerston advanced a remarkably flexible precept for involvement short of intervention:

if by interference is meant intermeddling, and intermeddling in every way, and to every extent, short of actual military force, then I must affirm that there is nothing in such interference, which the laws of nations may not in certain cases permit.

Just as a bystander might interfere 'to prevent a breach of the law', Palmerston insisted, so any country could 'interpose to prevent a flagrant violation of the laws of the community of nations'.[27] On becoming Foreign Secretary, from late 1830, Palmerston failed to persuade his Whig cabinet colleagues to authorize British involvement and so he resorted to covert assistance to Miguel's opponents.[28] In July 1833 Captain Charles Napier, having been dismissed from the Royal Navy the day before news of the engagement reached London, defeated Miguel's fleet off Cape St Vincent.[29] By mid-October, having recognized Maria II as queen, the British sent more arms to her adherents and opened the way for the passage of 2,500 volunteers to fight for her cause; the volunteers were described as 'Belgians' even though no more than 400 of them were non-British.[30] The following March Miguel gave up all claims to the throne and quit Portugal for ever, leading to the restoration of the 15-year-old Maria and a declaration that she was of age to reign.[31]

The political contest in Portugal from 1823 to 1834 demonstrated the severe limitations, irrespective of Palmerston's rhetoric, on British ability and willingness to intervene. Despite the close military alliance forged from 1809 to 1814, Canning's claims about the country's vital importance to Britain, and key ministers' willingness to deploy a deterrent force in Lisbon, Parliament evinced no enthusiasm for an assertive policy. The critical political shift which led to Miguel's defeat was not British policy, but the change of regime in France in 1830. Louis Philippe's constitutional and non-clericalist government no longer backed absolutism in Spain, and no longer, through that route, provided encouragement and support for absolutism in Portugal. For his part, Wellington as premier in 1828–30 justified non-intervention on the grounds that the threat to stability came then not from French intervention but from purely internal rivalries. But it has been pointed out that the main constraint upon British policy was not an attachment to a European balance of power. More pertinently, the British government lacked the military means to intervene and feared that Parliament, enmeshed in a protracted political crisis, would not accept intervention.[32]

The other factor shaping British political reluctance to re-enter the peninsula was, of course, the collapse of Spain's Latin American empire. British interest in opening and developing trade with Spanish Latin America informed Britain's relations with Spain from the 1780s. Once Spain allied itself to France, ministers sought to exclude France from Latin America. Britain was wary from 1807 onwards about encouraging Latin American rebellions, yet could exert little direct influence because most centres of economic and political strength were far inland, beyond the reach of British naval power.[33] The mainland colony most accessible to the sea – Rio de la Plata – held only 400,000 of Spanish America's 17 million people in the 1800s. A military expedition to its main town of Buenos Aires in 1806 stimulated extraordinary public interest in trading with the River Plate region of what is today Argentina. As revolts and revolutions spread in the 1810s and especially from 1820, the British worked to increase their influence with the Spanish colonies in revolt, and to separate political developments in Latin America from those in the Iberian peninsula; few whites living in the empire had been born in Spain and they were often much resented by the colonial whites. When George Canning became Foreign Secretary in 1822, at the height of the revolutionary upsurge, he gave greater urgency and prominence to what was already an established policy of edging towards recognizing Latin American states' independence. Wellington, however, opposed giving political recognition to revolutionary leaders such as Simon Bolivar, on the grounds that such recognition raised an objectionable precedent at a time when the British authorities continued to confront potential revolutionaries in Ireland. But by 1825 Canning persuaded or cajoled his cabinet colleagues to accord British diplomatic recognition, driven by a desire to extend commercial access, to Buenos Aires, Colombia and Mexico. This came after two years of a booming London market for bonds issued to the new governments and for investment in mining. British exports to Latin America were running at double their late eighteenth-century totals.[34] Wellington continued to complain about the inconsistency of Canning's policy, and queried the credibility of Canning's concerns about French intentions towards Spanish Latin America when France intervened in Spain. After all, British commercial interests had already benefited once the Latin American revolutions of 1808–11 opened the continent to direct British trade, and the most important market for British exports in Latin America was the Portuguese Empire in Brazil, which was only tangentially affected by the threat from French intervention in Spain.[35]

The collapse of Spain between the 1780s and the 1820s marked one of the great shifts of international power in European history. The British destroyed the Spanish navy; the French helped undermine the Spanish army, although an inefficient officer corps, lack of charismatic generalship and deeply particularist politics contributed much to that decline; and Spanish royal policy, colonial nationalism and determined local leadership broke the Latin American empire. The fact that France from 1823 to 1828 exerted considerable sway over Spain was less worrying than such dominance would have been earlier, because the one Spanish war-fighting asset which would have threatened the British if in French hands, its navy, had been reduced to insignificance. Equally important, the British had gained access to Latin America essentially by watching and waiting. On the other hand, safeguarding Portugal had proved frustrating to ministers and had involved them in devising or implementing some curious expedients to bypass Parliament and secure troops for its defence.

Mediterranean involvement

If British involvement in the decline of the Spanish American empire accentuated one element in wartime policy, Britain's interest in the Ottoman Empire's fate grew out of geostrategic concerns developed during the long wars. Although Britain had established trading interests in the eastern Mediterranean before the 1790s, the attempt by Napoleon to gain control of Egypt and extend French power along the coast of what is nowadays Lebanon and Syria gave an entirely new strategic significance to the region. British interest acquired further political momentum with the rising in April 1821 of Greeks attempting to overthrow Turkish rule. The Greeks primarily looked to Russia for aid on the grounds of shared Orthodox religious faith and because Russia, at least initially, was not committed to maintaining a strong Ottoman Empire. It was said that Tsar Alexander I saw the Greek revolt as a way of providing an outlet for the restless ambitions of the Russian army. But the Russian position was bound to be ambiguous since the absolutist tsar of an empire composed of widely divergent people was scarcely likely to be a wholehearted advocate of Greek independence secured by a popular revolt. Many Greek nationalists, having in the 1810s exaggerated the extent of Russian support for their cause, came by 1824 to suspect that Alexander was more interested in Russian success against the Ottomans than in an independent Greece. British interest in the Greek cause – and there were many private citizens who held strong philhellene sympathies – became more significant to the Greeks as suspicions of Russian commitments increased in the mid-1820s. Initial British official reactions manifested little concern for the Greeks' aspirations, with Canning describing the Greeks, who were deeply divided between Westernizers and traditionalists, as 'a most rascally set'. The underlying concern was instead to limit Russian gains and to support the Ottoman Empire as a major regional power and buffer against Russian expansionism. Canning in 1823 made Britain the first power to recognize the Greeks as belligerents, but sought to retain ultimate Turkish suzerainty and to limit the growth of Russian influence in any new political dispensation which might emerge.[36]

In 1825, following years of sometimes vicious fighting, a Turkish force under Ibrahim Pasha – son of the viceroy of Egypt, Mehemet Ali – landed in the Morea, or Peloponnese peninsula, to crush the successful rising there. Rumours that the Pasha had extensive plans for ethnic cleansing in that region, as well as intensified philhellene public pressure, led Britain, in April 1826, to join Russia in offering to broker a diplomatic settlement involving a self-governing Greece under Turkish sovereignty. Although Turkey settled some border disputes with Russia later in the year, the Turkish government declined to compromise when the Greeks dropped their claim to complete independence. By early 1827 the British ambassador at Constantinople, Stratford Canning, the Foreign Secretary's cousin, concluded that only force would budge the Turks. In July 1827, following the Egyptian army's capture of Athens, Britain, France and Russia agreed to mediate once the Ottoman Empire and the Greeks negotiated an armistice, and to work to achieve a self-governing Greece under Turkish sovereignty. A secret clause in the allies' agreement committed them to using force to end the fighting between Turkey and the Greeks if necessary. Allied naval intervention was intended to prevent Ibrahim Pasha from reinforcing the Morea from Egypt. The British felt that a collaborative approach would help them control especially Russian and also French naval involvement in the region, which would have occurred irrespective of British involvement. They went out of their way to offer naval supplies from Malta to their new partners, partly to forestall any ambitions those partners might have to secure naval bases of their own in the eastern Mediterranean.[37]

On 11 September, Vice Admiral Sir Edward Codrington's fleet arrived off Navarino Bay – easily accessible from the British-held Ionian islands – as part of the allied effort to keep Ibrahim's forces and the Greeks in the Morea apart. The Egyptian contingent had arrived there only a few days before Codrington. Once joined by the French, the allies met Ibrahim to stress the seriousness of the situation and of their orders. But Ibrahim, after putting to sea on 2 October with the intention of making for the eastern Morea, returned to his anchorage when warned off by the British, whose orders authorized them to engage the Egyptian force on the high seas to prevent the redeployment of Ottoman troops. On 15 October the Russian squadron arrived, and the allies faced the dilemma that blockading the bay all winter would be costly and would expose the blockading fleets to dispersal by storms, thereby enabling Ibrahim to escape and reinforce or resupply Turkish operations in the eastern Morea and the islands. Codrington focused on operational issues, claiming to have repeatedly if fruitlessly tried to negotiate with Ibrahim. He argued that, having overcome his allies' mutual distrust, he persuaded them that the only place from which the allies could watch Ibrahim's fleet safely, or secure his adherence to the armistice suggested since August, was within Navarino Bay. On 20 October, Codrington led the allies past the Turkish guns commanding the narrow entrance and entered the broad bay. The allied fleet consisted of ten ships of the line (four of them British), ten frigates (three British) and four smaller British warships. The Turkish fleet was far larger, but did not include many battle ships: three line ships, seventeen frigates, and sixty-nine smaller gunships, accompanying forty-one transports conveying 4,000 troops. The Turks probably carried 2,240 guns to the allies' 1,276, mostly of lighter weight and lesser calibre dispersed over many smaller vessels. Although the guns were smaller, the naval firepower afloat at Navarino Bay compared with the 1,502 guns borne by the successful British battle fleet at St Vincent. The Turkish fleet was anchored in a defensive crescent and prepared for any confrontation that might ensue.[38]

The battle of Navarino was the last major naval engagement of the age of sail, the only battle fought after Trafalgar which followed Nelsonian precepts of annihilating an enemy, and the only large-scale battle the Royal Navy fought before Jutland in 1916. Yet Codrington had no orders to seek out and destroy the Ottoman expeditionary force, operating instead under instructions to intercept it at sea and to restrict its movements.[39] The entry of the allied fleet into Navarino Bay occurred in an atmosphere of high tension and some concluded that Codrington deliberately provoked a fight. One cabinet minister described him as 'a madman and a rogue'. A small British boat came under musket fire which killed a number of seamen and their young commanding officer, Lieutenant George Fitzroy, the son of a lieutenant general, grandson of a general and descendant of an illegitimate son of Charles II. Although it was rumoured that Fitzroy initiated this 'imprudent attack', the allies returned musket fire. Then an Egyptian ship fired on the French flagship, and the action became general, leading to a four-hour onslaught against the Turkish force. Codrington, who had served on Howe's flagship at the Glorious First of June in 1794 and commanded a line ship at Trafalgar, was described by a cabinet minister as an excellent and brave officer, but one likely to be 'hasty'.[40] Codrington repeated one of Nelson's celebrated orders: 'No captain can do very wrong who places his ship alongside that of an enemy.' When he informed Lady Codrington that their son had been struck during the fighting, he added that it was 'worth such a wound to have been in such a glorious battle'. Of the 130 Turkish ships in the bay, of all sizes and including the troop transports, some sixty were said to have been destroyed and all but sixteen of the rest were apparently driven ashore. Although the British line ships suffered casualties commensurate with the mid-range of losses sustained by such ships in a major battle, total allied losses from the four-hour battle were relatively minor.[41]

Reactions to this victory proved decidedly mixed. The Russians were delighted with the outcome, as were the French, despite some reservations.[42] In December the Russians went to war with Turkey, their advance on Adrianople in August 1829 forcing the Turks into recognizing Greek independence and negotiating the international boundaries for the new country. Yet the British government derived the least satisfaction from the victory. Although George IV promptly honoured and promoted officers serving in the British squadron, the Foreign Office queried the legitimacy of Codrington's actions and the procedures by which he arrived at his decision to go into battle. The government formally described the battle in January 1828 as an 'untoward event' and Codrington was recalled from his command in the Mediterranean in May 1828. The crippling of Muhammad Ali's naval power in the eastern Mediterranean helped protect British trade from possible Egyptian interference, while some politicians and publicists were enthusiastic for the Greek cause. But weakening the Ottomans ran counter to Wellington's growing distrust of Russian motives and Russian expansionism.[43] In fact, Britain in 1828-30 helped limit Russian gains.[44] The independent Greece which then emerged in 1832 was as reliant upon British and French as upon Russian support, and the new country of 750,000 people was to be ruled by a younger son of the King of Bavaria with a regency of three Bavarian senior functionaries backed up by 3,500 Bavarian troops.[45] To underscore the new monarchy's dependent status, a British warship conveyed the seventeen-year old King Otho to his new domain.

According to Professor Schroeder, the years 1823–29 were the most peaceful in Europe of any in the period 1815–48.[46] Yet, simply within Europe, British governments proactively applied force in those years to defend British interests and to deter France and Russia from making gains which disrupted or threatened to disrupt the balance of regional powers desired by Britain. In European terms, the British failed to thwart Russia and constrain France. In fact, the French re-assertion of power was remarkable. An army, commanded initially by Charles X's eldest son and heir, operated in Spain from 1823 to 1828 and stimulated a degree of working collaboration between royalist and Bonapartist officers within the French army. France then pulled off a considerable coup in the Mediterranean when Charles X decided in 1830 to distract attention from domestic political pressure for reform by seizing Algiers. Even though it failed to counterbalance the political effect of Charles's domestic policies, the expedition, involving the despatch of 38,000 troops and 4,500 horses in 572 naval and merchant ships, including eleven line ships and twenty-four frigates among the 121 armed vessels, has long been regarded as a demonstration of how effectively the Bourbons reasserted French power. *The Times*, in noting the sheer scale of the naval preparations, stressed also the inclusion of eleven steamers, 'a kind of force as yet new to naval warfare'.[47] The British government accepted that France had good grounds to seek redress for genuine grievances against the regency in Algiers, but objected to French unilateralism, especially since the Ottoman Empire, which held ultimate sovereignty over most of north Africa, had not been consulted. The British repeatedly sought assurances from the extreme right-wing government of the Prince de Polignac that France intended a punitive intervention not an invasion or actions to destroy the regime in Algiers. By 21 April 1830 the Foreign Secretary, Lord Aberdeen, confided to the ambassador in Paris:

A French army, the most numerous, it is believed, which in modern times has ever crossed the sea, is about to undertake the conquest of a territory which, from its geographical position, has always been considered as of the highest importance. No man can look without anxiety at the issue of an enterprise, the ultimate objects of which are still so uncertain and undefined.[48]

British protests failed to halt an invasion which led to a prolonged imperial venture in North Africa. The intervention meant that from 1823 to 1848 French forces were active operationally in Spain or Algeria in every year except 1829. Worse for Britain, the extension of Russian influence into the eastern Mediterranean was unwelcome in itself and was ominous alongside the growing threat posed by Russian expansion in central Asia to British India's frontiers. Already, in 1829, the minister responsible for India predicted an eventual clash between the British and the Russians on India's north-west border. Yet ministers acquiesced in French assertiveness and Russian interference in part because they believed the 'political nation' would be reluctant to accept the costs of more confrontational containment.

Military interventions and India

Similar restraint was officially desired in India. In 1823 General Lord Hastings left the governor-generalship, having earlier undertaken the most extensive campaign ever launched by the British in India. His successor, Lord Amherst, the nephew and heir of a field marshal, arrived at a time when the East India Company had enjoyed a very good financial year, had no desire for further military expeditions, and wanted to reduce spending.[49] Yet within two years the government in India engaged in two significant military campaigns initiated for quite different reasons.

The first concerned Burma where, it has been argued, borders were destabilized by both Indian and Burmese local expansionism. Burmese penetration into Assam in 1817–1822 caused friction, but greater anger in British India was provoked when the Burmese ejected a small British post from an island off the coast of Arakan where Indians were conducting a modest trade. Amherst preferred a negotiated resolution to this minor dispute, but his officials pressed him to authorize military retribution.[50] The cast of the official mind in India was perhaps reflected in an observation by Major General Sir John Malcolm, governor of Bombay, to Wellington in 1828: 'general wars . . . appear as necessary to keep armies in health and good order as the calculation of capital in the mercantile world'.[51] Major General Jasper Nicholls, later a commander-in chief in India, noted privately: 'we must fight whenever neighbouring nations think proper to throw down the gauntlet'.[52]

This readiness to fight flowed from excessively optimistic assumptions. A force of nearly 13,000 troops readily took the port of Rangoon in May 1824. But the local population failed to welcome the British as liberators with the enthusiasm anticipated, while British looting did nothing to dispel locals' distrust. The invasion coincided with the onset of the monsoon. Once the momentum of campaigning stalled, sickness became far more serious than had been envisaged, food supplies became more difficult to maintain, and the death toll from disease at Rangoon rose alarmingly. The British failed to break out of the city because the Burmese removed river boats when they evacuated the port, erected stockades on the roads inland, and simply abandoned any stockade when vigorously attacked and withdrew to another one.[53]

While the main British thrust was directed at Rangoon in the south, a British post of about 1,000 sepoys was attacked at Ramu on the frontier of eastern Bengal. In response, an additional force of 12,000 sepoys took possession of the western coastal province of Arakan in April 1825. But this army was far too severely weakened by illness to cross the Arakan mountains and move into central Burma. Meanwhile, the army from Rangoon, plentifully reinforced, consolidated its position only in December 1824 and began its advance, having organized sixty river boats to carry the guns, in February. While Prome fell in April 1825, the army failed to reach the capital, Ava, before the rainy season set in. But in 1825, unlike the previous year, supplies proved forthcoming from the local inhabitants. The British approached Ava only in January 1826, forcing the Burmese to agree to pay an indemnity, renounce any claims to Assam in their north, and cede Arakan to the west and their eastern province of Tenasserim to British India. Lord Combermere, the commander-in-chief of the army in India, discerned no advantage in holding the Tenasserim coast, but was overruled by the governor-general. The Court of Directors in London saw few gains in such acquisitions or from a war which had cost £4.8 million.[54] Wellington complained that he had insufficient information to evaluate 'whether there is now any trade or whether there is any prospect of any', and objected to these acquisitions on strategic grounds: 'In general I should say that we ought not to extend ourselves in those unwholesome countries, or involve ourselves in the political systems in that part of the world.' He preferred that such territories be exchanged for an island affording easy defence and yielding 'maritime advantages in naval affairs'.[55]

The British conduct of operations offered a customary mix of positives and negatives. The campaign was launched in aggressive, self-confident style and was conducted with determination and resilience even when initial optimism proved unfounded. Some engagements involved intense fighting and one military commentator later claimed that 'British operations . . . were, as usual, chiefly successful through bold and dashing attack . . . Our attacks were generally, as they ever should be in such regions, sharp, short, and decisive'. On the other hand, strategic planning was weakly informed by knowledge of the country and political and social conditions within it.[56] Despite initial confidence that British forces would galvanize local opposition to the regime, the campaign tended to be confined to routes where transport by water was the norm; coastal and river access to Arakan was vital in the west, and the central thrust depended largely on the Irrawaddy River. This intervention demonstrated once again the truism that military predominance came at a very high price, for Britain, the pre-eminent military power in Asia, took over twenty months and deployed about 25,000 troops to subdue a neighbour possessing only basic military capabilities.

The other unanticipated campaign of Amherst's governor-generalship involved the seizure of Bharatpur. Unlike Burma, Bharatpur was very familiar to the British, having embarrassed them in 1804–05 by its resistance to repeated and bloody assaults. A dispute over the succession of the raja erupted from August 1824, and a variety of British officials advised intervention to demonstrate British strength and resolve. In September 1825 Amherst cast aside his earlier reluctance to act and authorized intervention. Recalling the humiliating reversals of 1804–05, the army made huge preparations, gathering together 30,000 troops and much artillery. An artillery bombardment softened up the extensive defensive walls, and then three weeks of mining operations were capped by an assault on 18 January 1826. British losses proved relatively light, at fewer than 1,000 casualties for the entire siege, in sharp contrast to the heavy losses of 1804–05. Among British advantages, Bharatpur's defensive guns could not be readily manoeuvred and depressed in their angle of fire, and the attacking force enjoyed excellent access to nearby supplies of equipment and munitions from the storehouses and arsenals at Kanpur, Agra and Allahabad. Such plentiful support could be extensively tapped since it was to be paid for by charges made upon the British-backed candidate for the rulership.[57] Operations were concluded with high self-confidence among the generals, but probably owed their success to mining which went undetected by the defendants and which enabled the assailants to blow up a critical stretch of the defensive wall.[58] Combermere stressed the importance of the victory in the context of the limited military resources available for deployment in India, and in the hope that it would 'have a good effect upon the Burmese war'.[59]

These two challenging campaigns engaged about 55,000 soldiers in the mid-1820s, a period of allegedly general peace. Not surprisingly, the Court of Directors remained critical of governors-general and their territorial expansionism. There were concerns in London at the excessive increase in the size of the armies overall in India – reaching 290,834 men in 1825–26 – and particularly the large increase in the Bengal army. Concerns over size were in turn intensified by the rivalries between the different presidency armies.[60] But senior commanders insisted that their forces' fighting prowess be vigorously maintained. The commander-in-chief of the Bengal army, Major General Sir Jasper Nicholls, pressed for such improvements as more European regimental officers, more rapid promotion, and the broadening of sepoy recruitment by district and by caste, but asserted in 1827 that, given those enhancements, 'the Bengal army ought to be the finest colonial army in the world'.[61]

Conclusion

Imperial expansionism by the Great Powers was in some ways a surprising outcome from an age of revolutionary upheavals which entailed the dramatic loss of imperial possessions. The British lost their most important settler colonies in 1783; France lost its single most important colony, Saint Domingue, to an extraordinary internal insurgency in the 1790s; and Spain lost virtually all its American empire by 1830. Yet, despite the extent of territorial losses and the vigorous, compelling and indeed revolutionary challenge to the established order, Britain, France and a new participant, Russia, were all by 1830 committed to maintaining and expanding their empires by military means.

These expansionist thrusts occurred while the war-weary Great Powers in the 1820s tried to reconcile their differences by concerted diplomatic action as a distinctive *modus operandi* in international relations. But the British experience suggests that the new European order rested on political vigilance backed up by the local use of force or the threat to use force because French and Russian expansionism was not contained by negotiations and Britain was concerned at both countries' geopolitical agendas. For a country allegedly so strong internationally after 1815, Britain was frustrated in her projection of power overseas, with her role in the Iberian peninsula and in the eastern Mediterranean proving remarkably tentative, even though military and naval forces were deployed in both areas. The running was made by France in the first and Russia in the second. In India, Britain proved far more assertive and mounted two campaigns on a scale which would have been impossible in the 1790s. Even so, the British army in India found neither campaign straightforward and recognized the need to prepare militarily for future challenges. In 1828, the governor of Bombay, John Malcolm, informed Wellington that 'Persia is . . . at the fist of Russia' and that any negotiated Russian withdrawal from confrontation would prove merely temporary – 'We shall soon have the bear you are hugging for our Asiatic neighbour.' Dismissing the current Anglo-Russian rapprochement over Greece, Malcolm pressed upon the prime minister his claim to a military command in any impending Anglo-Russian war.[62] Whatever the long view, the contemporary anticipation of war, and preparation for it, did not recede.

Emphasizing a new consensus-building approach to European relations therefore plays down the continuing significance of extra-European power projection. Three of the five European Great Powers continued to pursue traditional forms of imperial aggrandizement. Russia not only confronted periodic challenges as a colonial power in Poland but maintained its expansionism into central Asia. France not only intervened in Spain but from 1830 embarked on a long imperialist war in Algeria. These actions did not flow from consensual international action.

They also revealed the limitations that Britain suffered as a world power. Frustrated at Russian and French expansionism, Britain could do nothing to check it. The post-war dilemmas Britain faced as a world power flowed from her experience of the years 1790–1815. On many issues, Britain had to act through the European concert after 1815 because she had no capacity to wage large-scale continental warfare. But the image of Britain as a global superpower, as distinct from a European power, seems equally misleading. Britain was rarely a dominant power in any one place in 1793–1815 but asserted herself by being locally powerful in many places. To depict Britain after 1815 as a great world power therefore misrepresents both the record of her achievements in the long wars of 1793–1815 and the nature of her imperial power later. During the long wars and after 1815, Britain was a regional power in many, though not all, contested areas of the world: in the North Sea area and the Low Countries, along the eastern Atlantic seaboard, in North America, in the Caribbean, in eastern Australia, in southern Africa, and in the Mediterranean. In India, the British became an increasingly hegemonic power from 1790 to 1818. In Latin America, her influence was commercial rather than military or naval. But in southern Europe, despite wartime initiatives in Italy and the huge commitment to the Iberian peninsula, Britain's post-war leverage was limited. Success at Waterloo did nothing to make Britain a player in the heartlands of Europe. The model of Britain as a world power needs therefore to be refined. Britain struggled almost everywhere to assert her power in 1790–1815. Few campaigns proved straightforward; few victories came without grievous costs. So, too, after 1815, British power proved very difficult to translate into clear geopolitical gains. But Britain remained uniquely capable of widespread power projection. It was the ability to intervene with moderate-sized military and naval forces in far more places than any other power could do that distinguished Britain as a power with global reach, even though Britain was no global superpower.

Notes and references

1 J.R. Jones, *Britain and the World, 1649–1815* (London, 1980), p. 117; Michael Duffy, ' World-wide war and British expansion, 1793–1815', in P.J. Marshall (ed.), *The Eighteenth Century* (Oxford, 1998), pp. 184–207, esp. pp. 184, 205; Jeremy Black, *Britain as a Military Power, 1688–1815* (London, 1999), p. 267; Peter Padfield, *Maritime Power and the Struggle for Freedom 1788–1851* (London, 2003), p. 351.

2 Felipe Fernandez-Armesto, 'Britain, the sea, the empire, the world' in David Cannadine (ed.), *Empire, the Sea and Global History: Britain's Maritime World c.1760–c.1840* (London, 2007), pp. 6–21, esp. pp. 15–16; Jeremy Black, *War and the World: Military Power and the Fate of Continents* (London, 1998).

3 Joseph S. Nye, Jr., *Soft Power: The Means to Success in World Politics* (New York, 2004); Paul W. Schroeder, *The Transformation of European Politics, 1763–1848* (Oxford, 1996), pp. 575–82; 797–804.

4 Schroeder, *The Transformation of European Politics*, p. 575.

5 J.R. Seeley, *The Expansion of England* (London, 1895 edn), pp. 23–24; John Lynn, *The Wars of Louis XIV, 1667–1714* (London, 1999), p. 364; Kenneth Bourne, *Palmerston: The Early Years, 1784–1841* (New York, 1982), p. 349.

6 Carl von Clausewitz, *On War*, edited and translated by Michael Howard and Peter Paret (Princeton, NJ, 1989), pp. 635–37.

7 C.J. Bartlett, *Castlereagh* (London, 1966), pp. 146–50.

8 Bartlett, *Castlereagh*, pp. 121, 136, 156.

9 Philip Mansel, *Louis XVIII* (London, 1981), pp. 163, 170–88; Dominique Bagge, *Les Idées Politiques en France sous la Restauration* (Paris, 1952), pp. 183–85.

10 Douglas Porch, *Army and Revolution: France 1815–1848* (London, 1974),
   pp. 31–33, 38; Pamela M. Pilbeam, *The 1830 Revolution in France*
   (Basingstoke, 1991), pp. 17–18; Duke of Wellington (ed.), *Despatches,
   Correspondence and Memoranda of Arthur, Duke of Wellington, KG . . .
   from 1818 to 1831*, 8 vols (London, 1867–80), Vol. II, pp. 64–5.

11 Bartlett, *Castlereagh*, pp. 134–35, 155–56; Glyndwr Williams, *The
   Expansion of Europe in the Eighteenth Century* (London, 1966),
   pp. 282–83.

12 Bartlett, *Castlereagh*, p. 136; Norman Gash, *Lord Liverpool* (London, 1984),
   pp. 107–15, 127–28 shows the prime minister's lack of ideological interest in
   empire and concerns over budgets.

13 Eric A. Walker, *A History of Southern Africa* (London, 1957 edn), p. 138.

14 Timothy E. Anna, *Spain and the Loss of America* (Lincoln, NE, 1983),
   pp. 113, 147, 158, 174–78, 189, 209, 215–21, 272–3; Brian Hamnett,
   A Concise History of Mexico (Cambridge, 1999), pp. 133–45; Carolyn Boyd,
   'The Military and Politics, 1808–1874' in Jose Alvarez Junco and Adrian
   Shubert (eds), *Spanish History since 1808* (London, 2000), pp. 64–79; Paul
   Johnson, *The Birth of the Modern: World Society 1815–1830* (London,
   1991), p. 639. Robert Harvey, *Liberators: South America's Savage Wars of
   Freedom, 1810–1830* (London, 2000) vividly describes an often-neglected
   aspect of the struggle for independence.

15 Mansel, *Louis XVIII*, pp. 393–95.

16 Wendy Hinde, *George Canning* (Oxford, 1989), pp. 322–23, 326–27.

17 Lieutenant Colonel Gurwood (ed.), *The Dispatches of Field Marshal the
   Duke of Wellington . . . from 1799 to 1815*, 12 vols (London, 1838),
   Vol. XII, p. 216.

18 Wellington (ed.), *Despatches*, Vol. II, pp. 30, 32.

19 Wellington (ed.), *Despatches*, Vol. II, pp. 32–33.

20 Wellington (ed.), *Despatches*, Vol. II, pp. 110–113.

21 Wellington (ed.), *Despatches*, Vol. II, pp. 281–84.

22 Hinde, *George Canning*, p. 422.

23 Hinde, *George Canning*, p. 375.

24 Hinde, *George Canning*, p. 421.

25 Hinde, *George Canning*, p. 424.

26 John Fortescue, *A History of the British Army*, 13 vols (London, 1900–30),
   Vol. XI, pp. 80–81.

27 Bourne, *Palmerston*, p. 299.

28 Bourne, *Palmerston*, pp. 388–95.

29 Charles C.F. Greville, *The Greville Memoirs: A Journal of the Reigns of George IV and King William IV*, ed. by Henry Reeve, 3 vols (London, 1874), Vol. III, pp. 9, 11.

30 Bourne, *Palmerston*, pp. 397–98.

31 H.V. Livermore, *A New History of Portugal* (Edinburgh, 1973), pp. 150–1.

32 P. Jupp, 'The foreign policy of Wellington's government, 1828–30' in C.M. Woolgar (ed.), *Wellington Studies III* (Southampton, 1999), pp. 152–83, esp. pp. 155–56, 173–74.

33 Bruce P. Lenman, 'Colonial wars and imperial instability, 1688–1793' in Marshall (ed.), *The Eighteenth Century*, pp. 151–68, esp. p. 159; Duffy, 'World-wide war', p. 194 in *idem*; Rory Miller, *Britain and Latin America in the Nineteenth and Twentieth Centuries* (London, 1993), pp. 34–36.

34 Hinde, *George Canning*, pp. 345–47, 350, 364–68, 372; John Lynch, *The Spanish American Revolutions 1808–1826* (New York, 1986 edn), pp. 12–14, 17–20; John Lynch, 'The River Plate republics from Independence to the Paraguayan War', and Tulio Donghi, 'Economy and society in post Independence Spanish America' in Leslie Bethell (ed.), *The Cambridge History of Latin America*, Vol. III, *From Independence to c.1870* (Cambridge, 1985), pp. 302–07, 639.

35 Wellington (ed.), *Despatches*, Vol. II, p. 394; Hinde, *George Canning*, p. 372; Miller, *Britain and Latin America*, pp. 40–44.

36 Hinde, *George Canning*, pp. 383–88; Richard Clogg, *A Short History of Modern Greece* (Cambridge, 1986 edn), pp. 50–65.

37 Hinde, *George Canning*, pp. 404–06, 408–10, 456–7; Wellington (ed.), *Despatches*, Vol. IV, pp. 39–40.

38 Afaf Lufti Al-Sayyid Marsot, *Egypt in the Reign of Muhammad Ali* (Cambridge, 1984), pp. 215–17; William Laird Clowes, *The Royal Navy: A History from the Earliest Times to the Present*, 7 vols (London, 1897–1903), Vol. V, p. 131; Vol. IV, p. 309; Vol. VII, p. 256; Lady Bourchier (ed.), *Memoir of the Life of Admiral Sir Edward Codrington*, 2 vols (London, 1873), Vol. II, pp. 64–67, 403–10.

39 D. Dakin, *The Greek Struggle for Independence, 1821–1833* (Berkeley, CA, 1973), p. 228.

40 Marsot, *Egypt in the Reign*, p. 216; Wellington (ed.), *Despatches*, Vol. IV, pp. 159, 182.

41 Clowes, *The Royal Navy*, Vol. VI, pp. 256, 260; Bourchier (ed.), *Memoir of the Life*, Vol. II, pp. 77–78.

42 Dakin, *The Greek Struggle for Independence*, p. 228.

43 Bourne, *Palmerston*, pp. 280–81; Marsot, *Egypt in the Reign*, p. 218; Bourchier (ed.), *Memoir of the Life*, Vol. II, pp. 115, 126–28; M.E.

Chamberlain, 'The soldier and the classicist: Wellington, Aberdeen and the Eastern Question, 1828–30' in C.M. Woolgar (ed.), *Wellington Studies III* (Southampton, 1999), pp. 136–51.

44 Schroeder, *The Transformation of European Politics*, pp. 657–64.

45 Dakin, *The Greek Struggle for Independence*, pp. 310–11.

46 Schroeder, *The Transformation of European Politics*, p. 63.

47 J.P.T. Bury, *France 1814–1940* (London, 1985 edn), pp. 42–43; Mansel, *Louis XVIII*, pp. 394–95; *The Times*, 14 April 1830, p. 2. Success in Algiers failed to win popular support for Charles's policies and left the regime short of troops in Paris when revolution broke out in July. Munro Price, *The Embattled Crown: France Between Revolutions, 1815–1848* (London, 2007), pp. 126–27, 136–38, 144–45.

48 'Papers relative to the occupation of Algiers, by the French' House of Commons, *Sessional Papers: Accounts and Papers* 1839 (155), pp. 47–52; quotation at p. 52.

49 Douglas M. Peers, *Between Mars and Mammon* (London, 1995), pp. 145–6.

50 Peers, *Between Mars and Mammon*, pp. 148–50.

51 Sir J. Malcolm to Duke of Wellington, 24 May 1828, WP1/933/5. Wellington paper, University of Southampton.

52 Peers, *Between Mars and Mammon*, p. 151.

53 Peers, *Between Mars and Mammon*, pp. 152–58; Colonel W.F.B. Laurie, *Our Burmese Wars and Relations with Burma* (Uckfield, 2005 reprint), pp. 459–60; Fortescue, *A History of the British Army*, Vol. XI, p. 349.

54 Charles Wynn to Duke of Wellington, 4 January 1827, WP1/879/9, Wellington papers, University of Southampton; Peers, *Between Mars and Mammon*, pp. 158–63, 182–93; Laurie, *Our Burmese War*, pp. 25, 39–41, 50.

55 Wellington (ed.), *Despatches*, Vol. V, p. 329.

56 Laurie, *Our Burmese Wars*, pp. 26, 40, 52, 67; Peers, *Between Mars and Mammon*, p. 152. Whereas Peers (pp. 155–56) lays a good deal of blame on the main expedition's commander, Fortescue credited him with holding the campaign together in very challenging circumstances. Fortescue, *A History of the British Army*, Vol. XI, pp. 351–52.

57 Peers, *Between Mars and Mammon*, pp. 128, 163–69.

58 John William Kaye, *The Life and Correspondence of Charles, Lord Metcalfe*, 2 vols (London, 1854), Vol. II, pp. 149, 151.

59 Wellington (ed.), *Despatches*, Vol. II, p. 76.

60 Peers, *Between Mars and Mammon*, pp. 214, 184–5, 188–91.

61 Wellington (ed.), *Despatches*, Vol. IV, p. 148.

62 Sir John Malcolm to the Duke of Wellington, 3 March 1828, WP1/921/8. Wellington papers, University of Southampton.

CHAPTER 19

Britain as a global power, 1815–30

The years after 1815 witnessed intense political challenges to Britain's military and naval world role. Fiscal restraint after decades of heavy borrowing, rather than imperial vision, drove government policy. Internal political turmoil as the country adjusted to post-war economic dislocation and then engaged in prolonged debates over political reform crowded out any meaningful debate about colonial mission, except for the pressure to end slavery in the West Indies. There were times, especially in 1819 and 1830–32, when political discontent so dwarfed any external agenda as to threaten revolution. Such facts of political life should not, however, disguise the continued commitment to imperial rule and the continued development of a particular military culture.

Despite pressures for retrenchment, Britain retained an extensive military and imperial role. Although the armed forces were greatly reduced after 1815, the numbers of ships and regiments provided an effective British presence in a wide range of locations. The empire was underpinned by the armed services' ability to exert authority at many critical points in the world. Britain was never a superpower, but rather a power capable of decisively influencing the balance of authority in numerous localities across the globe. Enough military and naval activity occurred to sustain a proficient officer corps accustomed to taking on considerable local responsibilities. Equally important, senior officers gained and commanded extensive administrative and political experience and remained closely connected with the political elite back in Britain. A vital legacy of the long wars was the emergence of a strong military culture which utilized the capacity of senior officers to command campaigns and to administer colonies. The proliferation of commitments in 1790–1815, continuing in the post-war years, meant that Britain was the most interventionist power in the post-war world. Such ubiquitous naval and military presence provided the framework for all other British activities, movements and initiatives on the world stage. It is appropriate therefore to explore the ways in which the British maintained their global role and interests by means of what was in effect an enclave empire.

Military and naval capabilities in the post-1815 world

The image of Britain as a Great Power after 1815 was highly ambiguous. Considerable activity in projecting power overseas was conditioned by parliamentary pressure and strong and popular radical campaigning for financial restraint. Retrenchment hit the armed services hard after 1815. The ministry cut the army from 150,591 effectives at the end of 1815 to 123,000 men for 1817, despite the argument canvassed by the commander-in-chief, the Duke of York, in favour of a peacetime army of over 152,000; any reductions below that, he warned, would leave the army unprepared for war, as it had been in the early 1790s. But parliamentary pressure for financial retrenchment and the declining need for troops in France and Ireland induced the government to act. In Ireland the force levels of 22,000 regulars and 4,000 other troops (including British militia) available in 1815 had been reduced to 20,000 by 1818, and the Chief Secretary for Ireland, Robert Peel, hoped to effect further reductions, relying on the permanent militia and the development of a domestic police force.[1] But concerns for security in Ireland recurred in the 1820s. In 1825, for example, Wellington urged that 'the state of Ireland was sufficient' reason for expanding the army, since any Irish rebellion would have to be crushed speedily to prevent the spread of disaffection.[2] Such concerns made little impact on the cabinet.

The navy suffered far worse cuts, with the government in 1817 reducing naval manpower to the level maintained in 1792 and the number of operational warships to 150 vessels, including those of the line and frigates. Despite the stock contention that warships could be kept 'in ordinary' until required, spending was also reduced on maintenance, ship repair and works at the dockyards. A force which engaged about 140,000 seamen and marines in 1814 was cut by three-quarters by 1816, although most sailors released from service presumably returned to work in merchant ships as the demand for commercial shipping, at least eventually, rose. During the years 1817–20 inclusive, only 23,000–24,000 sailors and marines were actually employed in the navy, of whom 6,000 were marines. Those numbers rose in 1824 and stayed at about 30,000 for the rest of the decade; in 1830 31,000 men were deployed, 9,000 being marines. The number of warships actually in commission slumped from 713 in early 1814 to 121 in 1818 and 134 in 1820. Even so, the number of naval officers in 1833 was nearly 150% larger than the number in 1792: 5,072 compared to 2,117. Most of them were lieutenants (3,218) and commanders (885), but 969 of them were in the higher and more influential ranks of captain or above. However, the vast majority of officers languished in reserve on half-pay, since only 542 naval officers were on active duty in 1833.[3]

The senior service fell victim to its own triumphs in the long wars. The 1770s and 1780s had witnessed a naval-building race which challenged British leadership at sea. Some 30% of all European and American naval tonnage in 1790 was possessed by Denmark, Holland and Spain; by 1815 those medium-sized navies' share of naval tonnage had shrunk to only 10%, as a result of the mauling they received from the Royal Navy. The destruction or capture of those countries' fleets explain why Britain's share of all naval tonnage swelled from 29.7% in 1775 and 28.4% in 1790 to a remarkable 44.4% in 1815. France still held 16.5% of naval tonnage, compared with 17.5% in 1775 and 19.4% in 1790, but had no potential western European allies possessing medium-sized fleets to supplement its own navy, as had happened in 1796–1805.[4] Equally important, the continued relative strength of the French fleet explained why the British ensured that Antwerp, whose naval yard was much larger by 1814 than British estimates had suggested and where the French apparently planned to complete eighteen line ships in 1814–15, was removed in 1815 from French control and reduced to exclusively civilian uses.[5]

Although the navy shrank, its size needs to be seen in context. For one thing, the armed services of the early nineteenth century did not employ large numbers of sailors and soldiers in administrative, technical or ordnance roles, so that the proportion of fighting men in the total manpower numbers was far greater than it would be in a modern navy or army. In 2006, for instance, at most 25% of British naval and army personnel were deployed at any one time in combat-related roles. Second, most ships in commission in peacetime were small warships, requiring relatively few crew. In 1836 the British had 114 ships on duty on stations across the globe, run by only 17,351 men. This provided for a substantial projection of power and for reasonably extensive opportunities for middle-ranking officers, and their men, to test their seafaring and technical skills. The importance of such experience and the high price at which it was acquired were demonstrated by the fact that, during the fifteen years from 1816 to 1830 inclusive, constant wear and tear cost the navy no fewer than forty-nine warships lost to storm, fire, wreck, and accident. Although the biggest ships lost were six frigates of 32 guns or more, the steady toll of small warships was a reminder of the recurrent hazards of this global service, with ships meeting their end off Newfoundland, Nova Scotia, Cuba, Jamaica, Barbados, Cape Verde Island, West Africa, Mauritius and Egypt, as well as elsewhere in the Mediterranean, in home waters and, for one small schooner, in the Arctic.[6]

This global naval activity was directed at protecting Britain's trading interests, countering piracy and containing the slave trade. The campaign against slave trading gave a distinct moral edge to the Royal Navy's role and gained public endorsement for the service. Such activities also gave scope to naval officers' enterprise in the pursuit of their careers. Significant bounties were originally provided for the capture of slaves, even though that form of prize-money was reduced in 1824 and again in the 1830s. The scope and public prominence of naval patrolling in West African waters was illustrated by the operations of the *Sybille*, the most successful anti-slaver warship up to 1830. This large frigate of 48 guns, under Captain F.A. Collier, went on station in 1828, together with the small armed vessels which attended her, and by September 1829 the flotilla had captured 4,445 slaves, each one attracting £10 prize-money to the command involved. In one encounter, a tender vessel, the *Black Joke*, of two guns and 55 men, chased and then engaged for 80 minutes a Spanish slaver armed with 14 guns; this minor engagement was challenging enough to incur six British casualties, two resulting in death, while 28 of the slaver's 80-man crew were killed or wounded. A Portuguese captain was approvingly quoted in the press for his view that it was 'mad to fire on de British flag – sure to be taken and hung up at de yard-arm'.[7] While, therefore, the navy was severely reduced after 1815, it operated effectively as a small-ship force with global reach.

A quite different pattern of post-war military provision emerged in India. At the end of the war against Mysore in 1793, the forces in India totalled 88,000. The East India Company's armies had grown to 192,000 by 1805. Following short-term reductions, they stood again at 194,000 in 1814 and expanded to 291,000 in 1826, with the biggest surge occurring during the Nepalese and Pindari campaigns in 1814–19. The recruitment of nearly 100,000 extra sepoys accounted for this growth. Only in the late 1820s, after the war in Burma and the campaign against Bharatpur, did the number of British army battalions serving in India rise. But the cessation of those hostilities led the East India Company to cut its armies back to 223,000 in 1830 and insist that it pay for only 20,000 UK army troops serving in India, as had been stipulated in the Company's charter renewal of 1813. Wellington as prime minister wanted to uphold the army's strength, despite parliament's wishes. He achieved at least something of his objective by retaining the number of battalions in India, while reducing the number of troops in each; he thus ensured that the command structure of senior officers and NCOs and the organizational apparatus of battalions and their depots were firmly in place to accommodate any future increase in troop numbers. Overall, the Indian armies were by 1830 back to their size of 1815, but this cutback still meant that the forces available in the subcontinent exceeded the regular armies embodied at any time before 1814 and represented a doubling of regular manpower since Richard Wellesley's arrival in 1797.[8]

Despite the reduction in the post-war armed services, Britain itself retained an army of sufficient strength to serve its global garrisoning needs. As shown in the table below, by the early 1830s over half the peacetime UK army served in the empire, while under one-quarter was stationed in England, Scotland and Wales.

Total effectives of cavalry and all types of infantry, January 1832

Great Britain	25,083
Ireland	20,077
India	18,364
Rest of overseas	30,853
TOTAL	94,377

Because India was so vast and the forces within it were so widely distributed, the most geographically concentrated British – as distinct from sepoy – forces overseas were stationed at Halifax (Nova Scotia), Gibraltar, Malta and the Ionian Islands, and the bases associated with protecting the route to India, at the Cape and on Mauritius and Ceylon. The military (and naval) presence in those relatively small centres of population offered a prominent reminder of the military character of the empire (see table).

Overseas distribution of the army, January 1832

	Total effectives
Canada	2,417
Nova Scotia	2,258
Windward and Leeward Islands	4,452
Bermuda	962
Jamaica and Honduras	3,122
Gibraltar	2,816
Malta	2,366
Ionian Islands	2,889
Cape of Good Hope	1,725
Mauritius	1,445
India	18,363
Ceylon	3,547
New South Wales	2,539

These forces enabled Britain, while acting with restraint in continental European affairs, to pursue her imperial ambitions in three ways. First, the end of war in Europe in April 1814 made little difference to the power politics of British India. By 1830, new strategic thinking about the threat of Russian expansionism towards Afghanistan, and the potential build-up of Russian influence there, opened a politico-military debate which increasingly disturbed and dominated British official India during the following ninety years. The second arena for military imperialism arose from frontier wars. Virtually all colonial governors in the 1810s and 1820s were senior army officers, and frontier defence provided an important part of their responsibilities. The most dramatic extension of frontiers came in southern Africa, where two campaigns, in 1811 and 1819, were launched against the Xhosa to the east and north of Cape Colony. This expansionism, accompanied by the promotion of white settlement, had a profound long-term impact on the scale and direction of British involvement in the region beyond the colony it had acquired from the Dutch. Other frontier conflicts, if less dramatic, were locally important in reducing indigenous people's military capability and territorial rulership. For example, small forces of regulars combined with local levies in the colonies which later became parts of Australia to exert a disproportionate impact on the Aboriginal population.[9]

The third distinctive element in the extension of British power was the continuing accumulation of bases and the installation of defensive lines.

The most notable acquisition proved to be Singapore, in 1819, although its naval potential was less significant in this initial move than its position commanding south Asian trading routes. Major defensive works were also undertaken on the Canadian frontier with the USA from the late 1820s. Lieutenant General Sir George Murray, the Secretary of State for War and the Colonies, emphasized in 1828 to Wellington, then prime minister, that the defences of Canada and Bermuda especially needed strengthening, since those colonies were vulnerable to sudden American attack.[10] Added to this was the daily activity of the Royal Navy in patrolling the high seas and policing the slave trade. Even in its vastly reduced numerical state after 1815, the navy, capable of applying force locally in support of civil authority, provided a ubiquitous reminder of the flexibility of British power projection.

Military and naval leadership

One unpredictable development from the late eighteenth century was the establishment of a cohort of senior officers and administrators committed to an imperial mission. Expanding overseas interests seemed to critics in the 1780s to spawn increasing corruption within the ruling elites. To counter such criticisms, British officials first promoted the defensive view that, if individual European malfeasance was bad, indigenous Indian regimes were systemically worse. This argument was then extended into an insistence that the British offered higher standards of good governance to displace the oppressions of oriental despotism. An increasing number of East India Company army officers were deployed to civil administrative and advisory posts to improve the quality of governance. Such service presumably also offered welcome variety, since the majority of East India Company officers never returned permanently to Britain. A sample of 201 cadets appointed to the Bengal army before 1783 indicates that at least 96 died in India or at sea, while many others stayed in India on retirement. A further sample of 155 cadets appointed in 1798–1810 shows that 91 of them, or nearly 60%, had died in the subcontinent or at sea by 1837.[11]

Just as the government of India blended military and civil attributes and personnel, so the development of an imperial mission and the related promotion of martial ideals was accompanied at home by a restatement of traditional notions of social and political authority. There were three ways in which the British establishment was strengthened by the long wars and used its involvement in those wars to portray itself more assertively as a legitimate ruling caste. Those concerned the local links between global militarism and the landed elite, the professional competence of the military and naval senior command, and the special role of the monarchy.

The more widespread dissemination of conditional militarism owed much to the landed elite's deep involvement with the local recruitment and leadership of the militia, while the interaction of aristocratic pride and national identity occurred also in the commemoration of heroic leaders. Landowners linked themselves and their families to heroes and their deeds. At Stowe, the palatial country seat of the head of the powerful Grenville family, there were monuments to, among other things, naval victories and the worldwide explorations of Captain Cook. At The Hirsel, the Earl of Home dedicated a monument to his eldest son and heir when he was killed in America in 1781. At Wentworth Woodhouse, Lord Rockingham erected a monument to a fellow Whig, Admiral Augustus Keppel, to celebrate his exoneration by a court martial. At Chatsworth, the Dukes of Devonshire, leading Whigs, erected monuments to both Nelson and Wellington, both of whom were Tories; their commemoration indicated that pride in national achievements was neither a partisan matter nor a phenomenon connected with, or buttressing the prestige of, the monarchy. At Shrewsbury, a column 151 feet high bearing a statue of Lord Hill, a local landowner and Peninsular War general, was built in 1814–16 to dominate the main road from London to Holyhead, the principal ferry port for Ireland. At the farther end of the newly constructed section of this major thoroughfare, a similar monument was erected to another local grandee, the Marquess of Anglesey, who commanded the cavalry at Waterloo.[12] Less ostentatiously but with equally clear intent to impress, locally prominent families installed monuments and wall tablets in churches across the country in memory of family members who died on active duty.

Sustaining a global military and naval role required an effective officer caste, possessing energy, ambition, skill and self-belief, all married to a willingness to take decisions and risks. The peculiarities of the British officer class did not guarantee such outcomes, but they fostered them. The long wars of 1793–1815 boosted officers' numbers and status. For the navy, initiative and vigour had been fostered not just by Nelsonian heroics but also by the financial rewards and honours available. About £40 million was distributed in naval prize-money during the wars of 1793–1815, compared with the total naval costs of those wars of £334 million.[13] Most of this money helped senior officers fund gentry or upper-middle-class lifestyles and clearly incentivized initiative and aggression. Those who rose highest in the army – notably Cornwallis, Lake and Wellington – made their mark in their first commands by their vigour, initiative and offensive-mindedness. Many middle-ranking officers of both services showed extraordinary determination on debilitating campaigns and exemplary courage in battle. Just as Napoleon did, British commanders expected and rewarded heroic leadership among their middle-ranking officers.

Of course, most military activity was routine rather than heroic. The challenges the British faced as a global power called for a substantial administrative commitment within the senior command. An indication of this demand is provided by the geographical distribution of general officers assigned to active duties in March 1813, just before the final, central European stage of the war began (see table). A large minority of senior officers were assigned to home defence, with most of them commanding small numbers of regulars buttressed by larger numbers of embodied militia; the latter would increase during national emergencies. For example, eight generals served in the Scottish command, with one major general each at Glasgow, Perth and Aberdeen, while the rest were stationed in and around Edinburgh, where the headquarters were located. Overseas, the administration of military affairs in numerous small colonies absorbed much senior manpower. The Caribbean islands and Bermuda were assigned twenty-nine generals, with every island colony being commanded by a senior officer, most of them reporting to the Commander-in-Chief, West Indies, at Barbados. In contrast, only ten generals from the British army served in India itself, because the East India Company organized its own officer corps. Equally striking, nearly 30% of British generals – fifty-eight of them – served in Ireland and the Caribbean (plus Bermuda), areas which, at this stage, do not figure in the history of the long wars. The commitment to defending colonies loomed far larger in the allocation of resources than is usually indicated in histories of the long wars.

General officers on active duty, 1 March 1813[14]

England	43
Scotland	8
Ireland	29
Total home staff	*80*

Iberian peninsula	49
Caribbean and Bermuda	29
Sicily and Malta	18
India and Ceylon	13
Canada and Nova Scotia	11
Cape of Good Hope	4
Total overseas stations	*124*

Gaining and holding this disparate empire required close inter-service cooperation. Some celebrated commanders did not succour such working relationships. For example, Lord Hood, in his operations on Corsica, and Nelson, in vainly trying to secure an expeditionary force for mainland Italy in 1799, failed to establish effective working relations with army commanders in the Mediterranean.[15] But, although some conjoint operations degenerated into inter-service recriminations, the army and navy generally developed the experience and the capacity to work together to run amphibious expeditions through *ad hoc* arrangements despite the absence of formal systems of joint command. Sir Charles Grey and Sir John Jervis ensured that the West Indies expedition of 1794 went smoothly. Elphinstone's capture of Cape Town in 1795 was achieved by soldiers and sailors working closely together. The landing of Abercromby's army in Egypt in 1801 was regarded as an exemplary case of inter-service cooperation. Attacks launched as far apart as Washington DC, New Orleans, Martinique, Buenos Aires, Mauritius, Burma, and Java all resulted from cooperation between the two services, often in joint operations on land as well as in transporting forces over great distances and landing them at appropriate points to optimum effect.

Given the demands upon commanders operating independently at great distances from London, senior officers were typically selected on the basis of considerable and relevant experience for their posts. The long period of the Duke of York's service as commander-in-chief, from 1795 to 1827 with one short break, meant that Horse Guards acquired a great deal of tacit knowledge of the aptitudes, performance and capabilities of officers of the rank of lieutenant colonel and above. Careful selection did not protect the service from the over-promotion of senior officers who failed to cope with the demands of higher command. But few systems of promotion, even those apparently based on 'objective' criteria and review can be certain to achieve this. Difficulties in predicting an officer's efficiency in a promoted post flowed from the changing mix of personal and professional attributes which made up effective command. In some instances, strong strategic appreciation might be needed, in others acute political insight, and in yet others a quick readiness to take risks. The absence of the last was probably the most common failing in military historians' eyes, but here one has to take into account the often oppressive responsibility borne by isolated commanders of small forces, brought together at great expense and representing a significant military outlay for a country unaccustomed to raising large armies. It was said at the time, and has been emphasized subsequently, that Wellington 'made' the British army, or rescued its reputation through its performance in the Peninsular

War.[16] The importance of York's reforms and the training provided at the newly established Royal Military Academy to this revival has also been stressed.

Yet the contemporary self-image of the army at Waterloo emphasized the strong professional commitment developed by officers acquiring their training in the 1780s and 1790s, long before Wellington made any impact. For example, the *Royal Military Panorama*'s series of monthly biographies of twenty leading generals serving at the very peak of the Peninsular War triumphs in 1812–14 emphasized continuity of service and the steady accretion of leadership skills. Of the generals in this pantheon, seven had served in America or elsewhere during the War for American Independence, from among the eleven who were commissioned at that time. Of the twenty, no fewer than thirteen had served in Flanders at some point in the period 1793–95, in what has often been regarded as one of the most disastrous interventions staged by the British army. Meanwhile another two were serving at Toulon in 1793 and one in the West Indies in 1793–95.[17] These biographical articles thus created a narrative of military expertise flourishing in 1812–14 which had been steadily developed through the fostering of leaders' talents, initiative and application from the 1770s and especially from the early 1790s onwards.

Past service was matched by the importance of political qualifications in selecting officers for high command. Commanders in North America were often selected on the basis of their having lived or served in North America and their fluency in French, as an indication of a capacity to reach out to the French majority in Quebec. For senior appointments to India, experience of other, non-European campaigning was usually required. Political experience, while no guarantor of success, was sometimes deemed helpful. Cornwallis and Hastings (both of whom had fought in America during the Revolution) were senior generals with political weight who took on the dual role of governor-general and commander-in-chief in India, and Lord William Bentinck eventually acquired both posts there. Understanding political realities, gained through family and personal connections to politicians and through membership of parliament, ensured that commanders grasped the limitations placed by political constraints upon them. The interconnectedness was illustrated, for example, when, in response to Napoleon's invasion of Russia, the government appointed the commander-in-chief in Scotland, General Lord Cathcart, as ambassador to Russia and British military commissioner to the Tsar's army. Apart from having extensive operational experience, Cathcart had long been an active Tory in politics and spoke Russian.

The close connection between military and political experience partly explains the considerable infusion of prominent officers into senior posts in government after 1815. Wellington regularly placed officers who had served under him in positions requiring political judgement and administrative skills and energy. He regarded his former ADC, Lord Fitzroy Somerset, younger son of the Duke of Beaufort, as 'a very able man, and the best man of business he was acquainted with'. Bishop Heber in India praised the commander-in-chief, Lord Combermere (recommended by Wellington) for 'his good sense, his readiness in dispatch of business, and his accessibility'.[18] When Wellington became prime minister in 1828, three of his twelve cabinet ministers had direct connections with his earlier career in the peninsula, while another, Lord Aberdeen, was the elder brother of one of his ADCs there. In addition, the quartermaster general of the peninsular army, Sir George Murray, joined the cabinet when another minister resigned. The network extended far more widely, as the table indicating the more prominent appointments held by the duke's former close associates in army command shows.

Wellington's former senior military subordinates in post in 1828–30

Lt. Gen. Sir George Murray, MP – Quartermaster General in the peninsula	Secretary of State for War and the Colonies, 1828–30
Gen. the Marquess of Anglesey – Commanded cavalry and artillery at Waterloo	Lord Lieutenant of Ireland, 1828–29
Maj. Gen. Sir Henry Hardinge, MP – 1808–14 peninsula with Prussian army, 1815	Secretary at War, 1828–30
Gen. Lord Hill – Lt. Gen. in the peninsula	Succeeded Wellington as Commander-in-Chief, Army, 1828–42
Lt. Gen. Sir Lowry Cole – Divisional commander in the peninsula	Governor of Cape Colony, 1828–33
Maj. Gen. Sir John Colborne – Battalion commander (52nd) in the peninsula	Lt. Governor of Upper Canada, 1828–36
Lt. Gen. Sir Charles Colville – Divisional commander in the peninsula and Belgium	Governor of Mauritius, 1828–34
Gen. Viscount Beresford – Commanded Portuguese army in the peninsula	Master-General of the Ordnance (a cabinet post), 1828–30
Lt. Gen. Sir John Byng – Commanded brigade in the peninsula	Commander-in-Chief, Ireland, 1828–31

Already in post

Gen. Lord Combermere – Cavalry commander in the peninsula	Commander-in-Chief, India, 1825–30
Lt. Gen. Sir Thomas Bradford – Brigade commander in the peninsula	Commander-in-Chief, Bombay, 1825–29
Lt. Gen. Sir George Walker – Divisional commander in the peninsula	Commander-in-Chief, Madras, 1826–31

Among Wellington's twelve divisional commanders of 1814, five held senior posts in 1828; three others were dead and another, a Hanoverian count, was ineligible for appointment. This was a remarkably high representation for generals with peninsular service.[19] One of the most glaring defects of the wars of 1775–83 – the system of command – was addressed if not resolved by Wellington's approach to appointments.

Senior colonial posts required political and administrative skills, as well as military abilities and the personal 'representational' presence provided by senior officers. Within the Australian colonies, for example, of the thirty-four governors, lieutenant-governors and senior administrators serving in New South Wales, Tasmania and Victoria in the years 1788 to 1855, only three were civilians. Most early governors worked their way up through their army careers. Of the ten governors of the Cape Colony from 1807 to 1854, nine were generals, the exception being the 1st Earl of Caledon (whose family had made a fortune in India and owned a northern Irish estate). Of the seven acting governors holding office for short periods between gubernatorial terms or while governors were absent, all were army officers and only one held a rank below that of general.[20] In India – where British military leadership except at the top was least affected by an aristocratic presence – the governor-generalship was held by two generals for seventeen of the twenty-two years during the period 1813–35, and Lord Amherst, the exception in this period, was the nephew and heir of a field marshal and presided over two major wars. Wellington's favoured candidate to succeed Amherst during a political crisis in 1825 was Sir Thomas Munro, a highly experienced senior official in the subcontinent who was 'peculiarly conversant in Indian warfare'.[21] It was common for relatively junior officers, in the rank of captain and major, to be seconded, sometimes for lengthy periods, to highly responsible jobs in civil administration or as official representatives of the East India Company at the courts of Indian rulers. By 1830, only 40% of European officers in the Bengal army were with their regiments.[22] Such administrative service did not detract from British officers' professional development, but instead extended their knowledge and skills and exercised their talents and initiative in an array of posts, often far more demanding, as well as financially rewarding, than routine regimental duties.

The projection of power and the maintenance of empire depended upon the development of habits of independent command. Indeed, the British probably succeeded far better than did the French in fostering such qualities in their middling-level commanders. A French commentator, having travelled widely in England after the wars, concluded that stern discipline and strict management helped explain the Royal Navy's success. During operations, orders were carried out keenly and with precision, with 'the calmness of force, the result of experience and good management'.[23] No fewer than 665 captains commanded frigates of 28–44 guns, ships which usually offered scope for independent action, during the wars of 1793–1815. The average length of command was a demanding three-and-a-half years and 9% of frigate commanders held their places for seven years or more.[24] Although the Royal Navy experienced numerous promotions for distinguished service, the average length of service in command meant that a turnover of active-duty officers could be maintained; after the late 1790s, rarely more than half the navy's captains were on active duty, including shore duties, in any one wartime year.[25] As for the army, in March 1813, many of the 207 generals on active duty were scattered in widely distributed commands. For example, in the Caribbean region, twenty-nine generals were distributed in nineteen different island and mainland colonies. Again, of the five generals attached to the Nova Scotia command two served at the headquarters in Halifax and one each commanded within the separate colonies of Newfoundland, New Brunswick, and Cape Breton. The British Isles were divided into twenty-two military districts, each with its own command structure. Some of those districts were wartime backwaters, with generals assigned to them being almost entirely held in reserve or semi-retired; but others, such as the separate commands of Guernsey, Jersey, and the Isle of Wight, were in the frontline of any potential French attack.

This distribution of command reflected the realities of geography and communications, but placed considerable onus on cooperation and co-ordination. Big strides were made in forging a more cohesive command system in India, so that campaigns under Cornwallis and the far-flung operations under Lord Wellesley's governorship were well coordinated, suffering relatively little from the divisions between commands which plagued the early 1780s. At the highest level, the importance of unity of command and cohesion in decision-making between the army commander and the political head of government in India was well illustrated by Wellington in 1826. The duke, as a member of the cabinet, wrote firmly to Lord Combermere, one of his subordinates in the peninsula, about official minutes the latter produced as commander-in-chief in India. Those minutes concerned 'purely political' issues and matters already decided. Wellington warned the general that:

> *any publick and continued difference of opinion between the Governor General and the Commander in Chief is prejudicial to the publick interests and cannot be allowed to exist . . . It shakes the authority of government to its very foundations, and while such difference continues every little man who takes part with either one or the other becomes of importance. The interests of the party are the great object, those of the publick are laid aside and forgotten, and even injured with impunity.*
>
> *God forbid that I should desire you to approve those measures of which you disapprove, or withhold from the Governor General your real opinions. But let them be your opinions. Discuss them with him in private fairly and candidly before you do so upon record, and avoid to record [sic] your difference of opinion by minute if it should be possible. The Commander in Chief is the first executive servant of the government. He is the right hand of the Governor General and he must be his friend and support his authority or one or both must be recalled. Rely upon it that in this country of law and civil government the military authority in such a contest will go to the wall.*[26]

This was a compelling observation on a state which had accorded the highest honours, rewards and respect to men of the sword.

The last element of the governing establishment to benefit from the long wars was the crown itself. The experience of war and threats of invasion had probably increased the monarchy's popularity as an institution by the late 1790s. This was partly because the classic contemporary criticism of monarchy – that it joined together civil and military power in ways that threatened subjects' rights – seemed by then to be equally applicable to republics. Dispensing with monarchs did not remove the problem. In the 1790s the new American republic periodically expressed fears of the possibility of Caesarism, arising from George Washington's military leadership during the war of independence and his role as presiding umpire during the country's emergence to political nationhood. While these fears may have been provoked more by some of Washington's colleagues' attitudes and aspirations than by any personal ambitions of the first president himself, the dilemma remained that military power, if concentrated in the federal government instead of being left in the hands of the states' militias, might undermine the republic. It was the French republic, however, which failed in its attempts by various methods, including the liberal guillotining of army commanders, to curtail generals' power, and the French Revolution, by coming to depend so completely on warfare for its survival, succumbed in 1799 to Caesarism in the shape of Napoleon Bonaparte.

By contrast, the British achieved a balance, which proved enduring, between military effectiveness and civilian control. In this period of almost uninterrupted warfare and campaigning, the heads of state remained unmilitaristic. The relationship between aristocratic and monarchical ideals and imperialism and militarism was double-edged for the British, for success in war could not be allowed to dilute the insistence upon civilian political primacy. An example of this arose in 1795 when the Prince of Wales pressed his father for a prominent army command in case of a French invasion. George III suggested that his eldest son and direct heir should not serve in such a capacity: 'There cannot be a doubt that the English do view with a jealous eye any decided predilection in those on or naturaly (*sic*) to mount the Throne to military pursuits, and I certainly feel the force of that opinion as strongly as any one.' While the king emphasized that his younger sons had 'no other situation in the State or occupation' than military ones, the heir apparent should hold no higher military rank than that of regimental colonel, which entailed no active duties. In confining himself to that ceremonial role, the prince was reminded that 'the approbation of the public ought to be your first object' and that the king expected that his dominions should long be 'governed by my lineal successors and on the same liberal sentiments of their ancestors', inspired by 'the intention of rendering their subjects prosperous and happy'.[27]

George III dressed in uniform when the occasion required, but he understood the need to mediate military and naval authority with civilian constraints and lacked military education or interests, being more of a politician in his public role than a 'general *manqué*'. George IV, both as Prince Regent and as king, loved to don uniforms and fantasized about having had the military career denied him by his father; he claimed in later life to have commanded the cavalry at Waterloo. But, as king, he proved too isolated politically, ineffectual in conducting the business of government, drugged, and derided in his personal behaviour to threaten to lend a militaristic character to the regime. No doubt if the American rebellion had collapsed in late 1776, or if the Duke of York had secured the command of the allied armies in Flanders in 1793 and led them in triumph to Paris, the British monarchy would have gained an immense boost in prestige and power. But it seems improbable that the British parliament would have enlarged the regular army in peacetime or expanded the army's scope. The intricate bureaucratic and financial checks and balances which made up the army's complex internal organization were intended to make it a weak player in domestic politics and ensure that it remained internally divided and politically manageable.

Yet for those politicians engaged in detailed week-by-week administration the reality seemed radically different. Palmerston, who laboured as the junior minister responsible for the army's administration from 1809 to 1828, saw the diffuse system as an opening for military influence, not a check upon it. He informed the chancellor of the exchequer in 1833:

The present confused and unconstitutional system dates only from the command of the Duke of York. He was a strong man; son of one King & brother of the other; heir presumptive; a political leader; he commanded too in time of war, when all men's minds took a military turn, & were accustomed to defer to military authority; he was always at the head of the army (except during a short interval) and took advantage of every opportunity to push on his encroachments; he had to do with a frequent succession of Secretaries of [sic] War, each of whom had to learn his duties and his powers, and many of whom had their pickets driven in, before they had well got into their saddle . . . Liverpool disliked facing him, as much as a boy fears his schoolmaster . . . and thus the Commander in Chief grew to be head of a great civil as well as military department without any direct contact with Parliament so as to render him practically responsible. There never was so much power wielded with so little parliamentary responsibility as that which since 1795 has been exercised by the Commander in Chief.[28]

Palmerston concentrated on powers acquired in the administrative and contracting activities of the British army, demonstrating that what seemed much later to have been a politically constricted institution was thought at the time to need evermore vigilant scrutiny.[29] Such sentiments help explain the fear expressed in 1830 from the other side by Major General Lord FitzRoy Somerset, Military Secretary at the Horse Guards, that members of the new Whig cabinet sought to crush the army.[30]

Conclusion

The making of the British Empire from 1790 to 1830 resulted from a multiplicity of factors. British interests in the wider world reflected British subjects' extraordinary range of motives and impulses to explore, engage with, emigrate to, evangelize in, export to, and exploit lands beyond their shores. Recent historiography has recognized the complexity and ambiguity of those myriad and often intensely felt interactions between individuals and the world stage – shaped as they were by class, gender, economic imperatives, and intellectual, cultural, political and moral concerns – which made Britain's global role so dynamic and so difficult to categorize.[31] The British state's interest in the world expanded partly because British people found more reasons and opportunities to enter upon that stage. But the state's interest in the world also took persistently coercive and protective forms in the shape of military and naval power. Those principal instruments – and the elites controlling their use – protected the sea routes, secured the harbours, cleared the political path to settlement, imposed legal and regulatory frameworks, and combated European rivals and indigenous opponents alike. In the 1830s about 65,000 British soldiers and sailors served outside the British Isles at any one time, far exceeding any other home-based group involved in any manner in imperial initiatives, be they commercial, governmental, philanthropic, or pastoral. They were supplemented by 200,000 Indian sepoys. The empire rested ultimately on force.

The extensive study of the projection of British power demonstrates the inadequacy of strategic analyses which argue or imply that the acquisition of economic, financial and political advantages by one state over its competitors enables that state to develop naval and military superiority. Turning such advantages into concrete territorial or diplomatic gains, and then maintaining those gains, required far more than the routine application of superior means. Success on the plains of Hindustan, in the valleys of Nepal, across the Great Lakes of North America, amidst the swelling seas of Biscay, or upon the slopes of Waterloo depended upon the discipline, determination, courage and resilience displayed by the men, the NCOs and the officers of the armed services. So-called hegemonic power looked decidedly less omnipotent when it repeatedly depended on what the officers and men of a warship or battalion, or small collections of warships and battalions, could achieve or threaten to achieve in challenging or even desperate circumstances, often against considerable odds and at great distances from centres of authority or concentrated force.

In practice, British military effectiveness was transformed between the early 1790s and the mid-1810s. In 1791, the Madras army had struggled in managing an invasion of Mysore. By 1818, the armies of British India had campaigned throughout the country and tackled far more difficult scenarios than that offered by Mysore. Again, in 1793–95 a small British army played a subsidiary and ultimately humiliating role in operations in the Low Countries. In 1815, the British contribution to Napoleon's final defeat was far more prominent and even distinguished, even though the French army at Waterloo was small compared with those France fielded in eastern and central Europe in 1812–13. More importantly, British forces were deployed throughout the world in a steady demonstration of power. Yet Britain's relative strength varied considerably between these different sectors. A brief review of the balance of power in eight regions where the British actively pursued their interests in the post-war years indicates the variability of British influence and the continuing challenges they faced.

In the Iberian peninsula the British in the early 1780s had fought hard to defend Gibraltar in one of the greatest sieges of the eighteenth century. In comparison with that, their position after 1815 looked immensely secure. Yet they did not find it easy to influence Spanish policy and ended up as spectators to an impressive demonstration of French power in the 1820s. The Portuguese government was far more amenable to British pressure but, even so, British interventions were hesitant and intermittent. As a second sphere of regional power-broking, the Mediterranean saw an accretion of British power through the acquisition of Malta and the Ionian Islands, but the implementation of policy in the late 1820s depended upon joint action by the Great Powers. The experiment in Sicily yielded no longer-term strategic benefit. Moreover, it could be argued that the British slipstreamed into strong military positions in Portugal and Sicily only when the French broke the authority of the indigenous governments of those states. Farther afield, in the New World, the British continued to feel challenged, if only potentially, by the USA and upgraded an extensive line of fortifications as a precautionary measure. In terms of military power on land and small-force naval power, the British were certainly not the clear superior to their southern neighbour. In the Caribbean, Britain's predominance in international relations was assured by the campaigns of the 1790s, the subsequent sequence of reconquests and, most importantly, by the emasculation of so many other colonial powers' navies. The advantages of naval power gave the British leverage in Latin America, but did not yield anything approaching decisive sway. By contrast, the Royal Navy ensured British superiority in the tiny colonies of what later became

Australia. Across the Indian Ocean, British naval and military strength guaranteed Cape Colony against European rivals, but the forces available proved sufficient only to pressurize, not to overwhelm, the Xhosa of the eastern Cape frontier.

In India, British power expanded out of all recognition. From 1780 until 1792, much British military effort concentrated on countering Mysore's expansionism. From 1799 onwards, the British engaged in a series of major wars which carried them to clear paramountcy. Large-scale campaigning occurred in almost one year in every three between 1790 and 1830. The British eliminated any residual threats from European rivals by the end of 1799, but the imposition of British rule and a system of subsidiary alliances, considerably advanced in 1803–05, was not brought about without challenge. And while the British found it relatively easy to create a stable internal political order in India, they still found themselves stretched when they confronted local rivals or instability on their borders.

This military and naval assertiveness did not slacken with the advent of peace. Among the eight regions noted here, the British in the years 1815–30 conducted major campaigns in India, a minor campaign in southern Africa, and punitive raids in Australia. But they also deployed force in Portugal and in the Mediterranean and increased military preparations in Canada. Only two of these regions did not witness direct military or naval action. The scale of these operations differed widely and reflected the differential impact of Britain as a regional power.

A review of the most prominent episodes in British power projection overseas taken from the entire period from 1790 to 1830 demonstrates how, in garrison duties, peacekeeping, patrolling, campaigning and war-making across the globe, Britain was probably the most persistently, and certainly the most widely, interventionist power of the age. If the operations of the militia within the United Kingdom, the regular army, the armies assembled by the East India Company, and the navy are taken together, it is probable that no other state applied force so constantly and that British officers deployed in independent commands served in more varied environments, and proved more professionally proficient, than any comparable officer corps in the world. The British experience demonstrated that an expansionist commercial power could also act as a militarily assertive power without destroying its commercial and civilian character.

In terms of military management, this global reach created distinct problems. Those responsible for running the army and navy sought to standardize and replicate facilities, procedures and rituals as soldiers and sailors moved from base to base and garrison to garrison. But the sheer

range and variety of campaigning worked against rigorous standardization. The British had to be extraordinarily flexible in forming local alliances.
In Mysore in 1791, they failed to secure cavalry support from the Marathas,
whereas they won such backing in the following year. In 1803–05, they
waged a complex war within a shifting framework of alliances among
the principal Maratha chiefs. The campaigns of the 1810s saw a similar
changing system of alliances within the Maratha confederacy, and new
local diplomatic initiatives among the tribal and regional rulers of Nepal.
The state system within India was multilayered and fluid during the period
1790–1819, and one factor in British readiness to resort to war was the
drive to bring stability to that system. Southern Europe might superficially
seem more straightforward in terms of alliances, Naples and Portugal
being fairly constant allies. But the politics of coalition-building always
needed careful diplomatic attention. In 1793, Britain failed to secure a
sufficient number of troops from southern European allies to maintain its
position at Toulon. Again, the demands made upon regional allies differed
widely in 1808–14. Portugal provided the enclave at and around Lisbon
and became a source of soldiers. Naples offered a base in Sicily, but not a
military recruiting ground. Spain proved a very testing ally beyond ready
British control. Even farther afield, the British raised Native American
allies in 1812 to contain American probes along and across the Canadian
frontier. On top of this range of local alliances, Britain had also to try her
hand at the frustrating task of forging and then holding together alliances
with the Great Powers of Europe. The array of politico-military strategies
pursued by Britain was far more varied and complex than that needed by
France or the leading eastern European powers.

So, too, there was no single model of interaction between the British
and indigenous populations overseas. The British took over Toulon by the
invitation of local monarchists, but were unable to extend that enclave
into a wider anti-republican constituency. Ireland saw the army both in
combative mode, in 1797–98, and in the role of guarantor of stability
and indeed peace. In India, of course, British campaigning depended
upon a sophisticated indigenous military labour market, elaborate systems
of supply run by local merchants, and a broad range of commercial and
political collaborations. The subsidiary alliance system, for example,
enmeshed the British in a range of geopolitical alliances which possessed
the additional advantage of casting the East India Company in the role of
coadjutor rather than conqueror. Even when penetrating into unfamiliar
territory, as in Nepal, an army's progress was accompanied by detailed
negotiations with the local rulers, involving their transfer of political

attachment and troops to the British cause. In the Peninsular War, Wellington tried to control at least the economic exchanges between his army and the indigenous population, but the relationship went through the entire gamut of potential interactions from friendship to misunderstandings, confrontations, and outright hostility. Success in Canada rested on ensuring trust between the British and the French Catholic majority.

Similar variety applied as much to fighting as to the relationships the British established with overseas peoples. There was no set model for military engagement. In the Caribbean, the main challenge was to pursue opponents into the interior, to maintain mobility between the islands and, severest of all, to preserve physical health. In Ireland, large numbers of troops were deployed in 1797–99 to suppress civil rebellion. Egypt in 1801 witnessed a brilliant landing delivered by exceptionally well-prepared troops, promptly followed up by a victory in battle. Against Mysore, siege capabilities came to the fore, whereas formal battle involving artillery and regular infantry, supported by high levels of mobility, proved decisive in the Maratha wars. Land–sea operations were vital to island-hopping in the Caribbean, the taking of Cape Town, and incursions in North America. The Iberian peninsula honed British skills in the conduct of traditional battle. From 1808 to 1815, the British fought thirteen battles against the French in the peninsula and south-western France and won them all.[32] No other country approached that record of success. But even this achievement is underscored by the small scale of British military operations. Only at Bussaco, Vitoria and Waterloo did the French engage more than 50,000 troops in the battles won by the British. That contrasts with more than 150,000 troops brought by Napoleon to the fields of battle at Wagram (1809), Smolensk (1812), Bautzen and Leipzig (1813).

The British experience of war-fighting was more frequent and successful than is normally allowed, but it remained limited in scale. Over the period 1790–1815, the British fought a battle of some significance, on either land or sea, in eighteen of the twenty-six years; and they launched significant expeditions or invasions in six of the other years. Apart from the French, no other power remotely rivalled that record of persistent power projection. Aside from the naval commitments at Toulon, the Glorious First of June, and Trafalgar, and perhaps St Vincent, none of these battles involved large forces according to the measures of the time. The British army emerged as extraordinarily adept at a wide range of types of warfare. Despite the charge of amateurism often levelled against it, the army proved exceptionally determined in sustained campaigning. Back in June 1781, the British commander-in-chief in India, Sir Eyre

Coote, lamented his immobility against the forces of Haidar Ali of Mysore:

he will pursue his uniform plan of harassing me . . . which he can practice with Impunity, by means of his immense Bodies of Cavalry which are too powerful to be opposed by the small number I have got, and too rapid in their motions to be even come at by Infantry. Had I but a good Body of Cavalry I am satisfied I should long ere now have made some impression upon him.[33]

Thus, following the very hard-fought battle outside Porto Novo (1 July 1781), the British had no cavalry with which to take Haidar Ali's guns and stores. Although the British drove Haidar Ali from the coast in a sequence of testing battles, they never staged a pursuit, the key, in Clausewitz's analysis of war, to decisive victory.

By contrast, the keys to victory against Mysore in 1790–92, the Marathas in 1803–05 and 1817–19, the Americans in 1812–15, and the French in 1808–14 were resilience and the organization and courage to stick to the task of wearing down an opponent. Although they worked hard at their technical skills and at improving their artillery, British forces did not awe their enemies through superior numbers, dashing gallantry or technological edge. They ground them down by persistence and the application of flexible approaches to war-fighting. Nor should the British achievement at sea be overshadowed by an emphasis upon the handful of great battles so devastatingly fought. The Royal Navy's perennial success was achieved through extraordinarily tenacious blockading and ubiquitous small-ship warfare. In so many varied ways, Britain became a global power through her ability to fight small and medium-level campaigns virtually anywhere on land or sea from widely distributed enclaves.

We began this study by considering the limitations upon British overseas power projection. In 1790 those limitations were ideological as well as practical. There were deep and widespread fears of standing armies and the relationship between military power and the strength of the aristocracy and especially the monarchy. The utility of war, and indeed empire, to a commercial nation seemed dubious. Moreover, Britain's recent record in war indicated no obvious prowess on the field of Mars and only faltering and tardy success in the realm of Neptune. By the 1820s, radical hostility to standing armies and aristocratic and monarchical influence remained. But the aristocracy had been strengthened by the long wars. The middle-class stake in the services had also grown out of all recognition. While the political elite did not spend generously on the peacetime armed services, they maintained a sufficiently large army and navy to sustain the higher ranks dominated by the aristocracy and gentry and the newfound status and position of the expanded and heavily middle-class officer corps as a whole. India, with its vastly expanded army, played an important part in this process. In relation to the empire, the key ingredients for the success of the British forces were their ubiquity, their mobility, and their localism. No other country projected its power in so many parts of the world. While inserting their forces so widely, the British maintained a level of mobility which reinforced the military and naval impact of their presence. The more they moved around – as, for example, within India – the more numerous and the more threatening the forces seemed. But, at the same time, the empire rested upon particular enclaves, not on the military control of great swathes of territory. It was the regular movement between enclaves, be they ports stretched across the globe, or garrisons within, say, Ireland or India, which proclaimed British military and naval presence and capabilities. Britain held down extensive territories by patrolling or policing or maintaining alliance systems from enclaves of relatively small but locally formidable power.

All this was possible because British militarism was subtly modulated. The naval and military elite came from and was integrated into the upper-middle and landowning classes in ways which strengthened aristocratic prestige and power and gentlemanly values. The dominant role of the landed gentry and aristocracy in the armed forces did not produce, or revive, a ruling establishment in Britain that looked militaristic, sounded militaristic, or aggressively advanced the interests of the army and navy in parliament. But the use of naval and military power, especially overseas, proved more politically acceptable, within the restraints of a constitutional and representative political system, because of that. The attack on war as an instrument of policy, on the grounds that war enhanced the power of aristocracy and monarchy, was vindicated by the legacy of the long wars. Nineteenth-century radicals remained edgily hostile to the army as a result of this linkage. But adherence to parliamentary accountability ensured legitimacy to the officer corps and safeguarded the state from acquiring a reputation for undue militarism. Among the greatest legacies of Britain's surge of global power projection were the development of types of military proficiency and the creation of a form of civilianized militarism which have endured, if far less prominently than of old, to this day. Richard Cobden, one of Victorian Britain's leading advocates of free trade and peace, made the point in lamenting the public reaction to Wellington's arrival at the Great Exhibition in 1851: 'the frenzy of admiration and enthusiasm which took possession of a hundred thousand people of all classes was one of the most impressive lessons I ever had of the real tendencies of the English character'.[34] This was not the whole truth or the sole truth, but it was, assuredly, an important and too frequently neglected part of the truth.

Notes and references

1 Norman Gash, *Mr Secretary Peel* (London, 1961), pp. 188–89.

2 Duke of Wellington (ed.), *Despatches, Correspondence, and Memoranda of Arthur, Duke of Wellington, KG . . . from 1818 to 1831*, 8 vols (London, 1867–80), Vol. II, pp. 391–92.

3 Michael Lewis, *The Navy in Transition 1814–64: A Social History* (London, 1965), pp. 66, 69; 'Returns of the number of Midshipmen promoted to be Lieutenants', House of Commons, *Sessional Papers: Accounts and Papers* 1833 (57), p. 282.

4 Jan Glete, *Navies and Nations: Warships, Navies and State Building in Europe and America, 1500–1860*, 2 vols (Stockholm, 1993), Vol. I, p. 312.

5 Sir Richard Vesey Hamilton (ed.), *Letters and Papers of Admiral of the Fleet Sir Thos. Martin Byam*, 3 vols (London, 1901), Vol. III, p. 16.

6 Lewis, *The Navy in Transition*, p. 236; William Laird Clowes, *The Royal Navy: A History*, 7 vols (London, 1897–1903), Vol. VI, pp. 506–07.

7 *The Times*, 14 February 1829, p. 4; 20 April 1829, p. 2; 23 November 1829, p. 3.

8 House of Commons *Sessional Papers 6 December 1831 to 16 August 1832*, Vol. 13, p. 195; Douglas M. Peers, *Between Mars and Mammon* (London, 1995), pp. 221, 233.

9 John Connor, *The Australian Frontier Wars 1788–1838* (Sydney, 2002), pp. 59–64, 90–101. Regular officers and small detachments of regular troops were deployed with locally raised forces.

10 Wellington (ed.), *Despatches*, Vol. V, pp. 79–80.

11 I used cadets appointed to the Bengal army whose surnames began with M in both periods. *Alphabetical List of the Officers of the Indian Army* (London, 1838), pp. 168–87.

12 John Newman and Nicholas Pevsner, *Shropshire* (London, 2006), pp. 578–79.

13 Richard Hill, *The Prizes of War: The Naval Prize System in the Napoleonic Wars, 1793–1815* (Stroud, 1998), pp. 246–47. There were occasions when

seamen could secure from prize-money multiples of their annual pay of £20, after deductions and allowing for such benefits as they received (*ibid.*, pp. 177–78).

14 Tables at front of *Royal Military Panorama or Officers' Companion*, Vol. I (March 1813).

15 Roger Knight, *The Pursuit of Victory: The Life and Achievement of Horatio Nelson* (London, 2005), pp. 167–72; Nicholas Harris Nicholas, *The Dispatches and Letters of Vice Admiral Lord Viscount Nelson*, 7 vols (London, 1998 reprint), Vol. III, pp. 469–70, Vol. IV, pp. 14–15.

16 Anthony Clayton, *The British Officer* (Harlow, 2006), pp. 55–71.

17 *The Royal Military Panorama or Officer's Companion*, Vol. I (London, 1812–13), pp. 8–9, 302–03, 400, 498; Vol. II, (1813), pp. 3–4, 101–02, 200, 297–99, 395–96, 496–99, 592; Vol. III (1813–14), pp. 4–5, 102, 217–19, 315, 511, 518–21; Vol. IV (1814), pp. 3–4, 102–03.

18 Charles C.F. Greville, *The Greville Memoirs: A Journal of the Reigns of George IV and King William IV* ed. by Henry Reeves, 3 vols (London, 1874), Vol. III, p. 186; Reginald Heber, *Narrative of a Journey through the Upper Provinces of India, 1824–1825*, 2 vols (London, 1828), Vol. II, p. 264.

19 See also, Zoe Laidlaw, *Colonial Connections, 1815–1845: Patronage, the Information Revolution and Colonial Government* (Manchester, 2005), pp. 21–27.

20 Eric A. Walker, *A History of Southern Africa* (London, 1957 edn), p. xviii.

21 Wellington (ed.), *Despatches*, Vol. II, p. 517.

22 Peers, *Between Mars and Mammon*, p. 79.

23 Charles Dupin, *A Tour through the Naval and Military Establishments of Great Britain*, translated (London, 1822), p. 38–39.

24 Tom Wareham, 'The duration of frigate command during the Revolutionary and Napoleonic Wars', *The Mariner's Mirror*, 86 (2000), 412–423.

25 N.A.M. Rodger, 'Commissioned officers' careers in the Royal Navy, 1690–1815', *Journal of Maritime Research* (June 2001).

26 Wellington (ed.), *Despatches*, Vol. III, pp. 501–02.

27 A. Aspinall (ed.), *The Later Correspondence of George III*, 5 vols (Cambridge, 1968), Vol. II, p. 329.

28 Kenneth Bourne, *Palmerston: The Early Years 1784–1841* (London, 1982), p. 180.

29 The potential domestic threat posed by a successful army is discussed by P.J. Marshall, 'Empire and British identity: The maritime dimension', in David Cannadine (ed.), *Empire, the Sea and Global History: Britain's Maritime World*, c.1760–c.1840 (London, 2007), pp. 41–59, esp. pp. 55–56.

30 Somerset to Wellington, 26 December 1830, WPI/1157/12, Wellington papers, University of Southampton.

31 Boyd Hilton, *A Mad, Bad, and Dangerous People? England 1783–1846* (Oxford, 2006), pp. 239–250.

32 Vimiero, Corunna, Talavera, Bussaco, Fuentes de Onoro, Albuera, Salamanca, Vitoria, Bidassoa, Nivelle, Toulouse, Quatre-Bras, Waterloo.

33 *First Report from the Committee of Secrecy*, (n.p., 1782) pp. 43–4, Appendix 18.

34 Michael Howard, *War and the Liberal Conscience* (Oxford, 1981), p. 45.

Index

Abercromby, Sir Ralph 98–9, 115, 116, 141, 145, 405
Abercromby, Sir Robert 164, 178
Aboukir Bay 137–8
Addington, Henry 147
administration 476–7, 480
Afghanistan 179, 183–4, 469
Agra 206–7
Alexandria 147
Ali, Haidar 43, 45
Aligarh 205
alliances 243, 319, 373, 441, 484
allied armies
   command and coordination 348
   France 285
   losses 303
   management 360
   military campaigning 36
   mixed nationalities 359
   Peninsular War 302
   Portugal 270
   retreat 77–8
   troop numbers 78–9, 283
Almeida 265
American Civil War 37
American colonies 4–5
American navy 331
American War (1776–83) 11, 27, 79–80
Ancien Régime 34, 37
Andalucia 276
Anglican Church of Ireland 112
Anglo Portuguese army 280
Annual Register for 1783 82, 429
Annual Register for 1795 356, 410
Anson, Admiral George 10
Arakan 456, 457
aristocracy

battle experience 486
casualties 433
France 422
legacy 428–35
militarism 419
officer corps 36, 471
political reform 421
raising battalions 427
aristocratic power 420–4
aristocrats 34, 44
Armstrong, John (Secretary of War, USA) 330
army recruits 42, 68, 111, 281
artillery
   Agra 207
   Aligarh 205
   battle of Argaum 204
   battle of Mehidpur 378
   battle of Waterloo 352–3, 359–60
   Ciudad Rodrigo 274
   effectiveness 33
   Ireland 127
   Maratha wars 209–10
   Mysore 165
   Nepalese war 367, 368
   New Orleans 338–9
   Seringapatam 187
Ashti 380
Asirgah 381
Assam 455
Association for the Preservation of Liberty and Property against Republicans and Levellers (APLP) 67
Austria
   alliance with Britain 136
   alliance with Britain collapses 142
   attacks France 140
   negotiations with France 304

Austria (*continued*)
  Poland 76
  settles with France 140, 243, 256
  troop numbers 350
  war with France 73–5, 138
authority 41, 43–4, 50, 428

Badajoz 274
Baird, Sir David, Baronet 187–8, 259
balance of power
  British influence 464
  Caribbean 96
  changing 218
  Europe 63, 229, 443
  India 175, 183, 198
  Ireland 119
  military 280
  military power 282
  naval power 65
  West Indies 70, 96–7
Baldwin, Stanley (Prime Minister,
  Britain) 3
Baltic sea 248
Baltimore 334–5, 336
Bangalore 162
Bank of England 28
Baring, Sir Francis 100
barracks 401, 403
Bartlett, Thomas 116
battle experience 45, 288, 340, 426
battle of Argaum 203–4
battle of Assaye 201–3
battle of Busaco 266
battle of Deig 216
battle of Leipzig (1813) 35
battle of Ligny 351
battle of Mehidpur 378
battle of Navarino 452–3
battle of New Orleans 320
battle of Nive 302
battle of Nivelle river 306
battle of Quatre Bras 351
battle of Salamanca 275
battle of St Vincent 103
battle of Trafalgar 241
battle of Vinegar Hill 124
battle of Vitoria 270, 283–4
battle of Waterloo 349–54, 358,
  426

battle of Wavre 348
battle tactics
  battle of Argaum 203–4
  battle of Waterloo 350, 357
  British army 78
  Jumna river 206
  Laswari 207
  Maida river 245
  Maratha wars 210, 213, 221
  Peninsular War 297
  reform 34
  training 33
battle training 32
battlefield performance 46–7
Bayly, Christopher 9, 173, 423
Bayonne 307
Belgium 140, 355, 356
Bengal 156, 157, 404, 458
Bentham, Jeremy
  Plan of Parliamentary Reform
    360–1
Bentinck, General Lord William Henry
  Cavendish 125, 272, 284, 404,
  441–2
Beresford, William 47
Beresford, William Carr 262, 270,
  294
Berkeley, Vice Admiral George 292
Bermuda 334
Bharatpur 217, 218, 457
Black, Jeremy 439
Bladensburg 335
Blake, Joaquim 289
blockading 293, 324, x
Blücher, Marshal Gebhard von 351–2,
  355
Board of Control 155
Bombay presidency 164, 167, 404
Bonaparte, Joseph 256, 273, 283
Bonaparte, Napoleon
  abdication 308, 354
  battle of Waterloo 360
  battle tactics 37, 357–8
  command systems 358
  Congress of Vienna 30
  Continental System 247
  control over Spain 255
  declared Emperor 422
  Egypt 136–7, 177

escaped Elba 347
expansionism 229, 236, 361
French army 349
Iberian Peninsula 280
invades Russia 281
Italian campaigns 102
negotiations with Britain 106, 147
Saint Domingue 232
Spain 306
tariff protectionism 148
troop numbers 260, 299–300
war with Austria 104
Bond, Brian 37
border tensions 366
border wars 158–9
Boydell, John (Lord Mayor of London)
    28
Brazil 255, 269
Brewer, John 395
Britain
    global reach 460
    Greece 451
    interventionist power 483
    isolation 63, 104
    Mediterranean 138
    negotiations with France 105–6
    world role 464
British advantages 293–7
British aristocracy 423
British army
    Bonaparte, Napoleon 347
    bravery 51
    counter-insurgency 126
    deployment of troops 355
    effectiveness 280, 385
    Egypt 142
    fragmented 398
    global power 52
    integration 210
    Ireland 109–10
    kudos 401
    landowners 427–8
    military efficiency 354–61
    mobility 198
    morale 388
    overseas distribution 469
    Pune 375
    regimentalism 405–8
    reputation 47–8, 144–5, 473–4

at sea 410
    size 480
    slaves 97
    support 48
    Toulon 85
British Empire
    balance of power 479
    colonies gained in war 443
    commerce 10–11
    enclaves 413, 465
    frontier defence 469
    India 365
British forces
    aid Portugal 446–7
    discipline 481
    fragmented 412
    Lisbon 257
    Mediterranean 450–5
    organization 396
    reduced 465
    reduced in size 364
    resilience 486
    rituals 403
    segregated from local populations
        404
    troop numbers 486–7
British influence 449, 482
British militarism 41–4
British military power 178
British officers 36
British overstretch 218–22
British power 439, 440, 469–70
British presence 409
British rule 44
British successes 293, 382–4
Broach 208
Brooke, Colonel Arthur 336
Brussels 348, 349–50
Burgos 276, 282
Burke, Edmund 66, 67, 80, 110
Burma 455

Cadiz 256–7, 267, 269, 286
Cain, P.J. 27
Cairo 146
Calcutta 404
Calcutta Monthly Journal 368
Calder, Sir Robert 237–8
Calvert, Harry 45

campaigns
  Caribbean 92
  Europe 63–4
  India 456–7
  New Orleans 336
  planning 387–8
  preparations for war 459
  successes 42
Canada 327, 341, 342, 401, 470, 485
Canning, George 364–5
Cape Colony 100, 101, 149, 233, 402, 469
Cape of Good Hope 100–2
Caribbean
  British influence 482
  British successes 104, 106
  command and coordination 232
  French colonies 319
  French power 91
  illness 42, 94
  indigenous peoples 16–17
  military operations 94–9
  mobility 485
  naval dockyards 401
  naval warfare xiv
  policy 26
  Royal Navy 91–4
  slaves as troops 42
  troop numbers 27
  warfare 100
casualties
  Aligarh 205
  Badajoz 274
  Baltic sea 143
  battle of Argaum 204
  battle of Assaye 202
  battle of Ligny 351
  battle of Mehidpur 378–9
  battle of Navarino 453
  battle of Salamanca 275
  battle of Trafalgar 240
  battle of Vitoria 284
  battle of Waterloo 352, 358
  Bharatpur 217, 457
  British Empire 433
  British forces 282
  Egypt 145
  final campaign 302
  Fort Erie 333

  French 267
  illness 98, 296
  Jumna river 206
  Kalanga 367
  La Coruña 260–1
  Laswari 207
  Nagpur 378
  Naples 246
  New Orleans 338
  Pyrenees 285
  regiments 407
  slaves rescued 467
  Spanish armies 288–90
  Talavera 263–4
  Toulouse 308
  war of 1812 342
Catholic Defenders 112
Catholic emancipation 126
cavalry
  battle of Assaye 202
  British army 357
  effectiveness 385
  Hyderabad 176
  India 486
  Maratha wars 209–10
  Marathas 388
  Sultan, Tipu (Mysore) 165, 186
  troop numbers 468t
Ceylon 46, 147, 402–3
Chalmers, George (Secretary of the Board of Trade) 67–8, 71
Chamber of Deputies (Paris) 353–4
Chandler, David 261
Charleroi 348
Chatham 399, 400
Churchill, Winston 15
City of London Corporation 28
Ciudad Rodrigo 265, 273–4, 276
civil expenditure 125
civil unrest 431–2
civil wars 43
Clarke, Major General Alured 101
Clausewitz, Carl von 10, 62–3, 75, 426, 440–1
Clay, Henry (Congressman) 322
Close, Barry 202
Cobbett, William 171, 285–6, 397
Cobden, Richard 487–8
Cochrane, Vice Admiral Sir Alexander 335, 337

Cockburn, Rear Admiral George 335
Codrington, Rear Admiral Edward 335, 452–3
coffee 92
Coimbatore 160
collaboration 44, 451–2
Colley, Linda 10
Collier, Captain F.A. 467
Collingwood, Cuthbert 39, 239
colonial governance 5, 93, 97
colonial posts 476
colonial warfare 65, 70, 441
    80–81, 80–1
colonies 458, 464
colours 405
command and coordination
    allied armies 348
    army and navy 85, 101, 292, 334, 340
    authority 50
    British army 45, 384
    Caribbean 95
    distribution 477–8
    efficiency 211
    frustration 355
    Ireland 118, 127
    Mysore campaigns 184
    officer corps 293–4
commerce 3, 5, 99
Compton, Herbert 201
Confederation of the Rhine 236
Congress of Vienna 30
conscription 35, 37, 41, 296, 300
Continental System
    Bonaparte, Napoleon 247
    Iberian Peninsula 281
    limited 319
    naval activity 326
    Portugal 255
    Spain 291
    undermined 269, 323
    war of 1812 321
Conway, Stephen 11, 12
Cookson, Professor J.E. 12
Cooper, Randolph 208–9
Coote, Lieutenant-General Sir Eyre 43, 45–6
Copenhagen 248
Cork 113, 401
Cormack, William 50

Cornwallis, Admiral William 231
Cornwallis, Charles (Marquess Cornwallis)
    act of union 125–6
    balance of power 175
    battle experience 44
    command 32
    Humbert, General Jean Joseph Amable 123–4
    India 7, 155–6
    Indian army 158, 220–1
    Ireland 120–1
    Irish defence 129
    local populations 43
    Mysore 159
    peace settlement 166–7
    reconstruction 122
    returns to India 218–19
    strategy 162
    subsidiary alliance system 385–6
    Yorktown 45
Corsica 102
Cortes 286–7, 290–1, 308–9, 310
County Kildare 117
County Wexford 117
Craig, Major General Sir James 100–1, 102, 178, 183, 244
Crawford, Lieutenant Colonel Robert 127–8

Davout, Louis-Nicolas 354
Deccan, The xvii
Decline and Fall of the Roman Empire 5
defence 8, 13, 129–30, 427
Delhi 205–6, 211
Denmark 143
desertion 166, 406
Diez, Juan Martin 299
diplomacy
    battle 348
    Europe 242–3
    expansionism 458
    Greek uprising 451
    India 172
    Maratha wars 221–2
    Mediterranean 230
    Portugal 301
    United States of America 1812 319
Dirom, Alexander 406

discipline 46–7, 408
drilling 31, 46–7
Dublin 116–17
Duffy, Michael 99, 439
Duke of Richmond *see* Lennox, Charles,
    Duke of Richmond
Duke of Wellington *see* Wellesley,
    Major-General Sir Arthur (later Duke
    of Wellington)
Duke of York *see* Frederick, Prince, Duke
    of York
Duncan, Admiral Adam 104–5
Dundas, David 356–7
Dundas, Henry
    colonial warfare 69–70
    Egypt 144
    empire 51
    expansionism 62
    France 176
    incompetence 16
    India 137
    Indian army 158
    Ireland 119
    Low Countries 66
    Marathas 189
    strategic priorities 83
    troop numbers 194
    volunteers 235
Dundas, Ralph 117
Dupin, Charles 27
Dutch army 356
Dutch settlements 98, 100–2
dysentery 33, 296

East India Company
    armies 155, 178
    Cape Colony 100
    Chatham 400
    expansionism 387, 455
    governance 470
    government 385
    Indian army 157, 213
    indigenous troops 42
    infrastructure 404
    land rights 366
    Maratha princes 193–7
    military reputation 171
    Nagpur 378
    officer corps 476

Pindari/Maratha war 382
Pindari threat 373
political power 26
President of the Board of Control 6
Rao II, Baji 195–6
regimental system 406
revenue collection 174, 188
revenues 166, 220
Secret Committee 219
Sindhia, Daulat Rao 208
state system 172
subsidiary alliance system 385
troop numbers 165, 408, 468
Wellesley, Richard 28
eastern front 379
economic development 4, 62, 68,
    173–4, 404
economic interest 92
economic reforms 272
Eden, William, Baron Auckland 124
Edmonstone, N.B. 374
Egypt 135, 137, 144–7, 149
Ehrman, John 84
El Empecinado *see* Diez, Juan Martin
elephants 368
Eliott, General George Augustus
    48–9
Elliott, Gilbert 85
Elphinstone, Mountstuart 375, 379–80,
    384
Elphinstone, Admiral Sir George,
    Viscount Keith 100–1, 140, 141–42,
    231
empire
    constricted 8
    France 91
    global 49
    importance 421
    military character 468
    power 477
    scattered interests 81–2
    stakeholders 26–31, 52
    troop numbers 64
    viability 25
    war 49–52
*Empire: How Britain Made the Modern
    World* 9
employment 400
enclaves 413, 487

Europe
    alliances 236, 484–5
    balance of power 63
    British influence 459–60
    challenges 235
    financial subsidies 64–5
    Great Powers 106
    soft power 439–40
European waters xii
expansion 3–4, 7, 25
expansionism
    aristocracy 428, 430
    authority 50
    British Empire 439, 481
    British militarism 19, 44, 193
    command 424
    commerce 483
    East India Company 378
    France 74, 91, 135
    Grenville, William Wyndham, Baron
        29
    Gurkhas 366
    India 155, 166, 220, 387, 458
    military expenditure 395
    military experience 432
    North America 322
    power 30
    security 62
    warfare 419
experience 15–16, 32, 92, 475–6
exports 269, 321–2, 324, 325, 332,
    449–50
    from Britain 71–2

Fadnis, Nana 175
Ferdinand VII, King of Spain 308
Ferguson, Niall
    Empire: How Britain Made the
        Modern World 9
financial subsidies
    Austria 261
    to Europe 347, 349, 355
    to Holland 442
    Portugal 264, 272
    Spain 296
First World War 37
Fitzwilliam, William Wentworth, Earl
    114
Flanders 73

Floyd, Lieutenant-Colonel John 163
Foley, Captain Thomas 137
Fort Erie 333
Fortescue, John 15, 110, 126, 162,
    385
Fouché, Joseph 353
Fox, Charles James 4, 15, 66
Foy, Maximilien 270, 275
France
    admiration 12
    colonies 232
    comparisons 31–8
    continental order 440
    empire 276–7
    European supremacy 109
    expansionism 148, 459
    financial penalties 442
    Hanover 235
    India 172, 176
    invaded by allied armies 302–3
    invades Algiers 454–5
    invades Naples 138
    invasion by Britain 280
    Ireland 111, 122–3
    military campaigning 76–7
    naval power 70
    negotiations with Britain 105–6
    Peninsular War 302–8
    Portugal 265–6
    reduced aristocracy 422
    in Spain 454
    Spanish guerrillas 299
    threat in India 180
    threat to Britain 61–2, 233
    threats in India 176–7
    war 65, 66
    withdrawal from Portugal 267
    withdrawal from Spain 280
Franks, General Tommy 38
Frederick II, the Great, King of Prussia
    31, 35, 63
Frederick, Prince, Duke of York
    head of the army 355
    Irish defence 129
    Royal Military College 294
    troops for Ireland 14
    war with France 73, 74–5
    withdrawal from Netherlands
        141

French army
  battle experience 356
  French Revolution 34–6, 422
  losses 300
  morale 354
  Spain 284, 297–8
  surrenders Cairo 146
  troop numbers 264
French forces 281
French military 25
French navy 84, 92, 96, 104, 257
French possessions 93, 442–3
French Revolution 31, 479
Frost, Alan 9
Fullerton, Colonel William 157, 158

Gardner, Alan, Baron 39
Gates, David 261
general officers 472
Genoa 140
George III (King, Britain)
  Catholic emancipation 126
  civilianized army 7
  command and coordination 45
  Egypt 145
  Mediterranean 137
  peace settlement 149
  peerages 425
  Royal Navy 82
  West Indies 81, 232
German army 37–8, 303, 350
Germany 37
Gibbon, Edward
  Decline and Fall of the Roman
    Empire 5
Gibraltar 32–3, 48, 102, 256
Gillespie, Major-General Rollo 367–8
Glengarry Volunteers 329
global infrastructure 395–6
Glorious First of June 425
Gneisenau, Graf von (Prussian Chief of
  Staff) 351–2
Godwin, William 425
  Enquiry Concerning Political Justice
    424
Gordon, George, Marquis of Huntly
  121
Gordon Highlanders 121, 407
Gore, Captain John 231

government 101–2, 173–4, 254, 298,
  432, 478
Grant, Charles 100
Grattan, Henry 113
Gravina, Admiral Don Frederico 237
Great Lakes 321
Great Powers 106, 310–11, 349, 458,
  465
Greece 450–1, 453–4
Grenville, William Wyndham, Baron 29,
  84, 140, 148
Greville, Charles 431
Grey, General Sir Charles 402
Grey, Sir Charles 93, 94–5
Grouchy, Marquis Emmanuel 348, 352,
  353
Guadeloupe 95, 96
Gulf War (1991) 38
gunpowder 380, 381
Gurkhas 364, 366, 371

Hamilton, Alexander 3, 10, 11–12
Hamilton, Sir William 140
Hamilton-Williams, David 347
Hanoverians 356
harbours 402–3
Hardy, Sir Charles 82
Harris, James Edward, Earl of
  Malmesbury 75, 105
Harris, Major-General George 180, 183,
  184–5
Harrison, Major-General William H.
  330, 331, 332
Harvey, Arnold 16
Haslar Naval Hospital 399
Hastings, Francis Rawdon, Marquis of
  366, 371–2, 373, 377, 382, 387
Hastings, Warren 46, 156
Haythornthwaite, Philip J. 347
Heber, Bishop Walter 404–5, 409
Hely-Hutchinson, General John 123,
  146
heroism 424–5, 457, 471–2
Hickey, Donald 339
higher command 25
Hill, Sir Rowland 283
Hindustan 157
Hislop, Lieutenant-General Sir Thomas
  377, 378, 382–3

Hobart, Robert, Earl of Buckinghamshire 234–5
Hobsbawm, Eric 31
Holkar, Jaswant Rao 175–6, 195, 214–18, 373, 378
Holkar war xviii
Holland, Edward John (Governor, Madras) 159
Hood, Samuel, Viscount 69, 83, 85
Hope, Lieutenant-General Sir John 307
Hopkins, A.G. 27
Horse Guards 119, 288
hospital 198
Hull, William 330
Humbert, General Jean Joseph Amable 123–4
Hyderabad 175, 176, 182

Iberian Peninsula 64, 254, 268, 291, 458
    map xix
illness 94–5, 271, 296, 298, 357, 456
    West Indies 98
imperial policy 3, 469
imperialism 4–10
India
    British armies 36
    British influence 459
    British military challenges 155–8
    British possessions 1783 xvi
    British possessions 1818 xxii
    British power 459
    British presence 387
    British rule 51
    command systems 46
    economic development 173–4
    empire 222
    expansionism 483
    government 371, 470
    indigenous peoples 17
    military competitiveness 176
    military interventions 455–8
    military leadership 476
    military presence 468
    military provision 467–8
    mobility 486
    paramountcy 364–5, 440
    Pindari threat 371–5

    political culture 365
    protection 142
    regimental system 405
    subsidiary alliance system 484
    troop numbers 64, 408
    war 174
    warfare 171
    Wellesley, Richard 28
India Act (1784) 155
Indian army 158
Indian nationals 385
Indian society 172–3
indigenous peoples 17
Industrial Revolution 428
infantry 179, 187, 209
    troop numbers 468
infrastructure 395, 396–405
Ingram, Edward 16, 179–80
Inquiry into the Wealth of Nations 5
international relations 66, 73, 439, 444–50, 458
international trade 255
invasion 13, 111, 237, 397
Ionian Islands 248
Ireland
    army recruits 15
    barracks 396–7, 398
    civil unrest 485
    direct rule 126
    discontent 110–13
    France 109, 233–4
    invasion 122–4
    landowners 29
    map xv
    suppression 130
    troop numbers 407–8, 465
    troops 14
    volunteers 234
Irish Government 110
isolation 73, 104
Italy 280

Jackson, Major-General Andrew 320, 337, 338
Jaithak 370
Jamaica 93, 96, 98, 336, 401–2
Jefferson, Thomas 120
Jefferson, Thomas, President USA 321, 322

Jenkinson, Robert Banks, Earl of
Liverpool *see* Liverpool, Robert Banks
Jenkinson, Earl of
Jervis, John, Earl of St Vincent 39, 94–5,
102–3, 136, 137, 140
Jones, J.R. 439

Kalanga 369
Kamaun 370
Kathmandu 367
Khan, Ali 176, 178
Kinsale 401
Kirkpatrick, William 176, 179
Knox, Thomas 115–16

La Coruña 260, 292
Lake Champlain 333
Lake Erie 331
Lake, Major-General Gerard
battle of Vinegar Hill 45, 120, 124
Delhi 211
French threat in India 199
Holkar, Jaswant Rao 214–16
Humbert, General Jean Joseph
Amable 123–4
India 401
Ireland 115–16
northern campaigns 1803 204–5
Wexford 120
Lake Ontario 331
landowners
defence 427
expansionism 428, 435
military experience 432
military skills 420
power 30–1
Prussian army 421
Langford, Paul 424
Laswari 207, 211
Latin American colonies 449, 459
leadership
aristocracy 434
British army 384, 430
British Empire 413
British forces 339
Indian army 157
Nepalese war 366
regimental system 358
Spanish forces 288

war 419
Waterloo campaign 354
Wellesley, Major-General Sir Arthur
(later Duke of Wellington) 359
League of Armed Neutrality 142–3
Lenman, Bruce 16
Lennox, Charles, Duke of Richmond 69,
72
Lisbon 257, 276, 292
Liverpool, Robert Banks Jenkinson,
Earl of
Bonaparte, Napoleon 281
conspiracy 376
East India Company 26
Latin American colonies 310
peace settlement 147
Pindari threat 372
Portugal 262
Portuguese government 272
possible evacuation of Portugal
268–9
war of 1812 320
local populations 43, 271, 305, 328,
396, 404
logistics 34, 233
losses 407, 453, 457
Low Countries 66, 69, 72–6, 262
Lynn, John 61

Macartney, George, Earl Macartney 45,
46, 102
Mackenzie, John, Lord Macleod 43
Madeira 255–6
Madison, James, President USA 320
Madras 44–5, 157, 220, 372, 404
Madras presidency 197–8
Madrid 275, 283
Maida river 245
malaria 42, 95, 99, 296
Malcolm, John 215, 381, 455
Malta 137, 140, 142, 148, 229
Mandara (Egypt) 145
manpower 113–17
Maratha wars 218–22
Marathas
alliance with Britain 179
British intervention 196
conspiracy 376
defeated by Britain 364

Gwalior 157
  military campaigning 36
  mobility 218
  north west frontier 183
  northern campaigns 1803 204–8
  Pindari 373
  Pindari threat 371
  politics 197
  principalities 172
  revenues 166
  southern campaign 200–4
  succession disputes 175
  system collapse 195
  tax system 173
  war 197–200
Marley, Major-General Bennett 367,
  369
Marmaris (Turkey) 145
Marmont, Marshal Auguste de 275
Martinique 93, 95
Mauritius 176, 181
Maxwell, Lieutenant Colonel Patrick
  202
Mediterranean
  British bases 319
  British domination 242–8
  British presence 230
  initiatives 1798–9 136–40
  Royal Navy 83–5, 242
  Russian influence 455
  Spanish challenge Britain 102
Medows, Major-General William
  159–61
mercenaries 176, 209
merchant ships 27, 321, 323, 325
Metcalfe, Charles 373, 387
Middleton, Sir Charles 70–1
militarism 3, 4, 13, 425, 440, 470–1
military campaigning 31–2, 64, 76–9,
  296
military capabilities 465–70
military capability 349
military commitment 63–4
military competence 50
military competitiveness 176
military criticism 40
military culture 49, 365, 434, 464
military effectiveness 208–13, 321, 413,
  482

military efficiency 354–61
military ethos 44–9
military expenditure
  barracks 397
  expansionism 387
  India 156, 178
  Ireland 124–5
  reduced 364, 420
  regimental system 407–8
  weapons 250
military experience 355
military hospitals 296
military incompetence 15–18, 259, 262,
  300–1
military infrastructure 403
military intelligence
  battle of Quatre Bras 358
  defects 162
  India 384
  Maratha wars 213
  Nepalese war 369
  southern campaign 203
  training 294–5
  Wellesley, Major-General
    Sir Arthur (later Duke of
    Wellington) 301
military leadership 38–40, 423,
  470–80
military management 483–4
military performance 339–42
military policing 124–6
military power 246, 421, 479, 481, x
military service 29, 424–8
military strategy 295
military success 155
military training 33
militias
  Britain 234
  Canada 329, 340–1
  growth 68
  Ireland 114, 398
  leadership 423
  New Orleans 338
  North America 328
  opposition 11
  Portugal 270
  United States of America 422–3
  violence 129
Mina, Francisco Espoz y 299

mobilization
  allied armies 349
  British forces 216–17, 234
  defensive 65
  forces 42
  North America 328
  Spanish armies 297
Moltke, Helmuth von 37
monarchy 442, 470–1, 478, 479
Monroe, James (Secretary of State, USA) 335
Monson, Colonel Wiliam 216
Moore, Sir John
  Alexandria 147
  command and coordination 259–60
  Gordon, George, Marquis of Huntly 121
  Ireland 125, 128–9
  Peninsular War 47
  Portugal 258
  St Lucia 98
  Sweden 249
  Wexford 120
morale 395, 408, 413
Mughal empire 173–4
Muir, Rory 36, 281, 360
Mulgrave, Henry Phipps, Earl of 355
Munro, Thomas
  balance of power 183
  French threat in India 181
  India 197
  Pindari/Maratha war 384
  Pindari threat 374–5
  politics 30
  revenue collectors 382
  subsidiary alliance system 386
Murat, Marshal Joachim 255, 350
Murray, David see Stormont, Viscount
Murray, Sir John 282, 292
Mysore
  campaigns 155, 183–6
  fourth war 171
  Hindu rulers 188
  international context 171–9
  invades Madras 44–5
  invasion 158–65
  invasions 36
  strategy 168, 179–80
  war 182–3
Mysore campaigns 186–9

Napier, Sir William 52, 260
Naples 137–8, 139, 243, 246–7
Napoleon see Bonaparte, Napoleon
national debt 28, 35, 67, 219–20, 420
national identity 10–15, 471
national populations 35
Native Americans 329–30, 337
naval capabilities 465–70
naval dockyards 399, 430–1
naval effectiveness 413
naval guns 240, 452
naval leadership 470–80
naval power
  battle of Trafalgar 242
  British 70, 72, 440, x
  Europe 65
  French 79
  global reach 230
  Great Lakes 332
  lack of pressure 17
  Lake Erie 331
  limitations 140–4
  North America 319
  Royal Navy 322, 481
naval tonnage 326, 400, 466
naval warfare 65, 79–83, 102–6, 324, 333–4
Navarino Bay 452
Nawab of Arcot 172
Neapolitan troops 85
Nelson, Horatio, Viscount (Admiral)
  attacks Copenhagen 143
  battle of St Vincent 103
  blockades Cadiz 238–9
  Bonaparte, Napoleon 137
  Corsica 102
  dies 240
  funeral 28
  Mediterranean 83, 138–9
Nepal 36, 365–71
Netherlands 79, 100, 140, 348, 350
Netherlands Campaign
  map xi
  Waterloo xxi
New Orleans 334, 338, 339
Ney, Michel 353–4
Niagara River 330
Nicolls, Colonel Jasper 370, 371, 455, 458

North America 16–17, 32, 319, 484,
    xiv, xx
North, Frederick North, Lord 80
northern campaigns 1803 204–8
Nugent, Major-General George 119
Nye, Joseph 439

Ochterlony, Major-General David
    366–7, 368–9, 370–1
officer corps
    accountability 487
    aristocrats 44
    battle experience 46, 487
    British army 38, 293
    civil unrest 432
    civilianized army 6
    commitment to European wars 474
    comparisons 25
    half-pay 364
    incompetence 40
    independence 483
    India 468
    Ireland 110
    local knowledge 340
    military activity 464
    peace time 431
    Portugal 270
    prestige 432
    promotion 297
    regimental system 406
    Royal Military College 47
    Royal Navy 466–7
    shortages in Canada 329
    successes 50
O'Hara, Brigadier-General Charles 44,
    45
organization 155, 405
Orthez 307
Ottoman empire 142, 451
overseas policy 440, 444
Oxford History of the British Empire 9

Padfield, Peter 439
Paine, Tom
    Common Sense 5, 67
    Rights of Man, The 67, 106, 424
Pakenham, Sir Edward 338
Palmer, William 194–5
Paris 347, 348, 349, 353
Parsons, Sir Lawrence (MP) 110

Pathan warriors 372
peace settlement 147–9, 166–7
Peel, Sir Robert 398
Pellew, Captain Edward 71
Peninsular War
    assessment 297–302
    British army 310
    British offensives 1812 273–7
    British support 48
    costs 268
    final campaign 302–8
    regimental system 405
    regular armies 288
    senior command 356
    setbacks 17
    Spanish military contribution 285–91
    Wellesley, Major-General Sir Arthur
        (later Duke of Wellington) 301–2
Perceval, Spencer 67
Perry, Commodore Oliver H. 331
Phillip, Captain Arthur 403
Pindari/Maratha war 375–9, 385
Pindari threat 371–5
Pitt, William, Lord Chatham 84, 399
Pitt, William, the Younger
    British army 47–8
    Caribbean 97
    Catholic emancipation 126
    City of London Corporation 28
    East India Company 26, 155
    France 61–2
    French monarchy 74
    government falls 135
    incompetence 16
    military strategy 73
    peace settlement 148–9
    Toulon 69
    volunteers 235
    war 4
planning 212, 215–16
plantation economy 26, 93
Poland 76
policy instrument 19, 25, 28, 441, 481
policy-makers 18
policy making 6, 40, 144, 262, 361, 464
political culture 365
political emancipation 112
political influence 18–19
political leadership 288, 423
political organization 301

political reform 112, 114, 420, 464
politicians 434–5
politics 28–9, 30, 49, 173, 174
Pondicherry 159, 176
population 113, 196, 402, 404
Portsmouth 399
Portugal
    allied armies 303, 310
    British forces 254, 263
    British influence 447–9
    defence 255–61
    demands on British government 284
    French invasion 446–7
    international relations 444–50
    Portuguese army 270
    renewed commitment 261–73
    trading interests 269
Potomac River 336
power 6, 30, 62, 298–9
Pratt, Sir John Jeffreys, Marquess
    Camden 115, 128
predatory raiding 158–9
presidencies
    revenues 220
President of the Board of Control 6
Prevost, Sir George 327, 333–4,
    339–40
Prinsep, Henry Thoby 383
Pritzler, Theophilus 380–1
privateering 92, 325
prize money 65, 95, 188, 467
Procter, Major General Henry 331
professionalism 429–30
professionalization 44, 47
promotion 46, 406–7, 412, 422
Protestant Orange orders 112, 114
Prussia 74, 75–6, 256, 304, 421
Prussian army 347, 350, 351, 353
public celebrations 68
Pune 175, 375, 376–7
Pye, Sir Thomas 83
Pyrenees 284–5

Quarterly Review 51–2, 385
Quebec 327

raids 372, 384
Randolph, John 325
Rangoon 456

Rao II, Baji
    conflict 375
    East India Company 195
    escaped Ashti 380
    internal exile 381
    military intelligence 384
    prolonged campaign 1818–19
        379–82
    Pune 376–7
    succession disputes 175
rebellion
    counter-insurgency 128
    death toll 124
    ex-slaves 96
    Ireland 110, 117–21
    military significance 126–31
    Saint Domingue 99
recruitment
    American army 329
    British army 408
    expansion 397
    foreign nationals 42
    French army 300, 349
    military 11, 295
    militias 471
    Portugal 272
    regimental system 406, 412
    regiments 426
    sepoys 468
    wartime 14, 45
    yeomans 115
regimental pride 47
regimental system 349, 358, 395, 411,
    413
regimentalism 405–8
regiments 408, 412
regional power 459
regular armies 288
reinforcements 157–8, 369
repression 119, 121, 129
republicanism 5, 122
reputation 17–18, 47–8, 178, 405
resources 323, 457–8, 472
revenues
    Agra 207
    Andalucia 276
    Caribbean 80
    East India Company 177, 378
    expansionism 387

Hyderabad to East India Company
    182
India 156–7, 220
rituals 403–4, 408–11, 412
rivalries 197
Rodger, N.A.M. 63, 81, 242
Rodney, Sir George 80–1
role
    aristocracy 424
    British 61, 464, x
    British Empire 433, 481
    Spanish armies 298
Roosevelt, Theodore 341
Ross, Lieutenant Colonel Robert 245
Ross, Major-General Robert 335, 336
Rothenburg, Gunther 37
Roy, Kaushik 209
Royal Arsenal 399
Royal Artillery Barracks 399
Royal Edinburgh Volunteer Light
    Dragoons 13
Royal Horse Artillery 127
Royal Hospital, Chelsea 398
Royal Military Academy 399, 474
Royal Military Asylum 398
Royal Military College 47, 294
Royal Military Panorama or Officer's
    Companion 429
Royal Naval Hospital 399
Royal Navy
    American ships harassed 322
    Anglo-Russian campaign 141
    aristocracy 433–4
    battle experience 83
    battle of St Vincent 103
    battle success 82
    Bay of Biscay 293
    blockades Cadiz 257
    blockading 231, 321, 323, 325, 332,
        342
    British waters 400
    colonial warfare 70, 80–1
    command and coordination 81
    competence 39
    Copenhagen 248
    expenditure 35, 326, 395
    frigate warfare 319
    frigates 324
    global power 52

    Greek uprising 452
    Iberian Peninsula 269
    instrument of war 79–80
    Ireland 109
    losses 231, 326–7
    Mediterranean 242, 247
    naval officers 326, 477
    naval operations 41
    North America fleet 324
    political pressure 102
    Portugal 255
    prize money 471
    reduced numbers 465
    Saint Domingue 232
    sea power 69
    size 326
    slave trade 9
    successes 486
    superiority 482–3
    Trafalgar campaign 237–42
    troop movements 292
    victories 16
    West Indies 91, 93
Royal William Yard 399
Russia
    attacks France 140
    Bonaparte, Napoleon 300
    expansionism 459, 469
    foreign policy 143
    Greece 450–1
    invasion by France 36
    League of Armed Neutrality 142–3
    Malta 142
    negotiations with France 304
    protects Malta 137
    war with France 138
    war with Turkey 453
Russian army 350
Russian influence 455

Sahib, Apa 378, 381
sailors 11, 465–7
Saint Domingue 93, 95, 98, 99, 149, 232
Salamanca 283
Sanchez, Lieutenant General Ricardo 38
Sandwich, John Montagu, Earl of 26,
    81, 82
Satara 379
Saumarez, Captain James 71

Schroeder, Paul W. 347, 439, 454
Scotland 11, 14
Scott, Sir Walter 13, 356, 360
sea power 69, 280, 291–3
Secretary of State for War and the
    Colonies 6, 119
security 62
Seeley, J.R. 8, 11, 365
senior command
    administration 472
    aristocracy 425–7
    aristocrats 419
    battle experience 356
    competence 39, 294, 470–1
    corruption 470
    experience 464
    independent operations 473
    landowners 420
    qualifications 474
sepoy soldiers 208–9
Seringapatam 162–3, 165–8, 186
Seven Years' War (1756–63) 11
Shore, Sir John 178
Sicily 136, 230, 244, 247, 272, 282
Sindhia, Daulat Rao
    forces destroyed 207–8
    negotiations with Britain 199
    northern campaigns 1803 205
    Pindari threat 373
    succession disputes 175
    threat to British India 200
    war with Holkar, Jaswant Rao 195
Sindhia, Mahadji 175
Singapore 470
Singleton Copley, John 48
slavery
    abolition 10, 464
    Caribbean 26–7, 94
    New Orleans 334, 336–7
    Spain 310
    West Indian Regiments 97
slaves 26, 42, 93, 99, 337, 402
Smith, Adam 27
    Inquiry into the Wealth of Nations 5
Smith, Brigadier-General Lionel 379
Smith, Sir Harry 342, 360
Society of United Irishmen
    command and coordination 128
    French assistance 118

infiltration 116
march on Dublin 117
political emancipation 111
political reform 112–13
rebellion 233
recruitment 114
republicanism 122
surrender 121
soldiers 11, 13–14, 406
Soult, Nicolas Jean de Dieu
    battle of Nive 302
    battle of Nivelle river 306
    evacuates Andalucia 275
    La Coruña 260
    losses 305–6
    Peninsular War 47
    replaces Joseph Bonaparte 284
    Wellesley, Major-General Sir Arthur
        (later Duke of Wellington) 307
South Africa 42–3
South America 256
southern campaign 200–4
Spain
    allied armies 36
    allied to France 79, 102
    British commitment 264–5
    collapse 450
    declares war on Britain 98
    demands on British government
        284
    financial subsidies 297
    French army 36
    French intervention 445
    importance to France 280–1
    international relations 444–50
    Latin American colonies 309
    military contribution 285–91
    outnumbers French troops 281
    post-war settlement 308–11
    relations with Britain 280
    resists France 256, 257–8, 261, 267,
        273
    revolution 298
    taken by France 264
    victories 280
Spanish armies 288–9, 303, 304, 309,
    444
    military resistance 290
Spanish colonies 444

Spanish empire 286
Spanish troops 85
Spencer, George John, Earl (first Lord
    of the Admiralty) 104–5, 148, 149,
    176
St Lucia 93, 95, 96, 98
St Paul's Cathedral 28
St Vincent 103
stakeholders 26–31, 92
standardization 396
standing armies 5, 11
Stewart, Major-General James 116
Stewart, Robert, Viscount Castlereagh
    British army 51
    diplomacy 420
    foreign policy 441
    Holkar, Jaswant Rao 214
    landowners 29
    Peninsular diplomacy 311
    Spanish colonies 309–10
Stormont, Viscount 3
Strachan, Sir Richard, Baronet 39
Strachey, Edward 202
strategy
    Bathurst, Henry, Earl 332
    British army 332
    choices 249
    collapse 76–7
    Egypt 144
    Elphinstone, Mountstuart 380
    Europe 229, 230
    evaluation 264
    French 265
    French navy 92
    Iberian Peninsula 269, 301
    India 179–83
    lack of analysis 401
    Maratha wars 212–13
    Mysore 167–8
    naval 323
    North America 319
    Oxford History of the British Empire
        9
    Pindari war 374
    sea power 293
    southern campaign 200–1
    Spain 263
    war against France 66–72
    war of 1812 321, 335, 339

Stuart, Charles 301
Stuart, Lieutenant-General James 51,
    180–1
Stuart, Major-General Charles 138
Stuart, Major-General James 46
Stuart, Major-General Sir John 244–6,
    247
subsidiary alliance system
    India 196–7, 222, 365
    maintained 220
    military expenditure 387
    Rao II, Baji 375–6
    reliability 385
succession disputes 175
Suchet, Louis 284
sugar 27, 92, 99
Sullivan, Major-General John
    Nepalese war 367
Sultan, Tipu (Mysore)
    alliance with France 181
    dies 186
    French help 176
    India 29
    reduced power 187
    warfare 159–61
    warlord 177–8
supplies
    British army 163–4, 186
    failures 295
    gunpowder 380, 381
    importance 211–12
    Marathas 199
    Portuguese army 271
    Russian campaign 300
    sea power 292
    southern campaign 200
    unreliable 290
    Wellesley, Major-General Sir Arthur
        (later Duke of Wellington) 284
suppression 130
Surtees, John 338
Surtees, William 408, 411
Sweden 249

tactics 382–3, 384
Talavera 263–4
Talleyrand-Perigord, Charles-Maurice
    353
tax system 173, 196

Tecumseh 330, 331–2
Third Coalition 236
Thompson, E.P. 397
Thornborough, Sir Edward 39
Times, The
   Algiers 454
   French trade 95
   Glorious First of June 400–1
   Marathas 376
   Saint Domingue 232
   war of 1812 320, 323
Tod, Lieutenant-Colonel James 386–7
Tone, Wolfe 124
Toulon 69, 84, 85, 102
Toulouse 307
trading interests
   Baltic sea 248
   Britain 319
   Britain and Russia 142
   British exports 269
   British India 174
   Cadiz 269
   Caribbean 92
   Continental System 247
   imports to Britain 92
   inter-colonial 93–4
   Latin American colonies 449
   Mediterranean 450
   Portugal 255
   protection 71–2
   Royal Navy 467
   Spanish America 285, 286
   war 230
Trafalgar 239–40
Trafalgar campaign 237–42
training
   British army 210, 408
   high command 38–9
   junior officers 294
   military 31
   multi-ethnic forces 43
   officer corps 47
   regimental system 412
Travancore 159
Treaty of Alliance 310
Treaty of Ghent 339
Treaty of Vienna 310
Trinidad 98–9, 147
troop movements 292, 409, 413

troop numbers
   Algiers 454
   allied armies 78–9, 270–1
   Arakan 457
   Badajoz 274
   Baltimore 336
   barracks 397
   battle of Ligny 351
   battle of Mehidpur 378
   battle of Waterloo 350, 352, 358, 359
   Bayonne 307
   Bharatpur 457
   British army 42–3, 68, 234, 330, 333
   British Empire 481
   British forces 36, 73–4
   Canada 327–8, 341
   Cape Colony 101
   Caribbean 27, 94, 233
   Europe 236, 485
   European war 69
   Flanders 355
   France 282
   French army 306
   French superiority 78–9
   guerrilla forces 299
   Iberian Peninsula 64, 268
   illness 95, 99
   India 64, 156–7, 182, 194, 458, 467–8
   indigenous peoples 42
   Ireland 14–15, 110, 113–14, 118–19, 127, 130
   Lake, Major-General Gerard 211
   losses 145, 303
   Maratha princes 200
   Maratha wars 212
   Marathas war 198
   Mediterranean 247
   military campaigning 33, 64
   Mysore 188
   Mysore campaigns 185
   Nagpur 378
   Nepalese war 367, 369
   North America 328–9
   northern campaigns 1803 205
   Peninsular War 295, 296
   Pindari/Maratha war 377, 382
   Pindari war 374

Portugal 258, 262, 270–1, 281–2
Prussia 75
Rangoon 456
reduced 219, 364, 465
River Thames (Canada) 331
Royal Navy 292
Scotland 14–15
Spain 259–60, 263, 281–2, 284, 289, 290
Spanish armies 84–5
West Indies 95, 96–7, 402
troops 27, 73, 84, 121, 127, 193–4
Turkey 137, 145
Turner, Wesley B. 341

Ulster 119
United Provinces 79
United Services Club 434
United States of America 40, 422, 479
  see also North America
Upper Canada 319

victories
  Ashti 380
  battle of Vitoria 284
  British army 298
  public celebrations 68
  public support 41
  at sea 16
  Vimiero 258
Villeneuve, Vice Admiral Pierre 237, 238
Vimiero 258, 411
Vinegar Hill 124
violence 117, 128, 131
Vitoria 281–5
volunteers
  aid Portugal 448
  Americans 341
  aristocracy 427
  Canada 329
  citizens' defence force 11
  militias 68
  national defence 12, 13–14, 234
  New Orleans 338
  training 408

war
  aristocracy 424
  British conduct 281

British experience 485
challenges 231–6
colonial warfare 65
commerce 4
empire 49–52
Holkar, Jaswant Rao 214–18
morality 40
national debt 67
national identity 10–15
peripheral activity 8
Pindari 373–4
policy instrument 19, 25, 174, 441
principles 44
promotion 407
successes 97
United States of America 1812 319
war of 1812 320–2, 323–31, 332–9
warfare 84, 91, 143–4, 196, 419, 424
Warren, Commodore Sir John 124
Warren, Sir John Borlase 324, 337
warships
  French navy 84, 104, 241–2
  Great Lakes 332
  Greek uprising 452
  losses 232, 324–5
  numbers increased 231, 326
  reduced 465–7
  Royal Navy 41, 65, 141
  war of 1812 323
  West Indies 93
wartime mobilization 14
Washington DC 335, 336
Waterloo 17 *see also* battle of
  map xxi
weapons
  Agra 207
  Aligarh 205
  Asirgah 381
  battle of Busaco 266
  battle of Deig 216
  battle of Trafalgar 240
  battle of Waterloo 352
  distribution 127
  Lee-Enfield rifle 359
  Maratha wars 213
  seized at Vitoria 284
  into Spain 259
  Spain 289
  supplies 250

Webbe, Josias 180, 184
Webster, Lieutenant-Colonel James 44
Wedderburn, Alexander, Baron 84
Weigley, Russell 16, 36–7
Wellesley, Henry 286, 301, 401
Wellesley, Major-General Sir Arthur
    (later Duke of Wellington) 17, 30, 47
    allied armies 348–9
    battle of Quatre Bras 351
    battle of Waterloo 352, 357, 360
    Bonaparte, Napoleon 354
    British army 51
    British forces 265–6
    co-operation with Spanish 263
    command and coordination 292, 350
    Cortes 287
    French power 287–8
    French threat in India 181
    Holkar, Jaswant Rao 214
    India 7, 401
    invasion of France 302–8
    Ireland 398
    lack of preparedness 355
    Marathas 195–6
    marches on Madrid 275
    Mauritius 176–7
    Mysore campaigns 184
    officer corps 294
    Portugal 258, 261, 262–3
    Portuguese enclave 270
    Portuguese government 272
    preparations for war 198
    recognition of Portuguese effort 303
    regimental system 406
    removed from India 219
    Salamanca 283
    senior command 1828–30 475, 476
    Seringapatam 188
    Spanish advance 273–4
    Spanish incompetence 300–1
    strategy 269, 306–7
    subsidiary alliance system 385
    Sultan, Tipu (Mysore) 178
    tactics 297
    Toulouse 307–8
    visits Madrid 309
    Vitoria 283
    war 199
Wellesley, Richard, Lord Mornington,
    later Marquess
    Foreign Secretary 264
    Holkar, Jaswant Rao 214
    India 28–9, 179–80
    Maratha wars 210
    Mysorean defeat 194
    Sultan, Tipu (Mysore) 181–2
Wellington, Duke of see Wellesley,
    Major General Sir Arthur 17, 30, 47
West, Benjamin 240–1
West India Committee 27
West Indian Regiments 97
West Indies 70, 81, 91, 92, 402
Wexford 118
Whigs 421, 423
Winder, Brigadier general William 335
Windham, William (Secretary of State for
    War and the Colonies) 246
Winkfield Plain 408–9
withdrawal 260, 267
Wood, Major-General J.S. 369

yellow fever 42, 95, 99
Yeo, Sir James 324, 334
yeomanry 110, 114–15, 124, 129,
    398
Yorke, Charles (Secretary at War)
    234–5
Yorktown 32, 45, 46, 80